T0156081

Pro TBB

C++ Parallel Programming with Threading Building Blocks

Michael Voss
Rafael Asenjo
James Reinders

Pro TBB: C++ Parallel Programming with Threading Building Blocks

Michael Voss
Austin, Texas, USA

Rafael Asenjo
Málaga, Spain

James Reinders
Portland, Oregon, USA

ISBN-13 (pbk): 978-1-4842-4397-8
https://doi.org/10.1007/978-1-4842-4398-5

ISBN-13 (electronic): 978-1-4842-4398-5

Copyright © 2019 by Intel Corporation

Managing Director, Apress Media LLC: Welmoed Spahr
Acquisitions Editor: Natalie Pao
Development Editor: James Markham
Coordinating Editor: Jessica Vakili

Cover designed by eStudioCalamar

Cover image designed by Freepik (www.freepik.com)

Distributed to the book trade worldwide by Springer Science+Business Media New York, 233 Spring Street, 6th Floor, New York, NY 10013. Phone 1-800-SPRINGER, fax (201) 348-4505, e-mail orders-ny@springer-sbm.com, or visit www.springeronline.com. Apress Media, LLC is a California LLC and the sole member (owner) is Springer Science + Business Media Finance Inc (SSBM Finance Inc). SSBM Finance Inc is a **Delaware** corporation.

For information on translations, please e-mail rights@apress.com, or visit http://www.apress.com/rights-permissions.

Apress titles may be purchased in bulk for academic, corporate, or promotional use. eBook versions and licenses are also available for most titles. For more information, reference our Print and eBook Bulk Sales web page at http://www.apress.com/bulk-sales.

Any source code or other supplementary material referenced by the author in this book is available to readers on GitHub via the book's product page, located at www.apress.com/978-1-4842-4397-8. For more detailed information, please visit http://www.apress.com/source-code.

Printed on acid-free paper.

Table of Contents

About the Authors

Michael Voss is a Principal Engineer in the Intel Architecture, Graphics and Software Group at Intel. He has been a member of the TBB development team since before the 1.0 release in 2006 and was the initial architect of the TBB flow graph API. He is also one of the lead developers of Flow Graph Analyzer, a graphical tool for analyzing data flow applications targeted at both homogeneous and heterogeneous platforms. He has co-authored over 40 published papers and articles on topics related to parallel programming and frequently consults with customers across a wide range of domains to help them effectively use the threading libraries provided by Intel. Prior to joining Intel in 2006, he was an Assistant Professor in the Edward S. Rogers Department of Electrical and Computer Engineering at the University of Toronto. He received his Ph.D. from the School of Electrical and Computer Engineering at Purdue University in 2001.

Rafael Asenjo, Professor of Computer Architecture at the University of Malaga, Spain, obtained a PhD in Telecommunication Engineering in 1997 and was an Associate Professor at the Computer Architecture Department from 2001 to 2017. He was a Visiting Scholar at the University of Illinois in Urbana-Champaign (UIUC) in 1996 and 1997 and Visiting Research Associate in the same University in 1998. He was also a Research Visitor at IBM T.J. Watson in 2008 and at Cray Inc. in 2011. He has been using TBB since 2008 and over the last five years, he has focused on productively exploiting heterogeneous chips leveraging TBB as the orchestrating framework. In 2013 and 2014 he visited UIUC to work on CPU+GPU chips. In 2015 and 2016 he also started to research into CPU+FPGA chips while visiting U. of Bristol. He served as General Chair for ACM PPoPP'16 and as an Organization Committee member as well as a Program Committee member for several HPC related conferences (PPoPP, SC, PACT, IPDPS, HPCA, EuroPar, and SBAC-PAD). His research interests include heterogeneous programming models and architectures, parallelization of irregular codes and energy consumption.

James Reinders is a consultant with more than three decades experience in Parallel Computing, and is an author/co-author/editor of nine technical books related to parallel programming. He has had the great fortune to help make key contributions to two of the world's fastest computers (#1 on Top500 list) as well as many other supercomputers, and software developer tools. James finished 10,001 days (over 27 years) at Intel in mid-2016, and now continues to write, teach, program, and do consulting in areas related to parallel computing (HPC and AI).

Acknowledgments

Two people offered their early and continuing support for this project – Sanjiv Shah and Herb Hinstorff. We are grateful for their encouragement, support, and occasional gentle pushes.

The real heroes are reviewers who invested heavily in providing thoughtful and detailed feedback on draft copies of the chapters within this book. The high quality of their input helped drive us to allow more time for review and adjustment than we initially planned. The book is far better as a result.

The reviewers are a stellar collection of users of TBB and key developers of TBB. It is rare for a book project to have such an energized and supportive base of help in refining a book. Anyone reading this book can know it is better because of these kind souls: Eduard Ayguade, Cristina Beldica, Konstantin Boyarinov, José Carlos Cabaleiro Domínguez, Brad Chamberlain, James Jen-Chang Chen, Jim Cownie, Sergey Didenko, Alejandro (Alex) Duran, Mikhail Dvorskiy, Rudolf (Rudi) Eigenmann, George Elkoura, Andrey Fedorov, Aleksei Fedotov, Tomás Fernández Pena, Elvis Fefey, Evgeny Fiksman, Basilio Fraguela, Henry Gabb, José Daniel García Sánchez, Maria Jesus Garzaran, Alexander Gerveshi, Darío Suárez Gracia, Kristina Kermanshahche, Yaniv Klein, Mark Lubin, Anton Malakhov, Mark McLaughlin, Susan Meredith, Yeser Meziani, David Padua, Nikita Ponomarev, Anoop Madhusoodhanan Prabha, Pablo Reble, Arch Robison, Timmie Smith, Rubén Gran Tejero, Vasanth Tovinkere, Sergey Vinogradov, Kyle Wheeler, and Florian Zitzelsberger.

We sincerely thank all those who helped, and we apologize for any who helped us and we failed to mention!

Mike (along with Rafa and James!) thanks all of the people who have been involved in TBB over the years: the many developers at Intel who have left their mark on the library, Alexey Kukanov for sharing insights as we developed this book, the open-source contributors, the technical writers and marketing professionals that have worked on documentation and getting the word out about TBB, the technical consulting engineers and application engineers that have helped people best apply TBB to their problems, the managers who have kept us all on track, and especially the users of TBB that have always provided the feedback on the library and its features that we needed to figure out where

ACKNOWLEDGMENTS

to go next. And most of all, Mike thanks his wife Natalie and their kids, Nick, Ali, and Luke, for their support and patience during the nights and weekends spent on this book.

Rafa thanks his PhD students and colleagues for providing feedback regarding making TBB concepts more gentle and approachable: José Carlos Romero, Francisco Corbera, Alejandro Villegas, Denisa Andreea Constantinescu, Angeles Navarro; particularly to José Daniel García for his engrossing and informative conversations about C++11, 14, 17, and 20, to Aleksei Fedotov and Pablo Reble for helping with the OpenCL_ node examples, and especially his wife Angeles Navarro for her support and for taking over some of his duties when he was mainly focused on the book.

James thanks his wife Susan Meredith – her patient and continuous support was essential to making this book a possibility. Additionally, her detailed editing, which often added so much red ink on a page that the original text was hard to find, made her one of our valued reviewers.

As coauthors, we cannot adequately thank each other enough. Mike and James have known each other for years at Intel and feel fortunate to have come together on this book project. It is difficult to adequately say how much Mike and James appreciate Rafa! How lucky his students are to have such an energetic and knowledgeable professor! Without Rafa, this book would have been much less lively and fun to read. Rafa's command of TBB made this book much better, and his command of the English language helped correct the native English speakers (Mike and James) more than a few times. The three of us enjoyed working on this book together, and we definitely spurred each other on to great heights. It has been an excellent collaboration.

We thank Todd Green who initially brought us to Apress. We thank Natalie Pao, of Apress, and John Somoza, of Intel, who cemented the terms between Intel and Apress on this project. We appreciate the hard work by the entire Apress team through contract, editing, and production.

Thank you all,

Mike Voss, Rafael Asenjo, and James Reinders

Preface

Think Parallel

We have aimed to make this book useful for those who are new to parallel programming as well as those who are expert in parallel programming. We have also made this book approachable for those who are comfortable only with C programming, as well as those who are fluent in C++.

In order to address this diverse audience without "dumbing down" the book, we have written this Preface to level the playing field.

What Is TBB

TBB is a solution for writing parallel programs in C++ which has become the most popular, and extensive, support for parallel programming in C++. It is widely used and very popular for a good reason. More than 10 years old, TBB has stood the test of time and has been influential in the inclusion of parallel programming support in the C++ standard. While C++11 made major additions for parallel programming, and C++17 and C++2x take that ever further, most of what TBB offers is much more than what belongs in a language standard. TBB was introduced in 2006, so it contains support for pre-C++11 compilers. We have simplified matters by taking a modern look at TBB and assuming C++11. Common advice today is "if you don't have a C++11 compiler, get one." Compared with the 2007 book on TBB, we think C++11, with lambda support in particular, makes TBB both richer and easier to understand and use.

TBB is simply the best way to write a parallel program in C++, and we hope to help you be very productive in using TBB.

Organization of the Book and Preface

This book is organized into four major sections:

I. Preface: Background and fundamentals useful for understanding the remainder of the book. Includes motivations for the TBB parallel programming model, an introduction to parallel programming, an introduction to locality and caches, an introduction to vectorization (SIMD), and an introduction to the features of C++ (beyond those in the C language) which are supported or used by TBB.

II. Chapters 1–8: A book on TBB in its own right. Includes an introduction to TBB sufficient to do a great deal of effective parallel programming.

III. Chapters 9–20: Include special topics that give a deeper understanding of TBB and parallel programming and deal with nuances in both.

IV. Appendices A and B and Glossary: A collection of useful information about TBB that you may find interesting, including history (Appendix A) and a complete reference guide (Appendix B).

Think Parallel

For those new to parallel programming, we offer this Preface to provide a foundation that will make the remainder of the book more useful, approachable, and self-contained. We have attempted to assume only a basic understanding of C programming and introduce the key elements of C++ that TBB relies upon and supports. We introduce parallel programming from a practical standpoint that emphasizes what makes parallel programs most effective. For experienced parallel programmers, we hope this Preface will be a quick read that provides a useful refresher on the key vocabulary and thinking that allow us to make the most of parallel computer hardware.

After reading this Preface, you should be able to explain what it means to "Think Parallel" in terms of decomposition, scaling, correctness, abstraction, and patterns. You will appreciate that locality is a key concern for all parallel programming. You will understand the philosophy of supporting task programming instead of thread programming – *a revolutionary development in parallel programming supported by TBB*. You will also understand the elements of C++ programming that are needed above and beyond a knowledge of C in order to use TBB well.

The remainder of this Preface contains five parts:

(1)   An explanation of the motivations behind TBB (begins on page xxi)

(2)   An introduction to parallel programming (begins on page xxvi)

(3)   An introduction to locality and caches – we call "Locality and the Revenge of the Caches" – the one aspect of hardware that we feel essential to comprehend for top performance with parallel programming (begins on page lii)

(4)   An introduction to vectorization (SIMD) (begins on page lx)

(5)   An introduction to the features of C++ (beyond those in the C language) which are supported or used by TBB (begins on page lxii)

Motivations Behind Threading Building Blocks (TBB)

TBB first appeared in 2006. It was the product of experts in parallel programming at Intel, many of whom had decades of experience in parallel programming models, including OpenMP. Many members of the TBB team had previously spent years helping drive OpenMP to the great success it enjoys by developing and supporting OpenMP implementations. Appendix A is dedicated to a deeper dive on the history of TBB and the core concepts that go into it, including the breakthrough concept of task-stealing schedulers.

Born in the early days of multicore processors, TBB quickly emerged as the most popular parallel programming model for C++ programmers. TBB has evolved over its first decade to incorporate a rich set of additions that have made it an obvious choice for parallel programming for novices and experts alike. As an open source project, TBB has enjoyed feedback and contributions from around the world.

TBB promotes a revolutionary idea: parallel programming should enable the programmer to expose opportunities for parallelism without hesitation, and the underlying programming model implementation (TBB) should map that to the hardware at runtime.

Understanding the importance and value of TBB rests on understanding three things: (1) program using tasks, not threads; (2) parallel programming models do not need to be messy; and (3) how to obtain scaling, performance, and performance portability with portable low overhead parallel programming models such as TBB. We will dive into each of these three next because they are so important! It is safe to say that the importance of these were underestimated for a long time before emerging as cornerstones in our understanding of how to achieve effective, and structured, parallel programming.

Program Using Tasks Not Threads

Parallel programming should always be done in terms of *tasks*, not *threads*. We cite an authoritative and in-depth examination of this by Edward Lee at the end of this Preface. In 2006, he observed that "For concurrent programming to become mainstream, we must discard threads as a programming model."

Parallel programming expressed with *threads* is an exercise in mapping an application to the specific number of parallel execution threads on the machine we happen to run upon. Parallel programming expressed with *tasks* is an exercise in exposing opportunities for parallelism and allowing a runtime (e.g., TBB runtime) to map tasks onto the hardware at runtime without complicating the logic of our application.

Threads represent an execution stream that executes on a hardware thread for a time slice and may be assigned other hardware threads for a future time slice. Parallel programming in terms of threads fail because they are too often used as a one-to-one correspondence between threads (as in execution threads) and threads (as in hardware threads, e.g., processor cores). A hardware thread is a physical capability, and the number of hardware threads available varies from machine to machine, as do some subtle characteristics of various thread implementations.

In contrast, *tasks* represent *opportunities* for parallelism. The ability to subdivide tasks can be exploited, as needed, to fill available threads when needed.

With these definitions in mind, a program written in terms of threads would have to map each algorithm onto specific systems of hardware and software. This is not only a distraction, it causes a whole host of issues that make parallel programming more difficult, less effective, and far less portable.

Whereas, a program written in terms of tasks allows a runtime mechanism, for example, the TBB runtime, to map tasks onto the hardware which is actually present at runtime. This removes the distraction of worrying about the number of actual hardware threads available on a system. More importantly, in practice this is the only method which opens up nested parallelism effectively. This is such an important capability, that we will revisit and emphasize the importance of nested parallelism in several chapters.

Composability: Parallel Programming Does Not Have to Be Messy

TBB offers *composability* for parallel programming, and that changes everything. Composability means we can mix and match features of TBB without restriction. Most notably, this includes nesting. Therefore, it makes perfect sense to have a `parallel_for` inside a `parallel_for` loop. It is also okay for a `parallel_for` to call a subroutine, which then has a `parallel_for` within it.

Supporting composable nested parallelism turns out to be highly desirable because it exposes more opportunities for parallelism, and that results in more scalable applications. OpenMP, for instance, is not composable with respect to nesting because each level of nesting can easily cause significant overhead and consumption of resources leading to exhaustion and program termination. This is a huge problem when you consider that a library routine may contain parallel code, so we may experience issues using a non-composable technique if we call the library while already doing parallelism. No such problem exists with TBB, because it is composable. TBB solves this, in part, by letting use expose opportunities for parallelism (tasks) while TBB decides at runtime how to map them to hardware (threads).

This is the key benefit to coding in terms of tasks (available but nonmandatory parallelism (see "relaxed sequential semantics" in Chapter 2)) instead of threads (mandatory parallelism). If a `parallel_for` was considered mandatory, nesting would cause an explosion of threads which causes a whole host of resource issues which can easily (and often do) crash programs when not controlled. When `parallel_for` exposes available nonmandatory parallelism, the runtime is free to use that information to match the capabilities of the machine in the most effective manner.

We have come to expect composability in our programming languages, but most parallel programming models have failed to preserve it (fortunately, TBB does preserve composability!). Consider "if" and "while" statements. The C and C++ languages allow them to freely mix and nest as we desire. Imagine this was not so, and we lived in a world where a function called from within an if statement was forbidden to contain a while statement! Hopefully, any suggestion of such a restriction seems almost silly. TBB brings this type of composability to *parallel programming* by allowing parallel constructs to be freely mixed and nested without restrictions, and without causing issues.

Scaling, Performance, and Quest for Performance Portability

Perhaps the most important benefit of programming with TBB is that it helps create a performance portable application. We define performance portability as the characteristic that allows a program to maintain a similar "percentage of peak performance" across a variety of machines (different hardware, different operating systems, or both). We would like to achieve a high percentage of peak performance on many different machines without the need to change our code.

We would also like to see a 16× gain in performance on a 64-core machine vs. a quad-core machine. For a variety of reasons, we will almost never see ideal speedup (never say never: sometimes, due to an increase in aggregate cache size we can see more than ideal speedup – a condition we call superlinear speedup).

WHAT IS SPEEDUP?

Speedup is formerly defined to be the time to run sequentially (not in parallel) divided by the time to run in parallel. If my program runs in 3 seconds normally, but in only 1 second on a quad-core processor, we would say it has a speedup of 3×. Sometimes, we might speak of efficiency which is speedup divided by the number of processing cores. Our 3× would be 75% efficient at using the parallelism.

The ideal goal of a 16× gain in performance when moving from a quad-core machine to one with 64 cores is called linear *scaling* or perfect *scaling*.

To accomplish this, we need to keep all the cores busy as we grow their numbers – something that requires considerable available parallelism. We will dive more into this concept of "available parallelism" starting on page xxxvii when we discuss Amdahl's Law and its implications.

For now, it is important to know that TBB supports high-performance programming and helps significantly with performance portability. The high-performance support comes because TBB introduces essentially no overhead which allows scaling to proceed without issue. Performance portability lets our application harness available parallelism as new machines offer more.

In our confident claims here, we are assuming a world where the slight additional overhead of dynamic task scheduling is the most effective at exposing the parallelism and exploiting it. This assumption has one fault: if we can program an application to perfectly match the hardware, without any dynamic adjustments, we may find a few percentage points gain in performance. Traditional High-Performance Computing (HPC) programming, the name given to programming the world's largest computers for intense computations, has long had this characteristic in highly parallel scientific computations. HPC developer who utilize OpenMP with static scheduling, and find it does well with their performance, may find the dynamic nature of TBB to be a slight reduction in performance. Any advantage previously seen from such static scheduling is becoming rarer for a variety of reasons. All programming including HPC programming, is increasing in complexity in a way that demands support for nested and dynamic parallelism support. We see this in all aspects of HPC programming as well, including growth to multiphysics models, introduction of AI (artificial intelligence), and use of ML (machine learning) methods. One key driver of additional complexity is the increasing diversity of hardware, leading to heterogeneous compute capabilities within a single machine. TBB gives us powerful options for dealing with these complexities, including its flow graph features which we will dive into in Chapter 3.

It is clear that effective parallel programming requires a separation between exposing parallelism in the form of tasks (programmer's responsibility) and mapping tasks to hardware threads (programming model implementation's responsibility).

Introduction to Parallel Programming

Before we dive into demystifying the terminology and key concepts behind parallel programming, we will make a bold claim: parallel is more intuitive than sequential. Parallelism is around us every day in our lives, and being able to do a single thing step by step is a luxury we seldom enjoy or expect. Parallelism is not unknown to us and should not be unknown in our programming.

Parallelism Is All Around Us

In everyday life, we find ourselves thinking about parallelism. Here are a few examples:

- Long lines: When you have to wait in a long line, you have undoubtedly wished there were multiple shorter (faster) lines, or multiple people at the front of the line helping serve customers more quickly. Grocery store check-out lines, lines to get train tickets, and lines to buy coffee are all examples.

- Lots of repetitive work: When you have a big task to do, which many people could help with at the same time, you have undoubtedly wished for more people to help you. Moving all your possessions from an old dwelling to a new one, stuffing letters in envelopes for a mass mailing, and installing the same software on each new computer in your lab are examples. The proverb "*Many hands make light work*" holds true for computers too.

Once you dig in and start using parallelism, you will Think Parallel. You will learn to think first about the parallelism in your project, and only then think about coding it.

Yale Pat, famous computer architect, observed:

A Conventional Wisdom Problem is the belief that

Thinking in Parallel is Hard

Perhaps (All) Thinking is Hard!

How do we get people to believe that:

Thinking in parallel is natural

(we could not agree more!)

Concurrent vs. Parallel

It is worth noting that the terms *concurrent* and *parallel* are related, but subtly different. Concurrent simply means "happening during the same time span" whereas parallel is more specific and is taken to mean "happening at the same time (at least some of the time)." Concurrency is more like what a single person tries to do when multitasking, whereas parallel is akin to what multiple people can do together. Figure P-1 illustrates the concepts of concurrency vs. parallelism. When we create effective parallel programs, we are aiming to accomplish more than just concurrency. In general, speaking of concurrency will mean there is not an expectation for a great deal of activity to be truly parallel – which means that two workers are not necessarily getting more work done than one could in theory (see tasks A and B in Figure P-1). Since the work is not done sooner, concurrency does not improve the latency of a task (the delay to start a task). Using the term parallel conveys an expectation that we improve latency and throughput (work done in a given time). We explore this in more depth starting on page xxxv when we explore limits of parallelism and discuss the very important concepts of Amdahl's Law.

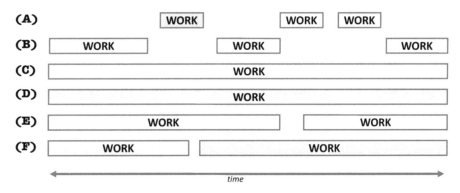

Figure P-1. *Parallel vs. Concurrent: Tasks (A) and (B) are concurrent relative to each other but not parallel relative to each other; all other combinations are both concurrent and parallel*

Enemies of parallelism: locks, shared mutable state, synchronization, not "Thinking Parallel," and forgetting that algorithms win.

Enemies of Parallelism

Bearing in mind *the enemies of parallel programming* will help understand our advocacy for particular programming methods. Key parallel programming enemies include

- Locks: In parallel programming, locks or mutual exclusion objects (mutexes) are used to provide a thread with exclusive access to a resource – blocking other threads from simultaneously accessing the same resource. Locks are the most common explicit way to ensure parallel tasks update shared data in a coordinated fashion (as opposed to allowing pure chaos). We hate locks because they serialize part of our programs, limiting scaling. The sentiment "we hate locks" is on our minds throughout the book. We hope to instill this mantra in you as well, without losing sight of when we must synchronize properly. Hence, a word of caution: we actually do love locks when they are needed, because without them disaster will strike. This love/hate relationship with locks needs to be understood.

- Shared mutable state: Mutable is another word for "can be changed." Shared mutable state happens any time we share data among multiple threads, and we allow it to change while being shared. Such sharing either reduces scaling when synchronization is needed and used correctly, or it leads to correctness issues (race conditions or deadlocks) when synchronization (e.g., a lock) is incorrectly applied. Realistically, we need shared mutable state when we write interesting applications. Thinking about careful handling of shared mutable state may be an easier way to understand the basis of our love/hate relationship with locks. In the end, we all end up "managing" shared mutable state and the mutual exclusion (including locks) to make it work as we wish.

- *Not* "Thinking Parallel": Use of clever bandages and patches will not make up for a poorly thought out strategy for scalable algorithms. Knowing where the parallelism is available, and how it can be exploited, should be considered before implementation. Trying to add parallelism to an application, after it is written, is fraught with peril. Some preexisting code may shift to use parallelism relatively well, but most code will benefit from considerable rethinking of algorithms.

- *Forgetting* that algorithms win: This may just be another way to say "Think Parallel." The choice of algorithms has a profound effect on the scalability of applications. Our choice of algorithms determine how tasks can divide, data structures are accessed, and results are coalesced. The optimal algorithm is really the one which serves as the basis for optimal solution. An optimal solution is a combination of the appropriate algorithm, with the best matching parallel data structure, and the best way to schedule the computation over the data. The search for, and discovery of, algorithms which are better is seemingly unending for all of us as programmers. Now, as parallel programmers, we must add *scalable* to the definition of *better* for an algorithm.

Locks, can't live with them, can't live without them.

Terminology of Parallelism

The vocabulary of parallel programming is something we need to learn in order to converse with other parallel programmers. None of the concepts are particularly hard, but they are very important to internalize. A parallel programmer, like any programmer, spends years gaining a deep intuitive feel for their craft, despite the fundamentals being simple enough to explain.

We will discuss decomposition of work into parallel tasks, scaling terminology, correctness considerations, and the importance of locality due primarily to cache effects.

When we think about our application, how do we find the parallelism?

At the highest level, parallelism exists either in the form of data to operate on in parallel, or in the form of tasks to execute in parallel. And they are *not* mutually exclusive. In a sense, all of the important parallelism is in data parallelism. Nevertheless, we will introduce both because it can be convenient to think of both. When we discuss scaling, and Amdahl's Law, our intense bias to look for *data* parallelism will become more understandable.

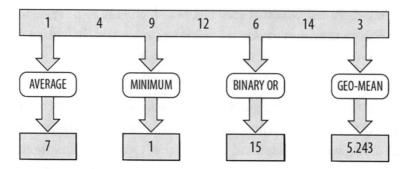

Figure P-2. *Task parallelism*

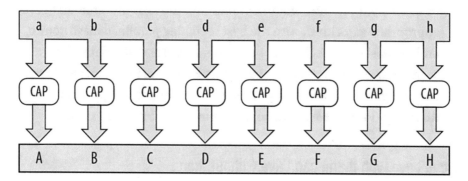

Figure P-3. *Data parallelism*

Terminology: Task Parallelism

Task parallelism refers to different, independent tasks. Figure P-2 illustrates this, showing an example of mathematical operations that can each be applied to the same data set to compute values that are independent. In this case, the average value, the minimum value, the binary OR function, and the geometric mean of the data set are computed. Finding work to do in parallel in terms of task parallelism becomes limited by the number of independent operations we can envision.

Earlier in this Preface, we have been advocating using *tasks* instead of *threads*. As we now discuss *data* vs. *task* parallelism, it may seem a bit confusing because we use the word *task* again in a different context when we compare *task parallelism* vs. *data parallelism*. For either type of parallelism, we will program for either in terms of *tasks* and not *threads*. This is the vocabulary used by parallel programmers.

Terminology: Data Parallelism

Data parallelism (Figure P-3) is easy to picture: take lots of data and apply the same transformation to each piece of the data. In Figure P-3, each letter in the data set is capitalized and becomes the corresponding uppercase letter. This simple example shows that given a data set and an operation that can be applied element by element, we can apply the same task in parallel to each element. Programmers writing code for supercomputers love this sort of problem and consider it so easy to do in parallel that it has been called *embarrassingly parallel*. A word of advice: if you have lots of data parallelism, do not be embarrassed – take advantage of it and be very happy. Consider it *happy parallelism*.

When comparing the effort to find work to do in parallel, an approach that focuses on data parallelism is limited by the amount of data we can grab to process. Approaches based on task parallelism alone are limited by the different task types we program. While both methods are valid and important, it is critical to find parallelism in the data that we process in order to have a truly scalable parallel program. Scalability means that our application can increase in performance as we add hardware (e.g., more processor cores) provided we have enough data. In the age of big data, it turns out that big data and parallel programming are made for each other. It seems that growth in data sizes is a reliable source of additional work. We will revisit this observation, a little later in this Preface, when we discuss Amdahl's Law.

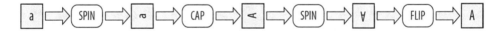

Figure P-4. *Pipeline*

Figure P-5. *Imagine that each position is a different car in different stages of assembly, this is a pipeline in action with data flowing through it*

Terminology: Pipelining

While task parallelism is harder to find than data parallelism, a specific type of task parallelism is worth highlighting: *pipelining*. In this kind of algorithm, many independent tasks need to be applied to a stream of data. Each item is processed by each stage, as shown by the letter A in (Figure P-4). A stream of data can be processed more quickly when we use a pipeline, because different items can pass through different stages at the same time, as shown in Figure P-5. In these examples, the time to get a result may not be faster (referred to as the *latency* measured as the time from input to output) but the *throughput* is greater because it is measured in terms of completions (output) per unit of time. Pipelines enable parallelism to increase *throughput* when compared with a sequential (serial) processing. A pipeline can also be more sophisticated: it can reroute data or skip steps for chosen items. TBB has specific support for simple pipelines (Chapter 2) and very complex pipelines (Chapter 3). Of course, each step in the pipeline can use data or task parallelism as well. The composability of TBB supports this seamlessly.

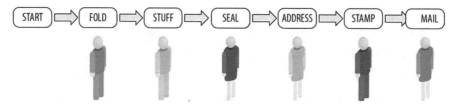

Figure P-6. *Pipelining – each person has a different job*

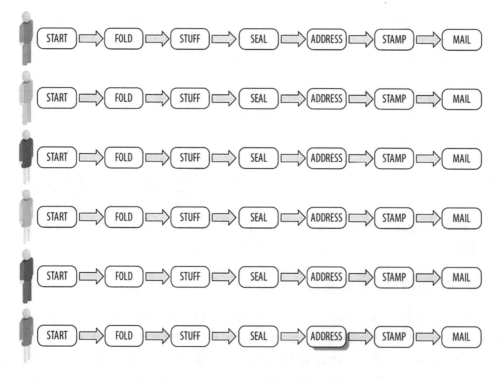

Figure P-7. *Data Parallelism – each person has the same job*

Example of Exploiting Mixed Parallelism

Consider the task of folding, stuffing, sealing, addressing, stamping, and mailing letters. If we assemble a group of six people for the task of stuffing many envelopes, we can arrange each person to specialize in and perform their assigned task in a pipeline fashion (Figure P-6). This contrasts with data parallelism, where we divide up the supplies and give a batch of everything to each person (Figure P-7). Each person then does all the steps on their collection of materials.

Figure P-7 is clearly the right choice if every person has to work in a different location far from each other. That is called *coarse-grained* parallelism because the interactions between the tasks are infrequent (they only come together to collect envelopes, then leave and do their task, including mailing). The other choice shown in Figure P-6 approximates what we call *fine-grained* parallelism because of the frequent interactions (every envelope is passed along to every worker in various steps of the operation).

Neither extreme tends to fit reality, although sometimes they may be close enough to be useful. In our example, it may turn out that addressing an envelope takes enough time to keep three people busy, whereas the first two steps and the last two steps require only one person on each pair of steps to keep up. Figure P-8 illustrates the steps with the corresponding size of the work to be done. We can conclude that if we assigned only one person to each step as we see done in Figure P-6, that we would be "starving" some people in this pipeline of work for things to do – they would be idle. You might say it would be hidden "underemployment." Our solution, to achieve a reasonable balance in our pipeline (Figure P-9) is really a hybrid of data and task parallelism.

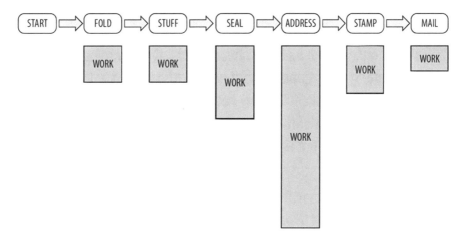

Figure P-8. *Unequal tasks are best combined or split to match people*

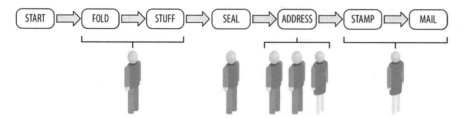

Figure P-9. *Because tasks are not equal, assign more people to addressing letters*

Achieving Parallelism

Coordinating people around the job of preparing and mailing the envelopes is easily expressed by the following two conceptual steps:

1. Assign people to tasks (and feel free to move them around to balance the workload).

2. Start with one person on each of the six tasks but be willing to split up a given task so that two or more people can work on it together.

The six tasks are folding, stuffing, sealing, addressing, stamping, and mailing. We also have six people (resources) to help with the work. That is exactly how TBB works best: we define tasks and data at a level we can explain and then split or combine data to match up with resources available to do the work.

The first step in writing a parallel program is to consider where the parallelism is. Many textbooks wrestle with task and data parallelism as though there were a clear choice. TBB allows any combination of the two that we express.

Far from decrying chaos – we love the chaos of lots of uncoordinated tasks running around getting work done without having to check-in with each other (synchronization). This so-called "loosely coupled" parallel programming is great! More than locks, we hate synchronization because it makes tasks wait for other tasks. Tasks exist to work – not sit around waiting!

If we are lucky, our program will have an abundant amount of data parallelism available for us to exploit. To simplify this work, TBB requires only that we specify tasks and how to split them. For a completely data-parallel task, in TBB we will define one task to which we give all the data. That task will then be split up automatically to use the available hardware parallelism. The implicit synchronization (as opposed to synchronization we directly ask for with coding) will often eliminate the need for using locks to achieve synchronization. Referring back to our enemies list, and the fact that we hate locks, the implicit synchronization is a good thing. What do we mean by "implicit" synchronization? Usually, all we are saying is that synchronization occurred but we did not explicitly code a synchronization. At first, this should seem like a "cheat." After all, synchronization still happened – and someone had to ask for it! In a sense, we are counting on these implicit synchronizations being more carefully planned and implemented. The more we can use the standard methods of TBB, and the less we explicitly write our own locking code, the better off we will be – in general.

By letting TBB manage the work, we hand over the responsibility for splitting up the work and synchronizing when needed. The synchronization done by the library for us, which we call implicit synchronization, in turn often eliminates the need for an explicit coding for synchronization (see Chapter 5).

We strongly suggest starting there, and only venturing into explicit synchronization (Chapter 5) when absolutely necessary or beneficial. We can say, from experience, even when such things seem to be necessary – they are not. You've been warned. If you are like us, you'll ignore the warning occasionally and get burned. We have.

People have been exploring decomposition for decades, and some patterns have emerged. We'll cover this more later when we discuss design patterns for parallel programming.

Effective parallel programming is really about keeping all our tasks busy getting useful work done all the time – and hunting down and eliminating idle time is a key to our goal: scaling to achieve great speedups.

Terminology: Scaling and Speedup

The scalability of a program is a measure of how much speedup the program gets as we add more computing capabilities. Speedup is the ratio of the time it takes to run a program without parallelism vs. the time it takes to run in parallel. A speedup of 4× indicates that the parallel program runs in a quarter of the time of the serial program. An example would be a serial program that takes 100 seconds to run on a one-processor machine and 25 seconds to run on a quad-core machine.

As a goal, we would expect that our program running on two processor cores should run faster than our program running on one processor core. Likewise, running on four processor cores should be faster than running on two cores.

Any program will have a point of diminishing returns for adding parallelism. It is not uncommon for performance to even drop, instead of simply leveling off, if we force the use of too many compute resources. The granularity at which we should stop subdividing a problem can be expressed as a *grain size*. TBB uses a notion of *grain size* to help limit the splitting of data to a reasonable level to avoid this problem of dropping in performance. Grain size is generally determined automatically, by an automatic partitioner within TBB, using a combination of heuristics for an initial guess and dynamic refinements as execution progresses. However, it is possible to explicitly manipulate the grain size settings if we want to do so. We will not encourage this in this book, because we seldom will do better in performance with explicit specifications than the automatic partitioner in TBB, it tends to be somewhat machine specific, and therefore explicitly setting grain size reduces performance portability.

As Thinking Parallel becomes intuitive, structuring problems to scale will become second nature.

How Much Parallelism Is There in an Application?

The topic of how much parallelism there is in an application has gotten considerable debate, and the answer is "it depends."

It certainly depends on the size of the problem to be solved and on the ability to find a suitable algorithm (and data structures) to take advantage of the parallelism. Before multicore processors, this debate centered on making sure we wrote efficient and worthy programs for expensive and rare parallel computers. The definition of size, the efficiency required, and the expense of the computer have all changed with the emergence of multicore processors. We need to step back and be sure we review the ground we are standing on. The world has changed.

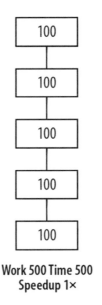

Work 500 Time 500
Speedup 1×

Figure P-10. *Original program without parallelism*

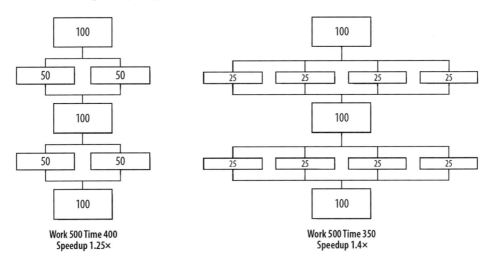

Work 500 Time 400
Speedup 1.25×

Work 500 Time 350
Speedup 1.4×

Figure P-11. *Progress on adding parallelism*

Amdahl's Law

Renowned computer architect, Gene Amdahl, made observations regarding the maximum improvement to a computer system that can be expected when only a portion of the system is improved. His observations in 1967 have come to be known as Amdahl's Law. It tells us that if we speed up everything in a program by 2×, we can expect the resulting program to run 2× faster. However, if we improve the performance of only 2/5th of the program by 2×, the overall system improves only by 1.25×.

Amdahl's Law is easy to visualize. Imagine a program, with five equal parts, that runs in 500 seconds, as shown in Figure P-10. If we can speed up two of the parts by 2× and 4×, as shown in Figure P-11, the 500 seconds are reduced to only 400 (1.25× speedup) and 350 seconds (1.4× speedup), respectively. More and more, we are seeing the limitations of the portions that are not speeding up through parallelism. No matter how many processor cores are available, the serial portions create a barrier at 300 seconds that will not be broken (see Figure P-12) leaving us with only 1.7× speedup. If we are limited to parallel programming in only 2/5th of our execution time, we can never get more than a 1.7× boost in performance!

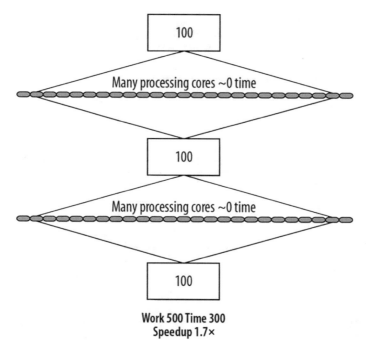

Work 500 Time 300
Speedup 1.7×

Figure P-12. *Limits according to Amdahl's Law*

Parallel programmers have long used Amdahl's Law to predict the maximum speedup that can be expected using multiple processors. This interpretation ultimately tells us that a computer program will never go faster than the sum of the parts that do not run in parallel (the serial portions), no matter how many processors we have.

Many have used Amdahl's Law to predict doom and gloom for parallel computers, but there is another way to look at things that shows much more promise.

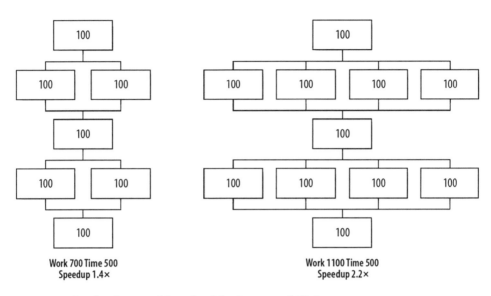

Figure P-13. *Scale the workload with the capabilities*

Gustafson's Observations Regarding Amdahl's Law

Amdahl's Law views programs as fixed, while we make changes to the computer. But experience seems to indicate that as computers get new capabilities, applications change to take advantage of these features. Most of today's applications would not run on computers from 10 years ago, and many would run poorly on machines that are just 5 years old. This observation is not limited to obvious applications such as video games; it applies also to office applications, web browsers, photography, and video editing software.

More than two decades after the appearance of Amdahl's Law, John Gustafson, while at Sandia National Labs, took a different approach and suggested a reevaluation of Amdahl's Law. Gustafson noted that parallelism is more useful when we observe that workloads grow over time. This means that as computers have become more powerful, we have asked them to do more work, rather than staying focused on an unchanging workload. For many problems, as the problem size grows, the work required for the parallel part of the problem grows faster than the part that cannot be parallelized (the serial part). Hence, as the problem size grows, the serial fraction decreases, and, according to Amdahl's Law, the scalability improves. We can start with an application that looks like Figure P-10, but if the problem scales with the available parallelism, we are likely to see the advancements illustrated in Figure P-13. If the sequential parts still take the same amount of time to perform, they become less and less important as a percentage of the whole. The algorithm eventually reaches the conclusion shown in Figure P-14. Performance grows at the same rate as the number of processors, which is called linear or order of n scaling, denoted as O(n).

Even in our example, the efficiency of the program is still greatly limited by the serial parts. The efficiency of using processors in our example is about 40% for large numbers of processors. On a supercomputer, this might be a terrible waste. On a system with multicore processors, one can hope that other work is running on the computer in parallel to use the processing power our application does not use. This new world has many complexities. In any case, it is still good to minimize serial code, whether we take the "glass half empty" view and favor Amdahl's Law or we lean toward the "glass half full" view and favor Gustafson's observations.

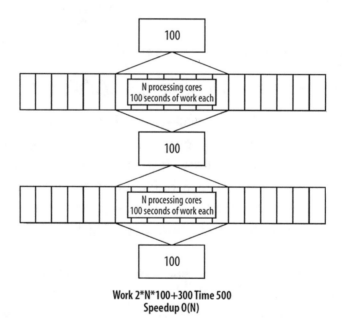

Figure P-14. *Gustafson saw a path to scaling*

Both Amdahl's Law and Gustafson's observations are correct, and they are not at odds. They highlight a different way to look at the same phenomenon. Amdahl's Law cautions us that if we simply want an existing program to run faster with the same workload, we will be severely limited by our serial code. When we envision working on a larger workload, Gustafson has pointed out we have hope. History clearly favors programs getting more complex and solving larger problems, and this is when parallel programming pays off.

The value of parallelism is easier to prove if we are looking forward than if we assume the world is not changing.

Making today's application run faster by switching to a parallel algorithm without expanding the problem is harder than making it run faster on a larger problem. The value of parallelism is easier to prove when we are not constrained to speeding up an application that already works well on today's machines.

Some have defined scaling that requires the problem size to grow as *weak scaling*. It is ironic that the term *embarrassingly parallel* is commonly applied to other types of scaling, or *strong scaling*. Because almost all true scaling happens only when the problem size scales with the parallelism available, we should just call that *scaling*. Nevertheless, it is common to apply the term *embarrassing scaling* or *strong scaling* to scaling that occurs without growth in the problem size and refer to scaling that depends on expanding data sizes as *weak scaling*. As with embarrassing parallelism, when we have embarrassing scaling, we gladly take advantage of it and we are not embarrassed. We generally expect scaling to be the so-called *weak scaling*, and we are happy to know that any scaling is good and we will simply say that our algorithms *scale* in such cases.

The scalability of an application comes down to increasing the work done in parallel and minimizing the work done serially. Amdahl motivates us to reduce the serial portion, whereas Gustafson tells us to consider larger problems.

What Did They Really Say?

Here is what Amdahl and Gustafson actually said in their famous papers, which have generated much dialog ever since:

> *...the effort expended on achieving high parallel processing rates is wasted unless it is accompanied by achievements in sequential processing rates of very nearly the same magnitude.*
>
> —Amdahl, 1967

> *...speedup should be measured by scaling the problem to the number of processors, not by fixing the problem size.*
>
> —Gustafson, 1988

Serial vs. Parallel Algorithms

One of the truths in programming is this: the best serial algorithm is seldom the best parallel algorithm, and the best parallel algorithm is seldom the best serial algorithm.

This means that trying to write a program that runs well on a system with one processor core, and also runs well on a system with a dual-core processor or quad-core processor, is harder than just writing a good serial program or a good parallel program.

Supercomputer programmers know from practice that the work required grows quickly as a function of the problem size. If the work grows faster than the sequential overhead (e.g., communication, synchronization), we can fix a program that scales poorly just by increasing the problem size. It's not uncommon at all to take a program that won't scale much beyond 100 processors and scale it nicely to 300 or more processors just by doubling the size of the problem.

Strong scaling means we can solve the same problem faster on a parallel system. Weak scaling means we can solve more interesting problems using multiple cores in the same amount of time that we solved the less interesting problems using a single core.

To be ready for the future, write parallel programs and abandon the past. That's the simplest and best advice to offer. Writing code with one foot in the world of efficient single-threaded performance and the other foot in the world of parallelism is the hardest job of all.

One of the truths in programming is this: the best serial algorithm is seldom the best parallel algorithm, and the best parallel algorithm is seldom the best serial algorithm.

What Is a Thread?

If you know what a thread is, feel free to skip ahead to the section "Safety in the Presence of Concurrency." It's important to be comfortable with the concept of a thread, even though the goal of TBB is to abstract away thread management. Fundamentally, we will still be constructing a threaded program, and we will need to understand the implications of this underlying implementation.

All modern operating systems are multitasking operating systems that typically use a preemptive scheduler. Multitasking means that more than one program can be active at a time. We may take it for granted that we can have an e-mail program and a web browser program running at the same time. Yet, not that long ago, this was not the case.

A preemptive scheduler means the operating system puts a limit on how long one program can use a processor core before it is forced to let another program use it. This is how the operating system makes it appear that our e-mail program and our web browser are running at the same time when only one processor core is actually doing the work.

Generally, each program runs relatively independent of other programs. In particular, the memory where our program variables will reside is completely separate from the memory used by other processes. Our e-mail program cannot directly assign a new value to a variable in the web browser program. If our e-mail program can communicate with our web browser – for instance, to have it open a web page from a link we received in e-mail – it does so with some form of communication that takes much more time than a memory access.

This isolation of programs from each other has value and is a mainstay of computing today. Within a program, we can allow multiple threads of execution to exist in a single program. An operating system will refer to the program as a *process*, and the threads of execution as (operating system) *threads*.

All modern operating systems support the subdivision of processes into multiple threads of execution. Threads run independently, like processes, and no thread knows what other threads are running or where they are in the program unless they synchronize explicitly. The key difference between threads and processes is that the threads within a process share all the data of the process. Thus, a simple memory access can set a variable in another thread. We will refer to this as "shared mutable state" (changeable memory locations that are shared) – and we will decry the pain that sharing can cause in this book. Managing the sharing of data, is a multifaceted problem that we included in our list of enemies of parallel programming. We will revisit this challenge, and solutions, repeatedly in this book.

We will note, that it is common to have shared mutable state between processes. It could be memory that each thread maps into their memory space explicitly, or it could be data in an external store such as a database. A common example would be airline reservation systems, which can independently work with different customers to book their reservations – but ultimately, they share a database of flights and available seats. Therefore, you should know that many of the concepts we discuss for a single process can easily come up in more complex situations. Learning to think parallel has benefits beyond TBB! Nevertheless, TBB is almost always used within a single process with multiple threads, with only some flow graphs (Chapter 3) having some implications beyond a single process.

Each thread has its own *instruction pointer* (a register pointing to the place in the program where it is running) and stack (a region of memory that holds subroutine return addresses and local variables for subroutines), but otherwise a thread shares its memory with all of the other threads in the same process. Even the stack memory of each thread is accessible to the other threads, though when they are programmed properly, they don't step on each other's stacks.

Threads within a process that run independently but share memory have the obvious benefit of being able to share work quickly, because each thread has access to the same memory as the other threads in the same process. The operating system can view multiple threads as multiple processes that have essentially the same permissions to regions of memory. As we mentioned, this is both a blessing and a curse – this "shared mutable state."

Programming Threads

A process usually starts with a single thread of execution and is allowed to request that more threads be started. Threads can be used to logically decompose a program into multiple tasks, such as a user interface and a main program. Threads are also useful for programming for parallelism, such as with multicore processors.

Many questions arise when we start programming to use threads. How should we divide and assign tasks to keep each available processor core busy? Should we create a thread each time we have a new task, or should we create and manage a pool of threads? Should the number of threads depend on the number of cores? What should we do with a thread running out of tasks?

These are important questions for the implementation of multitasking, but that doesn't mean we should answer them. They detract from the objective of expressing the goals of our program. Likewise, assembly language programmers once had to worry about memory alignment, memory layout, stack pointers, and register assignments. Languages such as Fortran and C were created to abstract away those important details and leave them to be solved by compilers and libraries. Similarly, today we seek to abstract away thread management so that programmers can express parallelism directly.

TBB allows programmers to express parallelism at a higher level of abstraction. When used properly, TBB code is implicitly parallel.

A key notion of TBB is that we should break up the program into many more tasks than there are processors. We should specify as much parallelism as practical and let TBB runtime choose how much of that parallelism is actually exploited.

What Is SIMD?

Threading is not the only way for a processor to do more than one thing at a time! A single instruction can do the same operation on multiple data items. Such instructions are often called vector instructions, and their use is called vectorization of code (or vectorization for short). The technique is often referred to as Single Instruction Multiple Data (SIMD). The use of vector instructions to do multiple things at once is an important topic which we will discuss later in this Preface (starting on page lxi).

Safety in the Presence of Concurrency

When code is written in such a way that runs may have problems due to the concurrency, it is said not to be thread-safe. Even with the abstraction that TBB offers, the concept of thread safety is essential. Thread-safe code is code that is written in a manner to ensures it will function as desired even when multiple threads use the same code. Common mistakes that make code not thread-safe include lack of synchronization to control access to shared data during updates (this can lead to corruption) and improper use of synchronization (can lead to deadlock, which we discuss in a few pages).

Any function that maintains a persistent state between invocations requires careful writing to ensure it is thread-safe. We need only to do this to functions that might be used concurrently. In general, functions we may use concurrently should be written to have no side effects so that concurrent use is not an issue. In cases where global side effects are truly needed, such as setting a single variable or creating a file, we must be careful to call for mutual exclusion to ensure only one thread at a time can execute the code that has the side effect.

We need to be sure to use thread-safe libraries for any code using concurrency or parallelism. All the libraries we use should be reviewed to make sure they are thread-safe. The C++ library has some functions inherited from C that are particular problems because they hold internal state between calls, specifically `asctime`, `ctime`, `gmtime`, `localtime`, `rand`, and `strtok`. We need to check the documentation when using these functions to see whether thread-safe versions are available. The C++ Standard Template Library (STL) container classes are, in general, not thread-safe (see Chapter 6 for some current container solutions from TBB for this problem, or Chapter 5 for synchronization to use in conjunction with items that are otherwise not thread-safe).

Mutual Exclusion and Locks

We need to think about whether concurrent accesses to the same resources will occur in our program. The resource we will most often be concerned with is data held in memory, but we also need to think about files and I/O of all kinds.

If the precise order that updates of shared data matters, then we need some form of synchronization. The best policy is to decompose our problem in such a way that synchronization is infrequent. We can achieve this by breaking up the tasks so that they can work independently, and the only synchronization that occurs is waiting for all the tasks to be completed at the end. This synchronization "when all tasks are complete" is commonly called a barrier synchronization. Barriers work when we have very coarse-grained parallelism because barriers cause all parallel work to stop (go serial) for a moment. If we do that too often, we lose scalability very quickly per Amdahl's Law.

For finer-grained parallelism, we need to use synchronization around data structures, to restrict both reading and writing by others, while we are writing. If we are updating memory based on a prior value from memory, such as incrementing a counter by ten, we would restrict reading and writing from the time that we start reading the initial value until we have finished writing the newly computed value. We illustrate a simple way to do this in Figure P-15. If we are only reading, but we read multiple related data, we would use synchronization around data structures to restrict writing while we read. These restrictions apply to other tasks and are known as *mutual exclusion*. The purpose of *mutual exclusion* is to make a set of operations appear *atomic* (indivisible).

TBB implements portable mechanisms for *mutual exclusion*. There are fundamentally two approaches: atomic (indivisible) operations for very simple and common operations (such as increment), and a general lock/unlock mechanism for longer sequences of code. These are all discussed in Chapter 5.

Thread A	Thread B	Value of X
LOCK (X)	*(wait)*	44
Read X (44)	*(wait)*	44
add 10	*(wait)*	44
Write X (54)	*(wait)*	54
UNLOCK (X)	*(wait)*	54
	LOCK (X)	54
	Read X (54)	54
	subtract 12	54
	Write X (42)	42
	UNLOCK (X)	**42**

Figure P-15. *Serialization that can occur when using mutual exclusion*

Consider a program with two threads that starts with X = 44. Thread A executes X = X + 10. Thread B executes X = X - 12. If we add locking (Figure P-15) so that only Thread A or Thread B can execute its statement at a time, we always end up with X = 42. If both threads try to obtain a lock at the same time, one will be excluded and will have to wait before the lock is granted. Figure P-15 shows how long Thread B might have to wait if it requested the lock at the same time as Thread A but did not get the lock because Thread A held it first.

Instead of locks, which are used in Figure P-15, we could use a small set of operations that the system guarantees to appear to be *atomic* (indivisible). We showed locks first, because they are a general mechanism that allows any sequence of code to appear to be atomic. We should always keep such sequences as short as possible because they degrade scaling per Amdahl's Law (see page xxxvi). If a specific atomic operation (e.g., increment) is available, we would use that because it should be the quickest method and therefore degrade scaling the least.

Thread A	Thread B	Value of X
	Read X (44)	44
	subtract 12	44
	Write X (32)	32
Read X (32)		32
add 10		32
Write X (42)		**42**

Thread A	Thread B	Value of X
Read X (44)		44
add 10	Read X (44)	44
Write X (54)	subtract 12	54
	Write X (32)	**32**

Thread A	Thread B	Value of X
	Read X (44)	44
Read X (44)	subtract 12	44
add 10	Write X (32)	32
Write X (54)		**54**

RACE – A first, B second   DESIRED   RACE – B first, A second

Figure P-16. *Race conditions can lead to problems when we have no mutual exclusion. A simple fix here would be to replace each Read-operation-Write with the appropriate atomic operation (atomic increment or atomic decrement).*

As much as we hate locks, we need to concede that without them, things are even worse. Consider our example without the locks, a *race condition* exists and at least two more results are possible: X=32 or X=54 (Figure P-16). We will define this very important concept of *race condition* very soon starting on page l. The additional incorrect results are now possible because each statement reads X, does a computation, and writes to X. Without locking, there is no guarantee that a thread reads the value of X before or after the other thread writes a value.

Correctness

The biggest challenge of learning to Think Parallel is understanding correctness as it relates to concurrency. Concurrency means we have multiple threads of control that may be active at one time. The operating system is free to schedule those threads in different ways. Each time the program runs, the precise order of operations will potentially be different. Our challenge as a programmer is to make sure that every legitimate way the operations in our concurrent program can be ordered will still lead to the correct result. A high-level abstraction such as TBB helps a great deal, but there are a few issues we have to grapple with on our own: potential variations in results when programs compute results in parallel, and new types of programming bugs when locks are used incorrectly.

Computations done in parallel often get different results than the original sequential program. Round-off errors are the most common surprise for many programmers when a program is modified to run in parallel. We should expect numeric results, when using floating-point values, to vary when computations are changed to run in parallel because floating-point values have limited precision. For example, computing (A+B+C+D) as ((A+B)+(C+D)) enables A+B and C+D to be computed in parallel, but the final sum may be different from other evaluations such as $(((A+B)+C)+D)$. Even the parallel results can differ from run to run, depending on the order of the operations actually taken during program execution. Such nondeterministic behavior can often be controlled by reducing runtime flexibility. We will mention such options in this book, in particular the options for deterministic reduction operations (Chapter 16). Nondeterminism can make debugging and testing much more difficult, so it is often desirable to force deterministic behavior. Depending on the circumstances, this can reduce performance because it effectively forces more synchronization.

A few types of program failures can happen only in a program using concurrency because they involve the coordination of tasks. These failures are known as *deadlocks* and *race conditions*. Determinism is also a challenge since a concurrent program has many possible paths of execution because there can be so many tasks operating independently.

Although TBB simplifies programming so as to reduce the chance for such failures, they are still possible even with TBB. Multithreaded programs can be nondeterministic as a result of race conditions, which means the same program with the same input can follow different execution paths each time it is invoked. When this occurs, failures do not repeat consistently, and debugger intrusions can easily change the failure, thereby making debugging frustrating, to say the least.

Tracking down and eliminating the source of unwanted nondeterminism is not easy. Specialized tools such as Intel Advisor can help, but the first step is to understand these issues and try to avoid them.

There is also another very common problem, which is also an implication of nondeterminism, when moving from sequential code to parallel code: instability in results. Instability in results means that we get different results because of subtle changes in the order in which work is done. Some algorithms may be unstable, whereas others simply exercise the opportunity to reorder operations that are considered to have multiple correct orderings.

Next, we explain three key errors in parallel programming and solutions for each.

Deadlock

Deadlock occurs when at least two tasks wait for each other and each will not resume until the other task proceeds. This happens easily when code requires the acquisition of multiple locks. If Task A needs Lock R and Lock X, it might get Lock R and then try to get Lock X. Meanwhile, if Task B needs the same two locks but grabs Lock X first, we can easily end up with Task A wanting Lock X while holding Lock R, and Task B waiting for Lock R while it holds only Lock X. The resulting impasse can be resolved only if one task releases the lock it is holding. If neither task yields, deadlock occurs and the tasks are stuck forever.

Solution for Deadlock

Use implicit synchronization to avoid the need for locks. In general, avoid using locks, especially multiple locks at one time. Acquiring a lock and then invoking a function or subroutine that happens to use locks is often the source of multiple lock issues. Because access to shared resources must sometimes occur, the two most common solutions are to acquire locks in a certain order (always A and then B, for instance) or to release all locks whenever any lock cannot be acquired and begin again (after a random length delay).

Race Conditions

A race condition occurs when multiple tasks read from and write to the same memory without proper synchronization. The "race" may finish correctly sometimes and therefore complete without errors, and at other times it may finish incorrectly. Figure P-16 illustrates a simple example with three different possible outcomes due to a race condition.

Race conditions are less catastrophic than deadlocks, but more pernicious because they do not necessarily produce obvious failures and yet can lead to corrupted data (an incorrect value being read or written). The result of some race conditions can be a state unexpected (and undesirable) because more than one thread may succeed in updating only part of their state (multiple data elements).

Solution for Race Conditions

Manage shared data in a disciplined manner using the synchronization mechanisms described in Chapter 5 to ensure a correct program. Avoid low-level methods based on locks because it is so easy to get things wrong. Explicit locks should be used only as a last resort. In general, we are better off using the synchronization implied by the algorithm templates and task scheduler when possible. For instance, use parallel_ reduce (Chapter 2) instead of creating our own with shared variables. The join operation in `parallel_reduce` is guaranteed not to run until the subproblems it is joining are completed.

Instability of Results (Lack of Deterministic Results)

A parallel program will generally compute answers differently each time because it the many concurrent tasks operate with slight variations between different invocations, and especially on systems with differing number of processors. We explained this in our discussion of correctness starting on page xlviii.

Solution for Instability of Results

TBB offers ways to ensure more deterministic behavior by reducing runtime flexibility. While this can reduce performance somewhat, the benefits of determinism are often worth it. Determinism is discussed in Chapter 16.

Abstraction

When writing a program, choosing an appropriate level of abstraction is important. Few programmers use assembly language anymore. Programming languages such as C and C++ have abstracted away the low-level details. Hardly anyone misses the old programming method.

Parallelism is no different. We can easily get caught up in writing code that is too low level. Raw thread programming requires us to manage threads, which is time-consuming and error-prone.

Programming with TBB offers an opportunity to avoid thread management. This will result in code that is easier to create, easier to maintain, and more elegant. In practice, we find that this code is also more portable and performance portable. However, it does require thinking of algorithms in terms of what work can be divided and how data can be divided.

Patterns

Experienced parallel programmers know that there are common problems for which there are known solutions. All types of programming are like this – we have concepts such as stacks, queues, and linked lists in our vocabulary as a result. Parallel programming brings forward concepts such as map, reduce, and pipeline.

We call these *patterns*, and they can be adapted to our particular needs. Learning common patterns is a perfect way to learn from those who have gone before us. TBB implements solutions for key patterns, so we can implicitly learn them simply by learning TBB. We think patterns are an important enough concept, that we will discuss them in more depth in Chapter 8.

Locality and the Revenge of the Caches

Effective parallel programming requires that we have a sense of the importance of *locality*. The motivation for this requires that we speak briefly about the hardware, in particular memory *caches*. A "cache" is simply a hardware buffer of sorts that retains data we have recently seen or modified, closer to us so it can be accessed faster than if it was in the larger memory. The purpose of a cache is to make things faster, and therefore if our program makes better usage of caches our application may run faster.

We say "caches" instead of "cache" because modern computer design generally consists of multiple levels of caching hardware, each level of which is a cache. For our purposes, thinking of cache as a single collection of data is generally sufficient.

We do not need to understand *caches* deeply, but a high-level understanding of them helps us understand locality, the related issues with *sharing* of *mutable state*, and the particularly insidious phenomenon known as *false sharing*.

Important cache implications we must understand: locality, sharing and false-sharing. To understand these – we must understand caches and cache-lines. These are fundamental to all modern computer designs.

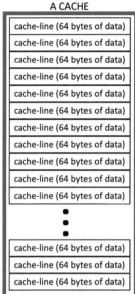

MAIN MEMORY

Memory is *much* larger than a cache.

Memory is *much* slower than a cache.

Lines in the cache hold copies of lines from locations scattered around the memory.

Lines are moved in/out of cache as needed for the more recent needs of the processing of data that is occurring.

A CACHE

cache-line (64 bytes of data)

It is sufficient for our purposes to consider caches as a single item and not worry about terms like L1 cache, L2 cache, etc.

In reality, modern designs usually have two, three or four levels of cache, with each level being smaller in capacity (size) but with higher throughput.

Modern design also often have separate caches for instructions and data, at least at innermost cache levels (smallest numbers, e.g., L1 caches).

Figure P-17. *Main memory and a cache*

Hardware Motivation

We would like to ignore the details of hardware implementation as much as possible, because generally the more we cater to a particular system the more we lose portability, and performance portability. There is a notable and important exception: caches (Figure P-17).

A memory *cache* will be found in all modern computer designs. In fact, most systems will have multiple levels of caches. It was not always this way; originally computers fetched data and instructions from memory only when needed and immediately wrote results into memory. Those were simpler times!

The speed of processors has grown to be much faster than main memory. Making all of memory as fast as a processor would simply prove too expensive for most computers. Instead, designers make small amounts of memory, known as *caches*, that operate as fast as the processor. The main memory can remain slower and therefore more affordable. The hardware knows how to move information in and out of caches as needed, thereby adding to the number of places where data is shuffled on its journey between memory and the processor cores. Caches are critical in helping overcome the mismatch between memory speed and processor speed.

Virtually all computers use caches only for a temporary copy of data that should eventually reside in memory. Therefore, the function of a memory subsystem is to move data needed as input to caches near the requesting processor core, and to move data produced by processing cores out to main memory. As data is read from memory into the caches, some data may need to be evicted from the cache to make room for the newly requested data. Cache designers work to make the data evicted be approximately the least recently used data. The hope is that data which has not been used recently is not likely to be needed in the near future. That way, caches keep in their precious space the data we are most likely to use again.

Once a processor accesses data, it is best to exhaust the program's use of it while it is still in the cache. Continued usage will hold it in the cache, while prolonged inactivity will likely lead to its eviction and future usage will need to do a more expensive (slow) access to get the data back into the cache. Furthermore, every time a new thread runs on a processor, data is likely to be discarded from the cache to make room for the data needed by the particular thread.

Locality of Reference

Consider it to be expensive to fetch data from memory the first time, but it is much cheaper to use the data for a period of time after it is fetched. This is because *caches* hold onto the information much like our own *short-term memories* allow us to remember things during a day that will be harder to recall months later.

A simple, and often cited, example of a matrix multiplication, C=AxB, with matrices A, B, and C of size nxn, is shown in Figure P-18.

```
for (i=0;i<n;i++)
  for(j=0;j<n;j++)
    for (k=0;k<n;k++)
      c[i][j] = c[i][j] + a[i][k] * b[k][j];
```

Figure P-18. *Matrix multiplication with poor locality of reference*

C and C++ store arrays in *row-major* order. Which means that the contiguous array elements are in the last array dimension. This means that c[i][2] and c[i][3] are next to each other in memory, while c[2][j] and c[3][j] will be far apart (n elements apart in our example).

By switching the looping order for j and k, as shown in Figure P-19, the speedup can be dramatic because the locality of reference is greatly increased. This does not fundamentally change the mathematical result, but it improves efficiency because the memory caches are utilized more effectively. In our example, the value of n needs to be large enough that the combined size of the matrices exceeds the size of the caches. If this is not the case, the order will not matter nearly as much because either order will fit within the caches. A value of n=10,000 would make each matrix have one hundred million elements. Assuming double precision floating-point value, the three matrices together will occupy 2.4GB of memory. This will start to cause cache effects on all machines at the time of this book's publication! Almost all computers would benefit fully from the switched ordering of indices yet almost all systems will see no effects at all when n is small enough for data to all fit in cache.

```
for (i=0;i<n;i++)
  for(k=0;k<n;k++)
    for (j=0;j<n;j++)
      c[i][j] = c[i][j] + a[i][k] * b[k][j];
```

Figure P-19. *Matrix multiplication with improved locality of reference*

Cache Lines, Alignment, Sharing, Mutual Exclusion, and False Sharing

Caches are organized in lines. And processors transfer data between main memory and the cache at the granularity of cache lines. This causes three considerations which we will explain: data alignment, data sharing, and false sharing.

The length of a cache line is somewhat arbitrary, but 512 bits is by far the most common today – that is, 64 bytes in size, or the size of eight double precision floating-point numbers or sixteen 32-bit integers.

Alignment

It is far better for any given data item (e.g., int, long, double, or short) to fit within a single cache line. Looking at Figure P-17 or Figure P-20, and consider if it were a single data item (e.g., double) stretching across two cache lines. If so, we would need to access (read or write) two caches lines instead of one. In general, this will take twice as much time. Aligning single data items to not span cache lines can be very important for performance. To be fair to hardware designers, some hardware has significant capabilities to lessen the penalty for data that is not aligned (often called misaligned data). Since we cannot count on such support, we strongly advise that data be aligned on its natural boundaries. Arrays will generally span cache lines unless they are very short; normally, we advise that an array is aligned to the alignment size for a single array element so that a single element never sits in two cache lines even though the array may span multiple cache lines. The same general advice holds for structures as well, although there may be some benefit to aligning small structures to fit entirely in a cache line.

A disadvantage of alignment is wasted space. Every time we align data, we are potentially skipping some memory. In general, this is simply disregarded because memory is cheap. If alignment occurs frequently, and can be avoided or rearranged to save memory, that can occasionally still be important. Therefore, we needed to mention the disadvantage of alignment. In general, alignment is critical for performance, so we should just do it. Compilers will automatically align variables, including array and structures to the element sizes. We need to explicitly align when using memory allocations (e.g., `malloc`) so we recommend how to do that in Chapter 7.

The real reason we explain alignment is so we can discuss sharing and the evils of false sharing.

Sharing

Sharing copies of immutable (unchangeable) data from memory is easy, because every copy is always a valid copy. Sharing immutable data does not create any special problems when doing parallel processing.

It is mutable (changeable) data that creates substantial challenges when doing parallel processing of the data. We did name *shared mutable state* as an enemy of parallelism! In general, we should minimize sharing of mutable (changeable) data between tasks. The less sharing, the less there is to debug and the less there is to go wrong. We know the reality is that sharing data allows parallel tasks to work on the same problem to achieve scaling, so we have to dive into a discussion about how to share data correctly.

Shared mutable (changeable) state creates two challenges: (1) ordering, and (2) false sharing. The first is intrinsic to parallel programming and is not caused by the hardware. We discussed *mutual exclusion* starting on page xlv and illustrated a key concern over correctness with Figure P-16. It is a critical topic that must be understood by every parallel programmer.

False Sharing

Because data is moved around in cache lines, it is possible for multiple ,completely independent variables or memory allocations to be all or partially within the same cache line (Figure P-20). This sharing of a cache line will not cause a program to fail. However, it can greatly reduce performance. A complete explanation of the issues that arise when sharing a cache line, for mutable data being used in multiple tasks, would take many pages. A simple explanation is updating data anywhere in a cache line can create slowdowns for all accesses in the cache line from other tasks.

Regardless of the details of why false sharing slows down machines, we know that well written parallel programs take measures to avoid false sharing. Even if one machine configuration suffers less than most, in order to be performance portable, we should always take measures to avoid false sharing.

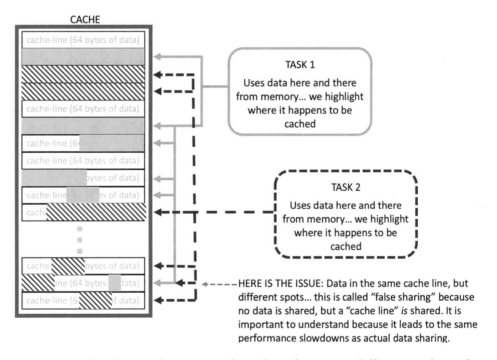

Figure P-20. *False sharing happens when data from two different tasks end up in the same cache line*

To illustrate why **false sharing** carries such a performance penalty, let's consider the extra overhead imposed on the caches and operating system when two threads access memory near each other. We'll assume for the sake of this example that a cache line contains 64 bytes, at least two threads are running on processors that share the cache, and our program defines an array that threads access and update based on their thread ID:

```
int my_private_counter[MAX_THREADS];
```

Two consecutive entries in my_private_counter are likely to be in the same cache line. Therefore, our example program can experience extra overhead due specifically to the false sharing caused by having data used by separate threads land in the same cache line. Consider two threads 0 and 1 running on core0 and core1 respectively, and the following sequence of events:

Thread 0 increments my_private_counter[0] which translates into reading the value in the core 0 private cache, incrementing the counter, and writing the result. More precisely, core 0 reads the whole line (say 64 bytes) including this counter into the cache and then updates the counter with the new value (usually only in the cache line).

Next, if thread 1 also increments my_private_counter[1], extra overhead due to false sharing is paid. It is highly likely that positions 0 and 1 of my_private_counter fall into the same cache line. If this is the case, when thread 1 in core1 tries to read their counter, the cache coherence protocol comes into play. This protocol works at the cache line level, and it will conservatively assume that thread 1 is reading the value written by thread 0 (as if thread 0 and thread 1 where truly sharing a single counter). Therefore, core 1 must read the cache line from core 0 (the slowest alternative would be to flush core 0 cache line to memory, from where core1 can read it). This is already expensive, but it is even worse when thread 1 increments this counter, invalidating the copy of the cache line in core0.

Now if thread 0 increments again my_private_counter[0], it does not find his counter in core 0's local cache because it was invalidated. It is necessary to pay the extra time to access core 1's version of the line that was updated most recently. Once again, if thread 0 then increments this counter, it invalidates the copy in core 1. If this behavior continues, the speed at which thread 0 and thread 1 will access their respective counters is significantly slower than in the case in which each counter lands in a different cache line.

This issue is called "false sharing" because actually each thread has a private (not shared) counter, but due to the cache coherence protocol working at cache line level, and both counters "sharing" the same cache line, the two counters seem to be shared from a hardware point of view.

Now you are probably thinking that a straightforward solution would be to fix the hardware implementation of the cache coherence protocol so that it works at word level instead of a line level. However, this hardware alternative is prohibitive, so hardware vendors ask us to solve the problem by software: Do your best to get each private counter falling in a different cache line so that it is clear to the hardware that the expensive cache coherence mechanism does not have to be dispatched.

We can see how a tremendous overhead can easily be imposed from false sharing of data. In our simple example, the right solution is to use copies of each element. This can be done in a number of ways, one of which would be to use the cache aligned allocator for the data needed for a given thread instead allocating them all together with the risk of false sharing.

Avoiding False Sharing with Alignment

In order to avoid false sharing (Figure P-20), we need to make sure that *distinctly different pieces of* mutable data that may be updated in parallel do not land in the same cache line. We do that with a combination of alignment and padding.

Alignment of data structures, such as arrays or structures, to a cache line boundary will prevent placement of the start of the data structure in a cache line used by something else. Usually, this means using a version of malloc that aligns to a cache line. We discuss memory allocation, including cache aligned memory allocators (e.g., `tbb::cache_aligned_allocator`), in Chapter 7. We can also explicitly align static and local variables with compiler directives (pragmas), but the need for that is far less common. We should note that performance slowdowns from false sharing from memory allocation are often somewhat nondeterministic, meaning that it may affect some runs of an application and not others. This can be truly maddening because debugging a nondeterministic issue is very challenging since we cannot count on any particular run of an application to have the issue!

TBB Has Caches in Mind

TBB is designed with caches in mind and works to limit the unnecessary movement of tasks and data. When a task has to be moved to a different processor, TBB moves the task with the lowest likelihood of having data in the cache of the old processor. These considerations are built into the work (task) stealing schedulers and therefore are part of the algorithm templates discussed in Chapters 1–3.

While dealing with caches has a role in many chapters, a few key chapters to note are

- Chapter 5 explains privatization and reduction.

- Chapter 7 covers important considerations for memory allocators to help with caches, including alignment and padding to avoid false sharing.

- Chapter 16 revisits data locality with an advanced discussion of options tuning for better locality.

For best performance, we need to keep data locality in mind when considering how to structure our programs. We should avoid using data regions sporadically when we can design the application to use a single set of data in focused chunks of time.

Introduction to Vectorization (SIMD)

Parallel programming is ultimately about harnessing the parallel computational capabilities of the hardware. Throughout this book, we focus on parallelism that exploits having multiple processor cores. Such hardware parallelism is exploited by thread-level (or abstractly task-level) parallelism, which is what TBB solves for us.

There is another class of very important hardware parallelism known as vector instructions, which are instructions that can do more computation (in parallel) than a regular instruction. For instance, a regular add instruction takes two numbers, adds them, and returns a single result. An eight-way vector add would be able to handle eight pairs of inputs, add each pair, and produce eight outputs. Instead of C=A+B in a regular add instruction, we get $C_0=A_0+B_0$ and $C_1=A_1+B_1$ and $C_2=A_2+B_2$ ... and $C_7=A_7+B_7$ from a single vector add instruction. This can offer 8× in performance. These instructions do require that we have eight of the same operations to do at once, which does tend to be true of numerically intensive code.

This ability to do multiple operations in a single instruction is known as Single Instruction Multiple Data (SIMD), one of four classification of computer architecture known by computer scientists as Flynn's taxonomy. The concept that a single instruction can operate on multiple data (e.g., the inputs to eight different additions) gives us parallelism that we will want to exploit.

Vectorization is the technology that exploits SIMD parallelism, and it is a technology which relies on compilers because compilers specialize in hardware instruction selection.

We could largely ignore vector parallelism in this book and say "it's a different subject with a different set of things to study" – but we won't! A good parallel program generally uses both task parallelism (with TBB) and SIMD parallelism (with a vectorizing compiler).

Our advice is this: Read Chapter 4 of this book! Learn about vectorizing capabilities of your favorite compiler and use them. `#pragma SIMD` is one such popular capability in compilers these days. Understand Parallel STL (Chapter 4 and Appendix B), including why it is generally not the best solution for effective parallel programming (Amdahl's Law favors parallelism being put at a higher level in the program than in STL calls).

While vectorization is important, using TBB offers superior speedup for most applications (if you consider choosing one or the other). This is because systems usually have more parallelism from cores than from SIMD lanes (how wide the vector instructions are), plus tasks are a lot more general than the limited number of operations that are available in SIMD instructions.

Good advice: Multitask your code first (use TBB);
vectorize second (use vectorization).

Best advice: Do both.

Doing both is generally useful when programs have computations that can benefit from vectorization. Consider a 32-core processor with AVX vector instructions. A multitasking program could hope to get a significant share of the theoretical maximum 32× in performance from using TBB. A vectorized program could hope to get a significant share of the theoretical maximum 4× in performance from using vectorization on double precision mathematical code. However, together the theoretical maximum jump in performance is 256× – this multiplicative effect is why many developers of numerically intensive programs always do both.

Introduction to the Features of C++ (As Needed for TBB)

Since the goal of parallel programming is to have an application scale in performance on machines with more cores, C and C++ both offer an ideal combination of abstraction with a focus on efficiency. TBB makes effective use of C++ but in a manner that is approachable to C programmers.

Every field has its own terminology, and C++ is no exception. We have included a glossary at the end of this book to assist with the vocabulary of C++, parallel programming, TBB, and more. There are several terms we will review here that are fundamental to C++ programmers: lambda functions, generic programming, containers, templates, Standard Template Library (STL), overloading, ranges, and iterators.

Lambda Functions

We are excited by the inclusion of lambda functions in the C++11 standard, which allow code to be expressed inline as an anonymous function. We will wait to explain them in Chapter 1 when we need them and will illustrate their usage.

Generic Programming

Generic programming is where algorithms are written to generically operate on any data type. We can think of them as using parameters which are "to-be-specified-later." C++ implements generic programming in a way that favors compile time optimization and avoids the necessity of runtime selection based on types. This has allowed modern C++ compilers to be highly tuned to minimize abstraction penalties arising from heavy use of generic programming, and consequently templates and STL. A simple example of generic programming is a sort algorithm which can sort any list of items, provided we supply a way to access an item, swap two items, and compare two items. Once we have put together such an algorithm, we can instantiate it to sort a list of integers, or floats, or complex numbers, or strings, provided that we define how the swap and the comparison is done for each data type.

A simple example of generic programming comes from considering support for complex numbers. The two elements of a complex number might be float, double, or long double types. Rather than declare three types of complex numbers and have three sets of functions to operate on the various types, with generic programming we can create the concept of a generic complex data type. When we declare an actual variable, we will use one of the following declarations which specifies the type of the elements we want in our complex number variables:

```
complex<float> my_single_precision_complex;

complex<double> my_double_precision_complex;

complex<long double> my_quad_precision_complex;
```

These are actually supported in the C++ Standard Template Library (STL – definition coming up on the next page) for C++ when we include the appropriate header file.

Containers

"Container" is C++ for "a struct" that organizes and manages a collection of data items. A C++ container combines both object-oriented capabilities (isolates the code that can manipulate the "struct") and generic programming qualities (the container is abstract, so it can operate on different data types). We will discuss containers supplied by TBB in Chapter 6. Understanding containers is not critical for using TBB, they are primarily supported by TBB for C++ users who already understand and use containers.

Templates

Templates are patterns for creating functions or classes (such as containers) in an efficient generic programming fashion, meaning their specification is flexible with types, but the actual compiled instance is specific and therefore free of overhead from this flexibility. Creating an effective template library can be a very involved task, but using one is not. TBB is a template library.

To use TBB, and other template libraries, we can really treat them as a collection of function calls. The fact that they are templates really only affects us in that we need to use a C++ compiler to compile them since templates are not part of the C language. Modern C++ compilers are tuned to minimize abstraction penalties arising from heavy use of templates.

STL

The C++ Standard Template Library (STL) is a software library for the C++ programming language which is part of the C++ programming standard. Every C++ compiler needs to support STL. STL provides four components called algorithms, containers, functions, and iterators.

The concept of "generic programming" runs deep in STL which relies heavily on templates. STL algorithms, such as sort, are independent of data types (containers). STL supports more complex data types including containers and associative arrays, which can be based upon any built-in type or user-defined type provided they support some elementary operations (such as copying and assignment).

Overloading

Operator overloading is an object-oriented concept which allows new data types (e.g., complex) to be used in contexts where built-in types (e.g., int) are accepted. This can be as arguments to functions, or operators such as = and +. C++ templates given us a generalized overloading which can be thought of extending overloading to function names with various parameters and or return value combinations. The goals of generic programming with templates, and object-oriented programming with overloading, are ultimately *polymorphism* – the ability to process data differently based on the type of the data, but reuse the code processing. TBB does this well – so we can just enjoy it as users of the TBB template library.

Ranges and Iterators

If you want to start a bar fight with C++ language gurus, pick either "iterators" or "ranges" and declare that one is vastly superior to the other. The C++ language committee is generally favoring to ranges as a higher-level interface and iterators for future standard revisions. However, that simple claim might start a bar fight too. C++ experts tell us that ranges are an approach to generic programming that uses the sequence abstraction as opposed to the iterator abstraction. Head spinning yet?

As users, the key concept behind an iterator or a range is much the same: a shorthand to denote a set (and some hints on how to traverse it). If we want to denote the numbers 0 to 999999 we can mathematically write this as [0,999999] or [0,1000000). Note the use of mathematical notation where [or] are inclusive and (or) note noninclusion of the number closest to the parenthesis. Using TBB syntax, we write `blocked_range<size_t>(0,1000000)`.

We love ranges, because they match perfectly with our desire to specify "possible parallelism" instead of mandatory parallelism. Consider a "parallel for" that planned to iterate a million times. We could immediately create a million threads to do the work in parallel, or we could create one thread with a range of [0,1000000). Such a range can be subdivided as needed to fill the available parallelism, and this is why we love ranges.

TBB supports and makes use of `iterators` and `ranges`, and we will mention that periodically in this book. There are plenty of examples of these starting in Chapter 2. We will show examples of how to use them, and we think those examples are easy to imitate. We will simply show which one to use where, and how, and not debate why C++ has them both. Understanding the deep C++ meanings of iterators vs. ranges will not improve our ability to use TBB. A simple explanation for now would be that iterators are less abstract that ranges, and at a minimum that leads to a lot of code using iterators which passes two parameters: `something.begin()` and `something.end()` when all we wanted to say was "use this range – begin to end."

Summary

We have reviewed how to "Think Parallel" in terms of decomposition, scaling, correctness, abstraction, and patterns. We have introduced *locality* as a key concern for all parallel programming. We have explained how using tasks instead of threads is a key revolutionary development in parallel programming supported by TBB. We have introduced the elements of C++ programming that are needed above and beyond a knowledge of C in order to use TBB well.

With these key concepts bouncing around in your head, you have begun to *Think Parallel*. You are developing an intuition about parallelism that will serve you well.

This Preface, the Index, and Glossary are key resources as you venture forth in the rest of this book to explore and learn parallel programming with TBB.

For More Information

- The C++ standard(s), https://isocpp.org/std/the-standard.

- "The Problem with Threads" by Edward Lee, 2006. IEEE Computer Magazine, May 2006, http://citeseerx.ist.psu.edu/viewdoc/download?doi=10.1.1.306.9963&rep=rep1&type=pdf, or U. C. Berkley Technical Report: www2.eecs.berkeley.edu/Pubs/TechRpts/2006/EECS-2006-1.pdf.

- All of the code examples used in this book are available at https://github.com/Apress/pro-TBB.

Part 1

CHAPTER 1

Jumping Right In: "Hello, TBB!"

Over 10 years after its first release, the Threading Building Blocks (TBB) library has become one of the most widely used C++ libraries for parallel programming. While it has retained its core philosophy and features, it continues to expand to address new opportunities and challenges as they arise.

In this chapter, we discuss the motivations for TBB, provide a brief overview of its main components, describe how to get the library, and then jump right into a few simple examples.

Why Threading Building Blocks?

Parallel programming has a long history, stretching back to the 1950s and beyond. For decades, scientists have been developing large-scale parallel simulations for supercomputers, and businesses have been developing enterprise applications for large multiprocessor mainframes. But a little over 10 years ago, the first multicore chips intended for desktops and laptops started to enter the marketplace. This was a game changer.

The number of processors in these first multicore desktop and laptop systems was small – only two cores – but the number of developers that had to become parallel programmers was huge. If multicore processors were to become mainstream, parallel programming had to become mainstream too, especially for developers who care about performance.

The TBB library was first released in September of 2006 to address the unique challenges of mainstream parallel programming. Its goal now, and when it was first introduced over 10 years ago, is to provide an easy and powerful way for developers to

© Intel Corporation 2019
M. Voss, R. Asenjo, J. Reinders, *Pro TBB*, https://doi.org/10.1007/978-1-4842-4398-5_1

build applications that continue to scale as new platforms, with different architectures and more cores, are introduced. This "future-proofing" has paid off as the number of cores in mainstream processors has grown from two in 2006 to more than 64 in 2018!

To achieve this goal of future-proofing parallel applications against changes in the number and capabilities of processing cores, the key philosophy behind TBB is to make it easy for developers to express the parallelism in their applications, while limiting the control they have over the mapping of this parallelism to the underlying hardware. This philosophy can seem counterintuitive to some experienced parallel programmers. If we believe parallel programming must get maximum performance at all costs by programming to the bare metal of a system, and hand-tuning and optimizing applications to squeeze out every last bit of performance, then TBB may not be for us. Instead, the TBB library is for developers that want to write applications that get great performance on today's platforms but are willing to give up a little performance to ensure that their applications continue to perform well on future systems.

To achieve this end, the interfaces in TBB let us express the parallelism in our applications but provide flexibility to the library so it can effectively map this parallelism to current and future platforms, and to adapt it to dynamic changes in system resources at runtime.

Performance: Small Overhead, Big Benefits for C++

We do not mean to make too big a deal about performance loss, nor do we wish to deny it. For simple C++ code written in a "Fortran" style, with a single layer of well-balanced parallel loops, the dynamic nature of TBB may not be needed at all. However, the limitations of such a coding style are an important factor in why TBB exists. TBB was designed to efficiently support nested, concurrent, and sequential composition of parallelism and to dynamically map this parallelism on to a target platform. Using a *composable* library like TBB, developers can build applications by combining components and libraries that contain parallelism without worrying that they will negatively interfere with each other. Importantly, TBB does not require us to restrict the parallelism we express to avoid performance problems. For large, complicated applications using C++, TBB is therefore easy to recommend without disclaimers.

The TBB library has evolved over the years to not only adjust to new platforms but also to demands from developers that want a bit more control over the choices the library makes in mapping parallelism to the hardware. While TBB 1.0 had very few performance controls for users, TBB 2019 has quite a few more – such as affinity controls, constructs for work isolation, hooks that can be used to pin threads to cores, and so on. The developers of TBB worked hard to design these controls to provide just the right level of control without sacrificing composability.

The interfaces provided by the library are nicely layered – TBB provides high-level templates that suit the needs of most programmers, focusing on common cases. But it also provides low-level interfaces so we can drill down and create tailored solutions for our specific applications if needed. TBB has the best of both worlds. We typically rely on the default choices of the library to get great performance but can delve into the details if we need to.

Evolving Support for Parallelism in TBB and C++

Both the TBB library and the C++ language have evolved significantly since the introduction of the original TBB. In 2006, C++ had no language support for parallel programming, and many libraries, including the Standard Template Library (STL), were not easily used in parallel programs because they were not thread-safe.

The C++ language committee has been busy adding features for threading directly to the language and its accompanying Standard Template Library (STL). Figure 1-1 shows new and planned C++ features that address parallelism.

	C++11/14	C++17	C++2x (proposed)
High level (events, messages, flow graphs)	`std::async`, `std::future`	`std::async`, `std::future`	resumable functions, executors
fork-join, threading	`std::thread` + synchronization	STL with `par` policy	Task block, for loop
SIMD / vectorization	None	STL with `par_unseq` policy	STL with `unseq` and `vec` policies, SIMD vector types

Figure 1-1. *The features in the C++ standard as well as some proposed features*

Even though we are big fans of TBB, we would in fact prefer if all of the fundamental support needed for parallelism is in the C++ language itself. That would allow TBB to utilize a consistent foundation on which to build higher-level parallelism abstractions. The original versions of TBB had to address a lack of C++ language support, and this is an area where the C++ standard has grown significantly to fill the foundational voids that TBB originally had no choice but to fill with features such as portable locks and atomics. Unfortunately, for C++ developers, the standard still lacks features needed for full support of parallel programming. Fortunately, for readers of this book, this means that TBB is still relevant and essential for effective threading in C++ and will likely stay relevant for many years to come.

It is very important to understand that we are not complaining about the C++ standard process. Adding features to a language standard is best done very carefully, with careful review. The C++11 standard committee, for instance, spent huge energy on a memory model. The significance of this for parallel programming is critical for every library that builds upon the standard. There are also limits to what a language standard should include, and what it should support. We believe that the tasking system and the flow graph system in TBB is not something that will directly become part of a language standard. Even if we are wrong, it is not something that will happen anytime soon.

Recent C++ Additions for Parallelism

As shown in Figure 1-1, the C++11 standard introduced some low-level, basic building blocks for threading, including `std::async`, `std::future`, and `std::thread`. It also introduced atomic variables, mutual exclusion objects, and condition variables. These extensions require programmers to do a lot of coding to build up higher-level abstractions – but they do allow us to express basic parallelism directly in C++. The C++11 standard was a clear improvement when it comes to threading, but it doesn't provide us with the high-level features that make it easy to write portable, efficient parallel code. It also does not provide us with tasks or an underlying work-stealing task scheduler.

The C++17 standard introduced features that raise the level of abstraction above these low-level building blocks, making it easier for us to express parallelism without having to worry about every low-level detail. As we discuss later in this book, there are still some significant limitations, and so these features are not yet sufficiently expressive or performant – there's still a lot of work to do in the C++ standard.

The most pertinent of these C++17 additions are the *execution policies* that can be used with the Standard Template Library (STL) algorithms. These policies let us choose whether an algorithm can be safely parallelized, vectorized, parallelized and vectorized, or if it needs to retain its original sequenced semantics. We call an STL implementation that supports these policies a Parallel STL.

Looking into the future, there are proposals that might be included in a future C++ standard with even more parallelism features, such as resumable functions, executors, task blocks, parallel for loops, SIMD vector types, and additional execution policies for the STL algorithms.

The Threading Building Blocks (TBB) Library

The Threading Building Blocks (TBB) library is a C++ library that serves two key roles: (1) it fills foundational voids in support for parallelism where the C++ standard has not sufficiently evolved, or where new features are not fully supported by all compilers, and (2) it provides higher-level abstractions for parallelism that are beyond the scope of what the C++ language standard will likely ever include. TBB contains a number of features, as shown in Figure 1-2.

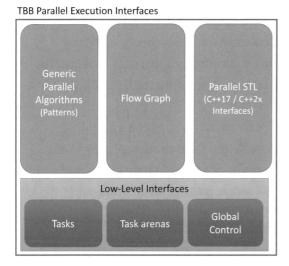
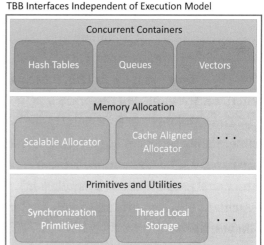

Figure 1-2. *The features of the TBB library*

These features can be categorized into two large groups: interfaces for expressing parallel computations and interfaces that are independent of the execution model.

Parallel Execution Interfaces

When we use TBB to create parallel programs, we express the parallelism in the application using one of the high-level interfaces or directly with tasks. We discuss tasks in more detail later in this book, but for now we can think of a TBB task as a lightweight object that defines a small computation and its associated data. As TBB developers, we express our application using tasks, either directly or indirectly through the prepackaged TBB algorithms, and the library schedules these tasks on to the platform's hardware resources for us.

It's important to note that as developers, we may want to express different kinds of parallelism. The three most common layers of parallelism that are expressed in parallel applications are shown in Figure 1-3. We should note that some applications may contain all three layers and others may contain only one or two of them. One of the most powerful aspects of TBB is that it provides high-level interfaces for each of these different parallelism layers, allowing us to exploit all of the layers using the same library.

The message-driven layer shown in Figure 1-3 captures parallelism that is structured as relatively large computations that communicate to each other through explicit messages. Common patterns in this layer include streaming graphs, data flow graphs, and dependency graphs. In TBB, these patterns are supported through the Flow Graph interfaces (described in Chapter 3).

The fork-join layer shown in Figure 1-3 supports patterns in which a serial computation branches out into a set of parallel tasks and then continues only when the parallel subcomputations are complete. Examples of fork-join patterns include functional parallelism (task parallelism), parallel loops, parallel reductions, and pipelines. TBB supports these with its Generic Parallel Algorithms (described in Chapter 2).

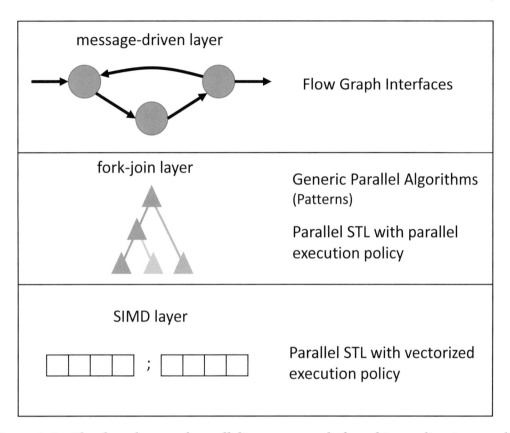

Figure 1-3. *The three layers of parallelism commonly found in applications and how they map to the high-level TBB parallel execution interfaces*

Finally, the Single Instruction, Multiple Data (SIMD) layer is where data parallelism is exploited by applying the same operation to multiple data elements simultaneously. This type of parallelism is often implemented using vector extensions such as AVX, AVX2, and AVX-512 that use the vector units available in each processor core. There is a Parallel STL implementation (described in Chapter 4) included with all of the TBB distributions that provides vector implementations, among others, that take advantage of these extensions.

TBB provides high-level interfaces for many common parallel patterns, but there may still be cases where none of the high-level interfaces matches a problem. If that's the case, we can use TBB tasks directly to build our own algorithms.

The true power of the TBB parallel execution interfaces comes from the ability to mix them together, something usually called "composability." We can create applications that have a Flow Graph at the top level with nodes that use nested Generic Parallel Algorithms. These nested Generic Parallel Algorithms can, in turn, use Parallel STL algorithms in their bodies. Since the parallelism expressed by all of these layers is exposed to the TBB library, this one library can schedule the corresponding tasks in an efficient and composable way, making best use of the platform's resources.

One of the key properties of TBB that makes it composable is that it supports *relaxed sequential semantics*. Relaxed sequential semantics means that the parallelism we express using TBB tasks is in fact only a hint to the library; there is no guarantee that any of the tasks actually execute in parallel with each other. This gives tremendous flexibility to the TBB library to schedule tasks as necessary to improve performance. This flexibility lets the library provide scalable performance on systems, whether they have one core, eight cores, or 80 cores. It also allows the library to adapt to the dynamic load on the platform; for example, if one core is oversubscribed with work, TBB can schedule more work on the other cores or even choose to execute a parallel algorithm using only a single core. We describe in more detail why TBB is considered a composable library in Chapter 9.

Interfaces That Are Independent of the Execution Model

Unlike the parallel execution interfaces, the second large group of features in Figure 1-2 are completely independent of the execution model and of TBB tasks. These features are as useful in applications that use native threads, such as `pthreads` or `WinThreads`, as they are in applications that use TBB tasks.

These features include concurrent containers that provide thread-friendly interfaces to common data structures like hash tables, queues, and vectors. They also include features for memory allocation like the TBB scalable memory allocator and the cache aligned allocator (both described in Chapter 7). They also include lower-level features such as synchronization primitives and thread-local storage.

Using the Building Blocks in TBB

As developers, we can pick and choose the parts of TBB that are useful for our applications. We can, for example, use just the scalable memory allocator (described in Chapter 7) and nothing else. Or, we can use concurrent containers (described in Chapter 6) and a few Generic Parallel Algorithms (Chapter 2). And of course, we can also choose to go all in and build an application that combines all three high-level execution interfaces and makes use of the TBB scalable memory allocator and concurrent containers, as well as the many other features in the library.

Let's Get Started Already!

Getting the Threading Building Blocks (TBB) Library

Before we can start using TBB, we need to get a copy of the library. There are a few ways to do this. At the time of the writing of this book, these ways include

- Follow links at `www.threadingbuildingblocks.org` or `https://software.intel.com/intel-tbb` to get a free version of the TBB library directly from Intel. There are precompiled versions available for Windows, Linux, and macOS. The latest packages include both the TBB library and an implementation of the Parallel STL algorithms that uses TBB for threading.

- Visit `https://github.com/intel/tbb` to get the free, open-source version of the TBB library. The open-source version of TBB is in no way a lite version of the library; it contains all of the features of the commercially supported version. You can choose to checkout and build from source, or you can click "releases" to download a version that has been built and tested by Intel. At GitHub, pre-built and tested versions are available for Windows, Linux, macOS, and Android. Again, the latest packages for the pre-built versions of TBB include both the TBB library and an implementation of Parallel STL that uses TBB for threading. If you want the source code for Parallel STL, you will need to download that separately from `https://github.com/intel/parallelstl`.

- You can download a copy of the Intel Parallel Studio XE tool suite `https://software.intel.com/intel-parallel-studio-xe`. TBB and a Parallel STL that uses TBB is currently included in all editions of this tool suite, including the smallest Composer Edition. If you have a recent version of the Intel C++ compiler installed, you likely already have TBB installed on your system.

We leave it to readers to select the most appropriate route for getting TBB and to follow the directions for installing the package that are provided at the corresponding site.

Getting a Copy of the Examples

All of the code examples used in this book are available at
`https://github.com/Apress/pro-TBB`. In this repository, there are directories for
each chapter. Many of the source files are named after the figure they appear in, for
example `ch01/fig_1_04.cpp` contains code that matches Figure 1-4 in this chapter.

Writing a First "Hello, TBB!" Example

Figure 1-4 provides a small example that uses a `tbb::parallel_invoke` to evaluate two
functions, one that prints `Hello` and the other that prints `TBB!` in parallel. This example
is trivial and will not benefit from parallelization, but we can use it to be sure that we
have set up our environment properly to use TBB. In Figure 1-4, we include the tbb.h
header to get access to the TBB functions and classes, all of which are in namespace tbb.
The call to `parallel_invoke` asserts to the TBB library that the two functions passed to
it are independent of each other and are safe to execute in parallel on different cores
or threads and in any order. Under these constraints, the resulting output may contain
either `Hello` or `TBB!` first. We might even see that there is no newline character between
the two strings and two consecutive newlines at the end of the output, since the printing
of each string and its `std::endl` do not happen atomically.

```cpp
#include <iostream>
#include <tbb/tbb.h>

int main() {
  tbb::parallel_invoke(
    []() { std::cout << " Hello " << std::endl; },
    []() { std::cout << " TBB! " << std::endl; }
  );
  return 0;
}
```

Figure 1-4. *A Hello TBB example*

Figure 1-5 provides an example that uses a Parallel STL `std::for_each` to apply a
function in parallel to two items in a `std::vector`. Passing a `pstl::execution::par`
policy to the `std::for_each` asserts that it is safe to apply the provided function in
parallel on different cores or threads to the result of dereferencing every iterator in the
range `[v.begin(), v.end())`. Just like with Figure 1-4, the output that results from
running this example might have either string printed first.

```
#include <iostream>
#include <vector>
#include <pstl/algorithm>
#include <pstl/execution>

int main() {
  std::vector<std::string> v = {" Hello ",
                                " Parallel STL! "};
  std::for_each(pstl::execution::par, v.begin(), v.end(),
    [](std::string &s) { std::cout << s << std::endl; }
  );
  return 0;
}
```

Figure 1-5. *A Hello Parallel STL example*

In both Figures 1-4 and 1-5, we use C++ *lambda expressions* to specify the functions. Lambda expressions are very useful when using libraries like TBB to specify the user code to execute as a task. To help review C++ lambda expressions, we offer a callout box "A Primer on C++ Lambda Expressions" with an overview of this important modern C++ feature.

A PRIMER ON C++ LAMBDA EXPRESSIONS

Support for lambda expressions was introduced in C++11. They are used to create anonymous function objects (although you can assign them to named variables) that can capture variables from the enclosing scope. The basic syntax for a C++ lambda expression is

> [*capture-list*] (*params*) -> *ret* { *body* }

where

- *capture-list* is a comma-separated list of captures. We capture a variable by value by listing the variable name in the capture-list. We capture a variable by reference by prefixing it with an ampersand, for example, &v. And we can use this to capture the current object by reference. There are also defaults: [=] is used to capture all automatic variables used in the body by value and the current object by reference, [&] is used to capture all automatic variables used in the body as well as the current object by reference, and [ ] captures nothing.

- *params* is the list of function parameters, just like for a named function.

- *ret* is the return type. If *->ret* is not specified, it is inferred from the return statements.

- *body* is the function body.

This next example shows a C++ lambda expression that captures one variable, i, by value and another, j, by reference. It also has a parameter k0 and another parameter l0 that is received by reference:

```
int i = 1, j = 10, k = 100, l = 1000;
auto lambdaExpression = [i, &j] (int k0, int &l0) -> int {
  j = 2 * j;
  k0 = 2 * k0;
  l0 = 2 * l0;
  return i + j + k0 + l0;
};

printValues(i, j, k, l);
std::cout << "First call returned " << lambdaExpression(k, l)
          << std::endl;
printValues(i, j, k, l);
std::cout << "Second call returned " << lambdaExpression(k, l)
          << std::endl;
printValues(i, j, k, l);
return 0;
```

Running the example will result in the following output:

```
i == 1
j == 10
k == 100
l == 1000
First call returned 2221
i == 1
j == 20
k == 100
l == 2000
Second call returned 4241
i == 1
j == 40
k == 100
l == 4000
```

We can think of a lambda expression as an instance of a function object, but the compiler creates the class definition for us. For example, the lambda expression we used in the preceding example is analogous to an instance of a class:

```
class Functor {
  int my_i;
  int &my_jRef;

public:
  Functor(int i, int &j) : my_i{i}, my_jRef{j} { }

  int operator()(int k0, int &l0) {
    my_jRef = 2 * my_jRef;
    k0 = 2 * k0;
    l0 = 2 * l0;
    return my_i + my_jRef + k0 + l0;
  }
};
```

Wherever we use a C++ lambda expression, we can substitute it with an instance of a function object like the preceding one. In fact, the TBB library predates the C++11 standard and all of its interfaces used to require passing in instances of objects of user-defined classes. C++ lambda expressions simplify the use of TBB by eliminating the extra step of defining a class for each use of a TBB algorithm.

Building the Simple Examples

Once we have written the examples in Figures 1-4 and 1-5, we need to build executable files from them. The instructions for building an application that uses TBB are OS and compiler dependent. However, in general, there are two necessary steps to properly configure an environment.

Steps to Set Up an Environment

1. We must inform the compiler about the location of the TBB headers and libraries. If we use Parallel STL interfaces, we must also inform the compiler about the location of the Parallel STL headers.

2. We must configure our environment so that the application can locate the TBB libraries when it is run. TBB is shipped as a dynamically linked library, which means that it is not directly embedded into our application; instead, the application locates and loads it at runtime. The Parallel STL interfaces do not require their own dynamically linked library but do depend on the TBB library.

We will now briefly discuss some of the most common ways to accomplish these steps on Windows and Linux. The instructions for macOS are similar to those for Linux. There are additional cases and more detailed directions in the documentation that ships with the TBB library.

Building on Windows Using Microsoft Visual Studio

If we download either the commercially supported version of TBB or a version of Intel Parallel Studio XE, we can integrate the TBB library with Microsoft Visual Studio when we install it, and then it is very simple to use TBB from Visual Studio.

To create a "Hello, TBB!" project, we create a project as usual in Visual Studio, add a ".cpp" file with the code contained in Figure 1-4 or Figure 1-5, and then go to the project's **Property Pages,** traverse to **Configuration Properties ➤ Intel Performance Libraries** and change **Use TBB** to **Yes**, as shown in Figure 1-6. This accomplishes step 1. Visual Studio will now link the TBB library into the project as it has the proper paths to the header files and libraries. This also properly sets the paths to the Parallel STL headers.

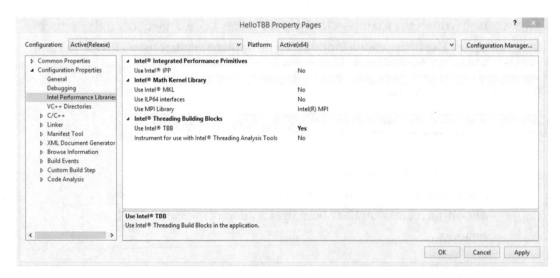

Figure 1-6. *Setting Use **TBB** to **Yes** in the project Property Pages in Visual Studio*

On Windows systems, the TBB libraries that are dynamically loaded by the application executable at runtime are the ".dll" files. To complete step 2 in setting up our environment, we need to add the location of these files to our PATH environment variable. We can do this by adding the path to either our Users or System PATH variable. One place to find these settings is in the Windows Control Panel by traversing **System and Security ➤ System ➤ Advanced System Settings ➤ Environment Variables**. We can refer to the documentation for our installation of TBB for the exact locations of the ".dll" files.

Note   Changes to the PATH variable in an environment only take effect in Microsoft Visual Studio after it is restarted.

Once we have the source code entered, have **Use TBB** set to **Yes**, and have the path to the TBB ".dll"s in our PATH variable, we can build and execute the program by entering **Ctrl-F5.**

Building on a Linux Platform from a Terminal

Using the Intel Compiler

When using the Intel C++ Compiler, the compilation process is simplified because the TBB library is included with the compiler and it supports a compiler flag –tbb that properly sets the include and library paths during compilation for us. Therefore, to compile our examples using the Intel C++ Compiler, we just add the –tbb flag to the compile line.

```
icpc –std=c++11 -tbb –o fig_1_04 fig_1_04.cpp
icpc –std=c++11 -tbb –o fig_1_05 fig_1_05.cpp
```

tbbvars and pstlvars Scripts

If we are not using the Intel C++ Compiler, we can use scripts that are included with the TBB and Parallel STL distributions to set up our environment. These scripts modify the CPATH, LIBRARY_PATH and LD_LIBRARY_PATH environment variables to include the directories needed to build and run TBB and Parallel STL applications. The CPATH variable adds additional directories to the list of directories the compiler searches when it looks for #include files. The LIBRARY_PATH adds additional directories to the list of directories the compiler searches when it looks for libraries to link against at compile time. And the LD_LIBRARY_PATH adds additional directories to the list of directories the executable will search when it loads dynamic libraries at runtime.

Let us assume that the root directory of our TBB installation is TBB_ROOT. The TBB library comes with a set of scripts in the ${TBB_ROOT}/bin directory that we can execute to properly set up the environment. We need to pass our architecture type [ia32|intel64|mic] to this script. We also need to add a flag at compile time to enable the use of C++11 features, such as our use of lambda expressions.

Even though the Parallel STL headers are included with all of the recent TBB library packages, we need to take an extra step to add them to our environment. Just like with TBB, Parallel STL comes with a set of scripts in the ${PSTL_ROOT}/bin directory. The PSTL_ROOT directory is typically a sibling of the TBB_ROOT directory. We also need to pass in our architecture type and enable the use of C++11 features to use Parallel STL.

The steps to build and execute the example in Figure 1-4 on a Linux platform with 64-bit Intel processors look like

```
source ${TBB_ROOT}/bin/tbbvars.sh intel64 linux auto_tbbroot
g++ -std=c++11 -o fig_1_04 fig_1_04.cpp -ltbb
./fig_1_04
```

The steps to build and execute the example in Figure 1-5 on a Linux platform with 64-bit Intel processors look like

```
source ${TBB_ROOT}/bin/tbbvars.sh intel64 linux auto_tbbroot
source ${PSTL_ROOT}/bin/pstlvars.sh intel64 auto_pstlroot
g++ -std=c++11 -o fig_1_05 fig_1_05.cpp -ltbb
./fig_1_05
```

Note   Increasingly, Linux distributions include a copy of the TBB library. On these platforms, the GCC compiler may link against the platform's version of the TBB library instead of the version of the TBB library that is added to the LIBRARY_PATH by the tbbvars script. If we see linking problems when using TBB, this might be the issue. If this is the case, we can add an explicit library path to the compiler's command line to choose a specific version of the TBB library.

For example:

```
g++ -L${TBB_ROOT}/lib/intel64/gcc4.7 -ltbb ...
```

We can add -Wl,--verbose to the g++ command line to generate a report of all of the libraries that are being linked against during compilation to help diagnose this issue.

Although we show commands for g++, except for the compiler name used, the command lines are the same for the Intel compiler (icpc) or LLVM (clang++).

Setting Up Variables Manually Without Using the **tbbvars** Script or the Intel Compiler

Sometimes we may not want to use the tbbvars scripts, either because we want to know exactly what variables are being set or because we need to integrate with a build system. If that's not the case for you, skip over this section unless you really feel the urge to do things manually.

Since you're still reading this section, let's look out how we can build and execute on the command line without using the tbbvars script. When compiling with a non-Intel compiler, we don't have the -tbb flag available to us, so we need to specify the paths to both the TBB headers and the shared libraries.

If the root directory of our TBB installation is TBB_ROOT, the headers are in ${TBB_ROOT}/include and the shared library files are stored in ${TBB_ROOT}/lib/${ARCH}/${GCC_LIB_VERSION}, where ARCH is the system architecture [ia32|intel64|mic] and the GCC_LIB_VERSION is the version of the TBB library that is compatible with your GCC or clang installation.

The underlying difference between the TBB library versions is their dependencies on features in the C++ runtime libraries (such as libstdc++ or libc++).

Typically to find an appropriate TBB version to use, we can execute the command gcc -version in our terminal. We then select the closest GCC version available in ${TBB_ROOT}/lib/${ARCH} that is not newer than our GCC version (this usually works even when we are using clang++). But because installations can vary from machine to machine, and we can choose different combinations of compilers and C++ runtimes, this simple approach may not always work. If it does not, refer to the TBB documentation for additional guidance.

For example, on a system with GCC 5.4.0 installed, we compiled the example in Figure 1-4 with

```
g++ -std=c++11 -o fig_1_04 fig_1_04.cpp       \
    -I ${TBB_ROOT}/include                     \
    -L ${TBB_ROOT}/lib/intel64/gcc4.7 -ltbb
```

And when using clang++, we used the same TBB version:

```
clang++ -std=c++11 -o fig_1_04 fig_1_04.cpp  \
    -I ${TBB_ROOT}/include                     \
    -L ${TBB_ROOT}/lib/intel64/gcc-4.7 -ltbb
```

To compile the example in Figure 1-5, we also need to add the path to the Parallel STL include directory:

```
g++ -std=c++11 -o fig_1_05 fig_1_05.cpp       \
    -I ${TBB_ROOT}/include                     \
    -I ${PSTL_ROOT}/include                    \
    -L ${TBB_ROOT}/lib/intel64/gcc4.7 -ltbb
```

Regardless of whether we have compiled with the Intel compiler, gcc, or clang++, we need to add the TBB shared library location to our LD_LIBRARY_PATH so that it can be found when the application runs. Again, assuming that the root directory of our TBB installation is TBB_ROOT, we can set this, for example, with

```
export LD_LIBRARY_PATH=${TBB_ROOT}/lib/${ARCH}/${GCC_LIB_VERSION}:${LD_LIBRARY_PATH}
```

Once we have compiled our application using the Intel compiler, gcc, or clang++ and have set our LD_LIBRARY_PATH as required, we can then run the applications from the command line:

```
./fig_1_04
```

This should result in an output similar to

```
Hello
Parallel STL!
```

A More Complete Example

The previous sections provide the steps to write, build, and execute a simple TBB application and a simple Parallel STL application that each print a couple of lines of text. In this section, we write a bigger example that can benefit from parallel execution using all three of the high-level execution interfaces shown in Figure 1-2. We do not explain all of the details of the algorithms and features used to create this example, but instead we use this example to see the different layers of parallelism that can be expressed with TBB. This example is admittedly contrived. It is simple enough to explain in a few paragraphs but complicated enough to exhibit all of the parallelism layers described in Figure 1-3. The final multilevel parallel version we create here should be viewed as a syntactic demonstration, not a how-to guide on how to write an optimal TBB application. In subsequent chapters, we cover all of the features used in this section in more detail and provide guidance on how to use them to get great performance in more realistic applications.

Starting with a Serial Implementation

Let's start with the serial implementation shown in Figure 1-7. This example applies a gamma correction and a tint to each image in a vector of images, writing each result to a file. The highlighted function, `fig_1_7`, contains a for-loop that processes the elements of a vector by executing `applyGamma`, `applyTint`, and `writeImage` functions on each image. The serial implementations of each of these functions are also provided in Figure 1-7. The definitions of the image representation and some of the helper functions are contained in `ch01.h`. This header file is available, along with all of the source code for the example, at `https://github.com/Apress/threading-building-blocks`.

```
#include <iostream>
#include <vector>
#include <tbb/tbb.h>
#include "ch01.h"

using ImagePtr = std::shared_ptr<ch01::Image>;

ImagePtr applyGamma(ImagePtr image_ptr, double gamma);
ImagePtr applyTint(ImagePtr image_ptr, const double *tints);
void writeImage(ImagePtr image_ptr);
```

```
void fig_1_7(const std::vector<ImagePtr> &image_vector) {
  const double tint_array[] = {0.75, 0, 0};
  for (ImagePtr img : image_vector) {
    img = applyGamma(img, 1.4);
    img = applyTint(img, tint_array);
    writeImage(img);
  }
}
```

```
ImagePtr applyGamma(ImagePtr image_ptr, double gamma) {
  auto output_image_ptr =
    std::make_shared<ch01::Image>(image_ptr->name() + "_gamma",
      ch01::IMAGE_WIDTH, ch01::IMAGE_HEIGHT);
  auto in_rows = image_ptr->rows();
  auto out_rows = output_image_ptr->rows();
  const int height = in_rows.size();
  const int width = in_rows[1] - in_rows[0];

  for ( int i = 0; i < height; ++i ) {
    for ( int j = 0; j < width; ++j ) {
      const ch01::Image::Pixel &p = in_rows[i][j];
      double v = 0.3*p.bgra[2] + 0.59*p.bgra[1] + 0.11*p.bgra[0];
      double res = pow(v, gamma);
      if(res > ch01::MAX_BGR_VALUE) res = ch01::MAX_BGR_VALUE;
      out_rows[i][j] = ch01::Image::Pixel(res, res, res);
    }
  }
  return output_image_ptr;
}
```

```
ImagePtr applyTint(ImagePtr image_ptr, const double *tints) {
  auto output_image_ptr =
    std::make_shared<ch01::Image>(image_ptr->name() + "_tinted",
      ch01::IMAGE_WIDTH, ch01::IMAGE_HEIGHT);
  auto in_rows = image_ptr->rows();
  auto out_rows = output_image_ptr->rows();
  int height = in_rows.size();
  const int width = in_rows[1] - in_rows[0];

  for ( int i = 0; i < height; ++i ) {
    for ( int j = 0; j < width; ++j ) {
      const ch01::Image::Pixel &p = in_rows[i][j];
      std::uint8_t b = (double)p.bgra[0] +
```

Figure 1-7. *A serial implementation of an example that applies a gamma correction and a tint to a vector of images*

```
                         (ch01::MAX_BGR_VALUE-p.bgra[0])*tints[0];
        std::uint8_t g = (double)p.bgra[1] +
                         (ch01::MAX_BGR_VALUE-p.bgra[1])*tints[1];
        std::uint8_t r = (double)p.bgra[2] +
                         (ch01::MAX_BGR_VALUE-p.bgra[2])*tints[2];
        out_rows[i][j] =
          ch01::Image::Pixel(
            (b > ch01::MAX_BGR_VALUE) ? ch01::MAX_BGR_VALUE : b,
            (g > ch01::MAX_BGR_VALUE) ? ch01::MAX_BGR_VALUE : g,
            (r > ch01::MAX_BGR_VALUE) ? ch01::MAX_BGR_VALUE : r
          );
      }
    }
    return output_image_ptr;
  }

  void writeImage(ImagePtr image_ptr) {
    image_ptr->write( (image_ptr->name() + ".bmp").c_str());
  }

  int main(int argc, char* argv[]) {
    std::vector<ImagePtr> image_vector;

    for ( int i = 2000; i < 20000000; i *= 10 )
      image_vector.push_back(ch01::makeFractalImage(i));

    tbb::tick_count t0 = tbb::tick_count::now();
    fig_1_7(image_vector);
    std::cout << "Time : " << (tbb::tick_count::now()-t0).seconds()
              << " seconds" << std::endl;
    return 0;
  }
```

Figure 1-7. (*continued*)

Both the applyGamma function and the applyTint function traverse across the rows
of the image in an outer for-loop and the elements of each row in an inner for-loop.
New pixel values are computed and assigned to the output image. The applyGamma
function applies a gamma correction. The applyTint function applies a blue tint to the
image. The functions receive and return std::shared_ptr objects to simplify memory
management; readers that are unfamiliar with std::shared_ptr can refer to the sidebar
discussion "A note on smart pointers." Figure 1-8 shows example outputs for an image
fed through the example code.

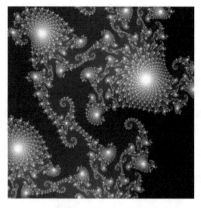

(a) Original (i==2000000)

(b) After gamma   (c) After gamma & tint

Figure 1-8. *Outputs for the example: (a) the original image generated by* ch01::
makeFractalImage(2000000), *(b) the image after it has been gamma corrected,
and (c) the image after it has been gamma corrected and tinted*

A NOTE ON SMART POINTERS

One of the most challenging parts of programming in C/C++ can be dynamic memory
management. When we use new/delete or malloc/free, we have to be sure we that we
match them up correctly to avoid memory leaks and double frees. Smart pointers including
unique_ptr, shared_ptr, and weak_ptr were introduced in C++11 to provide automatic,
exception-safe memory management. For example, if we allocate an object by using
make_shared, we receive a smart pointer to the object. As we assign this shared pointer to
other shared pointers, the C++ library takes care of reference counting for us. When there
are no outstanding references to our object through any smart pointers, then the object is

automatically freed. In most of the examples in this book, including in Figure 1-7, we use smart pointers instead of raw pointers. Using smart pointers, we don't have to worry about finding all of the points where we need to insert a free or delete – we can just rely on the smart pointers to do the right thing.

Adding a Message-Driven Layer Using a Flow Graph

Using a top-down approach, we can replace the outer loop in function fig_1_07 in Figure 1-7 with a TBB Flow Graph that streams images through a set of filters as shown in Figure 1-9. We admit that this is the most contrived of our choices in this particular example. We could have easily used an outer parallel loop in this case; or we could have merged the Gamma and Tint loop nests together. But for demonstration purposes, we choose to express this as a graph of separate nodes to show how TBB can be used to express message-driven parallelism, the top level of the parallelism in Figure 1-3. In Chapter 3, we will learn more about the TBB Flow Graph interfaces and discover more natural applications for this high-level, message-driven execution interface.

Figure 1-9. *A data flow graph that has four nodes: (1) a node that gets or generates images, (2) a node that applies the gamma correction, (3) a node that applies the tint, and (4) a node that writes out the resulting image*

By using the data flow graph in Figure 1-9, we can overlap the execution of different stages of the pipeline as they are applied to different images. For example, when a first image, img_0, completes in the gamma node, the result is passed to the tint node, while a new image img_1 enters the gamma node. Likewise, when this next step is done, img_0, which has now passed through both the gamma and tint nodes, is sent to the write node. Meanwhile, img_1 is sent to the tint node, and a new image, img_2, begins processing in the gamma node. At each step, the execution of the filters is independent of each other, and so these computations can be spread across different cores or threads. Figure 1-10 shows the loop from function fig_1_7 now expressed as a TBB Flow Graph.

```
void fig_1_10(const std::vector<ImagePtr> &image_vector) {
  const double tint_array[] = {0.75, 0, 0};

  tbb::flow::graph g;

  int i = 0;
  tbb::flow::source_node<ImagePtr> src (g,
    [&i, &image_vector] (ImagePtr &out) -> bool {
      if ( i < image_vector.size() ) {
        out = image_vector[i++];
        return true;
      } else {
        return false;
      }
    }, false);

  tbb::flow::function_node<ImagePtr, ImagePtr> gamma (g,
    tbb::flow::unlimited,
    [] (ImagePtr img) -> ImagePtr {
      return applyGamma(img, 1.4);
    }
  );

  tbb::flow::function_node<ImagePtr, ImagePtr> tint (g,
    tbb::flow::unlimited,
    [tint_array] (ImagePtr img) -> ImagePtr {
      return applyTint(img, tint_array);
    }
  );

  tbb::flow::function_node<ImagePtr> write (g,
    tbb::flow::unlimited,
    [] (ImagePtr img) {
      writeImage(img);
    }
  );

  tbb::flow::make_edge(src, gamma);
  tbb::flow::make_edge(gamma, tint);
  tbb::flow::make_edge(tint, write);
  src.activate();
  g.wait_for_all();
}
```

Figure 1-10. *Using a TBB Flow Graph in place of the outer for-loop*

As we will see in Chapter 3, several steps are needed to build and execute a TBB
Flow Graph. First, a graph object, g, is constructed. Next, we construct the nodes that
represent the computations in our data flow graph. The node that streams the images to

the rest of the graph is a `source_node` named `src`. The computations are performed by the `function_node` objects named `gamma`, `tint`, and `write`. We can think of a `source_node` as a node that has no input and continues to send data until it runs out of data to send. We can think of a `function_node` as a wrapper around a function that receives an input and generates an output.

After the nodes are created, we connect them to each other using edges. Edges represent the dependencies or communication channels between nodes. Since, in our example in Figure 1-10, we want the `src` node to send the initial images to the `gamma` node, we make an edge from the `src` node to the `gamma` node. We then make an edge from the `gamma` node to the `tint` node. And likewise, we make an edge from the `tint` node to the `write` node. Once we complete construction of the graph's structure, we call `src.activate()` to start the `source_node` and call `g.wait_for_all()` to wait until the graph completes.

When the application in Figure 1-10 executes, each image generated by the `src` node passes through the pipeline of nodes as described previously. When an image is sent to the `gamma` node, the TBB library creates and schedules a task to apply the `gamma` node's body to the image. When that processing is done, the output is fed to the `tint` node. Likewise, TBB will create and schedule a task to execute the `tint` node's body on that output of the `gamma` node. Finally, when that processing is done, the output of the `tint` node is sent to the `write` node. Again, a task is created and scheduled to execute the body of the node, in this case writing the image to a file. Each time an execution of the `src` node finishes and returns `true`, a new task is spawned to execute the `src` node's body again. Only after the `src` node stops generating new images and all of the images it has already generated have completed processing in the write node will the `wait_for_all` call return.

Adding a Fork-Join Layer Using a `parallel_for`

Now, let's turn our attention to the implementation of the `applyGamma` and `applyTint` functions. In Figure 1-11, we replace the outer `i`-loops in the serial implementations with calls to `tbb::parallel_for`. We use a `parallel_for` Generic Parallel Algorithm to execute across different rows in parallel. A `parallel_for` creates tasks that can be spread across multiple processor cores on a platform. This pattern is an example of the fork-join layer from Figure 1-3 and is described in more detail in Chapter 2.

```
ImagePtr applyGamma(ImagePtr image_ptr, double gamma) {
  auto output_image_ptr =
    std::make_shared<ch01::Image>(image_ptr->name() + "_gamma",
      ch01::IMAGE_WIDTH, ch01::IMAGE_HEIGHT);
  auto in_rows = image_ptr->rows();
  auto out_rows = output_image_ptr->rows();
  const int height = in_rows.size();
  const int width = in_rows[1] - in_rows[0];
```

```
  tbb::parallel_for( 0, height,
    [&in_rows, &out_rows, width, gamma](int i) {
      for ( int j = 0; j < width; ++j ) {
        const ch01::Image::Pixel &p = in_rows[i][j];
        double v = 0.3*p.bgra[2] + 0.59*p.bgra[1] + 0.11*p.bgra[0];
        double res = pow(v, gamma);
        if(res > ch01::MAX_BGR_VALUE) res = ch01::MAX_BGR_VALUE;
        out_rows[i][j] = ch01::Image::Pixel(res, res, res);
      }
    }
  );
  return output_image_ptr;
}
```

```
ImagePtr applyTint(ImagePtr image_ptr, const double *tints) {
  auto output_image_ptr =
    std::make_shared<ch01::Image>(image_ptr->name() + "_tinted",
      ch01::IMAGE_WIDTH, ch01::IMAGE_HEIGHT);
  auto in_rows = image_ptr->rows();
  auto out_rows = output_image_ptr->rows();
  const int height = in_rows.size();
  const int width = in_rows[1] - in_rows[0];
```

```
  tbb::parallel_for( 0, height,
    [&in_rows, &out_rows, width, tints](int i) {
      for ( int j = 0; j < width; ++j ) {
        const ch01::Image::Pixel &p = in_rows[i][j];
        std::uint8_t b = (double)p.bgra[0] +
                          (ch01::MAX_BGR_VALUE-p.bgra[0])*tints[0];
        std::uint8_t g = (double)p.bgra[1] +
                          (ch01::MAX_BGR_VALUE-p.bgra[1])*tints[1];
        std::uint8_t r = (double)p.bgra[2] +
                          (ch01::MAX_BGR_VALUE-p.bgra[2])*tints[2];
        out_rows[i][j] =
          ch01::Image::Pixel(
            (b > ch01::MAX_BGR_VALUE) ? ch01::MAX_BGR_VALUE : b,
            (g > ch01::MAX_BGR_VALUE) ? ch01::MAX_BGR_VALUE : g,
            (r > ch01::MAX_BGR_VALUE) ? ch01::MAX_BGR_VALUE : r
          );
      }
    }
  );
  return output_image_ptr;
}
```

Figure 1-11. *Adding* parallel_for *to apply the gamma correction and tint across rows in parallel*

Adding a SIMD Layer Using a Parallel STL Transform

We can further optimize our two computational kernels by replacing the inner j-loops with calls to the Parallel STL function `transform`. The `transform` algorithm applies a function to each element in an input range, storing the results into an output range. The arguments to `transform` are (1) the execution policy, (2 and 3) the input range of elements, (4) the beginning of the output range, and (5) the lambda expression that is applied to each element in the input range and whose result is stored to the output elements.

In Figure 1-12, we use the `unseq` execution policy to tell the compiler to use the SIMD version of the transform function. The Parallel STL functions are described in more detail in Chapter 4.

```cpp
#include <iostream>
#include <vector>
#include <tbb/tbb.h>
#include <pstl/algorithm>
#include <pstl/execution>
#include "ch01.h"

using ImagePtr = std::shared_ptr<ch01::Image>;
void writeImage(ImagePtr image_ptr);

ImagePtr applyGamma(ImagePtr image_ptr, double gamma) {
  auto output_image_ptr =
    std::make_shared<ch01::Image>(image_ptr->name() + "_gamma",
      ch01::IMAGE_WIDTH, ch01::IMAGE_HEIGHT);
  auto in_rows = image_ptr->rows();
  auto out_rows = output_image_ptr->rows();
  const int height = in_rows.size();
  const int width = in_rows[1] - in_rows[0];

  tbb::parallel_for( 0, height,
    [&in_rows, &out_rows, width, gamma](int i) {
      auto in_row = in_rows[i];
      auto out_row = out_rows[i];
      std::transform(pstl::execution::unseq, in_row, in_row+width,
        out_row, [gamma](const ch01::Image::Pixel &p) {
          double v = 0.3*p.bgra[2] + 0.59*p.bgra[1] + 0.11*p.bgra[0];
          assert(v > 0);
          double res = pow(v, gamma);
          if(res > ch01::MAX_BGR_VALUE) res = ch01::MAX_BGR_VALUE;
          return ch01::Image::Pixel(res, res, res);
        });
    }
  );
  return output_image_ptr;
}
```

Figure 1-12. *Using* `std::transform` *to add SIMD parallelism to the inner loops*

```
ImagePtr applyTint(ImagePtr image_ptr, const double *tints) {
  auto output_image_ptr =
    std::make_shared<ch01::Image>(image_ptr->name() + "_tinted",
      ch01::IMAGE_WIDTH, ch01::IMAGE_HEIGHT);
  auto in_rows = image_ptr->rows();
  auto out_rows = output_image_ptr->rows();
  const int height = in_rows.size();
  const int width = in_rows[1] - in_rows[0];

  tbb::parallel_for( 0, height,
    [&in_rows, &out_rows, width, tints](int i) {
      auto in_row = in_rows[i];
      auto out_row = out_rows[i];
      std::transform(pstl::execution::unseq, in_row, in_row+width,
        out_row, [tints](const ch01::Image::Pixel &p) {
        std::uint8_t b = (double)p.bgra[0] +
                        (ch01::MAX_BGR_VALUE-p.bgra[0])*tints[0];
        std::uint8_t g = (double)p.bgra[1] +
                        (ch01::MAX_BGR_VALUE-p.bgra[1])*tints[1];
        std::uint8_t r = (double)p.bgra[2] +
                        (ch01::MAX_BGR_VALUE-p.bgra[2])*tints[2];
        return ch01::Image::Pixel(
          (b > ch01::MAX_BGR_VALUE) ? ch01::MAX_BGR_VALUE : b,
          (g > ch01::MAX_BGR_VALUE) ? ch01::MAX_BGR_VALUE : g,
          (r > ch01::MAX_BGR_VALUE) ? ch01::MAX_BGR_VALUE : r
        );
      });
    }
  );
  return output_image_ptr;
}
```

Figure 1-12. (*continued*)

In Figure 1-12, each Image::Pixel object contains an array with four single byte elements, representing the blue, green, red, and alpha values for that pixel. By using the unseq execution policy, a vectorized loop is used to apply the function across the row of elements. This level of parallelization corresponds to the SIMD layer in Figure 1-3 and takes advantage of the vector units in the CPU core that the code executes on but does not spread the computation across different cores.

Note   Passing an execution policy to a Parallel STL algorithm does not guarantee parallel execution. It is legal for the library to choose a more restrictive execution policy than the one requested. It is therefore important to check the impact of using an execution policy – especially one that depends on compiler implementations!

While the examples we created in Figure 1-7 through Figure 1-12 are a bit contrived, they demonstrate the breadth and power of the TBB library's parallel execution interfaces. Using a single library, we expressed message-driven, fork-join, and SIMD parallelism, composing them together into a single application.

Summary

In this chapter, we started by explaining why a library such as TBB is even more relevant today than it was when it was first introduced over 10 years ago. We then briefly looked at the major features in the library, including the parallel execution interfaces and the other features that are independent of the execution interfaces. We saw that the high-level execution interfaces map to the common message-driven, fork-join, and SIMD layers that are found in many parallel applications. We then discussed how to get a copy of TBB and verify that our environment is correctly set up by writing, compiling, and executing very simple examples. We concluded the chapter by building a more complete example that uses all three high-level execution interfaces.

We are now ready to walk through the key support for parallel programming in the next few chapters: Generic Parallel Algorithms (Chapter 2), Flow Graphs (Chapter 3), Parallel STL (Chapter 4), Synchronization (Chapter 5), Concurrent Containers (Chapter 6), and Scalable Memory Allocation (Chapter 7).

CHAPTER 2

Generic Parallel Algorithms

What is the best method for scheduling parallel loops? How do we process data structures in parallel that do not support random-access iterators? What's the best way to add parallelism to applications that look like pipelines? If the TBB library only provided tasks and a task scheduler, we would need to answer these questions ourselves. Luckily, we don't need to plow through the many master's theses and doctoral dissertations written on these topics. The TBB library developers have already done this dirty work for us! They provide the best-known methods for addressing these scenarios as template functions and template classes, a group of features known as the TBB generic parallel algorithms. These algorithms capture many of the processing patterns that are the cornerstones of multithreaded programming.

> **Note** The TBB library developers have historically used the term generic parallel *algorithms* to describe this set of features. By *algorithm*, they do not mean a specific computation like matrix multiplication, LU decomposition, or even something like `std::find`, but instead they mean common execution patterns. It has been argued by some reviewers of this book that these features would therefore be more accurately referred to as *patterns* and not algorithms. However, to align with the terminology that the TBB library has been using for many years, we refer to these features as generic parallel *algorithms* in this book.

© Intel Corporation 2019
M. Voss, R. Asenjo, J. Reinders, *Pro TBB*, https://doi.org/10.1007/978-1-4842-4398-5_2

We should have a strong preference for using these prewritten algorithms, whenever they apply, instead of writing our own implementations. The developers of TBB have spent years testing and improving their performance! The set of algorithms included in the TBB library do not, of course, exhaustively cover every possible scenario, but if one of them does match our processing pattern, we should use it. The algorithms provided by TBB capture the majority of the scalable parallelism in applications. In Chapter 8, we discuss design patterns for parallel programming, such as those described in *Patterns for Parallel Programming by Mattson, Sanders and Massingill (Addison-Wesley)*, and how we can implement them using the TBB generic parallel algorithms.

As shown in Figure 2-1, all of the TBB generic algorithms start from a single thread of execution. When a thread encounters a parallel algorithm, it spreads the work associated with that algorithm across multiple threads. When all of the pieces of work are done, the execution merges back together and continues again on the initial single thread.

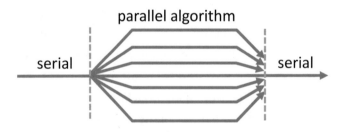

Figure 2-1. *The fork-join nature of the TBB parallel algorithms*

TBB algorithms provide a powerful but relatively easy parallel model to apply because they can often be added incrementally and with a fairly local view of the code under consideration. We can look for the most time-consuming region of a program, add a TBB parallel algorithm to speed up that region, then look for the next most time-consuming region, add parallelism there, and so on.

It must be understood however that TBB algorithms ***do not*** guarantee parallel execution! Instead, they only communicate to the library that parallel execution is allowed. If we look at Figure 2-1 from a TBB perspective, this means that all of the worker threads may participate in executing parts of the computation, only a subset of threads may participate, or just the master thread may participate. Programs and libraries that assume that the parallelism is optional, like TBB does, are referred to as having *relaxed sequential semantics*.

A parallel program has *sequential semantics* if executing it using only a single thread does not change the program's semantics. As we will note several times in this book though, the results of a sequential and parallel execution of a program may not always match exactly due to rounding issues and other sources of inexactness. We acknowledge these potential, nonsemantic differences by using the term *relaxed sequential semantics.* While models like TBB and the OpenMP API offer relaxed sequential semantics, some other models, such as MPI, let us write applications that have cyclic relationships that require parallel execution. The relaxed sequential semantics of TBB are an important part of what makes it useful for writing composable applications, as introduced in Chapter 1 and described in more detail in Chapter 9. For now, we should just remember that any of the algorithms described in this chapter will spread the work across one or more threads, but not necessarily all of the threads available in the system.

The set of algorithms available in the Threading Building Blocks 2019 distribution is shown in the table in Figure 2-2. They are all in namespace tbb and are available when the tbb.h header file is included. The basics of the **boldface** algorithms are covered in this chapter, with the other algorithms described in later chapters. We also provide a sidebar **Lambda expressions –vs- user-defined classes** that explains that while we almost exclusively use lambda expressions to pass code to the TBB algorithms in our examples in this book, these arguments can almost always be replaced by user-defined function objects if so desired.

Category	Generic Algorithm	Brief Description
Functional parallelism	**parallel_invoke**	Evaluates several functions in parallel.
Simple loops	**parallel_for**	Performs parallel iteration over a range of values.
	parallel_reduce	Computes a reduction over a range of values.
	parallel_deterministic_reduce	Computes a reduction over a range of values, with a deterministic split / join behavior.
	parallel_scan	Computes a parallel prefix over a range of values.
	parallel_for_each	A parallel implementation of std::for_each. Described in more detail in Chapter 4.
Complex loops	**parallel_do**	Processes work items in a container in parallel, with the ability to add additional work items dynamically.
Pipelines	pipeline	A class for performing pipelined execution of filters. Described in Appendix B.
	parallel_pipeline	A strongly typed function for performing pipelined execution of filters.
Sorting	parallel_sort	A function to perform a parallel sort of a sequence. Described in more detail in Chapter 4.

Figure 2-2. *The Generic Algorithms in the Threading Building Blocks library. The bold-face algorithms are described in more detail in this chapter.*

LAMBDA EXPRESSIONS –VS– USER-DEFINED CLASSES

Since the first release of TBB predates the C++11 standard that introduced lambda expressions into the language, the TBB generic algorithms do not require the use of lambda expressions. Sometimes we can use the same interface with lambda expressions or with function objects (functors). In other cases, there are two sets of interfaces for an algorithm: a set that is more convenient with lambda expressions and a set that is more convenient with user-defined objects.

For example, in place of

```
#include <vector>
#include <tbb/tbb.h>

void f(int v);

void sidebar_pfor_lambda(int N, const std::vector<int> &a) {
  tbb::parallel_for(0, N, 1,
    [&a](int i) {
        f(a[i]);
    }
  );
}
```

we can use a user-defined class and write

```
class Body {
  const std::vector<int> &myVector;
public:
  Body(const std::vector<int> &v) : myVector{v} {}
  void operator()(int i) const {
    f(myVector[i]);
  }
};

void sidebar_pfor_functor(int N, const std::vector<int> &a) {
  tbb::parallel_for(0, N, 1, Body{a});
}
```

Often the choice between using a lambda expression or a user-defined object is simply a matter of preference.

Functional / Task Parallelism

Perhaps the simplest algorithm provided by the TBB library is parallel_invoke, a function that allows us to execute as few as two functions in parallel, or as many as we wish to specify:

```
template<typename Func0, [...,] typename FuncN>
void parallel_invoke(const Func0& f0, [...,] const FuncN& fN);
```

The pattern name for this concept is *map* – which we will discuss more in Chapter 8 when we discuss patterns explicitly. The independence expressed by this algorithm/ pattern allows it to scale very well, making it the preferred parallelism to use when we can apply it. We will also see that `parallel_for`, because the loop bodies must be independent, can be used to similar effect.

A complete description of the interfaces available for `parallel_invoke` can be found in Appendix B. If we have a set of functions that we need to invoke and it is safe to execute the invocations in parallel, we use a `parallel_invoke`. For example, we can sort two vectors, v1 and v2, by calling a `serialQuicksort` on each vector, one after the other:

```
serialQuicksort(serial_v1.begin(), serial_v1.end());
serialQuicksort(serial_v2.begin(), serial_v2.end());
```

Or, since these calls are independent of each other, we can use a `parallel_invoke` to allow the TBB library to create tasks that can be executed in parallel by different worker threads to overlap the two calls, as shown in Figure 2-3.

```
#include <iostream>
#include <vector>
#include <tbb/tbb.h>

struct DataItem {
  int id;
  double value;
  DataItem(int i, double v) : id{i}, value{v} {}
};

using QSVector = std::vector<DataItem>;

void serialQuicksort(QSVector::iterator b, QSVector::iterator e);

void fig_2_3(QSVector &v1, QSVector &v2) {
  tbb::parallel_invoke(
    [&v1]() {serialQuicksort(v1.begin(), v1.end());},
    [&v2]() {serialQuicksort(v2.begin(), v2.end());}
  );
}
```

Figure 2-3. *Using* `parallel_invoke` *to execute two* `serialQuicksort` *calls in parallel*

If the two invocations of `serialQuicksort` execute for roughly the same amount of time and there are no resource constraints, this parallel implementation can be completed in half the time it takes to sequentially invoke the functions one after the other.

Note   We as developers are responsible for invoking functions in parallel only when they can be safely executed in parallel. That is, TBB will **not** automatically identify dependencies and apply synchronization, privatization, or other parallelization strategies to make the code safe. This responsibility is ours when we use `parallel_invoke` or any of the parallel algorithms we discuss in this chapter.

Using `parallel_invoke` is straightforward, but a single invocation of `parallel_invoke` is not very *scalable*. A scalable algorithm makes effective use of additional cores and hardware resources as they become available.

An algorithm shows *strong scaling* if it takes less time to solve a problem with a fixed size as additional cores are added. For example, an algorithm that shows good strong scaling may complete the processing of a given data set two times faster than the sequential algorithm when two cores are available but complete the processing of the same data set 100 times faster than the sequential algorithm when 100 cores are available.

An algorithm shows *weak scaling* if it takes the same amount of time to solve a problem with a fixed data set size *per processor* as more processors are added. For example, an algorithm that shows good weak scaling may be able to process two times the data than its sequential version in a fixed period of time using two processors and 100 times the data than its sequential version in that same fixed period of time when using 100 processors.

Using a `parallel_invoke` to execute two sorts in parallel will demonstrate neither strong nor weak scaling, since the algorithm can at most make use of two processors. If we have 100 processors available, 98 of them will be idle because we have not given them anything to do. Instead of writing code like our example, we should develop scalable applications that allow us to implement parallelism once without the need to revisit the implementation each time new architectures containing more cores become available.

Luckily, TBB can handle nested parallelism efficiently (described in detail in Chapter 9), and so we can create scalable parallelism by using `parallel_invoke` in recursive divide-and-conquer algorithms (a pattern we discuss in Chapter 8). TBB also includes additional generic parallel algorithms, covered later in this chapter, to target patterns that haven proven effective for achieving scalable parallelism, such as loops.

A Slightly More Complicated Example: A Parallel Implementation of Quicksort

A well-known example of a recursive divide-and-conquer algorithm is quicksort, as shown in Figure 2-4. Quicksort works by recursively shuffling an array around pivot values, placing the values that are less than or equal to the pivot value in the left partition of the array and the values that are greater than the pivot value in the right partition of the array. When the recursion reaches the base case, arrays of size one, the whole array has been sorted.

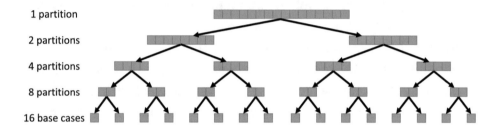

(a)   The recursive partitioning performed by quicksort

```
void serialQuicksort(QSVector::iterator b, QSVector::iterator e) {
  if (b >= e) return;

  // do shuffle
  double pivot_value = b->value;
  QSVector::iterator i = b, j = e-1;
  while (i != j) {
    while (i != j && pivot_value < j->value) --j;
    while (i != j && i->value <= pivot_value) ++i;
    std::iter_swap(i, j);
  }
  std::iter_swap(b, i);

  // recursive call
  serialQuicksort(b, i);
  serialQuicksort(i+1, e);
}
```

(b)   The source code for a serial implementation of quicksort

Figure 2-4.   *A serial implementation of quicksort*

We can develop a parallel implementation of quicksort as shown in Figure 2-5 by replacing the two recursive calls to `serialQuicksort` with a `parallel_invoke`. In addition to the use of `parallel_invoke`, we also introduce a cutoff value. In the original serial quicksort, we recursively partition all the way down to arrays of a single element.

Note   Spawning and scheduling a TBB task is not free – a rule of thumb is that a task should execute for at least 1 microsecond or 10,000 processor cycles in order to mitigate the overheads associated with task creation and scheduling. We provide experiments that demonstrate and justify this rule of thumb in more detail in Chapter 16.

To limit overheads in our parallel implementation, we recursively call parallel_invoke only until we dip below 100 elements and then directly call serialQuicksort instead.

```cpp
void parallelQuicksort(QSVector::iterator b, QSVector::iterator e) {
  const int cutoff = 100;

  if (e - b < cutoff) {
    serialQuicksort(b, e);
  } else {
    // do shuffle
    double pivot_value = b->value;
    QSVector::iterator i = b, j = e - 1;
    while (i != j) {
      while (i != j && pivot_value < j->value) --j;
      while (i != j && i->value <= pivot_value) ++i;
      std::iter_swap(i, j);
    }
    std::iter_swap(b, i);

    // recursive call
    tbb::parallel_invoke(
      [=]() { parallelQuicksort(b, i); },
      [=]() { parallelQuicksort(i + 1, e); }
    );
  }
}
```

Figure 2-5. *A parallel implementation of quicksort using* parallel_invoke

You may notice that the parallel implementation of quicksort has a big limitation – the shuffle is done completely serially. At the top level, this means we have an $O(n)$ operation that is done on a single thread before any of the parallel work can begin. This can limit the speedup. We leave it up to those that are interested to see how this limitation might be addressed by known parallel partitioning implementations (see the "For More Information" section at the end of this chapter).

Loops: **parallel_for**, **parallel_reduce**, and **parallel_scan**

For many applications, the execution time is dominated by time spent in loops. There are several TBB algorithms that express parallel loops, letting us quickly add scalable parallelism to the important loops in an application. The algorithms labeled as "Simple Loops" in Figure 2-2 are ones where the beginning and end of the iteration space can easily be determined by the time that the loop starts.

For example, we know there will be exactly N iterations in the following loop, so we classify it as a simple loop:

```
for (int i = 0; i < N; ++i)
  f(a[i]);
```

All of the simple loop algorithms in TBB are based on two important concepts, a *Range* and a *Body*. A Range represents a recursively divisible set of values. For a loop, a Range is typically the indices in the iteration space or the values that an iterator will take on as it iterates through a container. The Body is the function we apply to each value in the Range; in TBB, the Body is typically provided as a C++ lambda expression but can also be provided as a function object (see ***Lambda expressions –vs- user-defined classes***).

parallel_for: Applying a Body to Each Element in a Range

Let's start with a small serial for loop that applies a function to an element of an array in each iteration:

```
for (int i = 0; i < N; ++i)
  f(a[i]);
```

We can create a parallel version of this loop by using a parallel_for:

```
template<typename Index, typename Func>
Func parallel_for(Index first, Index last, [Index step,]
                  const Func& f);
```

A complete description of the interfaces available for `parallel_for` can be found in Appendix B. In the small example loop, the Range is the half-open interval [0, N), the step is 1, and the Body is `f(a[i])`. We can express this as shown in Figure 2-6.

```
#include <tbb/tbb.h>

void f(int v);

void fig_2_6(int N, const std::vector<int> &a) {
  tbb::parallel_for(0, N, 1, [a](int i) {
    f(a[i]);
  });
}
```

Figure 2-6. *Creating a parallel loop using* `parallel_for`

When TBB executes a `parallel_for`, the Range is divided up into chunks of iterations. Each chunk, paired with a Body, becomes a task that is scheduled onto one of the threads that participate in executing the algorithm. The TBB library handles the scheduling of tasks for us, so all we need to do is to use the `parallel_for` function to express that the iterations of the loop should be executed in parallel. In later chapters, we discuss tuning the behavior of TBB parallel loops. For now, let us assume that TBB generates a good number of tasks for the range size and number of available cores. In most cases, this is a good assumption to make.

It is important to understand that by using a `parallel_for`, we are asserting that it's safe to execute the iterations of the loop in any order and in parallel with each other. The TBB library does nothing to check that executing the iterations of a `parallel_for` (or in fact any of the generic algorithms) in parallel will generate the same results as a serial execution of the algorithm – it is our job as developers to be sure that this is the case when we choose to use a parallel algorithm. In Chapter 5, we discuss synchronization mechanisms in TBB that can be used to make some unsafe code, safe. In Chapter 6, we discuss concurrent containers that provide thread-safe data structures that can also sometimes help us make code thread-safe. But ultimately, we need to ensure when we use a parallel algorithm that any potential changes in read and write access patterns do not change the validity of the results. We also need to ensure that we are using only thread-safe libraries and functions from within our parallel code.

For example, the following loop is *not* safe to execute as a `parallel_for` since each iteration depends on the result of the previous iteration. Changing the order of execution of this loop will alter the final values stored in the elements of array a:

```
for (int i = 1; i < N; ++i)
  a[i] = a[i-1] + 1;
```

Imagine if the array a=$\{1,0,0,0,\ldots,0\}$. After executing this loop sequentially, it will hold $\{1,2,3,4,\ldots,N\}$. But if the loop executes out-of-order, the results will be different. A mental exercise, when looking for loops that are safe to execute in parallel, is to ask yourself whether the results will be the same if the loop iterations are executed all at once, or in random order, or in reverse order. In this case, if a=$\{1,0,0,0,\ldots,0\}$ and the iterations of the loop are executed in reverse order, a will hold $\{1,2,1,1,\ldots,1\}$ when the loop is complete. Obviously, execution order matters for this loop!

Formal descriptions of data dependence analysis are beyond the scope of this book but can be found in many compiler and parallel programming books, including *High-Performance Compilers for Parallel Computing* by Michael Wolfe (Pearson) and *Optimizing Compilers for Modern Architectures* by Allen and Kennedy (Morgan Kaufmann). Tools like Intel Inspector in Intel Parallel Studio XE can also be used to find and debug threading errors, including in applications that use TBB.

A Slightly More Complicated Example: Parallel Matrix Multiplication

Figure 2-7 shows a nonoptimized serial implementation of a matrix multiplication loop nest that computes C = AB for MxM matrices. We use this kernel here for demonstration purposes – if you ever need to use matrix multiply in a real application and do not consider yourself to be an optimization guru – you will almost certainly be better served by using a highly optimized implementation from a math library that implements the Basic Linear Algebra Subprograms (BLAS) like the Intel Math Kernel Library (MKL), BLIS, or ATLAS. Matrix multiplication is a good example here because it is a small kernel and performs a basic operation we are all familiar with. With these disclaimers covered, let us continue with Figure 2-7.

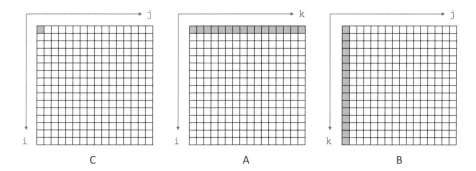

(a) The elements traversed by the first pass through the inner k-loop to calculate a single element of the C matrix.

```
void fig_2_7(int M, double *a, double *b, double *c) {
  for (int i = 0; i < M; ++i) {
    for (int j = 0; j < M; ++j) {
      int c_index = i*M+j;
      for (int k = 0; k < M; ++k) {
        c[c_index] += a[i*M + k] * b[k*M+j];
      }
    }
  }
}
```
(b) The serial implementation.

Figure 2-7. *A nonoptimized implementation of matrix multiplication*

We can quickly implement a parallel version of the matrix multiplication in Figure 2-7 by using `parallel_for` as shown in Figure 2-8. In this implementation, we make the outer i loop parallel. An iteration of the outer i loop executes the enclosed j and k loops and so, unless M is very small, will have enough work to exceed the 1 microsecond rule of thumb. It is often better to make outer loops parallel when possible to keep overheads low.

```
void fig_2_8(int M, double *a, double *b, double *c) {
  tbb::parallel_for( 0, M, [=](int i) {
    for (int j = 0; j < M; ++j) {
      int c_index = i*M+j;
      for (int k = 0; k < M; ++k) {
        c[c_index] += a[i*M + k] * b[k*M+j];
      }
    }
  });
}
```

Figure 2-8. *A simple* `parallel_for` *implementation of matrix multiply*

The code in Figure 2-8 quickly gets us a basic parallel version of matrix multiply. While this is a correct parallel implementation, it will leave a lot of performance on the table because of the way it is traversing the arrays. In Chapter 16, we will talk about the advanced features of `parallel_for` that can be used to tune performance.

`parallel_reduce`: Calculating a Single Result Across a Range

Another very common pattern found in applications is a reduction, commonly known as the "reduce pattern" or "map-reduce" because it tends to be used with a *map* pattern (see more about pattern terminology in Chapter 8).

A reduction computes a single value from a collection of values. Example applications include calculating a sum, a minimum value, or a maximum value.

Let's consider a loop that finds the maximum value in an array:

```
int max_value = std::numeric_limits<int>::min();
for (int i = 0; i < a.size(); ++i) {
  max_value = std::max(max_value,a[i]);
}
```

Computing a maximum from a set of values is an associative operation; that is, it's legal to perform this operation on groups of values and then combine those partial results, in order, later. Computing a maximum is also commutative, so we do not even need to combine the partial results in any particular order.

For loops that perform associative operations, TBB provides the function `parallel_reduce`:

```
template<typename Range, typename Value,
         typename Func, typename Reduction>
Value parallel_reduce(const Range& range, const Value& identity,
                        const Func& func, const Reduction& reduction);
```

A complete description of the `parallel_reduce` interfaces is provided in Appendix B.

Many common mathematical operations are associative, such as addition, multiplication, computing a maximum, and computing a minimum. Some operations are associative in theory but are not associative when implemented on real systems due to limitations in numerical representations. We should be aware of the implications of depending on associativity for parallelism (see ***Associativity and floating-point types***).

ASSOCIATIVITY AND FLOATING-POINT TYPES

In computer arithmetic, it is not always practical to represent real numbers with exact precision. Instead, floating-point types such as `float, double,` and `long double` are used as an approximation. The consequence of these approximations is that mathematical properties that apply to operations on real numbers do not necessarily apply to their floating-point counterparts. For example, while addition is associative and commutative on real numbers, it is neither of these for floating-point numbers.

For example, if we compute the sum of N real values, each of which is equal to 1.0, we would expect the result to be N.

```
float r = 0.0;
for (uint64_t i = 0; i < N; ++i)
  r += 1.0;
std::cout << "in-order sum == " << r << std::endl;
```

But there is a limited number of significant digits in the `float` representation and so not all integer values can be represented exactly. So, for example, if we run this loop with N == 10e6 (10 million), we will get an output of 10000000. But if we execute this loop with N == 20e6, we get an output of 16777216. The variable r simply cannot represent 16777217 since the standard `float` representation has a 24-bit mantissa (significand) and 16777217 requires 25 bits. When we add 1.0, the result rounds down to 16777216, and each subsequent addition of 1.0 also rounds down to 16777216. To be fair, at each step, the result of 16777216 is a good approximation of 16777217. It is the accumulation of these rounding errors that makes the final result so bad.

If we break this sum into two loops and combine partial results, we get the right answer in both cases:

```
float tmp1 = 0.0, tmp2 = 0.0;
for (uint64_t i = 0; i < N/2; ++i)
  tmp1 += 1.0;
for (uint64_t i = N/2; i < N; ++i)
  tmp2 += 1.0;
float r2 = tmp1 + tmp2;
std::cout << "associative sum == " << r2 << std::endl;
```

Why? Because r can represent larger numbers, just not always exactly. The values in tmp1 and tmp2 are of similar magnitude, and therefore the addition impacts the available significant digits in the representation, and we get a result that is a good approximation of 20 million. This example is an extreme case of how associativity can change the results of a computation using floating-point numbers.

The take-away of this discussion is that when we use a parallel_reduce, it uses associativity to compute and combine partial results in parallel. So, we may get different results when compared to a serial implementation when using floating-point numbers. And in fact, depending on the number of participating threads, the implementation of parallel_reduce may choose to create a different number of partial results from run to run. Therefore, we may also get different results from run to run in the parallel implementation, even on the same input.

Before we panic and conclude that we should never use a parallel_reduce, we should keep in mind that implementations that use floating-point numbers generally result in an approximation. Getting different results on the same input does not necessarily mean that at least one of the results is wrong. It just means that the rounding errors accumulated differently for two different runs. It is up to us as developers to decide whether or not the differences matter for an application.

If we want to ensure that we at least get the same results on each run on the same input data, we can choose to use a parallel_deterministic_reduce as described in Chapter 16. This deterministic implementation always creates the same number of partial results and combines them in the same order for the same input, so the approximation will be the same from run to run.

As with all of the simple loop algorithms, to use a TBB parallel_reduce, we need to provide a Range (range) and Body (func). But we also need to provide an Identity Value (identity) and a Reduction Body (reduction).

To create parallelism for a parallel_reduce, the TBB library divides the range into chunks and creates tasks that apply func to each chunk. In Chapter 16, we discuss how to use Partitioners to control the size of the chunks that are created, but for now, we can assume that TBB creates chunks of an appropriate size to minimize overheads and balance load. Each task that executes func starts with a value init that is initialized with identity and then computes and returns a partial result for its chunk. The TBB library combines these partial results by calling the reduction function to create a single final result for the whole loop.

The identity argument is a value that leaves other values unchanged when they are combined with it using the operation that is being parallelized. It is well known that the identity element with respect to addition (additive identity) is "0" (since x + 0 = x) and that the identity element with respect to multiplication (multiplicative identity) is "1" (since x * 1 = x). The reduction function takes two partial results and combines them.

Figure 2-9 shows how func and reduction functions may be applied to compute the maximum value from an array of 16 elements if the Range is broken into four chunks. In this example, the associative operation applied by func to the elements of the array is max() and the identity element is -∞, since max(x,-∞)=x. In C++, we can use std::max as the operation and std::numeric_limits<int>::min() as the programmatic representation of -∞.

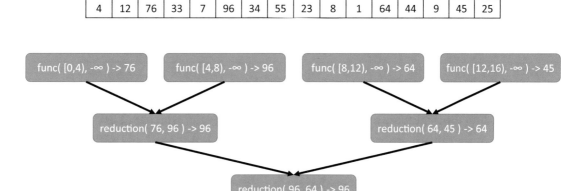

Figure 2-9. *How the func and* reduction *functions are called to compute a maximum value*

We can express our simple maximum value loop using a parallel_reduce as shown in Figure 2-10.

```
int fig_2_10(const std::vector<int> &a) {
  int max_value = tbb::parallel_reduce(
    /* the range = */ tbb::blocked_range<int>(0, a.size()),
    /* identity = */ std::numeric_limits<int>::min(),
    /* func = */
    [&](const tbb::blocked_range<int> &r, int init) -> int {
      for (int i = r.begin(); i != r.end(); ++i) {
        init = std::max(init, a[i]);
      }
      return init;
    },
    /* reduction = */
    [](int x, int y) -> int {
      return std::max(x,y);
    }
  );
  return max_value;
}
```

Figure 2-10. *Using* `parallel_reduce` *to compute a maximum value*

You may notice in Figure 2-10 that we use a `blocked_range` object for the Range, instead of just providing the beginning and ending of the range as we did with `parallel_for`. The `parallel_for` algorithm provides a simplified syntax that is not available with `parallel_reduce`. For `parallel_reduce`, we must pass a Range object directly, but luckily we can use one of the predefined ranges provided by the library, which include `blocked_range`, `blocked_range2d`, and `blocked_range3d` among others. These other range objects will be described in more detail in Chapter 16, and their complete interfaces are provided in Appendix B.

A `blocked_range`, used in Figure 2-10, represents a 1D iteration space. To construct one, we provide the beginning and ending value. In the Body, we use its `begin()` and `end()` functions to get the beginning and ending values of the chunk of values that this body execution has been assigned and then iterate over that subrange. In Figure 2-8, each individual value in the Range was sent to the `parallel_for` Body, and so there is no need for an `i`-loop to iterate over a range. In Figure 2-10, the Body receives a `blocked_range` object that represents a chunk of iterations, and therefore we still have an `i`-loop that iterates over the entire chunk assigned to it.

A Slightly More Complicated Example: Calculating π by Numerical Integration

Figure 2-11 shows an approach to calculate π by numerical integration. The height of each rectangle is calculated using the Pythagorean Theorem. The area of one quadrant of a unit circle is computed in the loop and multiplied by 4 to get the total area of the circle, which is equal to π.

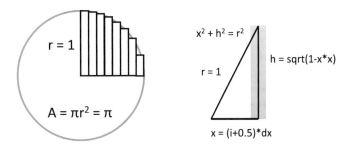

(a)   Using Numerical Integration to calculate π

```
#include <cmath>

double fig_2_11(int num_intervals) {
  double dx = 1.0 / num_intervals;
  double sum = 0.0;
  for (int i = 0; i < num_intervals; ++i) {
    double x = (i+0.5)*dx;
    double h = std::sqrt(1-x*x);
    sum += h*dx;
  }
  double pi = 4 * sum;
  return pi;
}
```

(b) The serial implementation

Figure 2-11. *A serial π calculation using the rectangular integral method*

The code in Figure 2-11 computes the sum of the areas of all of the rectangles, a reduction operation. To use a TBB `parallel_reduce`, we need to identify the `range`, body, `identity` value, and `reduction` function. For this example, the `range` is [0, num_intervals), and the body will be similar to the i-loop in Figure 2-11. The `identity` value is 0.0 since we are performing a sum. And the `reduction` body, which needs to combine partial results, will return the sum of two values. The parallel implementation using a TBB parallel_reduce is shown in Figure 2-12.

```cpp
#include <cmath>
#include <tbb/tbb.h>

double fig_2_12(int num_intervals) {
  double dx = 1.0 / num_intervals;
  double sum = tbb::parallel_reduce(
    /* range = */ tbb::blocked_range<int>(0, num_intervals),
    /* idenity = */ 0.0,
    /* func */
    [=](const tbb::blocked_range<int> &r, double init)
    -> double {
      for (int i = r.begin(); i != r.end(); ++i) {
        double x = (i + 0.5)*dx;
        double h = std::sqrt(1 - x*x);
        init += h*dx;
      }
      return init;
    },
    /* reduction */
    [](double x, double y) -> double {
      return x + y;
    }
  );
  double pi = 4 * sum;
  return pi;
}
```

Figure 2-12. *Implementation of pi using* `tbb::parallel_reduce`

As with parallel_for, there are advanced features and options that can be used with parallel_reduce to tune performance and to manage rounding errors (see **Associativity and floating-point types**). These advanced options are covered in Chapter 16.

parallel_scan: A Reduction with Intermediate Values

A less common, but still important, pattern found in applications is a scan (sometimes called a prefix). A scan is similar to a reduction, but not only does it compute a single value from a collection of values, it also calculates an intermediate result for each element in the Range (*the prefixes*). An example is a running sum of the values x_0, x_1, ... x_N. The results include each value in the running sum, y_0, y_1, ... y_N, and the final sum y_N.

$$y_0 = x_0$$

$$y_1 = x_0 + x_1$$

...

$$y_N = x_0 + x_1 + ... + x_N$$

A serial loop that computes a running sum from a vector v follows:

```
int serialImpl(const std::vector<int> &v,
               std::vector<int> &rsum) {
  int N = v.size();
  rsum[0] = v[0];
  for (int i = 1; i < N; ++i) {
    rsum[i] = rsum[i-1] + v[i];
  }
  int final_sum = rsum[N-1];
  return final_sum;
}
```

On the surface, a scan looks like a serial algorithm. Each prefix depends on the results computed in all of the previous iterations. While it might seem surprising, there are however efficient parallel implementations of this seemingly serial algorithm. The TBB parallel_scan algorithm implements an efficient parallel scan. Its interface requires that we provide a range, an identity value, a scan body, and a combine body:

```
template<typename Range, typename Value,
         typename Scan, typename Combine>
Value parallel_scan( const Range& range, const Value& identity,
                     const Scan& scan, const Combine& combine);
```

The range, identity value, and combine body are analogous to the range, identity value, and reduction body of parallel_reduce. And, as with the other simple loop algorithms, the range is divided by the TBB library into chunks and TBB tasks are created to apply the body (scan) to these chunks. A complete description of the parallel_scan interfaces is provided in Appendix B.

What is different about parallel_scan is that the scan body may be executed more than once on the same chunk of iterations – first in a *pre-scan* mode and then later in a *final-scan* mode.

In *final-scan* mode, the body is passed an accurate prefix result for the iteration that immediately precedes its subrange. Using this `value`, the body computes and stores the prefixes for each iteration in its subrange and returns the accurate prefix for the last element in its subrange.

However, when the scan body is executed in *pre-scan* mode, it receives a starting prefix value that is not the final value for the element that precedes its given range. Just like with `parallel_reduce`, a `parallel_scan` depends on associativity. In pre-scan mode, the starting prefix value may represent a subrange that precedes it, but not the complete range that precedes it. Using this value, it returns a (not yet final) prefix for the last element in its subrange. The returned value represents a partial result for the starting prefix combined with its subrange. By using these *pre-scan* and *final-scan* modes, it is possible to exploit useful parallelism in a scan algorithm.

How Does This Work?

Let's look at the running sum example again and think about computing it in three chunks A, B, and C. In a sequential implementation, we compute all of the prefixes for A, then B, and then C (three steps done in order). We can do better with a parallel scan as shown in Figure 2-13.

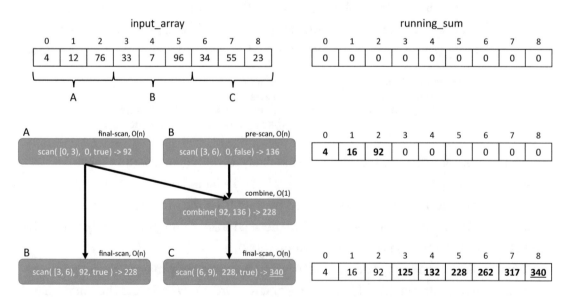

Figure 2-13. *Performing a scan in parallel to compute a sum*

First, we compute the scan of A in final-scan mode since it is the first set of values and so its prefix values will be accurate if it is passed an initial value of identity. At the same time that we start A, we start B in pre-scan mode. Once these two scans are done, we can now calculate accurate starting prefixes for both B and C. To B we provide the final result from A (92), and to C we provide the final-scan result of A combined with the pre-scan result of B (92+136 = 228).

The combine operation takes constant time, so it is much less expensive than the scan operations. Unlike the sequential implementation that takes three large steps that are applied one after the other, the parallel implementation executes final-scan of A and pre-scan of B in parallel, then performs a constant-time combine step, and then finally computes final-scan of B and C in parallel. If we have at least two cores and N is sufficiently large, a parallel prefix sum that uses three chunks can therefore be computed in about two thirds of the time of the sequential implementation. And parallel_prefix can of course execute with more than three chunks to take advantage of more cores.

Figure 2-14 shows an implementation of the simple partial sum example using a TBB parallel_scan. The range is the interval [1, N), the identity value is 0, and the combine function returns the sum of its two arguments. The scan body returns the partial sum for all of the values in its subrange, added to the initial sum it receives. However, only when its is_final_scan argument is true does it assign the prefix results to the running_sum array.

```
int fig_2_14(const std::vector<int> &v, std::vector<int> &rsum) {
  int N = v.size();
  rsum[0] = v[0];
  int final_sum = tbb::parallel_scan(
    /* range = */ tbb::blocked_range<int>(1, N),
    /* identity = */ (int)0,
    /* scan body */
    [&v, &rsum](const tbb::blocked_range<int> &r,
                int sum, bool is_final_scan) -> int {
      for (int i = r.begin(); i < r.end(); ++i) {
        sum += v[i];
        if (is_final_scan)
          rsum[i] = sum;
      }
      return sum;
    },
    /* combine body */
    [](int x, int y) {
      return x + y;
    }
  );
  return final_sum;
}
```

Figure 2-14. *Implementation of a running sum using* parallel_scan

A Slightly More Complicated Example: Line of Sight

Figure 2-15 shows a serial implementation of a line of sight problem similar to the one described in *Vector Models for Data-Parallel Computing, Guy E. Blelloch (The MIT Press)*. Given the altitude of a viewing point and the altitudes of points at fixed intervals from the viewing point, the line of sight code determines which points are visible from the viewing point. As shown in Figure 2-15, a point is not visible if any point between it and the viewing point, `altitude[0]`, has a larger angle Θ. The serial implementation performs a scan to compute the maximum Θ value for all points between a given point and the viewing point. If the given point's Θ value is larger than this maximum angle, then it is a visible point; otherwise, it is not visible.

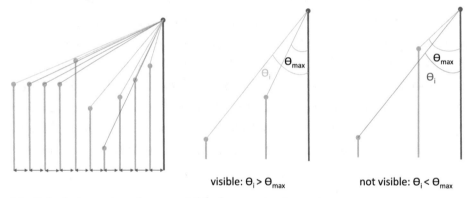

(a)   Calculating points that are visible from a viewing point.

```cpp
void fig_2_15(const std::vector<double> &altitude,
             std::vector<bool> &is_visible, double dx) {
  const int N = altitude.size();

  double max_angle = std::atan2(dx, altitude[0] - altitude[1]);
  double my_angle = 0.0;

  for (int i = 2; i < N; ++i ) {
    my_angle = std::atan2(i * dx, altitude[0] - altitude[i]);
    if (my_angle >= max_angle) {
      max_angle = my_angle;
    } else {
      is_visible[i] = false;
    }
  }
}
```

(b)   The serial implementation.

Figure 2-15.   *A line of sight example*

Figure 2-16 shows a parallel implementation of the line of sight example that uses a TBB `parallel_scan`. When the algorithm completes, the `is_visible` array will contain the visibility of each point (`true` or `false`). It is important to note that the code in Figure 2-16 needs to compute the maximum angle at each point in order to determine the point's visibility, but the final output is the visibility of each point, not the maximum angle at each point. Because the `max_angle` is needed but is not a final result, it is computed in both `pre-scan` and `final-scan` mode, but the `is_visible` values are stored for each point only during `final-scan` executions.

```
void fig_2_16(const std::vector<double> &altitude,
              std::vector<bool> &is_visible, double dx) {
  const int N = altitude.size();
  double max_angle = std::atan2(dx, altitude[0] - altitude[1]);

  double final_max_angle = tbb::parallel_scan(
    /* range = */ tbb::blocked_range<int>(1, N),
    /* identity */ 0.0,
    /* scan body */
    [&altitude, &is_visible, dx](const tbb::blocked_range<int> &r,
                                 double max_angle,
                                 bool is_final_scan) -> double {
      for (int i = r.begin(); i != r.end(); ++i) {
        double my_angle = atan2(i*dx, altitude[0] - altitude[i]);
        if (my_angle >= max_angle)
          max_angle = my_angle;
        if (is_final_scan && my_angle < max_angle)
          is_visible[i] = false;
      }
      return max_angle;
    },
    [](double a, double b) {
      return std::max(a,b);
    }
  );
}
```

Figure 2-16. *An implementation of the line of sight using* `parallel_scan`

Cook Until Done: parallel_do and parallel_pipeline

For some applications, simple loops get us full coverage of the useful parallelism. But for others, we need to express parallelism in loops where the range cannot be fully computed before the loop starts. For example, consider a while loop:

```
while(auto i = get_image()) {
  f(i);
}
```

This loop keeps reading in images until there are no more images to read. After each image is read, it is processed by the function f. We cannot use a parallel_for because we don't know how many images there will be and so cannot provide a range.

A more subtle case is when we have a container that does not provide random-access iterators:

```
std::list<image_type> my_images = get_image_list();
for (auto &i : my_list) {
  f(i);
}
```

Note   In C++, an iterator is an object that points to an element in a range of elements and defines operators that provide the ability to iterate through the elements of the range. There are different categories of iterators including *forward*, *bidirectional*, and *random-access* iterators. A random-access iterator can be moved to point to any element in the range in constant time.

Because a std::list does not support random access to its elements, we can obtain the delimiters of the range my_images.begin() and my_images.end(), but we cannot get to elements in between these points without sequentially traversing the list. The TBB library therefore cannot quickly (in constant time) create chunks of iterations to hand out as tasks since it cannot quickly point to the beginning and ending points of these chunks.

To handle complex loops like these, The TBB library provides two generic algorithms: parallel_do and parallel_pipeline.

parallel_do: Apply a Body Until There Are No More Items Left

A TBB parallel_do applies a Body to work items until there are no more items to process. Some work items can be provided up front when the loop begins, and others can be added by Body executions as they are processing other items.

The parallel_do function has two interfaces, one that accepts a first and last iterator and another that accepts a container. A complete description of the parallel_do interfaces is provided in Appendix B. In this section, we will look at the version that receives a container:

```
template<typename Container, typename Body>
void parallel_do(Container c, Body body);
```

As a simple example, let us start with a std::list of std::pair<int, bool> elements, each of which contains a random integer value and false. For each element, we will calculate whether or not the int value is a prime number; if so, we store true to the bool value. We will assume that we are given functions that populate the container and determine if a number is prime. A serial implementation follows:

```
using PrimesValue = std::pair<int, bool>;
using PrimesList = std::list<PrimesValue>;

bool isPrime(int n);

void serialImpl(PrimesList &values) {
  for (PrimesList::reference v : values) {
    if (isPrime(v.first))
      v.second = true;
  }
}
```

We can create a parallel implementation of this loop using a TBB parallel_do as shown in Figure 2-17.

```
void fig_2_17(PrimesList &values) {
  tbb::parallel_do(values,
    [](PrimesList::reference v) {
      if (isPrime(v.first))
        v.second = true;
    }
  );
}
```

Figure 2-17.   *An implementation of the prime number loop using a* parallel_do

The TBB parallel_do algorithm will safely traverse the container sequentially, while creating tasks to apply the body to each element. Because the container has to be traversed sequentially, a parallel_do is not as scalable as a parallel_for, but as long as the body is relatively large (> 100,000 clock cycles), the traversal overhead will be negligible compared to the parallel executions of the body on the elements.

In addition to handling containers that do not provide random access, the parallel_ do also allows us to add additional work items from within the body executions. If bodies are executing in parallel and they add new items, these items can be spawned in parallel too, avoiding the sequential task spawning limitations of parallel_do.

Figure 2-18 provides a serial implementation that calculates whether values are prime numbers, but the values are stored in a tree instead of a list.

```cpp
using PrimesValue = std::pair<int, bool>;

struct PrimesTreeElement {
  using Ptr = std::shared_ptr<PrimesTreeElement>;

  PrimesValue v;
  Ptr left;
  Ptr right;
  PrimesTreeElement(const PrimesValue &_v);
}

bool isPrime(int n);

void serialCheckPrimesElem(PrimesTreeElement::Ptr e) {
  if (e) {
    if (isPrime(e->v.first))
      e->v.second = true;
    if (e->left) serialCheckPrimesElem(e->left);
    if (e->right) serialCheckPrimesElem(e->right);
  }
}
```

Figure 2-18. *Checking for prime numbers in a tree of elements*

We can create a parallel implementation of this tree version using a parallel_do, as shown in Figure 2-19. To highlight the different ways to provide work items, in this implementation we use a container that holds a single tree of values. The parallel_do starts with only a single work item, but two items are added in each body execution, one to process the left subtree and the other to process the right subtree. We use the parallel_do_feeder.add method to add new work items to the iteration space. The class parallel_do_feeder is defined by the TBB library and is passed as the second argument to the body.

```
template<typename Item>
struct parallel_do_feeder {
  void add( const Item& item );
  // Supported since C++11
  void add( Item&& item );
};
```

The number of available work items increases exponentially as the bodies traverse down the levels of the tree. In Figure 2-19, we add new items through the feeder even before we check if the current element is a prime number, so that the other tasks are spawned as quickly as possible.

```
using PrimesValue = std::pair<int, bool>;

struct PrimesTreeElement {
  using Ptr = std::shared_ptr<PrimesTreeElement>;

  PrimesValue v;
  Ptr left;
  Ptr right;
  PrimesTreeElement(const PrimesValue & _v) : left{}, right{} {
    v.first = _v.first;
    v.second = _v.second;
  }
};

bool isPrime(int n);

void fig_2_19(PrimesTreeElement::Ptr root) {
  PrimesTreeElement::Ptr tree_array[] = {root};
  tbb::parallel_do(tree_array,
    [](PrimesTreeElement::Ptr e,
       tbb::parallel_do_feeder<PrimesTreeElement::Ptr>& feeder)
  {
      if (e) {
        if (e->left) feeder.add(e->left);
        if (e->right) feeder.add(e->right);
        if (isPrime(e->v.first))
          e->v.second = true;
      }
    }
  );
}
```

Figure 2-19. *Checking for prime numbers in a tree of elements using a TBB parallel_do*

We should note that the two uses we considered of `parallel_do` have the potential to scale for different reasons. The first implementation, without the feeder in Figure 2-17, can show good performance if each body execution has enough work to do to mitigate the overheads of traversing the list sequentially. In the second implementation, with the feeder in Figure 2-19, we start with only a single work item, but the number of available work items grows quickly as the bodies execute and add new items.

A Slightly More Complicated Example: Forward Substitution

Forward substitution is a method to solve a set of equations $Ax = b$, where A is an $n \times n$ lower triangular matrix. Viewed as matrices, the set of equations looks like

$$
\begin{bmatrix}
a_{11} & 0 & \cdots & 0 \\
a_{21} & a_{22} & \cdots & 0 \\
\vdots & \vdots & \ddots & \vdots \\
a_{n1} & a_{n2} & \cdots & a_{nn}
\end{bmatrix}
\begin{bmatrix}
x_1 \\
x_2 \\
\vdots \\
x_n
\end{bmatrix}
=
\begin{bmatrix}
b_1 \\
b_2 \\
\vdots \\
b_n
\end{bmatrix}
$$

and can be solved a row at a time:

$$x_1 = b_1 / a_{11}$$

$$x_2 = \left(b_2 - a_{21}x_1\right) / a_{22}$$

$$x_3 = \left(b_3 - a_{31}x_1 - a_{32}x_2\right) / a_{33}$$

$$\vdots$$

$$x_m = \left(b_n - a_{n1}x_1 - a_{n2}x_2 - \ldots - a_{nn-1}x_{n-1}\right) / a_{nn}$$

The serial code for a direct implementation of this algorithm is shown in Figure 2-20. In the serial code, b is destructively updated to store the sums for each row.

```
void fig_2_20(std::vector<double> &x,
              const std::vector<double> &a,
              std::vector<double> &b) {
  const int N = x.size();
  for (int i = 0; i < N; ++i) {
    for (int j = 0; j < i; ++j) {
      b[i] -= a[j + i*N] * x[j];
    }
    x[i] = b[i] / a[i + i*N];
  }
}
```

Figure 2-20. *The serial code for a direct implementation of forward substitution. This implementation is written to make the algorithm clear – not for best performance.*

Figure 2-21(a) shows the dependencies between the iterations of the body of the i,j loop nest in Figure 2-20. Each iteration of the inner j loop (shown by the rows in the figure) performs a reduction into b[i] and also depends on all of the elements of x that were written in earlier iterations of the i loop. We could use a parallel_reduce to parallelize the inner j loop, but there may not be enough work in the early iterations of the i loop to make this profitable. The dotted line in Figure 2-21(a) shows that there is another way to find parallelism in this loop nest by looking diagonally across the iteration space. We can exploit this parallelism by using a parallel_do to add iterations only as their dependencies are satisfied, similar to how we added new tree elements as we discovered them in Figure 2-19.

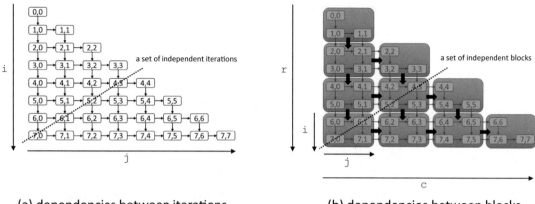

(a) dependencies between iterations   (b) dependencies between blocks

Figure 2-21. *The dependencies in forward substitution for a small 8 × 8 matrix. In (a), the dependencies between iterations are shown. In (b), the iterations are grouped into blocks to reduce scheduling overheads. In both (a) and (b), each block must wait for its neighbor above and its neighbor to its left to complete before it can safely execute.*

If we express the parallelism for each iteration separately, we will create tasks that are too small to overcome scheduling overheads since each task will only be a few floating-point operations. Instead, we can modify the loop nest to create blocks of iterations, as shown in Figure 2-21(b). The dependence pattern stays the same, but we will be able to schedule these larger blocks of iterations as tasks. A blocked version of the serial code is shown in Figure 2-22.

```
void fig_2_22(std::vector<double> &x, const std::vector<double> &a,
              std::vector<double> &b) {
  const int N = x.size();
  const int block_size = 512;
  const int num_blocks = N / block_size;

  for ( int r = 0; r < num_blocks; ++r ) {
    for ( int c = 0; c <= r; ++c ) {
      int i_start = r*block_size, i_end = i_start + block_size;
      int j_start = c*block_size, j_max = j_start + block_size - 1;
      for (int i = i_start; i < i_end; ++i) {
        int j_end = (i <= j_max) ? i : j_max + 1;
        for (int j = j_start; j < j_end; ++j) {
          b[i] -= a[j + i*N] * x[j];
        }
        if (j_end == i) {
          x[i] = b[i] / a[i + i*N];
        }
      }
    }
  }
}
```

Figure 2-22. *A blocked version of the serial implementation of forward substitution*

A parallel implementation that uses parallel_do is shown in Figure 2-23. Here, we use the interface of parallel_do that allows us to specify a beginning and ending iterator, instead of an entire container. You can see the details of this interface in Appendix B.

Unlike with the prime number tree example in Figure 2-19, we don't want to simply send every neighboring block to the feeder. Instead, we initialize an array of counters, ref_count, to hold the number of blocks that must complete before each block is allowed to start executing. Atomic variables will be discussed more in Chapter 5. For our purposes here, we can view these as variables that we can modify safely in parallel; in particular, the decrements are done in a thread-safe way. We initialize the counters so that the top-left element has no dependencies, the first column and the blocks along the diagonal have a single dependency, and all others have two dependencies. These counts match the number of predecessors for each block as shown in Figure 2-21.

```
void fig_2_23(std::vector<double> &x, const std::vector<double> &a,
              std::vector<double> &b) {
  const int N = x.size();
  const int block_size = 512;
  const int num_blocks = N / block_size;
  std::vector<tbb::atomic<char>> ref_count(num_blocks*num_blocks);
  for (int r = 0; r < num_blocks; ++r) {
    for (int c = 0; c <= r; ++c) {
      if (r == 0 && c == 0)
        ref_count[r*num_blocks + c] = 0;
      else if (c == 0 || r == c)
        ref_count[r*num_blocks + c] = 1;
      else
        ref_count[r*num_blocks + c] = 2;
    }
  }

  using BlockIndex = std::pair<size_t, size_t>;
  BlockIndex top_left(0,0);

  tbb::parallel_do( &top_left, &top_left+1 ,
    [&](const BlockIndex &bi,
        tbb::parallel_do_feeder<BlockIndex> &feeder) {
      size_t r = bi.first;
      size_t c = bi.second;
      int i_start = r*block_size, i_end = i_start + block_size;
      int j_start = c*block_size, j_max = j_start + block_size - 1;
      for (int i = i_start; i < i_end; ++i) {
        int j_end = (i <= j_max) ? i : j_max + 1;
        for (int j = j_start; j < j_end; ++j) {
          b[i] -= a[j + i*N] * x[j];
        }
        if (j_end == i) {
          x[i] = b[i] / a[i + i*N];
        }
      }
      // add successor to right if ready
      if (c + 1 <= r && --ref_count[r*num_blocks + c + 1] == 0) {
        feeder.add(BlockIndex(r, c + 1));
      }
      // add successor below if ready
      if (r + 1 < (size_t)num_blocks
          && --ref_count[(r+1)*num_blocks + c] == 0) {
        feeder.add(BlockIndex(r+1, c));
      }
    }
  );
}
```

Figure 2-23. *An implementation of forward substitution using* parallel_do

In the call to parallel_do in Figure 2-23, we initially provide only the top-left block, [&top_left, &top_left+1). But in each body execution, the if-statements at the bottom decrement the atomic counters of the blocks that are dependent on the block that was just processed. If a counter reaches zero, that block has all of its dependencies satisfied and is provided to the feeder.

Like the previous prime number examples, this example demonstrates the hallmark of applications that use parallel_do: the parallelism is constrained by the need to sequentially access a container or by the need to dynamically find and feed work items to the algorithm.

parallel_pipeline: Streaming Items Through a Series of Filters

The second generic parallel algorithm in TBB used to handle complex loops is parallel_ pipeline. A pipeline is a linear sequence of *filters* that transform *items* as they pass through them. Pipelines are often used to process data that stream into an application such as video or audio frames, or financial data. In Chapter 3, we will discuss the Flow Graph interfaces that let us build more complex graphs that include fan-in and fan-out to and from filters.

Figure 2-24 shows a small example loop that reads in arrays of characters, transforms the characters by changing all of the lowercase characters to uppercase and all of the uppercase characters to lowercase, and then writes the results in order to an output file.

```cpp
using CaseStringPtr = std::shared_ptr<std::string>;
CaseStringPtr getCaseString(std::ofstream &f);
void writeCaseString(std::ofstream &f, CaseStringPtr s);

void fig_2_24(std::ofstream &caseBeforeFile,
              std::ofstream &caseAfterFile) {
  while (CaseStringPtr s_ptr = getCaseString(caseBeforeFile)) {
    std::transform(s_ptr->begin(), s_ptr->end(), s_ptr->begin(),
      [](char c) -> char {
        if (std::islower(c))
          return std::toupper(c);
        else if (std::isupper(c))
          return std::tolower(c);
        else
          return c;
      }
    );
    writeCaseString(caseAfterFile, s_ptr);
  }
}
```

Figure 2-24. *A serial case change example*

The operations have to be done in order on each buffer, but we can overlap the execution of different filters applied to different buffers. Figure 2-25(a) shows this example as a pipeline, where the "write buffer" operates on $buffer_i$, while in parallel the "process" filter operates on $buffer_{i+1}$ and the "get buffer" filter reads in $buffer_{i+2}$.

(a) Three buffers are being processed in parallel by different filters.

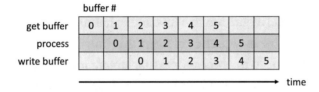

(b) In the steady-state, if all of the filters can work on only 1 item at a time, a maximum parallelism of 3 is possible.

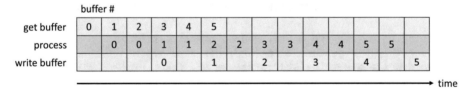

(c) Here the process filter takes 2 times longer than the other filters, and so the other filters are sometimes idle.

Figure 2-25.   *The case change example using a pipeline*

As illustrated in Figure 2-25(b), in the steady state, each filter is busy, and their executions are overlapped. However, as shown in Figure 2-25(c), unbalanced filters decrease speedup. The performance of a pipeline of serial filters is limited by the slowest serial stage.

The TBB library supports both serial and parallel filters. A parallel filter can be applied in parallel to different items in order to increase the throughput of the filter. Figure 2-26(a) shows the "case change" example, with the middle/process filter executing in parallel on two items. Figure 2-26(b) illustrates that if the middle filter takes twice as long as the other filters to complete on any given item, then assigning two threads to this filter will allow it to match the throughput of the other filters.

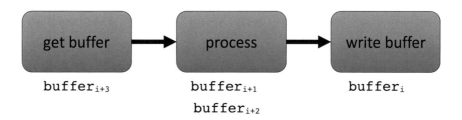

| get buffer | → | process | → | write buffer |

$buffer_{i+3}$ $buffer_{i+1}$ $buffer_i$
$buffer_{i+2}$

(a) A parallel filter can process more than one item in parallel.

buffer #

get buffer	0	1	2	3	4	5			
process		0	0	2	2	4	4		
			1	1	3	3	5	5	
write buffer				0	1	2	3	4	5

time →

(b) More threads can be provided to a parallel filter to increase its throughput to match the throughput of the other filters.

Figure 2-26. *The case change example using a pipeline with a parallel filter. By using two copies of the parallel filter, the pipeline maximizes throughput.*

A complete description of the parallel_pipeline interfaces is provided in Appendix B. The interface of parallel_pipeline we use in this section is shown as follows:

```
void parallel_pipeline( size_t max_number_of_live_tokens,
                        const filter_t<void,void>& filter_chain);
```

The first argument `max_number_of_live_tokens` is the maximum number of items that will be allowed to flow through the pipeline at any given time. This value is necessary to constrain resource consumption. For example, consider the simple three filter pipeline. What if the middle filter is a serial filter and it takes 1000 times longer than the filter that gets new buffers? The first filter might allocate 1000 buffers only to queue them up before the second filter – wasting a lot of memory.

The second argument to `parallel_pipeline` is `filter_chain`, a series of filters created by concatenating filters that are created using the `make_filter` function:

```
template<typename T, typename U, typename Func>
filter_t<T,U> make_filter(filter::mode mode, const Func& f );
```

The template arguments T and U specify the input and output types of the filter. The mode argument can be `serial_in_order`, `serial_out_of_order`, or parallel. And the f argument is the body of the filter. Figure 2-27 shows the implementation of the case change example using a TBB `parallel_pipeline`. A more complete description of the `parallel_pipeline` interfaces is provided in Appendix B.

We can note that the first filter, since its input type is `void`, receives a special argument of type `tbb::flow_control.` We use this argument to signal when the first filter in a pipeline is no longer going to generate new items. For example, in the first filter in Figure 2-27, we call `stop()` when the pointer returned by `getCaseString()` is `null`.

```cpp
void fig_2_27(int num_tokens, std::ofstream &caseBeforeFile,
              std::ofstream &caseAfterFile) {
  tbb::parallel_pipeline(
    /* tokens */ num_tokens,
    /* the get filter */
    tbb::make_filter<void, CaseStringPtr>(
      /* filter node */ tbb::filter::serial_in_order,
      /* filter body */
      [&](tbb::flow_control &fc) -> CaseStringPtr {
        CaseStringPtr s_ptr = getCaseString(caseBeforeFile);
        if (!s_ptr)
          fc.stop();
        return s_ptr;
      }) & // concatenation operation
    /* make the change case filter */
    tbb::make_filter<CaseStringPtr, CaseStringPtr>(
      /* filter node */ tbb::filter::parallel,
      /* filter body */
      [](CaseStringPtr s_ptr) -> CaseStringPtr {
        std::transform(s_ptr->begin(), s_ptr->end(), s_ptr->begin(),
          [](char c) -> char {
            if (std::islower(c))
              return std::toupper(c);
            else if (std::isupper(c))
              return std::tolower(c);
            else
              return c;
          });
        return s_ptr;
      }) & // concatenation operation
    /* make the write filter */
    tbb::make_filter<CaseStringPtr, void>(
      /* filter node */ tbb::filter::serial_in_order,
      /* filter body */
      [&](CaseStringPtr s_ptr) -> void {
        writeCaseString(caseAfterFile, s_ptr);
      })
  );
}
```

Figure 2-27. *The case change example using a pipeline with a parallel middle filter*

In this implementation, the first and last filters are created using the `serial_in_order` mode. This specifies that both filters should run on only one item at a time and that the last filter should execute the items in the same order that the first filter generated them in. A `serial_out_of_order` filter is allowed to execute the items in any order. The middle filter is passed `parallel` as its mode, allowing it to execute on different items in parallel. The modes supported by `parallel_pipeline` are described in more detail in Appendix B.

A Slightly More Complicated Example: Creating 3D Stereoscopic Images

A more complicated example of a pipeline is shown in Figure 2-28. A while loop reads in frame numbers, and then for each frame it reads a left and right image, adds a red coloring to the left image and a blue coloring to the right image. It then merges the resulting two images into a single red-cyan 3D stereoscopic image.

(a) Images are combined into a red-cyan 3D stereoscopic image. The original photograph was taken by Elena Adams.

```cpp
class PNGImage {
public:
  uint64_t frameNumber = -1;
  unsigned int width = 0, height = 0;
  std::shared_ptr<std::vector<unsigned char>> buffer;
  static const int numChannels = 4;
  static const int redOffset = 0;
  static const int greenOffset = 1;
  static const int blueOffset = 2;

  PNGImage() {}
  PNGImage(uint64_t frame_number, const std::string& file_name);
  PNGImage(const PNGImage &p);
  virtual ~PNGImage() {}
  void write() const;
};

int getNextFrameNumber();
PNGImage getLeftImage(uint64_t frameNumber);
PNGImage getRightImage(uint64_t frameNumber);
void increasePNGChannel(PNGImage& image, int channel_offset,
                        int increase);
void mergePNGImages(PNGImage& right, const PNGImage& left);
```

```cpp
void fig_2_28() {
  while (uint64_t frameNumber = getNextFrameNumber()) {
    auto left = getLeftImage(frameNumber);
    auto right = getRightImage(frameNumber);
    increasePNGChannel(left, PNGImage::redOffset, 10);
    increasePNGChannel(right, PNGImage::blueOffset, 10);
    mergePNGImages(right, left);
    right.write();
  }
}
```

(b) A serial implementation that reads images and applies the 3D effect.

Figure 2-28. *A red-cyan 3D stereoscopic sample application*

Similar to the simple case change sample, we again have a series of inputs that pass through a set of filters. We identify the important functions and convert them to pipeline filters: getNextFrameNumber, getLeftImage, getRightImage, increasePNGChannel (to left image), increasePNGChannel (to right image), mergePNGImages, and right.write(). Figure 2-29 shows the example drawn as a pipeline. The increasePNGChannel filter is applied twice, first on the left image and then on the right image.

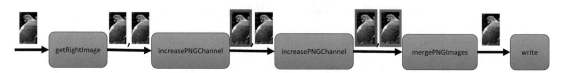

Figure 2-29. *The 3D stereoscopic sample application as a pipeline*

The parallel implementation using a TBB parallel_pipeline is shown in Figure 2-30.

```cpp
void fig_2_30() {
  using Image = PNGImage;
  using ImagePair = std::pair<PNGImage, PNGImage>;
  tbb::parallel_pipeline(
    /* tokens */ 8,
    /* make the left image filter */
    tbb::make_filter<void, Image>(
      /* filter type */ tbb::filter::serial_in_order,
      [&](tbb::flow_control &fc) -> Image {
        if (uint64_t frame_number = getNextFrameNumber()) {
          return getLeftImage(frame_number);
        } else {
          fc.stop();
          return Image{};
        }
      }) &
    tbb::make_filter<Image, ImagePair>(
      /* filter type */ tbb::filter::serial_in_order,
      [&](Image left) -> ImagePair {
        return ImagePair(left, getRightImage(left.frameNumber));
      }) &
    tbb::make_filter<ImagePair, ImagePair>(
      /* filter type */ tbb::filter::parallel,
      [&](ImagePair p) -> ImagePair {
        increasePNGChannel(p.first, Image::redOffset, 10);
        return p;
      }) &
    tbb::make_filter<ImagePair, ImagePair>(
      /* filter type */ tbb::filter::parallel,
      [&](ImagePair p) -> ImagePair {
        increasePNGChannel(p.second, Image::blueOffset, 10);
        return p;
      }) &
    tbb::make_filter<ImagePair, Image>(
      /* filter type */ tbb::filter::parallel,
      [&](ImagePair p) -> Image {
        mergePNGImages(p.second, p.first);
        return p.second;
      }) &
    tbb::make_filter<Image, void>(
      /* filter type */ tbb::filter::parallel,
      [&](Image img) {
        img.write();
      })
  );
}
```

Figure 2-30. *The stereoscopic 3D example implemented using parallel_pipeline*

The TBB `parallel_pipeline` function imposes a linearization of the pipeline filters. The filters are applied one after the other as the input from the first stage flows through the pipeline. This is in fact a limitation for this sample. The processing of the left and right images is independent until the `mergeImageBuffers` filter, but because of the interface of `parallel_pipeline`, the filters must be linearized. Even so, only the filters that read in the images are serial filters, and therefore this implementation can still be scalable if the execution time is dominated by the later, parallel stages.

In Chapter 3, we introduce the TBB Flow Graph, which will allow us to more directly express applications that benefit from nonlinearized execution of filters.

Summary

This chapter offered a basic overview of the generic parallel algorithms provided by the TBB library, including patterns that capture functional parallelism, simple and complex loops, and pipeline parallelism. These prepackaged algorithms (patterns) provide well-tested and tuned implementations that can be applied incrementally to an application to improve performance.

The code shown in this chapter provides small examples that show how these algorithms can be used. In Part 2 of this book (starting with Chapter 9), we discuss how to get the most out of TBB by combining these algorithms in composable ways and tuning applications using the library features available for optimizing locality, minimizing overheads, and adding priorities. Part 2 of the book also discusses how to deal with exception handling and cancellation when using the TBB generic parallel algorithms.

We continue in the next chapter by taking a look at another one of TBB's high-level features, the Flow Graph.

For More Information

Here are some additional reading materials we recommend related to this chapter.

- We discussed design patterns for parallel programming and how these relate to the TBB generic parallel algorithms. A collection of design patterns can be found in

Timothy Mattson, Beverly Sanders, and Berna Massingill, *Patterns for Parallel Programming* (First ed.), 2004, Addison-Wesley Professional.

- When discussing the parallel implementation of quicksort, we noted that the partitioning was still a serial bottleneck. Papers that discuss parallel partitioning implementations include

P. Heidelberger, A. Norton and J. T. Robinson, "Parallel Quicksort using fetch-and-add," in *IEEE Transactions on Computers*, vol. 39, no. 1, pp. 133-138, Jan 1990.

P. Tsigas and Y. Zhang. A simple, fast parallel implementation of quicksort and its performance evaluation on SUN enterprise 10000. In 11th Euromicro Workshop on Parallel, Distributed and Network-Based Processing (PDP 2003), pages 372–381, 2003.

- You can learn more about data dependence analysis in a number of compiler or parallel programming books, including

Michael Joseph Wolfe, *High-Performance Compilers for Parallel Computing,* 1995, Addison-Wesley Longman Publishing Co., Inc., Boston, MA, USA.

Kennedy and John R. Allen, *Optimizing Compilers for Modern Architectures,* 2001, Morgan Kaufmann Publishers Inc., San Francisco, CA, USA.

- When we discussed matrix multiplication, we noted that unless we are optimization gurus, we should typically prefer to use prepackaged implementations of linear algebra kernels when available.

Such packages include

The Basic Linear Algebra Subprograms (BLAS) at `www.netlib.org/blas/`

The Intel Math Kernel Library (Intel MKL) at `https://software.intel.com/mkl`

Automatically Tuned Linear Algebra Software (ATLAS) found at `http://math-atlas.sourceforge.net/`

The FLAME project researches and develops dense linear algebra libraries. Their BLIS software framework can be used to create high-performance BLAS libraries. The FLAME project can be found at `www.cs.utexas.edu/~flame`.

- The line of sight example in this chapter was implemented using parallel scan based on the description provided in

  Vector Models for Data-Parallel Computing, Guy E. Blelloch (The MIT Press).

The photograph used in Figures 2-28a, 2-29, and 3-7, was taken by Elena Adams, and is used with permission from the Halide project's tutorials at `http://halide-lang.org`.

CHAPTER 3

Flow Graphs

In Chapter 2, we introduced a set of algorithms that match patterns we often come across in applications. Those are great! And we should use those whenever we can. Unfortunately, not all applications fit nicely into one of those boxes; they can be messy. When things start to get messy, we can become control freaks and try to micromanage everything or just decide to "go with the flow" and react to things as they come along. TBB lets us choose either path.

In Chapter 10, we discuss how to use tasks directly to create our own algorithms. There are both high-level and low-level interfaces to tasks, so if we use tasks directly, we can choose to become control freaks if we really want to.

In this chapter, however, we look at the Threading Building Blocks Flow Graph interface. Most of the algorithms in Chapter 2 are geared toward applications where we have a big chunk of data up front and need to create tasks to divide up and process that data in parallel. The Flow Graph is geared toward applications that react as data becomes available, or toward applications that have dependences that are more complicated than can be expressed by a simple structure. The Flow Graph interfaces have been successfully used in a wide range of domains including in image processing, artificial intelligence, financial services, healthcare, and games.

The Flow Graph interfaces let us express programs that contain parallelism that can be expressed as graphs. In many cases, these applications stream data through a set of filters or computations. We call these *data flow graphs*. Graphs can also express before-after relationships between operations, allowing us to express dependency structures that cannot be easily expressed with a parallel loop or pipeline. Some linear algebra computations, for example, Cholesky decomposition, have efficient parallel implementations that avoid heavyweight synchronization points by tracking dependencies on smaller operations instead. We call graphs that express these before-after relationships *dependency graphs*.

© Intel Corporation 2019
M. Voss, R. Asenjo, J. Reinders, *Pro TBB*, https://doi.org/10.1007/978-1-4842-4398-5_3

In Chapter 2, we were introduced to two generic parallel algorithms that, like a Flow Graph, do not require all of the data to be known ahead of time, parallel_do and parallel_pipeline. These algorithms are very effective when they apply; however, both of these algorithms have limitations that a Flow Graph does not have. A parallel_do has only a single body function that is applied to each input item as it becomes available. A parallel_pipeline applies a linear series of filters to input items as they flow through a pipeline. At the end of Chapter 2, we looked at a 3D stereoscopic example that had more parallelism than could be expressed by a linear series of filters. The Flow Graph APIs let us express more complicated structures than either parallel_do or parallel_pipeline.

In this chapter, we start with a discussion about why graph-based parallelism is important and then discuss the basics of the TBB Flow Graph API. After that, we explore an example of each of the two major types of flow graphs: a data flow graph and a dependency graph.

Why Use Graphs to Express Parallelism?

An application that is expressed as a graph of computations exposes information that can be effectively used at runtime to schedule its computations in parallel. We can look at the code in Figure 3-1(a) as an example.

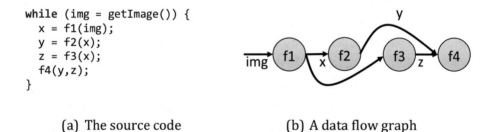

```
while (img = getImage()) {
    x = f1(img);
    y = f2(x);
    z = f3(x);
    f4(y,z);
}
```

(a) The source code   (b) A data flow graph

Figure 3-1. *An application that can be expressed as a data flow graph*

In each iteration of the while loop in Figure 3-1(a), an image is read and then passed through a series of filters: f1, f2, f3, and f4. We can draw the flow of data between these filters as shown in Figure 3-1(b). In this figure, the variables that were used to pass the data returned from each function are replaced by edges from the node that generates the value to the node(s) that consume the values.

For now, let's assume that the graph in Figure 3-1(b) captures all of the data that is shared between these functions. If so, we (and in turn a library like TBB) can infer a lot about what is legal to execute in parallel as shown in Figure 3-2.

Figure 3-2 shows the types of parallelism that can be inferred from the data flow graph representation of our small example. In the figure, we stream four images through the graph. Since there are no edges between nodes f2 and f3, they can be executed in parallel. Executing two different functions in parallel on the same data is an example of *functional parallelism* (task parallelism). If we assume that the functions are side-effect-free, that is, they do not update global states and only read from their incoming message and write to their outgoing message, then we can also overlap the processing of different messages in the graph, exploiting *pipeline parallelism*. And finally, if the functions are *thread-safe*, that is, we can execute each function in parallel with itself on different inputs, then we can also choose to overlap the execution of two different images in the same node to exploit *data parallelism*.

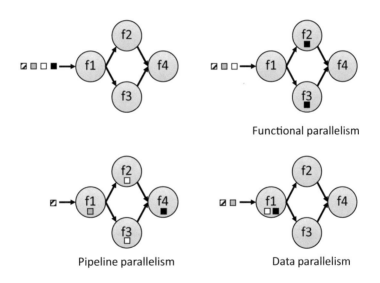

Functional parallelism

Pipeline parallelism   Data parallelism

Figure 3-2. *The kinds of parallelism that can be inferred from the graph*

When we express our application as a graph using the TBB flow graph interface, we provide the library with the information it needs to take advantage of these different kinds of parallelism so it can map our computation to the platform hardware to improve performance.

The Basics of the TBB Flow Graph Interface

The TBB flow graph classes and functions are defined in flow_graph.h and are contained within the tbb::flow namespace. The all-encompassing tbb.h also includes flow_graph.h, so if we use that header, we do not need to include anything else.

To use a flow graph, we first create a *graph* object. We then create *nodes* to perform operations on messages that flow through the graph, such as applying user computations, joining, splitting, buffering, or reordering messages. We use *edges* to express the message channels or dependencies between these nodes. Finally, after we have assembled a graph from the graph object, node objects, and edges, we feed *messages* into the graph. Messages can be primitive types, objects, or pointers to objects. If we want to wait for processing to complete, we can use the graph object as a handle for that purpose.

Figure 3-3 shows a small example that performs the five steps needed to use a TBB Flow Graph. In this section, we will discuss each of these steps in more detail.

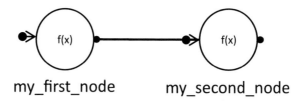

(a) A two node graph

```
#include <iostream>
#include <tbb/tbb.h>

void fig_3_3() {
  // step 1: construct the graph
  tbb::flow::graph g;

  // step 2: make the nodes
  tbb::flow::function_node<int, std::string> my_first_node(g,
    tbb::flow::unlimited,
    []( const int &in ) -> std::string {
      std::cout << "first node received: " << in << std::endl;
      return std::to_string(in);
    }
  );

  tbb::flow::function_node<std::string> my_second_node(g,
    tbb::flow::unlimited,
    []( const std::string &in ) {
      std::cout << "second node received: " << in << std::endl;
    }
  );

  // step 3: add edges
  tbb::flow::make_edge(my_first_node, my_second_node);

  // step 4: send messages
  my_first_node.try_put(10);

  // step 5: wait for graph to complete
  g.wait_for_all();
}
```

(b) The source-code for a two-node graph

Figure 3-3. *An example flow graph with two nodes*

Step 1: Create the Graph Object

The first step to create a flow graph is to construct a graph object. In the flow graph interface, a graph object is used for invoking whole graph operations such as waiting for all tasks related to the graph's execution to complete, resetting the state of all nodes in the graph, and canceling the execution of all nodes in the graph. When building a graph, each node belongs to exactly one graph, and edges are made between nodes in the same graph. Once we have constructed the graph, then we need to construct the nodes that implement the computations of the graph.

Step 2: Make the Nodes

The TBB flow graph interface defines a rich set of node types (Figure 3-4) that can roughly be broken into three groups: functional node types, control flow node types (includes join node types), and buffering node types. A detailed review of the interfaces provided by the graph class and the interfaces provided by all node types can be found in the "Flow Graph: nodes" section of Appendix B. It is not expected that you read these tables in detail now, but instead, that you know that you can reference them as node types are used in this and subsequent chapters.

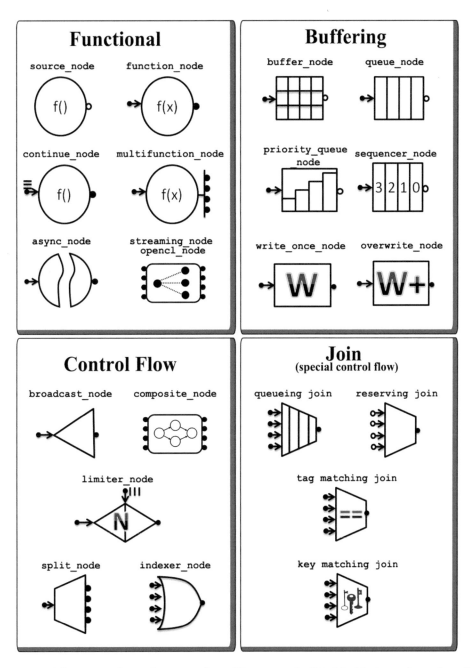

Figure 3-4. *Flow graph node types (see Chapters 3, 17, 18, 19; interface details in Appendix B)*

Like all of the functional nodes, a function_node takes a lambda expression as one of its arguments. We use these body arguments in functional nodes to provide the code we want to apply to incoming messages. In Figure 3-3, we defined the first node to receive an int value, print the value, and then convert it to a std::string, returning the converted value. This node is reproduced as follows:

```
tbb::flow::function_node<int, std::string> my_first_node(g,
  tbb::flow::unlimited,
  [](const int &in) -> std::string {
    std::cout << "first node received: " << in << std::endl;
    return std::to_string(in);
  }
);
```

Nodes are typically connected to each other by edges, but we can also explicitly send a message to a node. For example, we can send a message to my_first_node by calling try_put on it:

```
my_first_node.try_put(10);
```

This causes the TBB library to spawn a task to execute the body of my_first_node on the int message 10, resulting in output such as

```
first node received: 10
```

Unlike the functional nodes, where we provide a body argument, the control flow node types perform predefined operations that join, split, or direct messages as they flow through a graph. For example, we can create a join_node that joins together inputs from multiple input ports to create an output of type std::tuple<int, std::string, double> by providing a tuple type, the join policy, and a reference to the graph object:

```
join_node<tuple<int, std::string, double>,
          queueing> j(g);
```

This join_node, j, has three input ports and one output port. Input port 0 will accept messages of type int. Input port 1 will accept messages of type std::string. Input port 2 will accept messages of type double. There will be a single output port that broadcasts messages of type std::tuple<int, std::string, double>.

A join_node can have one of four join policies: queueing, reserving, key_matching, and tag_matching. For the queueing, key_matching, and tag_matching policies, the join_node buffers incoming messages as they arrive at each of its input ports. The queueing policy stores incoming messages in per-port queues, joining the messages into a tuple using a first-in-first-out approach. The key_matching and tag_matching policies store the incoming messages in per-port maps and join messages based on matching keys or tags.

A reserving join_node does not buffer the incoming messages at all. Instead, it tracks the state of the preceding buffers – when it believes that there are messages available for each of its input ports, it tries to reserve an item for each input port. A reservation prevents any other node from consuming the item while the reservation is held. Only if the join_node can successfully acquire a reservation on an element for each input port does it then consume these messages; otherwise, it releases all of the reservations and leaves the messages in the preceding buffers. If a reserving join_node fails to reserve all of the inputs, it tries again later. We will see use cases of this reserving policy in Chapter 17.

The buffering node types buffer messages. Since the functional nodes, function_node and multifunction_node, contain buffers at their inputs and source_node contains a buffer at its output, buffering nodes are used in limited circumstances – typically in conjunction with a reserving join_node (see Chapter 17).

Step 3: Add Edges

After we construct a graph object and nodes, we use make_edge calls to set up the message channels or dependencies:

```
make_edge(predecessor_node, successor_node);
```

If a node has more than one input port or output port, we use the input_port and output_port function templates to select the ports:

```
make_edge(output_port<0>(predecessor_node),
          input_port<1>(successor_node));
```

In Figure 3-3, we made an edge between my_first_node and my_second_node in our simple two-node graph. Figure 3-5 shows a slightly more complicated flow graph that has four nodes.

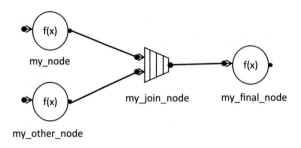

(a) A four node graph

```
void fig_3_5() {
  // step 1: construct the graph
  tbb::flow::graph g;
  // step 2: make the nodes
  tbb::flow::function_node<int, std::string> my_node(g,
    tbb::flow::unlimited,
    []( const int &in ) -> std::string {
      std::cout << "received: " << in << std::endl;
      return std::to_string(in);
    }
  );
  tbb::flow::function_node<int, double> my_other_node(g,
    tbb::flow::unlimited,
    [](const int &in) -> double {
      std::cout << "other received: " << in << std::endl;
      return double(in);
    }
  );
  tbb::flow::join_node<std::tuple<std::string, double>,
                       tbb::flow::queueing> my_join_node(g);
  tbb::flow::function_node<std::tuple<std::string, double>,
                           int> my_final_node(g,
    tbb::flow::unlimited,
    [](const std::tuple<std::string, double> &in) -> int {
      std::cout << "final: " << std::get<0>(in)
                << " and " << std::get<1>(in) << std::endl;
      return 0;
    }
  );
  // step 3: add the edges
  make_edge(my_node, tbb::flow::input_port<0>(my_join_node));
  make_edge(my_other_node, tbb::flow::input_port<1>(my_join_node));
  make_edge(my_join_node, my_final_node);
  // step 4: send messages
  my_node.try_put(1);
  my_other_node.try_put(2);
  // step 5: wait for the graph to complete
  g.wait_for_all();
}
```

(b) The source-code for a four node graph with a `join_node`.

Figure 3-5. *An example flow graph with four nodes*

The first two nodes in Figure 3-5 generate results that are joined together into a tuple by a queueing join_node, my_join_node. When the edges are made to the input ports of the join_node, we need to specify the port number:

```
make_edge(my_node, tbb::flow::input_port<0>(my_join_node));
make_edge(my_other_node, tbb::flow::input_port<1>(my_join_node));
```

The output of the join_node, a std::tuple<std::string, double>, is sent to my_final_node. We do not need to specify a port number when there is only a single port:

```
make_edge(my_join_node, my_final_node);
```

Step 4: Start the Graph

The fourth step in creating and using a TBB flow graph is to start the graph execution. There are two main ways that messages enter a graph either (1) through an explicit try_put to a node or (2) as the output of a source_node. In both Figure 3-3 and Figure 3-5, we call try_put on nodes to start messages flowing into the graph.

A source_node is constructed by default in the active state. Whenever an outgoing edge is made, it immediately starts sending messages across the edge. Unfortunately, we believe this is error prone, and so we always construct our source nodes in the inactive state, that is, pass false as the is_active argument. To get messages flowing after our graph is completely constructed, we call the activate() function on all of our inactive nodes

Figure 3-6 demonstrates how a source_node can be used as a replacement for a serial loop to feed messages to a graph. In Figure 3-6(a), a loop repeatedly calls try_put on a node my_node, sending messages to it. In Figure 3-6(b), a source_node is used for the same purpose.

The return value of a source_node is used like the boolean condition in a serial loop – if true, another execution of the loop body is performed; otherwise, the loop halts. Since a source_node's return value is used to signal the boolean condition, it returns its output value by updating the argument provided to its body. In Figure 3-6(b), the source_node replaces the count loop in Figure 3-6(a).

```
void loop_with_try_put() {
  const int limit = 3;
  tbb::flow::graph g;
  tbb::flow::function_node<int> my_node(g, tbb::flow::unlimited,
    [](int i) {
      std::cout << i << std::endl;
    }
  );
  for (int count = 0; count < limit; ++count) {
    int value = count;
    my_node.try_put(value);
  }
  g.wait_for_all();
}
```

(a) using a for-loop and explicit calls to `try_put`

```
void fig_3_6() {
  tbb::flow::graph g;
  int count = 0;
  tbb::flow::source_node<int> my_src(g,
    [&count](int &i) -> bool {
      const int limit = 3;
      if (count < limit) {
        i = count++;
        return true;
      } else {
        return false;
      }
    },
    false);
  tbb::flow::function_node<int> my_node(g,
    tbb::flow::unlimited,
    [](int i) {
      std::cout << i << std::endl;
    }
  );
  tbb::flow::make_edge(my_src, my_node);
  my_src.activate();
  g.wait_for_all();
}
```

(b) using a `source_node` instead of a loop

Figure 3-6. *In (a), a loop sends the int values 0, 1, and 2 to a node my_node. In (b), a source_node sends the int values 0, 1, and 2 to the node my_node.*

The main advantage of using a source_node, instead of loop, is that it responds to other nodes in the graph. In Chapter 17, we discuss how a source_node can be used in conjunction with a reserving join_node or a limiter_node to control how many messages are allowed to enter a graph. If we use a simple loop, we can flood our graph with inputs, forcing nodes to buffer many messages if they cannot keep up.

Step 5: Wait for the Graph to Complete Executing

Once we have sent messages into a graph either using `try_put` or a `source_node`, we wait for the execution of the graph to complete by calling `wait_for_all()` on the graph object. We can see these calls in Figure 3-3, Figure 3-5, and Figure 3-6.

If we build and execute the graph in Figure 3-3, we see an output like

```
first node received: 10
second node received: 10
```

If we build and execute the graph in Figure 3-5, we see an output like

```
other received: received: 21

final: 1 and 2
```

The output from Figure 3-5 looks a little jumbled, and it is. The first two function nodes execute in parallel, and both are streaming to `std::cout`. In our output, we see a combination of the two outputs jumbled together because we broke the assumption we made earlier in this chapter when we discussed graph-based parallelism – our nodes are not side-effect-free! These two nodes execute in parallel, and both affect the state of the global `std::cout` object. In this example, that's ok since this output is printed just to show the progress of the messages through the graph. But it is an important point to remember.

The final `function_node` in Figure 3-5 only executes when both values from the preceding function nodes are joined together by the `join_node` and are passed to it. This final node therefore executes by itself, and so it streams the expected final output to `std::cout`: "final: 1 and 2".

A More Complicated Example of a Data Flow Graph

In Chapter 2, we introduced an example that applied a red-cyan 3D stereoscopic effect to pairs of left and right images. In Chapter 2, we parallelized this example with a TBB `parallel_pipeline`, but in doing so admitted that we left some parallelism on the table by linearizing the pipeline stages. An example output is shown in Figure 3-7.

Figure 3-7. *A left and right image are used to generate a red-cyan stereoscopic image. The original photograph was taken by Elena Adams.*

Figure 3-8 shows the data and control dependencies in the serial code that was shown in Figure 2-28. The data dependencies are shown as solid lines and the control dependencies as dotted lines. From this diagram, we can see that the calls to getLeftImage followed by increasePNGChannel do not depend on the calls to getRightImage followed by increasePNGChannel. Consequently, these two series of calls can be made in parallel with each other. We can also see that mergePNGImages cannot proceed until increasePNGChannel has completed on both the left and right images. And finally, write must wait until the call to mergePNGImages is finished.

Unlike in Chapter 2, where we used a linear pipeline, using a TBB flow graph we can now more accurately express the dependencies. To do so, we need to first understand the constraints in our application that preserve correct execution. For example, each iteration of the while loop does not start until the previous iteration is complete, but this may be just a side effect of using a serial while loop. We need to determine which constraints are truly necessary.

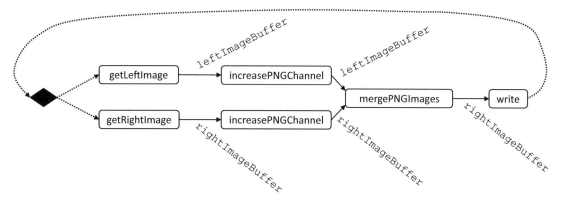

Figure 3-8. *The control and data dependencies from the code sample in Figure 2-28, where the solid lines represent data dependencies and the dotted lines represent control dependencies*

In this example, let us assume that the images represent frames that are read in order, either from a file or from a camera. Since the images must be read in order, we cannot make multiple calls to getLeftImage or multiple calls to getRightImage in parallel; these are serial operations. We can, however, overlap a call to getLeftImage with a call to getRightImage because these functions do not interfere with each other. Beyond these constraints though, we will assume that increasePNGChannel, mergePNGImages, and write are safe to execute on different inputs in parallel (they are both side-effect-free and thread-safe). Therefore, the iterations of the while loop cannot be executed completely in parallel, but there is some parallelism that we can exploit both within and across iterations as long as the constraints we have identified here are preserved.

Implementing the Example as a TBB Flow Graph

Now, let's step through the construction of a TBB flow graph that implements our stereoscopic 3D sample. The structure of the flow graph we will create is shown in Figure 3-9. This diagram looks different than Figure 3-8, because now the nodes represent TBB flow graph node objects and the edges represent TBB flow graph edges.

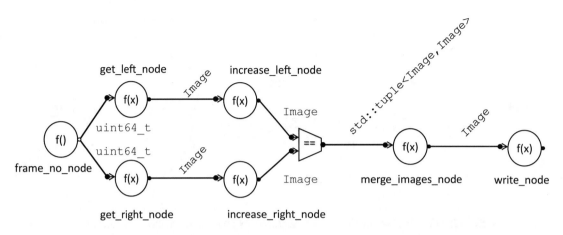

Figure 3-9. *A graph that represents the calls in Figure 2-28. The circles encapsulate the functions from Figure 2-28. The edges represent intermediate values. The trapezoid represents a node that joins messages into a two-tuple.*

Figure 3-10 shows the stereoscopic 3D example implemented using the TBB flow graph interfaces. The five basic steps are outlined in boxes. First, we create a graph object. Next, we create the eight nodes, including a source_node, several function_node instances, and a join_node. We then connect the nodes using calls to make_edge. After making the edges, we activate the source node. Finally, we wait for the graph to complete.

In the diagram in Figure 3-9, we see that frame_no_node is the source of inputs for the graph, and in Figure 3-10, this node is implemented using a source_node. As long as the body of a source_node continues to return true, the runtime library will continue to spawn new tasks to execute its body, which in turn calls getNextFrameNumber().

As we noted earlier, the getLeftImage and getRightImage functions must execute serially. In the code in Figure 3-10, we communicate this constraint to the runtime library by setting the concurrency constraint for these nodes to flow::serial. For these nodes, we use class function_node. You can see more details about function_node in Appendix B. If a node is declared with flow::serial, the runtime library will not spawn the next task to execute its body until any outstanding body task is finished.

```
tbb::flow::graph g;
```

```
tbb::flow::source_node<uint64_t> frame_no_node(g,
  [] (uint64_t &frame_number) -> bool {
    if (frame_number = getNextFrameNumber())
      return true;
    else
      return false;}, false);
tbb::flow::function_node<uint64_t, Image> get_left_node(g, tbb::flow::serial ,
  [] (uint64_t frame_number) -> Image {
  return getLeftImage(frame_number);});
tbb::flow::function_node<uint64_t, Image> get_right_node(g, tbb::flow::serial,
  [] (uint64_t frame_number) -> Image {
  return getRightImage(frame_number);});
tbb::flow::function_node<Image, Image> increase_left_node(g,
  tbb::flow::unlimited ,
  [] (Image left) -> Image {
    increasePNGChannel(left, Image::redOffset, 10);
    return left;});
tbb::flow::function_node<Image, Image> increase_right_node(g,
  tbb::flow::unlimited,
  [] (Image right) -> Image {
    increasePNGChannel(right, Image::blueOffset, 10);
    return right;});
tbb::flow::join_node<std::tuple<Image, Image>, tbb::flow::tag_matching >
  join_images_node(g, [] (Image left) { return left.frameNumber; },
                      [] (Image right) { return right.frameNumber; } );
tbb::flow::function_node<std::tuple<Image, Image>, Image>
merge_images_node(g, tbb::flow::unlimited,
  [] (std::tuple<Image, Image> t) -> Image {
    auto &l = std::get<0>(t);
    auto &r = std::get<1>(t);
    mergePNGImages(r, l);
    return r;});
tbb::flow::function_node<Image> write_node(g, tbb::flow::unlimited,
  [] (Image img) {
    img.write();});
```

```
tbb::flow::make_edge(frame_no_node, get_left_node);
tbb::flow::make_edge(frame_no_node, get_right_node);
tbb::flow::make_edge(get_left_node, increase_left_node);
tbb::flow::make_edge(get_right_node, increase_right_node);
tbb::flow::make_edge(increase_left_node,
                    tbb::flow::input_port<0>(join_images_node));
tbb::flow::make_edge(increase_right_node,
                    tbb::flow::input_port<1>(join_images_node));
tbb::flow::make_edge(join_images_node, merge_images_node);
tbb::flow::make_edge(merge_images_node, write_node);
```

```
frame_no_node.activate();
```

```
g.wait_for_all();
```

Figure 3-10. *The stereoscopic 3D example as a TBB flow graph*

In contrast, the `increase_left_node` and the `increase_rigt_node` objects are constructed with a concurrency constraint of `flow::unlimited.` The runtime library will immediately spawn a task to execute the body of these nodes whenever an incoming message arrives.

In Figure 3-9, we see that the `merge_images_node` function needs both a right and left image. In the original serial code, we were ensured that the images would be from the same frame, because the while loop only operated on one frame at a time. In our flow graph version, however, multiple frames may be pipelined through the flow graph and therefore may be in progress at the same time. We therefore need to ensure that we only merge left and right images that correspond to the same frame.

To provide our `merge_images_node` with a pair of matching left and right images, we create the `join_images_node` with a `tag_matching` policy. You can read about `join_node` and its different policies in Appendix B. In Figure 3-10, `join_images_node` is constructed to have two input ports and to create a tuple of `Image` objects based on matching their `frameNumber` member variables. The call to the constructor now includes two lambda expressions that are used to obtain the tag values from the incoming messages on the two input ports. The `merge_images_node` accepts a tuple and generates a single merged image.

The last node created in Figure 3-10 is `write_node`. It is a `flow::unlimited` `function_node` that receives `Image` objects and calls `write` to store each incoming buffer to an output file.

Once constructed, the nodes are connected to each other using calls to `make_edge` to create the topology shown in Figure 3-9. We should note that nodes that have only a single input or output do not require a port to be specified. However, for nodes such as `join_images_node` that have multiple input ports, port accessor functions are used to pass specific ports to the `make_edge` call.

Finally, in Figure 3-10, the `frame_no_node` is activated and a call to `wait_for_all` is used to wait for the graph to complete executing.

Understanding the Performance of a Data Flow Graph

It is important to note that, unlike in some other data flow frameworks, the nodes in a TBB flow graph are not implemented as threads. Instead, TBB tasks are spawned reactively as messages arrive at nodes and concurrency limits allow. Once tasks are spawned, they are then scheduled across the TBB worker threads using the same work-stealing approach used by the TBB generic algorithms (see Chapter 9 for details about work-stealing schedulers).

There are three main factors that can limit the performance of a TBB flow graph: (1) the serial nodes, (2) the number of worker threads, and (3) the overhead from the parallel execution of TBB tasks.

Let's consider how our 3D stereoscopic graph might be mapped to TBB tasks and how these tasks might perform. Nodes frame_no_node, get_left_node, and get_right_node are flow::serial nodes. The remaining nodes are flow::unlimited.

Serial nodes can cause worker threads to become idle, because they limit the availability of tasks. In our stereoscopic 3D example, the images are read in order. Once each image has been read, the processing of the image can begin immediately and can be overlapped with any other work in the system. Therefore, these three serial nodes are the ones limiting task availability in our graph. If the time to read these images dominates the rest of the processing, we will see very little speedup. If, however, the processing time is much larger than the time to read the images, we may see a significant speedup.

If the image reads are not our limiting factor, the performance is then limited by the number of worker threads and the overhead of parallel execution. When we use a flow graph, we pass data between nodes that may execute on different worker threads and, likewise, processor cores. We also overlap the execution of different functions. Both the passing of data across threads and the execution of functions simultaneously on different threads can affect memory and cache behavior. We will discuss locality and overhead optimizations in more detail in Part 2 of this book.

The Special Case of Dependency Graphs

The TBB flow graph interfaces support both data flow and dependency graphs. Edges in a data flow graph are channels over which data passes between nodes. The stereoscopic 3D example that we constructed earlier in this chapter is an example of a data flow graph – Image objects pass over the edges from node to node in the graph.

Edges in a dependency graph represent before-after relationships that must be satisfied for a correct execution. In a dependency graph, data is passed from node to node through shared memory and is not communicated directly by messages that travel over the edges. Figure 3-11 shows a dependency graph for making a peanut butter and jelly sandwich; the edges communicate that a node cannot begin until **_all_** of its predecessors have completed.

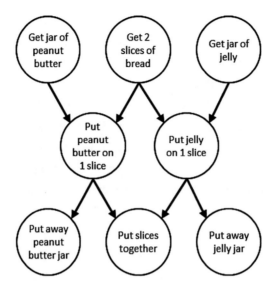

Figure 3-11. *A dependency graph for making a peanut butter and jelly sandwich. The edges here represent before-after relationships.*

To express dependency graphs using the TBB flow graph classes, we use class continue_node for the nodes and pass messages of type continue_msg. The primary difference between a function_node and continue_node is how they react to messages. You can see the details of continue_node in Appendix B.

When a function_node receives a message, it applies its body to that message – either by spawning a task immediately or by buffering the message until it is legal to spawn a task to apply the body. In contrast, a continue_node counts the number of messages it receives. When the number of messages it has received is equal to the number of predecessors it has, it spawns a task to execute its body and then resets its messages-received count. For example, if we were to implement Figure 3-11 using continue_nodes, the "Put slices together" node would execute each time it received two continue_msg objects, since it has two predecessors in the graph.

continue_node objects count messages and do not track that each individual predecessor has sent a message. For example, if a node has two predecessors, it will execute after it receives two messages, regardless of where the messages originated. This makes the overhead of these nodes much lower but also requires that dependency graphs are acyclic. Also, while a dependency graph can be executed repeatedly to completion, it is not safe to stream continue_msg objects into it. In both cases, when there is a cycle or if we stream items into a dependency graph, the simple counting mechanism means that the node might mistakenly trigger because it counts messages received from the same successor when it really needs to wait for inputs from different successors.

Implementing a Dependency Graph

The steps for using a dependency graph are the same as for a data flow graph; we create a graph object, make nodes, add edges, and feed messages into the graph. The main differences are that only continue_node and broadcast_node classes are used, the graph must be acyclic, and we must wait for the graph to execute to completion each time we feed a message into the graph.

Now, let us build an example dependency graph. For our example, let's implement the same forward substitution example that we implemented in Chapter 2 using a TBB parallel_do. You can refer to the detailed description of the serial example in that chapter.

The serial tiled implementation of this example is reproduced in Figure 3-12.

```
void fig_3_12(std::vector<double> &x, const std::vector<double> &a,
              std::vector<double> &b) {
  const int N = x.size();
  const int block_size = 512;
  const int num_blocks = N / block_size;

  for ( int r = 0; r < num_blocks; ++r ) {
    for ( int c = 0; c <= r; ++c ) {
      int i_start = r*block_size, i_end = i_start + block_size;
      int j_start = c*block_size, j_max = j_start + block_size - 1;
      for (int i = i_start; i < i_end; ++i) {
        int j_end = (i <= j_max) ? i : j_max + 1;
        for (int j = j_start; j < j_end; ++j) {
          b[i] -= a[j + i*N] * x[j];
        }
        if (j_end == i) {
          x[i] = b[i] / a[i + i*N];
        }
      }
    }
  }
}
```

Figure 3-12. *The serial blocked code for a direct implementation of forward substitution. This implementation is written to make the algorithm clear – not for best performance.*

In Chapter 2, we discussed the dependencies between the operations in this example and noted, as shown again in Figure 3-13, that there is a wavefront of parallelism that can be seen diagonally across the computation. When using a `parallel_do`, we created a 2D array of atomic counters and had to manually track when each block could be safely fed to the `parallel_do` algorithm for execution. While effective, this was cumbersome and is error-prone.

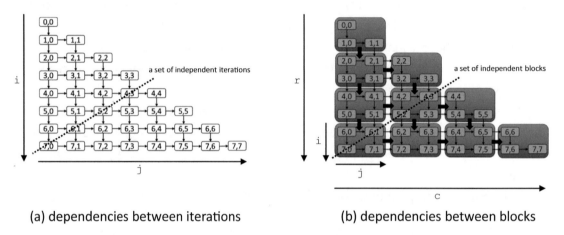

(a) dependencies between iterations   (b) dependencies between blocks

Figure 3-13.   *The dependencies in forward substitution for a small 8 × 8 matrix. In (a), the dependencies between iterations are shown. In (b), the iterations are grouped into blocks to reduce scheduling overheads. In both (a) and (b), each node must wait for its neighbor above and its neighbor to its left to complete before it can execute.*

In Chapter 2, we noted that we might also use a `parallel_reduce` to express parallelism in this example. We can see such an implementation in Figure 3-14.

```
void fig_3_14(std::vector<double> &x, const std::vector<double> &a,
              std::vector<double> &b) {
  const int N = x.size();
  for (int i = 0; i < N; ++i) {
    b[i] -= tbb::parallel_reduce(tbb::blocked_range<int>(0,i), 0.0,
      [&a, &x, i, N] (const tbb::blocked_range<int> &b, double init)
        -> double {
        for (int j = b.begin(); j < b.end(); ++j) {
          init += a[j + i*N] * x[j];
        }
        return init;
      },
      std::plus<double>()
    );
    x[i] = b[i] / a[i + i*N];
  }
}
```

Figure 3-14. *Using a* `parallel_reduce` *to make forward substitution parallel*

However, as we can see in Figure 3-15, the main thread must wait for each `parallel_` `reduce` to complete before it can move on to the next one. This synchronization between the rows adds unnecessary synchronization points. For example, once block 1,0 is done, it is safe to immediately start working on 2,0, but we must wait until the fork-join `parallel_reduce` algorithm is done until we move on to that row.

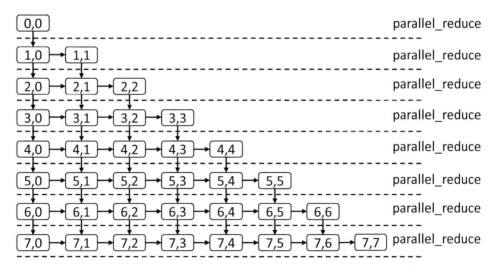

Figure 3-15. *The main thread must wait for each* `parallel_reduce` *to complete before it can move to the next* `parallel_reduce`, *introducing synchronization points*

Using a dependency graph, we simply express the dependencies directly and allow the TBB library to discover and exploit the available parallelism in the graph. We do not have to maintain counts or track completions explicitly like in the `parallel_do` version in Chapter 2, and we do not introduce unneeded synchronization points like in Figure 3-14.

Figure 3-16 shows a dependency graph version of this example. We use a `std::vector` nodes to hold a set of `continue_node` objects, each node representing a block of iterations. To create the graph, we follow the common pattern: (1) create a graph object, (2) create nodes, (3) add edges and (4) feed a message into the graph, and (5) wait for the graph to complete. However, we now create the graph structure using a loop nest as shown in Figure 3-16. The function `createNode` creates a new `continue_node` object for each block, and the function `addEdges` connects the node to the neighbors that must wait for its completion.

```
#include <iostream>
#include <memory>
#include <vector>
#include <tbb/tbb.h>

using Node = tbb::flow::continue_node<tbb::flow::continue_msg>;
using NodePtr = std::shared_ptr<Node>;

NodePtr createNode(tbb::flow::graph &g, int r, int c, int block_size,
                   std::vector<double> &x,
                   const std::vector<double> &a,
                   std::vector<double> &b);

void addEdges(std::vector<NodePtr> &nodes, int r, int c,
              int block_size, int num_blocks);

void fig_3_16(std::vector<double> &x, const std::vector<double> &a,
              std::vector<double> &b) {
  const int N = x.size();
  const int block_size = 1024;
  const int num_blocks = N / block_size;

  std::vector<NodePtr> nodes(num_blocks*num_blocks);
  tbb::flow::graph g;
  for (int r = num_blocks - 1; r >= 0; --r) {
    for (int c = r; c >= 0; --c) {
      nodes[r*num_blocks + c] =
        createNode(g, r, c, block_size, x, a, b);

      addEdges(nodes, r, c, block_size, num_blocks);
    }
  }
  nodes[0]->try_put(tbb::flow::continue_msg());

  g.wait_for_all();
}
```

Figure 3-16. *A dependency graph implementation of the forward substitution example*

In Figure 3-17, we show the implementation of the createNode. In Figure 3-18, we show the implementation of the addEdges functions.

```
NodePtr createNode(tbb::flow::graph &g, int r, int c, int block_size,
                   std::vector<double> &x,
                   const std::vector<double> &a,
                   std::vector<double> &b) {
  const int N = x.size();
  return std::make_shared<Node>(g,
    [r, c, block_size, N, &x, &a, &b]
    (const tbb::flow::continue_msg &msg) {
      int i_start = r*block_size, i_end = i_start + block_size;
      int j_start = c*block_size, j_max = j_start + block_size - 1;
      for (int i = i_start; i < i_end; ++i) {
        int j_end = (i <= j_max) ? i : j_max + 1;
        for (int j = j_start; j < j_end; ++j) {
          b[i] -= a[j + i*N] * x[j];
        }
        if (j_end == i) {
          x[i] = b[i] / a[i + i*N];
        }
      }
      return msg;
    }
  );
}
```

Figure 3-17. *The* createNode *function implementation*

The continue_node objects created in createNode use a lambda expression that encapsulates the inner two loops from the blocked version of forward substitution shown in Figure 3-12. Since no data is passed across the edges in a dependency graph, the data each node needs is accessed via shared memory using the pointers that are captured by the lambda expression. In Figure 3-17, the node captures by value the integers r, c, N, and block_size as well as references to the vectors x, a and b.

In Figure 3-18, the function addEdges uses make_edge calls to connect each node to its right and lower neighbors, since they must wait for the new node to complete before they can execute. When the loop nest in Figure 3-16 is finished, a dependency graph similar to the one in Figure 3-13 has been constructed.

```
void addEdges(std::vector<NodePtr> &nodes, int r, int c,
              int block_size, int num_blocks) {
  NodePtr np = nodes[r*num_blocks + c];
  if (c + 1 < num_blocks && r != c)
    tbb::flow::make_edge(*np, *nodes[r*num_blocks + c + 1]);
  if (r + 1 < num_blocks)
    tbb::flow::make_edge(*np, *nodes[(r + 1)*num_blocks + c]);
}
```

Figure 3-18. *The* addEdges *function implementation*

As shown in Figure 3-16, once the complete graph is constructed, we start it by sending a single `continue_msg` to the upper left node. Any `continue_node` that has no predecessors will execute whenever it receives a message. Sending a message to the top left node starts the dependency graph. Again, we use `g.wait_for_all()` to wait until the graph is finished executing.

Estimating the Scalability of a Dependency Graph

The same performance limitations that apply to data flow graphs also apply to dependency graphs. However, because dependency graphs must be acyclic, it is easier to estimate an upper bound on scalability for them. In this discussion, we use notation introduced by the Cilk project at MIT (see, e.g., *Blumofe, Joerg, Kuszmaul, Leiserson, Randall and Zhou, "Cilk: An Efficient Multithreaded Runtime System," In the Proceedings of the Principles and Practice of Parallel Programming, 1995*).

We denote the sum of the times to execute all nodes in a graph as T_1; the 1 means that this is the time it takes to execute the graph if we have only one thread of execution. And we denote the time to execute the nodes along the critical (longest) path as T_∞ since this is the minimum possible execution time even if we had an infinite number of threads available. The maximum speedup achievable through parallelism in a dependency graph is then T_1/T_∞. When executing on a platform with P processors, the execution time can never be smaller than the largest of T_1/P and T_∞.

For example, let us assume for simplicity that every node in Figure 3-13(a) takes the same amount of time to execute. We will call this time t_n. There are 36 nodes (the number of rows * the number of columns) in the graph, and so $T_1 = 36t_n$. The longest path from `0,0` to `7,7` contains 15 nodes (the number of rows + the number of columns – 1), and so for this graph $T_\infty = 15t_n$. Even if we had an infinite number of processors, the nodes along the critical path must be executed in order and cannot be overlapped. Therefore, our maximum speedup for this small 8×8 graph is $36t_n/15t_n = 2.4$. However, if we have a larger set of equations to solve, let's assume a 512×512 matrix, there would be 512×512=131,328 nodes and 512+512-1=1023 nodes along the critical path, for a maximum speedup of $131,328/1023 \approx 128$.

When possible, if you are considering implementing a dependency graph version of a serial application, it is good practice to profile your serial code, collect the time for each would-be node, and estimate the critical path length. You can then use the simple calculation described previously to estimate the upper bound on the achievable speedup.

Advanced Topics in TBB Flow Graphs

The TBB flow graph has a rich set of nodes and interfaces, and we have really only begun to scratch this surface with this chapter. In Chapter 17, we delve deeper into the API to answer some important questions, including

- How do we control resource usage in a flow graph?

- When do we need to use buffering?

- Are there antipatterns to avoid?

- Are there effective patterns to mimic?

Also, flow graph enables asynchronous, and heterogeneous, capabilities that we will explore in Chapters 18 and 19.

Summary

In this chapter, we learned about the classes and functions in the `tbb::flow` namespace that let us develop data flow and dependency graphs. We first discussed why expressing parallelism using graphs is useful. We then learned the basics of the TBB flow graph interface, including a brief overview of the different categories of nodes that are available in the interface. Next, we built, step by step, a small data flow graph that applies a 3D stereoscopic effect to sets of left and right images. Afterward, we discussed how these nodes are mapped to TBB tasks and what the limitations are on the performance of flow graphs. Next, we looked at dependency graphs, a special case of data flow graphs, where edges communicate dependency messages instead of data messages. We also built a forward substitution example as a dependency graph and discussed how to estimate its maximum speedup. Finally, we noted some of the important advanced topics that will be covered later in this book.

The photograph used in Figures 2-28a, 2-29, and 3-7, was taken by Elena Adams, and is used with permission from the Halide project's tutorials at `http://halide-lang.org`.

CHAPTER 4

TBB and the Parallel Algorithms of the C++ Standard Template Library

To use the Threading Building Blocks (TBB) library effectively, it is important to understand how it supports and augments the C++ standard. We discuss three aspects of TBB's relationship with standard C++ in this chapter:

1. The TBB library has often included parallelism-related features that are new to the C++ standard. Including such features in TBB provides developers early access to them before they are widely available in all compilers. In this vein, all pre-built distributions of TBB now include Intel's implementation of the parallel algorithms of the C++ Standard Template Library (STL). These implementations use TBB tasks to implement multithreading and use SIMD instructions to implement vectorization. Discussion of Parallel STL makes up the bulk of this chapter.

2. The TBB library also provides features that are not included in the C++ standard but make expressing parallelism easier for developers. The generic parallel algorithms and flow graph are examples of these. In this chapter, we discuss custom iterators that have been included in TBB to widen the applicability of the Parallel STL algorithms.

© Intel Corporation 2019
M. Voss, R. Asenjo, J. Reinders, *Pro TBB*, https://doi.org/10.1007/978-1-4842-4398-5_4

3. Finally, we note throughout the chapter that some additions to the C++ standard may displace the need for certain TBB features. However, we also note that TBB has value that will likely not be subsumed by the C++ standard for the foreseeable future. The features that TBB provides that will be of continuing benefit include its work-stealing task scheduler, its thread-safe containers, its flow graph API, and its scalable memory allocators for example.

Does the C++ STL Library Belong in This Book?

Does a chapter about additions to the C++ Standard Template Library really belong in a book about TBB? Yes, indeed it does! TBB is a C++ library for parallelism, and it does not exist in a vacuum. We need to understand how it relates to the C++ standard.

The execution policies we discuss in this chapter are similar in some ways to the TBB parallel algorithms covered in Chapter 2 because they let us express that an algorithm is safe to execute in parallel — but they ***do not*** prescribe the exact implementation details. If we want to mix TBB algorithms and Parallel STL algorithms in an application and still have efficient, composable parallelism (see Chapter 9), we benefit from using a Parallel STL implementation that uses TBB as its parallel execution engine! Therefore, when we talk about the parallel execution policies in this chapter, we will focus on TBB-based implementations. When we use a Parallel STL that uses TBB underneath, then Parallel STL becomes just another path for us to use TBB tasks in our code.

Back in Figure 1-3 in Chapter 1, we noted that many applications have multiple levels of parallelism available, including a Single Instruction Multiple Data (SIMD) layer that is best executed on vector units. Exploiting this level of parallelism can be critical as demonstrated by the performance results for the binomial options application shown in in Figure 4-1. Vector parallelism can only improve performance by a small factor when used alone; it's limited by the vector width. Figure 4-1 reminds us, however, that the multiplicative effect of using both task parallelism and vector parallelism should not be overlooked.

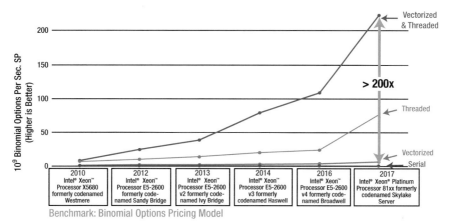

Benchmark results were obtained prior to implementation of recent software patches and firmware updates that are intended to address exploits referred to as "Spectre" and "Meltdown." Implementation of these updates may make these results inapplicable to your device or system.

Software and workloads used in performance tests may have been optimized for performance only on Intel microprocessors. Performance tests, such as SYSmark and MobileMark, are measured using specific computer systems, components, software, operations, and functions. Any change to any of those factors may cause the results to vary. You should consult other information and performance tests to assist you in fully evaluating your contemplated purchases, including the performance of that product when combined with other products. For more complete information, visit Performance Benchmark Test Disclosure.

Figure 4-1. *The performance of a binomial options pricing application when executed serial, vectorized, threaded, and vectorized and threaded*

In Chapter 1, we implemented an example that used a top-level TBB flow graph layer to introduce threading, nested generic TBB parallel algorithms within the graph nodes to get more threading, and then nested STL algorithms that use vector policies in the bodies of the parallel algorithms to introduce vectorization. When we combine TBB with Parallel STL and its execution policies, we not only get composable messaging and fork-join layers, but we also gain access to the SIMD layer.

It is for these reasons that execution policies in the STL library are an important part of our exploration of TBB!

TBB AND THE C++ STANDARD

The team that develops TBB is a strong proponent of support for threading in the C++ language itself. In fact, TBB has often included parallelism features modeled after those proposed for standardization in C++ to allow developers to migrate to these interfaces before they are widely supported by mainstream compilers. An example of this is `std::thread`. The developers of TBB recognized the importance of `std::thread` and so made an implementation available as a migration path for developers before it was available in all of the C++ standard libraries, injecting the feature directly into the `std` namespace. Today, TBB's implementation of `std::thread` simply includes the platform's implementation of `std::thread` if available and only falls back to its own implementation if the platform's standard C++ library does not include an implementation. A similar story can be told for other now-standard C++ features like atomic variables, mutex objects, and `std::condition_variable`.

A Parallel STL Execution Policy Analogy

To help think about the different execution policies that are provided by the Parallel STL library, we can visualize a multilane highway as shown in Figure 4-2. As with most analogies, this is not perfect, but it can help us see the benefits of the different policies.

We can think of each lane in a multilane highway as a thread of execution, each person as an operation to accomplish (i.e., the person needs to get from point A to point B), each car as a processor core, and each seat in the car as an element in a (vector) register. In a *serial execution*, we only use a single lane of the highway (a single thread) and each person gets their own car (we are not using vector units). Whether people are traveling the same route or not, they each take their own car and all travel in the same lane.

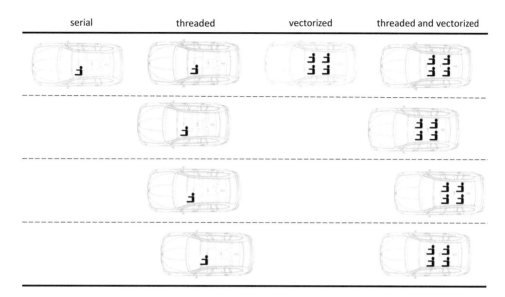

Figure 4-2. *A multilane highway analogy for the execution policies in Parallel STL*

In a *threaded execution*, we use more than one lane of the highway (i.e., more than one thread of execution). Now, we get more tasks accomplished per unit of time, but still, no carpooling is allowed. If several people are coming from the same starting point and traveling to the same destination, they each take their own car. We are more effectively utilizing the highway, but our cars (cores) are being used inefficiently.

A *vectorized execution* is like carpooling. If several people need to travel the same exact route, they share a car. Many modern processors support vector instructions, for example SSE and AVX in Intel processors. If we don't use vector instructions, we are underutilizing our processors. The vector units in these cores can apply the same operation to multiple pieces of data simultaneously. The data in vector registers are like people sharing a car, they take the same exact route.

Lastly, a threaded and vectorized execution is like using all the lanes in the highway (all of the cores) and also carpooling (using the vector units in each core).

A Simple Example Using `std::for_each`

Now that we have a general idea about execution policies but before we get into all of the gory details, let's start by applying a function `void f(float &e)` to all of the elements in a vector `v` as shown in Figure 4-3(a). Using `std::for_each`, one of the algorithms in the C++ STL library, we can do the same thing, as shown in Figure 4-3(b). Just like with a range-based for, the for_each iterates from v.begin() to v.end() and invokes the lambda expression on each item in the vector. This is the default sequenced behavior of for_each.

With Parallel STL, however, we can inform the library that it is okay to relax these semantics in order to exploit parallelism or, as shown in Figure 4-3(c), we can make it explicitly known to the library that we want the sequenced semantics. When using Intel's Parallel STL, we need to include both the algorithms and the execution policy headers into our code, for example:

```
#include <pstl/execution>
#include <pstl/algorithm>
```

In C++17, leaving out the execution policy or passing in the sequenced_policy object, seq, results in the same default execution behavior: it *appears as if* the lambda expression is invoked on each item in the vector in order. We say "as if" because the hardware and compiler are permitted to parallelize the algorithm, but only if doing so is invisible to a standard-conforming program.

The power of Parallel STL comes from the other execution policies that relax this sequenced constraint. We say that the operations can be overlapped or vectorized from within a single thread of execution by using the unsequenced_policy object, unseq, as shown in Figure 4-3(d). The library can then overlap operations in a single thread, for example, by using Single Instruction Multiple Data (SIMD) extensions such as SSE or AVX to vectorize the execution. Figure 4-4 shows this behavior using side-by-side boxes to indicate that these operations execute simultaneously using vector units. The unseq execution policy allows "carpooling."

```
for (auto &i : v ) {
  f(i);
}
(a) a for loop

std::for_each(v.begin(), v.end(),
 [](float &i) {
   f(i);
 }
);
(b) std::for_each and no execution policy

std::for_each(pstl::execution::seq, v.begin(), v.end(),
  [](float &i) {
    f(i);
  }
);
(c) std::for_each and seq execution policy

std::for_each(pstl::execution::unseq, v.begin(), v.end(),
  [](float &i) {
    f(i);
  }
);
(d) std::for_each and unseq execution policy

std::for_each(pstl::execution::par, v.begin(), v.end(),
  [](float &i) {
    f(i);
  }
);
(e) std::for_each and par execution policy

std::for_each(pstl::execution::par_unseq, v.begin(), v.end(),
  [](float &i) {
    f(i);
  }
);
(f) std::for_each and par_unseq execution policy
```

Figure 4-3. *A simple loop implemented with* std::for_each *and using various Parallel STL execution policies*

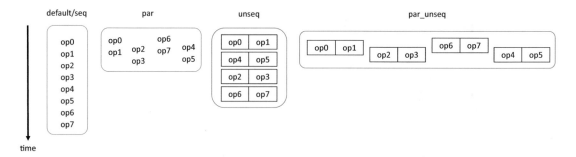

Figure 4-4. *Applying operations using different execution policies*

In Figure 4-3(e), we tell the library that it is safe to execute this function on all of the elements in the vector using multiple threads of execution using the `parallel_policy` object, `par`. As shown in Figure 4-4, the `par` policy allows the operations to be spread across different threads of execution, but, within each thread, the operations are not overlapped (i.e., they are not vectorized). Thinking back to our multilane highway example, we are now using all of the lanes in the highway but are not yet carpooling.

Finally, in Figure 4-3(f), the `parallel_unsequenced_policy` object, `par_unseq`, is used to communicate that the application of the lambda expression to the elements can be both parallelized and vectorized. In Figure 4-4, the `par_unseq` execution uses multiple threads of execution *and* overlaps operations within each thread. We are now fully utilizing all of the cores in our platform and effectively utilizing each core by making use of its vector units.

In practice, we must be careful when we use execution policies. Just like with the generic TBB parallel algorithms, when we use an execution policy to relax the execution order for an STL algorithm, we are asserting to the library that this relaxation is legal and profitable. The library does not check that we are correct. Likewise, the library does not guarantee that performance is not degraded by using a certain execution policy.

Another point to notice in Figure 4-3 is that the STL algorithms themselves are in namespace `std`, but the execution policies, as provided by Intel's Parallel STL, are in namespace `pstl::execution`. If you have a fully compliant C++17 compiler, other implementations that may not use TBB will be selected if you use the standard execution policies in the `std::execution` namespace.

What Algorithms Are Provided in a Parallel STL Implementation?

The C++ Standard Template Library (STL) primarily includes operations that are applied to sequences. There are some outliers like `std::min` and `std::max` that can be applied to values, but for the most part, the algorithms, such as `std::for_each, std::find, std::transform, std::copy,` and `std::sort`, are applied to sequences of items. This focus on sequences is convenient when we want to operate on containers that support iterators, but can be somewhat cumbersome if we want to express something that does not operate on containers. Later in this chapter, we will see that sometimes we can "think outside the box" and use custom iterators to make some algorithms act more like general loops.

Explaining what each STL algorithm does is beyond the scope of this chapter and book. There are entire books written about the C++ Standard Template Library and how to use it, including *The C++ Standard Library: A Tutorial and Reference by Nicolai Josuttis (Addison-Wesley Professional).* In this chapter, we only focus on what the execution policies, first introduced in C++17, mean for these algorithms and how they can be used together with TBB.

Most of the STL algorithms specified in the C++ standard have overloads in C++17 that accept execution polices. In addition, a few new algorithms were added because they are especially useful in parallel programs or because the committee wanted to avoid changes in semantics. We can find exactly which algorithms support execution policies by looking at the standard itself or online at web sites like `http://en.cppreference.com/w/cpp/algorithm`.

How to Get and Use a Copy of Parallel STL That Uses TBB

Detailed instructions for downloading and installing Intel's Parallel STL are provided in Chapter 1 in the section "Getting the Threading Building Blocks (TBB) Library." If you download and install a pre-built copy of TBB 2018 update 5 or later, whether a commercially license copy obtained through Intel or an open-source binary distribution downloaded from GitHub, then you also get Intel's Parallel STL. Parallel STL comes with all of the pre-built TBB packages.

If however, you want to build the TBB library from sources obtained from GitHub, then you will need to download the Parallel STL sources from GitHub separately, since the source code for the two libraries are maintained in separate repositories `https://github.com/intel/tbb` and `https://github.com/intel/parallelstl`.

As we have already seen, Parallel STL supports several different execution policies, some that support parallelized execution, some that support vectorized execution, and some that support both. Intel's Parallel STL supports parallelism with TBB and vectorization using OpenMP 4.0 SIMD constructs. To get the most out of Intel's Parallel STL, you must have a C++ compiler that supports C++11 and OpenMP 4.0 SIMD constructs – and of course you also need TBB. We strongly recommend using the Intel compiler that comes with any version of Intel Parallel Studio XE 2018 or later. Not only do these compilers include both the TBB library and support OpenMP 4.0 SIMD constructs, but they also include optimizations that were specifically included to increase performance for some C++ STL algorithms when used with the unseq or par_ unseq execution policies.

To build an application that uses Parallel STL on the command line, we need to set the environment variables for compilation and linkage. If we installed Intel Parallel Studio XE, we can do this by calling the suite-level environment scripts such as compilervars.{sh|csh|bat}. If we just installed Parallel STL, then we can set the environment variables by running pstlvars.{sh|csh|bat} in <pstl_install_dir>/ {linux|mac|windows}/pstl/bin. Additional instructions are provided in Chapter 1.

Algorithms in Intel's Parallel STL

Intel's Parallel STL does not yet support all execution policies for every single STL algorithm. An up-to-date list of which algorithms are provided by the library and which policies each algorithm supports can be found at https://software.intel.com/en-us/ get-started-with-pstl.

Figure 4-5 shows the algorithms and execution policies that were supported at the time this book was written.

Algorithm Categories	
Non-modifying sequence operations	**header: \<algorithm>**
`adjacent_find, all_of, any_of, count, count_if, find, find_end, find_first_of, find_if, find_if_not, for_each, for_each_n, mismatch, none_of, search, search_n`	
Modifying sequence operations	**header: \<algorithm>**
`copy, copy_if, copy_n, fill, fill_n, generate, generate_n, move, remove, remove_copy, remove_copy_if, remove_if, replace, replace_copy, replace_copy_if, replace_if, reverse, reverse_copy, rotate, rotate_copy, shuffle, swap_ranges, transform, unique*, unique_copy`	
Partitioning operations	**header: \<algorithm>**
`is_partitioned, partition*, partition_copy, stable_partition*`	
Sorting operations	**header: \<algorithm>**
`is_sorted, is_sorted_until, nth_element*, partial_sort*, partial_sort_copy*, sort*, stable_sort*`	
Operations on sorted ranges	**header: \<algorithm>**
`includes*, inplace_merge*, merge*, set_difference*, set_intersection*, set_symmetric_difference*, set_union*`	
Heap operations	**header: \<algorithm>**
`is_heap, is_heap_until`	
Minimum/maximum operations	**header: \<algorithm>**
`max_element, min_element, minmax_element`	
Comparison operations	**header: \<algorithm>**
`equal, lexicographical_compare`	
Numeric operations	**header: \<numeric>**
`adjacent_difference, exclusive_scan, inclusive_scan, reduce, transform_exclusive_scan, transform_inclusive_scan, transform_reduce`	
Operations on uninitialized memory	**header: \<memory>**
`uninitialized_copy, uninitialized_copy_n, uninitialized_default_construct, uninitialized_default_construct_n, uninitialized_fill, uninitialized_fill_n, uninitialized_move, uninitialized_move_n, uninitialized_value_construct, uninitialized_value_construct_n`	

* Supports threading but not SIMD execution

Figure 4-5. *The algorithms that support execution policies in Intel's Parallel STL as of January 2019. Additional algorithms and policies may be supported later. See* `https://software.intel.com/en-us/get-started-with-pstl` *for updates.*

Figure 4-6 shows the policies supported by Intel's Parallel STL including those that are part of the C++17 standard as well as those that have been proposed for inclusion in a future standard. The C++17 policies let us select a sequenced execution (seq), a parallel execution using TBB (par), or a parallel execution using TBB that is also vectorized (par_unseq). The unsequenced (unseq) policy let us select an implementation that is only vectorized.

Policy	Standard	Class	Global Object
sequenced	C++17	`sequenced_policy`	`seq`
parallel	C++17	`parallel_policy`	`par`
parallel + unsequenced	C++17	`parallel_unsequenced_policy`	`par_unseq`
unsequenced	Proposed	`unsequenced_policy`	`unseq`

Figure 4-6. *The execution policies supported by Intel's Parallel STL*

Capturing More Use Cases with Custom Iterators

Earlier in this chapter, we introduced a simple use of `std::for_each` and showed how the different execution policies can be used with it. Our simple example with `par_unseq` in Figure 4-3(f) looked like

```
std::for_each(pstl::execution::par_unseq, v.begin(), v.end(),
  [](float &i) {
    f(i);
  }
);
```

At first glance, the `for_each` algorithm appears fairly limited, it visits the elements in a sequence and applies a unary function to each element. When used on a container in this expected way, it is in fact limited in applicability. It does not, for example, accept a range like the TBB `parallel_for`.

However, C++ is a powerful language, and we can use STL algorithms in creative ways to stretch their applicability. As we discussed earlier in Chapter 2, an iterator is an object that points to an element in a range of elements and defines operators that provide the ability to iterate through the elements of the range. There are different categories of iterators including *forward*, *bidirectional*, and *random-access* iterators. Many standard C++ containers provide `begin` and `end` functions that return iterators that let us traverse the elements of the containers. One common way to apply STL algorithms to more use cases is by using *custom* iterators. These classes implement the iterator interface but are not included in the C++ Standard Template Library.

Three commonly used custom iterators are included in the TBB library to assist in using the STL algorithms. These iterator types are described in Figure 4-7 and are available in the iterators.h header or through the all-inclusive tbb.h header file.

Type	Description
template<typename IntType> class counting_iterator;	A random access iterator that maintains an internal counter that changes based on the arithmetic operations performed on the iterator. The operator*() function returns the current counter value. It is commonly used to obtain an index into a container or set of containers.
template<typename... Types> class zip_iterator;	A random access iterator that iterates over several iterators simultaneously. The operator*() function returns a tuple of the dereferenced values of the individual iterators.
template<typename UnaryFunc, typename Iter> class transform_iterator;	A random access iterator that applies a transformation to a sequence. The operator*() function applies a unary transformation function to the value returned by dereferencing the underlying iterator.

Figure 4-7. *The custom iterator classes available in TBB*

As an example, we can pass custom iterators to std::for_each to make it act more like a general for loop. Let's consider the simple loop shown in Figure 4-8(a). This loop writes a[i]+b[i]*b[i] back to a[i] for each i in the range [0,n).

```cpp
std::vector<float> a(n, 1.0), b(n, 3.0);

for (int i = 0; i < n; ++i) {
  a[i] = a[i] + b[i]*b[i];
}
```
(a) The initial serial for loop

```cpp
std::for_each(tbb::counting_iterator<int>(0),
              tbb::counting_iterator<int>(n),
  [&a, &b](int i) {
    a[i] = a[i] + b[i]*b[i];
  });
```
(b) Using tbb::counting_iterator

```cpp
auto begin = tbb::make_zip_iterator(a.begin(), b.begin());
auto end = tbb::make_zip_iterator(a.end(), b.end());

std::for_each(begin, end,
  [](const std::tuple<float&, float&>& v) {
    float &a = std::get<0>(v);
    float b = std::get<1>(v);
    a = a + b*b;
  });
```
(c) Using tbb::zip_iterator

```cpp
auto zbegin = tbb::make_zip_iterator(a.begin(), b.begin());
auto zend = tbb::make_zip_iterator(a.end(), b.end());
auto square_b = [](const std::tuple<float &, float &>& v) {
  float b = std::get<1>(v);
  return std::tuple<float &, float>(std::get<0>(v), b*b);
};
auto begin = tbb::make_transform_iterator(zbegin, square_b);
auto end = tbb::make_transform_iterator(zend, square_b);

std::for_each(begin, end,
  [](const std::tuple<float&, float>& v) {
    float &a = std::get<0>(v);
    a = a + std::get<1>(v);
  });
```
(d) Using tbb::transform_iterator

Figure 4-8. *Using* std::for_each *with custom iterators*

In Figure 4-8(b), the `counting_iterator` class is used to create something like a range. The arguments passed to the `for_each` lambda expression will be the integer values from 0 to n-1. Even though the `for_each` still iterates over only a single sequence, we use these values as an index into the two vectors, a and b.

In Figure 4-8(c), the `zip_iterator` class is used to iterate over the a and b vectors simultaneously. The TBB library provides a `make_zip_iterator` function to simplify construction of the iterators:

```
template<typename... T>
zip_iterator<T...> make_zip_iterator(T&&... args);
```

In Figure 4-8(c), we still use only a single sequence in the call to `for_each`. But now, the argument passed to the lambda expression is a `std::tuple` of references to `float`, one from each vector.

Finally, in Figure 4-8(d), we add uses of the `transform_iterator` class. We first combine the two sequences from vector a and b into a single sequence using the `zip_iterator` class, like we did in Figure 4-8(c). But, we also create a lambda expression, which we assign to `square_b`. The lambda expression will be used to transform the `std::tuple` of references to `float` that are obtained by dereferencing the `zip_iterator`. We pass this lambda expression to our calls to the `make_tranform_iterator` function:

```
template<typename UnaryFunc, typename Iter>
transform_iterator<UnaryFunc, Iter>
make_transform_iterator(Iter it, UnaryFunc unary_func);
```

When the `transform_iterator` objects in Figure 4-8(d) are dereferenced, they receive an element from the underlying `zip_iterator`, square the second element of the tuple, and create a new `std::tuple` that contains a reference to the `float` from a and the squared value from b. The argument passed to the `for_each` lambda expression includes an already squared value, and so the function does not need to compute `b[i]*b[i]`.

Because custom iterators like those in Figure 4-7 are so useful, they are not only available in the TBB library but also through other libraries such as the Boost C++ libraries (`www.boost.org`) and Thrust (`https://thrust.github.io/doc/group__fancyiterator.html`). They are currently not available directly in the C++ Standard Template Library.

Highlighting Some of the Most Useful Algorithms

With the preliminaries out of the way, we can now discuss the more useful and general algorithms provided by Parallel STL in more depth, including for_each, transform, reduce, and transform_reduce. As we discuss each algorithm, we point out analogs in the TBB generic algorithms. The advantage of the Parallel STL interfaces over the TBB-specific interfaces is that Parallel STL is part of the C++ standard. The disadvantage of the Parallel STL interfaces is that they are less expressive and less tunable than the generic TBB algorithms. We point out some of these drawbacks as we talk about the algorithms in this section.

std::for_each, std::for_each_n

We've already talked a lot about for_each in this chapter. In addition to for_each, Parallel STL also provides a for_each_n algorithm that only visits the first n elements. Both algorithms for_each and for_each_n have several interfaces; the ones that accept execution policies are as follows:

```
template<class ExecutionPolicy, class ForwardIt,
         class UnaryFunction>
void for_each( ExecutionPolicy&& policy,
               ForwardIt first, ForwardIt last,
               UnaryFunction f);

template<class ExecutionPolicy, class ForwardIt, class Size,
         class UnaryFunction>
ForwardIt for_each_n(ExecutionPolicy&& policy,
                     ForwardIt first, Size n, UnaryFunction f);
```

Combined with custom iterators, for_each can be quite expressive, as we demonstrated earlier in Figure 4-8. We can, for example, take the simple matrix multiplication example from Chapter 2 and re-implement it in Figure 4-9 using the counting_iterator class.

```
std::for_each(
  /* policy */ pstl::execution::par,
  /* first */  tbb::counting_iterator<int>(0),
  /* last */   tbb::counting_iterator<int>(M),
  [&a, &b, &c, M](int i) {
    for (int j = 0; j < M; ++j) {
      int c_index = i*M + j;
      for (int k = 0; k < M; ++k) {
        c[c_index] += a[i*M + k] * b[k*M + j];
      }
    }
  }
);
```

Figure 4-9. *Using* `std::for_each` *with* `tbb::counting_iterator` *to create a parallel version of matrix multiplication*

If we use an STL that uses TBB underneath, like Intel's Parallel STL, the par policy is implemented using a `tbb::parallel_for`, and so the performance of `std::for_each` and `tbb::parallel_for` will be similar for a simple example like this.

This of course begs a question. If `std::for_each` uses a `tbb::parallel_for` to implement its par policy but is a standard interface and also gives us access to the other policies, shouldn't we just *always* use `std::for_each` instead of a `tbb::parallel_for`?

Unfortunately, no. Not all code is as simple as this example. If we are interested in an effective threaded implementation, it's typically better to use a `tbb::parallel_for` directly. Even for this matrix multiplication example, as we noted back in Chapter 2, our simple implementation is not optimal. In Part 2 of this book, we discuss important optimization hooks available in TBB that we can use to tune our code. We will see in Chapter 16 that these hooks result in significant performance gains. Unfortunately, most of these advanced features cannot be applied when we use a Parallel STL algorithm. The standard C++ interfaces simply do not allow for them.

When we use a Parallel STL algorithm and choose a standard policy such as par, unseq, or par_unseq, we get whatever the implementation decides to give us. There are proposals for additions to C++, like executors, that may address this limitation sometime in the future. But for now, we have little control over STL algorithms. When using TBB generic algorithms, such as `parallel_for`, we have access to the rich set of optimization features described in Part 2 of this book, such as partitioners, different types of blocked ranges, grainsizes, affinity hints, priorities, isolation features, and so on.

For some simple cases, a standard C++ Parallel STL algorithm might be just as good as its TBB counterpart, but in more realistic scenarios, TBB provides us with the flexibility and control we need to get the performance we want.

std::transform

Another useful algorithm in Parallel STL is transform. It applies a unary operation to the elements from one sequence or a binary operation to the elements from two input sequences and writes the results to the elements in a single output sequence. The two interfaces that support parallel execution policies are as follows:

```
template< class ExecutionPolicy, class ForwardIt1, class ForwardIt2,
          class UnaryOperation >
ForwardIt2 transform(ExecutionPolicy&& policy, ForwardIt1 first1,
                     ForwardIt1 last1, ForwardIt2 d_first,
                     UnaryOperation unary_op);

template< class ExecutionPolicy, class ForwardIt1, class ForwardIt2,
          class ForwardIt3, class BinaryOperation >
ForwardIt3 transform(ExecutionPolicy&& policy, ForwardIt1 first1,
                     ForwardIt1 last1, ForwardIt2 first2,
                     ForwardIt3 d_first,
                     BinaryOperation binary_op);
```

In Figure 4-8, we used for_each and custom iterators to read from two vectors and write back to a single output vector, computing a[i] = a[i] + b[i]*b[i] in each iteration. This is a great candidate for std::transform as we can see in Figure 4-10. Because transform has an interface that supports two input sequences and one output sequence, this matches our example well.

```
std::vector<float> a(n, 1.0), b(n, 3.0);

std::transform(pstl::execution::par_unseq,
  /* in1 range */ a.begin(), a.end(),
  /* in2 first */ b.begin(),
  /* out first */ a.begin(),
  [](float ae, float be) -> float {
    return ae + be*be;
  }
);
```

Figure 4-10. *Using* std::transform *to add two vectors*

As with `std::for_each`, the applicability of this algorithm when used in a typical way is limited because there is at most two input sequences and only a single output sequence. If we have a loop that writes to more than one output array or container, it's awkward to express that with a single call to transform. Of course, it's possible – almost anything is in C++ – but it requires using custom iterators, like `zip_iterator`, and some pretty ugly code to access the many containers.

std::reduce

We discussed reductions when we covered `tbb::parallel_reduce` in Chapter 2. The Parallel STL algorithm `reduce` performs a reduction over the elements of a sequence. Unlike `tbb::parallel_reduce` however, it provides only a reduction operation. In the next section, we discuss `transform_reduce`, which is more like `tbb::parallel_reduce` because it provides both a transform operation and a reduce operation. The two interfaces to `std::reduce` that support parallel execution policies are as follows:

```
template<class ExecutionPolicy, class ForwardIt, class T>
T reduce(ExecutionPolicy&& policy,
          ForwardIt first, ForwardIt last, T init);

template<class ExecutionPolicy, class ForwardIt, class T,
          class BinaryOp>
T reduce(ExecutionPolicy&& policy, ForwardIt first,
          ForwardIt last, T init, BinaryOp binary_op);
```

The `reduce` algorithm performs a generalized sum of the elements of the sequence using `binary_op` and the identity value `init`. In the first interface, `binary_op` is not an input parameter, and `std::plus<>` is used by default. A generalized sum means a reduction where the elements can be grouped and rearranged in arbitrary order – so this algorithm assumes that the operation is both associative and commutative. Because of this, we can have the same floating-point rounding issues that we discussed in the sidebar in Chapter 2.

If we want to sum the elements in a vector, we can use `std::reduce` and any of the execution policies, as shown in Figure 4-11.

```
std::vector<float> a(n, 1.0);

float sum = std::reduce(pstl::execution::seq, a.begin(), a.end());
sum += std::reduce(pstl::execution::unseq, a.begin(), a.end());
sum += std::reduce(pstl::execution::par, a.begin(), a.end());
sum += std::reduce(pstl::execution::par_unseq, a.begin(), a.end());
```

Figure 4-11. *Using* `std::reduce` *to sum the elements of a vector four times*

std::transform_reduce

As mentioned in the previous section, `transform_reduce` is similar to a `tbb::parallel_reduce` because it provides both a transform operation and reduce operation. However, as with most STL algorithms, it can be applied to only one or two input sequences at a time:

```
template<class ExecutionPolicy, class ForwardIt,
class T, class BinaryOp, class UnaryOp>
T transform_reduce(ExecutionPolicy&& policy,
                   ForwardIt first, ForwardIt last,
                   T init, BinaryOp binary_op, UnaryOp unary_op);

template<class ExecutionPolicy,
        class ForwardIt1, class ForwardIt2,
        class T, class BinaryOp1, class BinaryOp2>
T transform_reduce(ExecutionPolicy&& policy,
                   ForwardIt1 first1, ForwardIt1 last1,
                   ForwardIt2 first2, T init,
                   BinaryOp1 binary_op1, BinaryOp2 binary_op2);
```

An important and common kernel we can implement with a `std::transform_reduce` is an inner product. It is so commonly used for this purpose that there is an interface that uses `std::plus<>` and `std::multiplies<>` for the two operations by default:

```
template<class ExecutionPolicy,
        class ForwardIt1, class ForwardIt2, class T>
T transform_reduce(ExecutionPolicy&& policy,
                   ForwardIt1 first1, ForwardIt1 last1,
                   ForwardIt2 first2, T init);
```

The serial code for an inner product of two vectors, a and b, is shown in Figure 4-12(a). We can use a `std::transform_reduce` and provide our own lambda expressions for the two operations as shown in Figure 4-12(b). Or, like in Figure 4-12(c), we can rely on the default operations.

```
float v = 0.0;
for (int i = 0; i < n; ++i) {
  v += a[i]*b[i];
}
```
(a) serial code for an inner product of two vectors

```
std::transform_reduce(pstl::execution::par,
  /* in1 range */ a.begin(), a.end(),
  /* in2 range */ b.begin(),
  /* init */ 0.0,
  /* op1, the reduce */
  [](float ae, float be) -> float {
    return ae + be;
  },
  /* op2, the transform */
  [](float ae, float be) -> float {
    return ae * be;
  }
);
```
(b) std::transform_reduce with both operations specified

```
std::transform_reduce(pstl::execution::par,
  /* in1 range */ a.begin(), a.end(),
  /* in2 range */ b.begin(),
  /* init */ 0.0
);
```
(c) std::transform_reduce with default operations

Figure 4-12. *Using* std::transform_reduce *to calculate an inner product*

And again, as with the other Parallel STL algorithms, if we think slightly outside of the box, we can use custom iterators, like counting_iterator, to use this algorithm to process more than just elements in containers. For example, we can take the calculation of pi example that we implemented with tbb::parallel_reduce in Chapter 2 and implement it using a std::transform_reduce, as shown in Figure 4-13.

```
float fig_4_13() {
  constexpr float dx = 1.0 / num_intervals;
  float sum = std::transform_reduce(
    /* policy */ std::execution::par_unseq,
    /* first */ tbb::counting_iterator<int>(0),
    /* last */  tbb::counting_iterator<int>(num_intervals),
    /* init = */ 0.0,
    /* reduce */
    [](float x, float y) -> float {
      return x + y;
    },
    /* transform */
    [=](int i) -> float {
      float x = (i + 0.5)*dx;
      float h = sqrt(1 - x*x);
      return h*dx;
    }
  );
  return 4 * sum;
}
```

Figure 4-13. Using $std::transform\_reduce$ to calculate pi

Using a Parallel STL algorithm like std::transform_reduce instead of a tbb::parallel_reduce carries with it the same pros and cons as the other algorithms we've described. It uses a standardized interface so is potentially more portable. However, it doesn't allow us to use the optimization features that are described in Part 2 of this book to optimize its performance.

A Deeper Dive into the Execution Policies

The execution policies in Parallel STL let us communicate the constraints that we want to apply to the ordering of the operations during the execution of the STL algorithm. The standard set of policies did not come out of thin air – it captures the relaxed constraints necessary for executing efficient parallel/threaded or SIMD/vectorized code.

If you are happy enough to think of the sequenced_policy as meaning sequential execution, the parallel_policy as meaning parallel execution, the unsequenced_policy as meaning vectorized execution, and the parallel_unsequenced_policy as meaning parallel and vectorized execution, then you can skip the rest of this section. However, if you want to understand the subtleties implied by these policies, keep reading as we dive into the details.

The `sequenced_policy`

The `sequenced_policy` means that an algorithm's execution *appears as if* (1) all of the *element access functions* used by the algorithm are invoked on the thread that called the algorithm and (2) the invocations of the element access functions are not interleaved (i.e., they are sequenced with respect to each other within a given thread). An element access function is any function invoked during the algorithm that accesses the elements, such as functions in the iterators, comparison or swap functions, and any other user-provided functions that are applied to the elements. As mentioned earlier, we say "as if" because the hardware and compiler are permitted to break these rules, but only if doing so is invisible to a standard-conforming program.

One thing to note is that many of the STL algorithms do not specify that operations are applied in any specific sequence order even in the sequenced case. For example, while `std::for_each` does specify that the elements of a sequence are accessed in order in the sequenced case, `std::transform` does not. The `std::transform` visits all of the elements in a sequence, but not in any particular order. Unless stated otherwise, a sequenced execution means that the invocations of the element access functions are *indeterminately sequenced* in the calling thread. If two function calls are "indeterminately sequenced," it means that one of the function calls executes to completion before the other function call starts executing – but it doesn't matter which function call goes first. The result is that the library may not be able to interleave the execution of the operations from the two functions, preventing the use of SIMD operations for example.

The "as if" rule can sometimes lead to unexpected performance results. For example, a `sequenced_policy` execution may perform just as well as an `unsequenced_policy` because the compiler vectorizes both. If you get confusing results, you may want to inspect your compiler's optimization reports to see what optimizations have been applied.

The parallel_policy

The `parallel_policy` allows the element access functions to be invoked in the calling thread or from other threads created by the library to assist in parallel execution. However, any calls from within the same thread are sequenced with respect to each other, that is, the execution of access functions on the same thread cannot be interleaved.

When we use Intel's Parallel STL library, the `parallel_policy` is implemented using TBB generic algorithms and tasks. The threads that execute the operations are the main thread and the TBB worker threads.

The unsequenced_policy

The `unsequenced_policy` asserts that all of the element access functions must be invoked from the calling thread. However, within the calling thread, the execution of these functions can be interleaved. This relaxation of the sequenced constraint is important since it allows the library to aggregate operations in different function invocations into single SIMD instructions or to overlap operations.

SIMD parallelism can be implemented with vector instructions introduced through assembly code, compiler intrinsics, or compiler pragmas. In Intel's Parallel STL implementation, the library uses OpenMP SIMD pragmas.

Because the executions of the element access functions can be interleaved in a single thread, it is unsafe to use mutex objects in them (mutex objects are described in more detail in Chapter 5). Imagine, for example, interleaving several lock operations from different functions before executing any of the matching unlock operations.

The parallel_unsequenced_policy

As we might guess after learning about the preceding policies, the `parallel_unsequenced_policy` weakens execution constraints in two ways: (1) element access functions may be invoked by the calling thread or by other threads created to help with parallel execution and (2) the function executions within each thread may be interleaved.

Which Execution Policy Should We Use?

When we choose an execution policy, we first have to be sure it doesn't relax constraints to a point that the values computed by the algorithm will be wrong.

For example, we can use a `std::for_each` to compute `a[i] = a[i] + a[i-1]` for a vector a, but the code depends on the sequenced order of `for_each` (which, unlike some other indeterminately sequenced algorithms, applies the operator to the items in order):

```
float previous_value = 0.0;
std::for_each(
  pstl::execution::par, a.begin(), a.end(),
    [&](float &in)  {
       float p = previous_value;
       previous_value = in;
       in += p;
  }
);
```

This sample stores the last value into the previous_value variable, which has been captured by reference by the lambda expression. This sample only works if we execute the operations in order within a single thread of execution. Using any of the policy objects other than seq will yield incorrect results.

But let's assume we do our due diligence and we know which policies are legal for our operations and the STL algorithm we are using. How do we choose between a sequenced_policy execution, an unsequenced_policy execution, a parallel_policy execution, or a parallel_unsequenced_policy execution?

Unfortunately, there's not a simple answer. But there are some guidelines we can use:

- We should use threaded execution only when the algorithm has enough work to profit from parallel execution. We discuss rules of thumb for when to use tasks or not in Chapter 16 in Part 2 of this book. These rules apply here as well. A parallel execution has some overhead, and if the work isn't large enough we will only add overhead with no performance gain.

- Vectorization has lower overhead and therefore can be used effectively for small, inner loops. Simple algorithms may benefit from vectorization when they do not benefit from threading.

- Vectorization can have overhead too though. To use vector registers in a processor, the data has to be packed together. If our data is not contiguous in memory or we cannot access it with a unit stride, the compiler may have to generate extra instructions to gather the data into the vector registers. In such cases, a vectorized loop may perform worse than its sequential counterpart. You should read compiler vectorization reports and look at runtime profiles to makes sure you don't make things worse by adding vectorization.

- Because we can switch policies easily with Parallel STL, the best
  option may be to profile your code and see which policy performs
  best for your platform.

Other Ways to Introduce SIMD Parallelism

Outside of using the parallel algorithms in the C++ STL, there are several ways to
introduce SIMD parallelism into applications. The easiest, and preferred route, is to use
optimized domain-specific or math-kernel libraries whenever possible. For example,
the Intel Math Kernel Library (Intel MKL) provides highly tuned implementations of
many math functions, like those found in BLAS, LAPACK, and FFTW. These functions
take advantage of both threading and vectorization when profitable – so if we use these,
we get both threading and vectorization for free. Free is good! Intel MLK supports
TBB-based execution for many of its functions, so if we use these TBB versions they will
compose well with the rest of our TBB-based parallelism.

Of course, we might need to implement algorithms that are not available in any
prepackaged library. In that case, there are three general approaches to adding vector
instructions: (1) inline assembly code, (2) `simd` intrinsics, and (3) compiler-based
vectorization.

We can use inline assembly code to inject specific assembly instructions, including
vector instructions, directly into our applications. This is a low-level approach that is
both compiler and processor dependent and therefore is the least portable and most
error-prone. But, it does give us complete control over the instructions that are used (for
better or worse). We use this approach as a last resort!

An only slightly better approach is to use SIMD intrinsics. Most compilers provide a
set of intrinsic functions that let us inject platform-specific instructions without resorting
to inline assembly code. But other than making it easier to inject the instructions, the
end result is still compiler and platform dependent and error-prone. We generally avoid
this approach too.

The final approach is to rely on compiler-based vectorization. At one extreme, this
can mean fully automated vectorization, where we turn on the right compiler flags, let
the compiler do its thing, and hope for the best. If that works, great! We get the benefits

of vectorization for free. Remember, free is a good thing. However, sometimes we need to give guidance to the compiler so that it can (or will) vectorize our loops. There are some compiler specific ways to provide guidance, such as the Intel compiler's `#pragma ivdep` and `#pragma vector always` and some standardized approaches, such as using the OpenMP `simd` pragmas. Both fully automatic and user-guided compiler vectorization are much more portable than inserting platform-specific instructions directly into our code through inline assembly code or compiler intrinsics. In fact, even Intel's Parallel STL library uses OpenMP `simd` pragmas to support vectorization in a portable way for the `unseq` and `parallel_unseq` policies.

We provide links to learn more about the options for adding vector instructions in the "For More Information" section at the end of this chapter.

Summary

In this chapter, we provided an overview of Parallel STL, what algorithms and execution policies it supports, and how to get a copy that uses Threading Building Blocks as its execution engine. We then discussed the custom iterator classes provided by TBB that increase the applicability of the STL algorithms. We continued by highlighting some of the most useful and general algorithms for parallel programming: `std::for_each`, `std::transform`, `std::reduce`, and `std::transform_reduce`. We demonstrated that some of the samples we implemented in Chapter 2 can also be implemented with these algorithms. But we also warned that the STL algorithms are still not as expressive as TBB and that the important performance hooks we discuss in Part 2 of this book cannot be used with Parallel STL. While Parallel STL is useful for some simple cases, its current limitations make us hesitant to recommend it broadly for threading. That said, TBB tasks are not a path to SIMD parallelism. The `unseq` and `parallel_unseq` policies provided by Intel's Parallel STL, which is included with all of the recent TBB distributions, augment the threading provided by TBB with support for easy vectorization.

For More Information

Vladimir Polin and Mikhail Dvorskiy, "Parallel STL: Boosting Performance of C++ STL Code: C++ and the Evolution Toward Parallelism," The Parallel Universe Magazine, Intel Corporation, Issue 28, pages 5–18, 2017.

Alexey Moskalev and Andrey Fedorov, "Getting Started with Parallel STL," `https://software.intel.com/en-us/get-started-with-pstl`, March 29, 2018.

Pablo Halpern, Arch D Robison, Robert Geva, Clark Nelson and Jen Maurer, "Vector and Wavefront Policies," Programming Language C++ (WG21), P0076r3, `http://open-std.org/JTC1/SC22/WG21/docs/papers/2016/p0076r3.pdf`, July 7, 2016.

The Intel 64 and IA-32 Architectures Software Developer Manuals: `https://software.intel.com/en-us/articles/intel-sdm`.

The Intel Intrinsics Guide: `https://software.intel.com/sites/landingpage/IntrinsicsGuide/`.

CHAPTER 5

Synchronization: Why and How to Avoid It

Let us underscore this up front: if you don't need to use the synchronization features described in this chapter, so much the better. Here, we cover synchronization mechanisms and alternatives to achieve mutual exclusion. "Synchronization" and "exclusion" should have quite a negative connotation for parallel programmers caring about performance. These are operations that we want to avoid because they cost time and, in some cases, processor resources and energy. If we can rethink our data structures and algorithm so that it does not require synchronization nor mutual exclusion, this is great! Unfortunately, in many cases, it is impossible to avoid synchronization operations, and if this is your case today, keep reading! An additional take-home message that we get from this chapter is that careful rethinking of our algorithm can usually result in a cleaner implementation that does not abuse synchronization. We illustrate this process of rethinking an algorithm by parallelizing a simple code following first a naïve approach that resorts to mutexes, evolve it to exploit atomic operations, and then further reduce the synchronization between threads thanks to privatization and reduction techniques. In the latter of these, we show how to leverage thread local storage (TLS) as a way to avoid highly contended mutual exclusion overhead. In this chapter, we assume you are, to some extent, familiarized with the concepts of "lock," "shared mutable state," "mutual exclusion," "thread safety," "data race," and other synchronization-related issues. If not, a gentle introduction to them is provided in the Preface of this book.

M. Voss, R. Asenjo, J. Reinders, *Pro TBB*, https://doi.org/10.1007/978-1-4842-4398-5_5

A Running Example: Histogram of an Image

Let's us start with a simple example that can be implemented with different kinds of mutual exclusion (mutex) objects, atomics, or even by avoiding most of the synchronization operations altogether. We will describe all these possible implementations with their pros and cons, and use them to illustrate the use of mutexes, locks, atomic variables, and thread local storage.

There are different kinds of histograms, but an image histogram is probably the most widely used, especially in image and video devices and image processing tools. For example, in almost all photo editing applications, we can easily find a palette that shows the histogram of any of our pictures, as we see in Figure 5-1.

 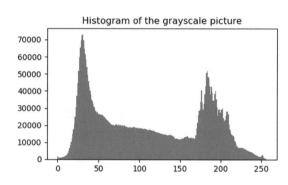

Figure 5-1. *Grayscale picture (of Ronda, Málaga) and its corresponding image histogram*

For the sake of simplicity, we will assume grayscale images. In this case, the histogram represents the number of pixels (y-axis) with each possible brightness value (x-axis). If image pixels are represented as bytes, then only 256 tones or brightness values are possible, with zero being the darkest tone and 255 the lightest tone. In Figure 5-1, we can see that the most frequent tone in the picture is a dark one: out of the 5 Mpixels, more than 70 thousand have the tone 30 as we see at the spike around x=30. Photographers and image professionals rely on histograms as an aid to quickly see the pixel tone distribution and identify whether or not image information is hidden in any blacked out, or saturated, regions of the picture.

In Figure 5-2, we illustrate the histogram computation for a 4×4 image where the pixels can only have eight different tones from 0 to 7. The bidimensional image is usually represented as a unidimensional vector that stores the 16 pixels following a row-major order. Since there are only eight different tones, the histogram only needs eight elements, with indices from 0 to 7. The elements of the histogram vector are sometime called "bins" where we "classify" and then count the pixels of each tone. Figure 5-2 shows the histogram, hist, corresponding to that particular image. The "4" we see stored in bin number one is the result of counting the four pixels in the image with tone 1. Therefore, the basic operation to update the value of the bins while traversing the image is hist[<tone>]++.

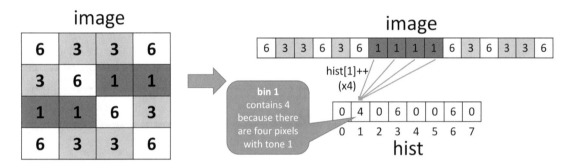

Figure 5-2. *Computing the histogram, hist, from an image with 16 pixels (each value of the image corresponds to the pixel tone)*

From an algorithmic point of view, a histogram is represented as an array of integers with enough elements to account for all possible tone levels. Assuming the image is an array of bytes, there are now 256 possible tones; thus, the histogram requires 256 elements or bins. The sequential code that computes the histogram of such an image is presented in Figure 5-3.

```cpp
int main() {
  constexpr long int n = 1000000;
  constexpr int num_bins = 256;

  // Initialize random number generator
  std::random_device seed;      // Random device seed
  std::mt19937 mte{seed()};     // mersenne_twister_engine
  std::uniform_int_distribution<> uniform{0,num_bins};
  // Initialize image
  std::vector<uint8_t> image; // empty vector
  image.reserve(n);             // image vector prealocated
  std::generate_n(std::back_inserter(image), n,
                  [&] { return uniform(mte); }
              );

  // Initialize histogram
  std::vector<int> hist(num_bins);

  // Serial execution
  tbb::tick_count t0 = tbb::tick_count::now();
  std::for_each(image.begin(), image.end(),
      [&hist] (uint8_t i) { hist[i]++; }
  );
  tbb::tick_count t1 = tbb::tick_count::now();
  double t_serial = (t1 - t0).seconds();

  std::cout << "Serial time: " << t_serial << std::endl;
  return 0;
}
```

Figure 5-3. *Code listing with the sequential implementation of the image histogram computation. The relevant statements are highlighted inside a box.*

If you already understand everything in the previous code listing, you will probably want to skip the rest of this section. This code first declares the vector image of size n (say one million for a Megapixel image) and, after initializing the random number generator, it populates the image vector with random numbers in the range [0,255] of type uint8_t. For this, we use a Mersenne_twister_engine, mte, which generates random numbers uniformly distributed in the range [0, num_bins) and inserts them into the image vector. Next, the hist vector is constructed with num_bins positions (initialized to zero by default). Note that we declared an empty vector image for which we later reserved n integers instead of constructing image(n). That way we avoid traversing the vector first to initialize it with zeros and once again to insert the random numbers.

The actual histogram computation could have been written in C using a more traditional approach:

```
for (int i = 0; i < N; ++i) hist[image[i]]++;
```

which counts in each bin of the histogram vector the number of pixels of every tonal value. However, in the example of Figure 5-3, we fancied showing you a C++ alternative that uses the STL for_each algorithm and may be more natural for C++ programmers. Using the for_each STL approach, each actual element of the image vector (a tone of type uint8_t) is passed to the lambda expression, which increments the bin associated with the tone. For the sake of expediency, we rely on the tbb::tick_count class in order to account for the number of seconds required in the histogram computation. The member functions now and seconds are self-explanatory, so we do not include further explanation here.

An Unsafe Parallel Implementation

The first naïve attempt to parallelize the histogram computation consists on using a tbb::parallel_for as shown in Figure 5-4.

```
// Parallel execution
std::vector<int> hist_p(num_bins);

t0 = tbb::tick_count::now();
parallel_for(tbb::blocked_range<size_t>{0, image.size()},
             [&](const tbb::blocked_range<size_t>& r)
             {
               for (size_t i = r.begin(); i < r.end(); ++i)
                 hist_p[image[i]]++;
             });
t1 = tbb::tick_count::now();
double t_parallel = (t1 - t0).seconds();

std::cout << "Serial: "   << t_serial   << ", ";
std::cout << "Parallel: " << t_parallel << ", ";
std::cout << "Speed-up: " << t_serial/t_parallel << std::endl;

if (hist != hist_p)
    std::cerr << "Parallel computation failed!!" << std::endl;
return 0;
```

Figure 5-4. *Code listing with the **unsafe** parallel implementation of the image histogram computation*

In order to be able to compare the histogram resulting from the sequential implementation of Figure 5-3, and the result of the parallel execution, we declare a new histogram vector hist_p. Next, the crazy idea here is to traverse all the pixels in parallel... why not? Aren't they independent pixels? To that end, we rely on the parallel_for template that was covered in Chapter 2 to have different threads traverse different chunks of the iteration space and, therefore, read different chunks of the image. However, this is not going to work: the comparison of vectors hist and hist_p (yes, hist!=hist_p does the right thing in C++), at the end of Figure 5-4, reveals that the two vectors are different:

```
c++ -std=c++11 -O2 -o fig_5_4 fig_5_4.cpp -ltbb
./fig_5_4
Serial: 0.606273, Parallel: 6.71982, Speed-up: 0.0902216
Parallel computation failed!!
```

A problem arises because, in the parallel implementation, different threads are likely to increment the same shared bin at the same time. In other words, our code is not thread-safe (or unsafe). More formally, as it is, our parallel unsafe code exhibits "undefined behavior" which also means that our code is not correct. In Figure 5-5 we illustrate the problem supposing that there are two threads, A and B, running on cores 0 and 1, each one processing half of the pixels. Since there is a pixel with brightness 1 in the image chunk assigned to thread A, it will execute hist_p[1]++. Thread B also reads a pixel with the same brightness and will also execute hist_p[1]++. If both increments coincide in time, one executed on core 0 and the other on core 1, it is highly likely that we miss an increment.

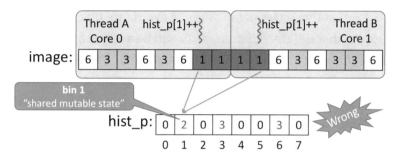

Figure 5-5. *Unsafe parallel update of the shared histogram vector*

This happens because the increment operation is not atomic (or indivisible), but on the contrary it usually consists of three assembly level operations: load the variable from memory into a register, increment the register, and store the register back into memory.[1] Using a more formal jargon, this kind of operation is known as a Read-Modify-Write or RMW operation. Having concurrent writes to a shared variable is formally known as shared mutable state. In Figure 5-6, we illustrate a possible sequence of machine instructions corresponding to the C++ instruction `hist_p[1]++`.

`hist_p[1]++` →	R1 on Core 0	R1 on Core 1	Time or cycle
`load R1, @(hist_p+1)`	1	1	X
`add R1, R1, #1`	2	2	X+1
`store R1, @(hist_p+1)`	2	2	X+2

Figure 5-6. *Unsafe update of a shared variable or shared mutable state*

If at the time of executing these two increments we have already found one previous pixel with brightness `1`, `hist_p[1]` contains a value of one. This value could be read and stored in private registers by both threads which will end up writing two in this bin instead of three, which is the correct number of pixels with brightness 1 that have been encountered thus far. This example is somehow oversimplified, not taking into account caches and cache coherence, but serve us to illustrate the data race issue. A more elaborated example is included in the Preface (see Figures P-15 and P-16).

---

[1]Due to the very essence of the von Neumman architecture, the computational logic is separated from the data storage so the data must be moved into where it can be computed, then computed and finally moved back out to storage again.

We might think that this series of unfortunate events are unlikely to happen, or even if they happen, that slightly different result will be acceptable when running the parallel version of the algorithm. Is not the reward a faster execution? Not quite: as we saw in the previous page, our unsafe parallel implementation is ~10× slower than the sequential one (running with four threads on a quad-core processor and with n equal to one thousand million pixels). The culprit is the cache coherency protocol that was introduced in the Preface (see "Locality and the Revenge of the Caches" section in the Preface). In the serial execution, the histogram vector is likely to be fully cached in the L1 cache of the core running the code. Since there are a million pixels, there will be a million of increments in the histogram vector, most of them served at cache speed.

Note   On most Intel processors, a cache line can hold 16 integers (64 bytes). The histogram vector with 256 integers will need just 16 cache lines if the vector is adequately aligned. Therefore, after 16 cache misses (or much less if prefetching is exercised), all histogram bins are cached and each one accessed in only around three cycles (that's *very* fast!) in the serial implementation (assuming a large enough L1 cache and that the histogram cache lines are never evicted by other data).

On the other hand, in the parallel implementation, all threads will fight to cache the bins in per-core private caches, but when one thread writes in one bin on one core, the cache coherence protocol invalidates the 16 bins that fit in the corresponding cache line in all the other cores. This invalidation causes the subsequent accesses to the invalidated cache lines to cost an order of magnitude more time than the much desired L1 access time. The net effect of this ping-pong mutual invalidation is that the threads of the parallel implementation end up incrementing un-cached bins, whereas the single thread of the serial implementation almost always increments cached bins. Remember once again that the one-megapixel image requires one million increments in the histogram vector, so we want to create an increment implementation that is as fast as possible. In this parallel implementation of the histogram computation, we find both false sharing (e.g., when thread A increments hist_p[0] and thread B increments hist_p[15], due to both bins land in the same cache line) and true sharing (when both threads, A and B, increment hist_p[i]). We will deal with false and true sharing in subsequent sections.

A First Safe Parallel Implementation: Coarse-Grained Locking

Let's first solve the problem of the parallel access to a shared data structure. We need a mechanism that prevents other threads from reading and writing in a shared variable when a different thread is already in the process of writing the same variable. In more layman terms, we want a fitting room where a single person can enter, see how the clothes fit, and then leaves the fitting room for the next person in the queue. Figure 5-7 illustrates that a closed door on the fitting room excludes others. In parallel programming, the fitting room door is called a mutex, when a person enters the fitting room he acquires and holds a lock on the mutex by closing and locking the door, and when the person leaves they release the lock by leaving the door open and unlocked. In more formal terms, a mutex is an object used to provide mutual exclusion in the execution of a protected region of code. This region of code that needs to be protected with mutual exclusion is usually known as a "critical section." The fitting room example also illustrates the concept of contention, a state where the resource (a fitting room) is wanted by more than one person at a time, as we can see in Figure 5-7(c). Since the fitting room can be occupied just by a single person at a time, the use of the fitting room is "serialized." Similarly, anything protected by a mutex can reduce the performance of a program, first due to the extra overhead introduced by managing the mutex object, and second and more importantly because the contention and serialization it can elicit. A key reason we want to reduce synchronization as much as possible is to avoid contention and serialization which in turns limits scaling in parallel programs.

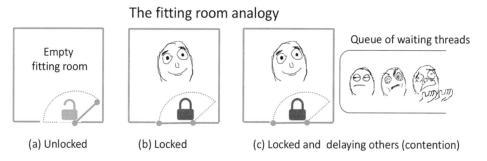

Figure 5-7. *Closing a door on a fitting room excludes others*

In this section, we focus on the TBB mutex classes and related mechanisms for synchronization. While TBB predates C++11, it is worth noting that C++11 did standardize support for a mutex class, although it is not as customizable as the ones in the TBB library. In TBB, the simplest mutex is the `spin_mutex` that can be used after including `tbb/spin_mutex.h` or the all-inclusive `tbb.h` header file. With this new tool in our hands, we can implement a safe parallel version of the image histogram computation as we can see in Figure 5-8.

```
#include <tbb/spin_mutex.h>

// Parallel execution
using my_mutex_t = tbb::spin_mutex;
my_mutex_t my_mutex;

parallel_for(tbb::blocked_range<size_t>{0, image.size()},
             [&](const tbb::blocked_range<size_t>& r)
             {
                 my_mutex_t::scoped_lock my_lock{my_mutex};
                 for (size_t i = r.begin(); i < r.end(); ++i)
                   hist_p[image[i]]++;
             });
```

Figure 5-8. *Code listing with our first safe parallel implementation of the image histogram computation that uses coarse-grained locking*

The object `my_lock` that acquires a lock on `my_mutex`, when it is created automatically unlocks (or releases) the lock in the object destructor, which is called when leaving the object scope. It is therefore advisable to enclose the protected regions with additional braces, {}, to keep the lifetime of the lock as short as possible, so that the other waiting threads can take their turn as soon as possible.

Note   If in the code of Figure 5-8 we forget to put a name to the lock object, for example:

```
// was my_lock{my_mutex}
my_mutex_t::scoped_lock {my_mutex};
```

the code compiles without warning, but the scope of the `scoped_lock` ends at the semicolon. Without the name of the object (`my_lock`), we are constructing an anonymous/unnamed object of the `scoped_lock` class, and its lifetime ends at the semicolon because no named object outlives the definition. This is not useful, and the critical section is *not* protected with mutual exclusion.

A more explicit, but **not recommended**, alternative of writing the code of Figure 5-8 is presented in Figure 5-9.

```
parallel_for(tbb::blocked_range<size_t>{0, image.size()},
             [&](const tbb::blocked_range<size_t>& r)
             {
                 my_mutex_t::scoped_lock my_lock;
                 my_lock.acquire(my_mutex);
                 for (size_t i = r.begin(); i < r.end(); ++i)
                     hist_p[image[i]]++;
                 my_lock.release();
             });
```

Figure 5-9. *A discouraged alternative for acquiring a lock on a mutex*

C++ pundits favor the alternative of Figure 5-8, known as "Resource Acquisition Is Initialization," RAII, because it frees us from remembering to release the lock. More importantly, using the RAII version, the lock object destructor, where the lock is released, is also called in case of an exception so that we avoid leaving the lock acquired due to the exception. If in the version of Figure 5-9 an exception is thrown before the `my_lock.release()` member function is called, the lock is also released anyway, because the destructor is invoked and there, the lock is released. If a lock leaves its scope but was previously released with the `release()` member function, then the destructor does nothing.

Back to our code of Figure 5-8, you are probably wondering, "but wait, haven't we serialized our parallel code with a coarse-grained lock?" Yes, you are right! As we can see in Figure 5-10, each thread that wants to process its chunk of the image first tries to acquire the lock on the mutex, but only one will succeed and the rest will impatiently wait for the lock to be released. Not until the thread holding the lock releases it, can a different thread execute the protected code. Therefore, the `parallel_for` ends up being executed serially! The good news is that now, there are no concurrent increments of the histogram bins and the result is finally correct. Yeah!

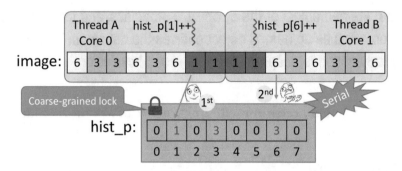

Figure 5-10. *Thread A holds the coarse-grained lock to increment bin number one, while thread B waits because the whole histogram vector is locked*

Actually, if we compile and run our new version, what we get is a parallel execution a little bit slower than the sequential one:

```
c++ -std=c++11 -O2 -o fig_5_8 fig_5_8.cpp -ltbb
./fig_5_8
Serial: 0.61068, Parallel: 0.611667, Speed-up: 0.99838
```

This approach is called coarse-grained locking because we are protecting a coarse-grained data structure (actually the whole data structure – the histogram vector – in this case). We could partition the vector in several sections and protect each section with its own lock. That way, we would increase the concurrency level (different threads accessing different sections can proceed in parallel), but we would have increased the complexity of the code and the memory required for each of the mutex objects.

A word of caution is in order! Figure 5-11 shows a common mistake of parallel programming newbies.

```
//my_mutex_t my_mutex;    **now declared in the body**
parallel_for(tbb::blocked_range<size_t>{0, image.size()},
        [&](const tbb::blocked_range<size_t>& r)
        {
            my_mutex_t my_mutex;
            my_mutex_t::scoped_lock my_lock{my_mutex};
            for (size_t i = r.begin(); i < r.end(); ++i)
                hist_p[image[i]]++;
        });
```

Figure 5-11. *Common mistake made by parallel programming newbies*

This code compiles without errors nor warnings, so what is wrong with it? Back to our fitting-room example, our intention was to avoid several people entering in the fitting-room at the same time. In the previous code, my_mutex is defined inside the parallel section, and there will be a mutex object per task, each one locking its own mutex, which does not prevent concurrent access to the critical section. As we can see in Figure 5-12, the newbie code essentially has a separate door for each person into the same fitting room! That is not what we want! The solution is to declare my_mutex once (as we did in Figure 5-8) so that all accesses have to enter the fitting room through the same door.

Figure 5-12. *A fitting room with more than one door*

Before tackling a fine-grained locking alternative, let's discuss two aspects that deserve a comment. First, the execution time of the "parallelized-then-serialized" code of Figure 5-8 is greater than the time needed by the serial implementation. This is due to the "parallelization-then-serialization" overhead, but also due to a poorer exploitation of the caches. Of course, there is no false sharing nor true sharing, because in our serialized implementation there is no "sharing" whatsoever! Or is there? In the serial implementation, only one thread accesses a cached histogram vector. In the coarse-grained implementation, when one thread processes its chunk of the image, it will cache the histogram in the cache of the core where the thread is running. When the next thread in the queue can finally process its own chunk, it may need to cache the histogram in a different cache (if the thread is running on a different core). The threads are still sharing the histogram vector, and more cache misses will likely occur with the proposed implementation than with the serial one.

The second aspect that we want to mention is the possibility of configuring the mutex behavior by choosing one of the possible mutex flavors that are shown in Figure 5-13. It is therefore recommended to use

```
using my_mutex_t = <mutex_flavor>
```

or the equivalent C-ish alternative

typedef <mutex_flavor> my_mutex_t;

and then use my_mutex_t onward. That way, we can easily change the mutex flavor in a single program line and experimentally evaluate easily which flavor suits us best. It may be necessary to also include a different header file, as indicated in Figure 5-13, or use the all-inclusive tbb.h.

Mutex flavor	Scalable	Fair	Recursive	Long Wait	Size
mutex (mutex.h)	OS depend.	OS dep.	no	blocks	≥ 3 words
recursive_mutex (recursive_mutex.h)	OS depend.	OS dep.	yes	blocks	≥ 3 words
spin_mutex (spin_mutex.h)	no	no	no	yields	1 byte
speculative_spin_mutex (spin_mutex.h)	HW depend.	no	no	yields	2 cache lines
queuing_mutex (queuing_mutex.h)	yes	yes	no	yields	1 word
spin_rw_mutex (spin_rw_mutex.h)	no	no	no	yields	1 word
speculative_spin_rw_mutex (spin_rw_mutex.h)	HW depend.	no	no	yields	3 cache lines
queuing_rw_mutex (queuing_rw_mutex.h)	yes	yes	no	yields	1 word
null_mutex (null_mutex.h)	moot	yes	yes	never	empty
null_rw_mutex (null_rw_mutex.h)	moot	yes	yes	never	empty

Figure 5-13. *Different mutex flavors and their properties*

Mutex Flavors

In order to understand the different flavors of mutex, we have to first describe the properties that we use to classify them:

- **Scalable** mutexes do not consume excessive core cycles nor memory bandwidth while waiting to have their turn. The motivation is that a waiting thread should avoid consuming the hardware resources that may be needed by other nonwaiting threads.

- **Fair** mutexes use a FIFO policy for the threads to take their turn.

- **Recursive** mutexes allow that a thread already holding a lock on a mutex can acquire another lock on the same mutex. Rethinking your code to avoid mutexes is great, doing it to avoid recursive mutexes is almost a must! Then, why does TBB provide them? There may be corner cases in which recursive mutexes are unavoidable. They may also come in handy when we can't be bothered or have no time to rethink a more efficient solution.

In the table in Figure 5-13, we also include the size of the mutex object and the behavior of the thread if it has to wait for a long time to get a lock on the mutex. With regard to the last point, when a thread is waiting its turn it can busy-wait, block, or yield. A thread that blocks will be changed to the blocked state so that the only resource required by the thread is the memory that keeps its sleeping state. When the thread can finally acquire the lock, it wakes up and moves back to the ready state where all the ready threads wait for their next turn. The OS scheduler assigns time slices to the ready threads that are waiting in a ready-state queue. A thread that yields while waiting its turn to hold a lock is kept in the ready state. When the thread reaches the top of the ready-state queue, it is dispatched to run, but if the mutex is still locked by other thread, it again gives away its time slice (it has nothing else to do!) and goes back to the ready-state queue.

Note   Note that in this process there may be two queues involved: (i) the ready-state queue managed by the OS scheduler, where ready threads are waiting, not necessarily in FIFO order, to be dispatched to an idle core and become running threads, and (ii) the mutex queue managed by the OS or by the mutex library in user space, where threads wait their turn to acquire a lock on a queueing mutex.

If the core is not oversubscribed (there is only one thread running in this core), a thread that yields because the mutex is still locked will be the only one in the ready-state queue and be dispatched right away. In this case, the yield mechanism is virtually equivalent to a busy-wait.

Now that we understand the different properties that can characterize the implementation of a mutex, let's delve into the particular mutex flavors that TBB offers.

mutex and **recursive_mutex** are TBB wrappers around the OS-provided mutex mechanism. Instead of the "native" mutex, we use TBB wrappers because they add exception-safe and identical interfaces to the other TBB mutexes. These mutexes block on long waits, so they waste fewer cycles, but they occupy more space and have a longer response time when the mutex becomes available.

spin_mutex, on the contrary, never blocks. It spins busy-waiting in the user space while waiting to hold a lock on a mutex. The waiting thread will yield after a number of tries to acquire the loop, but if the core is not oversubscribed, this thread keeps the core wasting cycles and power. On the other hand, once the mutex is released, the response time to acquire it is the fastest possible (no need to wake up and wait to be dispatched to run). This mutex is not fair, so no matter for how long a thread has been waiting its turn, a quicker thread can overtake it and acquire the lock if it is the first to find the mutex unlocked. A free-for-all prevails in this case, and in extreme situations, a weak thread can starve, never getting the lock. Nonetheless, this is the recommended mutex flavor under light contention situations because it can be the fastest one.

queueing_mutex is the scalable and fair version of the spin_mutex. It still spins, busy-waiting in user space, but threads waiting on that mutex will acquire the lock in FIFO order, so starvation is not possible.

speculative_spin_mutex is built on top of Hardware Transactional Memory (HTM) that is available in some processors. The HTM philosophy is to be optimistic! HTM lets all threads enter a critical section at the same time hoping that there will be no shared memory conflicts! But what if there are? In this case, the hardware detects the conflict and rolls back the execution of one of the conflicting threads, which has to retry the execution of the critical section. In the coarse-grained implementation shown in Figure 5-8, we could add this simple line:

```
using my_mutex_t = speculative_spin_mutex;
```

and then, the parallel_for that traverses the image becomes parallel once again. Now, all threads are allowed to enter the critical section (to update the bins of the histogram for a given chunk of the image), but only if there is an actual conflict updating one of the bins, one of the conflicting threads has to retry the execution. For this to work efficiently, the protected critical section has to be small enough so that conflicts and retries are rare, which is not the case in the code of Figure 5-8.

spin_rw_mutex, queueing_rw_mutex, and **speculative_spin_rw_mutex** are the Reader-Writer mutex counterparts of the previously covered flavors. These implementations allow multiple readers to read a shared variable at the same time. The lock object constructor has a second argument, a boolean, that we set to false if we will only read (not write) inside the critical section:

```
using rwmutex_t = spin_rw_mutex;
rwmutex_t my_mutex;
{
  rwmutex_t::scoped_lock my_lock{my_mutex,/*is_writer=*/false};
  // A reader lock is acquired so multiple
  // concurrent reads are allowed

}
```

If for any reason, a reader lock has to be promoted to a writer lock, TBB provides an upgrade_to_writer() member function that can be used as follows:

```
bool success=my_lock.upgrade_to_writer();
```

which returns true if the my_lock is successfully upgraded to a writer lock without releasing the lock, or false otherwise.

Finally, we have **null_mutex** and **null_rw_mutex** that are just dummy objects that do nothing. So, what's the point? Well, we can find these mutexes useful if we pass a mutex object to a function template that may or may not need a real mutex. In case the function does not really need the mutex, just pass the dummy flavor.

A Second Safe Parallel Implementation: Fine-Grained Locking

Now that we know a lot about the different flavors of mutexes, let's think about an alternative implementation of the coarse-grained locking one in Figure 5-8. One alternative is to declare a mutex for every bin of the histogram so that instead of locking the whole data structure with a single lock, we only protect the single memory position that we are actually incrementing. To do that, we need a vector of mutexes, fine_m, as the one shown in Figure 5-14.

```
using my_mutex_t=tbb::spin_mutex;
std::vector<my_mutex_t> fine_m(num_bins);
parallel_for(tbb::blocked_range<size_t>{0, image.size()},
          [&](const tbb::blocked_range<size_t>& r)
          {
            for (size_t i = r.begin(); i < r.end(); ++i){
              int tone=image[i];
              my_mutex_t::scoped_lock my_lock{fine_m[tone]};
              hist_p[tone]++;
            }
          });
```

Figure 5-14. *Code listing with a second safe parallel implementation of the image histogram computation that uses fine-grained locking*

As we see in the lambda used inside the parallel_for, when a thread needs to increment the bin hist_p[tone], it will acquire the lock on fine_m[tone], preventing other threads from touching the same bin. Essentially "you can update other bins, but not this particular one." This is illustrated in Figure 5-15 where thread A and thread B are updating in parallel different bins of the histogram vector.

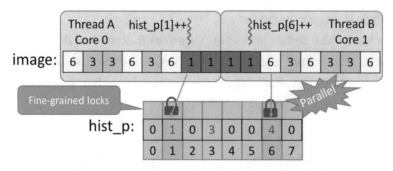

Figure 5-15. *Thanks to fine-grained locking, we exploit more parallelism*

However, from a performance standpoint, this alternative is not really an optimal one (actually it is the slowest alternative up to now):

```
c++ -std=c++11 -O2 -o fig_5_14 fig_5_14.cpp -ltbb
./fig_5_14
Serial: 0.59297, Parallel: 26.9251, Speed-up: 0.0220229
```

Now we need not only the histogram array but also an array of mutex objects of the same length. This means a larger memory requirement, and moreover, more data that will be cached and that will suffer from false sharing and true sharing. Bummer!

In addition to the lock inherent overhead, locks are at the root of two additional problems: convoying and deadlock. Let's cover first "convoying." This name comes from the mental image of all threads convoying one after the other at the lower speed of the first one. We need an example to better illustrate this situation, as the one depicted in Figure 5-16. Let's suppose we have threads 1, 2, 3, and 4 executing on the same core the same code, where there is a critical section protected by a spin mutex A. If these threads hold the lock at different times, they run happily without contention (situation 1). But it may happen that thread 1 runs out of its time slice before releasing the lock, which sends A to the end of the ready-state queue (situation 2).

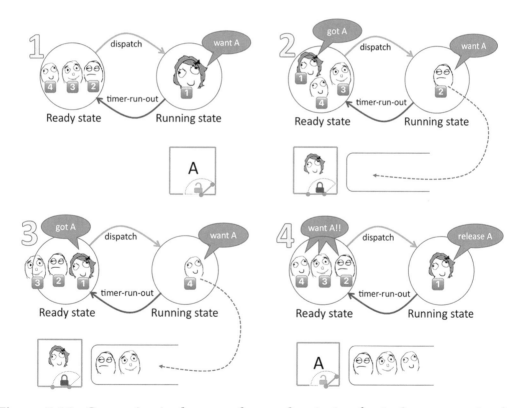

Figure 5-16. *Convoying in the case of oversubscription (a single core running four threads, all of them wanting the same mutex A)*

Threads 2, 3, and 4 will now get their corresponding time slices, but they cannot acquire the lock because 1 is still the owner (situation 3). This means that 2, 3, and 4 can now yield or spin, but in any case, they are stuck behind a big truck in first gear. When 1 is dispatched again, it will release the lock A (situation 4). Now 2, 3, and 4 are all poised to fight for the lock, with only one succeeding and the others waiting again. This situation is recurrent, especially if now threads 2, 3, and 4 need more than a time slice to run their protected critical section. Moreover, threads 2, 3, and 4 are now inadvertently coordinated, all running in step the same region of the code, which leads to a higher probability of contention on the mutex! Note that convoying is especially acute when the cores are oversubscribed (as in this example where four threads compete to run on a single core) which also reinforces our recommendation to avoid oversubscription.

An additional well-known problem arising from locks is "deadlock." Figure 5-17(a) shows a nightmare provoking situation in which nobody can make progress even when there are available resources (empty lines that no car can use). This is deadlock in real life, but get this image out of your head (if you can!) and come back to our virtual world of parallel programming. If we have a set of N threads that are holding a lock and also waiting to acquire a lock already held by any other thread in the set, our N threads are deadlocked. An example with only two threads is presented in Figure 5-17(b): thread 1 holds a lock on mutex A and is waiting to acquire a lock on mutex B, but thread 2 is already holding the lock on mutex B and waiting to acquire the lock on mutex A. Clearly, no thread will progress, forever doomed in a deadly embrace! We can avoid this unfortunate situation by not requiring the acquisition of a different mutex if the thread is already holding one. Or at least, by having all threads always acquire the locks in the same order.

(a) Deadlock in real life   (b) Deadlock in virtual life

Figure 5-17. Deadlock situations

We can inadvertently provoke deadlock if a thread already holding a lock calls a function that also acquires a different lock. The recommendation is to eschew calling a function while holding a lock if we don't know what the function does (usually advised as don't call other people's code while holding a lock). Alternatively, we should carefully check that the chain of subsequent functions call won't induce deadlock. Ah! and we can also avoid locks whenever possible!

Although convoying and deadlock are not really hitting our histogram implementation, they should have helped to convince us that locks often bring more problems than they solve and that they are not the best alternative to get high parallel performance. Only when the probability of contention is low and the time to execute the critical section is minimal are locks a tolerable choice. In these cases, a basic `spin_lock` or `speculative_spin_lock` can yield some speedup. But in any other cases, the scalability of a `lock based` algorithm is seriously compromised and the best advice is to think out of the box and devise a new implementation that does not require a mutex altogether. But, can we get fine-grained synchronization without relying on several mutex objects, so that we avoid the corresponding overheads and potential problems?

A Third Safe Parallel Implementation: Atomics

Fortunately, there is a less expensive mechanism to which we can resort to get rid of mutexes and locks in many cases. We can use atomic variables to perform atomic operations. As was illustrated in Figure 5-6, the increment operation is not atomic but divisible into three smaller operations (load, increment, and store). However, if we declare an atomic variable and do the following:

```
#include <tbb/atomic.h>
tbb::atomic<int> counter;
counter++;
```

the increment of the atomic variable *is* an atomic operation. This means that any other thread accessing the value of counter will "see" the operation as if the increment is done in a single step (not as three smaller operations, but as a single one). This is, any other "sharp-eyed" thread will either observe the operation completed or not, but it will never observe the increment half-complete.

Atomic operations do not suffer from convoying or deadlock[2] and are faster than mutual exclusion alternatives. However, not all operations can be executed atomically, and those that can, are not applicable to all data types. More precisely, atomic<T> supports atomic operations when T is an integral, enumeration, or pointer data type. The atomic operations supported on a variable x of such a type atomic<T> are listed in Figure 5-18.

=x	read the value of x
x=	write the value of x, and return it
x.fetch_and_store(y)	do $x=y$ and return the old value of x
x.fetch_and_add(y)	do $x+=y$ and return the old value of x
x.compare_and_swap(y,z)	if x equals z, then do $x=y$. In either case, return old value of x.

Figure 5-18. *Fundamental operations on atomic variables*

---

[2]Atomic operations cannot be nested, so they cannot provoke deadlock.

With these five operations, a good deal of derived operations can be implemented. For example, x++, x--, x+=..., and x-=... are all derived from x.fetch_and_add().

Note   As we have already mentioned in previous chapters, C++ also incorporated threading and synchronization features, starting at C++11. TBB included these features before they were accepted in the C++ standard. Although starting at C++11, std::mutex and std::atomic, among others, are available, TBB still provides some overlapping functionalities in its tbb::mutex and tbb::atomic classes, mainly for compatibility with previously developed TBB-based applications. We can use both flavors in the same code without problem, and it is up to us to decide if one or the other is preferable for a given situation. Regarding std::atomic, some extra performance, w.r.t. tbb::atomic, can be wheedle out if used to develop lock-free algorithms and data structures on "weakly-ordered" architectures (as ARM or PowerPC; in contrast, Intel CPUs feature a strongly-ordered memory-model). In the last section of this chapter, "For More Information," we recommend further readings related to memory consistency and C++ concurrency model where this topic is thoroughly covered. For our purpose here, suffice it to say that fetch_and_store, fetch_and_add, and compare_and_swap adhere by default to the sequential consistency (memory_order_seq_cst in C++ jargon), which can prevent some out-of-order execution and therefore cost a tiny amount of extra time. To account for that, TBB also offers release and acquire semantic: acquire by default in atomic read (...=x); and release by default in atomic write (x=...). The desired semantic can also be specified using a template argument, for example, x.fetch_and_add<release> enforces only the release memory order. In C++11, other more relaxed memory orders are also allowed (memory_order_relaxed and memory_order_consume) which in particular cases and architectures can allow for more latitude on the order of reads and writes and squeeze a small amount of extra performance. Should we want to work closer to the metal for the ultimate performance, even knowing the extra coding and debugging burden, then C++11 lower level features are there for us, and yet we can combine them with our higher-level abstractions provided by TBB.

Another useful idiom based on atomics is the one already used in the wavefront example presented in Figure 2-23 (Chapter 2). Having an atomic integer `refCount` initialized to "y" and several threads executing this code:

```
if (--refCount==0) {… /* body */… };
```

will result in only the y-th thread executing the previous line entering in the "body."

Of these five fundamental operations, `compare_and_swap` (CAS) can be considered as the mother of all atomic read-modify-write, RMW, operations. This is because all atomic RMW operations can be implemented on top of a CAS operation.

Note   Just in case you need to protect a small critical section and you are already convinced of dodging locks at any rate, let's dip our toes into the details of the CAS operation a little bit. Say that our code requires to atomically multiply a shared integer variable, v, by 3 (don't ask us why! we have our reasons!). We are aiming for a lock-free solution, though we know that multiplication is not included as one of the atomic operations. Here is where CAS comes in. First thing is to declare v as an atomic variable:

`tbb::atomic<uint_32_t> v;`

so now we can call `v.compare_and_swap(new_v, old_v)` which **atomically** does

```
ov=v; if (ov==old_v) v=new_v; return ov;
```

This is, if and only if v is equal to `old_v`, we can update v with the new value. In any case, we return ov (the shared v used in the "==" comparison). Now, the trick to implement our "times 3" atomic multiplication is to code what is dubbed CAS loop:

```
void fetch_and_triple(tbb::atomic<uint32_t>& v)
{
    uint32_t old_v;
    do {
      old_v=v; //take a snapshot
    } while (v.compare_and_swap(old_v * 3, old_v)!=old_v);
}
```

Our new `fetch_and_triple` is thread-safe (can be safely called by several threads at the same time) even when it is called passing the same shared atomic variable. This function is basically a do-while loop in which we first take a snapshot of the shared variable (which is key to later compare if other thread has managed to modify it). Then, atomically, **if no other thread has changed v** (v==old_v), we do update it (v=old_v*3) and return v. Since in this case v == old_v (again: no other thread has changed v), we leave the do-while loop and return from the function with our shared v successfully updated.

However, after taking the snapshot, it is possible that **other thread updates v**. In this case, v!=old_v which implies that (i) we do not update v and (ii) we stay in the do-while loop hoping that lady luck will smile on us next time (when no other greedy thread dares to touch our v in the interim between the moment we take the snapshot and we succeed updating v). Figure 5-19 illustrates how v is always updated either by thread 1 or thread 2. It is possible that one of the threads has to retry (as thread 2 that ends up writing 81 when initially it was about to write 27) one or more times, but this shouldn't be a big deal in well-devised scenarios.

The two caveats of this strategy are (i) it scales badly and (ii) it may suffer from the "ABA problem" (there is background on the classic ABA problem in Chapter 6 on page 201). Regarding the first one, consider P threads contending for the same atomic, only one succeeds with P-1 retrying, then another succeeds with P-2 retrying, then P-3 retrying, and so on, resulting in a quadratic work. This problem can be ameliorated resorting to an "exponential back off" strategy that multiplicatively reduces the rate of consecutive retries to reduce contention. On the other hand, the ABA problem happens when, in the interim time (between the moment we take the snapshot and we succeed updating v), a different thread changes v from value A to value B and back to value A. Our CAS loop can succeed without noticing the intervening thread, which can be problematic. Double check you understand this problem and its consequences if you need to resort to a CAS loop in your developments.

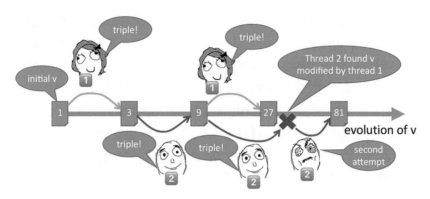

Figure 5-19. *Two threads concurrently calling to our* `fetch_and_triple` *atomic function implemented on top of a CAS loop*

But now it is time to get back to our running example. A re-implementation of the histogram computation can now be expressed with the help of atomics as shown in Figure 5-20.

```
#include <tbb/atomic.h>

// Parallel execution
std::vector<tbb::atomic<int>> hist_p(num_bins);
t0 = tbb::tick_count::now();
parallel_for(tbb::blocked_range<size_t>{0, image.size()},
             [&](const tbb::blocked_range<size_t>& r)
             {
               for (size_t i = r.begin(); i < r.end(); ++i)
                 hist_p[image[i]]++;
             });
```

Figure 5-20. *Code listing with a third safe parallel implementation of the image histogram computation that uses atomic variables*

In this implementation, we get rid of the mutex objects and locks and declare the vector so that each bin is a `tbb::atomic<int>` (initialized to 0 by default). Then, in the lambda, it is safe to increment the bins in parallel. The net result is that we get parallel increments of the histogram vector, as with the fine-grained locking strategy, but at a lower cost both in terms of mutex management and mutex storage.

However, performance wise, the previous implementation is still way too slow:

```
c++ -std=c++11 -O2 -o fig_5_20 fig_5_20.cpp -ltbb
./fig_5_20
Serial: 0.614786, Parallel: 7.90455, Speed-up: 0.0710006
```

In addition to the atomic increment overhead, false sharing and true sharing are issues that we have not addressed yet. False sharing is tackled in Chapter 7 by leveraging aligned allocators and padding techniques. False sharing is a frequent showstopper that hampers parallel performance, so we highly encourage you to read in Chapter 7 the recommended techniques to avoid it.

Great, assuming that we have fixed the false sharing problem, what about the true sharing one? Two different threads will eventually increment the same bin, which will be ping-pong from one cache to other. We need a better idea to solve this one!

A Better Parallel Implementation: Privatization and Reduction

The real problem posed by the histogram reduction is that there is a single shared vector to hold the 256 bins that all threads are eager to increment. So far, we have seen several implementations that are functionally equivalent, like the coarse-grained, fine-grained, and atomic-based ones, but none of those are totally satisfactory if we also consider nonfunctional metrics such as performance and energy.

The common solution to avoid sharing something is to privatize it. Parallel programming is not different in this respect. If we give a private copy of the histogram to each thread, each one will happily work with its copy, cache it in the private cache of the core in which the thread is running, and therefore increment all the bins at the cache speed (in the ideal case). No more false sharing, nor true sharing, nor nothing, because the histogram vector is not shared any more.

Okay, but then... each thread will end up having a partial view of the histogram because each thread has only visited some of the pixels of the full image. No problem, now is when the reduction part of this implementation comes into play. The final step after computing a privatized partial version of the histogram is to reduce all the contributions of all the threads to get the complete histogram vector. There is still some synchronization in this part because some threads have to wait for others that have not finished their local/private computations yet, but in the general case, this solution ends up being much less expensive than the other previously described implementations. Figure 5-21 illustrates the privatization and reduction technique for our histogram example.

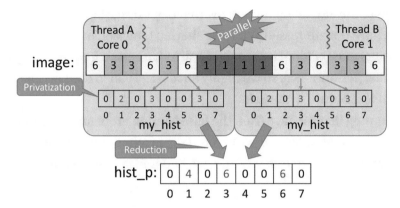

Figure 5-21. *Each thread computes its local histogram, `my_hist`, that is later reduced in a second step.*

TBB offers several alternatives to accomplish privatization and reduction operations, some based on thread local storage, TLS, and a more user-friendly one based on the reduction template. Let's go first for the TLS version of the histogram computation.

Thread Local Storage, TLS

Thread local storage, for our purposes here, refers to having a per-thread privatized copy of data. Using TLS, we can reduce accesses to shared mutable state between threads and also exploit locality because each private copy can be (sometimes partially) stored in the local cache of the core on which the thread is running. Of course, copies take up space, so they should not be used to excess.

An important aspect of TBB is that we do not know how many threads are being used at any given time. Even if we are running on a 32-core system, and we use `parallel_for` for 32 iterations, we cannot assume there will be 32 threads active. This is a critical factor in making our code composable, which means it will work even if called inside a parallel program, or if it calls a library that runs in parallel (see Chapter 9 for more details). Therefore, we do not know how many thread local copies of data are needed even in our example of a `parallel_for` with 32 iterations. The template classes for thread local storage in TBB are here to give an abstract way to ask TBB to allocate, manipulate, and combine the right number of copies without us worrying about how many copies that is. This lets us create scalable, composable, and portable applications.

TBB provides two template classes for thread local storage. Both provide access to a local element per thread and create the elements (lazily) on demand. They differ in their intended use models:

- Class enumerable_thread_specific, ETS, provides thread local storage that acts like an STL container with one element per thread. The container permits iterating over the elements using the usual STL iteration idioms. Any thread can iterate over all the local copies, seeing the other threads local data.

- Class combinable provides thread local storage for holding per-thread subcomputations that will later be reduced to a single result. Each thread can only see its local data or, after calling combine, the combined data.

enumerable_thread_specific, ETS

Let's see first, how our parallel histogram computation can be implemented thanks to the enumerable_thread_specific class. In Figure 5-22, we see the code needed to process in parallel different chunks of the input image and have each thread write on a private copy of the histogram vector.

```
#include <tbb/enumerable_thread_specific.h>

// Parallel execution
using vector_t = std::vector<int>;
using priv_h_t = tbb::enumerable_thread_specific<vector_t>;
priv_h_t priv_h{num_bins};
parallel_for(tbb::blocked_range<size_t>{0, image.size()},
             [&](const tbb::blocked_range<size_t>& r)
             {
                  priv_h_t::reference my_hist = priv_h.local();
                  for (size_t i = r.begin(); i < r.end(); ++i)

                    my_hist[image[i]]++;
             });
//Sequential reduction of the private histograms
vector_t hist_p(num_bins);

for(auto i=priv_h.begin(); i!=priv_h.end(); ++i){
  for (int j=0; j<num_bins; ++j) hist_p[j]+=(*i)[j];
}
```

Figure 5-22. *Parallel histogram computation on private copies using class* enumerable_thread_specific

We declare first an `enumerable_thread_specific` object, `priv_h`, of type `vector<int>`. The constructor indicates that the vector size is `num_bins` integers. Then, inside the `parallel_for`, an undetermined number of threads will process chunks of the iteration space, and for each chunk, the body (a lambda in our example) of the `parallel_for` will be executed. The thread taking care of a given chunk calls `my_hist = priv_h.local()` that works as follows. If it is the first time this thread calls the `local()` member function, a new private vector is created for this thread. If on the contrary, it is not the first time, the vector was already created, and we just need to reuse it. In both cases, a reference to the private vector is returned and assigned to `my_hist`, which is used inside the `parallel_for` to update the histogram counts for the given chunk. That way, a thread processing different chunks will create the private histogram for the first chunk and reuse it for the subsequent ones. Quite neat, right?

At the end of the `parallel_for`, we end up with undetermined number of private histograms that need to be combined to compute the final histogram, `hist_p`, accumulating all the partial results. But how can we do this reduction if we do not even know the number of private histograms? Fortunately, an `enumerable_thread_specific` not only provides thread local storage for elements of type T, but also can be iterated across like an STL container, from beginning to end. This is carried out at the end of Figure 5-22, where variable i (of type `priv_h_t::const_iterator`) sequentially traverses the different private histograms, and the nested loop j takes care of accumulating on `hist_p` all the bin counts.

If we would rather show off our outstanding C++ programming skills, we can take advantage of that fact that `priv_h` is yet another STL container and write the reduction as we show in Figure 5-23.

```
for (auto& i:priv_h) { // i traverses all private vectors
  std::transform(hist_p.begin(),      // source 1 begin
                 hist_p.end(),        // source 1 end
                 i.begin(),           // source 2 begin
                 hist_p.begin(),      // destination begin
                 std::plus<int>() );// binary operation
}
```

Figure 5-23. *A more stylish way of implementing the reduction*

Since the reduction operation is a frequent one, `enumerable_thread_specific` also offers two additional member functions to implement the reduction: `combine_each()` and `combine()`. In Figure 5-24, we illustrate how to use the member function `combine_each` in a code snippet that is completely equivalent to the one in Figure 5-23.

```
priv_h.combine_each([&](vector_t a)
{ // for each priv histogram a
   std::transform(hist_p.begin(),      // source 1 begin
                  hist_p.end(),        // source 1 end
                  a.begin(),           // source 2 begin
                  hist_p.begin(),      // destination begin
                  std::plus<int>() );// binary operation
});
```

Figure 5-24. *Using* combine_each() *to implement the reduction*

The member function combine_each() has this prototype:

```
template<typename Func> void combine_each(Func f)
```

and as we see in Figure 5-24, Func f is provided as a lambda, where the STL transform algorithm is in charge of accumulating the private histograms into hist_p. In general, the member function combine_each calls a unary functor for each element in the enumerate_thread_specific object. This combine function, with signature void(T) or void(const T&), usually reduces the private copies into a global variable.

The alternative member function combine() does return a value of type T and has this prototype:

```
template<typename Func> T combine(Func f)
```

where a binary functor f should have the signature T(T,T) or T(const T&,const T&). In Figure 5-25, we show the reduction implementation using the T(T,T) signature that, for each pair of private vectors, computes the vector addition into vector a and return it for possible further reductions. The combine() member function takes care of visiting all local copies of the histogram to return a pointer to the final hist_p.

```
vector_t hist_p = priv_h.combine(
  [](vector_t a, vector_t b) -> vector_t
    {
      std::transform(a.begin(),          // source 1 begin
                     a.end(),            // source 1 end
                     b.begin(),          // source 2 begin
                     a.begin(),          // destination begin
                     std::plus<int>() );// binary operation
      return a;
    });
```

Figure 5-25. *Using* combine() *to implement the same reduction*

And what about the parallel performance?

```
c++ -std=c++11 -O2 -o fig_5_22 fig_5_22.cpp -ltbb
./fig_5_22
Serial: 0.668987, Parallel: 0.164948, Speed-up: 4.05574
```

Now we are talking! Remember that we run these experiments on a quad-core machine, so the speedup of 4.05 is actually a bit super-linear (due to the aggregation of L1 caches of the four cores). The three equivalent reductions shown in Figures 5-23, 5-24, and 5-25 are executed sequentially, so there is still room for performance improvement if the number of private copies to be reduced is large (say that 64 threads are computing the histogram) or the reduction operation is computationally intensive (e.g., private histograms have 1024 bins). We will also address this issue, but first we want to cover the second alternative to implement thread local storage.

combinable

A combinable<T> object provides each thread with its own local instance, of type T, to hold thread local values during a parallel computation. Contrary to the previously described ETS class, a combinable object cannot be iterated as we did with priv_h in Figures 5-22 and 5-23. However, combine_each() and combine() member functions are available because this combinable class is provided in TBB with the sole purpose of implementing reductions of local data storage.

In Figure 5-26, we re-implement once again the parallel histogram computation, now relying on the combinable class.

```
#include <tbb/combinable.h>

using vector_t = std::vector<int>;
tbb::combinable<vector_t>priv_h{[](){return vector_t(num_bins);}};

parallel_for(tbb::blocked_range<size_t>{0, image.size()},
             [&](const tbb::blocked_range<size_t>& r)
             {
                 vector_t& my_hist = priv_h.local();
                 for (size_t i = r.begin(); i < r.end(); ++i)
                   my_hist[image[i]]++;
             });


//Sequential reduction of the private histograms
vector_t hist_p(num_bins);
priv_h.combine_each([&](vector_t a)
  { // for each priv histogram a
    std::transform(hist_p.begin(),      // source 1 begin
                   hist_p.end(),        // source 1 end
                   a.begin(),           // source 2 begin
                   hist_p.begin(),      // destination begin
                   std::plus<int>() );// binary operation
  });
```

Figure 5-26. *Re-implementing the histogram computation with a* `combinable` *object*

In this case, `priv_h` is a combinable object where the constructor provides a lambda with the function that will be invoked each time `priv_h.local()` is called. In this case, this lambda just creates an empty vector of `num_bins` integers. The `parallel_for`, which updates the per-thread private histograms, is quite similar to the implementation shown in Figure 5-22 for the ETS alternative, except that `my_hist` is just a reference to a vector of integers. As we said, now we cannot iterate the private histograms by hand as we did in Figure 5-22, but to make up for it, member functions `combine_each()` and `combine()` work pretty much the same as the equivalent member functions of the ETS class that we saw in Figures 5-24 and 5-25. Note that this reduction is still carried out sequentially, so it is only appropriate when the number of objects to reduce and/or the time to reduce two objects is small.

ETS and combinable classes have additional member functions and advanced uses which are documented in Appendix B.

The Easiest Parallel Implementation: Reduction Template

As we covered in Chapter 2, TBB already comes with a high-level parallel algorithm to easily implement a parallel_reduce. Then, if we want to implement a parallel reduction of private histograms, why don't we just rely on this parallel_reduce template? In Figure 5-27, we see how we use this template to code an efficient parallel histogram computation.

```
#include <tbb/parallel_reduce.h>

  // Parallel execution
    using vector_t = std::vector<int>;
    using image_iterator = std::vector<uint8_t>::iterator;
    t0 = tbb::tick_count::now();
    vector_t hist_p = parallel_reduce (
      /*range*/
      tbb::blocked_range<image_iterator>{image.begin(), image.end()},

      /*identity*/
      vector_t(num_bins),

      // 1st Lambda: Parallel computation on private histograms
      [](const tbb::blocked_range<image_iterator>& r, vector_t v) {
        std::for_each(r.begin(), r.end(),
          [&v](uint8_t i) {v[i]++;});
        return v;
      },

      // 2nd Lambda: Parallel reduction of the private histograms
      [](vector_t a, const vector_t & b) -> vector_t {
        std::transform(a.begin(),          // source 1 begin
                       a.end(),            // source 1 end
                       b.begin(),          // source 2 begin
                       a.begin(),          // destination begin
                       std::plus<int>() );// binary operation
        return a;
      });
```

Figure 5-27. *Code listing with a better parallel implementation of the image histogram computation that uses privatization and reduction*

The first argument of `parallel_reduce` is just the range of iterations that will be automatically partitioned into chunks and assigned to threads. Somewhat oversimplifying what is really going on under the hood, the threads will get a private histogram initialized with the identity value of the reduction operation, which in this case is a vector of bins initialized to 0. The first lambda is taking care of the private and local computation of the partial histograms that results from visiting just some of the chunks of the image. Finally, the second lambda implements the reduction operation, which in this case could have been expressed as

```
[](vector_t a, const vector_t & b) -> vector_t {
    for (int i=0; i<num_bins; ++i) a[i] += b[i];
    return a;
  }
```

which is exactly what the `std::transform` STL algorithm is doing. The execution time is similar to the one obtained with ETS and combinable:

```
c++ -std=c++11 -O2 -o fig_5_27 fig_5_27.cpp -ltbb
./fig_5_27
Serial: 0.594347, Parallel: 0.148108, Speed-up: 4.01293
```

In order to shed more light on the practical implications of the different implementations of the histogram we have discussed so far, we collect in Figure 5-28 all the speedups obtained on our quad-core processor. More precisely, the processor is a Core i7-6700HQ (Skylake architecture, sixth generation) at 2.6 GHz, 6 MB L3 cache, and 16 GB RAM.

Implementation:	Unsafe	Coarse	Fine	Atomic	TLS	Reduction
Speedup:	0.09	0.99	0.02	0.07	4.05	4.01

Figure 5-28. *Speedup of the different histogram implementations on an Intel Core i7-6700HQ (Skylake)*

We clearly identify three different sets of behaviors. Unsafe, fine-grained locking, and atomic solutions are way slower with four cores than in sequential (way slower here means more than one order of magnitude slower!). As we said, frequent synchronization due to locks and false sharing/true sharing is a real issue, and having histogram bins going back and forth from one cache to the other results in very disappointing speedups. Fine-grained solution is the worst because we have false sharing and true sharing for both the histogram vector and the mutex vector. As a single representative of its own kind, the coarse-grained solution is just slightly worse than the sequential one. Remember that this one is just a "parallelized-then-serialized" version in which a coarse-grained lock obliges the threads to enter the critical section one by one. The small performance degradation of the coarse-grained version is actually measuring the overhead of the parallelization and mutex management, but we are free from false sharing or true sharing now. Finally, privatization+reduction solutions (TLS and `parallel_reduction`) are leading the pack. They scale pretty well, even more than linearly, since the `parallel_reduction`, being a bit slower due to the tree-like reduction, does not pay off in this problem. The number of cores is small, and the time required for the reduction (adding to 256 `int` vectors) is negligible. For this tiny problem, the sequential reduction implemented with TLS classes is good enough.

Recap of Our Options

For the sake of backing up all the different alternatives that we have proposed to implement just a simple algorithm like the histogram computation one, let's recap and elaborate on the pros and cons of each alternative. Figure 5-29 illustrates some of our options with an even simpler vector addition of 800 numbers using eight threads. The corresponding sequential code would be similar to

```
sum = 0;
for (int i = 0; i < N; ++i) sum += vec[i];
```

As in "The Good, the Bad and the Ugly," the "cast" of this chapter are "The Mistaken, the Hardy, the Laurel, the Nuclear, the Local and the Wise":

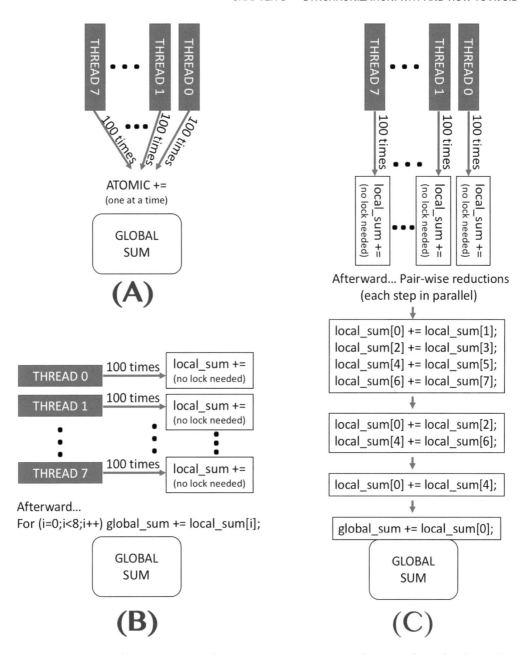

Figure 5-29. *Avoid contention when summing 800 numbers with eight threads: (A) atomic: protecting a global sum with atomic operations, (B) local: using* enumerable_thread_specific, *(C) wise: use* parallel_reduce.

- The Mistaken: We can have the eight threads incrementing a global counter, sum_g, in parallel without any further consideration, contemplation, or remorse! Most probably, sum_g will end up being incorrect, and the cache coherence protocol will also ruin performance. You have been warned.

```
long long sum_g = 0;
parallel_for(tbb::blocked_range<size_t>{0, N},
  [&](const tbb::blocked_range<size_t>& r)
  {
    for (int i=r.begin(); i<r.end(); ++i) sum_g+=vec[i];
  });
```

- The Hardy: If we use coarse-grained locking, we get the right result, but usually we also serialize the code unless the mutex implements HTM (as the speculative flavor does). This is the easiest alternative to protect the critical section, but not the most efficient one. For our vector sum example, we will illustrate the coarse-grained locking by protecting each vector chunk accumulation, thus getting a coarse-grained critical section.

```
parallel_for(tbb::blocked_range<size_t>{0, N},
  [&](const tbb::blocked_range<size_t>& r){
    my_mutex_t::scoped_lock mylock{my_mutex};
    for (int i=r.begin(); i<r.end(); ++i) sum_g+=vec[i];
  });
```

- The Laurel: Fine-grained locking is more laborious to implement and typically requires more memory to store the different mutexes that protect the fine-grained sections of the data structure. The silver lining though is that the concurrency among threads is increased. We may want to assess different mutex flavors to choose the best one in the production code. For the vector sum, we don't have a data structure that can be partitioned so that each part can be independently protected. Let's consider a fine-grained implementation the following one in which we have a lighter critical section (in this case is as serial as the coarse-grained one, but threads compete for the lock at finer granularity).

```
parallel_for(tbb::blocked_range<size_t>{0, N},
  [&](const tbb::blocked_range<size_t>& r){
    for (int i=r.begin(); i<r.end(); ++i){
      my_mutex_t::scoped_lock mylock{my_mutex};
      sum_g+=vec[i];
    }
  });
```

- The Nuclear: In some cases, atomic variables can come to our rescue. For example, when the shared mutable state can be stored in an integral type and the needed operation is simple enough. This is less expensive than the fine-grained locking approach and the concurrency level is on par. The vector sum example (see Figure 5-29(A)) would be as follows, in this case, as sequential as the two previous approaches and with the global variable as highly contended as in the finer-grained case.

```
tbb::atomic<long long> sum_a{0};
parallel_for(tbb::blocked_range<size_t>{0, N},
  [&](const tbb::blocked_range<size_t>& r)
  {
    for (int i=r.begin(); i<r.end(); ++i) sum_a+=vec[i];
  });
```

- The Local: Not always can we come up with an implementation in which privatizing local copies of the shared mutable state saves the day. But in such a case, thread local storage, TLS, can be implemented thanks to enumerate_thread_specific, ETS, or combinable classes. They work even when the number of collaborating threads is unknown and convenient reduction methods are provided. These classes offer enough flexibility to be used in different scenarios and can suit our needs when a reduction over a single iteration space does not suffice. To compute the vector sum, we present in the following an alternative in which the private partial sums, priv_s, are later accumulated sequentially, as in Figure 5-29(B).

```
using priv_s_t = tbb::enumerable_thread_specific<long long>;
priv_s_t priv_s{0};
parallel_for(tbb::blocked_range<size_t>{0, N},
  [&](const tbb::blocked_range<size_t>& r)
  { priv_s_t::reference my_s = priv_s.local();
    for (int i=r.begin(); i<r.end(); ++i) my_s+=vec[i];
  });
long long sum_p = 0;
for (auto& i:priv_s) {sum_p+=i;}
```

- The Wise: When our computation fits into a reduction pattern, it is highly recommendable to relay on the parallel_reduction template instead of hand-coding the privatization and reduction using the TBB thread local storage features. The following code may look more intricate than the previous one, but wise software architects devised clever tricks to fully optimize this common reduction operation. For instance, in this case the reduction operation follows a tree-like approach with complexity $O(\log n)$ instead of $O(n)$, as we see in Figure 5-29(C). Take advantage of what the library puts in your hands instead of reinventing the wheel. This is certainly the method that scales best for a large number of cores and a costly reduction operation.

```
sum_p = parallel_reduce(tbb::blocked_range<size_t>{0, N}, 0,
  [&](const tbb::blocked_range<size_t>&r,const long long &mysum)
    {
      long long res = mysum;
      for (int i=r.begin(); i<r.end(); ++i) res+=vec[i];
      return res;
    },
  [&](const long long& a, const long long& b)
    {
      return a+b;
    });
```

As with the histogram computation, we also evaluate the performance of the different implementations of the vector addition of size 10^9 on our Core i7 quad-core architecture, as we can see in Figure 5-30. Now the computation is an even finer-grained one (just incrementing a variable), and the relative impact of 10^9 lock-unlock operations or atomic increments is higher, as can be seen in the speedup (deceleration more properly speaking!) of the atomic (Nuclear) and fine-grained (Laurel) implementations. The coarse-grained (Hardy) implementation takes a slightly larger hit now than in the histogram case. The TLS (Local) approach is only 1.86× faster than the sequential code. Unsafe (Mistaken) is now 3.37× faster than sequential, and now the winner is the `parallel_reduction` (Wise) implementation that delivers a speedup of 3.53× for four cores.

Implementation:	Mistaken	Hardy	Laurel	Nuclear	Local	Wise
Speedup:	3.37	0.92	0.0008	0.01	1.86	3.53

Figure 5-30. *Speedup of the different implementations of the vector addition for N=10⁹ on an Intel Core i7-6700HQ (Skylake)*

You might wonder why we went through all these different alternatives to end up recommending the last one. Why did we not just go directly to the `parallel_reduce` solution if it is the best one? Well, unfortunately, parallel life is hard, and not all parallelization problems can be solved with a simple reduction. In this chapter, we provide you with the devices to leverage synchronization mechanisms if they are really necessary but also show the benefits of rethinking the algorithm and the data structure if at all possible.

Summary

The TBB library provides different flavors of mutexes as well as atomic variables to help us synchronize threads when we need to access shared data safely. The library also provides thread local storage, TLS, classes (as ETS and `combinable`) and algorithms (as `parallel_reduction`) that help us avoid the need for synchronization. In this chapter, we walked through the epic journey of parallelizing an image histogram computation. For this running example, we saw different parallel implementations starting from an incorrect one and then iterated through different synchronization alternatives, like coarse-grained locking, fine-grained-locking, and atomics, to end up with some alternative implementations that do not use locks at all. On the way, we stopped at some remarkable spots, presenting the properties that allow us to characterize mutexes, the different kinds of mutex flavors available in the TBB library, and common problems that usually arise when relying on mutexes to implement our algorithms. Now, at the end of the journey, the take-home message from this chapter is obvious: do not use locks unless performance is not your target!

For More Information

Here are some additional reading materials we recommend related to this chapter:

- C++ Concurrency in action, Anthony Williams, Manning Publications, Second Edition, 2018.

- A Primer on Memory Consistency and Cache Coherence, Daniel J. Sorin, Mark D. Hill, and David A. Wood, Morgan & Claypool Publishers, 2011.

Photo of Ronda, Málaga, in Figure 5-1, taken by author Rafael Asenjo, used with permission.

Memes shown within Chapter 5 figures used with permission from 365psd.com "33 Vector meme faces."

Traffic jam in Figure 5-17 drawn by Denisa-Adreea Constantinescu while a PhD student at the University of Malaga, used with permission.

CHAPTER 6

Data Structures for Concurrency

In the previous chapter, we shared how much we dislike locks. We dislike them because they tend to make our parallel programs less effective by limiting scaling. Of course, they can be a "necessary evil" when needed for correctness; however, we are well advised to structure our algorithms to minimize the need for locks. This chapter gives us some tools to help. Chapters 1–4 focused on scalable algorithms. A common characteristic is that they avoided or minimized locking. Chapter 5 introduced explicit synchronization methods, including locks, for when we need them. In the next two chapters, we offer ways to avoid using explicit synchronization by relying on features of TBB. In this chapter, we will discuss data structures with a desire to avoid locks. This chapter discusses concurrent containers to help address critical data structure considerations for concurrency. A related topic, the use of thread local storage (TLS), was already covered in Chapter 5.

This chapter and the next chapter cover the key pieces of TBB that help coordination of data between threads while avoiding the explicit synchronization found in Chapter 5. We do this to nudge ourselves toward coding in a manner that has proven ability to scale. We favor solutions where the implementations have been carefully crafted by the developers of TBB (to help motivate the importance of this for correctness, we discuss the A-B-A problem starting on page 200). We should remain mindful that the choice of algorithm can have a profound effect on parallel performance and the ease of implementation.

© Intel Corporation 2019
M. Voss, R. Asenjo, J. Reinders, *Pro TBB*, https://doi.org/10.1007/978-1-4842-4398-5_6

CHOOSE ALGORITHMS WISELY: CONCURRENT CONTAINERS ARE NOT A CURE-ALL

Parallel data access is best when it stems from a clear parallelism strategy, a key part of which is proper choice of algorithms. Controlled access, such as that offered by concurrent containers, comes at a cost: making a container "highly concurrent" is not free and is not even always possible. TBB offers concurrent containers when such support can work well in practice (queues, hash tables, and vectors). TBB does not attempt to support concurrency for containers such as "lists" and "trees," where fine-grained sharing will not scale well – the better opportunity for parallelism lies in revising algorithms and/or data structure choices.

Concurrent containers offer a thread-safe version for containers where concurrent support can work well in parallel programs. They offer a higher performance alternative to using a serial container with a coarse-grained lock around it, as discussed in the previous chapter (Chapter 5). TBB containers generally provide fine-grained locking, or lockless implementations, or sometimes both.

Key Data Structures Basics

If you are familiar with hash tables, unordered maps, unordered sets, queues, and vectors, then you may want to skip this section and resume reading with the "Concurrent Containers". To help review the key fundamentals, we provide a quick introduction to key data structures before we jump into talking about how TBB supports these for parallel programming.

Unordered Associative Containers

Unordered associative containers, in simple English, would be called a *collection*. We could also call them "sets." However, technical jargon has evolved to use the words map, set, and hash tables for various types of collections.

Associative containers are data structures which, given a *key*, can find a *value*, associated with that *key*. They can be thought of as a fancy array, we call them an "associative array." They take indices that are more complex than a simple series of numbers. Instead of `Cost[1]`, `Cost[2]`, `Cost[3]`, we can think of `Cost[Glass of Juice]`, `Cost[Loaf of Bread]`, `Cost[Puppy in the Window]`.

Our associative containers can be specialized in two ways:

1. **Map vs. Set:** Is there a *value*? Or just a *key*?

2. **Multiple values:** Can two items with the same *keys* be inserted in the same collection?

Map vs. Set

What we call a "map" is really just a "set" with a value attached. Imagine a basket of fruits (Apple, Orange, Banana, Pear, Lemon). A *set* containing fruits could tell us if we had a particular type of fruit in the basket. A simple *yes* or *no*. We could add a fruit type into the basket or remove it. A *map* adds to this a value, often a data structure itself with information. With a *map* of a fruit type into a collection (fruit basket), we could choose to keep a count, a price, and other information. Instead of a simple *yes* or *no*, we can ask about Cost[Apple] or Ripeness[Banana]. If the value is a structure with multiple fields, then we could query multiple things such as cost, ripeness, and color.

Multiple Values

Inserting something into a map/set using the same *key* as an item already in the map is not allowed (ensuring uniqueness) in the regular "map" or "set" containers but is allowed in the "multimap" and "multiset" versions. In the "multiple" versions, duplicates are allowed, but we lose the ability to look up something like Cost[Apple] because the *key* Apple is no longer unique in a map/set.

Hashing

Everything we have mentioned (associative arrays, map/set, single/multiple) is commonly implemented using *hash* functions. To understand what a *hash* function is, it is best to understand its motivation. Consider an associative array LibraryCardNumber[Name of Patron]. The array LibraryCardNumber returns the library card number for a patron given the name (specified as a string of characters) that is supplied as the index. One way to implement this associative array would be with a linked list of elements. Unfortunately, looking up an element would require searching the list one by one for a match. That might require traversing the entire list, which is highly inefficient in a parallel program because of contention over access to the share list structure. Even without parallelism, when inserting an item verification that there is no other entry with the same *key* requires searching the entire list. If the list has thousands or millions of patrons, this can easily require excessive amounts of time. More exotic data structures, such as trees, can improve some but not all these issues.

Imagine instead, a vast array in which to place data. This array is accessed by a traditional `array[integer]` method. This is very fast. All we need, is a magical *hash* function that takes the index for the associative array (*Name of Patron*) and turns it into the `integer` we need.

Unordered

We did start with the word *unordered* as a qualifier for the type of *associative containers* that we have been discussing. We could certainly sort the keys and access these containers in a given order. Nothing prevents that. For example, the *key* might be a person's name, and we want to create a phone directory in alphabetical order.

The word *unordered* here does not mean we cannot be programming with an ordering in mind. It does mean that the data structure (container) itself does not maintain an order for us. If there is a way to "walk" the container (*iterate* in C++ jargon), the only guarantee is that we will visit each member of the container once and only once, but the order is not guaranteed and can vary run-to-run, or machine-to-machine, and so on.

Concurrent Containers

TBB provides highly concurrent container classes that are useful for all C++ threaded applications; the TBB concurrent container classes can be used with any method of threading, including TBB of course!

The C++ Standard Template Library was not originally designed with concurrency in mind. Typically, C++ STL containers do not support concurrent updates, and therefore attempts to modify them concurrently may result in corrupted containers. Of course, STL containers can be wrapped in a coarse-grained `mutex` to make them safe for concurrent access by letting only one thread operate on the container at a time. However, that approach eliminates concurrency and thereby restricts parallel speedup if done in performance critical code. Examples of protecting with mutexes were shown in Chapter 5, to protect increments of elements in a histogram. Similar protection of non-thread-safe STL routines can be done to avoid correctness issues. If not done in performance critical sections, then performance impact may be minimal. This is an important point: conversion of containers to TBB concurrent containers should be motivated by need. Data structures that are used in parallel should be designed for concurrency to enable scaling for our applications.

The concurrent containers in TBB provide functionality similar to containers provided by the Standard Template Library (STL), but do so in a thread-safe way. For example, the `tbb::concurrent_vector` is similar to the `std::vector` class but lets us safely grow the vector in parallel. We don't need a concurrent container if we only read from it in parallel; it is only when we have parallel code that modifies a container that we need special support.

TBB offers several container classes, meant to replace corresponding STL containers in a compatible manner, that permit multiple threads to simultaneously invoke certain methods on the same container. These TBB containers offer a much higher level of concurrency, via one or both of the following methods:

- Fine-grained locking: Multiple threads operate on the container by locking only those portions they really need to lock (as the histogram examples in Chapter 5 showed us). As long as different threads access different portions, they can proceed concurrently.

- Lock-free techniques: Different threads account and correct for the effects of other interfering threads.

It is worth noting that TBB concurrent containers do come at a small cost. They typically have higher overheads than regular STL containers, and therefore operations on them may take slightly longer than on the STL containers. When the possibility of concurrent access exists, concurrent containers should be used. However, if concurrent access is not possible, the use of STL containers is advised. This is, we use concurrent containers when the speedup from the additional concurrency that they enable outweighs their slower sequential performance.

The interfaces for the containers remain the same as in STL, except where a change is required in order to support concurrency. We might jump ahead for a moment and make this a good time to consider a classic example of why some interfaces are not thread-safe – *and this is an important point to understand!* The classic example (see Figure 6-9) is the need for a new *pop-if-not-empty* capability (called `try_pop`) for queues in place of relying on a code sequence using STL *test-for-empty* followed by a *pop* if the test returned not-empty. The danger in such STL code is that another thread might be running, empty the container (after original thread's test, but before pop) and therefore create a race condition where the *pop* may actually block. That means the STL code is not thread-safe. We could throw a lock around the whole sequence to prevent modification of the queue between our test and our pop, but such locks are known to destroy performance when used in parallel parts of an application. Understanding this simple example (Figure 6-9) will help illuminate what is required to support parallelism well.

Like STL, TBB containers are templated with respect to an allocator argument. Each container uses that allocator to allocate memory for user-visible items. The default allocator for TBB is the scalable memory allocator supplied with TBB (discussed in Chapter 7). Regardless of the allocator specified, the implementation of the container may also use a different allocator for strictly internal structures.

TBB currently offers the following concurrent containers:

- Unordered associative containers

  – Unordered map (including unordered multimap)

  – Unordered set (including unordered multiset)

  – Hash table

- Queue (including bounded queue and priority queue)

- Vector

WHY DO TBB CONTAINERS ALLOCATOR ARGUMENTS DEFAULT TO TBB?

Allocator arguments are supported with all TBB containers, and they default to the TBB scalable memory allocators (see Chapter 7).

The containers default to using a mix of `tbb::cache_aligned_allocator` and `tbb:tbb_allocator`. We document the defaults in this chapter, but Appendix B of this book and the TBB header files are resources for learning the defaults. There is no requirement to link in the TBB scalable allocator library (see Chapter 7), as the TBB containers will silently default to using `malloc` when the library is not present. However, we should link with the TBB scalable allocator because the performance will likely be better from just linking in – especially easy using it as a proxy library as explained in Chapter 7.

Class name *and C++11 connection notes*	Concurrent traversal and insertion.	Keys have a value associated with them.	Support concurrent erasure	Built-in locking.	No visible locking (lock-free interface).	Identical items allowed to be inserted.	[] and at accessors
`concurrent_hash_map` *Predates C++11.*	✓	✓	✓	✓	✗	✗	✗
`concurrent_unordered_map` *Closely resembles the C++11 unordered_map.*	✓	✓	✗	✗	✓	✗	✓
`concurrent_unordered_multimap` *Closely resembles the C++11 unordered_multimap.*	✓	✓	✗	✗	✓	✓	✗
`concurrent_unordered_set` *Closely resembles the C++11 unordered_set.*	✓	✗	✗	✗	✓	✗	✗
`concurrent_unordered_multiset` *Closely resembles the C++11 unordered_multiset.*	✓	✗	✗	✗	✓	✓	✗

Figure 6-1. *Comparison of concurrent unordered associative containers*

Concurrent Unordered Associative Containers

Unordered associative containers are a group of class templates that implement hash table variants. Figure 6-1 lists these containers and their key differentiating features. Concurrent unordered associative containers can be used to store arbitrary elements, such as integers or custom classes, because they are templates. TBB offers implementations of unordered associative containers that can perform well concurrently.

A hash map (also commonly called a hash table) is a data structure that maps keys to values using a hash function. A hash function computes an index from a key, and the index is used to access the "bucket" in which value(s) associated with the key are stored.

Choosing a good hash function is very important! A perfect hash function would assign each key to a unique bucket so there will be no *collisions* for different keys. In practice, however, hash functions are not perfect and will occasionally generate the same index for more than one key. These collisions require some form of accommodation by the hash table implementation, and this will introduce some overhead – hash functions should be designed to minimize collisions by hashing inputs into a nearly even distribution across the buckets.

The advantage of a hash map comes from the ability to, in the average case, provide $O(1)$ time for searches, insertions, and keys. The advantage of a TBB hash map is support for concurrent usage both for correctness and performance. This assumes that a good hash function is being used – one that does not cause many collisions for the keys that are used. The theoretical worst case of $O(n)$ remains whenever an imperfect hash function exists, or if the hash table is not well-dimensioned.

Often hash maps are, in actual usage, more efficient than other table lookup data structures including search trees. This makes hash maps the data structure of choice for many purposes including associative arrays, database indexing, caches, and sets.

concurrent_hash_map

TBB supplies concurrent_hash_map, which maps keys to values in a way that permits multiple threads to concurrently access values via find, insert, and erase methods. As we will discuss later, tbb:: concurrent_hash_map was designed for parallelism, and therefore its interfaces are thread-safe unlike the STL map/set interfaces we will cover later in this chapter.

The keys are unordered. There is at most one element in a concurrent_hash_map for each key. The key may have other elements in flight but not in the map. Type HashCompare specifies how keys are hashed *and* how they are compared for equality. As is generally expected for hash tables, if two keys are equal, then they must hash to the same hash code. This is why HashCompare ties the concept of comparison and hashing into a single object instead of treating them separately. Another consequence of this is that we need to not change the hash code of a key while the hash table is nonempty.

A `concurrent_hash_map` acts as a container of elements of type `std::pair<const Key,T>`. Typically, when accessing a container element, we are interested in either updating it or reading it. The template class `concurrent_hash_map` supports these two purposes respectively with the classes `accessor` and `const_accessor` that act as smart pointers. An accessor represents update (write) access. As long as it points to an element, all other attempts to look up that key in the table block until the accessor is done. A `const_accessor` is similar, except that it represents read-only access. Multiple accessors can point to the same element at the same time. This feature can greatly improve concurrency in situations where elements are frequently read and infrequently updated.

We share a simple example of code using the `concurrent_hash_map` container in Figures 6-2 and 6-3. We can improve the performance of this example by reducing the lifetime of the element access. The methods `find` and `insert` take an `accessor` or `const_accessor` as an argument. The choice tells `concurrent_hash_map` whether we are asking for update or read-only access. Once the method returns, the access lasts until the `accessor` or `const_accessor` is destroyed. Because having access to an element can block other threads, try to shorten the lifetime of the `accessor` or `const_accessor`. To do so, declare it in the innermost block possible. To release access even sooner than the end of the block, use method `release`. Figure 6-5 shows a rework of the loop body from Figure 6-2 that uses `release` instead of depending upon destruction to end thread lifetime. The method `remove(key)` can also operate concurrently. It implicitly requests write access. Therefore, before removing the key, it waits on any other extant accesses on key.

```cpp
#include <tbb/concurrent_hash_map.h>
#include <tbb/blocked_range.h>
#include <tbb/parallel_for.h>
#include <string>

// Structure that defines hashing and comparison operations for
user's type.
struct MyHashCompare {
  static size_t hash( const std::string& x ) {
    size_t h = 0;
    for( const char* s = x.c_str(); *s; ++s )
      h = (h*17)^*s;
    return h;
  }
  //! True if strings are equal
  static bool equal( const std::string& x, const std::string& y
) {
    return x==y;
  }
};

// A concurrent hash table that maps strings to ints.
typedef tbb::concurrent_hash_map<std::string,int,MyHashCompare>
StringTable;

// Function object for counting occurrences of strings.
struct Tally {
  StringTable& table;
  Tally( StringTable& table_ ) : table(table_) {}
  void operator()(
    const tbb::blocked_range<std::string*> range ) const {
    for( std::string* p=range.begin(); p!=range.end(); ++p ) {
      StringTable::accessor a;
      table.insert( a, *p );
      a->second += 1;
    }
  }
};
```

Figure 6-2. *Hash Table example, part 1 of 2*

```
const size_t N = 10;

std::string Data[N] = { "Hello", "World", "TBB", "Hello",
      "So Long", "Thanks for all the fish", "So Long",
      "Three", "Three", "Three" };

void main() {
  // Construct empty table.
  StringTable table;

  // Put occurrences into the table
  tbb::parallel_for(
      tbb::blocked_range<std::string*>( Data, Data+N, 1000 ),
      Tally(table) );

  // Display the occurrences using a simple walk
  // (note: concurrent_hash_map does not offer const_iterator)
  // see a problem with this code???
  // read "Iterating thorough these structures is
  // asking for trouble" coming up in a few pages
  for( StringTable::iterator i=table.begin();
       i!=table.end();
       ++i )
    printf("%s %d\n",i->first.c_str(),i->second);
}
```

Figure 6-3. *Hash Table example, part 2 of 2*

```
              Three 3
              So Long 2
              Hello 2
              TBB 1
              World 1
              Thanks for all the fish 1
```

Figure 6-4. *Output of the example program in Figures 6-2 and 6-3*

```
for( std::string* p=range.begin(); p!=range.end(); ++p ) {
  StringTable::accessor a;
  table.insert( a, *p );
  a->second += 1;
  a.release();
}
```

Figure 6-5. *Revision to Figure 6-2 to reduce accessor lifetime hoping to improve scaling*

PERFORMANCE TIPS FOR HASH MAPS

- Always specify an initial size for the hash table. The default of one will scale horribly! Good sizes definitely start in the hundreds. If a smaller size seems correct, then using a lock on a small table will have an advantage in speed due to cache locality.

- Check your hash function – and be sure that there is good pseudo-randomness in the low-order bits of the hash value. In particular, you should not use pointers as keys because generally a pointer will have a set number of zero bits in the low-order bits due to object alignment. If this is the case, it is strongly recommended that the pointer be divided by the size of the type it points too, thereby shifting out the always zero bits in favor of bits that vary. Multiplication by a prime number, and shifting out some low order bits, is a strategy to consider. As with any form of hash table, keys that are equal must have the same hash code, and the ideal hash function distributes keys uniformly across the hash code space. Tuning for an optimal hash function is definitely application specific, but using the default supplied by TBB tends to work well.

- Do not use accessors if they can be avoided and limit their lifetime as much as possible when accessors are needed (see example of this in Figure 6-5). They are effectively fine-grained locks, inhibit other threads while they exist, and therefore potentially limit scaling.

- Use the TBB memory allocator (see Chapter 7). Use `scalable_allocator` as the template argument for the container if you want to enforce its usage (not allow a fallback to malloc) – at least a good sanity check during development when testing performance.

Concurrent Support for `map/multimap` and `set/multiset` Interfaces

Standard C++ STL defines `unordered_set`, `unordered_map`, `unordered_multiset`, and `unordered_multimap`. Each of these containers differs only by the constraints which are placed on their elements. Figure 6-1 is a handy reference to compare the five choices we have for concurrent map/set support including the `tbb::concurrent_hash_map` which we used in our code examples (Figures 6-2 through 6-5).

STL does not define anything called "hash" because C++ did not originally define a hash table. Interest in adding hash table support to STL was widespread, so there were widely used versions of STL that were extended to include hash table support, including those by SGI, gcc, and Microsoft. Without a standard, there ended up being variation in what "hash table" or "hash maps" came to mean to C++ programmers in terms of capabilities and performance. Starting with C++11, a hash table implementation was added to the STL, and the name `unordered_map` was chosen for the class to prevent confusion and collisions with pre-standard implementations. It could be said that the name `unordered_map` is more descriptive as it hints at the interface to the class and the unordered nature of its elements.

The original TBB hash table support predates C++11, called `tbb::concurrent_hash_map`. This hash function remains quite valuable and did not need to change to match the standard. TBB now includes support for `unordered_map` and `unordered_set` support to mirror the C++11 additions, with the interfaces augmented or adjusted only as needed to support concurrent access. Avoiding a few parallel-unfriendly interfaces is part of the "nudging us" to effective parallel programming. Appendix B has an exhaustive coverage of the details, but the three noteworthy adjustments for better parallel scaling are as follows:

- Methods requiring C++11 language features (e.g., `rvalue` references) are omitted.

- The erase methods for C++ standard functions are prefixed with `unsafe_` to indicate that they are not concurrency safe (because concurrent erasure is only supported for `concurrent_hash_map`). This does not apply to `concurrent_hash_map` because it *does* support concurrent erasure.

- The bucket methods (count of buckets, max count of buckets, size of buckets, and support to iterate through the buckets) are prefixed with unsafe_ as a reminder that they are not concurrency safe with respect to insertion. They are supported for compatibility with STL but should be avoided if possible. If used, they should be protected from being used concurrently with insertions occurring. These interfaces do not apply to concurrent_hash_map because the TBB designers avoided such functions.

Built-In Locking vs. No Visible Locking

The containers concurrent_hash_map and concurrent_unordered_* have some differences concerning the locking of accessed elements. Therefore, they may behave very differently under contention. The accessors of concurrent_hash_map are essentially locks: accessor is an exclusive lock, and const_accessor is a shared lock. Lock-based synchronization is built into the usage model for the container, protecting not only container integrity but to some degree data integrity as well. Code in Figure 6-2 uses an accessor when performing an insert into the table.

Iterating Through These Structures Is Asking for Trouble

We snuck in some concurrency unsafe code at the end of Figure 6-3 when we iterated through the hash table to dump it out. If insertions or deletions were made while we walked the table, this could be problematic. In our defense, we will just say "it is debug code – we do not care!" But, experience has taught us that it is all too easy for code like this to creep into non-debug code. Beware!

The TBB designers left the iterators available for concurrent_hash_map for debug purposes, but they purposefully did not tempt us with iterators as return values from other members.

Unfortunately, STL tempts us in ways we should learn to resist. The concurrent_ unordered_* containers are different than concurrent_hash_map – the API follows the C++ standard for associative containers (keep in mind, the original TBB concurrent_ hash_map predates any standardization by C++ for concurrent containers). The operations to add or find data return an iterator, so this tempts us to iterate with it. In a parallel program, we risk this being simultaneously with other operations on the map/set. If we give into temptation, protecting data integrity is completely left to us as programmers, the API of the container does not help. One could say that the C++ standard containers offer additional flexibility but lack the built-in protection that concurrent_hash_map offers. The STL interfaces are easy enough to use concurrently, if we avoid the temptation to use the iterators returned from an add or find operation for anything other than referencing the item we looked up. If we give into the temptation (we should not!), then we have a lot of thinking to do about concurrent updates in our application. Of course, if there are no updates happening – only lookups – then there are no parallel programming issues with using the iterators.

Concurrent Queues: Regular, Bounded, and Priority

Queues are useful data structures where items are added or removed from the queue with operations known as push (add) and pop (remove). The unbounded queue interfaces provide a "try pop" which tells us if the queue was empty and no value was popped from the queue. This steers us away from writing our own logic to avoid a blocking pop by testing empty – an operation that is not thread-safe (see Figure 6-9). Sharing a queue between multiple threads can be an effective way to pass work items from thread to thread – a queue holding "work" to do could have work items added to request future processing and removed by tasks that want to do the processing.

Normally, a queue operates in a first-in-first-out (FIFO) fashion. If I start with an empty queue, do a push(10) and then a push(25), then the first pop operation will return 10, and the second pop will return a 25. This is much different than the behavior of a stack, which would usually be last-in-first-out. But, we are not talking about stacks here!

We show a simple example in Figure 6-6 which clearly shows that the pop operations return the values in the same order as the push operations added them to the queue.

```cpp
#include <tbb/concurrent_queue.h>
#include <tbb/concurrent_priority_queue.h>
#include <iostream>

int myarray[10] = { 16, 64, 32, 512, 1, 2, 512, 8, 4, 128 };

void pval(int test, int val) {
  if (test) {
    std::cout << " " << val;
  } else {
    std::cout << " ***";
  }
}

void simpleQ() {
  tbb::concurrent_queue<int> queue;
  int val;

  for( int i=0; i<10; ++i )
    queue.push(myarray[i]);

  std::cout << "Simple  Q   pops are";

  for( int i=0; i<10; ++i )
    pval( queue.try_pop(val), val );

  std::cout << std::endl;
}

int main() {
  simpleQ();
//  boundedQ();
//  prioQ();
//  prioQgt();
  return 0;
}

Output is:
Simple  Q   pops are 16 64 32 512 1 2 512 8 4 128
```

Figure 6-6. *Example of using the simple (FIFO) queue*

There are two twists offered for queues: *bounding* and *priorities*. Bounding adds the concept of enforcing a limit on the size of a queue. This means that a push might not be possible if the queue is full. To handle this, the bounded queue interfaces offer us ways to have a push wait until it can add to the queue, or have a "try to push" operation that does the push if it can or lets us know the queue was full. A bounded queue is by default unbounded! If we want a bounded queue, we need to use concurrent_bounded_queue and call method set_capacity to set the size for the queue. We show in Figure 6-7 a simple usage of bounded queue in which only the first six items pushed made it into the queue. We could add a test on try_push and do something. In this case, we have the program print ******* when the pop operation finds that the queue was empty.

```
void boundedQ() {
  tbb::concurrent_bounded_queue<int> queue;
  int val;

  queue.set_capacity(6);

  for( int i=0; i<10; ++i )
    queue.try_push(myarray[i]);

  std::cout << "Bounded Q   pops are";

  for( int i=0; i<10; ++i )
    pval( queue.try_pop(val), val );

  std::cout << std::endl;
}

Output of the expanded program is:
Simple  Q    pops are 16 64 32 512 1 2 512 8 4 128
Bounded Q    pops are 16 64 32 512 1 2 *** *** *** ***
```

Figure 6-7. *This routine expands our program to show bounded queue usage*

A priority adds a twist to first-in-first-out by effectively sorting items in the queue. The default priority, if we do not specify one in our code, is std::less<T>. This means that a pop operation will return the highest valued item in the queue.

Figure 6-8 shows two examples of priority usage, one defaulting to std:: less<int> while the other specifying std::greater<int> explicitly.

```
void prioQ() {
  tbb::concurrent_priority_queue<int> queue;
  int val;

  for( int i=0; i<10; ++i )
    queue.push(myarray[i]);

  std::cout << "Prio    Q   pops are";

  for( int i=0; i<10; ++i )
    pval( queue.try_pop(val), val );

  std::cout << std::endl;
}

void prioQgt() {
  tbb::concurrent_priority_queue<int,std::greater<int>> queue;
  int val;

  for( int i=0; i<10; ++i )
    queue.push(myarray[i]);

  std::cout << "Prio    Qgt pops are";

  for( int i=0; i<10; ++i )
    pval( queue.try_pop(val), val );

  std::cout << std::endl;
}

Output of the expanded program is:
Simple  Q   pops are 16 64 32 512 1 2 512 8 4 128
Bounded Q   pops are 16 64 32 512 1 2 *** *** *** ***
Prio    Q   pops are 512 512 128 64 32 16 8 4 2 1
Prio    Qgt pops are 1 2 4 8 16 32 64 128 512 512
```

Figure 6-8. *These routines expand our program to show priority queueing*

As our examples in the prior three figures show, to implement these three variations on queues, TBB offers three container classes: concurrent_queue, concurrent_bounded_queue, and concurrent_priority_queue. All concurrent queues permit multiple threads to concurrently push and pop items. The interfaces are similar to STL std::queue or std::priority_queue except where it must differ to make concurrent modification of a queue safe.

The fundamental methods on a queue are push and try_pop. The push method works as it would with a std::queue. It is important to note that there is not support for front or back methods because they would not be safe in a concurrent environment since these methods return a reference to an item in the queue. In a parallel program, the front or back of a queue could be changed by another thread in parallel making the use of front or back meaningless.

Similarly, pop and testing for empty are not supported for unbounded queues – instead the method try_pop is defined to pop an item if it is available and return a true status; otherwise, it returns no item and a status of false. The test-for-empty and pop methods are combined into a single method to encourage thread-safe coding. For bounded queues, there is a non-blocking try_push method in addition to the potentially blocking push method. These help us avoid the size methods to inquire about the size of the queue. Generally, the size methods should be avoided, especially if they are holdovers from a sequential program. Since the size of a queue can change concurrently in a parallel program, the size method needs careful thought if it is used. For one thing, TBB can return a negative value for size methods when the queue empty and there are pending pop methods. The empty method is true when size is zero or less.

Bounding Size

For concurrent_queue and concurrent_priority_queue, capacity is unbounded, subject to memory limitations on the target machine. The concurrent_bounded_queue offers controls over bounds – a key feature being that a push method will block until the queue has room. A bounded queue is useful in slowing a supplier to match the rate of consumption instead of allowing a queue to grow unconstrained.

concurrent_bounded_queue is the only concurrent_queue_* container that offers a pop method. The pop method will block until an item becomes available. A push method can be blocking only with a concurrent_bounded_queue so this container type also offers a non-blocking method called try_push.

This concept of bounding to rate match, to avoid overflowing memory or overcommitting cores, also exists in Flow Graph (see Chapter 3) through the use of a limiter_node.

Priority Ordering

A priority queue maintains an ordering in the queue based on the priorities of individual queued items. As we mentioned earlier, a normal queue has a first-in-first-out policy, whereas a priority queue sorts its items. We can provide our own Compare to change the ordering from the default of `std::less<T>`. For instance, using `std::greater<T>` causes the smallest element to be the next to retrieved for a pop method. We did exactly that in our example code in Figure 6-8.

Staying Thread-Safe: Try to Forget About Top, Size, Empty, Front, Back

It is important to note that there is no `top` method, and we probably should avoid using `size` and `empty` methods. Concurrent usage means that the values from all three can change due to push/pop methods in other threads. Also, the `clear` and `swap` methods, while supported, are not thread-safe. TBB forces us to rewrite code using `top` when converting a `std::priority_queue` usage to `tbb::concurrent_priority_queue` because the element that would be returned could be invalidated by a concurrent pop. Because the return values are not endangered by concurrency, TBB does support `std::priority_queue` methods of `size`, `empty`, and `swap`. However, we recommend carefully reviewing the wisdom of using either function in a concurrent application, since a reliance on either is likely to be a hint that the code that needs rewriting for concurrency.

std:: code, not thread safe	tbb:: code, thread safe

<pre>#include <iostream>
#include <queue>
 	
void main() {
  int sum (0);
  int item;
 	
  std::priority_queue<int> myPQ;
 	
  for(int i=0; i<10001; i+=1) {
    myPQ.push(i);
  }
 	
  while(!myPQ.empty()) {
    sum += myPQ.top();
    myPQ.pop();
  }
 	
  // prints "total: 50005000"
  std::cout << "total: "
            << sum << '\n';
}</pre>
	<pre>#include <iostream>
	
	#include <tbb/concurrent_priority_queue.h>
	#include <tbb/parallel_for.h>
	
	void main() {
	  int sum (0);
	  int item;
	
	  tbb::concurrent_priority_queue<int> myPQ;
	
	  tbb::parallel_for(0,10001,1,
	    [&](size_t i){myPQ.push(i);});
	
	  while(myPQ.try_pop(item))
	    sum += item;
	
	  // prints "total: 50005000"
	  std::cout << "total: "
	            << sum << '\n';
	}</pre>

Figure 6-9. *Motivation for* try_pop *instead of* top *and* pop *shown in a side-by-side comparison of STL and TBB priority queue code. Both will total 50005000 in this example without parallelism, but the TBB scales and is thread-safe.*

Iterators

For debugging purposes alone, all three concurrent queues provide limited iterator support (iterator and const_iterator types). This support is intended solely to allow us to inspect a queue during debugging. Both iterator and const_iterator types follow the usual STL conventions for forward iterators. The iteration order is from least recently pushed to most recently pushed. Modifying a queue invalidates any iterators that reference it. The iterators are relatively slow. They should be used only for debugging. An example of usage is shown in Figure 6-10.

```
#include <tbb/concurrent_queue.h>
#include <iostream>

int main() {
  tbb::concurrent_queue<int> queue;
  for( int i=0; i<10; ++i )
    queue.push(i);
  for( tbb::concurrent_queue<int>::const_iterator
      i(queue.unsafe_begin());
      i!=queue.unsafe_end();
      ++i )
    std::cout << *i << " ";
  std::cout << std::endl;
  return 0;
}
Output of this program is:
0 1 2 3 4 5 6 7 8 9
```

Figure 6-10. Sample debugging code for iterating through a concurrent queue – note the unsafe_ *prefix on* begin *and* end *to emphasize the debug-only non-thread-safe nature of these methods.*

Why to Use This Concurrent Queue: The A-B-A Problem

We mentioned at the outset of this chapter that there is significant value in having containers that have been written by parallelism experts for us to "just use." None of us should want to reinvent good scalable implementations for each application. As motivation, we diverge to mention the A-B-A problem – a classic computer science example of parallelism gone wrong! At first glance, a concurrent queue might seem easy enough to simply write our own. It is not. Using the concurrent_queue from TBB, or any other well-researched and well-implemented concurrent queue, is a good idea. Humbling as the experience can be, we would not be the first to learn it is not as easy as we could naively believe. The update idiom (compare_and_swap) from Chapter 5 is inappropriate if the A-B-A problem (see sidebar) thwarts our intent. This is a frequent problem when trying to design a non-blocking algorithm for linked data structures, including a concurrent queue. The TBB designers have a solution to the A-B-A problem already packaged in the solutions for concurrent queues. We can just rely upon it. Of course, it is open source code so you can hunt around in the code to see the solution if you are feeling curious. If you do look in the source code, you'll see that arena management (subject of Chapter 12) has to deal with the ABA problem as well. Of course, you can just use TBB without needing to know any of this. We just wanted to emphasize that working out concurrent data structures is not as easy as it might appear – hence the love we have for using the concurrent data structures supported by TBB.

THE A-B-A PROBLEM

Understanding the A-B-A problem is a key way to train ourselves to think through the implications of concurrency when designing our own algorithms. While TBB avoids the A-B-A problems while implementing concurrent queues and other TBB structures, it is a reminder that we need to "Think Parallel."

The A-B-A problem occurs when a thread checks a location to be sure the value is *A* and proceeds with an update only if the value was *A*. The question arises whether it is a problem if other tasks change the same location in a way that the first task does not detect:

1.   A task reads a value *A* from `globalx`.

2.   Other tasks change `globalx` from *A* to *B* and then back to *A*.

3.   The task in step 1 does its `compare_and_swap`, reading *A* and thus not detecting the intervening change to *B*.

If the task erroneously proceeds under an assumption that the location has not changed since the task first read it, the task may proceed to corrupt the object or otherwise get the wrong result.

Consider an example with linked lists. Assume a linked list $W(1) \rightarrow X(9) \rightarrow Y(7) \rightarrow Z(4)$, where the letters are the node locations and the numbers are the values in the nodes. Assume that some task transverses the list to find a node *X* to dequeue. The task fetches the next pointer, `X.next` (which is *Y*) with the intent to put it in `W.next`. However, before the swap is done, the task is suspended for some time.

During the suspension, other tasks are busy. They dequeue *X* and then happen to reuse that same memory and queue a new version of node *X* as well as dequeueing Y and adding Q at some point in time. Now, the list is $W(1) \rightarrow X(2) \rightarrow Q(3) \rightarrow Z(4)$.

Once the original task finally wakes up, it finds that `W.next` still points to *X*, so it swaps out `W.next` to become *Y*, thereby making a complete mess out of the linked list.

Atomic operations are the way to go if they embody enough protection for our algorithm. If the A-B-A problem can ruin our day, we need to find a more complex solution. `tbb::concurrent_queue` has the necessary additional complexity to get this right!

When to NOT Use Queues: Think Algorithms!

Queues are widely used in parallel programs to buffer consumers from producers. Before using an explicit queue, we need to consider using `parallel_do` or `pipeline` instead (see Chapter 2). These options are often more efficient than queues for the following reasons:

- Queues are inherently bottlenecks because they must maintain an order.

- A thread that is popping a value will stall if the queue is empty until a value is pushed.

- A queue is a passive data structure. If a thread pushes a value, it could take time until it pops the value, and in the meantime the value (and whatever it references) becomes *cold* in cache. Or worse yet, another thread pops the value, and the value (and whatever it references) must be moved to the other processor core.

In contrast, `parallel_do` and `pipeline` avoid these bottlenecks. Because their threading is implicit, they optimize use of worker threads so that they do other work until a value shows up. They also try to keep items *hot* in cache. For example, when another work item is added to a `parallel_do`, it is kept local to the thread that added it unless another idle thread can steal it before the *hot* thread processes it. This way, items are more often processed by the *hot* thread thereby reducing delays in fetching data.

Concurrent Vector

TBB offers a class called `concurrent_vector`. A `concurrent_vector<T>` is a dynamically growable array of T. It is safe to grow a `concurrent_vector` even while other threads are also operating on elements of it, or even growing it themselves. For safe concurrent growing, `concurrent_vector` has three methods that support common uses of dynamic arrays: `push_back`, `grow_by`, and `grow_to_at_least`.

Figure 6-11 shows a simple usage of `concurrent_vector`, and Figure 6-12 shows, in the dump of the vector contents, the effects of parallel threads having added concurrently. The outputs from the same program would prove identical if sorted into numerical order.

When to Use tbb::concurrent_vector Instead of std::vector

The key value of `concurrent_vector<T>` is its ability to grow a vector concurrently and its ability to guarantee that elements do not move around in memory.

202

concurrent_vector does have more overhead than std::vector. So, we should use concurrent_vector when we need the ability to dynamically resize it while other accesses are (or might be) in flight or require that an element never move.

```cpp
#include <iostream>

#include <tbb/concurrent_vector.h>
#include <tbb/parallel_for.h>

void oneway() {
// Create a vector containing integers
    tbb::concurrent_vector<int> v = {3, 14, 15, 92};

    // Add more integers to vector IN PARALLEL
    for( int i = 100; i < 1000; ++i ) {
      v.push_back(i*100+11);
      v.push_back(i*100+22);
      v.push_back(i*100+33);
      v.push_back(i*100+44);
    }

    // Iterate and print values of vector (debug use only)
    for(int n : v) {
      std::cout << n << std::endl;
    }
}

void allways() {
// Create a vector containing integers
    tbb::concurrent_vector<int> v = {3, 14, 15, 92};

    // Add more integers to vector IN PARALLEL
    tbb::parallel_for( 100, 999, [&](int i){
      v.push_back(i*100+11);
      v.push_back(i*100+22);
      v.push_back(i*100+33);
      v.push_back(i*100+44);
    });

    // Iterate and print values of vector (debug use only)
    for(int n : v) {
      std::cout << n << std::endl;
    }
}
```

Figure 6-11. *Concurrent vector small example*

3	3
14	14
15	15
92	92
10011	10011
. . .	. . .
84911	72611
84922	91211
84933	87111
84944	72622
85011	91222
85022	87122
85033	72633
85044	91233
. . .	. . .
99933	99833
99944	99844

Figure 6-12. *The left side is output generated while using for (not parallel), and the right side shows output when using parallel_for (concurrent pushing into the vector).*

Elements Never Move

A concurrent_vector never moves an element until the array is cleared, which can be an advantage over the STL std::vector even for single-threaded code. Unlike a std::vector, a concurrent_vector never moves existing elements when it grows. The container allocates a series of contiguous arrays. The first reservation, growth, or assignment operation determines the size of the first array. Using a small number of elements as initial size incurs fragmentation across cache lines that may increase element access time. shrink_to_fit() merges several smaller arrays into a single contiguous array, which may improve access time.

Concurrent Growth of concurrent_vectors

While concurrent growing is fundamentally incompatible with ideal exception safety, concurrent_vector does offer a practical level of exception safety. The element type must have a destructor that never throws an exception, and if the constructor can throw an exception, then the destructor must be nonvirtual and work correctly on zero-filled memory.

The push_back(x) method safely appends x to the vector. The grow_by(n) method safely appends n consecutive elements initialized with T(). Both methods return an iterator pointing to the first appended element. Each element is initialized with T(). The following routine safely appends a C string to a shared vector:

```
void Append( concurrent_vector<char>& vector,
             const char* string ) {
    size_t n = strlen(string)+1;
    std::copy( string, string+n, vector.grow_by(n) );
}
```

grow_to_at_least(n) grows a vector to size n if it is shorter. Concurrent calls to the growth methods do not necessarily return in the order that elements are appended to the vector.

size() returns the number of elements in the vector, which may include elements that are still undergoing concurrent construction by methods push_back, grow_by, or grow_to_at_least. The previous example uses std::copy and iterators, not strcpy and pointers, because elements in a concurrent_vector might not be at consecutive addresses. It is safe to use the iterators while the concurrent_vector is being grown, as long as the iterators never go past the current value of end(). However, the iterator may reference an element undergoing concurrent construction. Therefore, we are required to synchronize construction and access.

Operations on concurrent_vector are concurrency safe with respect to growing, not for clearing or destroying a vector. Never invoke clear() if there are other operations in flight on the concurrent_vector.

Summary

In this chapter, we discussed three key data structures (hash/map/set, queues, and vectors) that have support in TBB. This support from TBB offers thread-safety (okay to run concurrently) as well as an implementation that scales well. We offered advice on things to avoid, because they tend to cause trouble in parallel programs – including using the iterators returned by map/set for anything other than the one item that was looked up. We reviewed the A-B-A problem both as a motivation for using TBB instead of writing our own and as an excellent example of the thinking we need to do when parallel programs share data.

As with other chapters, the complete APIs are detailed in Appendix B, and the code shown in figures is all downloadable.

Despite all the wonderful support for parallel use of containers, we cannot emphasize enough the concept that thinking through algorithms to minimize synchronization of any kind is critical to high performance parallel programming. If you can avoid sharing data structures, by using `parallel_do`, `pipeline`, `parallel_reduce`, and so on, as we mentioned in the section "When to NOT Use Queues: Think Algorithms!" – you may find your programs scale better. We mention this in multiple ways throughout this book, because thinking this through is important for the most effective parallel programming.

CHAPTER 7

Scalable Memory Allocation

This chapter discusses a *critical* part of any parallel program: scalable memory allocation, which includes use of new as well as explicit calls to malloc, calloc, and so on. Scalable memory allocation can be used regardless of whether we use any other part of Threading Building Blocks (TBB). In addition to interfaces to use directly, TBB offers a "proxy" method to automatically replace C/C++ functions for dynamic memory allocation, which is an easy, effective, and popular way to get a performance boost without any code changes. This is important and workvs regardless of how "modern" you are in your usage of C++, specifically whether you use the modern and encouraged std::make_shared, or the now discouraged new and malloc. The performance benefits of using a scalable memory allocator are significant because they directly address issues that would otherwise limit scaling and risk false sharing. TBB was among the first widely used scalable memory allocators, in no small part because it came free with TBB to help highlight the importance of including memory allocation considerations in any parallel program. It remains extremely popular today and is one of the best scalable memory allocators available.

Modern C++ programming (which favors smart pointers), combined with parallel thinking, encourages us to use TBB scalable memory allocators explicitly with std::allocate_shared or implicitly with std::make_shared.

© Intel Corporation 2019
M. Voss, R. Asenjo, J. Reinders, *Pro TBB*, https://doi.org/10.1007/978-1-4842-4398-5_7

Modern C++ Memory Allocation

While performance is especially interesting for parallel programming, *correctness* is a critical topic for *all* applications. Memory allocation/deallocation issues are a significant source of bugs in applications, and this has led many additions to the C++ standard and a shift in what is considered modern C++ programming!

Modern C++ programming *encourages* use of managed memory allocation with introduction of smart pointers in C++11 (make_shared, allocate_shared, etc.) and *discourages* extensive use of malloc or new. We have used std::make_shared in examples since the very first chapter of this book. The addition of std::aligned_alloc in C++17 provides for cache alignment to avoid false sharing but does not address scalable memory allocation. Many additional capabilities are in the works for C++20, but without explicit support for scalability.

TBB continues to offer this critical piece for parallel programmers: *scalable memory allocation*. TBB does this in a fashion that fits perfectly with all versions of C++ and C standards. The heart and soul of the support in TBB can be described as *memory pooling by threads*. This pooling avoids performance degradations caused by memory allocations that do not seek to avoid unnecessary shifting of data between caches. TBB also offers scalable memory allocation combined with cache alignment, which offers the scalable attribute above what one can expect from simply using std::aligned_alloc. Cache alignment is not a default behavior because indiscriminate usage can greatly expand memory usage.

As we will discuss in this chapter, the use of scalable memory allocation can be critical to performance. std::make_shared does not provide for the specification of an allocator, but there is a corresponding std::allocate_shared, which does allow specification of an allocator.

This chapter focuses on scalable memory allocators, which should then be used in whatever manner of C++ memory allocation is chosen for an application. Modern C++ programming, with parallel thinking, would encourage use to use std::allocate_shared explicitly with TBB scalable memory allocators, or use std::make_shared implicitly with TBB by overriding the default new to use the TBB scalable memory allocator. Note, std::make_shared is not affected by the new operator for a particular class because it actually allocates a larger block of memory to handle both the contents for a class and its extra space for bookkeeping (specifically, the atomic that is added to make it a smart pointer). That is why overriding the default new (to use the TBB allocator) will be sufficient to affect std::make_shared.

Manner of Use	Summary	Figure listing interfaces
C/C++ proxy	Most popular usage. Automatic replacements of standard memory allocation methods. No code changes required.	**Figure 7.4** has a list of functions replaced by the proxy library.
C++ classes	C++ standard interfaces (`std:allocator`).	List of classes in **Figure 7.12**.
C++ classes	C++ standard interfaces (`std:allocator`).	List of classes in **Figure 7.14**.
Performance optimization tweaks	Ways to tweak performance (across any manner of usage) to meet particular needs, including use of large pages. Useful when optimizing for the ultimate in performance.	Functional interfaces and an environment variable listed in **Figure 7.18**.

Figure 7-1. *Ways to use the TBB scalable memory allocator*

Scalable Memory Allocation: What

This chapter is organized to discuss the scalable memory capabilities of TBB in four categories as listed in Figure 7-1. Features from all four categories can be freely mixed; we break them into categories only as a way to explain all the functionality. The C/C++ proxy library is by far the most popular way to use the scalable memory allocator.

The scalable memory allocator is cleanly separate from the rest of TBB so that our choice of memory allocator for concurrent usage is independent of our choice of parallel algorithm and container templates.

Scalable Memory Allocation: Why

While most of this book shows us how to improve our programs speed by doing work in parallel, memory allocations and deallocations that are not thread-aware can undo our hard work! There are two primary issues at play in making careful memory allocation critical in a parallel program: contention for the allocator and cache effects.

When ordinary, nonthreaded allocators are used, memory allocation can become a serious bottleneck in a multithreaded program because each thread competes for a global lock for each allocation and deallocation of memory from a single global heap. Programs that run this way are not scalable. In fact, because of this contention, programs that make intensive use of memory allocation may actually slow down as the number of processor cores increases! Scalable memory allocators solve this by using more sophisticated data structures to largely avoid contention.

The other issue, caching effects, happens because the use of memory has an underlying mechanism in hardware for the caching of data. Data usage in a program will therefore have an implication on where data needs to be cached. If we allocate memory for thread B and the allocator gives us memory that was recently freed by thread A, it is highly likely that we are inadvertently causing data to be copied from cache to cache, which may reduce the performance of our application needlessly. Additionally, if memory allocations for separate threads are placed too closely together they can share a cache line. We can describe this sharing as *true sharing* (sharing the same object) or *false sharing* (no objects are shared, but objects happen to fall in the same cache line). Either type of sharing can have particularly dramatic negative consequences on performance, but *false sharing* is of particular interest because it can be avoided since no sharing was intended. Scalable memory allocators avoid false sharing by using class `cache_aligned_allocator<T>` to always allocate beginning on a cache line and maintaining per-thread heaps, which are rebalanced from time to time if needed. This organization also helps with the prior contention issue.

The benefits of using a scalable memory allocator can easily be a 20-30% performance, and we have even heard of 4X program performance in extreme cases by simply relinking with a scalable memory allocator.

Avoiding False Sharing with Padding

Padding is needed if the internals of a data structure cause issues due to false sharing. Starting in Chapter 5, we have used a histogram example. The buckets of the histogram and the locks for the buckets are both possible data structures which are packed tightly enough in memory to have more than one task updating data in a single cache line.

The idea of padding, in a data structure, is to space out elements enough that we do not share adjacent elements that would be updated via multiple tasks.

Regarding false sharing, the first measure we have to take is to rely on the `tbb::cache_aligned_allocator`, instead of `std::allocator` or `malloc`, when declaring the shared histogram (see Figure 5-20) as shown in Figure 7-2.

```
std::vector<tbb::atomic<int>,
   tbb::cache_aligned_allocator<tbb::atomic<int>>> hist_p(num_bins);
```

Figure 7-2. *Simple histogram vector of atomics*

However, this is just aligning the beginning of the histogram vector and ensuring that hist_p[0] will land at the beginning of a cache line. This means that hist_p[0], hist_p[1], ... , hist_p[15] are stored in the same cache line, which translates into false sharing when a thread increments hist_p[0] and another thread increments hist_p[15]. To solve this issue, we need to assure that each position of the histogram, each bin, is occupying a full cache line, which can be achieved using a padding strategy shown in Figure 7-3.

```
struct bin {    // sizeof(bin) = 64 bytes (cache line size)
  tbb::atomic<int> count;  // 4 bytes
  uint32_t padding[15];    // 60 bytes
};
std::vector<bin, tbb::cache_aligned_allocator<bin>> hist_p(num_bins);
for (size_t i = r.begin(); i < r.end(); ++i)
  hist_p[image[i]].count++;
```

Figure 7-3. *Getting rid of false sharing using padding in the histogram vector of atomics*

As we can see in Figure 7-3, the array of bins, hist_p, is now a vector of structs, each one containing the atomic variable, but also a dummy array of 60 bytes that will fill the space of a cache line. This code is, therefore, architecture dependent. In nowadays Intel processors, the cache line is 64 bytes, but you can find false sharing safe implementations that assume 128 bytes. This is because cache prefetching (caching line "i+1" when cache line "i" is requested) is a common technique, and this prefetching is somehow equivalent to cache lines of size 128 bytes.

Our false-sharing-free data structure does occupy 16 times more space than the original one. It is yet another example of the space-time trade-off that frequently arises in computer programming: now we occupy more memory, but the code is faster. Other examples are smaller code vs. loop unrolling, calling functions vs. function inlining, or processing of compressed data vs. uncompressed data.

Wait! was not the previous implementation of the bin struct a bit pedestrian? Well, it certainly was! A less hardwired solution would be this one:

```
struct bin {    // sizeof(bin) = 64 bytes (cache line size)
  tbb::atomic<int> count;            // 4 bytes
  uint8_t padding[64-sizeof(count)]; // 60 bytes
};
```

Since sizeof() is evaluated at compile time, we can use the same struct for other padded data structures in which the actual payload (count in this case) has a different size. But we know a better solution that is available in the C++ standard:

```
struct bin {      // sizeof(bin) = 64 bytes (cache line size)
  alignas(64) tbb::atomic<int> count;
};
std::vector<bin, tbb::cache_aligned_allocator<bin>>
    hist_p(num_bins);
```

This warrants that each bin of hist_p is occupying a full cache line thanks to the alignas() method. Just one more thing! We love to write portable code, right? What if in a different or future architecture cache line size is different. No problem, the C++17 standard has the solution we are looking for:

```
struct bin {  // sizeof(bin) = cache line (implement. defined)
  // available starting in C++17
  alignas(std::hardware_destructive_interference_size)
      tbb::atomic<int> count;
};
```

Great, assuming that we have fixed the *false sharing* problem, what about the true sharing one?

Two different threads will eventually increment the same bin, which will be ping-pong from one cache to other. We need a better idea to solve this one! We showed how to deal with this in Chapter 5 when we discussed *privatization and reduction*.

Scalable Memory Allocation Alternatives: Which

These days, TBB is not the only option for scalable memory allocations. While we are very fond of it, we will introduce the most popular options in this section. When using TBB for parallel programming, it is essential that we use a scalable memory allocator whether it is the one supplied by TBB or another. Programs written using TBB can utilize any memory allocator solution.

TBB was the first popular parallel programming method to promote scalable memory allocation alongside the other parallel programming techniques because the creators of TBB understood the importance of including memory allocation considerations in any parallel program. The TBB memory allocator remains extremely popular today and is definitely still one of the best scalable memory allocators available.

The TBB scalable memory allocator can be used regardless of whether we use any other part of Threading Building Blocks (TBB). Likewise, TBB can operate with any scalable memory allocator.

The most popular alternatives to the TBB scalable memory allocator are `jemalloc` and `tcmalloc`. Like the scalable memory allocator in TBB, there are alternatives to `malloc` that emphasize fragmentation avoidance while offering scalable concurrency support. All three are available open source with liberal licensing (BSD or Apache).

There are some people who will tell you that they have compared `tbbmalloc` for their application with `tcmalloc` and `jeamalloc` and have found it to be superior for their application. This is very common. However, there are some people who choose `jemalloc` or `tcmalloc` or `llalloc` even when using the rest of TBB extensively. This works too. The choice is yours to make.

`jemalloc` is the FreeBSD `libc` allocator. More recently, additional developer support features such as heap profiling and extensive monitoring/tuning hooks have been added. `jemalloc` is used by Facebook.

`tcmalloc` is part of Google's `gperftools`, which includes `tcmalloc` and some performance analysis tools. `tcmalloc` is used by Google.

`llalloc` from Lockless Inc. is available freely as an open-source lockless memory allocator or can be purchased for use with closed-source software.

The behavior of individual applications, and in particular patterns of memory allocations and releases, make it impossible to pick a single fits-all winner from these options. We are confident that any choice of `TBBmalloc, jemalloc, and tcmalloc` will be far superior to a default `malloc` function or `new` operator if they are of the nonscalable variety (FreeBSD uses `jemalloc` as its default malloc).

Compilation Considerations

When compiling with programs with the Intel compilers or gcc, it is best to pass in the following flags:

> -fno-builtin-malloc (on Windows: /Qfno-builtin-malloc)
>
> -fno-builtin-calloc (on Windows: /Qfno-builtin-calloc)
>
> -fno-builtin-realloc (on Windows: /Qfno-builtin-realloc)
>
> -fno-builtin-free (on Windows: /Qfno-builtin-free)

This is because a compiler may make some optimizations assuming it is using its own built-in functions. These assumptions may not be true when using other memory allocators. Failure to use these flags may not cause a problem, but it is not a bad idea to be safe. It might be wise to check the compiler documentation of your favorite compiler.

Most Popular Usage (C/C++ Proxy Library): How

Using the proxy methods, we can globally replace new/delete and malloc/calloc/realloc/free/etc. routines with a dynamic memory interface replacement technique. This automatic way to replace malloc and other C/C++ functions for dynamic memory allocation is by far the most popular way to use the TBB scalable memory allocator capabilities. It is also very effective.

We can replace malloc/calloc/realloc/free/ etc. (see Figure 7-4 for a complete list) and new/delete by using the tbbmalloc_proxy library. Using this method is easy and sufficient for most programs. The details of the mechanism used on each operating system vary a bit, but the net effect is the same everywhere. The library names are shown in Figure 7-5; a summary of the methods is shown in Figure 7-6.

	Linux	macOS	Windows
Replaceable global C++ operators `new` and `delete`	YES	YES	YES
Standard C library functions: `malloc, calloc, realloc, free`	YES	YES	YES
Standard C library functions (added in C11): `aligned_alloc`	YES		
Standard POSIX* function: `posix_memalign`	YES	YES	
Depending on the platform, other functions are also replaced (a list, current as of publication, follows below – any additions/changes will be in the TBB Developer Guide)			

GNU C library (glibc) specific functions:
`malloc_usable_size, __libc_malloc,`
`__libc_calloc, __libc_memalign, __libc_free,`
`__libc_realloc, __libc_pvalloc, __libc_valloc`
	YES		

Microsoft* C run-time library functions:
`_msize, _aligned_malloc, _aligned_realloc,`
`_aligned_free, _aligned_msize`
			YES

`valloc`			
`malloc_size`		YES	
`memalign, pvalloc, mallopt`	YES		

Figure 7-4. *List of routines replaced by proxy*

	Release version library	**Debug version library**
Linux	`libtbbmalloc_proxy.so.2`	`libtbbmalloc_proxy_debug.so.2`
macOS	`libtbbmalloc_proxy.dylib`	`libtbbmalloc_proxy_debug.dylib`
Windows	`tbbmalloc_proxy.dll`	`tbbmalloc_proxy_debug.dll`

Figure 7-5. *Names of the proxy library*

	Injection "by proxy"
Linux	`LD_PRELOAD` (**Figure 7.7**)
macOS	`DYLD_INSERT_LIBRARIES` (**Figure 7.7**)
Windows	See **Figure 7.8**

Figure 7-6. *Ways to use the proxy library*

Linux: malloc/new Proxy Library Usage

On Linux, we can do the replacement either by loading the proxy library at program load time using the LD_PRELOAD environment variable (without changing the executable file, as shown in Figure 7-7), or by linking the main executable file with the proxy library (-ltbbmalloc_proxy). The Linux program loader must be able to find the proxy library and the scalable memory allocator library at program load time. For that, we may include the directory containing the libraries in the LD_LIBRARY_PATH environment variable or add it to /etc/ld.so.conf. There are two limitations for dynamic memory replacement: (1) glibc memory allocation hooks, such as __malloc_hook, are not supported, and (2) Mono (an open source implementation of Microsoft's .NET Framework based) is not supported.

macOS: malloc/new Proxy Library Usage

On macOS, we can do the replacement either by loading the proxy library at program load time using the DYLD_INSERT_LIBRARIES environment variable (without changing the executable file, as shown in Figure 7-7), or by linking the main executable file with the proxy library (-ltbbmalloc_proxy). The macOS program loader must be able to find the proxy library and the scalable memory allocator library at program load time. For that, we may include the directory containing the libraries in the DYLD_LIBRARY_PATH environment variable.

```
# On Linux:
export LD_PRELOAD=libtbbmalloc_proxy.so.2

# On macOS:
export DYLD_INSERT_LIBRARIES=$TBBROOT/lib/libtbbmalloc_proxy.dylib

# There is no simple "DLL injection" on Windows, although
# there is a Wikipedia article "DLL injection" discussing
# more complicated ways to inject a DLL.  We recommend using
# the methods we outline in Figure 7.8 instead.
```

Figure 7-7. *Environment variables to inject the TBB scalable memory allocator*

Implementation insight for the curious (not required reading): TBB has a clever way of overcoming the fact that using DYLD_INSERT_LIBRARIES requires using flat namespaces in order to access the shared library symbols. Normally, if an application was built with two-level namespaces, this method would not work, and forcing usage of flat namespaces would likely lead to a crash. TBB avoids this by arranging things such that when the libtbbmalloc_proxy library is loaded into the process; its static constructor is called and registers a *malloc zone* for TBB memory allocation routines. This allows redirecting memory allocation routine calls from a standard C++ library into TBB scalable allocator routines. This means that the application does not need to use TBB malloc library symbols; it continues to call standard libc routines. Thus, there are no problems with namespaces. The macOS *malloc zones* mechanism also allows applications to have several memory allocators (e.g., used by different libraries) and manage memory correctly. This guarantees that Intel TBB will use the same allocator for allocations and deallocations. It is a safeguard against crashes due to calling a deallocation routine for a memory object allocated from another allocator.

Windows: malloc/new Proxy Library Usage

On Windows, we must modify our executable. We can either force the proxy library to be loaded by adding an #include in our source code, or use certain linker options as shown in Figure 7-8. The Windows program loader must be able to find the proxy library and the scalable memory allocator library at program load time. For that, we may include the directory containing the libraries in the PATH environment variable.

Including tbbmalloc_proxy.h> to a source of any binary (which is loaded during application startup):

```
#include <tbb/tbbmalloc_proxy.h>
```

or add the following parameters to the linker options for the binary (which is loaded during application startup). They can be specified for the EXE file or a DLL that is loaded upon application startup:

> *For win32:*
>   `tbbmalloc_proxy.lib /INCLUDE:"___TBB_malloc_proxy"`
> *For win64:*
>   `tbbmalloc_proxy.lib /INCLUDE:"__TBB_malloc_proxy"`

Figure 7-8. *Ways to use the proxy library on Windows (note: win32 has an additional underscore vs. win64)*

Testing our Proxy Library Usage

As a simple double check to see that our program is taking advantage of a faster allocation, we can use the test program in Figure 7-9 on a multicore machine. In Figure 7-10, we show how we run this little test and the timing differences we saw on a quadcore virtual machine running Ubuntu Linux. In Figure 7-11, we show how we run this little test and the timing difference we saw on a quadcore iMac. On Windows, using the Visual Studio "Performance Profiler" on a quadcore Intel NUC (Core i7) we saw times of 94ms without the scalable memory allocator and 50ms with it (adding `#include <tbb/tbbmalloc_proxy.h>` into `tbb_mem.cpp`). All these runs show how this little test can verify that the injection of the scalable memory allocator is working (for `new`/`delete`) and yielding nontrivial performance boosts! A trivial change to use `malloc()` and `free()` instead shows similar results. We include it as `tbb_malloc.cpp` in the sample programs download associated with this book.

The example programs do use a lot of stack space, so "`ulimit -s unlimited`" (Linux/macOS) or "`/STACK:10000000`" (Visual Studio: Properties > Configuration Properties > Linker > System > Stack Reserve Size) will be important to avoid immediate crashes.

```
#include <cstdio>
#include <tbb/tbb.h>

const int N = 1000000;
double *a[N];

int main() {
  tbb::parallel_for( 0, N-1, [&](int i) { a[i] = new double; } );
  tbb::parallel_for( 0, N-1, [&](int i) { delete a[i];        } );
  return 0;
}
```

Figure 7-9. *Small test program (tbb_mem.cpp) for speed of new/delete*

```
% g++ -o tbb_mem tbb_mem.cpp -std=c++11 -ltbb -O3
% time ./tbb_mem

real    0m0.160s
user    0m0.072s
sys     0m0.048s
%
% export LD_PRELOAD=$TBBROOT/lib/libtbbmalloc_proxy.so.2
or alternativelly
% g++ -o tbb_mem tbb_mem.cpp -std=c++11 -ltbb -O3 -ltbbmalloc_proxy
% time ./tbb_mem

real    0m0.043s
user    0m0.048s
sys     0m0.028s
```

Figure 7-10. *Running and timing tbb_mem.cpp on a quadcore virtual Linux machine*

```
% time ./tbb_mem

real    0m0.046s
user    0m0.078s
sys     0m0.053s
%
% export DYLD_INSERT_LIBRARIES=$TBBROOT/lib/libtbbmalloc_proxy.dylib
%
% time ./tbb_mem

real    0m0.019s
user    0m0.032s
sys     0m0.009s
```

Figure 7-11. *Running and timing tbb_mem.cpp on a quadcore iMac (macOS)*

Family 1	`void *scalable_malloc (size_t size)`	`malloc` analogue.
	`void scalable_free (void *ptr)`	`free` analogue.
	`void *scalable_realloc (void *ptr, size_t size)`	`realloc` analogue.
	`void *scalable_calloc (size_t nobj, size_t size)`	`calloc` analogue complementing `scalable_malloc`.
	`int scalable_posix_memalign (void **memptr, size_t alignment, size_t size)`	`posix_memalign` analogue.
Family 2	`void *scalable_aligned_malloc (size_t size, size_t alignment)`	`posix_memalign` analogue.
	`void *scalable_aligned_realloc (void *ptr, size_t size, size_t alignment)`	`realloc` analogue complementing `scalable_malloc`
	`void scalable_aligned_free (void *ptr)`	`free` analogue for a previously allocated by `scalable_aligned_malloc` or `scalable_aligned_remalloc`
All Families	`size_t scalable_msize (void *ptr)`	`msize/malloc_size/malloc_usable_size` analogue. Returns the usable size of a memory block previously allocated by `scalable_x`, or 0 (zero) if ptr does not point to such a block.
	`int scalable_allocation_mode (int param, intptr_t value)`	Set TBB allocator-specific allocation modes. *Discussed in a section titled "Performance Tuning: some control knobs" near the end of this chapter.*
	`int scalable_allocation_command (int cmd, void *param)`	Call TBB allocator-specific commands. *Discussed in a section titled "Performance Tuning: some control knobs" near the end of this chapter.*

Figure 7-12. *Functions offered by the TBB scalable memory allocator*

C Functions: Scalable Memory Allocators for C

A set of functions, listed in Figure 7-12, provide a C level interface to the scalable memory allocator. Since TBB programming uses C++, these interfaces are not here for TBB users – they are here for use with C code.

Each allocation routine `scalable_x` behaves analogously to a library function x. The routines form the two families shown in the Figure 7-13. Storage allocated by a `scalable_x` function in one family must be freed or resized by a `scalable_x` function in the same family, and not by a C standard library function. Similarly, any storage allocated by a C standard library function, or C++ `new`, should not be freed or resized by a `scalable_x` function.

These functions are defined by the specific `#include <tbb/scalable_allocator.h>`".

Family	Allocation Routine	Deallocation Routine	Analogous Library

1	`scalable_malloc`
	`scalable_calloc`
	`scalable_realloc`
		`scalable_free`	C standard library

	`scalable_posix_memalign`		POSIX
2	`scalable_aligned_malloc` `scalable_aligned_realloc`	`scalable_aligned_free`	Microsoft C run-time

Figure 7-13. *Coupling of allocate-deallocate functions by families*

`tbb::aligned_space< T, N >`	Block of space aligned sufficiently large to construct an array T with N elements of type T. The elements are not constructed or destroyed by this class. Somewhat analogous, but not semantically compatible, with the C++ `aligned_storage` class.
`tbb::cache_aligned_allocator< T >`	Scalable memory allocation, aligned to begin on a cache line. Helps avoid false sharing, but alignment can come at some cost in additional memory consumption.
`tbb::memory_pool_allocator< T, P >`	The class is mainly intended to enable memory pools within STL containers. This is a "preview" feature as we write this book (likely to promote to a regular feature in the future). Use `#define` `TBB_PREVIEW_MEMORY_POOL 1` to enable.
`tbb::scalable_allocator< T >`	Scalable memory allocation. Calling this directly will fail if the TBBmalloc library is not available.
`tbb::tbb_allocator< T >`	The class selects `tbb::scalable_allocator` when available, and falls back on standard `malloc` when the TBBmalloc library is not available. Calling this will work even if the TBBmalloc library is not available.
`tbb::zero_allocator< T [ , Allocator ] >`	Forwards allocation requests to `Allocator` (defaults to `tbb_allocator`) and zeros the allocation before returning it.

Figure 7-14. *Classes offered by the TBB scalable memory allocator*

C++ Classes: Scalable Memory Allocators for C++

While the proxy library offers a blanket solution to adopting scalable memory allocation, it is all based on specific capabilities that we might choose to use directly. TBB offers C++ classes for allocation in three ways: (1) allocators with the signatures needed by the C++ STL `std::allocator<T>`, (2) memory pool support for STL containers, and (3) a specific allocator for aligned arrays.

Allocators with std::allocator<T> Signature

A set of classes, listed in Figure 7-14, provide a C++ level interface to the scalable memory allocator. TBB has four template classes (tbb_allocator, cached_aligned_ allocator, zero_allocator, and scalable_allocator) that support the same signatures as std::allocator<T> per the C++ standards. This includes supporting <void> in addition to <T>, per the C++11 and prior standards, which is deprecated in C++17 and will likely be removed in C++20. This means they can be passed as allocation routines to be used by STL templates such as vector. All four classes model an allocator concept that meets all the "Allocator requirements" of C++, but with additional guarantees required by the Standard for use with ISO C++ containers.

scalable_allocator

The scalable_allocator template allocates and frees memory in a way that scales with the number of processors. Using a scalable_allocator in place of std::allocator may improve program performance. Memory allocated by a scalable_allocator should be freed by a scalable_allocator, not by a std::allocator.

The scalable_allocator allocator template requires that the TBBmalloc library be available. If the library is missing, calls to the scalable_allocator template will fail. In contrast, if the memory allocator library is not available, the other allocators (tbb_allocator, cached_aligned_allocator, or zero_allocator) fall back on malloc and free.

This class is defined with #include <tbb/scalable_allocator.h> and is notably **not** included by the (usually) all-inclusive tbb/tbb.h.

tbb_allocator

The tbb_allocator template allocates and frees memory via the TBBmalloc library if it is available; otherwise, it reverts to using malloc and free. The cache_alligned_ allocator and zero_allocator use tbb_allocator; therefore, they offer the same fall back on malloc, but scalable_allocator does not and therefore will fail if the TBBmalloc library is unavailable. This class is defined with #include <tbb/tbb_ allocator.h>

zero_allocator

The zero_allocator allocates zeroed memory. A zero_allocator<T,A> can be instantiated for any class A that models the Allocator concept. The default for A is tbb_allocator. The zero_allocator forwards allocation requests to A and zeros the allocation before returning it. This class is defined with #include <tbb/tbb_allocator.h>.

cached_aligned_allocator

The cached_aligned_allocator template offers both scalability and protection against false sharing. It addresses false sharing by making sure each allocation is done on a separate cache line.

Use cache_aligned_allocator only if false sharing is likely to be a real problem (see Figure 7-2). The functionality of cache_aligned_allocator comes at some cost in space because it allocates in multiples of cache-line-size memory chunks, even for a small object. The padding is typically 128 bytes. Hence, allocating many small objects with cache_aligned_allocator may increase memory usage.

Trying both tbb_allocator and the cache_aligned_allocator and measuring the resulting performance for a particular application is a good idea.

Note that protection against false sharing between two objects is guaranteed only if both are allocated with cache_aligned_allocator. For instance, if one object is allocated by cache_aligned_allocator<T> and another object is allocated some other way, there is no guarantee against false sharing because cache_aligned_allocator<T> starts an allocation on a cache line boundary but does not necessarily allocate to the end of a cache line. If an array or structure is being allocated, since only the start of the allocation is aligned, the individual array or structure elements may land together on cache lines with other elements. An example of this, along with padding to force elements onto individual cache line, is show in Figure 7-3.

This class is defined with #include <tbb/cache_alligned_allocator.h>.

Memory Pool Support: memory_pool_allocator

Pool allocators are an extremely efficient method for providing allocation of numerous objects of fixed size P. Our first allocator usage is special and asks to reserve enough memory to store T objects of size P. Thereafter, when the allocator is used to provide a chunk of memory, it returns an offset mod *P* into the allocated chunk. This is far more efficient than calling operator new separately for each request because it avoids the bookkeeping overhead required of a general-purpose memory allocator that services numerous requests for different-sized allocations.

The class is mainly intended to enable memory pools within STL containers. This is a "preview" feature as we write this book (likely to promote to a regular feature in the future). Use #define TBB_PREVIEW_MEMORY_POOL 1 to enable while this is still a preview feature.

Support is provided by tbb::memory_pool_allocator and tbb:: memory_pool_allocator. These require

```
#define TBB_PREVIEW_MEMORY_POOL 1
#include <tbb/memory_pool.h>
```

Array Allocation Support: aligned_space

This template class (aligned_space) occupies enough memory and is sufficiently aligned to hold an array *T[N]*. Elements are not constructed or destroyed by this class; the client is responsible for initializing or destroying the objects. An aligned_space is typically used as a local variable or field in scenarios where a block of fixed-length uninitialized memory is needed. This class is defined with #include <tbb/aligned_space.h>.

Replacing new and delete Selectively

There are a number of reasons one might develop custom new/delete operators, including error checking, debugging, optimization, and usage statistics gathering.

We can think of new/delete as coming in variations for individual objects and for arrays of objects. Additionally, C++11 defines throwing, nonthrowing, and placement versions of each of these: either the global set (::operator new, ::operator new[], ::operator delete and ::operator delete[]) or the class specific sets (for class X, we have X::operator new, X::operator new[], X::operator delete and X::operator delete[]). Finally, C++17 adds an optional alignment parameter to all versions of new.

If we want to globally replace all the new/delete operators and do not have any custom needs, we would use the proxy library. This also has the benefit of replacing malloc/free and related C functions.

For custom needs, it is most common to overload the class-specific operators rather than the global operators. This section shows how to replace the global new/delete operators as an example which can be customized for particular needs. We show throwing and nonthrowing versions, but we did not override the placement versions since they do not actually allocate memory. We also did not implement versions with alignment (C++17) parameters. It is also possible to replace new/delete operators for individual classes using the same concepts, in which case you may choose to implement placement versions and alignment capabilities. All these are handled by TBB if the proxy library is used.

Figures 7-15 and 7-16 together show a method to replace new and delete, and Figure 7-17 demonstrates their usage. All versions of new and delete should be replaced at once, which amounts to four versions of new and four versions of delete. Of course, it is necessary to link with the scalable memory library.

Our example chooses to ignore any new handler because there are thread-safety issues, and it always throws std::bad_alloc(). The variation of the basic signature includes the additional parameter const std::nothrow_t& that means that this operator will not throw an exception but will return NULL if the allocation fails. These four nonthrowing exception operators can be used for C runtime libraries.

We do not have to initialize the task scheduler to be able to use the memory allocator. We do initialize it in this example because it uses parallel_for in order to demonstrate the use of memory allocation and deallocation in multiple tasks. Similarly, the only header file that is required for the memory allocator is tbb/tbb_allocator.h.

```
#include <tbb/parallel_for.h>
#include <tbb/tbb_allocator.h>

// No retry loop because we assume that
// scalable_malloc does all it takes to allocate
// the memory, so calling it repeatedly
// will not improve the situation at all
//
// No use of std::new_handler because it cannot be
// done in portable and thread-safe way
//
// We throw std::bad_alloc() when scalable_malloc
// returns NULL (we return NULL if it is a no-throw
// implementation)

void* operator new (size_t size) throw (std::bad_alloc)
{
    if (size == 0) size = 1;
    if (void* ptr = scalable_malloc (size))
        return ptr;
    throw std::bad_alloc (  );
}

void* operator new[] (size_t size) throw (std::bad_alloc)
{
    return operator new (size);
}

void* operator new (size_t size, const std::nothrow_t&) throw ()
{
    if (size == 0) size = 1;
    if (void* ptr = scalable_malloc (size))
        return ptr;
    return NULL;
}

void* operator new[] (size_t size, const std::nothrow_t&) throw ()
{
    return operator new (size, std::nothrow);
}
```

Figure 7-15. *Demonstration of replacement of new operators (tbb_nd.cpp)*

```
void operator delete (void* ptr) throw ()
{
    if (ptr != 0) scalable_free (ptr);
}

void operator delete[] (void* ptr) throw ()
{
    operator delete (ptr);
}

void operator delete (void* ptr, const std::nothrow_t&) throw ()
{
    if (ptr != 0) scalable_free (ptr);
}

void operator delete[] (void* ptr, const std::nothrow_t&) throw ()
{
    operator delete (ptr, std::nothrow);
}
```

Figure 7-16. *Continuation from the previous figure, replacement of delete operators*

```
int main (int argc, char** argv)
{
  const size_t size = 1000;
  const size_t chunk = 100;

  // scalable_malloc will be called to allocate
  // the memory for this array of integers
  int *p = new int[size];

  tbb::parallel_for (size_t{0}, size, [=](size_t chunk)
                     {
                       // scalable_malloc will be called
                       // to allocate the memory
                       // for this array of integers
                       int *p = new int [chunk];

                       // scalable_free will be called to
                       // deallocate the memory
                       // for this array of integers
                       delete[] p;
                     } );

  return 0;
}
```

Figure 7-17. *Driver program to demonstrate the new/delete replacements*

Performance Tuning: Some Control Knobs

TBB offers some special controls regarding allocations from the OS, huge page support, and flushing of internal buffers. Each of these is provided to fine-tune performance.

Huge pages (*large pages* on Windows) are used to improve the performance for programs that utilize a very large amount of memory. In order to use huge pages, we need a processor with support, an operating system with support, and then we need to do something so our application takes advantage of huge pages. Fortunately, most systems have all this available, and TBB includes support.

What Are Huge Pages?

In most cases, a processor allocates memory 4K bytes at a time in what are commonly called pages. Virtual memory systems use page tables to map addresses to actual memory locations. Without diving in too deep, suffice to say that the more pages of memory that an application uses, the more page descriptors are needed, and having a lot of page descriptors flying around causes performance issues for a variety of reasons. To help with this issue, modern processors support additional page sizes that are much larger than 4K (e.g., 4 MB). For a program using 2 GB of memory, 524,288 page descriptions are needed to describe the 2 GB of memory with 4K pages. Only 512 page descriptions are needed using 4 MB descriptors and only two if 1 GB descriptors are available.

TBB Support for Huge Pages

To use huge pages with TBB memory allocation, it should be explicitly enabled by calling `scalable_allocation_mode( TBBMALLOC_USE_HUGE_PAGES,1)`, or by setting the `TBB_MALLOC_USE_HUGE_PAGES` environment variable to 1. The environment variable is useful when substituting the standard malloc routines with the `tbbmalloc_proxy` library.

These provide ways to tweak the algorithms used for all usages of the TBB scalable memory allocator (regardless of the method of usage: proxy library, C functions, or C++ classes). The functions take precedence over any environment variable settings. These are definitely not for casual use, they are here for self-proclaimed "control freaks" and offer great ways to optimize performance for particular needs. We recommend careful evaluation of the performance impact on an application, in the target environment, when using these features.

Of course, both methods assume that the system/kernel is configured to allocate huge pages. The TBB memory allocator also supports pre-allocated and transparent huge pages, which are automatically allocated by the Linux kernel when suitable. Huge pages are not a panacea; they can have negative impact on performance if their usage is not well considered.

The functions, as listed in Figure 7-18, are defined with `#include <tbb/tbb_allocator.h>`.

`int scalable_allocation_mode (int mode, intptr_t value)`
 `mode =`
 `TBBMALLOC_USE_HUGE_PAGES` or
 `TBBMALLOC_SET_SOFT_HEAP_LIMIT`
	Set TBB allocator-specific allocation modes.

Environment variable: `TBB_MALLOC_USE_HUGE_PAGES`	A value of "1" (one) will enable the use of huge pages by the allocator if supported by the operating system.
`int scalable_allocation_command (int cmd, void *reserved)` `reserved` should be `zero`	Call TBB allocator-specific commands.

Figure 7-18. *Ways to refine TBB scalable memory allocator behaviors*

scalable_allocation_mode(int mode, intptr_t value)

The `scalable_allocation_mode` function may be used to adjust the behavior of the scalable memory allocator. The arguments, described in the following two paragraphs, control aspects of behavior of the TBB allocators. The function returns `TBBMALLOC_OK` if the operation succeeded, `TBBMALLOC_INVALID_PARAM` if mode is not one of those described in the following subsections, or if value is not valid for the given mode. A return value of `TBBMALLOC_NO_EFFECT` is possible for conditions described when they apply (see explanation of each function).

TBBMALLOC_USE_HUGE_PAGES

`scalable_allocation_mode(TBBMALLOC_USE_HUGE_PAGES,1)`

This function enables the use of huge pages by the allocator if supported by the operating system; a zero as the second parameter disables it. Setting the TBB_MALLOC_USE_HUGE_PAGES environment variable to one has the same effect as calling `scalable_allocation_mode` to enable this mode. The mode set with `scalable_allocation_mode` takes priority over the environment variable. The function will return TBBMALLOC_NO_ EFFECT if huge pages are not supported on the platform.

TBBMALLOC_SET_SOFT_HEAP_LIMIT

scalable_allocation_mode(TBBMALLOC_SET_SOFT_HEAP_LIMIT, size)

This function sets a threshold of size bytes on the amount of memory the allocator takes from the operating systems. Exceeding the threshold will urge the allocator to release memory from its internal buffers; however, it does not prevent the TBB scalable memory allocator from requesting more memory when needed.

int scalable_allocation_command(int cmd, void ∗param)

The scalable_allocation_command function may be used to command the scalable memory allocator to perform an action specified by the first parameter. The second parameter is reserved and must be set to zero. The function will return TBBMALLOC_OK if the operation succeeded, TBBMALLOC_INVALID_PARAM if reserved is not equal to zero, or if cmd is not a defined command (TBBMALLOC_CLEAN_ALL_BUFFERS or TBBMALLOC_CLEAN_ THREAD_BUFFERS). A return value of TBBMALLOC_NO_EFFECT is possible as we describe next.

TBBMALLOC_CLEAN_ALL_BUFFERS

scalable_allocation_command(TBBMALLOC_CLEAN_ALL_BUFFERS, 0)

This function cleans internal memory buffers of the allocator and possibly reduces memory footprint. It may result in increased time for subsequent memory allocation requests. The command is not designed for frequent use, and careful evaluation of the performance impact is recommended. The function will return TBBMALLOC_NO_EFFECT if no buffers were released.

TBBMALLOC_CLEAN_THREAD_BUFFERS

scalable_allocation_command(TBBMALLOC_CLEAN_THREAD_BUFFERS, 0)

This function cleans internal memory buffers but only for the calling thread. It may result in increased time for subsequent memory allocation requests; careful evaluation of the performance impact is recommended. The function will return `TBBMALLOC_NO_EFFECT` if no buffers were released.

Summary

Using a scalable memory allocator is an essential element in any parallel program. The performance benefits can be very significant. Without a scalable memory allocator, serious performance issues often arise due to contention for allocation, false sharing, and other useless cache to cache transfers. The TBB scalable memory allocation (`TBBmalloc`) capabilities include use of `new` as well as explicit calls to `malloc`, and so on, all of which can be used directly or they can all be automatically replaced via the proxy library capability of TBB. The scalable memory allocation in TBB can be used regardless of whether we use any other part of TBB; the rest of TBB can be used regardless of which memory allocator is used (`TBBmalloc, tcmalloc, jemalloc, malloc`, etc.). The `TBBmalloc` library remains extremely popular today and is definitely one of the best scalable memory allocators available.

## CHAPTER 8

Mapping Parallel Patterns to TBB

It has been said that history does not repeat, it rhymes.

It could be said that software rhymes as well. While we may not write the same code over and over, there are patterns that emerge in the problems we solve and the code we write. We can learn from similar solutions.

This chapter takes a look at patterns that have proven to be effective in solving problems in a scalable manner, and we connect them with how to implement them using TBB (Figure 8-1). In order to achieve scalable parallelization, we should focus on data parallelism; data parallelism is the best overall strategy for scalable parallelism. Our coding needs to encourage the subdivision of any task into multiple tasks, with the number of tasks able to grow with the overall problem size; an abundance of tasks enables better scaling. Assisted best by the patterns we promote in this chapter, coding to provide an abundance of tasks helps us achieve scalability in our algorithms.

We can learn to "Think Parallel" by seeing how others have done it effectively already. Of course, we can stand on the shoulders of giants and reach ever further.

This chapter is about learning from prior experiences of parallel programmers, and in the course of doing that, learning better how to use TBB. We talk in terms of patterns as inspiration and useful tools for "Thinking Parallel." We do not describe patterns to form a perfect taxonomy of programming.

Parallel Patterns vs. Parallel Algorithms

As we mentioned in Chapter 2, it has been suggested to us by reviewers of this book that "TBB parallel algorithms" should be referred to as *patterns* instead of algorithms. That may be true, but in order to align with the terminology that the TBB library has

© Intel Corporation 2019
M. Voss, R. Asenjo, J. Reinders, *Pro TBB*, https://doi.org/10.1007/978-1-4842-4398-5_8

been using for many years, we refer to these features as generic parallel *algorithms* throughout this book and in the TBB documentation. The effect is the same – they offer the opportunity for us to benefit from the experience of those who have explored optimal solutions to these patterns before us – not only to *use* them, but to be encouraged to prefer using these particular patterns (algorithms) over other possible approaches because they tend work best (achieve better scaling).

Pattern Concept	Pattern Name	TBB Template
Powerful boost to all patterns: The ability to nest without restriction patterns within patterns.	**nesting**	*all of TBB*
Best pattern to use: Division of work into uniform independent tasks.	**map**	`parallel_for,` `parallel_invoke`
Generalization of map with incremental task addition.	**workpile** *(generalized map with incremental task addition)*	`parallel_do`
Common operation: Division of work into independent tasks to compute partials results that are reduced (combined) into a final result.	**reduce**	`parallel_reduce`
Specialized reduction capability to do a computation of a prefix computation (also known as a scan) in parallel: `y[i]=y[i-1] op x[i]`	**scan** *sometimes called "prefix"*	`parallel_scan`
Classic and powerful: Control flow splits into two flows (tasks) which eventually rejoin.	**fork-join**	`parallel_invoke,` `task_group, flow_graph`

Specialization of fork-join: divide work into subtasks recursively.	**divide-and-conquer**	`parallel_for,`
		`parallel_reduce,`
		`parallel_invoke,`
		`task_group,    flow_graph,`
		`parallel_sort`

Specialization of fork-join: divide work into subtask recursively with pruning to reduce the need for exhaustive search. Cancellation support (Chapter 15) can very valuable for implementing.	**branch-and-bound**	`parallel_for,`
		`parallel_reduce,`
		`parallel_invoke,`
		`task_group, flow_graph`
		plus controls for
		cancellation (Chapter 15)

Deceivingly powerful: Tasks connected in a producer-consumer relationship in a regular, nonchanging data flow.	**pipeline**	`parallel_pipeline,` `flow_graph`
Handles real world messy flows well: Tasks connected in a producer-consumer relationship with an irregular, and possibly changing, interaction between tasks.	**Event Based Coordination**	`flow_graph`

Figure 8-1. *TBB templates that express important "Patterns that work"*

Patterns Categorize Algorithms, Designs, etc.

The value of object-oriented programming was described by the Gang of Four (Gamma, Helm, Johnson, and Vlissides) and their landmark work *Design Patterns: Elements of Reusable Object-Oriented Software* (Addison-Wesley). Many credit that book with bringing more order to the world of object-oriented programming. Their book gathered the collective wisdom of the community and boiled it down into simple "patterns" with names, so people could talk about them.

Patterns for Parallel Programming by Mattson, Sanders, and Massingill (Addison-Wesley) has similarly collected wisdom from the parallel programming community. Experts use common tricks and have their own language to talk about techniques. With parallel patterns in mind, programmers can quickly come up to speed in parallel programming just as object-oriented programmers have done with the famous Gang-of-Four book.

Patterns for Parallel Programming is longer than this book, and very dense reading, but with some help from author Tim Mattson, we can summarize how the patterns relate to TBB.

Tim et al. propose that programmers need to work through four design spaces to develop a parallel program:

1. Finding concurrency.

   For this design space, we work within our problem domain to identify available concurrency and expose it for use in the algorithm design. TBB simplifies this effort by encouraging us to find as many tasks as we can without having to worry about how to map them to hardware threads. We also provide information on how to best make the tasks split in half when the task is considered large enough. Using this information, TBB then automatically divides large tasks repeatedly to help spread work evenly among processor cores. An abundance of tasks leads to scalability for our algorithms.

2. Algorithm structures.

   This design space embodies our high-level strategy for organizing a parallel algorithm. We need to figure out how we want to organize our workflow. Figure 8-1 lists important patterns that we can consult to guide our selection toward a pattern that best suits our needs. These "patterns that work" are the focus of *Structured Parallel Programming* by McCool, Robison, and Reinders (Elsevier).

3. Supporting structures.

    This step involves the details for turning algorithm strategy
    into actual code. We consider how the parallel program will be
    organized and the techniques used to manage shared (especially
    mutable) data. These considerations are critical and have an
    impact that reaches across the entire parallel programming
    process. TBB is well designed to encourage the right level of
    abstraction, so this design space is satisfied by using TBB well
    (something we hope we teach in this book).

4. Implementation mechanisms.

    This design space includes thread management and synchronization.
    Threading Building Blocks handles all the thread management,
    leaving us free to worry only about tasks at a higher level of design.
    When using TBB, most programmers code to avoid explicit
    synchronization coding and debugging. TBB algorithms (Chapter 2)
    and flow graph (Chapter 3) aim to minimize explicit synchronization.
    Chapter 5 discusses synchronization mechanisms for when we do
    need them, and Chapter 6 offers containers and thread local storage to
    help limit the need for explicit synchronization.

    Using a pattern language can guide the creation of better parallel
    programming environments and help us make the best use of TBB
    to write parallel software.

Patterns That Work

Armed with the language of patterns, we should regard them as tools. We emphasize
patterns that have proven useful for developing the most scalable algorithms. We
know that two prerequisites for achieving parallel scalability are good data locality and
avoidance of overhead. Fortunately, many good strategies have been developed for
achieving these objectives and are accessible using TBB (see table in Figure 8-1).
Consideration of the need to be well tuned, to real machines, details are already
provided for within TBB including issues related to the implementation of patterns such
as granularity control and good use of cache.

In these terms, TBB handles the details of implementation, so that we can program at a higher level. This is what lets code written using TBB be portable, leaving machine-specific tuning inside of TBB. TBB in turn, by virtue of algorithms such as task-stealing, helps minimize the tuning needed to port TBB. The abstraction of the algorithm strategy into semantics and implementation has proven to work extremely well in practice. The separation makes it possible to reason about the high-level algorithm design and the low-level (and often machine-specific) details separately.

Patterns provide a common vocabulary for discussing approaches to problem solving and allow reuse of best practices. Patterns transcend languages, programming models, and even computer architectures, and we can use patterns whether or not the programming system we are using explicitly supports a given pattern with a specific feature. Fortunately, TBB was designed to emphasize proven patterns that lead to well-structured, maintainable, and efficient programs. Many of these patterns are in fact also deterministic (or can be run in a deterministic mode – see Chapter 16), which means they give the same result every time they are executed. Determinism is a useful property since it leads to programs that are easier to understand, debug, test, and maintain.

Data Parallelism Wins

The best overall strategy for scalable parallelism is data parallelism. Definitions of data parallelism vary. We take a wide view and define data parallelism as any kind of parallelism that grows as the data set grows or, more generally, as the problem size grows. Typically, the data is split into chunks and each chunk processed with a separate task. Sometimes, the splitting is flat; other times, it is recursive. What matters is that bigger data sets generate more tasks.

Whether similar or different operations are applied to the chunks is irrelevant to our definition. In general, data parallelism can be applied whether a problem is regular or irregular. Because data parallelism is the best strategy for scalable parallelism, hardware support for data parallelism is commonly found in all types of hardware – CPUs, GPUs, ASIC designs, and FPGA designs. Chapter 4 discussed support for SIMD precisely to connect with such hardware support.

The opposite of data parallelism is functional decomposition (also called task parallelism), an approach that runs different program functions in parallel. At best, functional decomposition improves performance by a constant factor. For example, if a program has functions f, g, and h, running them in parallel at best triples performance, and in practice less. Sometimes functional decomposition can deliver an additional bit of parallelism required to meet a performance target, but it should not be our primary strategy, because it does not scale.

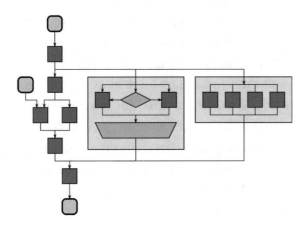

Figure 8-2. *Nesting pattern: a compositional pattern that allows other patterns to be composed in a hierarchy. Nesting is that any task block in a pattern can be replaced with a pattern with the same input and output configuration and dependencies.*

Nesting Pattern

Nesting (Figure 8-2) may seem obvious and normal, but in the parallel programming world it is not. TBB makes life simple – nesting just works, without severe oversubscription issues that other models such as OpenMP can have.

Two implications to emphasize what we get because of nesting support:

- We do not need to know if we are in a "parallel region" or a "serial region" when choosing if we should invoke a TBB template. Since using TBB just creates tasks, we do not have to worry about oversubscription of threads.

- We do not need to worry about calling a library, which was written with TBB, and controlling if it might use parallelism.

Nesting can be thought of as a meta-pattern because it means that patterns can be hierarchically composed. This is important for modular programming. Nesting is extensively used in serial programming for composability and information hiding but can be a challenge to carry over into parallel programming. The key to implementing nested parallelism is to specify optional, not mandatory, parallelism. This is one area that TBB excels compared to other models.

The importance of nesting was well understood when TBB was introduced in 2006, and it has always been well supported in all of TBB. In contrast, the OpenMP API was introduced in 1997 when we did not adequately foresee the critical importance of the nesting pattern for future machines. As a result, the nesting pattern is not supported throughout OpenMP. This can make OpenMP much more difficult to use for anything outside the world of applications which focus almost all work inside computationally intensive loop nests. These are the application types that dominated our thinking when creating OpenMP and its predecessors in the 1980s and 1990s. The nesting pattern, with modularity and composability, was key in our thinking when TBB was created (we credit the Cilk research work at MIT for the pioneering work that influenced our thinking heavily – see Appendix A for many more comments on influences, including Cilk).

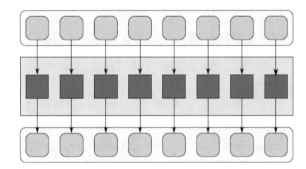

Figure 8-3. *Map pattern: a function is applied to all elements of a collection, usually producing a new collection with the same shape as the input.*

Map Pattern

The **map** pattern (Figure 8-3) is the most optimal pattern for parallel programming possible: dividing work into uniform independent parts that run in parallel with no dependencies. This represents a regular parallelization that is referred to as *embarrassing* parallelism. That is to say, the parallelism seems most obvious in cases where there is independent parallel work to be done. There is *nothing* embarrassing about getting great performance when an algorithm scales well! This quality makes the map pattern worth using whenever possible since it allows for both efficient parallelization and efficient vectorization.

A map pattern involves *no* shared mutable state between the parts; a map function (the independent work parts) must be "pure" in the sense that it must not modify shared state. Modifying shared (mutable) state would break perfect independence. This can result in nondeterminism from data races and result in undefined behavior including possible application failure. Hidden shared data can be present when using complex data structures, for instance `std::share_ptr`, which may have sharing implications.

Usages for map patterns include gamma correction and thresholding in images, color space conversions, Monte Carlo sampling, and ray tracing. Use `parallel_for` to implement map efficiently with TBB (example in Figure 8-4). Additionally, `parallel_invoke` can be used for a small amount of map type parallelism, but the limited amount will not provide much scalability unless parallelism also exists at other levels (e.g., inside the invoked functions).

```
tbb::parallel_for( size_t(0), n, [&](size_t i) {
  Foo(i);
} );
```

Figure 8-4. *Map pattern realized in parallel with* `parallel_for`

Workpile Pattern

The **workpile** pattern is a generalized map pattern where each instance (map function) can generate more instances. In other words, work can be added to the "pile" of things to do. This can be used, for example, in the recursive search of a tree, where we might want to generate instances to process each of the children of each node of the tree. Unlike the case with the map pattern, with the workpile pattern, the total number of instances of the map function is not known in advance nor is the structure of the work regular. This makes the workpile pattern harder to vectorize (Chapter 4) than the map pattern. Use `parallel_do` (Chapter 2) to implement workpile efficiently with TBB.

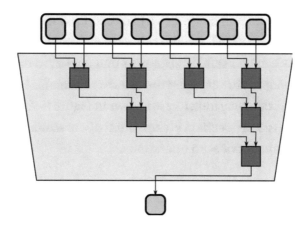

Figure 8-5. *Reduction pattern: subtasks produce subresults that are combined to form a final single answer.*

Reduction Patterns (Reduce and Scan)

The **reduce** pattern (Figure 8-5) can be thought of as a map operation where each subtask produces a subresult that we need to combine to form a final single answer. A reduce pattern combines the multiple subresults using an associative "combiner function." Because of the associativity of the combiner function, different orderings of the combining are possible run-to-run which is both a curse and a blessing. The blessing is that an implementation is free to maximize performance by combining in any order that is most efficient. The curse is that this offers a nondeterminism in the output if there are variations run-to-run in results due to rounding or saturation. Combining to find the maximum number or to find the boolean AND of all subresults does not suffer from these issues. However, a global addition using floating-point numbers will be nondeterministic due to rounding variations.

TBB offers both nondeterministic (highest performance) and deterministic (typically only a slight performance penalty) for reduction operations. The term deterministic refers only to the deterministic order of reduction run-to-run. If the combining function is deterministic, such as boolean AND, then the nondeterministic order of `parallel_reduce` will yield a deterministic result.

Typical combiner functions include addition, multiplication, maximum, minimum, and boolean operations AND, OR, and XOR. We can use `parallel_reduce` (Chapter 2) to implement nondeterministic reduction. We can use `parallel_deterministic_reduce` (Chapter 16) to implement deterministic reduction. Both allow us the ability to define our own combiner functions.

The **scan** pattern (Figure 8-6) computes a prefix computation (also known as a scan) in parallel (y[i]=y[i-1] op x[i]). As with other reductions, this can be done in parallel if op is associative. This can be useful in scenarios that appear to have inherently serial dependencies. Many people are surprised that there is a scalable way to do this at all. A sample of what serial code may look like is shown in Figure 8-7. A parallel version requires more operations than a serial version, but it offers scaling. TBB parallel_scan (Chapter 2) is used to implement scan operations.

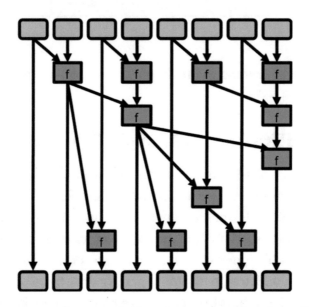

Figure 8-6. *Scan pattern: the complexity gives a visualization of the extra operations needed to offering scaling.*

```
void my_add_iscan(
    const float a[],      // input array
    float b[],            // output array
    size_t n ) {          // number of elements
    if (n>0) b[0]=a[0];   // equiv. to assuming b[i-1] is zero
    for (int i=1; i < n; ++i)
        b[i] = b[i-1] + a[i]; // iterations depends prior
}
```

Figure 8-7. *Serial code doing a scan operation*

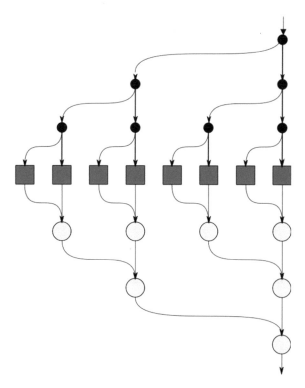

Figure 8-8. *Fork-join pattern: allows control flow fork into multiple parallel flows that rejoin later*

Fork-Join Pattern

The **fork-join** pattern (Figure 8-8) recursively subdivides a problem into subparts and can be used for both regular and irregular parallelization. It is useful for implementing a **divide-and-conquer** strategy (sometimes called a pattern itself) or a **branch-and-bound** strategy (also, sometimes called a pattern itself). A fork-join should not be confused with barriers. A barrier is a synchronization construct across multiple threads. In a barrier, each thread must wait for all other threads to reach the barrier before any of them leaves. A join also waits for all threads to reach a common point, but the difference is that after a barrier, all threads continue, but after a join, only one does. Work that runs independently for a while, then uses barriers to synchronize, and then proceeds independently again is effectively the same as using the map pattern repeatedly with barriers in between. Such programs are subject to Amdahl's Law penalties (see more in the Preface) because time is spent waiting instead of working (serialization).

We should consider `parallel_for` and `parallel_reduce` since they automatically implement capabilities that may do what we need if our needs are not too irregular. TBB templates `parallel_invoke` (Chapter 2), `task_group` (Chapter 10), and `flow_graph` (Chapter 3) are ways to implement the fork-join pattern. Aside from these direct coding methods, it is worth noting that fork-join usage and nesting support within the implementation of TBB makes it possible to get the benefits of fork-join and nesting without explicitly coding either. A `parallel_for` will automatically use an optimized fork-join implementation to help span the available parallelism while remaining composable so that nesting (including nested `parallel_for` loops) and other forms of parallelism can be active at the same time.

Divide-and-Conquer Pattern

The **fork-join** pattern can be considered the basic pattern, with **divide-and-conquer** being a strategy in how we fork and join. Whether this is a distinct pattern is a matter of semantics, and is not important for our purposes here.

A divide-and-conquer pattern applies if a problem can be divided into smaller subproblems recursively until a base case is reached that can be solved serially. Divide-and-conquer can be described as dividing (partitioning) a problem and then using the map pattern to compute solutions to each subproblem in the partition. The resulting solutions to subproblems are combined to give a solution to the original problem. Divide-and-conquer lends itself to parallel implementation because of ease of which work can be subdivided whenever more workers (tasks) would be advantageous.

The `parallel_for` and `parallel_reduce` implement capabilities that should be considered first when divide-and-conquer is desired. Also, divide-and-conquer can be implemented with the same templates which can serve as methods to implement the fork-join pattern (`parallel_invoke`, `task_group`, and `flow_graph`).

Branch-and-Bound Pattern

The **fork-join** pattern can be considered the basic pattern, with **branch-and-bound** being a strategy in how we fork and join. Whether this is a distinct pattern is a matter of semantics and is not important for our purposes here.

Branch-and-bound is a *nondeterministic* search method to find one satisfactory answer when many may be possible. Branch refers to using concurrency, and bound refers to limiting the computation in some manner – for example, by using an upper bound (such as the best result found so far). The name "branch and bound" comes from the fact that we recursively divide the problem into parts, then bound the solution in each part. Related techniques, such as alpha-beta pruning, are also used in state-space search in artificial intelligence including move evaluations for Chess and other games.

Branch-and-bound can lead to superlinear speedups, unlike many other parallel algorithms. However, whenever there are multiple possible matches, this pattern is nondeterministic because which match is returned depends on the timing of the searches over each subset. To get a superlinear speedup, the cancellation of in-progress tasks needs to be implemented in an efficient manner (see Chapter 15).

Search problems do lend themselves to parallel implementation, since there are many points to search. However, because enumeration is far too expensive computationally, the searches should be coordinated in some way. A good solution is to use a branch-and-bound strategy. Instead of exploring all possible points in the search space, we choose to repetitively divide the original problem into smaller subproblems, evaluate specific characteristics of the subproblems so far, set up constraints (bounds) according to the information at hand, and eliminate subproblems that do not satisfy the constraints. This elimination is often referred to as "pruning." The bounds are used to "prune" the search space, eliminating candidate solutions that can be proven will not contain an optimal solution. By this strategy, the size of the feasible solution space can be reduced gradually. Therefore, we will need to explore only a small part of the possible input combinations to find the optimal solution.

Branch-and-bound is a nondeterministic method and a good example of when nondeterminism can be useful. To do a parallel search, the simplest approach is to partition the set and search each subset in parallel. Consider the case where we only need one result, and any data that satisfies the search criteria is acceptable. In that case, once an item matching the search criteria is found, in any one of the parallel subset searches, the searches in the other subsets can be canceled.

Branch-and-bound can also be used for mathematical optimization, with some additional features. In mathematical optimization, we are given an objective function, some constraint equations, and a domain. The function depends on certain parameters. The domain and the constraint equations define legal values for the parameters. Within the given domain, the goal of optimization is to find values of the parameters that maximize (or minimize) the objective function.

The `parallel_for` and `parallel_reduce` implement capabilities that should be considered first when branch-and-bound is desired. Also, divide-and-conquer can be implemented with the same templates which can serve as methods to implement the fork-join pattern (`parallel_invoke`, `task_group` and `flow_graph`). Understanding TBB support for cancellation (see Chapter 15) may be particularly useful when implementing branch-and-bound.

Pipeline Pattern

The **pipeline** pattern (Figure 8-9) can be easily underestimated. The opportunities for parallelism through nesting and pipelining are enormous. A pipeline pattern connects tasks in a producer-consumer relationship in a regular, nonchanging data flow.

Conceptually, all stages of the pipeline are active at once, and each stage can maintain state which can be updated as data flows through them. This offers parallelism through pipelining. Additionally, each stage can have parallelism within itself thanks to nesting support in TBB. TBB `parallel_pipeline` (Chapter 2) supports basic pipelines. More generally, a set of stages could be assembled in a directed acyclic graph (a network). TBB `flow_graph` (Chapter 3) supports both pipelines and generalized pipelines.

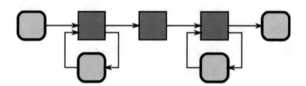

Figure 8-9. *Pipeline pattern: tasks connected in a regular nonchanging producer-consumer relationship*

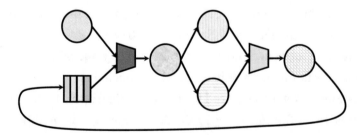

Figure 8-10. *Event-based coordination pattern: tasks connected in a producer-consumer relationship with an irregular, and possibly changing, interaction between tasks*

Event-Based Coordination Pattern (Reactive Streams)

The **event-based coordination** pattern (Figure 8-10) connects tasks in a producer-consumer relationship with an irregular, and possibly changing, interaction between tasks. Dealing with asynchronous activities is a common programming challenge.

This pattern can be easily underestimated for the same reasons many underestimate the scalability of a pipeline. The opportunities for parallelism through nesting and pipelining are enormous.

We are using the term "event-based coordination," but we are not trying to differentiate it from "actors," "reactive streams," "asynchronous data streams," or "event-based asynchronous."

The unique control flow aspects needed for this pattern led to the development of the flow_graph (Chapter 3) capabilities in TBB.

Examples of asynchronous events include interrupts from multiple real-time data feed sources such as image feeds or Twitter feeds, or user interface activities such as mouse events. Chapter 3 offers much more detail on flow_graph.

Summary

TBB encourages us to think about patterns that exist in our algorithmic thinking, and in our applications, and to map those patterns only onto capabilities that TBB offers. TBB offers support for patterns that can be effective for scalable applications, while proving an abstraction dealing with implementation details to keep everything modular and fully composable. The "super pattern" of nesting is very well supported in TBB, and therefore TBB offers composability not associated with many parallel programming models.

For More Information

TBB can be used to implement additional patterns which we did not discuss. We highlighted what we have found to be key patterns and their support in TBB, but one chapter can hardly compete with entire books on patterns.

Structured Parallel Programming by McCool, Robison, and Reinders (Elsevier, 2012) offers a hands-on coverage of "patterns that work." This is a book for programmers looking to have a more in-depth look at patterns with hands-on examples.

Patterns for Parallel Programming by Mattson, Sanders, and Massingill (Addison-Wesley, 2004) offers a much deeper, and more academic, look at patterns and their taxonomy and components.

Part 2

## CHAPTER 9

The Pillars of Composability

In this chapter, we discuss composability: what it is, what characteristics make Threading Building Blocks (TBB) a composable threading library, and how to use a library like TBB to create scalable applications. C++ is a composable language, and TBB adds parallelism in a way that maintains composability. Composability with TBB is highly valuable because it means we are free to expose opportunities for parallelism without worrying about overloading the system. If we do not expose parallelism, we limit scaling.

Ultimately, when we say that TBB is a composable parallel library, we mean that developers can mix and match code that uses TBB freely anywhere they want. These uses of TBB can be serial, one after the other; they can be nested; they can be concurrent; they can be all within a single monolithic application; they can be spread across disjoint libraries; or they can be in different processes that execute concurrently.

It might not be obvious that parallel programming models have often had restrictions that were difficult to manage in complex applications. Imagine if we could not use "`while`" statements within an "`if`" statement, even indirectly in functions we call. Before TBB, equally difficult restrictions existed for some parallel programming models, such as OpenMP. Even the newer OpenCL standard lacks full composability.

The most frustrating aspect of non-composable parallel programming models is that there is such a thing as requesting too much parallelism. This is horrible, and something TBB avoids. In our experience, naïve users of non-composable models often overuse parallelism – and their programs crash from explosions in memory usage or they slow down to a crawl due to unbearable synchronization overheads. Concern about these issues can lead experienced programmers to expose too little parallelism, resulting in load imbalances and poor scaling. Using a composable programming model avoids the need to worry about this difficult balancing act.

© Intel Corporation 2019
M. Voss, R. Asenjo, J. Reinders, *Pro TBB*, https://doi.org/10.1007/978-1-4842-4398-5_9

Composability makes TBB extraordinarily reliable to use in both simple and complex applications. Composability is a design philosophy that allows us to create programs that are more scalable because we can expose parallelism without fear. In Chapter 1, we introduced the idea of the three-layer cake of parallelism that is common in many applications, reproduced here as Figure 9-1.

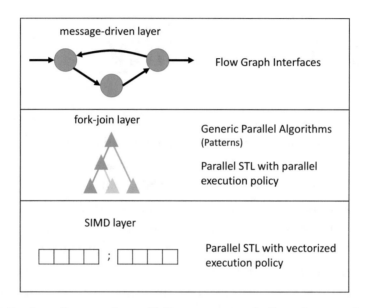

Figure 9-1. *The three layers of parallelism commonly found in applications and how they map to the high-level TBB parallel execution interfaces*

We covered the basics of the high-level interfaces shown in Figure 9-1 in the generic parallel algorithms in Chapter 2, the flow graph in Chapter 3, and Parallel STL in Chapter 4. Each of these high-level interfaces plays an important role in building up these layers of parallelism. And because they are all implemented using TBB tasks, and TBB is composable, we can safely combine them together to make complex, scalable applications.

What Is Composability?

Composability is, unfortunately, not a simple yes-or-no property of a programming model. Even though OpenMP has known composability issues for nested parallelism, it would be incorrect to label OpenMP as a non-composable programming model. If an application invokes OpenMP construct after OpenMP construct in series, this serial composition works just fine. It would likewise be an overstatement to say that TBB is a fully composable programming model that works well with all other parallel programming models in all situations. Composability is more accurately thought of as a measure of how well two programming models perform when composed in a specific way.

For example, let's consider two parallel programming models: model A and model B. Let's define T_A as the throughput of a kernel when it uses model A to express outer-level parallelism, and T_B as the throughput of the same kernel when it uses model B (without using model A) to express inner-level parallelism. If the programming models are composable, we would expect the throughput of the kernel using both outer and inner parallelism to be $T_{AB} >= max(T_A, T_B)$, How much greater T_{AB} is than $max(T_A, T_B)$ depends both on how efficiently the models compose with each other and on the physical properties of the targeted platform, such as the number of cores, the size of the memory, and so on.

Figure 9-2 shows the three general types of composition that we can use to combine software constructs: nested execution, concurrent execution, and serial execution. We say that TBB is a composable threading library because when a parallel algorithm using TBB is composed with other parallel algorithms in one of the three ways shown in Figure 9-2, the resulting code performs well, that is $T_{TBB+Other} >= max(T_{TBB}, T_{Other})$.

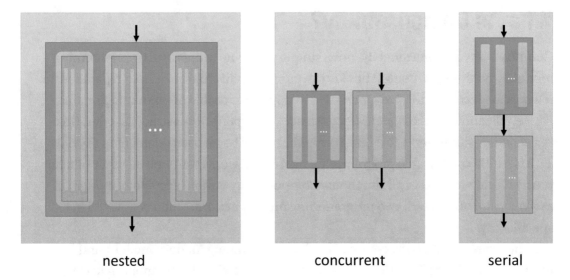

nested   concurrent   serial

Figure 9-2. *The ways in which software constructs can be composed*

Before we discuss the features of TBB that lead to good composability, let's look at each composition type, the issues that can arise, and what performance impacts we can expect.

Nested Composition

In a *nested* composition, the machine executes one parallel algorithm inside of another parallel algorithm. The intention of a nested composition is almost always to add additional parallelism, and it can even exponentially increase the amount of work that can be executed in parallel as shown in Figure 9-3. Handling nested parallelism effectively was a primary goal in the design of TBB.

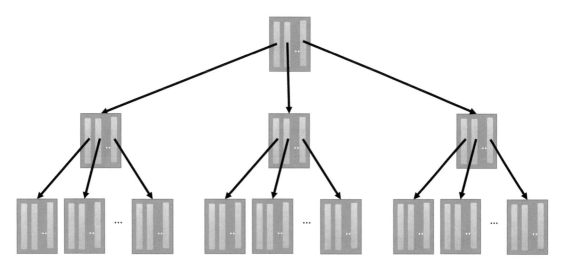

Figure 9-3. *Nested parallelism can lead to an exponential growth in the number of available parallel tasks (or when using a non-composable library, threads)*

In fact the algorithms provided by the TBB library in many cases depend on nested parallelism in order to create scalable parallelism. For example, in Chapter 2, we discussed how nested invocations of TBB's `parallel_invoke` can be used to create a scalable parallel version of quicksort. The Threading Building Blocks library is designed from the ground up to be an effective executor of nested parallelism.

In contrast to TBB, other parallel models may perform catastrophically bad in the presence of nested parallelism. A concrete example is the OpenMP API. OpenMP is a widely used programming model for shared-memory parallelism – and it is very effective for single level parallelism. However, it is a notoriously bad model for nested parallelism because mandatory parallelism is an integral part of its definition. In applications that have multiple levels of parallelism, each OpenMP parallel construct creates an additional team of threads. Each thread allocates stack space and also needs to be scheduled by the OS's thread scheduler. If the number of threads is very large, the application can run out of memory. If the number of threads exceeds the number of logical cores, the threads must share cores. Once the number of threads exceeds the number of cores, they tend to offer little benefit due to the oversubscription of the hardware resources, adding only overhead.

The most practical choice for nested parallelism with OpenMP is typically to turn off the nested parallelism completely. In fact, the OpenMP API provides an environment variable, `OMP_NESTED`, for the purpose of turning on or off nested parallelism. Because TBB has relaxed sequential semantics and uses tasks to express parallelism instead of threads, it can flexibly adapt parallelism to the available hardware resources. We can safely leave nested parallelism on with TBB – there's no need for a mechanism to turn off parallelism in TBB!

Later in this chapter, we discuss the key features of TBB that make it very effective at executing nested parallelism, including its thread pool and work-stealing task scheduler. In Chapter 8, we examine nesting as a very important recurring theme (pattern) in parallel programming. In Chapter 12, we discuss features that allow us to influence the behavior of the TBB library when executing nested parallelism in order to create isolation and improve data locality.

Concurrent Composition

As shown in Figure 9-4, *concurrent* composition is when the execution of parallel algorithms overlap in time. Concurrent composition can be used to intentionally add additional parallelism, or it can arise by happenstance when two unrelated applications (or constructs in the same program) execute concurrently on the same system. Concurrent and parallel execution are not always the same thing! As shown in Figure 9-3, *concurrent execution* is when multiple constructs execute during the same time frame, while *parallel execution* is when multiple constructs execute simultaneously. This means that parallel execution is a form of concurrent execution but concurrent execution is not always parallel execution. Concurrent composition improves performance when it is effectively turned into parallel execution.

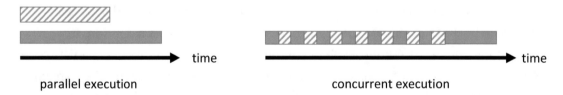

parallel execution   concurrent execution

Figure 9-4. *Parallel vs. concurrent execution*

A concurrent composition of the two loops in Figure 9-5 is when a parallel implementation of loop 1 executes concurrently with a parallel implementation of loop 2, whether in two different processes or in two different threads in the same process.

```
// loop 1                          // loop 2
for (int i = 0; i < N; ++i) {      for (int i = 0; i < M; ++i) {
  b[i] = f(a[i]);                    d[i] = g(c[i]);
}                                  }
```

Figure 9-5. *Two loops that execute concurrently*

When executing constructs concurrently, an arbitrator (a runtime library like TBB, the operating system or some combination of systems) is responsible for assigning system resources to the different constructs. If the two constructs require access to the same resources at the same time, then access to these resources must be interleaved.

Good performance for a concurrent composition might mean that the wall-clock execution time is as short as the time to execute the longest running construct, since all of the other constructs can execute in parallel with it (like in the parallel execution in Figure 9-4). Or, good performance might mean that the wall-clock execution time is no longer than the sum of the execution times of all the constructs if the executions need to be interleaved (like in the concurrent execution in Figure 9-4). But no system is ideal, and sources of both destructive and constructive interference make it unlikely that we get performance that exactly matches either of these cases.

First, there is the added cost of the arbitration. For example, if the arbitrator is the OS thread scheduler, then this would include the overheads of the scheduling algorithm; the overheads of preemptive multitasking, such as switching thread contexts; as well as the overheads of the OS's security and isolation mechanisms. If the arbitrator is a task scheduler in a user-level library like TBB, this cost is limited to the overheads of scheduling the tasks on to threads. If we express very fine-grained pieces of work, using many tasks scheduled on to a small set of threads has much lower scheduling overheads than using many threads directly, even though the tasks ultimately execute on top of threads.

Secondly, there is the performance impact from the concurrent use of shared system resources, such as the functional units, memory, and data caches. The overlapped execution of constructs can, for example, lead to changes in data cache performance – often an increase in cache misses but, in rare cases of constructive interference, possibly even a decrease in cache misses.

TBB's thread pool and its work-stealing task scheduler, discussed later in this chapter, help with concurrent composition as well, reduce arbitration overheads, and in many cases lead to task distributions that optimize resource usage. If TBB's default behaviors are not satisfactory, the features described in Chapters 11–14 can be used to mitigate negative impacts of resource sharing as needed.

Serial Composition

The final way to compose two constructs is to execute them serially, one after the other without overlapping them in time. This may seem like a trivial kind of composition with no implications on performance, but (unfortunately) it is not. When we use serial composition, we typically expect good performance to mean that there is no interference between the two constructs.

For example, if we consider the loops in Figure 9-6, the serial composition is to execute loop 3 followed by loop 4. We might expect that the time to complete each parallel construct when executed in series is no different than the time to execute that same construct alone. If the time it takes to execute loop 3 alone after parallelism is added using a parallel programming model A is $t_{3,A}$ and the time to execute loop 4 alone using a parallel programming model B is $t_{4,B}$, then we would expect the total time for executing the constructs in series is no more than the sum of the times of each construct, $t_{3,A} + t_{4,B}$.

```
// loop 3
for (int i = 0; i < N; ++i) {
  b[i] = f(a[i]);
}

// loop 4
for (int i = 0; i < N; ++i) {
  c[i] = f(b[i]);
}
```

Figure 9-6. Two loops that are executed one after the other

However, as with concurrent composition, there are sources of both destructive and constructive interference that can arise and cause actual execution times to diverge from this simple expectation.

In serial composition, the application must transition from one parallel construct to the next. Figure 9-7 shows ideal and nonideal transitions between constructs when using the same or different parallel programming models. In both ideal cases, there is no overhead, and we move immediately from one construct to the next. In practice, there is often some time required to clean up resources after executing a construct in parallel as well as some time required to prepare resources before the execution of the next construct.

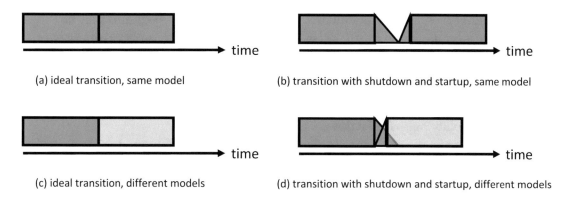

(a) ideal transition, same model

(b) transition with shutdown and startup, same model

(c) ideal transition, different models

(d) transition with shutdown and startup, different models

Figure 9-7. *Transitioning between the executions of different constructs*

When the same model is used, as shown in Figure 9-7(b), a runtime library may do work to shut down the parallel runtime only to have to immediately start it back up again. In Figure 9-7(d), we see that if two different models are used for the constructs, they may be unaware of each other, and so the shut-down of the first construct and the start-up, and even execution, of the next construct can overlap, perhaps degrading performance. Both of these cases can be optimized for – and TBB is designed with these transitions in mind.

And as with any composition, performance can be impacted by the sharing resources between the two constructs. Unlike with the nested or concurrent compositions, the constructs do not share resources simultaneously or in an interleaved fashion, but still, the ending state of the resources after one construct finishes can affect the performance of the next construct. For example, in Figure 9-6, we can see that loop 3 writes to array b and then loop 4 reads from array b. Assigning the same iterations in loop 3 and 4 to the same cores might increase data locality resulting in fewer cache misses. In contrast, an assignment of the same iterations to different cores can result in unnecessary cache misses.

The Features That Make TBB a Composable Library

The Threading Building Blocks (TBB) library is a composable library by design. When it was first introduced over 10 years ago, there was a recognition that as a parallel programming library targeted at all developers – not just developers of flat, monolithic applications – it had to address the challenges of composability head-on. The applications that TBB is used in are often modular and make use of third-party libraries that may, themselves, contain parallelism. These other parallel algorithms may be intentionally, or unintentionally, composed with algorithms that use the TBB library. In addition, applications are typically executed in multiprogrammed environments, such as on shared servers or on personal laptops, where multiple processes execute concurrently. To be an effective parallel programming library for all developers, TBB has to get composability right. And it does!

While it is not necessary to have a detailed understanding of the design of TBB in order to create scalable parallel applications using its features, we cover some details in this section for interested readers. If you are happy enough to trust that TBB does the right thing and are not too interested in how, then you can safely skip the rest of this section. But if not, read on to learn more about why TBB is so effective at composability.

The TBB Thread Pool (the Market) and Task Arenas

The two features of the Threading Building Blocks library that are primarily responsible for its composability are its *global thread pool (the market)* and *task arenas*. Figure 9-8 shows how the global thread pool and a single default task arena interact in an application that has a single main thread; for simplicity, we will assume that there are P=4 logical cores on the target system. Figure 9-8(a) shows that the application has 1 application thread (the main thread) and a global thread pool of workers that is initialized with P-1 threads. The workers in the global thread pool execute dispatchers (represented by the solid boxes). Initially, each thread in the global thread pool sleeps while waiting for an opportunity to participate in parallel work. Figure 9-8(a) also shows that a single default task arena is created. Each application thread that uses TBB is given its own task arena to isolate its work from the work of the other application threads. In Figure 9-8(a), there is only a single task arena, since there is only a single application thread. When the application thread executes a TBB parallel algorithm, it executes a dispatcher tied to that task arena until the algorithm is complete. While waiting for the algorithm to complete, the master thread can participate in executing tasks that are spawned into the arena. The main thread is shown filling the slot reserved for a master thread.

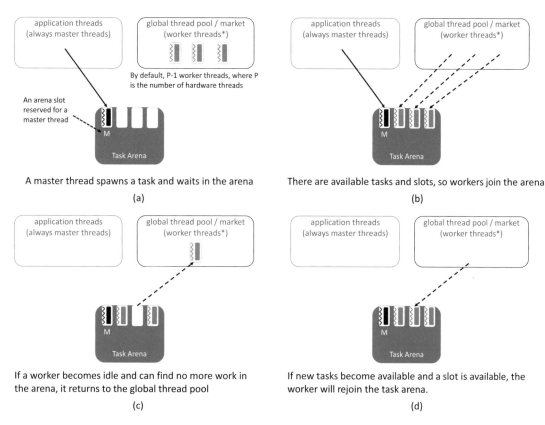

Figure 9-8. *In many applications, there is a single main thread, and the TBB library, by default, creates P-1 worker threads to participate in the execution of parallel algorithms*

When a master thread joins an arena and first spawns a task, the worker threads sleeping in the global thread pool wake up and migrate to the task arena as shown in Figure 9-8(b). When a thread joins a task arena, by filling one of its slots, its dispatcher can participate in executing tasks that are spawned by other threads in that arena, as well as spawn tasks that can be seen and stolen by the other threads' dispatchers that are connected to the arena. In Figure 9-8, there are just enough threads to fill the slots in the task arena, since the global thread pool creates P-1 threads and the default task arena has enough slots for P-1 threads. Typically, this is exactly the number of threads we want, since the main thread plus P-1 worker threads will fully occupy the cores in the machine without oversubscribing them. Once the task arena is fully occupied, the spawning of tasks does not wake up additional threads waiting in the global thread pool.

Figure 9-8(c) shows that when a worker thread becomes idle and can find no more work to do in its current task arena, it returns to the global thread pool. At that point, the worker could join a different task arena that needs workers if one is available, but in Figure 9-8, there is only a single task arena, so the thread will go back to sleep. If later more tasks become available, the threads that have returned to the global thread pool will wake back up and rejoin the task arena to assist with the additional work as shown in Figure 9-8(d).

The scenario outlined in Figure 9-8 represents the very common case of an application that has a single main thread and no additional application threads, and where no advanced features of TBB are used to change any defaults. In Chapters 11 and 12, we will discuss advanced TBB features that will allow us to create more complicated examples like the one shown in Figure 9-9. In this more complicated scenario, there are many application threads and several task arenas. When there are more task arena slots than worker threads, as is the case in Figure 9-8, the worker threads are divided in proportion to the need of each task arena. So, for example, a task arena with twice as many open slots as another task arena will receive roughly twice as many worker threads.

Figure 9-9 highlights a few other interesting points about task arenas. By default, there is one slot reserved for a master thread, like in Figure 9-8. However as shown by the right two task arenas in Figure 9-9, a task arena can be created (using advanced features that we discuss in later chapters) that reserves multiple slots for master threads or no slots at all for master threads. A master thread can fill any slot, while threads that migrate to an arena from the global thread pool cannot fill slots reserved for masters.

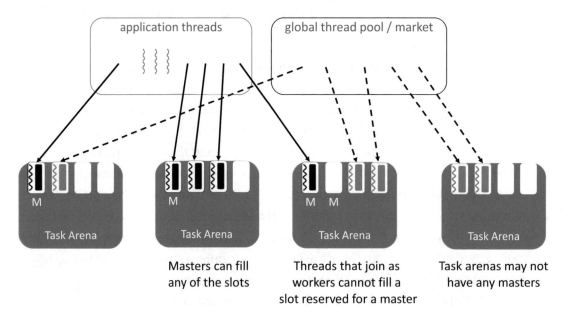

Figure 9-9. *A more complicated application with many native threads and task arenas*

Regardless of how complicated our application though, there is always a single global thread pool. When the TBB library is initialized, it allocates threads to the global thread pool. In Chapter 11, we discuss features that allow us to change the number of threads that are allocated to the global thread pool at initialization, or even dynamically, if we need to. But this limited set of worker threads is one reason that TBB is composable, since it prevents unintended oversubscription of the platform's cores.

Each application thread also gets its own implicit task arena. A thread cannot steal a task from a thread that is in another task arena, so this nicely isolates the work done by different application threads by default. In Chapter 12, we will discuss how application threads can choose to join other arenas if they want to – but by default they have their own.

The design of TBB makes applications and algorithms that use TBB tasks compose well when executed nested, concurrently, or serially. When nested, TBB tasks generated at all levels are executed within the same arena using only the limited set of worker threads assigned to the arena by the TBB library, preventing an exponential explosion in the number of threads. When run concurrently by different master threads, the worker threads are split between the arenas. And when executed serially, the worker threads are reused across the constructs.

Although the TBB library is not directly aware of the choices being made by other parallel threading models, the limited number threads it allocates in its global thread pool also limits its burden on those other models. We will discuss this in more detail later in this chapter.

The TBB Task Dispatcher: Work Stealing and More

The Threading Building Blocks scheduling strategy is often described as *work stealing*. And this is mostly true. Work stealing is a strategy that is designed to work well in dynamic environments and applications, where tasks are spawned dynamically and execution occurs on a multiprogrammed system. When work is distributed by work stealing, worker threads actively look for new work when they become idle, instead of having work passively assigned to them. This pay-as-you-go approach to work distribution is efficient because it does not force threads to stop doing useful work just so they can distribute part of their work to other idle threads. Work stealing moves these overheads on to the idle threads – which have nothing better to do anyway! Work-stealing schedulers stand in contrast to *work-sharing* schedulers, which assign tasks to worker threads up front when tasks are first spawned. In a dynamic environment, where tasks are spawned dynamically and some hardware threads may be more loaded than others, work-stealing schedulers are more reactive, resulting in better load balancing and higher performance.

In a TBB application, a thread participates in executing TBB tasks by executing a task dispatcher that is attached to a specific task arena. Figure 9-10 shows some of the important data structures that are maintained in each task arena and each per-thread task dispatcher.

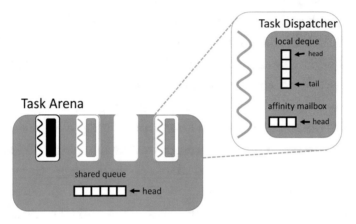

Figure 9-10. *The queues in a task arena and in the per-thread task dispatchers*

For the moment, let us ignore the shared queue in the task arena and the affinity mailbox in the task dispatcher and focus only on the local deque[1] in the task dispatcher. It is the local deque that is used to implement the work-stealing scheduling strategy in TBB. The other data structures are used to implement extensions to work stealing, and we will come back to those later.

In Chapter 2, we discussed the different kinds of loops that are implemented by the generic parallel algorithms included in the TBB library. Many of them depend on the concept of a Range, a recursively divisible set of values that represent the iteration space of the loop. These algorithms recursively divide a loop's Range, using *split tasks* to divide the Range, until they reach a good size to pair with the loop body to execute as a *body task*. Figure 9-11 shows an example distribution of tasks that implement a loop pattern. The top-level task t_0 represents the splitting of the complete Range, which is recursively split down to the leaves where the loop body is applied to each given subrange. With

---

[1]Deque means *double ended queue*, a data structure, not to be confused with dequeue, which is the action of removing items from a queue.

the distribution shown in Figure 9-11, each thread executes body tasks that execute across a contiguous set of iterations. Since nearby iterations often access nearby data, this distribution tends to optimize for locality. And because threads execute tasks within isolated task trees, once a thread gets an initial subrange to work on, it can execute on that tree without interacting much with the other threads.

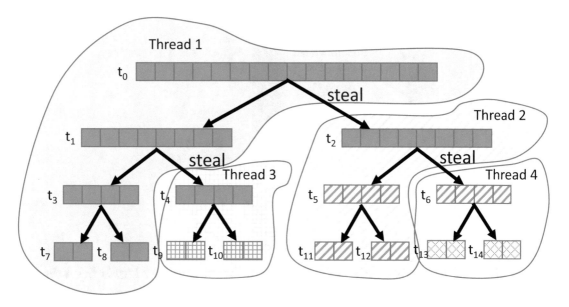

Figure 9-11. *A distribution of tasks that implements a loop pattern*

The TBB loop algorithms are examples of *cache-oblivious* algorithms. Perhaps, ironically, cache-oblivious algorithms are designed to highly optimize the use of CPU data caches – they just do this without knowing the details about cache or cache line sizes. As with the TBB loop algorithms, these algorithms are typically implemented using a divide-and-conquer approach that recursively divides data sets into smaller and smaller pieces that eventually fit into the data caches regardless of their sizes. We cover cache-oblivious algorithms in more detail in Chapter 16.

The TBB library task dispatchers use their local deques to implement a scheduling strategy that is optimized to work with cache-oblivious algorithms and create distributions like the one in Figure 9-11. This strategy is sometimes called a depth-first work, breadth-first steal policy. Whenever a thread *spawns* a new task – that is, makes it available to its task arena for execution – that task is placed at the head of its task dispatcher's local deque. Later, when it finishes the task it is currently working on and needs a new task to execute, it attempts to take work from the head of its local deque, taking the task it most recently spawned as shown in Figure 9-12. If, however, there is no task available in a task dispatcher's local deque, it looks for nonlocal work by randomly selecting another worker thread in its task arena. We call the selected thread a *victim* since the dispatcher is planning to steal a task from it. If the victim's local deque is not empty, the dispatcher takes a task from the tail of the victim thread's local deque, as shown in Figure 9-12, taking the task that was least recently spawned by that thread.

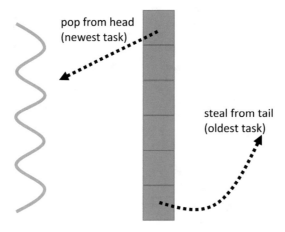

Figure 9-12. *The policy used by the task dispatcher to take local tasks from the head of the local deque but steal tasks from the tail of a victim thread's deque*

Figure 9-13 shows a snapshot of how tasks may be distributed by the TBB scheduling policy when executed using only two threads. The tasks shown in Figure 9-13 are a simplified approximation of a TBB loop algorithm. The TBB algorithm implementations are highly optimized and so may divide some tasks recursively without spawning tasks or use techniques like scheduler bypass (as described in Chapter 10). The example shown in Figure 9-13 assumes that each split and body task is spawned into the task arena – this is not really the case for the optimized TBB algorithms; however, this assumption is useful for illustrative purposes here.

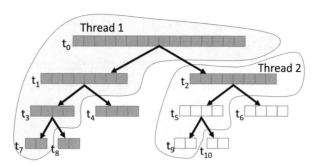

(a) tasks as distributed by work stealing across two threads

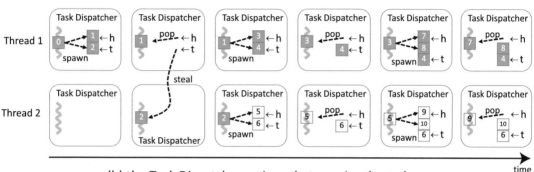

(b) the Task Dispatcher actions that acquire the tasks

Figure 9-13. *A snapshot of how tasks may be distributed across two threads and the actions the two task dispatchers took to acquire the tasks. Note: the actual implementations of TBB loop patterns use scheduler bypass and other optimizations that remove some spawns. Even so, the stealing and execution order will be similar to this figure.*

In Figure 9-13, Thread 1 starts with the root task and initially splits the Range into two large pieces. It then goes depth-first down one side of the task tree, splitting tasks until it reaches the leaf where it applies the body to a final subrange. Thread 2, which is initially idle, steals from the tail of Thread 1's local deque, providing itself with the second large piece that Thread 1 created from the original Range. Figure 9-13(a) is a snapshot in time, for example tasks t_4 and t_6 have not yet been taken by any thread. If two more worker threads are available, we can easily imagine that we get the distribution shown in Figure 9-11. At the end of the timeline in Figure 9-13(b), Thread 1 and 2 still have tasks in their local deques. When they pop the next task, they will grab the leaves that are contiguous with the tasks they just completed.

We shouldn't forget when looking at Figures 9-11 and 9-13 that the distribution shown is only one possibility. If the work per iteration is uniform and none of the cores are oversubscribed, we will likely get the equal distributions shown. Work stealing, however, means that if one of the threads is executing on an overloaded core, it will steal less often and subsequently acquire less work. The other threads will then pick up the slack. A programming model that only provides a static, equal division of iterations to cores would be unable to adapt to such a situation.

As we noted earlier, the TBB task dispatchers however are not just work-stealing schedulers. Figure 9-14 provides a simplified pseudo-code representation of the entire task dispatch loop. We can see lines commented as "execute the task," "take a task spawned by this thread," and "steal a task." These points implement the work-stealing strategy that we just outlined here, but we can see that there are other actions interleaved in the task dispatch loop as well.

The line labeled "scheduler bypass" implements an optimization used to avoid task scheduling overheads. If a task knows exactly which task the calling thread should execute next, it can directly return it, avoiding some of the overheads of task scheduling. As users of TBB, this is likely something we will not need to use directly, but you can learn more about in Chapter 10. The highly optimized TBB algorithms and flow graph do not use straightforward implementations like that shown in Figure 9-13 but instead rely on optimizations, like scheduler bypass, to provide best performance.

The line labeled "take a task with affinity for this thread" looks into the task dispatcher's affinity mailbox to find a task before it attempts to steal work from a random victim. This feature is used to implement task-to-thread affinity, which we describe in detail in Chapter 13.

And the line labeled "take a task from the arena's shared queue" in Figure 9-14 is used to support enqueued tasks – tasks that are submitted to the task arena outside of the usual spawning mechanism. These enqueued tasks are used for work that needs to be scheduled in a roughly first-in-first out order or for fire-and-forget tasks that need to be eventually executed but are not part of a structured algorithm. Task enqueuing will be covered in more detail in Chapter 10.

```
if this thread is a master
  t_next = the first task
else if this thread is a worker
  t_next = steal of task from a random thread's local deque
endif
do
  do
    do
      do
        do
          do
            // execute the task
            t = t_next
            t_next = t->execute()
          while t_next is a valid task // scheduler bypass
          if I'm a master and my algorithm is done
            return
          else if this was the last child of a parent task
            t_next = t->parent
          end if
        while t_next is a valid task
        // take a task spawned by this thread
        t_next = pop from end of local deque
      while t_next is a valid task
      // take a task with affinity for this thread
      t_next = get task from affinity mailbox
    while t_next is a valid task
    // take a task form the arena's shared queue
    t_next = pop from front (approximately) of shared queue
  while t_next t is a valid task
  // steal a task
  t_next = steal task from front of random thread's local deque
while t_next is a valid task

// I'm a worker and there's nothing left to do:
return myself to the global thread pool
```

Figure 9-14. *Pseudo-code for an approximation of the TBB task dispatch loop*

The TBB dispatcher shown in Figure 9-14 is a user-level, nonpreemptive task scheduler. An OS thread scheduler is much more complex, since it will need to deal with not only a scheduling algorithm but also thread preemption, thread migration, isolation, and security.

Putting It All Together

The previous sections describe the design that allows TBB algorithms and tasks to execute efficiently when composed in various ways. Earlier, we also claimed that TBB performs well when mixed with other parallel models too. With our newly acquired knowledge, let's revisit our composition types to convince ourselves that TBB is in fact a composable model because of its design.

In this discussion, we will compare against a hypothetical non-composable thread library, the Non-Composable Runtime (NCR). Our fictional NCR includes parallel constructs that require mandatory parallelism. Each NCR construct will require a team of P threads, which need to be exclusively used for the construct until it is finished – they cannot be shared by other concurrently executing or nested NCR constructs. NCR will also create its threads at the first use of a NCR construct but will not put its threads to sleep after its constructs end – it will keep them actively spinning, using up CPU cycles, so that they can respond as quickly as possible if another NCR construct is encountered. Behaviors like these are not uncommon in other parallel programming models. OpenMP parallel regions do have mandatory parallelism, which can lead to big trouble when the environment variable OMP_NESTED is set to "true." The Intel OpenMP runtime library also provides the option to keep the worker threads actively spinning between regions by setting the environment variable `OMP_WAIT_POLICY` to "active." To be fair, we should make it clear that the Intel OpenMP runtime defaults are `OMP_NESTED=false` and `OMP_WAIT_POLICY=passive`, so these non-composable behaviors are not the default. But as a point of comparison, we use NCR as a strawman to represent a very badly behaved, non-composable model.

Now, let's look out how well TBB composes with itself and with NCR. As a proxy for performance, we will look at oversubscription since the more oversubscribed a system is, the more scheduling and destructive sharing overheads it will likely incur. Figure 9-15 shows how our two models nest with themselves. When a TBB algorithm is nested inside of a TBB algorithm, all of the generated tasks will execute in the same arena and share the P threads. However, NCR shows an explosion in threads since each nested construct will need to assemble its own team of P threads, ultimately needing P^2 threads for even a two-level deep nesting.

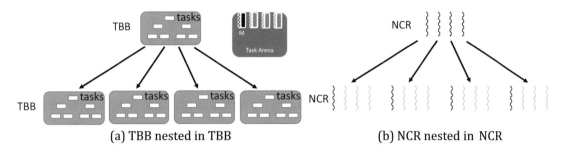

(a) TBB nested in TBB   (b) NCR nested in NCR

Figure 9-15. *The number of threads used for TBB nested in TBB and for a non-composable runtime (NCR) nested in NCR*

Figure 9-16 shows what happens when we combine the models. It doesn't matter how many threads execute TBB algorithms concurrently – the number of TBB worker threads will remain capped at P-1! When TBB is nested inside of NCR, we therefore use at most only 2P-1 threads: P threads from NCR, which will act like master threads in the nested TBB algorithms, and the P-1 TBB worker threads. If a NCR construct is nested inside of TBB however, each TBB task that executes a NCR construct will need to assemble a team of P threads. One of the threads might be the thread executing the outer TBB task, but the other P-1 threads will need to be created by or obtained from the NCR library. We therefore wind up with the P threads from TBB each executing in parallel and each using an additional P-1 threads, for a total of P^2 threads. We can see from Figures 9-15 and 9-16 that when TBB is nested inside of even a badly performed model, it behaves well – unlike a non-composable model like NCR.

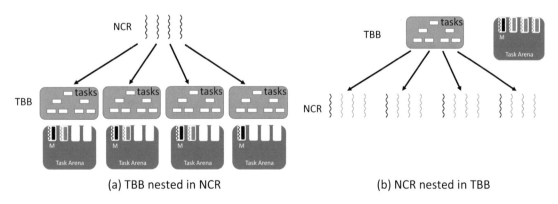

(a) TBB nested in NCR   (b) NCR nested in TBB

Figure 9-16. *When TBB and a non-composable runtime (NCR) are nested inside of each other*

When we look at concurrent execution, we need to consider both single-process concurrent, when parallel algorithms are executed by different threads in the same process concurrently, and multiprocess concurrency. The TBB library has single global thread pool per process – but does not share the thread pool across processes. Figure 9-17 shows the number of threads used for different combinations of concurrent executions for the single-process case. When TBB executes concurrently with itself in two threads, each thread gets its own implicit task arena, but these arenas share the P-1 worker threads; the total number of threads therefore is P+1. NCR uses a team of P threads per construct, so it uses 2P threads. And likewise, since TBB and NCR do not share thread pools, they will use 2P threads when executing concurrently in a single process.

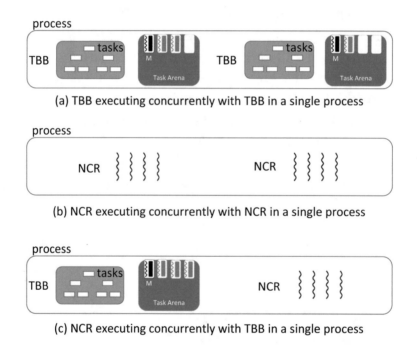

(a) TBB executing concurrently with TBB in a single process

(b) NCR executing concurrently with NCR in a single process

(c) NCR executing concurrently with TBB in a single process

Figure 9-17. *The number of threads used for concurrent executions of TBB algorithms and non-composable runtime (NCR) constructs in a single process*

Figure 9-18 shows the number of threads used for different combinations of concurrent executions for the multiprocess case. Since TBB creates a global thread pool per-process, it no longer has an advantage in this case over NCR. In all three cases, 2P threads are used.

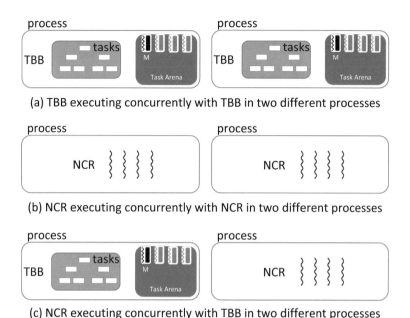

(a) TBB executing concurrently with TBB in two different processes

(b) NCR executing concurrently with NCR in two different processes

(c) NCR executing concurrently with TBB in two different processes

Figure 9-18. *The number of threads used for concurrent executions of TBB constructs and NCR constructs in two different processes*

Finally, let's consider the serial composition case, when one algorithm or construct is executed after another. Both TBB and NCR will compose well serially with other uses of their own libraries. If the delay is short, the TBB threads will still be in the task arena, since they actively search for work for a very short time once they run out of work. If the delay is long between TBB algorithms, the TBB worker threads will return to the global thread pool and migrate back to the task arena when new work becomes available. The overhead for this migration is very small, but non-negligible. Even so, typically the negative impact will be very low. Our hypothetical non-composable runtime (NCR) never sleeps, so it will always be ready to execute the next construct – no matter how long the delay. From a composability perspective, the more interesting cases are when we combine NCR and TBB together as shown in Figure 9-17. TBB quickly puts its threads to sleep after an algorithm ends, so it will not negatively impact an NCR construct that follows it. In contrast, the exceptionally responsive NCR library will keep it threads active, so a TBB algorithm that follows an NCR construct will be forced to fight these spinning threads for processor resources. TBB is clearly the better citizen because its design accounts for serial composability with other parallel models.

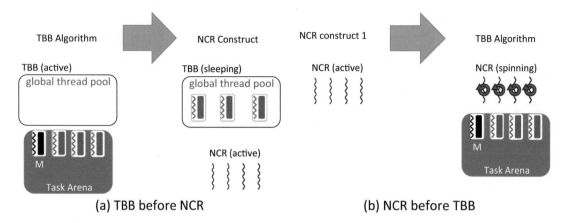

Figure 9-19. *The number of threads used for consecutive executions of TBB constructs and constructs that use mandatory parallelism*

Figures 9-15 through 9-19 demonstrate that TBB composes well with itself and its negative impact on other parallel models is limited due to its composable design. TBB algorithms efficiently compose with other TBB algorithms – but also are good citizens in general.

Looking Forward

In later chapters, we cover a number of topics that expand on themes raised in this chapter.

Controlling the Number of Threads

In Chapter 11, we describe how to use the `task_scheduler_init`, `task_arena`, and `global_control` classes to change the number of threads in the global thread pool and control the number of slots allocated to task arenas. Often, the defaults used by TBB are the right choice, but we can change these defaults if needed.

Work Isolation

In this chapter, we saw that each application thread gets its own implicit task arena by default to isolate its work from the work of other application threads. In Chapter 12, we discuss the function `this_task_arena::isolate`, which can be used in the uncommon situations when work isolation is necessary for correctness. We will also discuss class task_arena, which is used to create explicit task arenas that can be used to isolate work for performance reasons.

Task-to-Thread and Thread-to-Core Affinity

In Figure 9-10, we saw that each task dispatcher not only has a local deque but also has an affinity mailbox. We also saw in Figure 9-14 that when a thread has no work left in its local deque, it checks this affinity mailbox before it attempts random work stealing. In Chapter 13, we discuss ways to create task-to-thread affinity and thread-to-core-affinity by using the low-level features exposed by TBB tasks. In Chapter 16, we discuss features like Ranges and Partitioners that are used by the high-level TBB algorithms to exploit data locality.

Task Priorities

In Chapter 14, we discuss task priorities. By default, the TBB task dispatchers view all tasks as equally important and simply try to execute tasks as quickly as possible, favoring no specific tasks over others. However, the TBB library does allow developers to assign low, medium, and high priorities to tasks. In Chapter 14, we will discuss how to use these priorities and their implications on scheduling.

Summary

In this chapter, we stressed the importance of composability and highlighted that we get it automatically if we use TBB as our parallel programming model. We started this chapter by discussing the different ways in which parallel constructs might be composed with each other and the issues that stem from each type of composition. We then described the design of the TBB library and how this design leads to composable parallelism. We concluded by revisiting the different composition types and compared TBB to a hypothetical non-composable runtime (NCR). We saw that TBB composes well with itself but also is a good citizen when combined with other parallel models.

For More Information

Cilk is a parallel model and platform that was one of key inspirations for the initial TBB scheduler. It provides a space efficient implementation of a work-stealing scheduler as described in

> Robert D. Blumofe and Charles E. Leiserson. 1993. Space-efficient scheduling of multithreaded computations. In Proceedings of the twenty-fifth annual ACM symposium on Theory of computing (STOC '93). ACM, New York, NY, USA, 362–371.

TBB provides generic algorithms implemented using tasks that execute on top of threads. By using TBB, developers can use these high-level algorithms instead of using low-level threads directly. For a general discussion of why using threads directly as a programming model should be avoided, see

> Edward A. Lee, "The Problem with Threads." Computer, 39, 5 (May 2006), 33–42.

In some ways, we've used the OpenMP API as a strawman non-composable model in this chapter. OpenMP is in fact a very effective programming model that has a wide user base and is especially effective in HPC applications. You can learn more about OpenMP at

> www.openmp.org

CHAPTER 10

Using Tasks to Create Your Own Algorithms

One of the things that we like the most from TBB is its "multiresolution" nature. In the context of parallel programming models, multiresolution means that we can choose among different levels of abstraction to code our algorithm. In TBB, we have high-level templates, such as `parallel_for` or `pipeline` (see Chapter 2), that are ready to use when our algorithms fit into these particular patterns. But what if our algorithm is not that simple? Or what if the available high-level abstraction is not squeezing out the last drop of performance of our parallel hardware? Should we just give up and remain prisoners of the high-level features of the programing model? Of course not! There should be a capability to get closer to the hardware, a way to build our own templates from the ground up, and a way to thoroughly optimize our implementation using low-level and more tunable characteristics of the programming model. And in TBB, this capability exists. In this chapter, we will focus on one of the most powerful low-level features of TBB, the task programming interface. As we have said throughout the book, tasks are at the heart of TBB, and tasks are the building blocks used to construct the high-level templates such as `parallel_for` and `pipeline`. But there is nothing that prevents us from venturing into these deeper waters and starting to code our algorithms directly with tasks, from building our own high-level templates for future use on top of tasks, or as we describe in the next chapters, from fully optimizing our implementation by fine tuning the way in which tasks are executed. In essence, this is what you will learn by reading this chapter and the ones that follow. Enjoy the deep dive!

© Intel Corporation 2019
M. Voss, R. Asenjo, J. Reinders, *Pro TBB*, https://doi.org/10.1007/978-1-4842-4398-5_10

A Running Example: The Sequence

Task-based TBB implementations are particularly appropriate for algorithms in which a problem can be recursively divided into smaller subproblems following a tree-like decomposition. There are plenty of problems like these. The divide-and-conquer and branch-and-bound parallel patterns (Chapter 8) are examples of classes of such algorithms. If the problem is big enough, it usually scales well on a parallel architecture because it is easy to break it into enough tasks to fully utilize hardware and avoid load unbalance.

For the purpose of this chapter, we have chosen one of the simplest problems that can be implemented following a tree-like approach. The problem is known as the Fibonacci sequence, and it consists in computing the integer sequence that starts with zero and one, and afterward, every number in the sequence is the sum of the two preceding ones:

0, 1, 1, 2, 3, 5, 8, 13, 21, 34, 55, 89, 144, ...

Mathematically, the nth number in the sequence, F_n, can be computed recursively as

$$F_n = F_{n-1} + F_{n-2}$$

with initial values F_0=0 and F_1=1. There are several algorithms that compute F_n, but in the interest of illustrating how TBB tasks work, we chose the one presented in Figure 10-1, although it is not the most efficient one.

```
long fib(long n) {
  if(n<2)
    return n;
  else
    return fib(n-1)+fib(n-2);
}
```

Figure 10-1. *Recursive implementation of the computation of* F_n

Fibonacci number computation is a classic computer science example for showing recursion, but it is also a classic example in which a simple algorithm is inefficient. A more efficient method would be to compute

$$F_n = \begin{bmatrix} 1 & 1 \\ 1 & 0 \end{bmatrix}^{n-1}$$

and take the upper-left element. The exponentiation over the matrix can be done quickly via repeated squaring. But, we'll go ahead in this section and use the classic recursion example for teaching purposes.

The code presented in Figure 10-1 clearly resembles the recursive equation to compute $F_n = F_{n-1} + F_{n-2}$. While it may be easy to understand, we clarify it further in Figure 10-2 where we depict the recursive calling tree when calling fib(4).

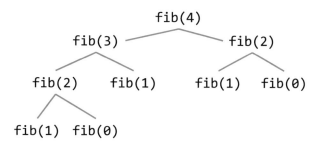

Figure 10-2. *Recursive calling tree for fib(4)*

The if (n<2) line at the beginning of the serial code of Figure 10-1 caters for what is called the *base case*, that is always needed in recursive codes to avoid infinite recursion, which is nice because we don't want to nuke the stack, do we?

We will parallelize this first sequential implementation using different task-based approaches, from simpler to more elaborated and optimized versions. The lessons we learn with these examples can be mimicked in other tree-like or recursive algorithms, and the optimizations we show can also be put to work to make the most out of our parallel architecture in similar situations.

The High-Level Approach: `parallel_invoke`

In Chapter 2, we already presented a high-level class that suits our needs when it comes to spawning parallel tasks: `parallel_invoke`. Relying on this class, we can come up with a first parallel implementation of the Fibonacci algorithm that we present in Figure 10-3.

```
#include <tbb/parallel_invoke.h>
long parallel_fib(long n) {
  if(n<2) {
    return n;
  }
  else {
    long x, y;
    tbb::parallel_invoke([&]{x=parallel_fib(n-1);},
                         [&]{y=parallel_fib(n-2);});
    return x+y;
  }
}
```

Figure 10-3. *Parallel implementation of Fibonacci using `parallel_invoke`*

The `parallel_invoke` member function recursively spawns `parallel_fib(n-1)` and `parallel_fib(n-2)` returning the result in stack variables x and y that are captured by reference in the two lambdas. When these two tasks finish, the caller task simply returns the sum of x+y. The recursive nature of the implementation keeps invoking parallel tasks until the base case is reached when n<2. This means that TBB will create a task even for computing `parallel_fib(1)` and `parallel_fib(0)`, that just return 1 and 0 respectively. As we have said throughout the book, we want to expose enough parallelism to the architecture creating a sufficiently large number of tasks, but at the same time tasks must also have a minimum degree of granularity (>1 microsecond, as we discuss in Chapters 16 and 17) so that task creation overhead pays off. This trade-off is usually implemented in this kind of algorithm using a "`cutoff`" parameter as we show in Figure 10-4.

```
long parallel_fib(long n) {
  if(n<cutoff) {
    return fib(n);
  }
  else {
    long x, y;
    tbb::parallel_invoke([&]{x=parallel_fib(n-1);},
                         [&]{y=parallel_fib(n-2);});
    return x+y;
  }
}
```

Figure 10-4. *Cutoff version of the* parallel_invoke *implementation*

The idea is to modify the base case so that we stop creating more tasks when n is not large enough (n<cutoff), and in this case we resort to the serial execution. Computing a suitable cutoff value requires some experimentation so it is advisable to write our code so that cutoff can be an input parameter to ease the search of a suitable one. For example, in our test bed, fib(30) only takes around 1 millisecond so this is a fine-grained-enough task to discourage further splitting. Thus, it makes sense to set cutoff=30, which results in calling the serial version of the code for tasks that receive n=29 and n=28, as we can see in Figure 10-5.

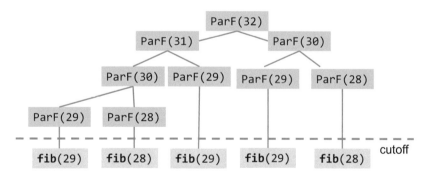

Figure 10-5. *Calling tree after invoking* parallel_fib(32) *–* ParF(32) *in the figure for the sake of saving space –* fib() *is the base case serially implemented*

If after looking at Figure 10-5 you think that it is silly to compute fib(29) in three different tasks and fib(28) in two additional ones, you are right, it is silly! As a disclaimer, we already said that this is not the optimal implementation but a commonly used recursive example that serves our educational interests. A clear optimization would be to implement recursion in a manner such that already computed Fibonacci numbers are not recomputed again, thus achieving the optimal O(log n) complexity, but this is not our goal today.

You may also be thinking, after looking at Figure 10-4, why in the world we are once again revisiting the parallel_invoke that was already covered way back in Chapter 2. Have we *really* reached the second, more advanced, section of this book? Yes! Well... where are the advanced features, the low-level knobs that we may need and the optimization opportunities that we love??? Okay, let's start diving into deeper waters!!!

The Highest Among the Lower: task_group

If we can get by without some of the task knobs and optimization features that will be presented later on, the task_group class can serve us well. This is a higher-level and easier to use class, a medium-level abstraction, if you will. A possible re-implementation of the Fibonacci code that relies on task_group is presented in Figure 10-6.

```
#include <tbb/task_group.h>
long parallel_fib(long n) {
  if(n<cutoff) {
    return fib(n);
  }
  else {
    long x, y;
    tbb::task_group g;
    g.run([&]{x=parallel_fib(n-1);}); // spawn a task
    g.run([&]{y=parallel_fib(n-2);}); // spawn another task
    g.wait();                  // wait for both tasks to complete
    return x+y;
  }
}
```

Figure 10-6. *Parallel Fibonacci based on* task_group

Apparently, this is just a more verbose way of implementing the code of Figure 10-4 where we used parallel_invoke. However, we would like to underscore that, differently from the parallel_invoke alternative, now we have a handle to a group of tasks, g, and as we will discuss later, this enables some additional possibilities as task cancellation. Also, by explicitly calling the member functions g.run() and g.wait(), we spawn the new tasks and wait for them to finish their computation at two different program points, whereas the parallel_invoke function has an implicit task barrier after the task spawning. To begin with, this separation between run() and wait() would allow for the caller thread to do some computation between spawning some tasks and waiting for them in the blocking call wait(). In addition, this class also offers other interesting member functions that can come handy in some situations:

- void run_and_wait(const Func& f), which is equivalent to {run(f); wait();}, but guarantees that f runs on the current thread. We will see later (in section "The Low-Level Task Interface: Part Two – Task Continuation") that there is a convenient trick to bypass the TBB scheduler. If we first call run(f), we basically spawn a task that gets enqueued in the worker thread local queue. When calling wait(), we call the scheduler that dequeues the just enqueued task if nobody else has stolen it in the meantime. The purpose of run_and_wait is twofold: first, we avoid the overhead of enqueueing-scheduling-dequeuing steps, and second, we avoid the potential stealing that can happen while the task is in the queue.

- void cancel(), which cancels all tasks in this task_group. Maybe the computation was triggered from a user interface, UI, that also includes a "cancel" button. If the user now presses this button, there is a way to stop the computation. In Chapter 15, we further elaborate on cancellation and exception handling.

- task_group_status wait(), which returns the final status of task group. Return values can be: complete (all tasks in the group have finished); canceled (task_group received a cancellation request); not_completed (not all tasks in the group have completed).

Note that, in our parallel implementation of Figure 10-6, each call to parallel_fib creates a new task_group so it is possible to cancel one branch without affecting the others, as we will see in Chapter 15. Having a single task_group also poses an additional downside: creating too many tasks in that single group results in task creation serialization and the ensuing loss of scalability. Consider for example we are tempted to write a code like this:

```
tbb::task_group g;
for (int i=0; i < n; i++) g.run([]{foo();});
g.wait();
```

As we see, n tasks will be spawn one after the other and by the same thread. The other worker threads will be forced to steal every task created by the one executing g.run(). This will certainly kill the performance, especially if foo() is a fine-grained task and the number of worker threads, nth, is high. The recommended alternative is the one used in Figure 10-6 where a recursive deployment of tasks is exercised. In that approach, the worker threads steal at the beginning of the computation, and ideally, in $\log_2$(nth) steps all nth worker threads are working in their own tasks that in turn enqueue more tasks in their local queues. For example, for nth=4, the first thread, A, spawns two tasks and starts working in one while thread B steals the other. Now, threads A and B spawn two tasks each (four in total) and start working in two of them, but the other two are stolen by threads C and D. From now on, all four threads are working and enqueueing more tasks in their local queues and stealing again only when they run out of local tasks.

BEWARE! ENTER AT YOUR OWN RISK: THE LOW-LEVEL TASKING INTERFACE

The task class has lots of features, which means there are lots of ways to make mistakes too. If the required parallel pattern is a common one, there is certainly an already available high-level template, implemented and optimized by clever developers on top of the tasking interface. This high-level algorithm is the recommended way to go in most cases. The purpose of the rest of the chapter is therefore serving two goals. In the first place, it provides you with the means to develop your own task-based parallel algorithm or high-level template if the ones already provided by TBB do not suit your needs. The second one is to uncover the low-level details of the TBB machinery so that you can understand some optimizations and tricks that will be mentioned in future chapters. For example, later chapters will refer back to this chapter to explain the way the `parallel_pipeline` and Flow Graph can better exploit locality thanks to a scheduling-bypassing technique. Here, we explain how this technique works and why it is beneficial.

The Low-Level Task Interface: Part One – Task Blocking

The TBB task class has plenty of features and knobs to fine-tune the behavior of our task-based implementation. Slowly but surely, we will introduce the different member functions that are available, progressively increasing the complexity of our Fibonacci implementation. As a starter, Figures 10-7 and 10-8 show the code required to implement the Fibonacci algorithms using low-level tasks. This is our baseline, using task blocking style, that will be optimized in subsequent versions.

```
#include <tbb/task.h>

long parallel_fib(long n) {
  long sum;
  FibTask& a = *new(tbb::task::allocate_root()) FibTask{n,&sum};
  tbb::task::spawn_root_and_wait(a);
  return sum;
}
```

Figure 10-7. `parallel_fib` *re-implementation using the task class*

The code of Figure 10-7 involves the following distinct steps:

1. Allocate space for the task. Tasks must be allocated by special member functions so that the space can be efficiently recycled when the task completes. Allocation is done by a special overloaded new and task::allocate_root member function. The _root suffix in the name denotes the fact that the task created has no parent. It is the root of a task tree.

2. Construct the task with the constructor FibTask{n,&sum} (the task definition is presented in the next figure), invoked by new. When the task is run in step 3, it computes the nth Fibonacci number and stores it into sum.

3. Run the task to completion with task::spawn_root_and_wait.

```
class FibTask: public tbb::task {
public:
  long const n;
  long* const sum;
  FibTask(long n_, long* sum_) : n{n_}, sum{sum_} {}
  tbb::task* execute() { // Overrides virtual function task::execute
    if(n<cutoff) {
      *sum = fib(n);
    }
    else {
      long x, y;
      FibTask& a = *new(tbb::task::allocate_child()) FibTask{n-1,&x};
      FibTask& b = *new(tbb::task::allocate_child()) FibTask{n-2,&y};
      // Set ref_count to "two children plus one for the wait".
      tbb::task::set_ref_count(3);
      // Start b running.
      tbb::task::spawn(b);
      // Start a running and wait for all children (a and b).
      tbb::task::spawn_and_wait_for_all(a);
      // Do the sum
      *sum = x+y;
    }
    return nullptr;
  }
};
```

Figure 10-8. *Definition of the FibTask class that is used in Figure 10-7*

The real work is done inside the class FibTask defined in Figure 10-8.
This is a relatively larger piece of code, compared to fib and the two previous
parallel implementations of parallel_fib. We were advised, this is a lower-level
implementation, and as such it is not as productive or friendly as a high-level
abstraction. To make up for the extra burden, we will see later how this class allows us to
get our hands dirty tweaking under the hood and tuning the behavior and performance
at our will.

Like all tasks scheduled by TBB, FibTask is derived from the class tbb::task. The
fields n and sum hold the input value and the pointer to the output, respectively. These are
initialized with the arguments passed to the constructor FibTask(long n_, long *sum_).

The execute member function does the actual computation. Every task must
provide a definition of execute that overrides the pure virtual member function
tbb::task::execute. The definition should do the work of the task and return either

`nullptr` or a pointer to the next task to run, as we saw in Figure 9-14. In this simple example, it returns `nullptr`.

The member function `FibTask::execute()` does the following:

1. Checks whether `n<cutoff` and resorts to the sequential version in this case.

2. Otherwise, the else branch is taken. The code creates and runs two child tasks that compute F_{n-1} and F_{n-2} respectively. Here, the inherited member function `allocate_child()` is used to allocate space for the task. Remember that the top-level routine `parallel_fib` used `allocate_root()` to allocate space for a task. The difference is that here the task is creating child tasks. This relationship is indicated by the choice of allocation method. The different allocation methods are listed in Appendix B, Figure B-76.

3. Calls `set_ref_count(3)`. The number 3 represents the two children and an additional implicit reference that is required by the member function `spawn_and_wait_for_all`. This `set_ref_count` member function initializes the `ref_count` attribute of each TBB task. Each time a child ends its computation, it decrements the `ref_count` attribute of its parent. Make sure to call `set_reference_count(k+1)` before spawning the k children if the task uses `wait_for_all` to be resumed after the children complete. Failure to do so results in undefined behavior. The debug version of the library usually detects and reports this type of error.

4. Spawns two child tasks. Spawning a task indicates to the scheduler that it can run the task whenever it chooses, possibly in parallel with executing other tasks. The first spawning, by the `tbb::task::spawn(b)` member function, returns immediately without waiting for the child task to start executing. The second spawning, by the member function `tbb::task::spawn_and_wait_for_all(a)`, is equivalent to `tbb::task::spawn(a); tbb::task::wait_for_all()`. The last member function causes the parent to wait until all currently allocated child tasks are finished. For this reason, we say this implementation follows what we call a task blocking style.

5. After the two child tasks complete, the ref_count attribute of the parent task has been decremented twice and now its value is one. This causes the parent task to resume just after the spawn_and_wait_for_all(a) call, so it computes x+y and stores it in *sum.

In Figure 10-9, we illustrate this task creation and execution when spawning the root_task FibTask(8, &sum) having set cutoff=7. Assuming a single thread executing all the tasks, and some simplification in the way the stack is used, in Figure 10-9 we have a streamlined representation of the computations carried out. When parallel_fib(8) is invoked, the variable sum is stored in the stack, and the root task is allocated on the heap and constructed with FibTask(8, &sum). This root task is executed by a worker thread which runs the overridden execute() member function. Inside this member function, two stack variables x and y are declared, and two new child tasks, a and b, are allocated and enqueued in the worker thread's local deque. In the constructor of these two tasks, we pass FibTask(7, &x) and FibTask(6, &y), which means that the variable member sum of the newly created tasks will point to FibTask(8) stack variables x and y, respectively.

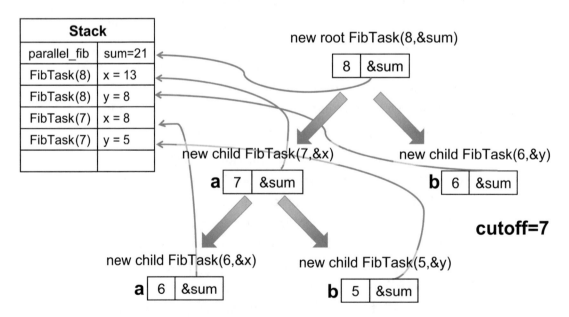

Figure 10-9. *Recursive calling tree for parallel_fib(8) with cutoff=7*

The member function execute() continues by setting ref_count of the task to 3, spawning first b and then a and waiting for both. At this point, the root task is suspended until it has no pending child. Remember that this is the task blocking style. The worker thread returns to the scheduler, where it will first dequeue task a (because it was enqueued last). This task a (FibTask(7,&x)) will recursively repeat the same process, suspending itself after allocating a new x and y on the stack and spawning FibTask(5,&x) and FibTask(6,&y). Since cutoff=7, these two new tasks will resort to the base case and call fib(5) and fib(6), respectively. FibTask(6,&x) is dequeued first, writes 8 to *sum (where sum points to x in FibTask(7) stack), and returns nullptr. Then, the FibTask(6,&x) is destroyed, but in the process, the ref_cont variable of the parent task (FibTask(7,&x)) is first decremented. The worker thread then dequeues FibTask(5,&y) that writes 5 to *sum (now alias of y in the stack) and also returns nullptr. This results in ref_count reaching the value 1, which wakes up the parent thread FibTask(7,&x) that just has to add 5+8, write it to *sum (alias of x in FibTask(8)) stack, and return nullptr. This decrements ref_count of the root task to 2. Next, the worker thread dequeues FibTask(6,&y) that calls fib(6), writes y=8 on the stack, returns, and dies. This finally leaves the root task without children (ref_count=1) so it can continue the execution just after the spawn_and_wait_for_all() member function, add 8+13, write to *sum (alias of sum in the stack of parallel_fib), and get destroyed. If you are exhausted after reading the description of all this process, so are we, but there is even a bit more so hold on for one more second. Now, imagine that there is more than one worker thread. Each one will have its own stack and fight to steal tasks. The result, 21, will be the same and, in essence, the same tasks will be executed, though now we don't know which thread will take care of each task. What we do know is that if the problem size and the number of tasks are large enough and if the cutoff is wisely set, then this parallel code will run faster than the sequential one.

Note   As we have seen, the TBB work-stealing scheduler evaluates a task graph. The graph is a directed graph where each node is a task. Each task points to its parent, also called successor, which is another task that is waiting on it to complete. If a task has no parent/successor, its parent reference points to nullptr. Method tbb::task::parent() gives you read-only access to the successor pointer. Each task has a ref_count that accounts for the number of tasks that have it as a successor (i.e., the number of children that the parent has to wait for before it can be triggered for execution).

And where are the much-vaunted knobs and tuning possibilities? Well, it is true that the code based on low-level tasks that we just discussed is doing pretty much the same as what we already implemented with the `parallel_invoke` and `task_group` classes, but at higher programming cost. Then, where is the bang for the buck? The task class has more member functions that will be covered soon, and the implementation discussed in this section is just the foundation on which more optimized version will be built. Stick with us and keep reading.

The Low-Level Task Interface: Part Two – Task Continuation

The task blocking style that we just presented can pose a problem if the body of the task requires many local variables. These variables sit on the stack and stay there until the task is destroyed. But the task is not destroyed until all its children are done. This is a potential showstopper if the problem is very large, and it is difficult to find a cutoff value without limiting the amount of available parallelism. This can happen when facing Branch and Bound problems that are used to find an optimal value by wisely traversing a search space following a tree-based strategy. There are cases in which the tree can be very large, unbalanced (some tree branches are deeper than other), and the depth of the tree is unknown. Using the blocking style for these problems can easily result in an explosion of the number of tasks and too much use of the stack space.

Another subtle inconvenience of the blocking style is due to the management of the worker thread that encounters the `wait_for_all()` call in a parent task. There is no point in wasting this worker thread waiting for the children tasks to finish, so we entrust it with the execution of other tasks. This means that when the parent task is ready to run again, the original worker thread that was taking care of it may be distracted with other duties and cannot respond immediately.

Note   *Continuation, continuation, continuation!!!* The authors of TBB, and other parallelism experts, love to encourage continuation style programming. Why??? It turns out that using it can be the difference between a working program that is relatively easy to write, and one that crashes from stack overflow. Worst yet, other than using continuations, code to solve such crashes can be hard to understand and gives parallel programming a bad name. Fortunately, TBB is designed to use continuations and encourages us to use continuations by default. Flow Graph (Chapters 3 and 17) encourages use of continue_node (and other nodes with potentials for scheduler bypass). The power of continuations (and task recycling, which we cover next) is worth knowing as a parallel programmer – you'll never want to let a task sit around waiting again (and wasting precious resources)!

To avoid this problem, we can adopt a different coding style, known as continuation passing. Figure 10-10 shows the definition of a new task that we call continuation task, and Figure 10-11 underscores in boxes the required changes in FibTask to implement the continuation-passing style.

```
class FibCont: public tbb::task {
public:
  long* const sum;
  long x, y;
  FibCont(long* sum_) : sum{sum_} {}
  tbb::task* execute(){
    *sum = x+y;
    return nullptr;
  }
};
```

Figure 10-10. *Continuation task* FibCont *for the Fibonacci example*

The continuation task FibCont also has an execute() member function, but now it only includes the code that has to be done once the children tasks are complete. For our Fibonacci example, after the children completion, we only need to add the results that they bring and return, and these are the only two lines of code after the spawn_and_wait_ for_all(a) in the code of Figure 10-8. The continuation task declares three member variables: a pointer to the final sum and the partial sum from the two children, x and y. The constructor FibCont(long∗ sum) initializes the pointer adequately. Now we have to modify our FibTask class to properly create and initialize the continuation task FibCont.

```
class FibTask: public tbb::task {
public:
  long const n;
  long* const sum;
  FibTask(long n_, long* sum_) : n{n_}, sum{sum_} {}
  tbb::task* execute() { // Overrides virtual function task::execute
    if(n<cutoff) {
      *sum = fib(n);
      return nullptr;
    }
    else {
      // long x, y; not needed anymore

      FibCont& c = *new(allocate_continuation()) FibCont{sum};
      FibTask& a = *new(c.allocate_child()) FibTask{n-1, &c.x};
      FibTask& b = *new(c.allocate_child()) FibTask{n-2, &c.y};
      // Set ref_count to "two children".
      c.set_ref_count(2);
      tbb::task::spawn(b);
      tbb::task::spawn(a);
      return nullptr;
    }
  }
};
```

Figure 10-11. *Following the continuation-passing style for parallel Fibonacci*

In Figure 10-11, besides the base case that does not change, we identify in the else part of the code that now, x and y private variables are not declared anymore and have been commented out. However, there is now a new task c of type FibCont&. This task is allocated using the allocate_continuation() function that is similar to allocate_child(), except that it transfers the parent reference of the calling task (this) to c and sets the parent attribute of this to nullptr. The reference count, ref_count, of this's parent does not change since the parent still has the same number of children, although one of the children has suddenly been mutated from the FibTask type to the FibCont one. If you are a happy parent, don't try this at home!

At this point, FibTask is still alive but we will do away with it soon. FibTask does not have a parent anymore, but it is in charge of some chores before dying. FibTask first creates two FibTask children, but watch out!

- The new tasks a and b are now children of c (not of this) because we allocate them using c.allocate_child() instead of just allocate_child(). In other words, c is now the successor of both a and b.

- The result of the children is not written in stack-stored variables any more. When initializing a, the constructor invoked now is FibTask(n-1,&c.x), so the pointer sum in the child task a (a.sum) is actually pointing to c.x. Likewise, b.sum points to c.y.

- The reference count of c (sort of an internal and private c.ref_count) is only set to two (c.set_ref_count(2)) since FibCont c has actually only two children (a and b).

Now children tasks a and b are ready to be spawned, and that's all the duties of FibTask. Now it can die in peace, and the memory it was occupying can be safely reclaimed. R.I.P.

Note   As we mentioned in the previous section, when following the blocking style, if a task A spawns k children and waits for them using the wait_for_all member function, A.ref_count has to be set to k+1. The extra "1" accounts for the additional work that task A has to finish before ending and dispatching A's parent. This extra "1" is not needed when following the continuation-passing style because A transfers the additional work to the continuation task C. In this case, C.ref_count has to be set exactly to k if it has k children.

To better illustrate how all this works now that we follow the continuation-passing style, Figures 10-12 and 10-13 contain some snapshots of the process.

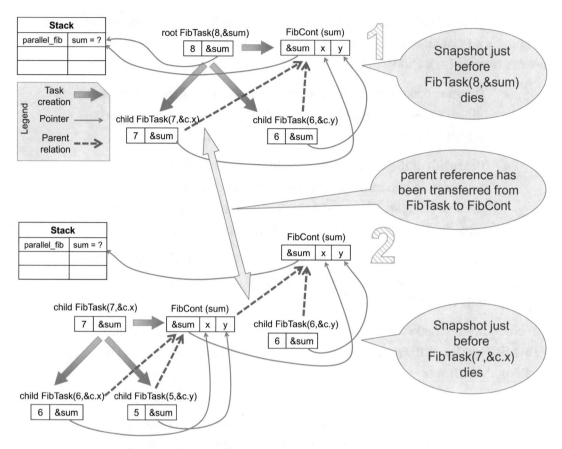

Figure 10-12. *The continuation-passing style for* `parallel_fib(8)` *with* `cutoff=7`

In the upper part of Figure 10-12, the root `FibTask(8,&sum)` has already created the continuation `FibCont(sum)` and tasks `FibTask(7,&c.x)` and `FibTask(6,&c.y)`, which are actually children of `FibCont`. In the stack, we see that we are only storing the final result sum that is local to `parallel_fib` function because x and y are not using stack space using this style. Now, x and y are member variables of `FibCont` and are stored in the heap. In the bottom part of this figure, we see that the original root task has disappeared with all the memory that it was using. In essence, we are trading stack space for heap space and `FibTask`'s objects by `FibCont`'s ones, which is beneficial if `FibCont` objects are smaller. We also see that the parent reference from `FibTask(7,&c.x)` to the root `FibCont(&sum)` has been transferred to the younger `FibCont`.

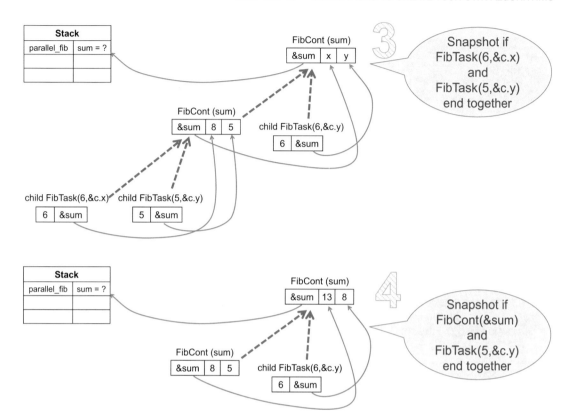

Figure 10-13. *The continuation-passing style example (continuation!!)*

In the top part of Figure 10-13, we start the unwinding part of the recursive algorithm. There is no trace of FibTask objects any more. Child tasks FibTask(6,&c.x) and FibTask(5,&c.y) have resorted to the base case (n<cutoff, assuming cutoff=7) and are about to return after having written *sum with 8 and 5, respectively. Each one of the children will return nullptr, so the worker thread takes control again and goes back to the work-stealing scheduler, decrements ref_count of the parent task, and checks whether or not ref_count is 0. In such a case, following the high-level description of the TBB task dispatch loop presented in Figure 9-14 of Chapter 9, the next task to take is the parent one (FibCont in this case). Contrary to the blocking style, this is now performed right away. In the bottom part of Figure 10-13, we see the two children of the original root task that have already written their results.

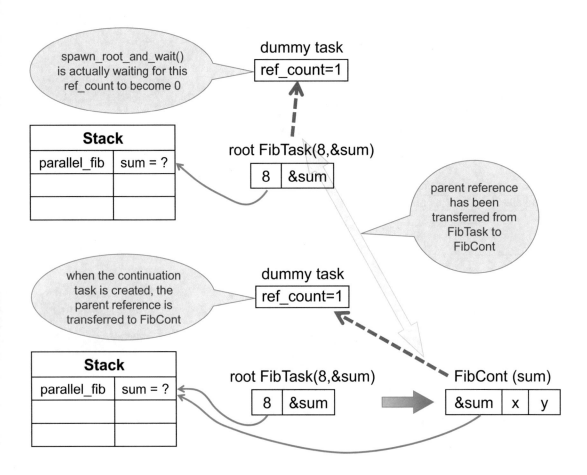

Figure 10-14. *parallel_fib waits for FibCont to complete thanks to a dummy task that has its own ref_count*

You may be wondering if the parallel_fib function is still waiting in the spawn_root_and_wait(a) to the first root task that was created, since this original FibTask was replaced by the first FibCont object and then died (see Figure 10-12). Well, indeed parallel_fib is still waiting because spawn_root_and_wait is designed to work correctly with continuation-passing style. An invocation of spawn_root_and_wait(x) does not actually wait for x to complete. Instead, it constructs a dummy successor of x and waits for the successor's ref_count to become 0. Because allocate_continuation forwards the parent reference to the continuation, the dummy successor's ref_count is not decremented until the continuation FibCont completes. This is illustrated in Figure 10-14.

Bypassing the Scheduler

Scheduler bypass is an optimization in which you directly specify the next task to run instead of letting the scheduler pick. Continuation-passing style often opens up an opportunity for scheduler bypass. For instance, in the continuation-passing example, it turns out that once `FibTask::execute()` returns, by the getting rules of the work-stealing scheduler described in Chapter 9, task a is always the next task taken from the ready pool because it was the last one being spawned (unless it has been stolen by another worker thread). More precisely, the sequence of events is as follows:

- Push task a onto the thread's deque.

- Return from member function `execute()`.

- Pop task a from the thread's deque, unless it is stolen by another thread.

Putting the task into the deque and then getting it back out incurs some overhead that can be avoided, or worse yet, permits stealing that can hurt locality without adding significant parallelism. To avoid both problems, make sure that `execute` does not spawn the task but instead returns a pointer to it as the result. This approach guarantees that the same worker thread immediately executes a, not some other thread. To that end, in the code of Figure 10-11, we need to replace these two lines as follows:

```
spawn(a);              ➜              //spawn(a); commented out!
return nullptr;                       return &a;
```

The Low-Level Task Interface: Part Three – Task Recycling

In addition to bypassing the scheduler, we might also want to bypass task allocation and deallocation. This opportunity frequently arises for recursive tasks that do scheduler bypass because the child is initiated immediately upon return just as the parent completes. Figure 10-15 shows the changes required to implement task recycling in the Fibonacci example.

```
class FibTask: public tbb::task {
public:
  long n;      // not const anymore
  long* sum;  // not const ptr anymore
  FibTask(long n_, long* sum_) : n{n_}, sum{sum_} {}
  tbb::task* execute() { // Overrides virtual function task::execute
    if(n<cutoff) {
      *sum = fib(n);
      return nullptr;
    }
    else {
      // long x, y; not needed anymore
      FibCont& c = *new(allocate_continuation()) FibCont{sum};
      FibTask& b = *new(c.allocate_child()) FibTask{n-2, &c.y};
      recycle_as_child_of(c);
      this->n -=1;
      this->sum = &c.x;
      // Set ref_count to "two children".
      c.set_ref_count(2);
      tbb::task::spawn(b);
      return this; // it was: return &a;
    }
  }
};
```

Figure 10-15. *Following the task recycling style for parallel Fibonacci*

The child that was previously called a is now the recycled this. The call recycle_as_child_of(c) has several effects:

- It marks this not to be automatically destroyed when execute returns.

- It sets the successor of this to be c. To prevent reference-counting problems, recycle_as_child_of has a prerequisite that this must have a nullptr successor (this's parent reference should point to nullptr). This is the case after allocate_continuation occurs.

Member variables have to be updated to mimic what was previously implemented using the constructor FibTask(n-1,&c.x). In this case, this->n is decremented (n -=1;), and this->sum is initialized to point to c.x.

When recycling, ensure that this's member variables are not used in the current execution of the task after the recycled task is spawned. This is the case in our example since the recycled task is actually not spawned and will only run after returning the pointer this. You can spawn the recycled task instead (i.e., spawn (*this); return nullptr;), as long as none of its member variables is used after the spawning. This restriction applies even to const member variables, because after the task is spawned, it might run and be destroyed before the parent progresses any further. A similar member function, task::recycle_as_continuation(), recycles a task as a continuation instead of as a child.

In Figure 10-16, we show the effect of recycling FibTask(8,&sum) as child of FibCont once the child has updated the member variables (8 becomes 7 and sum points to c.x).

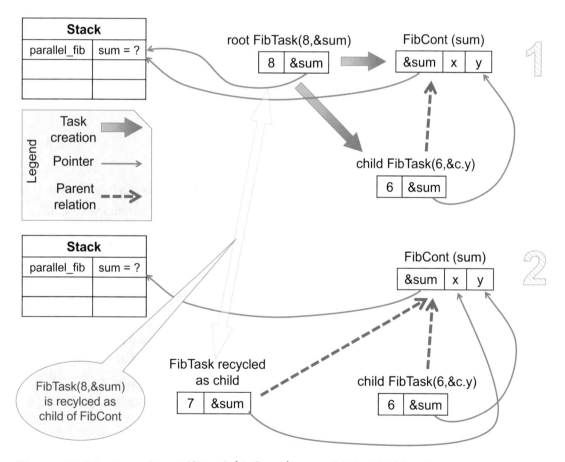

Figure 10-16. *Recycling* FibTask(8,&sum) *as a child of* FibCont

> **Note**   *Greener (and easier) parallel programming* ☺   The embracing of
> composability, continuations, and task recycling has a powerful impact on making
> parallel programming much easier simply by using TBB. Consider that recycling
> has gained favor around the world, and recycling of tasks really does help conserve
> energy too! *Join the movement for greener parallel programming – it doesn't hurt
> that it makes effective programming easier too!*

Scheduler bypassing and task recycling are powerful tools that can result in significant improvements and code optimizations. They are actually used to implement the high-level templates that were presented in Chapters 2 and 3, and we can also exploit them to design other tailored high-level templates that cater to our needs. Flow Graph (Chapter 3 and more coming in Chapter 17) encourages use of `continue_node` (and other nodes with potentials for scheduler bypass). In the next section, we present an example in which we leverage the low-level task API and evaluate its impact, but before that, check out our "checklist."

Task Interface Checklist

Resorting to the task interface is advisable for fork-join parallelism with lots of forks, so that the task stealing can cause sufficient breadth-first behavior to occupy threads, which then conduct themselves in a depth-first manner until they need to steal more work. In other words, the task scheduler's fundamental strategy is "breadth-first theft and depth-first work." The breadth-first theft rule raises parallelism sufficiently to keep threads busy. The depth-first work rule keeps each thread operating efficiently once it has sufficient work to do.

Remember though that it is not the simplest possible API, but one particularly designed for speed. In many cases, we face a problem that can be tackled using a higher-level interface, as the templates `parallel_for`, `parallel_reduce`, and so on do. If this is not the case and you need the extra performance offered by the task API, some of the details to remember are

- Always use `new(allocation_method)` `T` to allocate a task, where `allocation_method` is one of the allocation methods of class task (see Appendix B, Figure B-76). Do not create local or file-scope instances of a task.

- All siblings should be allocated before any start running, unless you are using `allocate_additional_child_of`. We will elaborate on this in the last section of the chapter.

- Exploit continuation passing, scheduler bypass, and task recycling to squeeze out maximum performance.

- If a task completes, and was not marked for re-execution (recycling), it is automatically destroyed. Also, its successor's reference count is decremented, and if it hits zero, the successor is automatically spawned.

One More Thing: FIFO (aka Fire-and-Forget) Tasks

So far, we have seen how tasks are spawned and the result of spawning a task: the thread that enqueues the task is likely the one dequeuing it in a LIFO (Last-in First-out) order (if no other thread steals the spawned task). As we said, this behavior has some beneficial implications in terms of locality and in restraining the memory footprint thanks to the "depth-first work." However, a spawned task can become buried in the local queue of the thread if a bunch of tasks are also spawned afterward.

If we prefer FIFO-like execution order, a task should be enqueued using the enqueue function instead of the spawn one, as follows:

```
class FifoTask : public tbb::task {
public:
  tbb::task *execute() {//do work}
};

FifoTask& t = *new(tbb::task::allocate_root()) FifoTask();
tbb::task::enqueue(t);
```

Our example `FifoTask` class derives from `tbb::task` and overrides the `execute()` member function as every normal task does. The four differences with spawned tasks are

- A spawned task can be postponed by the scheduler until it is waited upon, but an enqueued task will be eventually executed even if there is no thread explicitly waiting on the task. Even if the total number of worker threads is zero, a special additional worker thread is created to execute enqueued tasks.

- Spawned tasks are scheduled in a LIFO like order (most recently spawned is started next), but enqueued tasks are processed in roughly (not precisely) FIFO order (started in approximately the order they entered the queue – the "approximation" gives TBB some flexibility to be more efficient than a strict policy would allow).

- Spawned tasks are ideal for recursive parallelism in order to save memory space thanks to a depth-first traversal, but enqueued tasks can prohibitively consume memory for recursive parallelism since the recursion will expand in a breadth-first traversal.

- Spawned parent tasks should wait for their spawned children to complete, but enqueued tasks should not be waited upon because other enqueued tasks from unrelated parts of the program might have to be processed first. The recommended pattern for using an enqueued task is to have it asynchronously signal its completion. Essentially, enqueued tasks should be allocated as root, instead of as children that are then waited upon.

In Chapter 14, enqueued tasks are also illustrated in the context of prioritizing some tasks over others. Two additional use cases are also described in the Threading Building Blocks Design Patterns manual (see "For More Information" at the end of the chapter). There are two design patterns in which enqueued tasks come in handy. In the first one, a GUI thread must remain responsive even when a long running task is launched by the user. In the proposed solution, the GUI thread enqueues a task but does not wait for it to finish. The task does the heavy lifting and then notifies the GUI thread with a message before dying. The second design pattern is also related with assigning nonpreemptive priorities to different tasks.

Putting These Low-Level Features to Work

Let's switch to a more challenging application to evaluate the impact of different task-based implementation alternatives. Wavefront is a programming pattern that appears in scientific applications such as those based in dynamic programming or sequence alignment. In such a pattern, data elements are distributed on multidimensional grids representing a logical plane or space. The elements must be computed in order because they have dependencies among them. One example is the 2D wavefront that we show in Figure 10-17. Here, computations start at a corner of the matrix, and a sweep will progress across the plane to the opposite corner following a diagonal trajectory. Each antidiagonal represents the number of computations or elements that could be executed in parallel without dependencies among them.

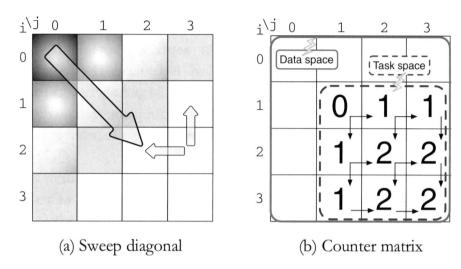

(a) Sweep diagonal   (b) Counter matrix

Figure 10-17. *Typical 2D wavefront pattern (a) and dependencies translated into a matrix of atomic counters (b)*

In the code of Figure 10-18, we compute a function for each cell of a nxn 2D grid. Each cell has a data dependence with two elements of the adjacent cells. For example, in Figure 10-17(a), we see that cell (2,3) depends on the north (1,3) and west (2,2) ones, since on each iteration of the i and j loops, cells that were calculated in previous iterations are needed: A[i,j] depends on A[i-1,j] (north dependency) and A[i,j-1] (west dependency). In Figure 10-18, we show the sequential version of the computation where array A has been linearized. Clearly, the antidiagonal cells are totally independent, so they can be computed in parallel. To exploit this parallelism (loops "i" and "j"), a task will carry out the computations corresponding to each cell inside the iteration space (or task space from now on), and independent tasks will be executed in parallel.

```
for (int i=1; i<n; ++i)
  for (int j=1; j<n; ++j)
    A[i*n+j] = foo(gs, A[i*n+j], A[(i-1)*n+j], A[i*n+j-1]);
```

Figure 10-18. *Code snippet for a 2D wavefront problem. Array A is the linearized view of the 2D grid.*

In our task parallelization strategy, the basic unit of work is the computation performed by function foo at each (i,j) cell of the matrix. Without loss of generality, we assume that the computational load for each cell will be controlled by the gs (grainsize) parameter of the foo function. That way, we can define the granularity of the tasks, and therefore, we can study the performance of different implementations depending on the task granularity, as well as situations with homogeneous or heterogeneous task workloads.

In Figure 10-17(b), the arrows show the data dependence flow for our wavefront problem. For example, after the execution of the upper left task (1, 1), which does not depend on any other task, two new tasks can be dispatched (the one below (2, 1) and the one to the right (1, 2)). This dependence information can be captured by a 2D matrix with counters, like the one we show in Figure 10-17(b). The value of the counters points out to how many tasks we have to wait for. Only the tasks with the corresponding counter nullified can be dispatched.

An alternative to implement this kind of wavefront computation is covered in the Intel TBB Design Patterns (see "For More Information") in which a General Graph of Acyclic tasks is implemented. This version is available along with the sources of this chapter under the name wavefront_v0_DAG.cpp. However, that version requires that all the tasks are preallocated beforehand and the implementation that we present next is more flexible and can be tuned to better exploit locality as we will see later. In Figure 10-19, we show our first task-based implementation that we call wavefront_v1_addchild. Each ready task first executes the task body, and then it will decrement the counters of the tasks depending on it. If this decrement operation ends up with a counter equal to 0, the task is also responsible of spawning the new independent task. Note that the counters are shared and will be modified by different tasks that are running in parallel. To account for this issue, the counters are atomic variables (see Chapter 5).

```
class Cell: public tbb::task {
  int i,j;
  int n;
  int gs;
  std::vector<double> &A;
  std::vector<std::atomic<int>> &counters;
public:
  Cell(int i_ ,int j_, int n_, int gs_,
       std::vector<double> &A_,
       std::vector<std::atomic<int>> &counters_) :
       i{i_},j{j_},n{n_},gs{gs_},A{A_},counters{counters_} {}
  task* execute(){
    A[i*n+j] = foo(gs, A[i*n+j], A[(i-1)*n+j], A[i*n+j-1]);
    if (j<n-1 && --counters[i*n+j+1]==0) // east cell ready
       spawn(*new(allocate_additional_child_of(*parent()))
             Cell{i,j+1,n,gs,A,counters});
    if (i<n-1 && --counters[(i+1)*n+j]==0) // south cell ready
       spawn(*new(allocate_additional_child_of(*parent()))
             Cell{i+1,j,n,gs,A,counters});
    return nullptr;
  }
};
```

Figure 10-19. *Excerpt from the code of the wavefront_v1_addchild version*

Note that in Figure 10-19, we use allocate_additional_child_of(*parent()) as the allocation method for the new tasks. By using this allocation method, we can add children while others are running. On the positive side, this allow us to save some coding that would have been necessary to ensure that all child tasks are allocated before any of them is spawned (since this depends on whether the east task, the south, or both are ready to be dispatched). On the negative side, this allocation method requires that the parent's ref_count is atomically updated (incremented when one "additional_child" is allocated and decremented when any child dies). Since we are using allocate_additional_child_of(*parent()), all created tasks will be children of the same parent. The first task of the task space is task (1, 1), and it is spawned with

```
tbb::task::spawn_root_and_wait(*new(tbb::task::allocate_root())
                  Cell{1,1,n,gs,A,counters});
```

and the parent of this root task is the dummy task that we already introduced in Figure 10-14. Then, all the tasks created in this code atomically update the ref_count of the dummy task.

Another caveat on using the allocate_additional_child_of allocation method is that the user (we) has to ensure that the parent's ref_count does not prematurely reach 0 before the additional child is allocated. Our code already accounts for this eventuality since a task, t, allocating an additional child, c, is already guaranteeing that the t parent's ref_count is at least one since t will only decrement its parent's ref_count when dying (i.e., after allocating c).

In Chapter 2, the parallel_do_feeder template was already presented to illustrate a different wavefront application: the forward substitution. This template essentially implements a work-list algorithm, in such a way that new tasks can be added dynamically to the work-list by invoking the parallel_do_feeder::add() member function. We call wavefront_v2_feeder to a version of the wavefront code that relies on parallel_do_feeder and, as in Figure 2-19 in Chapter 2, uses feeder.add() instead of the spawn calls in Figure 10-19.

If we want to avoid all child tasks pending from a single parent and fighting to atomically update its ref_count, we can implement a more elaborated version that mimics the blocking style explained earlier. Figure 10-20 shows the execute() member function in this case, where we first annotate whether the east, south, or both cells are ready to dispatch and then allocate and dispatch the corresponding tasks. Note that now we use the allocate_child() method, and each task has at most two descendants to wait upon. Although the atomic update of a single ref_count is not a bottleneck anymore, more tasks are in flight waiting for their children to finish (and occupying memory). This version will be named wavefront_v3_blockstyle.

```
task* execute(){
  A[i*n+j] = foo(gs, A[i*n+j], A[(i-1)*n+j], A[i*n+j-1]);
  int east = 0,south = 0;
  if (j<n-1 && --counters[i*n+j+1]==0) east=1;
  if (i<n-1 && --counters[(i+1)*n+j]==0) south=1;
  set_ref_count(1+east+south);
  if(east==1 && south==0)
    spawn_and_wait_for_all(*new(allocate_child())
                                Cell{i,j+1,n,gs,A,counters});
  if(east==0 && south==1)
    spawn_and_wait_for_all(*new(allocate_child())
                                Cell{i+1,j,n,gs,A,counters});
  if(east==1 && south==1) {
    //ensure all children are allocated before any is spawned
    Cell &a = *new(allocate_child()) Cell{i,j+1,n,gs,A,counters};
    Cell &b = *new(allocate_child()) Cell{i+1,j,n,gs,A,counters};
    spawn(a);
    spawn_and_wait_for_all(b);
  }
  return nullptr;
}
```

Figure 10-20. *execute() member function of the wavefront_v3_blockstyle version*

Now, let's also exploit continuation-passing and task recycling styles. In our wavefront pattern, each task has the opportunity to spawn two new tasks (east and south neighbors). We can avoid the spawn of one of them by returning a pointer to the next task, so instead of spawning a new task, the current task recycles into the new one. As we have explained, with this we achieve two goals: reducing the number of task allocations, calls to spawn(), as well as saving the time for getting new tasks from the local queue. The resulting version is called wavefront_v4_recycle, and the main advantage is that it reduces the number of spawns from n x n − 2n (the number of spawns in previous versions) to n − 2 (approximately the size of a column). See the companion source code to have a look at the complete implementation.

In addition, when recycling we can provide hints to the scheduler about how to prioritize the execution of tasks to, for example, guarantee a cache-conscious traversal of the data structure, which might help to improve data locality. In Figure 10-21, we see the code snippet of the wavefront_v5_locality version that features this optimization. We set the flag recycle_into_east if there is a ready to dispatch task to the east of the executing task. Otherwise, we set the flag recycle_into_south, if the south task is ready to dispatch. Later, according to these flags, we recycle the current task into the east or south tasks. Note that, since in this example the data structure is stored by rows, if both east and south tasks are ready, the data cache can be better exploited by recycling into the east task. That way, the same thread/core executing the current task is going to take care of the task traversing the neighbor data, so we make the most out of spatial locality. So, in that case, we recycle into the east task and spawn a new south task that would be executed later.

```
task* execute(){
  A[i*n+j] = foo(gs, A[i*n+j], A[(i-1)*n+j], A[i*n+j-1]);
  bool recycle_into_east=false;
  bool recycle_into_south=false;
  if (j<n-1 && --counters[i*n+j+1]==0) recycle_into_east=true;
  if (i<n-1 && --counters[(i+1)*n+j]==0){
      if (!recycle_into_east) recycle_into_south = true;
      else
        spawn(*new(allocate_additional_child_of(*parent()))
              Cell{i+1,j,n,gs,A,counters});
  }
  if (recycle_into_east) {
    recycle_as_child_of(*parent());
    j = j+1;
    return this;
  }
  else if(recycle_into_south){
    recycle_as_child_of(*parent());
    i=i+1;
    return this;
  }
  else return nullptr;
}
```

Figure 10-21.   *execute() member function of the wavefront_v5_locality version*

For huge wavefront problems, it may be relevant to reduce the footprint of each allocated task. Depending on whether or not you feel comfortable using global variables, you can consider storing the shared global state of all the tasks (n, gs, A, and counters) in global variables. This alternative is implemented in wavefront_v6_global, and it is provided in the directory with the source code of this chapter's examples.

Using the parameter gs that sets the number of floating-point operations per task, we found that for coarse-grained tasks that execute more than 2000 floating-point operations (FLOPs), there is not too much difference between the seven versions and the codes scale almost linearly. This is because the parallel overheads vanish in comparison with the large enough time needed to compute all the tasks. However, it is difficult to find real wavefront codes with such coarse-grained tasks. In Figure 10-22, we show the speedup achieved by versions 0 to 5 on a quad-core processor, more precisely, a Core i7-6700HQ (Skylake architecture, 6th generation) at 2.6 GHz, 6 MB L3 cache, and 16 GB RAM. Grain size, gs, is set to only 200 FLOPs and n=1024 (for this n, version 6 performs as version 5).

	Seq.	v0 DAG	v1 addchild	v2 feeder	v3 blockstyle	v4 recycle	v5 locality
Time (ms)	240	112	129	130	96	74	69
Speed-up	1	2.14	1.86	1.85	2.50	3.24	3.48

Figure 10-22. *Speedup on four cores of the different versions*

It is clear that TBB v5 is the best solution in this experiment. In fact, we measured speedups for other finer-grained sizes finding that the finer the granularity, the better the improvement of v4 and v5 in comparison with v1 and v2. Besides, it is interesting to see that a great deal of the improvement contribution is due to the recycling optimization, pointed out by the v4 enhancement over the v1 version. A more elaborated study was conducted by A. Dios in the papers that are listed at the end of the chapter.

Since the performance of the wavefront algorithms decreases as the task workload grain becomes finer, a well-known technique to counteract this trend is tiling (see the Glossary for a brief definition). By tiling, we achieve several goals: to better exploit locality since each task works within a space confined region of data for some time; to reduce the number of tasks (and therefore, the number of allocations and spawns); and to save some overhead in wavefront bookkeeping (memory space and the initialization time of the counter/dependence matrix, which is now smaller due to it requiring a counter per block-tile, and not one per matrix element). After coarsening the grain of the tasks via tiling, we are again free to go for v1 or v2 implementations, right? However, the downside of tiling is that it reduces the amount of independent task (they are coarser, but there are fewer of them). Then, if we need to scale our application to a large number of cores and the problem does not grow in size at the same pace, we probably have to squeeze until the last drop of available performance out of the TBB low-level features. In challenging situations like these, we have to demonstrate our outstanding command of TBB and that we have successfully honed our parallel programming skills.

Summary

In this chapter, we have delved into the task-based alternatives that can be particularly useful to implement recursive, divide and conquer, and wavefront applications, among others. We have used the Fibonacci sequence as a running example that we first implemented in parallel with the already discussed high-level `parallel_invoke`. We then started diving into deeper waters by using a medium-level API provided by the `task_group` class. It is though the task interface the one offering the larger degree of flexibility to cater for our specific optimization needs. TBB tasks are underpinning the other high-level templates that were presented in the first part of the book, but we can also get our hands on them to build our own patterns and algorithms, leveraging continuation passing, scheduler bypassing, and task recycling advanced techniques. For even more demanding developers, more possibilities are available thanks to task priorities, task affinity, and task enqueue features that will we cover in the next chapter. We can't wait to see what you can create and develop out of these powerful tools that are now in your hands.

For More Information

Here are some additional reading materials we recommend related to this chapter:

- A. Dios, R. Asenjo, A. Navarro, F. Corbera, E.L. Zapata, A case study of the task-based parallel wavefront pattern, Advances in Parallel Computing: Applications, Tools and Techniques on the Road to Exascale Computing, ISBN: 978-1-61499-040-6, Vol. 22, pp. 65–72, IOS Press BV, Amsterdam, 2012 (extended version available here: `www.ac.uma.es/~compilacion/publicaciones/UMA-DAC-11-02.pdf`).

- A. Dios, R. Asenjo, A. Navarro, F. Corbera, E.L. Zapata *High-level template for the task-based parallel wavefront pattern,* IEEE Intl. Conf. on High Performance Computing (HiPC 2011), Bengaluru (Bangalore), India, December 18–21, 2011. Implement a high-level template on top of TBB task to ease the implementation of wavefront algorithms.

- González Vázquez, Carlos Hugo, Library-based solutions for algorithms with complex patterns of parallelism, PhD report, 2015. `http://hdl.handle.net/2183/14385`. Describes three complex parallel patterns and addresses them by implementing high-level templates on top of TBB tasks.

- Intel TBB Design Patterns:

  - GUI thread: `http://software.intel.com/en-us/node/506119`

  - Priorities: `http://software.intel.com/en-us/node/506120`

  - Wavefront: `http://software.intel.com/en-us/node/506110`

CHAPTER 11

Controlling the Number of Threads Used for Execution

By default, the TBB library initializes its scheduler with what is typically the right number of threads to use. It creates one worker thread fewer than the number of logical cores on the platform, leaving one of the cores available to execute the main application thread. Because the TBB library implements parallelism using tasks that are scheduled on to these threads, this is usually the right amount of threads to have – there is exactly one software thread for each logical core, and the scheduling algorithms in TBB efficiently distribute tasks to these software threads using work stealing as described in Chapter 9.

Nevertheless, there are many scenarios in which we may justifiably want to change the default. Perhaps we are running scaling experiments and want to see how well our application performs with different numbers of threads. Or perhaps we know that several applications will always execute on our system in parallel, so we want to use only a subset of the available resources in our application. Or perhaps we know that our application creates extra native threads for rendering, AI, or some other purpose and we want to restrict TBB so that it leaves room on the system for those other native threads. In any case, if we want to change the default, we can.

There are three classes that can be used to influence how many threads participate in executing a specific TBB algorithm or flow graph. The interactions between these classes can be very complicated though! In this chapter, we focus on the common cases and best-known practices that will likely be enough for all but the most complicated applications. This level of detail will be sufficient for most readers, and the recommendations we make will be enough for almost all situations. Even so, readers

© Intel Corporation 2019
M. Voss, R. Asenjo, J. Reinders, *Pro TBB*, https://doi.org/10.1007/978-1-4842-4398-5_11

who want to understand the lowest level nuts-and-bolts of TBB are welcome to wade into the weeds in the TBB documentation to get into all of the details of the possible interactions between these classes if they choose. But if you follow the patterns outlined in this chapter, we don't think that will be necessary.

A Brief Recap of the TBB Scheduler Architecture

Before we begin talking about controlling the number of threads used in executing parallel algorithms, let's refresh our memory on the structure of the TBB scheduler shown in Figure 11-1. A more in-depth description of the TBB scheduler is found in Chapter 9.

The global thread pool (market) is where all of the worker threads start before migrating to task arenas. Threads migrate to task arenas that have tasks available to execute, and if there are not enough threads to fill all of the slots in all of the arenas, the threads fill slots in proportion to the number of slots in the arenas. For example, a task arena with twice as many slots as another arena will receive roughly twice as many workers.

Note   If task priorities are in use, worker threads will fully satisfy the requests from task arenas with higher priority tasks before filling slots in task arenas with lower priority tasks. We discuss task priorities in more detail in Chapter 14. For the rest of this chapter, we assume all tasks are of equal priority.

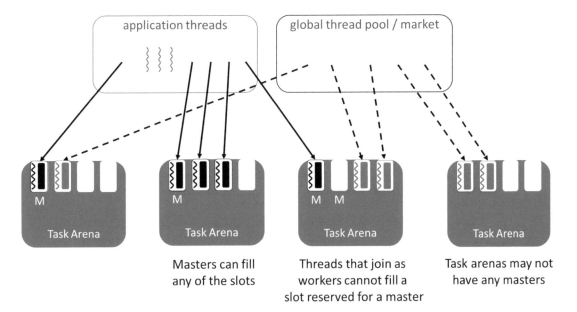

Figure 11-1. *The architecture of the TBB task scheduler*

Task arenas are created in one of two ways: (1) each master thread gets its own arena by default when it executes a TBB algorithm or spawns tasks and (2) we can explicitly create task arenas using class task_arena as described in more detail in Chapter 12.

If a task arena runs out of work, its worker threads return to the global thread pool to look for work to do in other arenas, or to sleep if there's no work in any arena.

Interfaces for Controlling the Number of Threads

The TBB library was first released over a decade ago, and it has evolved over that time to keep pace with the evolution of platforms and workloads. Now, TBB offers three ways to control threads: task_scheduler_init, task_arena, and global_control. In simple applications, we might be able to use just one of these interfaces to accomplish everything we need, but in more complex applications, we may need to use a combination of these interfaces.

Controlling Thread Count with **task_scheduler_init**

When the TBB library was first released, there was only a single interface for controlling the number of threads in an application: class task_scheduler_init. The interface of this class is shown in Figure 11-2.

A task_scheduler_init object can be used to (1) control when the task arena associated with a master thread is constructed and destroyed; (2) set the number of worker slots in that thread's arena; (3) set the stack size for each worker thread in the arena; and, if needed, (4) set an initial *soft* limit (see the side bar) on the number of threads available in the global thread pool.

```
class task_scheduler_init {
public:
  static const int automatic = /* implementation defined */;
  static const int deferred = /* implementation defined */;

  task_scheduler_init(int number_of_threads=automatic,
                      stack_size_type thread_stack_size=0);
  ~task_scheduler_init();

  void initialize(int number_of_threads=automatic);
  void initialize(int number_of_threads,
                  stack_size_type thread_stack_size);
  void terminate();

  static int default_num_threads ();
  bool is_active() const;

  // preview features
  void blocking_terminate();
  bool blocking_terminate(const std::nothrow_t&)
noexcept(true);
};
```

Figure 11-2. *The* task_scheduler_init *class interface*

Controlling Thread Count with **task_arena**

Later, as TBB was used on larger systems and in more complex applications, class task_arena was added to the library to create *explicit* task arenas as a way to isolate work. Work isolation is discussed in more detail in Chapter 12. In this chapter, we focus on how class task_arena lets us set the number of slots available in those explicit arenas. The functions in class task_arena used in this chapter are shown in Figure 11-3.

Using the task_arena constructor, we can set the total number of slots in the arena using the max_concurrency argument and the number of slots reserved exclusively for master threads using the reserved_for_masters argument. When we pass a functor to the execute method, the calling thread attaches to the arena, and any tasks spawned from within the functor are spawned into that arena.

```
class task_arena {
public:
  static const int automatic = implementation-defined;

  task_arena(int max_concurrency = automatic,
             unsigned reserved_for_masters = 1);

  template<typename F> auto execute(F& f) -> decltype(f());
  template<typename F> auto execute(const F& f) ->
decltype(f());
  template<typename F> void enqueue(F&& f);
  template<typename F> void enqueue(F&& f, priority_t p);
};
```

Figure 11-3. *The* task_arena *class interface*

SOFT AND HARD LIMITS

The global thread pool has both a *soft limit* and a *hard limit*. The number of worker threads available for parallel execution is equal to the minimum of the soft limit value and the hard limit value.

The soft limit is a function of the requests made by the task_scheduler_init and global_control objects in the application. The hard limit is a function of the number of logical cores, P, on the system. At the time of the writing of this book, there is a hard limit of 256 threads for platforms where P <= 64, 4P for platforms where 64 < P <= 128, and 2P for platforms where P > 128.

TBB tasks are executed non-preemptively on the TBB worker threads. So, oversubscribing a system with many more TBB threads than logical cores doesn't make a lot of sense – there are just more threads for the OS to manage. If we want more TBB threads than the *hard* limit allows, it is almost guaranteed that we are either using TBB incorrectly or trying to accomplish something that TBB was not designed for.

Controlling Thread Count with `global_control`

After class `task_arena` was introduced to the library, TBB users began requesting an interface to directly control the number of threads available in the global thread pool. The class `global_control` was only a *preview feature* until TBB 2019 Update 4 (it is now a full feature - meaning it is available by default without needing to enable with a preview macro definition) and is used to change the value of global parameters used by the TBB task scheduler – including the soft limit on the number of threads available in the global thread pool.

The class definition for class `global_control` is shown in Figure 11-4.

```
class global_control {
public:
  enum parameter {
    max_allowed_parallelism,
    thread_stack_size
  };
  global_control(parameter p, size_t value);
  ~global_control();
  static size_t active_value(parameter param);
};
```

Figure 11-4. *The global_control class interface*

Summary of Concepts and Classes

The concepts used in this chapter and the effects of the various classes are summarized in this section. Don't worry too much about understanding all of the details presented here. In the next section, we present best-known methods for using these classes to achieve specific goals. So, while the interactions described here may appear complicated, typical usage patterns are much simpler.

The scheduler: The TBB scheduler refers to the global thread pool and at least one task arena. Once a TBB scheduler is constructed, additional task arenas may be added to it, incrementing a reference count on the scheduler. As task arenas are destroyed, they decrement the reference count on the scheduler. If the last task arena is destroyed, the TBB scheduler is destroyed, including the global thread pool. Any future uses of TBB tasks will require construction of a new TBB scheduler. There is never more than one TBB scheduler active in a process.

The hard thread limit: There is a hard limit on the total number of worker threads that will be created by a TBB scheduler. This is a function of the hardware concurrency of the platform (see **Soft and Hard Limits** for more details).

The soft thread limit: There is a dynamic soft limit on the number of worker threads available to a TBB scheduler. A global_control object can be used to change the soft limit directly. Otherwise, the soft limit is initialized by the thread that creates the scheduler (see **Soft and Hard Limits** for more details).

The default soft thread limit: If a thread spawns a TBB task, whether directly by using the low-level interface or indirectly by using a TBB algorithm or flow graph, a TBB scheduler will be created if none exists at that time. If no global_control objects have set an explicit soft limit, the soft limit is initialized to P-1, where P is the platform's hardware concurrency.

global_control objects: A global_control object affects, during its lifetime, the soft limit on the number of worker threads that a TBB scheduler can use. At any point in time, the soft limit is the minimum value of all of the max_concurrency_limit values requested by the active global_control objects. If the soft limit was initialized before any of the active global_control objects were constructed, this initial value is also considered when finding the minimum value. When a global_control object is destroyed, the soft limit may increase if the destroyed object was the limiting max_concurrency_limit value. Creation of a global_control object does not initialize the TBB scheduler nor increment the reference count on the scheduler. When the last global_control object is destroyed, the soft limit is reset to the default soft thread limit.

task_scheduler_init objects: A task_scheduler_init object creates the task arena associated with a master thread, but only if one does not already exist for that thread. If one already exists, the task_scheduler_init object increments the reference count of the task arena. When a task_scheduler_init object is destroyed, it decrements the reference count, and if the new count is zero, the task arena is destroyed. If a TBB scheduler does not exist when a task_scheduler_init object is constructed, a TBB scheduler is created, and if the soft thread limit has not been set by a global_control object, it is initialized using the constructor's max_threads argument shown as follows:

P-1, where P is the number of logical cores	if max_threads <= P - 1
max_threads	otherwise

task_arena objects: A task_arena object creates an explicit task arena that is not associated with a specific master thread. The underlying task arena is not initialized immediately during the constructor but lazily on first use (in our illustrations in this chapter, we show the construction of the object not the underlying task arena representation). If a thread spawns or enqueues a task into an explicit task_arena before that thread has initialized its own implicit task arena, this action acts like a first use of the TBB scheduler for that thread – including all of the side effects of a default initialization of its implicit task arena and possible initialization of the soft limit.

The Best Approaches for Setting the Number of Threads

The combination of the task_scheduler_init, task_arena, and global_control classes provides a powerful set of tools for controlling the number of threads that can participate in the execution of parallel work in TBB.

The interaction of these objects can be confusing when combined in ways that fall outside of the expected patterns. Therefore, in this section, we focus on common scenarios and provide recommended approaches for using these classes. For simplicity in the figures that we show in this section, we assume that we are executing on a system that supports four logical cores. On such a system, the TBB library will, by default, create three worker threads, and there will be four slots in any default task arenas, with one slot reserved for a master thread. In our figures, we show the number of threads that are available in the global thread pool and the number of slots in the task arena(s). To reduce clutter in the figures, we do not show workers being assigned to slots. Downward arrows are used to indicate the lifetimes of objects. A large "X" indicates the destruction of an object.

Using a Single **task_scheduler_init** Object for a Simple Application

The simplest, and perhaps most common, scenario is that we have an application with a single main thread and no explicit task arenas. The application may have many TBB algorithms, including use of nested parallelism, but does not have more than one user-created thread – that is, the main thread. If we do nothing to control the number of threads managed by the TBB library, an implicit task arena will be created for the main thread when it first interacts with the TBB scheduler by spawning a task, executing a

TBB algorithm, or by using a TBB flow graph. When this default task arena is created, the global thread pool will be populated with one thread fewer than the number of logical cores in the system. This most basic case, with all default initializations, is illustrated for a system with four logical cores in Figure 11-5.

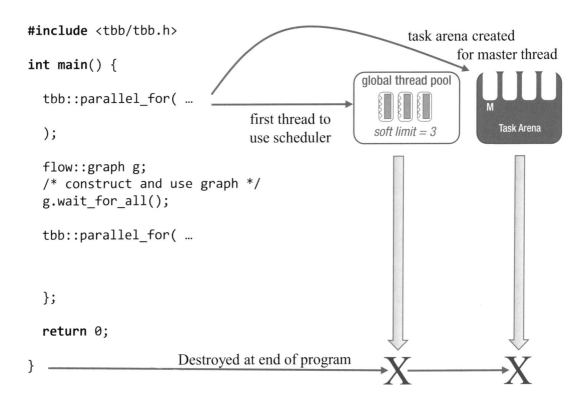

```
#include <tbb/tbb.h>

int main() {

    tbb::parallel_for( …

    );

    flow::graph g;
    /* construct and use graph */
    g.wait_for_all();

    tbb::parallel_for( …

    };

    return 0;

}
```

Figure 11-5. *Default initialization of the global thread pool and a single task arena for the main thread*

The sample code is available at Github in ch11/fig_11_05.cpp and is instrumented so that it prints a summary of how many threads participate in each section of the code. Many of the examples in this chapter are instrumented similarly. This instrumentation is not shown in the source code in the figures but is available in the code at Github. Running this example on a system with four logical cores results in output similar to

```
There are 4 logical cores.
4 threads participated in 1st pfor
4 threads participated in 2nd pfor
4 threads participated in flow graph
```

If we want different behavior in this simplest scenario, class task_scheduler_
init is sufficient for controlling the number of threads. All we need to do is create a
task_scheduler_init object before our first use of TBB tasks and pass to it the desired
number of threads we want our application to use. An example of this is shown in
Figure 11-6. The construction of this object creates the task scheduler, populates the
global thread pool (market) with an appropriate number of threads (at least enough to
fill the slots in the task arena[1]), and constructs a single arena for the main thread with
the requested number of slots. This TBB scheduler is destroyed when the single task_
scheduler_init object is destroyed.

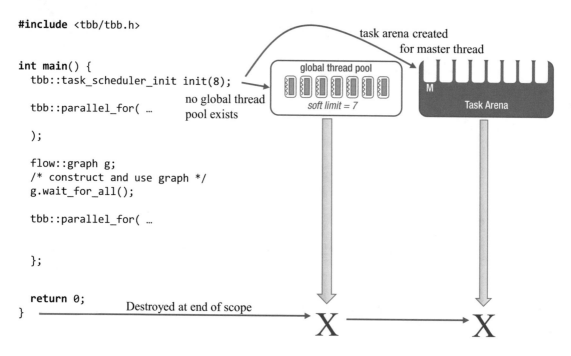

```
#include <tbb/tbb.h>

int main() {
  tbb::task_scheduler_init init(8);

  tbb::parallel_for( …

  );

  flow::graph g;
  /* construct and use graph */
  g.wait_for_all();

  tbb::parallel_for( …


  };

  return 0;
}
```

Figure 11-6. *Using a single* task_scheduler_init *object for a simple application*

---

[1]This is a slight oversimplification. See the earlier sidebar on soft and hard limits in this chapter to
learn more.

Executing the code for Figure 11-6 will result in an output:

```
There are 4 logical cores.
8 threads participated in 1st pfor
8 threads participated in 2nd pfor
8 threads participated in flow graph
```

> **Note**   Of course, statically coding the number of threads to use is a really bad idea. We are illustrating capabilities with easy to follow examples with specific numbers. In order to write portable and more timeless code, we would almost never recommend coding specific numbers.

Using More Than One `task_scheduler_init` Object in a Simple Application

A slightly more complicated use case is when we still have only a single application thread but we want to execute with different numbers of threads during different phases of the application. As long as we don't overlap the lifetimes of `task_scheduler_init` objects, we can change the number of threads during an application's execution by creating and destroying `task_scheduler_init` objects that use different `max_threads` values. A common scenario where this is used is in scaling experiments. Figure 11-7 shows a loop that runs a test on 1 through P threads. Here, we create and destroy a series of `task_scheduler_init` objects, and therefore TBB schedulers, that support different numbers of threads.

```
#include <iostream>
#include <tbb/tbb.h>

void run_test() {
  const int N =
    10*tbb::task_scheduler_init::default_num_threads();
  tbb::parallel_for(0, N, [](int) {
    tbb::tick_count t0 = tbb::tick_count::now();
    while ((tbb::tick_count::now() - t0).seconds() < 0.01);
  });
}

void fig_11_7() {
  const int P =
    tbb::task_scheduler_init::default_num_threads();
  for (int i = 1; i <= P; ++i) {
    tbb::tick_count t0 = tbb::tick_count::now();
    tbb::task_scheduler_init init(i);
    run_test();
    auto sec = (tbb::tick_count::now() - t0).seconds();
    std::cout << "Test using " << i << " threads took "
              << sec << "seconds" << std::endl;
  }
}
```

Figure 11-7. *A simple timing loop that runs a test using 1 through P threads*

In Figure 11-7, each time we create the task_scheduler_init object init, the library creates a task arena for the main thread with one slot reserved for a master thread and i-1 additional slots. At the same time, it sets the soft limit and populates the global thread pool with at least i-1 worker threads (remember that that if max_threads is < P-1, it still creates P-1 threads in the global thread pool). When init is destroyed, the TBB scheduler is destroyed, including the single task arena and the global thread pool.

The output from a run of the sample code, in which run_test() contains a parallel_for with 400 milliseconds of work, results in output similar to

```
Test using 1 threads took 0.401094seconds
Test using 2 threads took 0.200297seconds
Test using 3 threads took 0.140212seconds
Test using 4 threads took 0.100435seconds
```

Using Multiple Arenas with Different Numbers of Slots to Influence Where TBB Places Its Worker Threads

Let's now explore even more complicated scenarios, where we have more than one task arena. The most common way this situation arises is that our application has more than one application thread. Each of these threads is a master thread and gets its own implicit task arena. We can also have more than one task arena because we explicitly create arenas using class task_arena as described in Chapter 12. Regardless of how we wind up with multiple task arenas in an application, the worker threads migrate to task arenas in proportion to the number of slots they have. And the threads only consider task arenas that have tasks available to execute. As we noted earlier, we are assuming in this chapter that tasks are all of equal priority. Task priorities, which can affect how threads migrate to arenas, are described in more detail in Chapter 14.

Figure 11-8 shows an example with a total of three task arenas: two task arenas that are created for master threads (the main thread and thread t) and one explicit task arena, a. This example is contrived but shows code that is complicated enough to get our points across.

In Figure 11-8, there is no attempt to control the number of threads in the application or the number of slots in the task arenas. Therefore, each arena is constructed with the default number of slots, and the global thread pool is initialized with the default number of worker threads as shown in Figure 11-9.

```
void fig_11_8() {
  tbb::task_arena a;

  std::thread t([=]() {
    tbb::parallel_for(0, N, [](int) { /* do work */ });
  });

  a.execute([=]() { tbb::parallel_for(0, N,
    [](int) { /* do work */}
  );

  tbb::parallel_for(0, N, [](int) { /* do work */ });
  t.join();
}
```

Figure 11-8. *An application with three task arenas: the default arena for the main thread, an explicit* task_arena *a, and a default task arena for master thread* t

Because we now have more than one thread, we use the vertical position in
Figure 11-9 to indicate time; objects lower in the figure are constructed after objects
higher in the figure. The figure shows one possible execution order, and in our
illustration thread t is the first thread to spawn a task, by using a parallel_for, and so
it creates the TBB scheduler and the global thread pool. As complicated as the example
appears, the behavior is well defined.

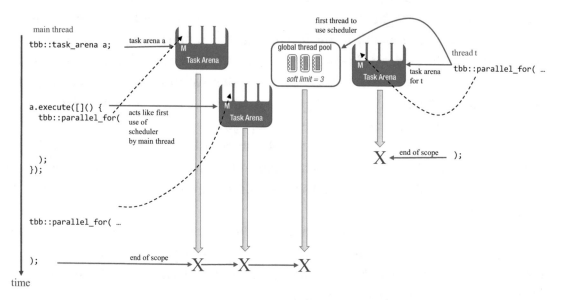

Figure 11-9. *A possible execution of the example with three task arenas*

As shown in Figure 11-9, the execution of the parallel_for algorithms in thread
t and task arena a might overlap. If so, the three threads in the global thread pool are
divided between them. Since there are three worker threads, one arena will initially get
one worker thread and the other one will initially get two worker threads. Which arena
gets fewer threads is up to the library's discretion, and when either of these arenas runs
out of work, the threads can migrate to the other arena to help finish the remaining work
there. After the call to a.execute completes in the main thread in Figure 11-9, the final
parallel_for executes within the main thread's default arena, with the main thread
filling its master slot. If at this point, the parallel_for in thread t is also complete, then
all three worker threads can migrate to the main thread's arena to work on the final
algorithm.

The default behavior shown in Figure 11-9 makes a lot of sense. We only have four logical cores in our system, so TBB initializes the global thread pool with three threads. When each task arena is created, TBB doesn't add more threads to the global thread pool because the platform still has the same number of cores. Instead, the three threads in the global thread pool are dynamically shared among the task arenas.

The TBB library assigns threads to task arenas in proportion to the number of slots they have. But we don't have to settle for task arenas with the default number of slots. We can control the number of slots in the different arenas by creating a task_scheduler_ init object for each application thread and/or by passing in a max_concurrency argument to explicit task_arena objects. A modified example that does this is shown in Figure 11-10.

```
void fig_11_10() {
  int N = 10*P;
  tbb::task_scheduler_init i4(4);

  tbb::task_arena a(3);

  std::thread t([=]() {
    tbb::task_scheduler_init i2(2);
    tbb::parallel_for(0, N, [](int) { /* do work */ });
  });

  a.execute([=]() {
    tbb::parallel_for(0, N, [](int) { /* do work */ });
  });

  tbb::parallel_for(0, N, [](int) { /* do work */ });
  t.join();
}
```

Figure 11-10. *An application with three task arenas: the default arena for the main thread will have a max concurrency of 4, the explicit* task_arena *a has a max concurrency of 3, and the default arena for master thread t has a max concurrency of 2.*

Now when we execute the application, the TBB library will only be able to provide at most one worker thread to thread t's arena since it only has a single slot for a worker, and the remaining two can be assigned to the parallel_for in arena a. We can see an example execution that shows this in Figure 11-11.

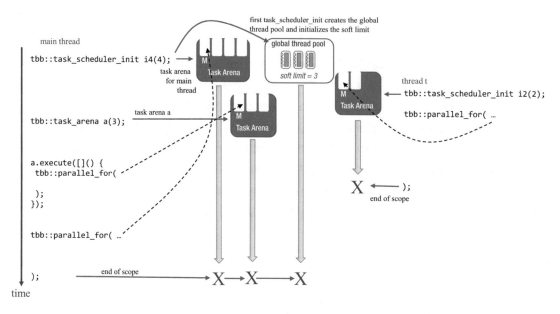

Figure 11-11. *A possible execution of the example with three task arenas after we have explicitly set the number of slots in the various arenas*

An execution of the sample code from Github, which tracks how many threads participates in each section, shows an output of

```
There are 4 logical cores.
3 threads participated in arena pfor
4 threads participated in main pfor
2 threads participated in std::thread pfor
```

Because we have limited the number of slots available to thread t, the other threads can no longer migrate from task_arena a to thread t after they finish their work. We need to be prudent when we limit slots. In this simple example, we have skewed execution in favor of task_arena a but have also restricted how many idle threads can assist thread t.

We have now controlled the number of slots for threads in task arenas but still relied on the default number of threads that TBB allocates in the global thread pool to fill these slots. If we want to change the number of threads that are available to the fill the slots, we need to turn to the class global_control.

Using `global_control` to Control How Many Threads Are Available to Fill Arena Slots

Let's revisit the example from the previous section one more time, but double the number of threads in the global thread pool. Our new implementation is shown in Figure 11-12.

```
void fig_11_12() {
  const int P =
tbb::task_scheduler_init::default_num_threads();
  int N = 10*P;

  auto mp = tbb::global_control::max_allowed_parallelism;
  int nt = 2*P;
  tbb::global_control gc(mp, nt);

  tbb::task_arena a(3*nt/4);

  std::thread t([=]() {
    tbb::task_scheduler_init i1(nt/4);
    tbb::parallel_for(0, N, [](int) { /* do work */ });
  });

  a.execute([=]() {
    tbb::parallel_for(0, N, [](int) { /* do work */ });
  });

  tbb::parallel_for(0, N, [](int) { /* do work */ });
  t.join();
}
```

Figure 11-12. *An application with three task arenas and a* global_control *object*

We now use a `global_control` object to set the number of threads in the global thread pool. Remember that a `global_control` object is used to affect global parameters used by the scheduler; in this case, we are changing the `max_allowed_parallelism` parameter. We also use a `task_scheduler_init` object in thread t and an argument to the `task_arena` constructor to set the maximum number of threads that can be assigned to each task arena. Figure 11-13 shows an example execution on our four-core machine. The application now creates seven worker threads (eight total threads minus the already available master thread), and the worker threads are divided up unequally between the explicit task_arena a and the default arena for thread t. Since we do nothing special for the main thread, the final parallel_for uses its default task arena with P slots.

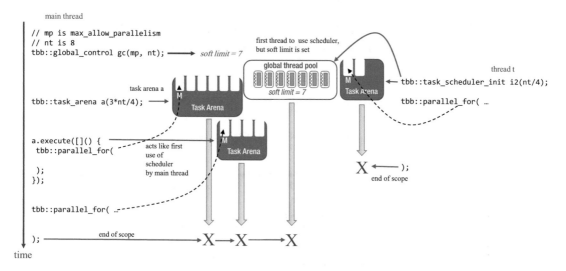

Figure 11-13. *A possible execution of the example with three task arenas after we have explicitly set the soft limit using a global_control object*

Executing the sample code for Figure 11-13 yields an output similar to

```
There are 4 logical cores.
6 threads participated in arena pfor
4 threads participated in main pfor
2 threads participated in std::thread pfor
```

Using **global_control** to Temporarily Restrict the Number of Available Threads

Another common scenario is to use a global_control object to temporarily change the number of threads for a specific phase of an application as shown in Figure 11-14. In this example, the master thread creates a thread pool and task arena that can support 12 worker threads by constructing a task_scheduler_init object. But a global_control object is used to restrict a specific parallel_for to only seven worker threads. While the task arena retains 12 slots during the whole application, the number of threads available in the thread pool is temporarily reduced, so at most seven of the slots in the task arena can be filled with workers.

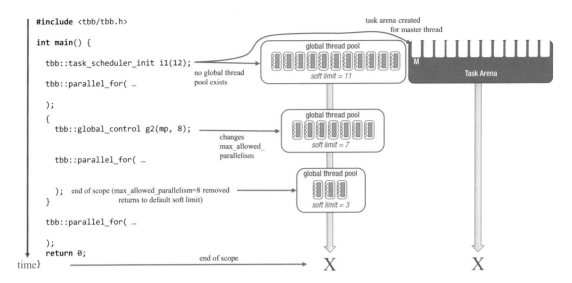

Figure 11-14. *Using a* `global_control` *object to temporarily change the number of threads available for a specific algorithm instance and then return to default setting*

When the `global_control` object is destroyed, the soft limit is recalculated, using any remaining `global_control` objects. Since there are none, the soft limit is set to the default soft limit. This perhaps unexpected behavior is important to note, since we need to create an outer `global_control` object if we want to maintain 11 threads in the global thread pool. We show this in Figure 11-15.

In Figures 11-14 and 11-15, we cannot use a `task_scheduler_init` object to temporarily change the number of threads because a task arena already exists for the main thread. If we create another `task_scheduler_init` object in the inner scope, it only increments the reference count on that task arena and does not create a new one. Therefore, we use a `global_control` object to restrict the number of threads that are available instead of reducing the number of arena slots.

If we execute the code in Figure 11-14, we see an output similar to

```
There are 4 logical cores.
12 threads participated in 1st pfor
8 threads participated in 2nd pfor
4 threads participated in 3rd pfor
```

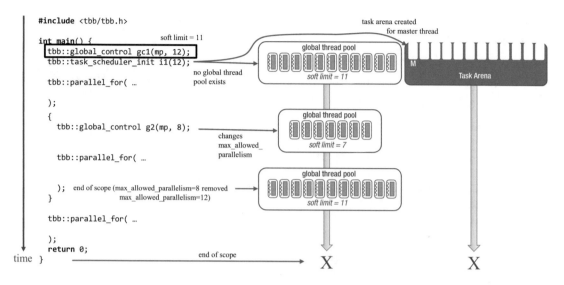

Figure 11-15. *Using* global_control *objects to temporarily change the number of threads available for a specific algorithm instance*

After adding an outer global_control object, as done in Figure 11-15, the resulting output is

```
There are 4 logical cores.
12 threads participated in 1st pfor
8 threads participated in 2nd pfor
12 threads participated in 3rd pfor
```

When NOT to Control the Number of Threads

When implementing a plugin or a library, its best to avoid using global_control objects. These objects affect global parameters, so our plugin or library function will change the number of threads available to all of the components in the application. Given the local view of a plugin or library, that's probably not something it should do. In Figure 11-14, we temporarily changed the number of threads in the global thread pool. If we did something like this from inside a library call, it would not only affect the number of threads available in the task arena of the calling thread, but every task arena in our application. How can a library function know this is the right thing to do? It very likely cannot.

We recommend that libraries do not meddle with global parameters and leave that only to the main program. Developers of applications that allow plugins should clearly communicate to plugin writers what the parallel execution strategy of the application is, so that they can implement their plugins appropriately.

SETTING THE STACK SIZE FOR WORKER THREADS

The `task_scheduler_init` and `global_control` classes can also be used to set the stack size for the worker threads. The interaction of multiple objects are the same as when used to set the number of threads, with one exception. When there is more than one `global_control` object that sets the stack size, the stack size is the *maximum*, not the minimum, of the requested values.

The second argument to the `task_scheduler_init` object is `thread_stack_size`. A value of 0, which is the default, instructs the scheduler to use the default for that platform. Otherwise, the provided value is used.

The `global_control` constructor accepts a parameter and value. If the parameter argument is `thread_stack_size,` then the object changes the value for the global stack size parameter. Unlike the `max_allowed_paralleism` value, the global `thread_stack_size` value is the maximum of the requested values.

Why change the default stack size?

A thread's stack has to be large enough for all of memory that is allocated on its stack, including all of the local variables on its call stack. When deciding how much stack is needed, we have to consider the local variables in our task bodies but also how recursive execution of task trees might lead to deep recursion, especially if we have implemented our own task-based algorithms using task blocking. If we don't remember how this style can lead to an explosion in stack usage, we can look back at the section, **The low-level task interface: part one/task blocking** in Chapter 10.

Since the proper stack size is application dependent, there is unfortunately no good rule of thumb to share. TBB's OS-specific default is already a best guess at what a thread typically needs.

Figuring Out What's Gone Wrong

The `task_scheduler_init`, `task_arena`, and `global_control` classes were introduced over time into the TBB library to solve specific problems. The `task_scheduler_init` class was sufficient in the early days of TBB, when few applications were parallel, and when they were, there was often only a single application thread. The `task_arena` class helped users manage isolation in applications as they became more complex. And the `global_control` class gave users better control of the global parameters used by the library to further manage complexity. Unfortunately, these features were not created together as part of one cohesive design. The result is that when used outside of the scenarios we have previously outlined, their behaviors can sometimes be nonintuitive, even if they are well defined.

The two most common sources of confusion are (1) knowing when a TBB scheduler is created by default and (2) races to set the global thread pool's soft limit.

If we create a `task_scheduler_init` object it either creates a TBB scheduler or else increments the reference count on the scheduler if it already exists. Which interfaces in the TBB library act like a first use of the TBB scheduler can be hard to keep straight. It's very clear that executing any of the TBB algorithms, using a TBB flow graph or spawning tasks, is a use of the TBB scheduler. But as we noted early, even executing tasks in an explicit `task_arena` is treated as a first use of the TBB scheduler, which impacts not only the explicit task arena, but may impact the calling thread's default task arena. What about using thread local storage or using one of the concurrent containers? These do not count. The best advice, other than paying close attention to the implications of the interfaces being used, is that if an application uses an unexpected number of threads – especially if it uses the default number of threads when you think you have changed the default – is to look for places where a default TBB scheduler may have been inadvertently initialized.

The second common cause of confusion is races to set the soft limit on the number of available threads. For example, if two application threads execute in parallel and both create a `task_scheduler_init` object, the first one to create its object will set the soft limit. In Figure 11-16, two threads executing concurrently in the same application both create `task_scheduler_init` objects – one requesting `max_threads=4` and the other `max_threads=8`. What happens with the task arenas is simple: each master thread gets its own task arena with the number of slots it requested. But what if the soft limit on the number of threads in the global thread pool has not been set yet? How many threads does the TBB library populate the global thread pool with? Should it create 3 or 7 or 3+7=10 or P-1 or ...?

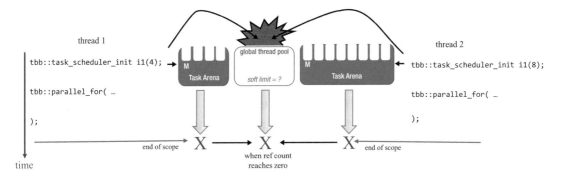

Figure 11-16. *The concurrent use of two* `task_scheduler_init` *objects*

As we outlined in our description of `task_scheduler_init`, it does none of these things. Instead, it uses whichever request comes first. Yes, you read that right! If thread 1 just so happens to create its `task_scheduler_init` object first, we get a TBB scheduler with a global thread pool with three worker threads. If thread 2 creates its `task_scheduler_init` object first, we get a thread pool with seven worker threads. Our two threads may be sharing three worker threads or seven worker threads; it all depends on which one wins the race to create the TBB scheduler first!

We shouldn't despair though; almost all of the potential pitfalls that come along with setting the number of threads can be addressed by falling back to the common usage patterns described earlier in this chapter. For example, if we know that our application may have a race like that shown in Figure 11-16, we can make our desires crystal clear by setting the soft limit in the main thread using a `global_control` object.

Summary

In this chapter, we provided a brief recap of the structure of the TBB scheduler before introducing the three classes used to control the number of threads used for parallel execution: `class task_scheduler_init`, `class task_arena`, and `class global_ control`. We then described common use cases for controlling the number of threads used by parallel algorithms – working from simple cases where there is a single main thread and a single task arena to more complex cases where there are multiple master threads and multiple task arenas. We concluded by pointing out that while there are potential gotchas in using these classes, we can avoid these by carefully using the classes to make our intention clear without relying on default behaviors or the winners of races.

CHAPTER 12

Using Work Isolation for Correctness and Performance

Anyone who has been around children (or who acts like a child) knows that sometimes the only way to stop children from bothering each other is to separate them. The same thing can be said of TBB tasks and algorithms. When tasks or algorithms just can't get along, we can separate them using *work isolation*.

For example, when using nested parallelism, we need – in some limited situations – to create work isolation in order to ensure correctness. In this chapter, we walk through scenarios where this need arises and then provide a set of rules for determining when we need isolation for correctness. We also describe how the `isolate` function is used to create work isolation.

In other cases, we may want to create work isolation so that we can constrain where tasks execute for performance reasons by using explicit task arenas. Creating isolation in these cases is a double-edged sword. On one hand, we will be able to control things like the number of threads that will participate in different task arenas as a way to favor some tasks over others, or to use hooks in the TBB library to pin the threads to specific cores to optimize for locality. On the other hand, explicit task arenas make it more difficult for threads to participate in work outside of the arena they are currently assigned to. We discuss how to use `class task_arena` when we want to create isolation for performance reasons. We will also caution that while `class task_arena` can be used to create isolation to address correctness problems too, its higher overhead makes it less desirable for that purpose.

Work isolation is a valuable feature when required and used properly, but, as we will see throughout this chapter it needs to be used cautiously.

© Intel Corporation 2019
M. Voss, R. Asenjo, J. Reinders, *Pro TBB*, https://doi.org/10.1007/978-1-4842-4398-5_12

Work Isolation for Correctness

The TBB scheduler is designed to keep worker threads, and their underlying cores, as busy as possible. If and when a worker thread becomes idle, it steals work from another thread so that it has something to do. When it steals, a thread is not aware of what parallel algorithm, loop or function originally created the task that it steals. Usually, where a task comes from is irrelevant, and so the best thing for the TBB library to do is to treat all available tasks equally and process them as quickly as possible.

However, if our application uses nested parallelism, the TBB library can steal tasks in a way that leads to an execution order that might not be expected by a developer. This execution order is not inherently dangerous; in fact, in most cases, it is exactly what we would like to happen. But if we make incorrect assumptions about how tasks may execute, we can create patterns that lead to unexpected or even disastrous results.

A small example that demonstrates this issue is shown in Figure 12-1. In the code, there are two `parallel_for` loops. In the body of the outer loop, a lock on mutex `m` is acquired. The thread that acquires this lock calls a second nested `parallel_for` loop while holding the lock. A problem arises if the thread that acquires the lock on `m` becomes idle before its inner loop is done; this can happen if worker threads steal away iterations but have not yet finished them when the master thread runs out of work. The master thread cannot simply exit the `parallel_for`, since it's not done yet. To be efficient, this thread doesn't just idly spin, waiting for the other threads to finish their work; who knows how long that could take? Instead, it keeps its current task on its stack and looks for additional work to keep itself busy until it can pick up where it left off. If this situation arises in Figure 12-1, there are two kinds of tasks in the system at the point that the thread is looking for work to steal – inner loop tasks and outer loop tasks. If the thread happens to steal and execute a task from the outer `parallel_for`, it will attempt to acquire a lock on `m` again. Since it already holds a lock on `m`, and a `tbb::spin_mutex` is not a recursive lock, there is a deadlock. The thread is trapped waiting for itself to release the lock!

```
#include <tbb/tbb.h>

void doWork();

void fig_12_1() {
  tbb::spin_mutex m;
  const int P =
    tbb::task_scheduler_init::default_num_threads();

  tbb::parallel_for(0, P,
    [&m](int) {
      const int N = 1000;
      tbb::spin_mutex::scoped_lock l{m};
      tbb::parallel_for(0, N, [](int j) { doWork();});
    }
  );
}
```

Figure 12-1. *Holding a lock while executing a nested* parallel_for

After seeing this example, two questions commonly arise: (1) does anyone really write code like this? And, (2) can a thread really wind up stealing a task from the outer loop? The answer to both of these questions is, unfortunately, yes.

People in fact do write code like this – almost always unintentionally though. One common way this pattern might arise is if a lock is held while a library function is called. A developer may assume they know what a function does, but if they are not familiar with its implementation, they can be wrong. If the library call contains nested parallelism, the case shown in Figure 12-1 can be the result.

And yes, work stealing can cause this example to deadlock. Figure 12-2 shows how our example might fall into this terrible state.

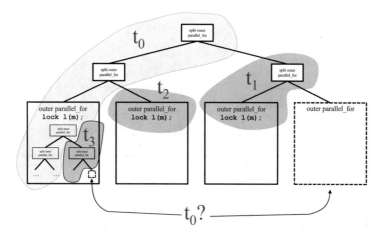

(a) t₀ can steal an outer or inner task

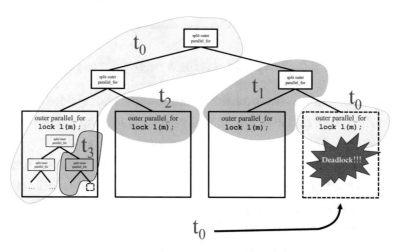

(b) t₀ takes the outer task and deadlocks

Figure 12-2. *One potential execution of the task tree generated by the code in Figure 12-1*

In Figure 12-2(a), thread t_0 starts the outer loop and acquires the lock on m. Thread t_0 then starts the nested `parallel_for` and executes the left half of its iteration space. While thread t_0 is busy, three other threads t_1, t_2, and t_3 participate in the execution of tasks in the arena. Threads t_1 and t_2 steal outer loop iterations and are blocked waiting to acquire the lock on m, which t_0 currently holds. Meanwhile, thread t_3 randomly selects t_0 to steal from and starts executing the right half of its inner loop. This is where things start to get interesting. Thread t_0 completes the left half of the inner loop's iterations and therefore will steal work to prevent itself from becoming idle. At this point it has two options: (1) if it randomly chooses thread t_3 to steal from, it will execute more of its own inner loop or (2) if it randomly chooses thread t_1 to steal from, it will execute one of the outer loop iterations. Remember that by default, the scheduler treats all tasks equally, so it doesn't prefer one over the other. Figure 12-2(b) shows the unlucky choice where it steals from thread t_1 and becomes deadlocked trying to acquire the lock it already holds since its outer task is still on its stack.

Another example that shows correctness issues is shown in Figure 12-3. Again, we see a set of nested `parallel_for` loops, but instead of a deadlock, we get unexpected results because of the use of thread local storage. In each task, a value is written to a thread local storage location, `local_i`, an inner `parallel_for` loop is executed, and then the thread local storage location is read. Because of the inner loop, a thread may steal work if it becomes idle, write another value to the thread local storage location, and then return to the outer task.

```cpp
#include <tbb/tbb.h>

void doWork();

thread_local int local_i = -1;

void fig_12_3() {
  const int P =
tbb::task_scheduler_init::default_num_threads();

    tbb::parallel_for(0, P,
      [](int i) {
        const int N = 1000;
        local_i = i;
        tbb::parallel_for(0, N, [](int j) {doWork();});
        if (local_i != i) {
          std::cout << "Unexpected local_i!!! ";
        }
      }
    );
  std::cout << std::endl;
}
```

Figure 12-3. *Nested parallelism that can cause unexpected results due to the use of thread local storage*

The TBB development team uses the term *moonlighting*[1] for situations in which a thread has unfinished child tasks in flight and steals unrelated tasks to keep itself busy. Moonlighting is usually a good thing! It means that our threads are not sitting around idle. It's only in limited situations when things go awry. In both of our examples, there was a bad assumption. They both assumed – not surprisingly – that because TBB has a non-preemptive scheduler, the same thread could never be executing an inner task and then start executing an outer task before it completed the inner task. As we've seen, because a thread can steal work while it's waiting in nested parallelism, this situation can in fact occur. This typically benign behavior is only dangerous if we incorrectly depend on the thread executing the tasks in a mutually exclusive way. In the first case, a lock was held while executing nested parallelism – allowing the thread to pause the inner task and pick up an outer task. In the second case, the thread accessed thread local storage before and after nested parallelism and assumed the thread would not moonlight in between.

As we can see, these examples are different but share a common misconception. In the blog "The Work Isolation Functionality in Intel Threading Building Blocks" that is listed in the "For More Information" section at the end of this chapter, Alexei Katranov provides a three-step checklist for deciding when work isolation is needed to ensure correctness:

1. Is nested parallelism used (even indirectly, through third party library calls)? If not, isolation is not needed; otherwise, go to the next step.

2. Is it safe for a thread to reenter the outer level parallel tasks (as if there was recursion)? Storing to a thread local value, re-acquiring a mutex already acquired by this thread, or other resources that should not be used by the same thread again can all cause problems. If reentrance is safe, isolation is not needed; otherwise, go to the next step.

3. Isolation is needed. Nested parallelism has to be called inside an isolated region.

---

[1] From Collins Dictionary: to work at a secondary job, esp. at night, and often illegitimately.

Creating an Isolated Region with `this_task_arena::isolate`

When we need isolation for correctness, we can use one of the `isolate` functions in the `this_task_arena` namespace:

```
namespace this_task_arena {
  // Supported until C++11
  template<typename F> void isolate(F& f);
  template<typename F> void isolate(const F& f);

  // Supported since C++11
  template<typename F> auto isolate(F& f) -> decltype(f());
  template<typename F> auto isolate(const F& f) ->
    decltype(f());
}
```

Figure 12-4 shows how to use this function to add an isolated region around the nested `parallel_for` from Figure 12-1. Within an isolated region, if a thread becomes idle because it must wait – for example at the end of a nested `parallel_for` – it will only be allowed to steal tasks spawned from within its own isolated region. This fixes our deadlock problem, because if a thread steals while waiting at the inner `parallel_for` in Figure 12-4, it will not be allowed to steal an outer task.

```cpp
#include <tbb/tbb.h>

void doWork();

void fig_12_4() {
  tbb::spin_mutex m;
  const int P =
tbb::task_scheduler_init::default_num_threads();

  tbb::parallel_for(0, P,
    [&m](int i) {
      const int N = 1000;
      tbb::spin_mutex::scoped_lock l{m};
      tbb::this_task_arena::isolate(
        [i]() {
          tbb::parallel_for(0, N, [](int j) {doWork();});
        }
      );
    }
  );
}
```

Figure 12-4. *Using the isolate function to prevent moonlighting in the case of nested parallelism*

When a thread becomes blocked within an isolated region, it will still randomly choose a thread from its task arena to steal from, but now must inspect tasks in that victim thread's deque to be sure it steals only tasks that originated from within its isolated region.

The main properties of this_task_arena::isolate are nicely summarized, again in Alexei's blog, as follows:

- The isolation only constrains threads that enter or join an isolated region. Worker threads outside of an isolated region can take any task including a task spawned in an isolated region.

- When a thread without isolation executes a task spawned in an isolated region, it joins the region of this task and becomes isolated until the task is complete.

- Threads waiting inside an isolated region cannot process tasks
  spawned in other isolated regions (i.e., all regions are mutually
  isolated). Moreover, if a thread within an isolated region enters a
  nested isolated region, it cannot process tasks from the outer isolated
  region.

Oh No! Work Isolation Can Cause Its Own Correctness Issues!

Unfortunately, we can't just indiscriminately apply work isolation. There are
performance implications, which we will get to later, but more importantly, work
isolation itself can cause deadlock if used incorrectly! Here we go again...

In particular, we have to be extra careful when we mix work isolation with TBB
interfaces that separate spawning tasks from waiting for tasks – such as task_group and
flow graphs. A task that calls a wait interface in one isolated region cannot participate in
tasks spawned in a different isolated region while it waits. If enough threads get stuck in
such a position, the application might run out of threads and forward progress will stop.

Let's consider the example function shown in Figure 12-5. In the function
splitRunAndWait, M tasks are spawned in task_group tg. But each spawn happens
within a *different* isolated region.

```
#include <tbb/tbb.h>

void doWork();

const int M =
2*tbb::task_scheduler_init::default_num_threads();

void splitRunAndWait() {
  tbb::task_group tg;

  for ( int i=0; i<M; ++i ) {
    tbb::this_task_arena::isolate( [&tg]{
      // Run in inner region
      tg.run( []{
        const int N = 10000;
        tbb::parallel_for(0,N,[](int i) {doWork();});
      });
    });
  }
  tg.wait();
}

void fig_12_5() {
  tbb::parallel_for( 0, M, []( int ) {
    splitRunAndWait();
  } );
}
```

Figure 12-5. *A function that calls* run *and* wait *on* task_group *tg. The call to* run *is made from within an isolated region.*

If we call function fig_12_5 directly, as is done in Figure 12-5, there is no problem. The call to tg.wait in splitRunAndWait is not inside of an isolated region itself, so the master thread and the worker threads can help with the different isolated regions and then move to other ones when they are finished.

But what if we change our main function to the one in Figure 12-6?

```
#include <tbb/tbb.h>

void doWork();

const int M =
2*tbb::task_scheduler_init::default_num_threads();

void splitRunAndWait() {
  tbb::task_group tg;

  for ( int i=0; i<M; ++i ) {
    tbb::this_task_arena::isolate( [&tg]{
      // Run in inner region
      tg.run( []{
        const int N = 10000;
        tbb::parallel_for(0,N,[](int i) {doWork();});
      });
    });
  }
  tg.wait();
}

void fig_12_6() {
  tbb::parallel_for( 0, M, []( int ) {
    tbb::this_task_arena::isolate( [] {
      splitRunAndWait();
    });
  });
}
```

Figure 12-6. *A function that calls* run *and* wait *on* task_group *tg. The call to* run *is made from within an isolated region.*

Now, the calls to splitRunAndWait are each made inside of different isolated regions, and subsequently the calls to tg.wait are made in those isolated regions. Each thread that calls tg.wait has to wait until its tg is finished but cannot steal any of the tasks that belong to its tg or any other task_group, because those tasks were spawned from different isolated regions! If M is large enough, we will likely wind up with all of our threads waiting in calls to tg.wait, with no threads left to execute any of the related tasks. So our application deadlocks.

If we use an interface that separates spawns from waits, we can avoid this issue by making sure that we always wait in the same isolated region from which we spawn the tasks. We could, for example, rewrite the code from Figure 12-6 to move the call to run out into the outer region as shown in Figure 12-7.

```cpp
#include <tbb/tbb.h>

void doWork();

const int M =
2*tbb::task_scheduler_init::default_num_threads();

void splitRunAndWait() {
  tbb::task_group tg;

  for ( int i=0; i<M; ++i ) {
    tg.run( [&tg]{
        tbb::this_task_arena::isolate( [&tg]{
        // Run in inner region
          const int N = 10000;
          tbb::parallel_for(0,N,[](int i) {doWork();});
        });
    });
  }
  tg.wait();
}

void fig_12_7() {
  tbb::parallel_for( 0, M, []( int ) {
      tbb::this_task_arena::isolate( [] {
        splitRunAndWait();
      });
  });
}
```

Figure 12-7. *A function that calls* run *and* wait *on* task_group *tg. The calls to* run *and* wait *are now both made outside of the isolated region.*

Now, even if our main function uses a parallel loop and isolation, we no longer have a problem, since each thread that calls tg.wait will be able to execute the tasks from its tg:

Even When It Is Safe, Work Isolation Is Not Free

In addition to potential deadlock issues, work isolation does not come for free from a performance perspective either, so even when it is safe to use, we need to use it judiciously. A thread that is not in an isolated region can choose any task when it steals, which means it can quickly pop the oldest task from a victim thread's deque. If the victim has no tasks at all, it can also immediately pick another victim. However, tasks spawned in an isolated region, and their children tasks, are tagged to identify the isolated region they belong to. A thread that is executing in an isolated region must scan a chosen victim's deque to find the oldest task that belongs to its isolated region – not just any old task will do. And the thread only knows if a victim thread has no tasks from its isolated region after scanning all of the available tasks and finding none from its region. Only then will it pick another victim to try to steal from. Threads stealing from within an isolated region have more overhead because they need to be pickier!

Using Task Arenas for Isolation: A Double-Edged Sword

Work isolation restricts a thread's options when it looks for work to do. We can isolate work using the isolate function as described in the previous section, or we can use class task_arena. The subset of the class task_arena interface relevant to this chapter is shown in Figure 12-8.

```
class task_arena {
public:
    task_arena(int max_concurrency = automatic,
               unsigned reserved_for_masters = 1);
    task_arena(const task_arena &s);
    explicit task_arena(task_arena::attach);
    ~task_arena();

    int max_concurrency() const;

    // Supported since C++11
    template<typename F> auto execute(F& f) -> decltype(f());
    template<typename F> auto execute(const F& f) ->
      decltype(f());
    template<typename F> void enqueue(F&& f);
    template<typename F> void enqueue(F&& f, priority_t p);
};
```

Figure 12-8. *A subset of the* class task_arena *public interface*

It almost never makes sense to use class task_arena instead of the isolate function to create isolation solely to ensure correctness. That said, there are still important uses for class task_arena. Let's look at the basics of class task_arena and, while doing so, uncover its strengths and weaknesses.

With the task_arena constructor, we can set the total number of slots for threads in the arena using the max_concurrency argument and the number of those slots that are reserved exclusively for master threads using the reserved_for_masters argument. More details on how task_arena can be used to control the number of threads used by computations are provided in Chapter 11.

Figure 12-9 shows a small example where a single task_arena ta2 is created, with max_concurrency=2, and a task that executes a parallel_for is executed in that arena.

```
void fig_12_9() {
  tbb::task_arena ta2{2};
  ta2.execute([&]() {
    const int N = 1000;
    tbb::parallel_for(0, N, [](int) {doWork();});
  });
}
```

Figure 12-9. *A task_arena that has a maximum concurrency of 2*

When a thread calls a task_arena's execute method, it tries to join the arena as a master thread. If there are no available slots, it enqueues the task into the task arena. Otherwise, it joins the arena and executes the task in that arena. In Figure 12-9, the thread will join task_arena ta2, start the parallel_for, and then participate in executing tasks from the parallel_for. Since the arena has a max_concurrency of 2, at most, one additional worker thread can join in and participate in executing tasks in that task arena. If we execute the instrumented example from Figure 12-9 available at Github, we see

```
There are 4 logical cores.
2 threads participated in ta2
```

Already we can start to see differences between isolate and class task_arena. It is true that only threads in ta2 will be able to execute tasks in ta2, so there is work isolation, but we were also able to set the maximum number of threads that can participate in executing the nested parallel_for.

Figure 12-10 takes this a step further by creating two task arenas, one with a max_concurrency of 2 and the other with a max_concurrency of 6. A parallel_invoke is then used to create two tasks, one that executes a parallel_for in ta2 and another that executes a parallel_for in ta6. Both parallel_for loops have the same number of iterations and spin for the same amount of time per iteration.

```
void fig_12_10() {
  const int N = 1000;

  tbb::task_arena ta2{2};
  tbb::task_arena ta6{6};
  double ta2_time = 0.0, ta6_time = 0.0;

  tbb::parallel_invoke(
    [&]() {
      ta2.execute([&]() {
        tbb::tick_count t0 = tbb::tick_count::now();
        tbb::parallel_for(0, N, [](int i) {doWork();});
        ta2_time = (tbb::tick_count::now() - t0).seconds();
      });
    },
    [&]() {
      ta6.execute([&]() {
        tbb::tick_count t0 = tbb::tick_count::now();
        tbb::parallel_for(0, N, [](int i) {doWork();});
        ta6_time = (tbb::tick_count::now() - t0).seconds();
      });
    }
  );
  std::cout << "ta2_time == " << ta2_time << std::endl
            << "ta6_time == " << ta6_time << std::endl;
}
```

Figure 12-10. *Using two* task_arena *objects to use six threads for one loop and two for another*

We have effectively divided up our eight threads into two groups, letting two of the threads work on the parallel_for in ta2 and six of the threads work on the parallel_ for in ta6. Why would we do this? Perhaps we think the work in ta6 is more critical.

If we execute the code in Figure 12-10 on a platform with eight hardware threads, we will see output similar to

```
ta2_time == 0.500409
ta6_time == 0.169082

There are 8 logical cores.
2 threads participated in ta2
6 threads participated in ta6
```

This is the key difference between using `isolate` and `task_arena` to create isolation. When using `task_arena`, we are almost always more concerned with controlling the threads that participate in executing the tasks, rather than in the isolation itself. The isolation is not created for correctness but instead for performance. An explicit `task_arena` is a double-edged sword – it lets us control the threads that participate in the work but also builds a very high wall between them. When a thread leaves an isolated region created by `isolate`, it is free to participate in executing any of the other tasks in its arena. When a thread runs out of work to do in an explicit `task_arena`, it must travel back to the global thread pool and then find another arena that has work to do and has open slots.

Note   We just offered a KEY rule of thumb: Use `isolate` primarily to aid in correctness; use `task_arenas` primarily for performance.

Let's consider our example in Figure 12-10 again. We created more slots in `task_arena` ta6. As a result, the `parallel_for` in ta6 completed much faster than the `parallel_for` in ta2. But after the work is done in ta6, the threads assigned to that arena return to the global thread pool. They are now idle but unable to help with the work in ta2 – the arena has only two slots for threads and they are already full!

The `class task_arena` abstraction is very powerful, but the high wall it creates between threads limits its practical applications. Chapter 11 discusses in more detail how `class task_arena` can be used alongside `class task_scheduler_init` and `class global_control` to control the number of threads that are available to specific parallel algorithms in a TBB application. Chapter 20 shows how we can use `task_arena` objects to partition work and schedule the work on specific cores in a Non-Uniform Memory Access (NUMA) platform to tune for data locality. In both chapters, we will see that `task_arena` is very useful but has drawbacks.

Don't Be Tempted to Use `task_arenas` to Create Work Isolation for Correctness

In the specific use cases described in Chapters 11 and 20, the number of threads and even their placement on to particular cores are tightly controlled – and therefore we want to have different threads in the different arenas. In the general case though, the need for `task_arena` objects to manage and migrate threads just creates overhead.

As an example, let's again look at a nested set of `parallel_for` loops, but now without a correctness problem. We can see the code and a possible task tree in Figure 12-11. If we execute this set of loops, all of the tasks will be spawned into the same task arena. When we used `isolate` in the previous section, all of the tasks were still kept in the same arena, but threads isolated themselves by inspecting tasks before they stole them to make sure they were allowed to take them according to isolation constraints.

```
#include <tbb/tbb.h>

void doWork();

const int N = 128;

void fig_12_11(int M) {
  tbb::parallel_for(0, M,
    [](int) {
      tbb::parallel_for(0, N, [](int j) {doWork();});
    }
  );
}
```

(a) source code for two nested `parallel_for` loops

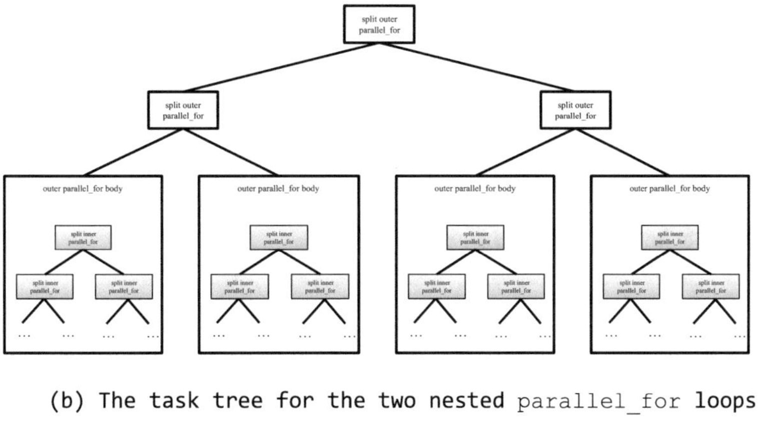

(b) The task tree for the two nested `parallel_for` loops

Figure 12-11. *An example of two nested `parallel_for` loops: (a) the source code and (b) the task tree*

Now, let's modify this simple nested loop example to create isolation using explicit task arena objects. If we want each thread that executes an iteration in the outer loop to only execute tasks from its own inner loop, which we easily achieved by using isolate in Figure 12-4, we can create local nested explicit task_arena instances within each outer body as shown in Figure 12-12(a) and Figure 12-12(b).

```cpp
#include <tbb/tbb.h>

void doWork();

const int N = 128;

void fig_12_12(int M) {
  tbb::parallel_for(0, M,
    [](int) {
      tbb::task_arena nested;
      nested.execute([]() {
        tbb::parallel_for(0, N, [](int j) {doWork();});
      });
    }
  );
}
```

(a) the source code

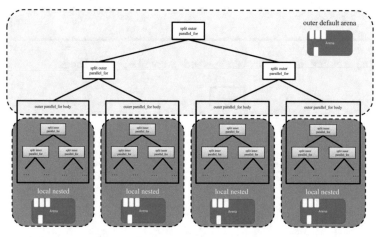

(b) the task tree with the task arenas they belong to

Figure 12-12. *Creating an explicit* task_arena *for each outer loop body execution. Now, while executing in the inner arena, threads will be isolated from the outer work and unrelated inner loops.*

If M == 4, there will be a total of five arenas, and when each thread calls nested.execute, it will be isolated from outer loop tasks as well as unrelated inner loop tasks. We have created a very elegant solution, right?

Of course not! Not only are we creating, initializing, and destroying several task_arena objects, these arenas need to be populated with worker threads. As described in Chapter 11, worker threads fill task arenas in proportion to the number of slots they have. If we have a system with four hardware threads, each arena will only get one thread! What's the point in that? If we have more threads, they will be evenly divided among the task arenas. As each inner loop finishes, its threads will return to the global thread pool and then migrate to another task arena that has not yet finished. This is not a cheap operation!

Having many task arenas and migrating threads between them is simply not an efficient way to do load balancing. Our toy example in Figure 12-12(b) is shown with only four outer iterations; if there were many iterations, we would create and destroy task_ arenas in each outer task. Our four worker threads would scramble around from task arena to task arena looking for work! Stick with the isolate function for these cases!

Summary

We have now learned how to separate TBB tasks and algorithms when they just can't get along. We saw that nested parallelism combined with the way that stealing occurs in TBB can lead to dangerous situations if we are not careful. We then saw that the this_task_ arena::isolate function can be used to address these situations, but it too must be used carefully or else we can create new problems.

We then discussed how we can use class task_arena when we want to create isolation for performance reasons. While class task_arena can be used to create isolation to address correctness, its higher overheads make it less desirable for that purpose. However, as we see in Chapters 11 and 20, class task_arena is an essential part of our toolbox when we want to control the number of threads used by an algorithm or to control the placement of threads on to cores.

For More Information

Alexei Katranov, "The Work Isolation Functionality in Intel Threading Building Blocks (Intel TBB)," `https://software.intel.com/en-us/blogs/2018/08/16/the-work-isolation-functionality-in-intel-threading-building-blocks-intel-tbb`.

CHAPTER 13

Creating Thread-to-Core and Task-to-Thread Affinity

When developing parallel applications with the Threading Building Blocks library, we create tasks by using the high-level execution interfaces or the low-level APIs. These tasks are scheduled by the TBB library onto software threads using work stealing. These software threads are scheduled by the Operating System (OS) onto the platform's cores (hardware threads). In this chapter, we discuss the features in TBB that let us influence the scheduling choices made by the OS and by TBB. *Thread-to-core affinity* is used when we want to influence the OS so that it schedules the software threads onto particular core(s). *Task-to-thread affinity* is used when we want to influence the TBB scheduler so that it schedules tasks onto particular software threads. Depending on what we are trying to achieve, we may be interested in one kind of affinity or the other, or a combination of both.

There can be different motivations for creating affinity. One of the most common motivations is to take advantage of data locality. As we have repeatedly noted in this book, data locality can have a huge impact on the performance of a parallel application. The TBB library, its high-level execution interfaces, its work-stealing scheduler, and its concurrent containers have all been designed with locality in mind. For many applications, using these features will lead to good performance without any manual tuning. Sometimes though, we will need to provide hints or take matters completely into our own hands so that the schedulers, in TBB and the OS, more optimally schedule work near its data. In addition to data locality, we might also be interested in affinity when using heterogeneous systems, where the capabilities of cores differ, or when software threads have different properties, such as higher or lower priorities.

© Intel Corporation 2019
M. Voss, R. Asenjo, J. Reinders, *Pro TBB*, https://doi.org/10.1007/978-1-4842-4398-5_13

In Chapter 16, the high-level features for data locality that are exposed by the TBB parallel algorithms are presented. In Chapter 17, the features for tuning cache and memory use in TBB flow graphs are discussed. In Chapter 20, we showed how to use features of the TBB library to tune for Non-Uniform Memory Access (NUMA) architectures. For many readers, the information in those chapters will be sufficient to accomplish the specific tasks they need to perform to tune their applications. In this chapter, we focus on the lower-level, fundamental support provided by the TBB's scheduler and tasks that are sometimes abstracted by the high-level features described in those chapters or sometimes used directly in those chapters to create affinity.

Creating Thread-to-Core Affinity

All of the major operating systems provide interfaces that allow users to set the affinity of software threads, including `pthread_setaffinity_np` or `sched_setaffinity` on Linux and `SetThreadAffinityMask` on Windows. In Chapter 20, we use the Portable Hardware Locality (hwloc) package as a portable way to set affinity across platforms. In this chapter, we do not focus on the mechanics of setting affinity – since these mechanics will vary from system to system – instead we focus on the hooks provided by the TBB library that allow us to use these interfaces to set affinity for TBB master and worker threads.

The TBB library by default creates enough worker threads to match the number of available cores. In Chapter 11, we discussed how we can change those defaults. Whether we use the defaults or not, the TBB library does not automatically affinitize these threads to specific cores. TBB allows the OS to schedule and migrate the threads as it sees fit. Giving the OS flexibility in where it places TBB threads is an intentional design choice in the library. In a multiprogrammed environment, an environment in which TBB excels, the OS has visibility of all of the applications and threads. If we make decisions about where threads should execute from within our limited view inside of a single application, we might make choices that lead to poor overall system resource utilization. Therefore, it is often better to not affinitize threads to cores and instead allow the OS to choose where the TBB master and worker threads execute, including allowing it to dynamically migrate threads during a program's execution.

However, like we will see in many chapters of this book, the TBB library provides features that let us change this behavior if we wish. If we want to force TBB threads to have affinity for cores, we can use the task_scheduler_observer class to do so (see **Observing the scheduler with the task_scheduler_observer class**). This class lets an application define callbacks that are invoked whenever a thread enters and leaves the TBB scheduler, or a specific task arena, and use these callbacks to assign affinity. The TBB library does not provide an abstraction to assist with making the OS-specific calls required to set thread affinity, so we have to handle these low-level details ourselves using one of the OS-specific or portable interfaces we mentioned earlier.

OBSERVING THE SCHEDULER WITH THE TASK_SCHEDULER_OBSERVER CLASS

The task_scheduler_observer class provides a way to observe when a thread starts or stops participating in task scheduling. The interface of this class is shown as follows:

```
class task_scheduler_observer {
public:
  task_scheduler_observer();
  virtual ~task_scheduler_observer();
  void observe( bool state=true );
  bool is_observing() const;
  virtual void on_scheduler_entry( bool is_worker ) {}
  virtual void on_scheduler_exit( bool is_worker } {}
};
```

To use the class, we create our own class that inherits from task_scheduler_observer and implements the on_scheduler_entry and on_scheduler_exit callbacks. When an instance of this class is constructed and its observe state is set to true, the entry and exit functions will be called whenever a master or worker thread enters or exits the global TBB task scheduler.

A recent extension to the class now allows us to pass a task_arena to the constructor. This extension was a preview feature prior to TBB 2019 Update 4 but is now fully supported. When a task_arena reference is passed, the observer will only receive callbacks for threads that enter and exit that specific arena:

```
explicit task_scheduler_observer(task_arena & a);
```

Figure 13-1 shows a simple example of how to use a task_scheduler_observer object to pin threads to cores on Linux. In this example, we use the sched_setaffinity function to set the CPU mask for each thread as it joins the default arena. In Chapter 20, we show an example that assigns affinity using the hwloc software package. In the example in Figure 13-1, we use tbb::this_task_arena::max_concurrency() to find the number of slots in the arena and tbb::this_task_arena::current_thread_index() to find the slot that the calling thread is assigned to. Since we know there will be the same number of slots in the default arena as the number of logical cores, we pin each thread to the logical core that matches its slot number.

```cpp
#include <iostream>
#include <sched.h>
#define TBB_PREVIEW_LOCAL_OBSERVER 1
#include <tbb/tbb.h>

thread_local int my_cpu = -1;
void doWork();

class pinning_observer : public tbb::task_scheduler_observer {
public:
    pinning_observer() { observe(true); }

    void on_scheduler_entry( bool is_worker ) {
        cpu_set_t *mask;
        auto number_of_slots =
          tbb::this_task_arena::max_concurrency();
        mask = CPU_ALLOC(number_of_slots);
        auto mask_size = CPU_ALLOC_SIZE(number_of_slots);

        auto slot_number =
          tbb::this_task_arena::current_thread_index();
        CPU_ZERO_S(mask_size, mask);
        CPU_SET_S(slot_number, mask_size, mask);
        if (sched_setaffinity( 0, mask_size, mask )) {
            std::cout << "Error in sched_setaffinity"
                        << std::endl;
        }
        // so we can see if it worked:
        my_cpu = sched_getcpu();
    }
};

void fig_13_1() {
  const int N = 100;

  std::cout << "Without pinning:" << std::endl;
  tbb::parallel_for(0, N, [](int) {doWork();});

  std::cout << std::endl
            << "With pinning:" << std::endl;
  pinning_observer p;
  tbb::parallel_for(0, N, [](int) {doWork();});
  std::cout << std::endl;
}
```

Figure 13-1. *Using a* `task_scheduler_observer` *to pin threads to cores on a Linux platform*

We can of course create more complicated schemes for assigning logical cores to threads. And, although we don't do this in Figure 13-1, we can also store the original CPU mask for each thread so that we can restore it when the thread leaves the arena.

As we discuss in Chapter 20, we can use the `task_scheduler_observer` class, combined with explicit `task_arena` instances, to create isolated groups of threads that are restricted to the cores that share the same local memory banks in a Non-Uniform-Memory Access (NUMA) system, a NUMA node. If we also control data placement, we can greatly improve performance by spawning the work into the arena of the NUMA node on which its data resides. See Chapter 20 for more details.

We should always remember that if we use thread-to-core affinity, we are preventing the OS from migrating threads away from oversubscribed cores to less-used cores as it attempts to optimize system utilization. If we do this in production applications, we need to be sure that we will not degrade multiprogrammed performance! As we'll mention several more times, only systems dedicated to running a single application (at a time) are likely to have an environment in which limiting dynamic migration can be of benefit.

Creating Task-to-Thread Affinity

Since we express our parallel work in TBB using tasks, creating thread-to-core affinity, as we described in the previous section, is only one part of the puzzle. We may not get much benefit if we pin our threads to cores, but then let our tasks get randomly moved around by work stealing!

When using the low-level TBB tasking interfaces introduced in Chapter 10, we can provide hints that tell the TBB scheduler that it should execute a task on the thread in a particular arena slot. Since we will likely use the higher-level algorithms and tasking interfaces whenever possible, such as `parallel_for`, `task_group` and flow graphs, we will rarely use these low-level interfaces directly however. Chapter 16 shows how the `affinity_partitioner` and `static_partitioner` classes can be used with the TBB loop algorithms to create affinity without resorting to these low-level interfaces. Similarly, Chapter 17 discusses the features of TBB flow graphs that affect affinity.

So while task-to-thread affinity is exposed in the low-level task class, we will almost exclusively use this feature through high-level abstractions. Therefore using the interfaces we describe in this section is reserved for TBB experts that are writing their own algorithms using the lowest-level tasking interfaces. If you're such an expert, or want to have a deeper understanding of how the higher-level interfaces achieve affinity, keep reading this section.

Figure 13-2 shows the functions and types provided by the TBB task class that we use to provide affinity hints.

```
typedef implementation-defined-unsigned-type affinity_id;
virtual void note_affinity( affinity_id id );
void set_affinity( affinity_id id );
affinity_id affinity() const;
```

Figure 13-2. *The functions in* tbb::task *that are used for task to thread affinity*

The type affinity_id is used to represent the slot in an arena that a task has affinity for. A value of zero means the task has no affinity. A nonzero value has an implementation-defined value that maps to an arena slot. We can set the affinity of task to an arena slot before spawning it by passing an affinity_id to its set_affinity function. But since the meaning of affinity_id is implementation defined, we don't pass a specific value, for example 2 to mean slot 2. Instead, we capture an affinity_id from a previous task execution by overriding the note_affinity callback function.

The function note_affinity is called by the TBB library before it invokes a task's execute function when (1) the task has no affinity but will execute on a thread other than the one that spawned it or (2) the task has affinity but it will execute on a thread different than the one specified by its affinity. By overriding this callback, we can track TBB stealing behavior so we can provide hints to the library to recreate this same stealing behavior in a subsequent execution of the algorithm, as we will see in the next example.

Finally, the affinity function lets us query a task's current affinity setting.

Figure 13-3 shows a class that inherits from tbb::task and uses the task affinity functions to record affinity_id values into a global array a. It only records the value when its doMakeNotes variable is set to true. The execute function prints the task id, the slot of the thread it is executing on, and the value that was recorded in the array for this task id. It prefixes its reporting with "hmm" if the task's doMakeNotes is true (it will then record the value), "yay!" if the task is executing in the arena slot that was recorded in array a (it was scheduled onto the same thread again), and "boo!" if it is executing in a different arena slot. The details of the printing are contained in the function printExclaim.

```cpp
#include <iostream>
#define TBB_PREVIEW_LOCAL_OBSERVER 1
#include <tbb/tbb.h>

const int numTasks = 8;
tbb::task::affinity_id a[numTasks];
void doWork();
void printExclaim(const std::string &str, int id,
                  int slot, int note);

class MyTask : public tbb::task {
  int taskId;
  bool doMakeNotes;
public:
  MyTask(int id, bool do_make_notes = true)
    : taskId(id), doMakeNotes(do_make_notes) { }

  void note_affinity(tbb::task::affinity_id id) override {
    if (doMakeNotes) a[taskId] = id;
  }

  tbb::task *execute() override {
    auto slot_number = tbb::this_task_arena::current_thread_index();
    tbb::task::affinity_id a_id = a[taskId];

    std::string exclaim = "yay!";
    if (a_id != 0 && slot_number != a_id-1) exclaim = "boo!";
    if (doMakeNotes) exclaim = "hmm.";
    printExclaim(exclaim, taskId, slot_number, a_id);

    doWork();
    return NULL;
  }
};

void executeTaskTree(const std::string &name, bool note_affinity,
                     bool set_affinity) {
  std::cout << name << std::endl << "id:slot:a[i]" << std::endl;
  tbb::task *root = new(tbb::task::allocate_root()) tbb::empty_task;
  root->set_ref_count(numTasks+1);
  for (int i = 0; i < numTasks; ++i) {
    tbb::task *t = new (root->allocate_child())
                     MyTask(i,note_affinity);

    if (set_affinity && a[i]) t->set_affinity(a[i]);
    tbb::task::spawn(*t);
  }
  root->wait_for_all();
}

void fig_13_3() {
  std::fill(a, a+numTasks, 0);
  executeTaskTree("note_affinity", true, false);
  executeTaskTree("without set_affinity", false, false);
  executeTaskTree("with set_affinity", false, true);
}
```

Figure 13-3. *Using the task affinity functions*

While the meaning of affinity_id is implementation defined, TBB is open source, and so we peaked at the implementation. We therefore know that the affinity_id is 0 if there is no affinity, but otherwise it is the slot index plus 1. We should not depend on this knowledge in production uses of TBB, but we depend on it in our example's execute function so we can assign the correct exclamation "yay!" or "boo!".

The function fig_13_3 in Figure 13-3 builds and executes three task trees, each with eight tasks, and assigns them ids from 0 to 7. This sample uses the low-level tasking interfaces we introduced in Chapter 10. The first task tree uses note_affinity to track when a task has been stolen to execute on some other thread than the master. The second task tree executes without noting or setting affinities. Finally, the last task tree uses set_affinity to recreate the scheduling recorded during the first run.

When we executed this example on a platform with eight threads, we recorded the following output:

```
note_affinity
id:slot:a[i]
hmm. 7:0:-1
hmm. 0:1:1
hmm. 1:6:6
hmm. 2:3:3
hmm. 3:2:2
hmm. 4:4:4
hmm. 5:7:7
hmm. 6:5:5

without set_affinity
id:slot:a[i]
yay! 7:0:-1
boo! 0:4:1
boo! 1:3:6
boo! 4:5:4
boo! 3:7:2
boo! 2:2:3
boo! 5:6:7
boo! 6:1:5
```

```
with set_affinity
id:slot:a[i]
yay! 7:0:-1
yay! 0:1:1
yay! 4:4:4
yay! 5:7:7
yay! 2:3:3
yay! 3:2:2
yay! 6:5:5
yay! 1:6:6
```

From this output, we see that the tasks in the first tree are distributed over the eight available threads, and the affinity_id for each task is recorded in array a. When the next set of tasks is executed, the recorded affinity_id for each task is not used to set affinity, and the tasks are randomly stolen by different threads. This is what random stealing does! But, when we execute the final task tree and use set_affinity, the thread assignments from the first run are repeated. Great, this worked out exactly as we wanted!

However, set_affinity only provides an affinity *hint* and the TBB library is actually free to ignore our request. When we set affinity using these interfaces, a reference to the task-with-affinity is placed in the targeted thread's affinity mailbox (see Figure 13-4). But the actual task remains in the local deque of the thread that spawned it. The task dispatcher only checks the affinity mailbox when it runs out of work in its local deque, as shown in the task dispatch loop in Chapter 9. So, if a thread does not check its affinity mailbox quickly enough, another thread may steal or execute its tasks first.

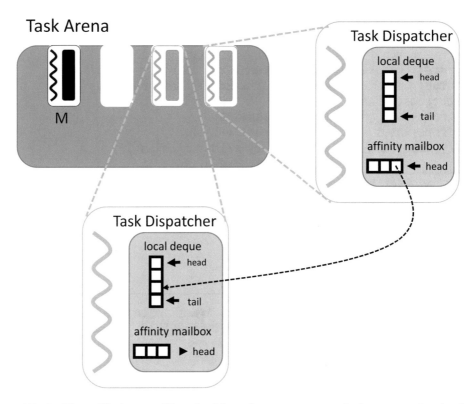

Figure 13-4. *The affinity mailbox holds reference to a task that remains in the local deque of the thread that spawned the task*

To demonstrate this, we can change how task affinities are assigned in our small example, as shown in Figure 13-5. Now, foolishly, we set all of the affinities to the same slot, the one recorded in a[2].

```
void executeTaskTree(const std::string &name, bool
note_affinity,
                         bool set_affinity) {
  std::cout << name << std::endl << "id:slot" << std::endl;
  tbb::task *root = new(tbb::task::allocate_root())
tbb::empty_task;
  root->set_ref_count(numTasks+1);
  for (int i = 0; i < numTasks; ++i) {
    tbb::task *t = new ( root->allocate_child() )
                      MyTask(i,note_affinity);
    if (set_affinity) t->set_affinity(a[2]);
    tbb::task::spawn(*t);
  }
  root->wait_for_all();
}

void fig_13_5() {
  std::fill(a, a+numTasks, 0);
  executeTaskTree("note_affinity", true, false);
  executeTaskTree("with set_affinity to a[2]", false, true);
}
```

Figure 13-5. *A function that first runs different groups of tasks, sometimes noting affinities and sometimes setting affinities. An example output is also shown.*

If the TBB scheduler honors our affinity requests, there will be a large load imbalance since we have asked it to mail all of the work to the same worker thread. But if we execute this new version of the example, we see:

```
id:slot
7:0
0:1
1:2
3:4
2:3
5:5
4:6
6:7
with set_affinity to a[2]
id:slot
7:0
0:3
2:4
1:6
5:1
6:5
3:7
4:2
```

Because affinity is only a hint, the other idle threads still find tasks, stealing them from the master thread's local deque before the thread in slot a[2] is able to drain its affinity mailbox. In fact, only the first task spawned, id==0, is executed by the thread in the slot previously recorded in a[2]. So, we still see our tasks distributed across all eight of the threads.

The TBB library has ignored our request and instead avoided the load imbalance that would have been created by sending all of these tasks to the same thread. This weak affinity is useful in practice because it lets us communicate affinities that *should* improve performance, but it still allows the library to adjust so that we don't inadvertently create a large load imbalance.

While we can use these task interfaces directly, we see in Chapter 16 that the loop algorithms provide a simplified abstraction, affinity_partitioner that luckily hides us from most of these low-level details.

When and How Should We Use the TBB Affinity Features?

We should use `task_scheduler_observer` objects to create thread-to-core affinity only if we are tuning for absolute best performance on a dedicated system. Otherwise, we should let the OS do its job and schedule threads as it sees fit from its global viewpoint. If we do choose to pin threads to cores, we should carefully weigh the potential impact of taking this flexibility away from the OS, especially if our application runs in a multiprogrammed environment.

For task-to-thread affinity, we typically want to use the high-level interfaces, like `affinity_partitioner` described in Chapter 16. The `affinity_partitioner` uses the features described in this chapter to track where tasks are executed and provide hints to the TBB scheduler to replay the partitioning on subsequent executions of the loop. It also tracks changes to keep the hints up to date.

Because TBB task affinities are just scheduler hints, the potential impact of misusing these interfaces is far less – so we don't need to be as careful when we use task affinities. In fact, we should be encouraged to experiment with task affinity, especially through the higher-level interfaces, as a normal part of tuning our applications.

Summary

In this chapter, we discussed how we can create thread-to-core and task-to-thread affinity from within our TBB applications. While TBB does not provide an interface for handling the mechanics of setting thread-to-core affinity, its `class task_scheduler_observer` provides a callback mechanism that allows us to insert the necessary calls to our own OS-specific or portable libraries that assign affinities. Because the TBB work-stealing scheduler randomly assigns tasks to software threads, thread-to-core affinity is not always sufficient on its own. We therefore also discussed the interfaces in TBB's `class task` that lets us provide affinity hints to the TBB scheduler about what software thread we want a task to be scheduled onto. We noted that we will most likely not use these interfaces directly, but instead use the higher-level interfaces described in Chapters 16 and 17. For readers that are interested in learning more about these low-level interfaces though, we provided examples that showed how we can use the `note_affinity` and `set_affinity` functions to implement task-to-thread affinity for code that uses the low-level TBB tasking interface.

Like with many of the optimization features of the TBB library, affinities need to be used carefully. Using thread-to-core affinity incorrectly can degrade performance significantly by restricting the Operating System's ability to balance load. Using the task-to-thread affinity hints, being just hints that the TBB scheduler can ignore, might negatively impact performance if used unwisely, but much less so.

For More Information

- Posix set/get CPU affinity of a thread, `http://man7.org/linux/man-pages/man3/pthread_setaffinity_np.3.html`

- SetThreadAffinityMask function, `https://docs.microsoft.com/en-us/windows/desktop/api/winbase/nf-winbase-setthreadaffinitymask`

- Portable Hardware Locality (hwloc), `www.open-mpi.org/projects/hwloc/`

CHAPTER 14

Using Task Priorities

The Threading Building Blocks scheduler is not a real-time scheduler, and therefore it is not suitable for use in *hard* real-time systems. In real-time systems, a task can be given a deadline by which it must complete, and the usefulness of the task degrades if it misses its deadline. In hard real-time systems, a missed deadline can lead to a total system failure. In soft real-time systems, a missed deadline is not catastrophic but leads to a decrease in quality of service. The TBB library has no support for assigning deadlines to tasks, but it does have support for task priorities. These priorities might be of use in applications that have soft real-time requirements. Whether or not they are sufficient requires understanding both the soft real-time demands of the application and the properties of TBB tasks and task priorities.

Beyond soft real-time use, task priorities can have other uses as well. For example, we may want to prioritize some tasks over others because doing so will improve performance or responsiveness. Perhaps we want to prioritize tasks that free memory over tasks that allocate memory, so that we reduce the memory footprint of our application. Or perhaps, we want to prioritize tasks that touch data already in our caches over tasks that will load new data into our caches.

In this chapter, we describe task priorities as supported by TBB tasks and the TBB task scheduler. Readers that are considering TBB for soft real-time applications can use this information to determine if TBB is sufficient for their requirements. Other readers might find this information useful if needed to implement performance optimizations that benefit from task priorities.

© Intel Corporation 2019
M. Voss, R. Asenjo, J. Reinders, *Pro TBB*, https://doi.org/10.1007/978-1-4842-4398-5_14

Support for Non-Preemptive Priorities in the TBB Task Class

Just like with the support for task affinities described in Chapter 13, TBB's support for priorities is enabled by functions in the low-level task class. The TBB library defines three priority levels: `priority_normal`, `priority_low`, and `priority_high` as shown in Figure 14-1.

```
namespace tbb {
  enum priority_t {
    priority_normal = implementation-defined,
    priority_low = implementation-defined,
    priority_high = implementation-defined
  };

  class task {
    // . . .
    static void enqueue( task&, priority_t );
    void set_group_priority ( priority_t );
    priority_t group_priority () const;
    // . . .
  };
}
```

Figure 14-1. *The types and functions in class task that support priorities*

In general, TBB executes tasks that are higher priority before tasks that are lower priority. But there are caveats.

The most important caveat is that TBB tasks are executed non-preemptively by TBB threads. Once a task has started to execute, it will execute to completion – even if a higher priority task has been spawned or enqueued. While this behavior may seem like a weakness, since it may delay the application's switch to higher priority tasks, it is also a strength because it helps us avoid some dangerous situations. Imagine if, for example, a task t_0 holds a lock on a shared resource and then higher priority tasks are spawned. If TBB doesn't allow t_0 to finish and release its lock, the higher priority tasks can deadlock if they block on the acquisition of a lock on this same resource. A more complicated but similar issue, *priority inversion*, was famously the cause of problems with the Mars Pathfinder rover in the late 1990s. In "What Happened on Mars?", Mike Jones suggests priority inheritance as a way to address these situations. With priority inheritance, a task that blocks higher priority tasks inherits the priority of the highest task it blocks. The TBB library does not implement priority inheritance or other complicated approaches since it avoids many of these issues due to its use of non-preemptive priorities.

The TBB library ***does not*** provide any high-level abstraction for setting ***thread priorities***. Because there is no high-level support in TBB for thread priorities, if we want to set thread priorities, we need to use OS-specific code to manage them – just as we did for thread-to-core affinity in Chapter 13. And just as with thread-to-core affinity, we can use `task_scheduler_observer` objects and invoke these OS-specific interfaces in the callbacks as threads enter and exit the TBB task scheduler, or a specific task arena. However, we warn developers to ***use extreme caution when using thread priorities***. If we introduce thread priorities, which are preemptive, we also invite back in all of the known pathologies that come with preemptive priorities, such as priority inversion.

Critical Rule of Thumb   Do not set different priorities for threads operating in the same arena. Weird things can and will happen because TBB treats threads within an arena as equals.

Beyond the non-preemptive nature of TBB task execution, there are a few other important limitations to mention about its support for task priorities. First, changes may not come into effect immediately on all threads. It's possible that some lower priority tasks may start executing even if there are higher priority tasks present. Second, worker threads may need to migrate to another arena to gain access to the highest priority tasks, and as we've noted before in Chapter 12, this can take time. Once workers have migrated, this may leave some arenas (that do not have high priority tasks) without worker threads. But, because master threads cannot migrate, the master threads will remain in those arenas, and they themselves are not stalled – they can continue to execute tasks from their own task arena even if they are of a lower priority.

Task priorities are not hints like TBB's support for task-to-thread affinity described in Chapter 13. Still, there are enough caveats to make task priorities weaker in practice than we may desire. In addition, the support for only three priority levels, low, normal, and high, can be quite limiting in complex applications. Even so, we will continue in the next section by describing the mechanics of using TBB task priorities.

Setting Static and Dynamic Priorities

Static priorities can be assigned to individual tasks that are enqueued to the shared queue (see enqueued tasks in Chapter 10). And *dynamic priorities* can be assigned to groups of tasks, through either the set_group_priority function or through a task_group_context object's set_priority function (see the task_group_context sidebar).

TASK_GROUP_CONTEXT: EVERY TASK BELONGS TO A GROUP

A task_group_context represents a group of tasks that can be canceled, or have their priority level set, together. All tasks belong to some group, and a task can be a member of only one of these groups at a time.

In Chapter 10, we allocated TBB tasks using special functions such as allocate_root(). There is an overload of this function that lets us assign a task_group_context to a newly allocated root task:

```
static proxy2 allocate_root( task_group_context& );
```

A task_group_context is also an optional argument to TBB high-level algorithms and to the TBB flow graph, for example:

```
template<typename Index, typename Func>
Func parallel_for(Index first, Index_type last, const Func& f,
                  partitioner[, task_group_context& group]] );

graph([task_group_context& context]);
```

We can assign groups at the task level during allocation but also through the higher-level interfaces, such as TBB algorithms and flow graphs. There are other abstractions, such as task_group, that let us group tasks for execution purposes. The purpose of task_group_context groups is to support cancellation, exception handling, and priorities.

When we use the `task::enqueue` function to provide a priority, the priority affects only that single task and cannot be changed afterward. When we assign a priority to a group of tasks, the priority affects all of the tasks in the group and the priority can be changed at any time by subsequent calls to `task::set_group_priority` or `task_group_context::set_priority`.

The TBB scheduler tracks the highest priority of ready tasks, including both enqueued and spawned tasks, and postpones (the earlier caveats aside) execution of lower priority tasks until all higher priority tasks are executed. By default, all tasks and groups of tasks are created with `priority_normal`.

Two Small Examples

Figure 14-2 shows an example that enqueues 25 tasks on a platform with P logical cores. Each task actively spins for a given duration. The first task in the `task_priority` function is enqueued with normal priority and is set to spin for roughly 500 milliseconds. The for-loop in the function then creates P low priority, P normal priority, and P high priority tasks, each of which will actively spin for roughly 10 ms. When each task executes, it records a message into a thread-local buffer. The high-priority task `ids` are prefixed with `H`, the normal task `ids` with `N` and the low priority tasks `ids` with `L`. At the end of the function, all of the thread local buffers are printed, providing an accounting of the order in which tasks were executed by the participating threads. The complete implementation of this example is available in the Github repository.

```cpp
#include <iostream>
#include <string>

#include <tbb/tbb.h>

void doWork(double sec);

class Spinner : public tbb::task {
public:
  Spinner(const char *m, int id, double len);
  tbb::task *execute() override;

private:
  std::string msg;
  int messageId;
  double length;
};

void enqueueTask(const char *msg,
                 int id,
                 double len,
                 tbb::priority_t
priority=tbb::priority_normal) {
  tbb::task::enqueue(*new( tbb::task::allocate_root())
                        Spinner(msg, id, len),
                   priority);
}

void fig_14_02() {
  int P = tbb::task_scheduler_init::default_num_threads();

  enqueueTask("N", 0, 0.5);
  doWork(0.01);

  for (int i = 0; i < P; ++i) {
    enqueueTask("L", i, 0.01, tbb::priority_low);
    enqueueTask("N", i+1, 0.01, tbb::priority_normal);
    enqueueTask("H", i, 0.01, tbb::priority_high);
  }
  doWork(1.0);
}
```

Figure 14-2. Enqueuing tasks with different priorities

Executing this example on a system with eight logical cores, we see the following output:

```
N:0                   ← thread 1
H:7 H:5 N:3 L:7  ← thread 2
H:2 H:1 N:8 L:5  ← thread 3
H:6 N:1 L:3 L:2  ← thread 4
H:0 N:2 L:6 L:4  ← thread 5
H:3 N:4 N:5 L:0  ← thread 6
H:4 N:7 N:6 L:1  ← thread 8
```

In this output, each row represents a different TBB worker thread. For each thread, the tasks it executes are ordered from left to right. The master thread never participates in the execution of these tasks at all, since it doesn't call wait_for_all, and so we only see seven rows. The first thread executes only the first long, normal priority task that executed for 500 milliseconds. Because TBB tasks are non-preemptive, this thread cannot abandon this task once it starts, so it continues to execute this task even when higher priority tasks become available. Otherwise though, we see that even though the for-loop mixes together the high, normal, and low priority task enqueues, the high priority tasks are executed first by the set of worker threads, then the normal tasks and finally the low priority tasks.

Figure 14-3 shows code that executes two parallel_for algorithms in parallel using two native threads, t0 and t1. Each parallel_for has 16 iterations and uses a simple_partitioner. As described in more detail in Chapter 16, a simple_partitioner divides the iteration space until a fixed grainsize is reached, the default being a grainsize of 1. In our example, each parallel_for will result in 16 tasks, each of which will spin for 10 milliseconds. The loop executed by thread t0 first creates a task_group_context and sets its priority to priority_high. The loop executed by the other thread, t1, uses a default task_group_context that has a priority_normal.

```
#include <iostream>
#include <thread>

#include <tbb/tbb.h>

void doWork(double sec);

void fig_14_03() {
  std::thread t0([]() {
    tbb::task_group_context tcg;
    tcg.set_priority(tbb::priority_high);
    tbb::parallel_for( 0, 16, [] (int) {
      // do high priority work
      doWork(0.01);
      std::cout << "High\n";
    }, tbb::simple_partitioner(), tcg );
  });

  std::thread t1( []() {
    tbb::parallel_for( 0, 16, [] (int) {
      // do normal priority work
      doWork(0.01);
      std::cout << "Normal\n";
    }, tbb::simple_partitioner());
  });

  t0.join();
  t1.join();
}
```

Figure 14-3. *Executing algorithms with different priorities*

An example output from the sample when executed on a platform with eight logical cores follows:

```
Normal
High
High
High
High
High
High
```

```
Normal
High
High
High
High
High
High
High
High
Normal
High
High
Normal
Normal
Normal
Normal
Normal
Normal
Normal
Normal
Normal
Normal
Normal
Normal
Normal
Normal
```

Initially, there are seven "High" tasks executed for every one "Normal" task. This is because thread t1, which started the parallel_for with normal priority, cannot migrate away from its implicit task arena. It can only execute the "Normal" tasks. The other seven threads however, execute only the "High" tasks until they are all completed. Once the high priority tasks are completed, the worker threads can migrate to thread t1's arena and help out.

Implementing Priorities Without Using TBB Task Support

What if low, normal, and high are not enough? One workaround is to spawn generic wrapper tasks that look to a priority queue, or other data structure, to find the work they should do. With this approach, we rely on the TBB scheduler to distribute these generic wrapper tasks across the cores, but the tasks themselves enforce priorities through a shared data structure.

Figure 14-4 shows an example that uses a `task_group` and a `concurrent_priority_queue`. When a piece of work needs to be done, two actions are taken: (1) a description of the work is pushed into the shared queue and (2) a wrapper task is spawned in the `task_group` that will pop and execute an item from the shared queue. The result is that there is exactly one task spawned per work item – but the specific work item that a task will process is not determined until the task executes.

```
#include <iostream>
#include <tbb/tbb.h>

class WorkItem {
public:
  WorkItem() { }
  WorkItem(int p) : priority(p) { }

  bool operator<(const WorkItem &b) const {
    if (priority < b.priority) return true;
    else return false;
  }

  void doWork();

private:
  int priority;
};

void fig_14_4() {
  tbb::concurrent_priority_queue<WorkItem> q;
  tbb::task_group g;

  const std::string prefix = "w";
  for (int i = 0; i < 16; ++i) {
    q.push(WorkItem(i));
    g.run([&q]() {
      WorkItem w;
      if (q.try_pop(w))
        w.doWork();
    });
  }
  g.wait();
}
```

Figure 14-4. *Using a concurrent priority queue to feed work to wrapper tasks*

A concurrent_priority_queue by default relies on operator< to determine ordering and so when we define work_item::operator< as shown in Figure 14-4, we will see an output that shows the items executing in decreasing order, from 15 down to 0:

```
WorkItem: 15
WorkItem: 14
WorkItem: 13
WorkItem: 12
```

```
WorkItem: 11
WorkItem: 10
WorkItem: 9
WorkItem: 8
WorkItem: 7
WorkItem: 6
WorkItem: 5
WorkItem: 4
WorkItem: 3
WorkItem: 2
WorkItem: 1
WorkItem: 0
```

If we change the operator to return true if (`priority > b.priority`), then we will see the tasks execute in increasing order from 0 to 15.

Using the generic-wrapper-task approach provides increased flexibility because we have complete control over how priorities are defined. But, at least in Figure 14-4, it introduces a potential bottleneck – the shared data structure accessed concurrently by the threads. Even so, when TBB task priorities are insufficient we might use this approach as a backup plan.

Summary

In this chapter, we provided an overview of task priority support in TBB. Using mechanisms provided by `class task`, we can assign low, normal, and high priorities to tasks. We showed that we can assign static priorities to tasks that are enqueued and dynamic priorities to groups of tasks using `task_group_context` objects. Since TBB tasks are executed non-preemptively by the TBB worker threads, the priorities in TBB are also non-preemptive. We briefly discussed the benefits and drawbacks of non-preemptive priorities, and also highlighted some of the other caveats we need to be aware of when using this support. We then provided a few simple examples that demonstrated how task priorities can be applied to TBB tasks and to algorithms.

Since there are many limitations to the task priority support in the library, we concluded our discussion with an alternative that used wrapper tasks and a priority queue.

The TBB scheduler is not a hard real-time scheduler. We see in this chapter though that there is some limited support for prioritizing tasks and algorithms. Whether these features are useful or not for soft real-time applications, or to apply performance optimizations, needs to be considered by developers on a case-by-case basis.

For More Information

Mike Jones, "What Happened on Mars?" a note sent on December 5, 1997. `www.cs.cmu.edu/afs/cs/user/raj/www/mars.html`.

L. Sha, R. Rajkumar, and J. P. Lehoczky. Priority Inheritance Protocols: An Approach to Real-Time Synchronization. In IEEE Transactions on Computers, vol. 39, pp. 1175-1185, Sep. 1990.

CHAPTER 15

Cancellation and Exception Handling

More or less frequently, we all get bitten by run-time errors, either in our sequential or parallel developments. To try to assuage the pain, we have learnt to capture them using error codes or a more high-level alternative like exception handling. C++, as most OO languages, supports exception handling, which, when conveniently exercised, enables the development of robust applications. Now, considering that TBB adds task-based parallelism on top of C++, it is perfectly understandable that developers should expect that exception handling is well supported. As we will see in this chapter, exception handling is indeed well and automatically supported in TBB. This means that in case of an error, perish the thought, our code can resort to an exception handler if such is available, or terminate the whole work otherwise. Implementing support in TBB was certainly nontrivial considering that

1. Exceptions can be thrown inside of tasks that are executed by a number of threads.

2. Cancellation of tasks has to be implemented in order to terminate the work that threw the exception.

3. TBB composability has to be preserved.

4. Exception management should not affect performance if no exception arises.

The implementation of exceptions within TBB meets all these requirements, including the support of task cancellation. As we said, task cancellation support is necessary since throwing an exception can result in the need to cancel the execution of

M. Voss, R. Asenjo, J. Reinders, *Pro TBB*, https://doi.org/10.1007/978-1-4842-4398-5_15

the parallel algorithm that has generated the exception. For example, if a `parallel_for` algorithm incurs in an out-of-bound or division by zero exception, the library may need to cancel the whole `parallel_for`. This requires TBB to cancel all of the tasks involved in processing chunks of the parallel iteration space and then jump to the exception handler. TBB's implementation of task cancellation seamlessly achieves the necessary cancellation of tasks involved in the offending `parallel_for` without affecting tasks that are executing unrelated parallel work.

Task cancellation is not only a requirement for exception handling but has a value in its own. Therefore, in this chapter, we begin by showing how cancellation can be leveraged to speed up some parallel algorithms. Although cancellation of TBB algorithms just work out-of-the-box, advanced TBB developers might want to know how to get full control of task cancellation and how it is implemented in TBB. We also try to satisfy advanced developers in this chapter (remember this is the advanced part of the book). The second part of this chapter moves on to cover exception handling. Again, exception handling "just works" without any added complication: relying on our well-known try-catch construction (as we do in sequential codes) is all we need to be ready to capture standard C++ predefined exceptions plus some additional TBB ones. And again, we don't settle for the basics in this respect either. To close the chapter, we describe how to build our own custom TBB exceptions and delve into how TBB exception handling and TBB cancellation interplay under the hood.

Even if you are skeptical of exception handling because you belong to the "error code" school of thought, keep reading and discover if we end up convincing you of the advantages of TBB exception handling when developing reliable, fault-tolerant parallel applications.

How to Cancel Collective Work

There are situations in which a piece of work has to be canceled. Examples range from external reasons (the user cancels the execution by pressing a GUI button) to internal ones (an item has been found, which alleviates the need for any further searching). We have seen such situations in sequential code, but they also arise in parallel applications. For example, some expensive global optimization algorithms follow a branch-and-bound parallel pattern in which the search space is organized as a tree and we may wish to cancel the tasks traversing some branches if the solution is likely to be found in a different branch.

Let's see how we can put cancellation to work with a somewhat contrived example: we want to find the position of the single -2 in a vector of integers, data. The example is contrived because we set data[500]=-2, so we do know the output beforehand (i.e., where –2 is stored). The implementation uses a parallel_for algorithm as we see in Figure 15-1.

```cpp
std::vector<int> data(n);
data[500] = -2;
int index = -1;
auto t1 = tbb::tick_count::now();
tbb::parallel_for(tbb::blocked_range<int>{0, n},
  [&](const tbb::blocked_range<int>& r){
      for(int i=r.begin(); i!=r.end(); ++i){
        if(data[i] == -2) {
          index = i;
          tbb::task::self().cancel_group_execution();
          break;
        }
      }
});
auto t2 = tbb::tick_count::now();
std::cout << "Index "      << index;
std::cout << " found in " << (t2-t1).seconds() << " seconds!\n";
```

Figure 15-1. *Finding the index in which –2 is stored*

The idea is to cancel all other concurrent tasks collaborating in the parallel_for when one of them finds that data[500]==-2. So, what does task::self().cancel_group_execution()? Well, task::self() returns a reference to the innermost task that the calling thread is running. Tasks have been covered in several chapters, but details were provided in Chapters 10–14. In those chapters, we saw some of the member functions included in the task class, and cancel_group_execution() is just one more. As the name indicates, this member function does not cancel just the calling task, but **all** the tasks belonging to the same group.

In this example, the group of tasks consists of all the tasks collaborating in the parallel_for algorithm. By canceling this group, we are stopping all its tasks and essentially interrupting the parallel search. Picture the task that finds data[500]==-2 shouting to the other sibling tasks "Hey guys, I got it! don't search any further!". In general, each TBB algorithm creates its own group of tasks, and every task collaborating in this TBB algorithm belongs to this group. That way, any task of the group/algorithm can cancel the whole TBB algorithm.

For a vector of size n=1,000,000,000, this loop consumes 0.01 seconds, and the output can be like

Index 500 found in 0.01368 seconds!

However, if task::self().cancel_group_execution() is commented out, the execution time goes up to 1.56 seconds on the laptop on which we happen to be writing these lines.

That's it. We are all set. That is all we need to know to do (basic) TBB algorithm cancellation. However, now that we have a clear motivation for canceling tasks (more than 100× speedup in the previous example!), we can also (optionally) dive into how task cancellation is working and some considerations to fully control which tasks actually get canceled.

Advanced Task Cancellation

In Chapter 14, the task_group_context concept was introduced. Every task belongs to one and only one task_group_context that, for brevity, we will call TGC from now on. A TGC represents a group of tasks that can be canceled or have their priority level set. In Chapter 14, some examples illustrated how to change the priority level of a TGC. We also said that a TGC object can optionally be passed to high-level algorithms like the parallel_for or flow graph. For instance, an alternative way to write the code of Figure 15-1 is sketched in Figure 15-2.

```
tbb::task_group_context tg;

...
tbb::parallel_for(tbb::blocked_range<int>{0, n},
  [&](const tbb::blocked_range<int>& r){
    for(int i=r.begin(); i!=r.end(); ++i){
      if(data[i] == -2){
        index = i;
        tg.cancel_group_execution();
        break;
      }
    }
}, tg);
```

Figure 15-2. *Alternative implementation of the code in Figure 15-1*

In this code, we see that a TGC, `tg`, is created and passed as the last argument of the `parallel_for`, and also used to call `tg.cancel_group_execution()` (now using a member function of the `task_group_context class`).

Note that the codes of Figures 15-1 and 15-2 are completely equivalent. The optional TGC parameter, `tg`, passed as the last argument of the `parallel_for`, just opens the door to more elaborated developments. For example, say that we also pass the same TGC variable, `tg`, to a `parallel_pipeline` that we launch in a parallel thread. Now, any task collaborating either in the `parallel_for` or in the `parallel_pipeline` can call `tg.cancel_group_execution()` to cancel both parallel algorithms.

A task can also query the TGC to which it belongs by calling the member function `group()` that returns a pointer to the TGC. That way, we can safely add this line inside the lambda of the `parallel_for` in Figure 15-2: `assert(task::self().group()==&tg);`. This means that the following three lines are completely equivalent and can be interchanged in the code of Figure 15-2:

```
tg.cancel_group_execution();
tbb::task::self().group()->cancel_group_execution();
tbb::task::self().cancel_group_execution();
```

When a task triggers the cancellation of the whole TGC, spawned tasks waiting in the queues are finalized without being run, but already running tasks will not be canceled by the TBB scheduler because, as you certainly remember, the scheduler is non-preemptive. This is, before passing the control to the `task::execute()` function, the scheduler checks the cancellation flag of the task's TGC and then decides if the task should be executed or the whole TGC canceled. But if the task already has the control, well, it has the control until it deigns to return it to the scheduler. However, in case we want to also do away with running tasks, each task can pool the canceling status using one of these two alternatives:

```
if (task::self().group()->is_group_execution_cancelled()) return;
if (task::self().is_cancelled()) return;
```

Next question: to which TGC are the new tasks assigned? Of course, we have the devices to fully control this mapping, but there is also a default behavior that is advisable to know. First, we cover how to manually map tasks into a TGC.

Explicit Assignment of TGC

As we have seen, we can create TGC objects and pass them to the high-level parallel algorithms (`parallel_for,...`) and to the low-level tasking API (`allocate_root()`). Remember that in Chapter 10 we also presented the `task_group` class as a medium-level API to easily create tasks sharing a TGC that can be canceled or assigned a priority simultaneously with a single action. All the tasks launched using the same `task_group::run()` member function will belong to the same TGC, and therefore one of the tasks in the group can cancel the whole gang.

As an example, consider the code of Figure 15-3 in which we rewrite the parallel search of a given value "hidden" in a `data` vector, and get the index in which it is stored. This time, we use a manually implemented divide-and-conquer approach using the `task_group` features (the `parallel_for` approach is actually doing something similar under the hood, even if we don't see it).

```cpp
int grainsize = 100;
std::vector<int> data;
int myindex=-1;
tbb::task_group g;

void SerialSearch(long begin, long end){
  for(int i=begin; i<end; ++i){
    if(data[i] == -2){
      myindex = i;
      g.cancel();
      break;
    }
  }
}

void ParallelSearch(long begin, long end){
  if((end-begin) < grainsize){ //cutoof equivalent
    return SerialSearch(begin, end);
  }
  else{
    long mid = begin + (end-begin)/2;
    g.run([&]{ParallelSearch(begin, mid);}); // spawn a task
    g.run([&]{ParallelSearch(mid, end);});   // spawn another task
  }
}

int main(int argc, char** argv)
{
  int n = (argc>1) ? atoi(argv[1]) : 1000;
  data.resize(n);
  data[n/2] = -2;

  auto t0 = tbb::tick_count::now();
  SerialSearch(0, n);
  auto t1 = tbb::tick_count::now();
  ParallelSearch(0, n);
  g.wait();       // wait for all spawned tasks
  auto t2 = tbb::tick_count::now();
  double t_s = (t1 - t0).seconds();
  double t_p = (t2 - t1).seconds();

  cout << "SerialSearch:   " << myindex << " Time: " << t_s << endl;
  cout << "ParallelSearch: " << myindex << " Time: " << t_p
       << " Speedup: "       << t_s/t_p << endl;
  return 0;
}
```

Figure 15-3. *Manual implementation of the parallel search using* task_group *class*

For the sake of expediency, the vector, data, the resulting index, myindex, and the task_group, g, are global variables. This code recursively bisections the search space until a certain grainsize (a cutoff value as we saw in Chapter 10). The function ParallelSearch(begin,end) is the one used to accomplish this parallel partitioning. When the grainsize becomes small enough (100 iterations in our example), the SequentialSearch(begin,end) is invoked. If the value we were looking for, –2, is found in one of the ranges traversed inside the SequentialSearch, all spawned tasks are canceled using g.cancel(). In our laptop with four cores, and for N equal to 10 million, this is the output of our algorithm:

```
SerialSearch:    5000000 Time: 0.012667
ParallelSearch: 5000000 Time: 0.000152 Speedup: 83.3355
```

5000000 is the index of the -2 value we have found. Looking at the speedup, we can be baffled by it running 83× faster than the sequential code. However, this is one of the situations in which we are witness to a parallel implementation having to carry out less work than the sequential counterpart: once a task finds the key, no more traversal of the vector Data is needed. In our run, the key is in the middle of the vector, N/2, and the sequential version has to get to that point, whereas the parallel version starts searching in parallel at different positions, for example, 0, N/4, N/2, N·3/4, and so on.

If your mind was blown by the achieved speedup, wait and see because we can do even better. Remember that cancel() cannot terminate already running tasks. But again, we can query from within a running task to check if a different task in the TGC has canceled the execution. To achieve this using the task_group class, we just need to insert:

```
if(g.is_canceling()) return;
```

at the beginning of the ParallelSearch() function. This apparently minor mod results in these execution times:

```
SerialSearch:    5000000 Time: 0.012634
ParallelSearch: 5000000 Time: 2e-06 Speedup: 6317
```

We wish we could always get that kind of parallel speedup in a quad-core machine!!

Note   Advanced and seldom needed: In addition to explicitly creating a `task_group`, setting the TGC for a TBB parallel algorithm, and setting the TCG for a root task using `allocate_root`, we can also change the TGC of any task using its member function:

> `void task::change_group(task_group_context& ctx);`

and because we can query any task's TGC using `task::group()`, we have full control to move any task to the TGC of any other task. For example, if two tasks have access to a TGC_X variable (say you have a global `task_group_context *TGC_X`) and a first task has previously executed this:

> `TGC_X=task::self().group();`

then a second one can execute this:

> `task::self().change_group(*TGC_X);`

Default Assignment of TGC

Now, what happens if we do not explicitly specify the TGC? Well, the default behavior has some rules:

- A thread that creates a `task_scheduler_init` (either explicitly or implicitly by using a TBB algorithm) creates its own TGC, tagged as "**isolated**." The first task executed by this thread belongs to that TGC and subsequent child tasks inherit the same parent's TGC.

- When one of these tasks invokes a parallel algorithm without explicitly passing a TGC as optional argument (e.g., `parallel_for`, `parallel_reduce`, `parallel_do`, `pipeline`, flow graph, etc.), a new TGC, now tagged as "**bound**," is implicitly created for the new tasks that will collaborate in this nested algorithm. This TGC is therefore a child *bound* to the isolated parent TGC.

- If tasks of a parallel algorithm invoke a nested parallel algorithm, a new bound child TGC is created for this new algorithm, where the parent is now the TGC of the invoking task.

An example of a forest of TGC trees automatically built by a hypothetical TBB code is depicted in Figure 15-4.

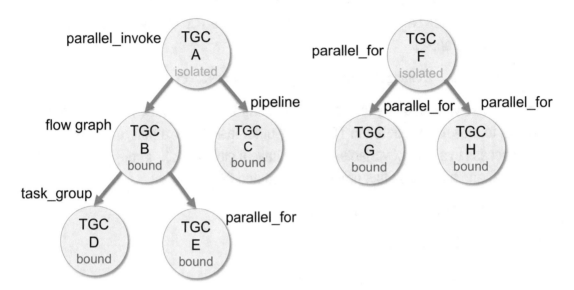

Figure 15-4. *A forest of TGC trees automatically created when running a hypothetical TBB code*

In our hypothetical TBB code, the user wants to nest several TBB algorithms but knows nothing about TGCs so he just calls the algorithms without passing the optional and explicit TGC object. In one master thread, there is a call to a `parallel_invoke`, which automatically initializes the scheduler creating one arena and the first isolated TGC, A. Then, inside the `parallel_invoke`, two TBB algorithms are created, a flow graph and a `pipeline`. For each of these algorithms, a new TGC, B and C in this case, is automatically created and bound to A. Inside one of the flow graph nodes, a `task_group` is created, and a `parallel_for` is instantiated in a different flow graph node. This results in two newly created TGCs, D and E, that are bound to B. This forms the first tree of our TGC forest, with an isolated root and where all the other TGCs are bound, that is, they have a parent. The second tree is built in a different master thread that creates a `parallel_for` with just two parallel ranges, and for each one a nested `parallel_for` is called. Again, the root of the tree is an isolated TGC, F, and the other TGCs, G and H, are bound. Note that the user just wrote the TBB code, nesting some TBB algorithms into other TBB algorithms. It is the TBB machinery creating the forest of TGCs for us. And do not forget about the tasks: there are several tasks sharing each TGC.

Now, what happens if a task gets canceled? Easy. The rule is that the whole TGC containing this task is canceled, but the cancellation also propagates downward. For example, if we cancel a task of the flow graph (TGC B), we will also cancel the task_group (TGC D) and the parallel_for (TGC E), as shown in Figure 15-5. It makes sense: we are canceling the flow graph, and everything created from there on. The example is somewhat contrived since it may be difficult to find a real application with this nesting of algorithms. However, it serves to illustrate how different TGCs are automatically linked in order to deal with the much vaunted TBB's composability.

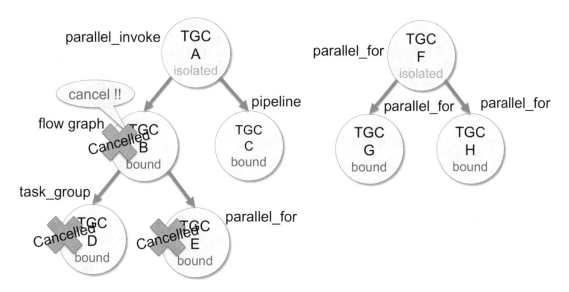

Figure 15-5. *Cancel is called from a task belonging to TGC B*

But wait, we may want to cancel the flow graph and the task_group but keep the parallel_for (TGC E) alive and kicking. Fine, this is also possible by manually creating an isolated TGC object and passing it as the last argument of the parallel for. To that end, we can write code similar to the one of Figure 15-6, where a function_node of the flow graph, g, exploits this possibility.

```
tbb::flow::function_node<float,float> node{g,…,[&](float a){
  tbb::task_group_context TGC_E(task_group_context::isolated);
  // nested parallel_for
  tbb::parallel_for(0, N, 1, [&](…){/*loop body*/}, TGC_E);
  return a;
}};
```

Figure 15-6. *Alternative to detach a nested algorithm from the tree of TGCs*

The isolated TGC object, TGC_E, is created on the stack and passed as the last argument to the parallel_for. Now, as depicted in Figure 15-7, even if a task of the flow graph cancels its TGC B, the cancellation propagates downward till TGC D but cannot reach TGC E because it has been created detached from the tree.

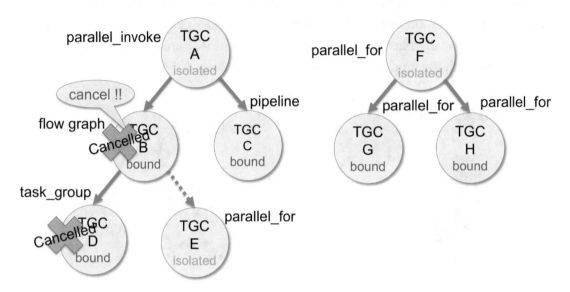

Figure 15-7. *TGC E is now isolated and won't be canceled*

More precisely, the isolated TGC E can now be the root of another tree in our forest of TGCs because it is an isolated TGC and it can be the parent of new TGCs created for deeper nested algorithms. We will see an example of this in the next section.

Summarizing, if we nest TBB algorithms without explicitly passing a TGC object to them, the default forest of TGCs will result in the expected behavior in case of cancellation. However, this behavior can be controlled at our will by creating the necessary number of TGC objects and passing them to the desired algorithms. For example, we can create a single TGC, A, and pass it to all the parallel algorithms invoked in the first thread of our hypothetical TBB example. In such a case, all tasks collaborating in all algorithms will belong to that TGC A, as depicted in Figure 15-8. If now a task of the flow graph gets canceled, not only the nested task_group and parallel_for algorithms are also canceled, but all the algorithms sharing the TGC A.

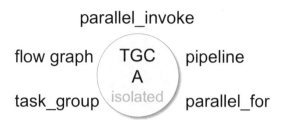

Figure 15-8. *After modifying our hypothetical TBB code so that we pass a single TGC A to all the parallel algorithms*

As a final note regarding cancellation, we want to underscore that efficiently keeping track of the forest of TGCs and how they get linked is quite challenging. The interested reader can have a look at the paper of Andrey Marochko and Alexey Kukanov (see the "For More Information" section) in which they elaborate on the implementation decisions and internal details. The main take-away is that great care was taken to ensure that TGC bookkeeping does not affect performance if cancellation is not required.

Exception Handling in TBB

Note   If C++ exception is not completely familiar, here is an example to help illustrate the fundamentals:

```
int main(){
  try{
    try{
      throw 5;
    }
    catch(int& n){
      cout << "Re-throwing value: "<< n << endl;
      throw;
    }
  }
  catch(int& e){
    cout<< "Value caught: "<< e << endl;
  }
  catch (...){
    cout << "Exception occurred\n";
  }
}
```

The output after running this code is

```
Re-throwing value: 5
Value caught: 5
```

As we can see, the first try block includes a nested try catch. This one throws as an exception as an integer with value 5. Since the catch block matches the type, this code becomes the exception handler. Here, we only print the value received and re-throw the exception upward. At the outer level there are two catch blocks, but the first one is executed because the argument type matches the type of the thrown value. The second catch in the outer level receives an ellipsis (...) so it becomes the actual handler if the exception has a type not considered in the preceding chain of catch functions. For example, if we throw 5.0 instead of 5, the output message would be "Exception occurred."

Now that we understand cancellation as the keystone mechanism supporting TBB exception management, let's go into the meat of the matter. Our goal is to master the development of bulletproof code that exercise exceptions, as the one in Figure 15-9.

```cpp
int main() {
  std::vector<int> data(1000);
  try{
    tbb::parallel_for(0, 2000, [&](int i) {data.at(i)++;});
  }
  catch(std::out_of_range& ex){
    std::cout << "Out_of_range: " << ex.what() << std::endl;
  }
  return 0;
}
```

Figure 15-9. *Basic example of TBB exception handling*

Okay, maybe it is not completely bulletproof yet, but for a first example it is good enough. The thing is that the vector data has only 1000 elements, but the parallel_for algorithm insists on walking till position 2000-1. To add insult to injury, data is not accessed using data[i], but using Data.at(i), which, contrary to the former, adds bound-checking and throws `std::out_of_range` objects if we don't toe the line. Therefore, when we compile and run the code of Figure 15-9, we will get

`Out_of_range: vector`

As we know, several tasks will be spawned to increment `data` elements in parallel. Some of them will try to increment at positions beyond 999. The task that first touches an out-of-range element, for example, `data.at(1003)++`, clearly has to be canceled. Then, the `std::vector::at()` member function instead of incrementing the inexistent 1003 position throws `std::out_of_range`. Since the exception object is not caught by the task, it is re-thrown upward, getting to the TBB scheduler. Then, the scheduler catches the exception and proceeds to cancel all concurrent tasks of the corresponding TGC (we already know how the whole TGC gets canceled). In addition, a copy of the exception object is stored in the TGC data structure. When all TGC tasks are canceled, the TGC is finalized, which re-throws the exception in the thread that started the TGC execution. In our example, this is the thread that called `parallel_for`. But the `parallel_for` is in a `try` block with a `catch` function that receives an `out_of_range` object. This means that the `catch` function becomes the exception handler which finally prints the exception message. The `ex.what()` member function is responsible of returning a string with some verbose information about the exception.

Note   Implementation detail. The compiler is not aware of the threading nature of a TBB parallel algorithm. This means that enclosing such algorithm in a try block results in only the calling thread (master thread) being guarded, but the worker threads will be executing tasks that can throw exceptions too. To solve this, the scheduler already includes try-catch blocks so that every worker thread is able to intercept exceptions escaping from its tasks.

The argument of the `catch()` function should be passed by reference. That way, a single catch function capturing a base class is able to capture objects of all derived types. For example, in Figure 15-9, we could have written **catch**(`std::exception& ex`) instead of **catch**(`std::out_of_range& ex`) because `std::out_of_range` is derived from `std::logic_failure` that in turn is derived from the base class `std::exception` and capturing by reference captures all related classes.

Not all C++ compilers support the exception propagation feature of C++11. More precisely, if the compiler does not support std::exception_ptr (as happen in a pre-C++11 compiler), TBB cannot re-throw an exact copy of the exception object. To make up for it, in such cases, TBB summarizes the exception information into a tbb::captured_exception object, and this is the one that can be re-thrown. There are some additional details regarding how different kinds of exceptions (std::exception, tbb::tbb_exception, or others) are summarized. However, since nowadays it is becoming difficult to get our hands on a compiler not supporting C++11, we will not pay extra attention to this TBB backward compatibility feature.

Tailoring Our Own TBB Exceptions

The TBB library already comes with some predefined exception classes that are listed in the table of Figure B-77.

However, in some cases, it is good practice to derive our own specific TBB exceptions. To this end, we could use the abstract class tbb::tbb_exception that we see in Figure 15-10. This abstract class is actually an interface since it declares five pure virtual functions that we are forced to define in the derived class.

```
class tbb_exception: public std::exception{
            virtual tbb_exception* move() throw() = 0;
            virtual void destroy() throw() = 0;
            virtual void throw_self() = 0;
            virtual const char* name() throw() = 0;
            virtual const char* what() throw() = 0;
    };
```

Figure 15-10. *Deriving our own exception class from tbb::tbb_exception*

The details of the pure virtual functions of the tbb_exception interface are

- move() should create a pointer to a copy of the exception object that can outlive the original. It is advisable to move the contents of the original, especially if it is going to be destroyed. The function specification throw() just after move() (as well as in destroy(), what(), and name()) is only to inform the compiler that this function won't throw anything.

- destroy() should destroy a copy created by move().

- throw_self() should throw *this.

- name() typically returns the RTTI (Run-time type information) name of the originally intercepted exception. It can be obtained using the typeid operator and std::type_info class. For example, we could return typeid(*this).name().

- what() returns a null-terminated string describing the exception.

However, instead of implementing all the virtual functions required to derive from tbb_exception, it is easier and recommended to build our own exception using the TBB class template, tbb::movable_exception. Internally, this class template implements for us the required virtual functions. The five virtual functions described before are now regular member functions that we can optionally override or not. There are however other available functions as we see in an excerpt of the signature:

```
template<typename ExceptionData>
class movable_exception: public tbb_exception{
public:
  movable_exception(const ExceptionData& src);
  ExceptionData& data() throw();
  ...
}
```

The movable_exception constructor and the data() member function will be explained with an example. Let's say that division by 0 is an exceptional event that we want to explicitly capture. In Figure 15-11, we present how we create our own exception with the help of the class template tbb::movable_exception.

```
class div_ex
{
  public:
    int it;
    explicit div_ex(int it_) : it{it_} {}
    const char* what() const throw(){
      return "Division by 0!";
    }
    const char* name() const throw(){
      return typeid(*this).name();
    }
};

int main(int argc, char** argv){
  int n = (argc>1) ? atoi(argv[1]): 1000;

  std::vector<float> data(n, 1.0);
  data[n/2] = 0.0;
  try {
    tbb::parallel_for(0, n, [&](int i){
      if (data[i]) data[i] = 1/data[i];
      else{
        tbb::movable_exception<div_ex> de{div_ex{i}};
        throw de;
      }
    });
  }
  catch(tbb::movable_exception<div_ex>& ex){
    std::cout << "Exception name: " << ex.data().name() << endl;
    std::cout << "Exception: "      << ex.data().what();
    std::cout << " at position: "   << ex.data().it << endl;
  }
  return 0;
}
```

Figure 15-11. *Convenient alternative to configure our own movable exception*

We create our custom class div_ex with the data that we want to move along with the exception. In this case, the payload is the integer it that will store the position at which division by 0 occurs. Now we are able to create an object, de, of the movable_exception class instantiated with the template argument div_ex as we do in the line:

```
tbb::movable_exception<div_ex> de{div_ex{i}};
```

where we can see that we pass a constructor of div_ex, div_ex{i}, as the argument to the constructor of movable_exception<div_ex>.

Later, in the catch block, we capture the exception object as ex, and use the ex. data() member function to get a reference to the div_ex object. That way, we have access to the member variables and member functions defined in div_ex, as name(), what(), and it. The output of this example when input parameter n=1000000 is

```
Exception name: div_ex
Exception: Division by 0! at position: 500000
```

Although we added what() and name() as member functions of our custom div_ex class, now they are optional, so we can get rid of them if we don't need them. In such a case, we can change the catch block as follows:

```
catch(tbb::movable_exception<div_ex>& ex){
  cout << "Division by 0 at pos: " << ex.data().it << endl;
}
```

since this exception handler will be executed only if receiving movable_ exception<div_ex> which only happens when a division by 0 is thrown.

Putting All Together: Composability, Cancellation, and Exception Handling

To close this chapter, let us go back to the composability aspects of TBB with a final example. In Figure 15-12, we have a code snippet showing a parallel_for that would traverse the rows of a matrix Data, were it not for the fact that it throws an exception (actually the string "oops") in the first iteration!! For each row, a nested, parallel_for should traverse the columns of Data also in parallel.

```
bool data[N][N];
int main(){
  try{
    tbb::parallel_for(0, N, 1,
      [&](int i) {
        tbb::task_group_context root{task_group_context::isolated};
        tbb::parallel_for(0, N, 1,
          [&](int j){
            data[i][j] = true;
          }
          //, root  //Uncomment and see!
        );
        throw "oops";
      });
  }

  catch(...){
    std::cout << "An exception captured " << std::endl;
  }

  return 0;
}
```

Figure 15-12. *A* parallel_for *nested in an outer* parallel_for *that throws an exception*

Say that four different tasks are running four different iterations i of the outer loop and calling to the inner parallel_for. In that case, we may end up with a tree of TGCs similar to the one of Figure 15-13.

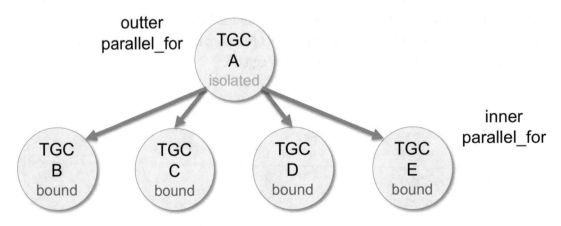

Figure 15-13. *A possible tree of TGCs for the code of Figure 15-12*

This means that when in the first iteration of the outer loop we get to the `throw` keyword, there are several inner loops in flight. However, the exception in the outer level propagates downward also canceling the inner parallel loops no matter what they are doing. The visible result of this global cancellation is that some rows that were in the process of changing the value from false to true were interrupted so these rows will have some true values and some false values.

But look, there is, per-row, an isolated `task_group_context` named `root`, thanks to this line:

```
tbb::task_group_context root(task_group_context::isolated);
```

Now, if we pass this TGC root as the last argument of the inner `parallel_for` uncommenting this line:

```
, root //Uncomment and see!
```

We get a different configuration of the TGC, as depicted in Figure 15-14.

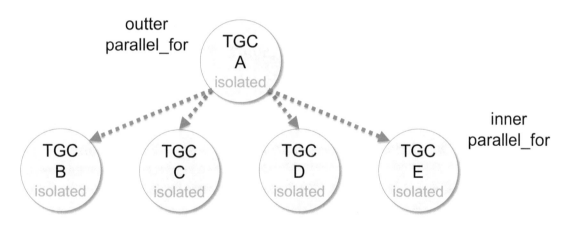

Figure 15-14. *Different configuration of the TGC*

In this new situation, the exception provokes cancellation of the TGC in which it is thrown, TGC A, but there are no children of TGC A to cancel. Now, if we check the values of the array `data` we will see that rows either have all true or all false elements, but not a mix as in the previous case. This is because once an inner loop starts setting a row with true values, it won't be canceled halfway.

In a more general case, if we can say so of our forest of TGC trees of Figure 15-4, what happens if a nested algorithm throws an exception that is not caught at any level? For example, let's suppose that in the tree of TGCs of Figure 15-15 an exception is thrown inside the flow graph (TGC B).

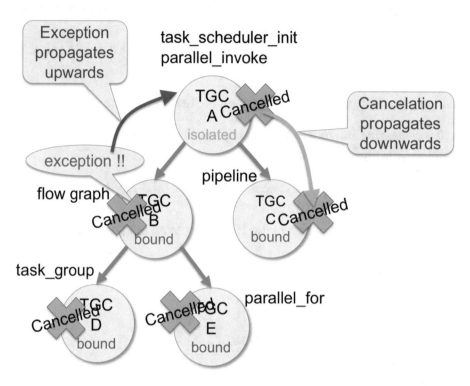

Figure 15-15. *The effect of an exception thrown in a nested TBB algorithm*

Of course, TGC B and descendent TGCs D and E are also canceled. We know that. But the exception propagates upward, and if at that level it is not caught either, it will provoke also the cancellation of the tasks in the TGC A, and because cancellation propagates downward, TGC C dies as well. Great! This is the expected behavior: a single exception, no matter at what level it is thrown, can gracefully do away with the whole parallel algorithm (as it would do with a serial one). We can prevent the chain of cancellations by either catching the exception at the desired level or by configuring the required nested algorithm in an isolated TGC. Isn't it neat?

Summary

In this chapter, we saw that canceling a TBB parallel algorithm and using exception handling to manage run-time error are straightforward. Both features just work right-out-of-the-box as expected if we resort to the default behavior. We also discussed an important feature of TBB, the task group context, TGC. This element is key in the implementation of the cancellation and exception handling in TBB and can be manually leveraged to get a closer control of these two features. We started covering the cancellation operation, explaining how a task can cancel the whole TGC to which it belongs. Then we reviewed how to manually set the TGC to which a task is mapped and the rules that apply when this mapping is not specified by the developer. The default rules result in the expected behavior: if a parallel algorithm is canceled, so are all the nested parallel algorithms. Then we moved on to exception handling. Again, the behavior of TBB exceptions resemble exceptions in sequential code, though the internal implementation in TBB is way more complex since an exception thrown in one task executed by one thread may end up being captured by a different thread. When the compiler supports C++11 features, an exact copy of the exception can be moved between threads, otherwise, a summary of the exception is captured in a `tbb::captured_exception` so that it can be re-thrown in a parallel context. We also described how to configure our own exception classes using the class template `tbb::movable_exception`. Finally, we closed the chapter by elaborating on how composability, cancellation, and exception handling interplay.

For More Information

Here are some additional reading materials we recommend related to this chapter:

- A. Marochko and A. Kukanov, Composable Parallelism Foundations in the Intel Threading Building Blocks Task Scheduler, Advances in Parallel Computing, vol 22, 2012.

- Deb Haldar, Top 15 C++ Exception handling mistakes and how to avoid them. `www.acodersjourney.com/2016/08/top-15-c-exception-handling-mistakes-avoid/`.

CHAPTER 16

Tuning TBB Algorithms: Granularity, Locality, Parallelism, and Determinism

In Chapter 2, we described the generic parallel algorithms provided by the TBB library and gave a few examples to show how they can be used. While doing so, we noted that the default behavior of the algorithms was often good enough but claimed that there were ways to tune performance if needed. In this chapter, we back up that claim by revisiting some TBB algorithms and talk about important features that can be used to change their default behaviors.

There are three concerns that will dominate our discussions. The first is granularity – the amount of work that a task does. The TBB library is efficient at scheduling tasks, but we need to think about the size of the tasks that our algorithms will create since task size can have a significant impact on performance, especially if the tasks are extremely small or extremely large. The second issue is data locality. As discussed in detail in the Preface, how an application uses caches and memory can make or break an application's performance. And the final issue is available parallelism. Our goal when using TBB is to introduce parallelism of course, but we cannot do it blindly without considering granularity and locality. Tuning an application's performance is often an exercise in balancing the trade-offs between these three concerns.

© Intel Corporation 2019
M. Voss, R. Asenjo, J. Reinders, *Pro TBB*, https://doi.org/10.1007/978-1-4842-4398-5_16

One of the key differences between the TBB algorithms and other interfaces like Parallel STL is that the TBB algorithms provide hooks and features that let us influence their behavior around these three concerns. The TBB algorithms are not just black boxes over which we have no control!

In this chapter, we will first discuss task granularity and arrive at a rule of thumb about how big is big enough when it comes to task size. We will then focus on the simple loop algorithms and how to use Ranges and Partitioners to control task granularity and data locality. We also have a brief discussion about determinism and its impact on flexibility when tuning for performance. We conclude the chapter by turning our attention to the TBB pipeline algorithm and discuss how its features affect granularity, data locality, and maximum parallelism.

Task Granularity: How Big Is Big Enough?

To let the TBB library have maximum flexibility in balancing the load across threads, we want to divide the work done by an algorithm into as many pieces as possible. At the same time, to minimize the overheads of work stealing and task scheduling, we want to create tasks that are as large as possible. Since these forces oppose each other, the best performance for an algorithm is found somewhere in the middle.

To complicate matters, the exact best task size varies by platform and application, and therefore there is no exact guideline that applies universally. Still, it is useful to have a ballpark number that we can use as a crude guideline. With these caveats in mind, we therefore offer the following rule of thumb:

RULE OF THUMB   TBB tasks should be on average greater than 1 microsecond to effectively hide the overheads of work stealing. This translates to several thousand CPU cycles – if you prefer using cycles, we suggest a 10,000 cycle rule of thumb.

It's important to keep in mind that not every task needs to be greater than 1 microsecond – in fact, that's often not possible. In divide and conquer algorithms for example, we might use small tasks to divide up the work and then use larger tasks at the leaves. This is how the TBB `parallel_for` algorithms works. TBB tasks are used to both split the range and to apply the body to the final subranges. The split tasks typically do very little work, while the loop body tasks are much larger. In this case, we can't make all of the tasks larger than 1 microsecond, but we can aim to make the average of the task sizes larger than 1 microsecond.

When we use algorithms like `parallel_invoke` or use TBB tasks directly, we are in complete control of the size of our tasks. For example, in Chapter 2, we implemented a parallel version of quicksort using a `parallel_invoke` and directed the recursive parallel implementation to a serial implementation once the array size (and therefore task execution time) fell below a cutoff threshold:

```
if (end - begin < cutoff) {
  serialQuicksort(begin, end);
}
```

When we use simple loop algorithms, like `parallel_for`, `parallel_reduce`, and `parallel_scan`, their range and partitioner arguments provide us with the control we need. We talk about these in more detail in the next section.

Choosing Ranges and Partitioners for Loops

As introduced in Chapter 2, a Range represents a recursively divisible set of values – typically a loop's iteration space. We use Ranges with the simple loop algorithms: `parallel_for`, `parallel_reduce`, `parallel_deterministic_reduce`, and `parallel_scan`. A TBB algorithm partitions its range and applies the algorithm's body object(s) to these subranges using TBB tasks. Combined with Partitioners, Ranges provide a simple, but powerful way to represent iterations spaces and control how they should be partitioned into tasks and assigned to worker threads. This partitioning can be used to tune task granularity and data locality.

To be a Range, a class must model the Range Concept shown in Figure 16-1. A Range can be copied, can be split using a *splitting constructor*, and may optionally provide a *proportional splitting constructor*. It also must provide methods to check if it is empty or divisible and provide a boolean constant that is true if it defines the proportional splitting constructor.

Pseudo-Signature	Semantics
R::R(const R&)	Copy constructor.
R::~R()	Destructor.
bool R::empty() const	True if range is empty.
bool R::is_divisible() const	True if range can be partitioned into two subranges.
R::R(R& r, split)	Basic splitting constructor. Splits r into two subranges.
R::R(R& r, proportional_split proportion)	**Optional.** Proportional splitting constructor. Splits r into two subranges in accordance with proportion.
static const bool R::is_splittable_in_proportion	**Optional.** If true, the proportional splitting constructor is defined for the range and may be used by parallel algorithms.

Figure 16-1. *The Range concept*

While we can define our own Range types, the TBB library provides the blocked ranges shown in Figure 16-2, which will cover most situations. For example, we can represent the iteration space of the following nested loop with a `blocked_range2d<int, int> r(i_begin, i_end, j_begin, j_end )`:

```
for (int i = i_begin; i < i_end, ++i )
  for (int j = j_begin; j < j_end; ++j )
    /* loop body */
```

Range Type	Constructor Arguments	Description
blocked_range	Value begin, Value end, [size_t grainsize]	Models a one-dimensional range.
blocked_range2d	RowValue row_begin, RowValue row_end, [size_type row_grainsize], ColValue col_begin, ColValue col_end, [size_type col_grainsize]	Models a two-dimensional range. After repeated splitting, the subranges approach the aspect ratio of the respective row and column grain sizes.
blocked_range3d	PageValue page_begin, PageValue page_end, [size_type page_grainsize], RowValue row_begin, RowValue row_end, [size_type row_grainsize], ColValue col_begin, ColValue col_end, [size_type col_grainsize]	Models a three-dimensional range. After repeated splitting, the subranges approach the aspect ratio of the respective page, row and column grain sizes.
blocked_rangeNd	const blocked_range<Value>& dim_0, ..., const blocked_range<Value>& dim_{N-1}	A preview feature that models an N-dimensional range. Requires C++11 support. After repeated splitting, the subranges approach the aspect ratio of the N blocked_range grain sizes.

Figure 16-2. *The blocked ranges provided by the TBB library*

For interested readers, we describe how to define a custom range type in the "Deep in the Weeds" section at the end of this chapter.

An Overview of Partitioners

Along with Ranges, TBB algorithms support Partitioners that specify how an algorithm should partition its Range. The different Partitioner types are shown in Figure 16-3.

Partitioner	Description	When Used with blocked_range(i,j,g)
simple_partitioner	Chunksize bounded by grain size.	$g/2 \leq chunksize \leq g$
auto_partitioner (default)	Automatic chunk size.	$g/2 \leq chunksize$
affinity_partitioner	Automatic chunk size, cache affinity and initial uniform distribution of iterations.	
static_partitioner	Deterministic chunk size, cache affinity and uniform distribution of iterations without load balancing. A uniform distribution is created unless the grainsize prevents P chunks from being created.	$\max(g/3,\ N/P) \leq chunksize$ *where:* *N is problem size* *P is number of resources*

Figure 16-3. *The partitioners provided by the TBB library*

A simple_partitioner is used to recursively divide a Range until its is_divisible method returns false. For the blocked range types, this means the range will be divided until its size is less than or equal to its grainsize. If we have highly tuned our grainsize (and we will talk about this in the next section), we want to use a simple_partitioner since it ensures that the final subranges respect the provided grainsizes.

An auto_partitioner uses a dynamic algorithm to sufficiently split a range to balance load, but it does not necessarily divide a range as finely as is_divisible allows. When used with the blocked range classes, the grainsize still provides a lower bound on the size of the final chunks but is much less important since the auto_partitioner can decide to use larger grainsizes. It is therefore commonly acceptable to use a grainsize of 1 and just let the auto_partitioner determine the best grainsize. In TBB 2019, the default Partitioner type used for parallel_for, parallel_reduce, and parallel_scan is an auto_partitioner with a grainsize of 1.

A static_partitioner distributes the range over the worker threads as uniformly as possible without the possibility for further load balancing. The work distribution and mapping to threads is deterministic and only depends on the number of iterations, the grainsize, and the number of threads. The static_partitioner has the lowest overhead of all partitioners, since it makes no dynamic decisions. Using a static_partitioner can also result in improved cache behavior since the scheduling pattern will be repeated across executions of the same loop. A static_partitioner however severely restricts load balancing so it needs to be used judiciously. In section "Using a static_ partitioner," we will highlight the strengths and weaknesses of static_partitioner.

The affinity_partitioner combines the best from auto_partitioner and static_partitioner and improves cache affinity if the same partitioner object is reused when a loop is re-executed over the same data set. The affinity_partitioner, like static_partitioner, initially creates a uniform distribution but allows for additional load balancing. It also keeps a history of which thread executes which chunk of the range and tries to recreate this execution pattern on subsequent executions. If a data set fits completely within the processors' caches, repeating the scheduling pattern can result in significant performance improvements.

Choosing a Grainsize (or Not) to Manage Task Granularity

At the beginning of this chapter, we talked about how important task granularity can be. When we use a blocked range type, we should always then highly tune our grainsize, right? Not necessarily. Selecting the right grainsize when using a blocked range can be extremely important – or almost irrelevant – it all depends on the Partitioner being used.

If we use a simple_partitioner, the grainsize is the sole determinant of the size of the ranges that will be passed to the body. When a simple_partitioner is used, the range is recursively subdivided until is_divisible returns false. In contrast, all of the other Partitioners have their own internal algorithms for deciding when to stop dividing ranges. Choosing a grainsize of 1 is typically sufficient for these other partitioners that use is_divisible as only a lower bound.

To demonstrate the impact of grainsize on the different Partitioners, we can use a simple parallel_for microbenchmark and vary the number of iterations in the loop (N), the grainsize, the execution time per loop iteration, and the Partitioner.

```
template< typename P >
static inline double executePfor(int num_trials, int N,
                                 int gs, P &p, double tpi) {
  tbb::tick_count t0;
  for (int t = -1; t < num_trials; ++t) {
    if (!t) t0 = tbb::tick_count::now();
    tbb::parallel_for (
      tbb::blocked_range<int>{0, N, gs},
      [tpi](const tbb::blocked_range<int> &r) {
        int e = r.end();
        for (int i = r.begin(); i < e; ++i) {
          spinWaitForAtLeast(tpi);
        }
      },
      p
    );
  }
  tbb::tick_count t1 = tbb::tick_count::now();
  return (t1 - t0).seconds()/num_trials;
}
```

Figure 16-4. *A function used to measure the time to execute a* `parallel_for` *with N iterations using a partitioner (p), a grainsize (gs), and time-per-iteration (tpi)*

All performance results presented in this chapter were collected on a single socket server with an Intel Xeon Processor E3-1230 with four cores supporting two hardware threads per core; the processor has a base frequency of 3.4 GHz, a shared 8 MB L3 cache, and per-core 256 KB L2 caches. The system was running SUSE Linux Enterprise Server 12. All samples were compiled using the Intel C++ Compiler 19.0 with Threading Building Blocks 2019, using the compiler flags "–std=c++11 –O2 –tbb".

Figure 16-5 shows the results of the program in Figure 16-4 when executed for $N=2^{18}$ using each of the Partitioner types available in TBB and with a range of grainsizes. We can see that for a very small `time_per_iteration` of 10 ns, the `simple_partitioner` approaches the other `partitioner`'s maximum performance when the grainsize is >= 128. As the time-per-iteration increases, the `simple_partitioner` approaches the maximum performance more quickly, since fewer iterations are needed to overcome scheduling overheads.

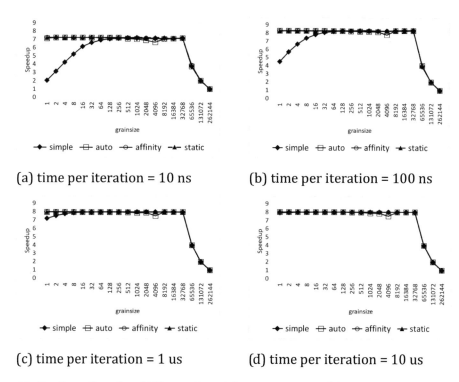

(a) time per iteration = 10 ns

(b) time per iteration = 100 ns

(c) time per iteration = 1 us

(d) time per iteration = 10 us

Figure 16-5. *Speedup for different Partitioner types and increasing grainsizes. The total number of iterations in the loop being tested is $2^{18} == 262144$*

For all of the Partitioner types shown in Figure 16-5 except `simple_partitioner`, we see maximum performance from a grainsize of 1 until 4096. Our platform has 8 logical cores and therefore we need a grainsize less than or equal to $2^{18}/8 == 32,768$ to provide at least one chunk to each thread; consequently, all of the Partitioners begin to tail off after a grainsize of 32768. We might also note that at a grainsize of 4096, the `auto_partitioner` and `affinity_partitioner` show drops in performance in all of the figures. This is because picking large grainsizes limits the choices available to these algorithms, interfering with their ability to complete their automated partitioning.

This small experiment confirms that the grainsize is critically important for `simple_partitioner`. We can use a `simple_partitioner` to manually select the size of our tasks, but when we do so, we need to be more accurate in our choices.

A second take-away is that efficient execution, with a speedup close to the linear upper bound, is seen when the body size approaches 1 us (10ns x 128 = 1.28 us). This result reinforces the rule of thumb we presented earlier in the chapter! This should not be surprising since experience and experiments like these are the reason for our rule of thumb in the first place.

Ranges, Partitioners, and Data Cache Performance

Ranges and Partitioners can improve data cache performance by enabling cache-oblivious algorithms or by enabling cache affinity. Cache-oblivious algorithms are useful when a data set is too large to fit into the data caches, but reuse of data within the algorithm can be exploited if it is solved using a divide and conquer approach. In contrast, cache affinity is useful when the data set completely fits into the caches. Cache affinity is used to repeatedly schedule the same parts of a range onto the same processors – so that the data that fits in the cache can be accessed again from the same cache.

Cache-Oblivious Algorithms

A cache-oblivious algorithm is an algorithm that achieves good (or even optimal) use of data caches without depending upon knowledge of the hardware's cache parameters. The concept is similar to loop tiling or loop blocking but does not require an accurate tile or block size. Cache-oblivious algorithms often recursively divide problems into smaller and smaller subproblems. At some point, these small subproblems begin to fit into a machine's caches. The recursive subdivision might continue all the way down to the smallest possible size or there may be a cutoff point for efficiency – but this cutoff point is **not** related to the cache size and typically creates patterns that access data sized well below any reasonable cache size.

Because *Cache-oblivious algorithms* are not at all disinterested in cache performance, we've heard many other suggested names, such as *cache agnostic* since these algorithms optimize for whatever cache they encounter; and *cache paranoid*, since they assume there can be infinite levels of caches. But cache oblivious is the name used in the literature and it has stuck.

Here, we will use matrix transposition as an example of an algorithm that can benefit from a cache-oblivious implementation. A non-cache-oblivious serial implementation of matrix transposition is shown in Figure 16-6.

```
void fig_16_6(int N, double *a, double *b) {
  for (int i = 0; i < N; ++i) {
    for (int j = 0; j < N; ++j) {
      b[j*N+i] = a[i*N+j];
    }
  }
}
```

Figure 16-6. *A serial implementation of a matrix transposition*

For simplicity, let's assume that four elements fit in a cache line in our machine. Figure 16-7 shows the cache lines that will be accessed during the transposition of the first two rows of the N×N matrix a. If the cache is large enough, it can retain all of the cache lines accessed in b during that transposition of the first row of a and not need to reload these during that transposition of the second row of a. But if it is not large enough, these cache lines will need to be reloaded – resulting in a cache miss at each access to the matrix b. In the figure, we show a 16×16 array but imagine if it was very large.

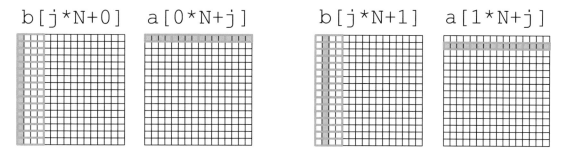

Figure 16-7. *The cache lines accessed when transposing the first two rows of the matrix a. For simplicity, we show four items in each cache line.*

A cache-oblivious implementation of this algorithm reduces the amount of data accessed between reuses of the same cache line or data item. As shown in Figure 16-8, if we focus on transposing only a small block of matrix a before moving on to other blocks of matrix a, we can reduce the number of cache lines that hold elements of b that need to be retained in the cache to get performance gains due to cache line reuse.

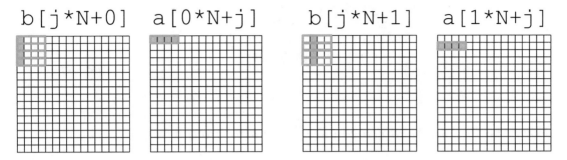

Figure 16-8. *Transposing a block at a time reduces the number of cache lines that need to be retained to benefit from reuse*

A serial implementation of a cache-oblivious implementation of matrix transposition is shown in Figure 16-9. It recursively subdivides the problem along the i and j dimensions and uses a serial for-loop when the range drops below a threshold.

```
void obliviousTranspose(int N, int ib, int ie, int jb, int je,
                        double *a, double *b, int gs) {
  int ilen = ie-ib;
  int jlen = je-jb;
  if (ilen > gs ||  jlen > gs) {
    if ( ilen > jlen ) {
      int imid = (ib+ie)/2;
      obliviousTranspose(N, ib, imid, jb, je, a, b, gs);
      obliviousTranspose(N, imid, ie, jb, je, a, b, gs);
    } else {
      int jmid = (jb+je)/2;
      obliviousTranspose(N, ib, ie, jb, jmid, a, b, gs);
      obliviousTranspose(N, ib, ie, jmid, je, a, b, gs);
    }
  } else {
    for (int i = ib; i < ie; ++i) {
      for (int j = jb; j < je; ++j) {
        b[j*N+i] = a[i*N+j];
      }
    }
  }
}
```

Figure 16-9. *A serial cache-oblivious implementation of a matrix transposition*

Because the implementation alternates between dividing in the i and j direction, the matrix a is transposed using the traversal pattern shown in Figure 16-10, first completing block 1, then 2, then 3, and so on. If gs is 4 and our cache line size is 4, we get the reuse within each block that we showed in Figure 16-8. But if our cache line is 8 items instead of 4 (which is much more likely for real systems), we would get reuse not only within the smallest blocks but also across blocks. For example, if the data cache can retain all of the cache lines loaded during blocks 1 and 2, these will be reused when transposing blocks 3 and 4.

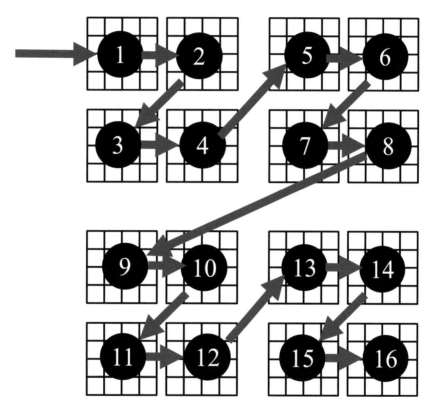

Figure 16-10. *A traversal pattern that computes the transpose for sub-blocks of a before moving on to other blocks*

This is the true power of cache-oblivious algorithms – we don't need to exactly know the sizes of the levels of the memory hierarchy. As the subproblems get smaller, they fit in progressively smaller parts of the memory hierarchy, improving reuse at each level.

The TBB loop algorithms and the TBB scheduler are designed to specifically support cache-oblivious algorithms. We can therefore quickly implement a cache-oblivious parallel implementation of matrix transposition using a parallel_for, a blocked_range2d, and a simple_partitioner as shown in Figure 16-11. We use a blocked_range2d because we want the iteration space subdivided into two-dimensional blocks.

And we use a `simple_partitioner` because we only get the benefits from reuse if the blocks are subdivided down to sizes smaller than the cache size; the other Partitioner types optimize load balancing and so may choose larger range sizes if those are sufficient to balance load.

```
double fig_16_11(int N, double *a, double *b, int gs) {
  tbb::tick_count t0 = tbb::tick_count::now();
  tbb::parallel_for(
    tbb::blocked_range2d<int,int>{0, N, gs, 0, N, gs},
    [N, a, b](const tbb::blocked_range2d<int,int> &r) {
      int ie = r.rows().end();
      int je = r.cols().end();
      for (int i = r.rows().begin(); i < ie; ++i) {
        for (int j = r.cols().begin(); j < je; ++j) {
          b[j*N+i] = a[i*N+j];
        }
      }
    }, simple_partitioner()
  );
  tbb::tick_count t1 = tbb::tick_count::now();
  return (t1-t0).seconds();
}
```

Figure 16-11. *A cache-oblivious parallel implementation of matrix transposition that uses a* `simple_partitioner`, *a* `blocked_range2d`, *and a grainsize (gs)*

Figure 16-12 shows that the way the TBB `parallel_for` recursively subdivides ranges creates the same blocks that we want for our cache-oblivious implementation. The depth-first work and breadth-first stealing behavior of the TBB scheduler also means that the blocks will execute in an order similar to the one shown in Figure 16-10.

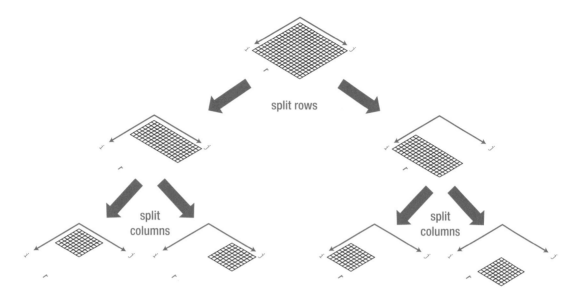

Figure 16-12. *The recursive subdivision of the blocked2d_range provides a division that matches the blocks we want for our cache-oblivious parallel implementation*

Figure 16-13 shows the performance of the serial cache-oblivious implementation in Figure 16-9, the performance of an implementation using a 1D `blocked_range`, and the performance of a `blocked_range2d` implementation similar to the one in Figure 16-11. We implemented our parallel versions so that we could change the grainsize and partitioner easily. The code for all of the versions is available in `fig_16_11.cpp`.

In Figure 16-13, we show the speedup of our implementations on an 8192×8192 matrix compared to the simple serial implementation from Figure 16-6.

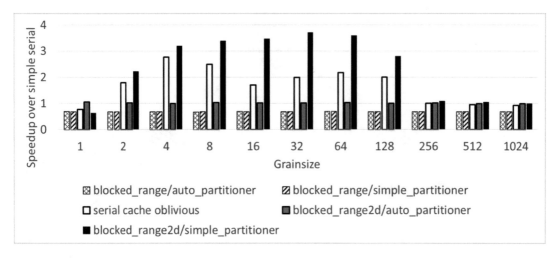

Figure 16-13. *The speedup on our test machine for N=8192 with various grainsizes and partitioners*

Matrix transposition is limited by the speed at which we can read and write data – there is no compute whatsoever. We can see from Figure 16-13 that our 1D `blocked_range` parallel implementations perform worse than our simple serial implementation, regardless of the grainsize we use. The serial implementation is already limited by the memory bandwidth – adding additional threads simply adds more pressure on the already-stressed memory subsystem and does nothing to help matters.

Our serial cache-oblivious algorithm reorders memory accesses, reducing the number of cache misses. It significantly outperforms the simple version. When we use a `blocked_range2d` in our parallel implementation, we similarly get 2D subdivisions. But as we see in Figure 16-13, only when we use a `simple_partitioner` does it fully behave like a cache-oblivious algorithm. In fact, our cache-oblivious parallel algorithm with a `blocked_range2d` and a `simple_partitioner` reduces pressure on the memory hierarchy to such a degree that now using multiple threads can improve performance over the serial cache-oblivious implementation!

Not all problems have cache-oblivious solutions, but many common problems do. It is worth the time to research problems to see if a cache-oblivious solution is possible and worthwhile. If so, the blocked range types and the `simple_partitioner` will make it very easy to implement one with TBB algorithms.

Cache Affinity

Cache-oblivious algorithms improve cache performance by breaking problems, which have data locality but do not fit into the cache, down into smaller problems that do fit into the cache. In contrast, cache affinity addresses the repeated execution of ranges across data that already fit in the cache. Since the data fits in the cache, if the same subranges are assigned to the same processors on subsequent executions, the cached data can be accessed more quickly. We can use either an affinity_partitioner or a static_partitioner to enable cache affinity for the TBB loop algorithms. Figure 16-14 shows a simple microbenchmark that adds a value to each element in a 1D array. The function receives a reference to the Partitioner – we need to receive the Partitioner as a reference to record history in the affinity_partitioner object.

```
template <typename Partitioner>
double fig_16_14(double v, int N, double *a, Partitioner &p) {
  tbb::parallel_for( tbb::blocked_range<int>(0, N, 1),
    [v, a](const tbb::blocked_range<int> &r) {
      int ie = r.end();
      for (int i = r.begin(); i < ie; ++i) {
        a[i] += v;
      }
    }, p
  );
}
```

Figure 16-14. *A function that uses a TBB* parallel_for *to add a value to all of the elements of a 1D array*

To see the impact of cache affinity we can execute this function repeatedly, sending in the same value for N and the same array a. When using an auto_partitioner, the scheduling of the subranges to threads will vary from invocation to invocation. Even if array a completely fits into the processors' caches, the same region of a may not fall on the same processor in subsequent executions:

```
for (int i = 0; i < M; ++i) {
  fig_16_14(v[i], N, a, tbb::auto_partitioner{});
}
```

If we use an affinity_partitioner however, the TBB library will record the task scheduling and use affinity hints to recreate it on each execution (see Chapter 13 for more information on affinity hints). Because the history is recorded in the Partitioner, we must pass the same Partitioner object on subsequent executions, and cannot simply create a temporary object like we did with auto_partitioner:

```
tbb::affinity_partitioner aff_p;
for (int i = 0; i < M; ++i) {
  fig_16_14(v[i], N, a, aff_p);
}
```

Finally, we can also use a static_partitioner to create cache affinity. Because the scheduling is deterministic when we use a static_partitioner, we do not need to pass the same partitioner object for each execution:

```
for (int i = 0; i < M; ++i) {
  fig_16_14(v[i], N, a, tbb::static_partitioner{});
}
```

We executed this microbenchmark on our test machine using N=100,000 and M=10,000. Our array of doubles will be $100,000 \times 8 = 800$ K in size. Our test machine has four 256 K L2 data caches, one per core. When using an affinity_partitioner, the test completed 1.4 times faster than when using the auto_partitioner. When using a static_partitioner, the test completed 2.4 times faster than when using the auto_ partitioner! Because the data was able to fit into the aggregate L2 cache size $(4 \times 256$ K = 1 MB), replaying the same scheduling had a significant impact on the execution time. In the next section, we'll discuss why the static_partitioner outperformed the auto_partitioner in this case and why we shouldn't be too surprised, or excited about that. If we increase N to 1,000,000 elements, we no longer see a large difference in the execution times since array a is now too large to fit in the caches of our test system – in this case, re-thinking the algorithm to implement tiling/blocking to exploit cache locality is necessary.

Using a static_partitioner

The static_partitioner is the lowest overhead partitioner, and it quickly provides a uniform distribution of a blocked range across the threads in an arena. Since the partitioning is deterministic, it also can improve cache behavior when a loop or a series of loops are executed repeatedly on the same range. In the previous section, we saw that it out-performed affinity_partitioner significantly for our microbenchmark. However, because it creates just enough chunks to provide one to each thread in the arena, there is no opportunity for work stealing to balance the load dynamically. In effect, the `static_partitioner` disables the TBB library's work-stealing scheduling approach.

There is a good reason though for TBB to include `static_partitioner`. As the number of cores increase, random work stealing becomes costlier; especially when transitioning from a serial part of an application to a parallel part. When the master thread first spawns new work into the arena, all of the worker threads wake up and as a *thundering herd* try to find work to do. To make matters worse, they don't know where to look and start randomly peeking into not only the master thread's deque, but each other's local deques too. Some worker thread will eventually find the work in the master and subdivide it, and another worker will eventually find this subdivided piece, subdivide it, and so on. And after a while, things will settle down and all of the workers will find something to do and will happily work from their own local deques.

But, if we already know that the workload is well balanced, that the system is not oversubscribed, and all our cores are equally powerful – do we really need all of this work-stealing overhead to just get a uniform distribution across the workers? Not if we use a `static_partitioner`! It is designed for just this case. It pushes tasks that uniformly distribute the range to the worker threads so that they don't have to steal tasks at all. When it applies, `static_partitioner` is the most efficient way to partition a loop.

But don't get too excited about `static_partitioner`! If the workload is not uniform or any of the cores are oversubscribed with additional threads, then using a `static_partitioner` can wreck performance. For example, Figure 16-15 shows the same microbenchmark configuration we used in Figure 16-5(c) to examine the impact of grainsize on performance. But Figure 16-15 shows what happens if we add a single extra thread running on one of the cores. For all but the `static_partitioner`, there is a small impact due to the extra thread. The `static_partitioner` however assumes that all of the cores are equally capable and uniformly distributes the work among them. As a result, the overloaded core becomes a bottleneck and the speedup takes a huge performance hit.

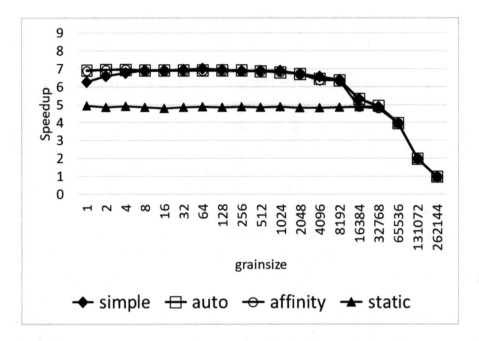

Figure 16-15. *Speedup for different Partitioner types and increasing grainsizes when an additional thread executes a spin loop in the background. The time-per-iteration is set to 1 us.*

Figure 16-16 shows a loop where the work increases with each iteration. If a static_ partitioner is used, the thread that gets the lowest set of iterations will have much less work to do than the unlucky thread that gets the highest set of iterations.

```
template <typename Partitioner>
double fig_16_16(int N, Partitioner &p) {
  tbb::parallel_for( tbb::blocked_range<int>(0, N, 1),
    [](const tbb::blocked_range<int> &r) {
      int ie = r.end();
      for (int i = r.begin(); i < ie; ++i) {
        spinForMicroseconds(i);
      }
    }, p
  );
}
```

Figure 16-16. *A loop where the work increases in each iteration*

If we run the loop in Figure 16-16 ten times using each partitioner type with N=1000, we see the following results:

```
auto_partitioner = 0.629974 seconds
affinity_partitioner = 0.630518 seconds
static_partitioner = 1.18314 seconds
```

The auto_partitioner and affinity_partitioner are able to rebalance the load across the threads, while the static_partitioner is stuck with its initial uniform, but unfair distribution.

The static_partitioner is therefore almost exclusively useful in High Performance Computing (HPC) applications. These applications run on systems with many cores and often in batch mode, where a single application is run at a time. If the work load does not need *any* dynamic load balancing, then static_partitioner will almost always outperform the other partitioners. Unfortunately, well-balanced workloads and single-user, batch-mode systems are the exception and not the rule.

Restricting the Scheduler for Determinism

In Chapter 2, we discussed **Associativity and floating-point types**. We noted that any implementation of floating-point numbers is an approximation, and so parallelism can lead to different results when we depend on properties like associativity or commutativity – those results aren't necessarily wrong; they are just different. Still, in the case of reduction, TBB provides a parallel_deterministic_reduce algorithm if we want to ensure that we get the same results for each execution on the same input data when executed on the same machine.

As we might guess, parallel_deterministic_reduce only accepts simple_partitioner or static_partitioner, since the number of subranges is deterministic for both of these partitioner types. The parallel_deterministic_reduce also always executes the same set of split and join operations on a given machine no matter how many threads dynamically participate in execution and how tasks are mapped to threads – the parallel_reduce algorithm may not. The result is that parallel_deterministic_reduce will always return the same result when run on the same machine – but sacrifices some flexibility to do so.

Figure 16-17 shows the speedup for the pi calculation example from Chapter 2 when implemented using `parallel_reduce` (r-auto, r-simple, and r-static) and `parallel_deterministic_reduce` (d-simple and d-static). The maximum speedup is similar for both; however, the `auto_partitioner` performs very well for `parallel_reduce`, and that is simply not an option with `parallel_deterministic_reduce`. If needed, we can implement a deterministic version of our benchmark but then must deal with the complications of choosing a good grainsize.

While `parallel_deterministic_reduce` will have some additional overhead because it must perform all of the splits and joins, this overhead is typically small. The bigger limitation is that we cannot use any of the partitioners that automatically find a chunk size for us.

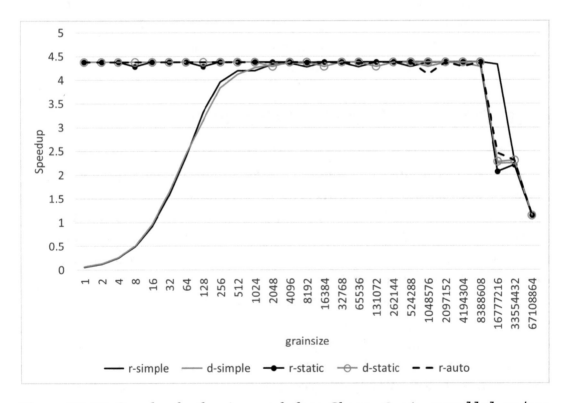

Figure 16-17. *Speedup for the pi example from Chapter 2 using `parallel_reduce` with an `auto_partitioner` (r-auto), a `simple_partitioner` (r-simple), and a `static_partitioner` (r-static); and `parallel_deterministic_reduce` with a `simple_partitioner` (d-simple) and a `static_partitioner` (d-static). We show results for grainsizes ranging from 1 to N.*

Tuning TBB Pipelines: Number of Filters, Modes, and Tokens

Just as with the loop algorithms, the performance of TBB pipelines is impacted by granularity, locality, and available parallelism. Unlike the loop algorithms, TBB pipelines do not support Ranges and Partitioners. Instead, the controls used to tune pipelines include the number of filters, the filter execution modes, and the number of tokens passed to the pipeline when it is run.

TBB pipeline filters are spawned as tasks and scheduled by the TBB library, and therefore, just as with the subranges created by the loop algorithms, we want the filter bodies to execute long enough to mitigate overheads but we also want ample parallelism. We balance these concerns by how we break our work into filters. The filters should also be well balanced in execution time since the slowest serial stage will be a bottleneck.

As described in Chapter 2, pipeline filters are also created with an execution mode: `serial_in_order`, `serial_out_of_order`, or `parallel`. When using `serial_in_order` mode, a filter can process at most one item at a time, and it must process them in the same order that the first filter generated them in. A `serial_out_of_order` filter is allowed to execute the items in any order. A `parallel` filter is allowed to execute on different items in parallel. We will look at how these different modes limit performance later in this section.

When run, we need to provide a `max_number_of_live_tokens` argument to a TBB pipeline, which constrains the number of items that are allowed to flow through the pipeline at any given time.

Figure 16-18 shows the structure of the microbenchmarks we will use to explore these different controls. In the figure, both pipelines are shown with eight filters – but we will vary this number in our experiments. The top pipeline has filters that use the same execution `mode,` and all have the same `spin_time` – so this represents a very well-balanced pipeline. The bottom pipeline has one filter than spins for `imbalance * spin_time` – we will vary this imbalance factor to see the impact of imbalance on speedup.

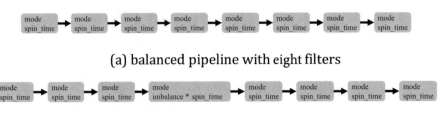

(a) balanced pipeline with eight filters

(b) unbalanced pipeline with eight filters

Figure 16-18. *A balanced pipeline microbenchmark and an imbalanced pipeline microbenchmark*

Understanding a Balanced Pipeline

Let's first consider how well our rule of thumb for task sizes applies to pipelines. Is a filter body of 1 microsecond sufficient to mitigate overheads? Figure 16-19 shows the speedup of our balanced pipeline microbenchmark when fed 8000 items while using only a single token. The results are shown for various filter execution times. Since there is only a single token, only a single item will be allowed to flow through the pipeline at a time. The result is a serialized execution of the pipeline (even when the filter execution mode is set to parallel).

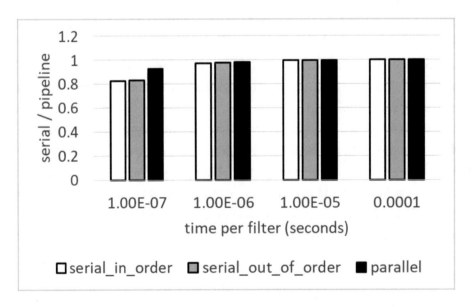

Figure 16-19. *The overhead seen by different filter execution modes when executing a balanced pipeline with eight filters, a single token, and 8000 items on our test machine*

When compared to a true serial execution, where we execute the proper number of spins in a for-loop, we see the impact of managing the work as a TBB pipeline. In Figure 16-19, we see that when the spin_time approaches 1 microsecond, the overhead is fairly low, and we get very close to the execution time of the true serial execution. It seems that our rule of thumb applies to a TBB pipeline too!

Now, let's look at how the number of filters affects performance. In a serial pipeline, the parallelism comes only from overlapping different filters. In a pipeline with parallel filters, parallelism is also obtained by executing the parallel filters simultaneously on different items. Our target platform supports eight threads, so we should expect at most a speedup of 8 for a parallel execution.

Figure 16-20 shows the speedup of our balanced pipeline microbenchmark when setting the number of tokens to 8. For both serial modes, the speedup increases with the number of filters. This is important to remember, since the speedup of a serial pipeline does not scale with the data set size like the TBB loop algorithms do. The balanced pipeline that contains all parallel filters however has a speedup of 8 even with only a single filter. This is because the 8000 input items can be processed in parallel in that single filter – there is no serial filter to become a bottleneck.

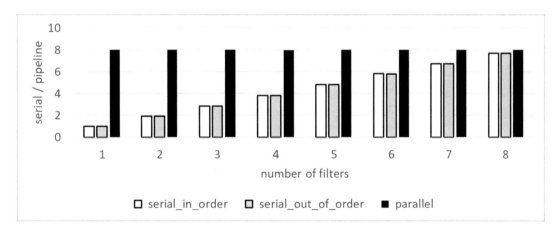

Figure 16-20. *The speedup achieved by the different filter execution modes when executing a balanced pipeline with eight tokens, 8000 items, and an increasing number of filters. The filters spin for 100 microseconds.*

In Figure 16-21, we see the speedup for our balanced pipeline when using eight filters but with varying numbers of tokens. Because our platform has eight threads, if we have fewer than eight tokens, there are not enough items in flight to keep all of the threads busy. Once we have at least eight items in the pipeline, all threads can participate. Increasing the number of tokens past eight has little impact on performance.

Figure 16-21. *The speedup achieved by the different filter execution modes when executing a balanced pipeline with eight filters, 8000 items, and an increasing number of tokens. The filters spin for 100 microseconds.*

Understanding an Imbalanced Pipeline

Now, let's look at the performance of the imbalanced pipeline from Figure 16-18. In this microbenchmark, all of the filters spin for `spin_time` seconds except for one of the filters that spins for `spin_time * imbalance` seconds. The work required to process N items as they pass through our imbalanced pipeline with eight filters is therefore

$$T_1 = N * \left(7 * spin\_time + spin\_time * imbalance \right)$$

In the steady state, a serial pipeline is limited by the slowest serial stage. The critical path length of this same pipeline when the imbalanced filter executes with serial mode is equal to

$$T_\infty = N * \max \left(spin\_time, spin\_time * imbalance \right)$$

Figure 16-22 shows the results of our imbalanced pipeline when executed on our test platform with different imbalance factors. We also include the theoretical maximum speedup, labeled as "work/critical path," calculated as

$$Speedup_{max} = \frac{7 * spin\_time + spin\_time * imbalance}{max(spin\_time, \ spin\_time * imbalance)}$$

Not unexpectedly, Figure 16-22 shows that serial pipelines are limited by their slowest filters – and the measured results are close to what our work/critical path length calculation predicts.

Figure 16-22. *The speedup achieved by the different filter execution modes when executing an imbalanced pipeline with eight filters, 8000 items, and different imbalance factors. Seven of the filters spin for 100 microseconds, and the other spins for* `imbalance * 100` *microseconds.*

In contrast, the parallel pipeline in Figure 16-22 is shown to not be limited by the slowest stage because the TBB scheduler can overlap the execution of the slowest filter with other invocations of that same filter. You may be wondering if increasing the number of tokens beyond eight will help, but in this case, no. Our test system has only eight threads, so we can at most overlap eight instances of the slowest filter. While there may be cases where a temporary load imbalance can be smoothed out by having more tokens than the number of threads, in our microbenchmark where the imbalance is a constant factor, we are in fact limited by the critical path length and the number of threads – and any number of additional tokens will not change that.

However, there are algorithms in which an insufficient number of tokens will hamper the automatic load balancing feature of the work-stealing TBB scheduler. This is the case when the stages are not well balanced and there are serial stages stalling the pipe. A. Navarro et al. demonstrated (see the "For More Information" section at the end of the chapter) that a pipeline algorithm implemented in TBB can yield optimal performance if appropriately configured with the right number tokens. She devised an analytical model based on queueing theory that helps in finding this key parameter. A major take-away of the paper is that when the number of tokens is sufficiently large, the work stealing in TBB emulates a global queue that is able to feed all the threads (in queueing theory, a theoretical centralized system with a single global queue served by all the resources is known to be the ideal case). However, in reality, a global single queue would exhibit contention when it is served by a large number of threads. The fundamental advantage of the TBB implementation is that it resorts to a distributed solution with one queue per thread that behaves as a global queue thanks to the work-stealing scheduler. This is, the decentralized TBB implementation performs like the ideal centralized system but without the bottleneck of the centralized alternative.

Pipelines and Data Locality and Thread Affinity

With the TBB loop algorithms, we used the blocked range types `affinity_partitioner` and `static_partitioner` to tune cache performance. The TBB `parallel_pipeline` function and the `pipeline` class have no similar options. But all is not lost! The execution order built into TBB pipelines is designed to enhance temporal data locality without the need to do anything special.

When a TBB master or worker thread completes the execution of a TBB filter, it executes the next filter in the pipeline unless that filter cannot be executed due to execution mode constraints. For example, if a filter f_0 generates an item i and its output is passed to the next filter f_1, the same thread that ran f_0 will move on to execute f_1 – unless that next filter is a `serial_out_of_order` filter and it is currently processing something else, or if it is a `serial_in_order` filter and item i is not the next item in line. In those cases, the item is buffered in the next filter and the thread will look for other work to do. Otherwise to maximize locality, the thread will follow the data it just generated and process that item by executing the next filter.

Internally, the processing of one item in the filter f_0 is implemented as a task executed by a thread/core. When the filter is done, the task recycles itself (see task recycling in Chapter 10) to execute the next filter f_1. Essentially, the dying task f_0 reincarnates into the new f_1 task, bypassing the scheduler – the same thread/core that executed f_0 will also execute f_1. In terms of data locality and performance, this is way better than what a regular/naive pipeline implementation would do: filter f_0 (served by one or several threads) enqueuing the item in filter f_1's queue (where f_1 is also served by one or several threads). This naive implementation wrecks locality because the item processed by filter f_0 on one core is likely to be processed on a different core by filter f_1. In TBB, if f_0 and f_1 fulfil the conditions mentioned previously, this will never happen. As a result, the TBB pipeline is biased toward finishing items that are already in-flight before injecting more items at the beginning of the pipeline; this behavior not only exploits data locality but uses less memory by reducing the size of the queues that are necessary for serial filters.

Unfortunately, TBB pipeline filters *do not* support affinity hints. There is no way to hint that we want a particular filter to execute on a particular worker thread. But, perhaps surprisingly, there is a hard affinity mechanism, `thread_bound_filter`. Using `thread_bound_filter` however requires using the more error-prone, type-unsafe `tbb::pipeline` interface, which we describe as part of the next section, "Deep in the Weeds."

Deep in the Weeds

This section covers some features that are rarely used by TBB users, but when needed, they can be extremely helpful. You might choose to skip this section and read it on demand if you ever need to create your own Range type or use a `thread_bound_filter` in a TBB pipeline. Or, if you really want to know as much as possible about TBB, read on!

Making Your Own Range Type

As mentioned earlier in this chapter, the blocked range types capture most common scenarios. Over our years of using TBB, we have personally only encountered a handful of situations in which it made sense to implement our own Range type. But if we need to, we can create our own range types by implementing classes that model the Range Concept described in Figure 16-1.

As an example of a useful but atypical range type, we can revisit the quicksort algorithm again, as shown in Figure 16-23.

```
struct SortData {
  int id;
  double value;
  SortData(int i, double v) : id(i), value(v) {}
  bool operator<(const SortData &other) const {
    return value < other.value;
  }
  bool operator==(const SortData &other) const {
    return value == other.value;
  }
};

using QSVector = std::vector<SortData>;

QSVector::iterator doShuffle(QSVector::iterator b,
                             QSVector::iterator e) {
  QSVector::iterator i = b, j = e-1;
  double pivot_value = b->value;
  while (i != j) {
    while (i != j && pivot_value < j->value) --j;
    while (i != j && i->value <= pivot_value) ++i;
    std::iter_swap(i, j);
  }
  std::iter_swap(b, i);
  return i;
}

void serialQuicksort(QSVector::iterator b,
                     QSVector::iterator e) {
  if (b >= e) return;
  QSVector::iterator i = doShuffle(b,e);
  serialQuicksort(b, i);
  serialQuicksort(i+1, e);
}
```

Figure 16-23. *The implementation of a serial quicksort*

Here, we will parallelize quicksort not as a recursive algorithm at all, but instead use a parallel_for and our own custom ShuffleRange. Our pforQuicksort implementation is shown in Figure 16-24.

```
class ShuffleRange {
  QSVector::iterator myBegin;
  QSVector::iterator myEnd;

public:
  static const bool is_splittable_in_proportion = false;
  static const int cutoff = 100;

  // constructors
  ShuffleRange(const QSVector::iterator b,
               const QSVector::iterator e )
    : myBegin(b), myEnd(e) { }

  ShuffleRange(const ShuffleRange &r)
    : myBegin(r.myBegin), myEnd(r.myEnd) { }

  ShuffleRange(ShuffleRange &r, tbb::split)
      : myBegin(r.myBegin), myEnd(r.myEnd) {
      QSVector::iterator b = r.myBegin;
      QSVector::iterator e = r.myEnd;
      QSVector::iterator i = doShuffle(b,e);
      r.myEnd = i;
      myBegin = i+1;
  }

  bool empty() const { return myBegin >= myEnd; }
  bool is_divisible() const { return myEnd-myBegin >= cutoff;
  }
  QSVector::iterator begin() const { return myBegin; }
  QSVector::iterator end() const { return myEnd; }
};

void pforQuicksort(QSVector::iterator b, QSVector::iterator e)
{
  tbb::parallel_for(ShuffleRange(b, e),
    [](const ShuffleRange &r) {
      serialQuicksort(r.begin(), r.end());
    },
    tbb::simple_partitioner()
  );
}
```

Figure 16-24. *Implementing a parallel quicksort using a* parallel_for *and a custom ShuffleRange that implements a Range*

In Figure 16-24, we can see that the `parallel_for` body lambda expression is the base case, where we call a `serialQuicksort`. We also use a `simple_partitioner`, which means that our range will be recursively divided until it returns false from its `is_divisible` method. All of the shuffling magic of quicksort therefore needs to happen in the `ShuffleRange` class as it splits itself into subranges. The class definition of `ShuffleRange` is also shown in Figure 16-24.

The `ShuffleRange` models the Range concept, defining a copy constructor, a splitting constructor, an `empty` method, an `is_divisible` method, and an `is_splittable_in_proportion` member variable that is set to `false`. This class also holds `begin` and `end` iterators that delineate the elements of the array and a `cutoff` value.

Let's start with `empty`. The range is empty if its `begin` iterator is at or past its `end` iterator.

We use our cutoff value to determine if the range should be further divided. Remember, we are using a `simple_partitioner`, so the `parallel_for` will keep dividing the ranges until `is_divisible` returns false. So, the `ShuffleRange is_divisible` implementation is just a check against this cutoff value.

Ok, now we can look at the heart of our implementation, the `ShuffleRange` splitting constructor shown in Figure 16-24. It receives a reference to the original `ShuffleRange` r that needs to be split and a `tbb::split` object that is used to distinguish this constructor from the copy constructor. The body of the constructor is the basic pivot and shuffle algorithm. It updates the original range r to be the left partition and the newly constructed `ShuffleRange` to be the right partition.

Executing our `pforQuicksort` on our test platform yields performance results that are very similar to the `parallel_invoke` implementation from Chapter 2. But this example shows just how flexible the Range Concept is. We may think of the recursive division of the range as negligible in a `parallel_for`, but in our `pforQuicksort` implementation it is not. We rely on the splitting of the `ShuffleRange` to do a substantial portion of the work.

The Pipeline Class and Thread-Bound Filters

As we noted in our earlier discussions in this chapter, affinity hints are not supported by `tbb::parallel_pipeline`. We cannot express that we prefer that a particular filter execute on a specific thread. However, there is support for thread-bound filters if we use the older, thread-unsafe `tbb::pipeline` class! These thread-bound filters are not processed at all by TBB worker threads; instead, we need to explicitly process items in these filters by calling their `process_item` or `try_process_item` functions directly.

Typically, a `thread_bound_filter` is not used to improve data locality, but instead it is used when a filter must be executed on a particular thread – perhaps because only that thread has the rights to access the resources required to complete the action implemented by the filter. Situations like this can arise in real applications when, for example, a communication or offload library requires that all communication happen from a particular thread.

Let's consider a contrived example that mimics this situation, where only the main thread has access to an opened file. To use a `thread_bound_filter,` we need to use the type unsafe class interfaces of `tbb::pipeline`. We cannot create a `thread_bound_filter` when using the `tbb::parallel_pipeline` function. We will soon see why it would never make sense to use a `thread_bound_filter` with the `parallel_pipeline` interface anyway.

In our example, we create three filters. Most of our filters will inherit from `tbb::filter`, overriding the `operator()` function:

```
namespace tbb {
    class filter {
    public:
        enum mode {
            parallel = implementation-defined,
            serial_in_order = implementation-defined,
            serial_out_of_order = implementation-defined
        };
        bool is_serial() const;
        bool is_ordered() const;
        virtual void* operator()( void* item ) = 0;
        virtual void finalize( void* item ) {}
        virtual ~filter();
    protected:
        explicit filter( mode );
    };
}
```

Our `SourceFilter`, shown in Figure 16-25, is a `serial_in_order` filter that inherits from `tbb::filter` and generates a series of numbers. The type unsafe interfaces implemented by `tbb::pipeline` require that we return the output of each filter as a `void *`. `NULL` is used to indicate the end of the input stream. We can easily see why the newer `parallel_pipeline` interface is preferred when it applies.

The second filter type we create, MultiplyFilter, multiplies the incoming value by 2 and returns it. It too will be a serial_in_order filter and inherit from tbb::filter.

Finally, BadWriteFilter implements a filter that will write the output to a file. This class also inherits from tbb::filter as shown in Figure 16-25.

The function fig_16_25 puts all of these classes together – while purposely introducing an error. It creates a three-stage pipeline using our filter classes and the tbb::pipeline interface. It creates a pipeline object and then adds each of the filters, one after the other. To run the pipeline, it calls void pipeline::run(size_t max_ number_of_live_tokens) passing in eight tokens.

As we should expect when we run this example, the BadWriteFilter wf sometimes executes on a thread other than the master, so we see the output

Error!
Done.

While this example may appear contrived, remember that we are trying to mimic real situations when execution on a specific thread is required. In this spirit, let's assume that we cannot simply make the ofstream accessible to all of the threads, but instead we must do the writes on the main thread.

```cpp
class SourceFilter : public tbb::filter {
public:
  SourceFilter(size_t n);
  void *operator() (void *) override;
private:
  size_t numItems;
};

class MultiplyFilter : public tbb::filter {
public:
  MultiplyFilter();
  void *operator() (void *v) override;
};

thread_local std::ofstream output;

class BadWriteFilter : public tbb::filter {
public:
  BadWriteFilter()
    : tbb::filter(tbb::filter::serial_in_order),
      issued_error(false) { }
  void *operator() (void *v) override {
    if (output.is_open()) {
      output << reinterpret_cast<size_t>(v) << std::endl;
    } else if (!issued_error) {
      std::cerr << "Error!" << std::endl;
      issued_error = true;
    }
  }
private:
  bool issued_error;
};

void fig_16_25() {
  output.open("output.txt", std::ofstream::out);

  SourceFilter sf(100);
  MultiplyFilter mf;
  BadWriteFilter wf;
  tbb::pipeline p;
  p.add_filter(sf);
  p.add_filter(mf);
  p.add_filter(wf);
  p.run(tbb::task_scheduler_init::default_num_threads());
  std::cout << "Done." << std::endl;
}
```

Figure 16-25. *A buggy example that fails if the* BadWriteFilter *tries to write to output from a worker thread*

Figure 16-26 shows how we can use a `thread_bound_filter` to work around this limitation. To do so, we create a filter class, `ThreadBoundWriteFilter`, that inherits from `thread_bound_filter`. In fact, other than changing what the class inherits from, the implementation of the filter class is the same as `BadWriteFilter`.

While the classes implementations are similar, our use of the filter must change significantly as shown in function `fig_16_26`. We now run the pipeline from a separate thread – we need to do this, because we must keep the main thread available to service the thread-bound filter. We also add a while-loop that repeatedly calls the `process_item` function on our `ThreadBoundWriteFilter` object. It is here that the filter is executed. The while-loop continues until a call to `process_item` returns `tbb::thread_bound_filter::end_of_stream` indicating that there are no more items to process.

Running the example in Figure 16-26, we see that we have fixed our problem:

`Done.`

```cpp
thread_local std::ofstream output;

class ThreadBoundWriteFilter : public tbb::thread_bound_filter {
  bool issued_error;
public:
  ThreadBoundWriteFilter()
    : tbb::thread_bound_filter(tbb::filter::serial_in_order) { }
  void *operator() (void *v) override {
    if (output.is_open()) {
        output << reinterpret_cast<size_t>(v) << std::endl;
    } else if (!issued_error) {
      std::cerr << "Error!" << std::endl;
      issued_error = true;
    }
  }
};

void fig_16_26() {
  output.open("output.txt", std::ofstream::out);

  SourceFilter sf(100);
  MultiplyFilter mf;
  ThreadBoundWriteFilter wf;

  tbb::pipeline p;
  p.add_filter(sf);
  p.add_filter(mf);
  p.add_filter(wf);

  std::thread t([&]() {
    p.run(tbb::task_scheduler_init::default_num_threads());
  });
  while (wf.process_item() !=
         tbb::thread_bound_filter::end_of_stream)
    continue;

  t.join();
  std::cout << "Done." << std::endl;
}
```

Figure 16-26. *An example that writes to output only from the master thread*

Summary

In this chapter, we delved deeper into the features that can be used to tune TBB algorithms. We formed our discussion around the three common concerns when tuning TBB applications: task granularity, available parallelism, and data locality.

For the loop algorithms, we focused on the blocked range types and the different Partitioner types. We found that we can use 1 microsecond as a general guide for how long tasks should execute to mitigate the overheads of task scheduling. This rough guideline holds true for both loop algorithms, like `parallel_for`, and also for the filter sizes in `parallel_pipeline`.

We discussed how the blocked range types can be used to control granularity but also to optimize for the memory hierarchy. We used `blocked_range2d` and a `simple_partitioner` to implement a cache-oblivious implementation of matrix transposition. We then showed how `affinity_partitioner` or `static_partitioner` can be used to replay the scheduling of range so that the same pieces of data are accessed repeatedly by the same threads. We showed that while `static_partitioner` is the best performing partitioner for well-balanced workloads when executing in batch mode, as soon as the load is imbalanced or the system is oversubscribed, it suffers from its inability to dynamically balance the load through work stealing. We then briefly revisited determinism, describing how `deterministic_parallel_reduce` can provide deterministic results, but only by forcing us to use a `simple_partitioner` and carefully choose a grainsize, or use a `static_partitioner` and sacrifice dynamic load balancing.

We next turned our attention to `parallel_pipeline` and how the number of filters, the execution modes, and the number of tokens impact performance. We discussed how balanced and imbalanced pipelines behave. Finally, we also noted that while TBB pipelines do not offer hooks for us to tune for cache affinity, it is designed to enable temporal locality by having threads follow items as they flow through a pipeline.

We concluded the chapter with some advanced topics, including how to create our own Range types and how to use a `thread_bound_filter`.

For More Information

For more information on cache-oblivious algorithms:

Matteo Frigo, Charles E. Leiserson, Harald Prokop, and Sridhar Ramachandran. 2012. Cache-Oblivious Algorithms. *ACM Trans. Algorithms* 8, 1, Article 4 (January 2012), 22 pages.

For a more in-depth discussion on pipeline parallelism:

> Angeles Navarro et al. "Analytical Modeling of Pipeline
> Parallelism," ACM-IEEE International Conference on Parallel
> Architectures and Compilation Techniques (PACT'09). 2009.

For more information on the thundering herd problem:

```
https://en.wikipedia.org/wiki/Thundering_herd_problem
```

CHAPTER 17

Flow Graphs: Beyond the Basics

This chapter contains some key tips on getting top performance from flow graphs in TBB. The less structured nature of the TBB flow graph APIs offers an expressiveness that requires some thinking to get the best scalable performance – we dive into details in this chapter that let us tune flow graphs to their full potential.

In Chapter 3, we introduced the classes and functions in the `tbb::flow` namespace and how they can be used to express simple data flow and dependency graphs. In this chapter, we discuss some of the more advanced questions and issues that arise when using TBB flow graphs. As in Chapter 16, much of our discussion will revolve around granularity, effective memory use, and creating sufficient parallelism. But because the flow graph APIs let us express parallelism that is less structured than the parallel algorithms described in Chapter 16, we will also discuss some dos and don'ts to be aware of when architecting a flow graph.

The section "Key FG Advice: Dos and Don'ts," starting on page 480, gives very specific rules of thumb that are invaluable when using flow graphs with TBB.

We conclude this chapter with a brief overview of the Flow Graph Analyzer (FGA), a tool available within Intel Parallel Studio XE. It has strong support for the graphical design and analysis of TBB flow graphs. While using FGA is not required when working with flow graphs, visualizing graphs during design and analysis can be very helpful. The tool is freely available to everyone, and we highly recommend it for anyone doing serious TBB flow graph work.

© Intel Corporation 2019
M. Voss, R. Asenjo, J. Reinders, *Pro TBB*, https://doi.org/10.1007/978-1-4842-4398-5_17

Optimizing for Granularity, Locality, and Parallelism

In this section, we focus on the same three concerns that drove our discussions in Chapter 16. We first look at the impact of node granularity on performance. Because flow graphs are used for less structured algorithms, we need to consider how parallelism is introduced as we discuss granularity – does the structure require a significant amount of stealing or is the generation of tasks spread well across the threads? Also, we may want to use some very small nodes in a flow graph simply because they make the design clearer – in such cases, we describe how a node with a `lightweight` execution policy can be used to limit overheads. The second issue we will address is data locality. Unlike the TBB parallel algorithms, the flow graph API does not provide abstractions like Ranges and Partitioners; instead, it is designed to enhance locality naturally. We will discuss how threads follow data to exploit locality. Our third issue is creating sufficient parallelism. Just as in Chapter 16, optimizing for granularity and locality sometimes comes at the cost of restricted parallelism – we need to be sure we walk this tightrope carefully.

Node Granularity: How Big Is Big Enough?

In Chapter 16, we discussed Ranges and Partitioners and how these can be used to ensure that the tasks created by the TBB generic algorithms are large enough to amortize scheduling overheads while still being small enough to provide enough independent work items for scalability. The TBB flow graph does not have support for Ranges and Partitioners, but we still need to be concerned about task granularity.

To see if our rule of thumb for 1 microsecond tasks that we introduced in Chapter 16 applies as well to flow graph nodes as it does to parallel algorithm bodies, we will explore a few simple microbenchmarks that capture the extremes that can exist in flow graphs. We will compare the execution times of four functions and use different amounts of work per node execution. We will refer to these functions as **Serial**, **FG loop**, **Master loop**, and **FG loop per worker**.

It is our belief that studying these examples (Figures 17-1 to 17-4) is critical to having an intuitive grasp of some key issues that differentiate highly scalable flow graph usage and disappointing uses of flow graph. The APIs themselves, fully documented in Appendix B, do not provide this education – we hope you will study these examples enough to grasp the concepts as we believe this will make you much better at getting the most out of using TBB flow graphs (peek at Figure 17-5 to see a quantification of the benefits on performance of understanding these!).

The **Serial** loop is our baseline and contains a for-loop that calls an active spin-wait function N times, as shown in Figure 17-1.

```
double fig_17_1(int num_trials, int N, double per_node_time) {
  tbb::tick_count t0, t1;
  for (int t = -1; t < num_trials; ++t) {
    if (!t) t0 = tbb::tick_count::now();
    for (int i = 0; i < N; ++i) {
      spinWaitForAtLeast(per_node_time);
    }
  }
  t1 = tbb::tick_count::now();
  return (t1-t0).seconds()/num_trials;
}
```

Figure 17-1. *Serial: A function that times the baseline serial loop*

The **FG loop** function is shown in Figure 17-2. This function builds a flow graph that has a single multifunction_node with an edge from its output to its input. A single message starts the cycle and the node then spin-waits and sends a message back to its input. The cycle repeats N-1 times. Because the node spins before sending the message back to its input, this graph is still a mostly serial loop – the bulk of the work in the body tasks will not overlap. However, because the message is sent before the body returns, there is still a small-time gap during which another thread can steal the task that the try_put generates. We can use this graph to see the basic overhead of the flow graph infrastructure.

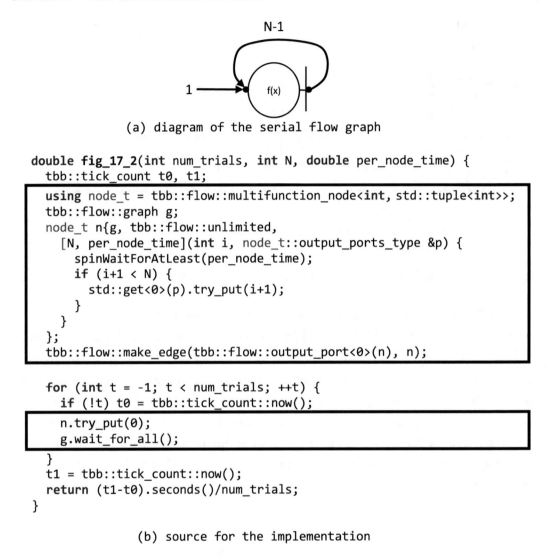

(a) diagram of the serial flow graph

```
double fig_17_2(int num_trials, int N, double per_node_time) {
  tbb::tick_count t0, t1;
  using node_t = tbb::flow::multifunction_node<int, std::tuple<int>>;
  tbb::flow::graph g;
  node_t n{g, tbb::flow::unlimited,
    [N, per_node_time](int i, node_t::output_ports_type &p) {
      spinWaitForAtLeast(per_node_time);
      if (i+1 < N) {
        std::get<0>(p).try_put(i+1);
      }
    }
  };
  tbb::flow::make_edge(tbb::flow::output_port<0>(n), n);

  for (int t = -1; t < num_trials; ++t) {
    if (!t) t0 = tbb::tick_count::now();
    n.try_put(0);
    g.wait_for_all();
  }
  t1 = tbb::tick_count::now();
  return (t1-t0).seconds()/num_trials;
}
```

(b) source for the implementation

Figure 17-2. *FG loop: A function that times a serial flow graph*

Our next microbenchmarking function, **Master loop** shown in Figure 17-3, does not create a cycle. It instead sends all N messages to the multifunction_node directly from the master thread in a serial loop. Since the multifunction_node has unlimited parallelism and the serial for-loop will send messages very quickly, there are a lot of parallel tasks created. However, because the master thread is the only thread that calls the try_put method on node n, all body tasks are spawned into the master thread's local deque. Worker threads that participate in executing this graph will be forced to steal each task they execute – and only after they have randomly selected the master as their victim. We can use this graph to see the behavior of a flow graph with sufficient parallelism but that requires an extreme amount of work-stealing.

(a) diagram of a parallel flow graph with N initial messages

```
double fig_17_3(int num_trials, int N, double per_node_time) {
  tbb::tick_count t0, t1;
  using node_t = tbb::flow::multifunction_node<int, std::tuple<int>>;
  tbb::flow::graph g;
  node_t n(g, tbb::flow::unlimited,
    [N, per_node_time](int i, node_t::output_ports_type &p) {
      spinWaitForAtLeast(per_node_time);
    }
  );

  for (int t = -1; t < num_trials; ++t) {
    if (!t) t0 = tbb::tick_count::now();
    for (int i = 0; i < N; ++i) {
      n.try_put(0);
    }
    g.wait_for_all();
  }
  t1 = tbb::tick_count::now();
  return (t1-t0).seconds();
}
```

(b) source for the implementation

Figure 17-3. *Master loop: A function that submits messages only from the master thread; workers must steal every task they execute*

Finally, Figure 17-4 shows the **FG loop per worker** function. This function spreads the tasks across the master and worker threads' local deques, since once a thread has stolen its initial task, it will then spawn tasks into its own local deque. We can use this graph to see the behavior of a flow graph with a very small amount of stealing.

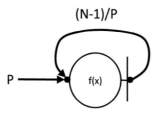

(a) diagram of a parallel flow graph with P initial messages

```
double fig_17_4(int num_trials, int P,
                int N_per_P, double per_node_time) {
  tbb::tick_count t0, t1;
```
```
  using node_t = tbb::flow::multifunction_node<int, std::tuple<int>>;
  tbb::flow::graph g;
  node_t n(g, tbb::flow::unlimited,
    [N_per_P, per_node_time](int i,
                             node_t::output_ports_type &p) {
      spinWaitForAtLeast(per_node_time);
      if (i+1 < N_per_P) {
        std::get<0>(p).try_put(i+1);
      }
    }
  );
  tbb::flow::make_edge(tbb::flow::output_port<0>(n), n);
```
```
  for (int t = -1; t < num_trials; ++t) {
    if (!t) t0 = tbb::tick_count::now();
```
```
    for (int p = 0; p < P; ++p) {
      n.try_put(0);
    }
    g.wait_for_all();
```
```
  }
  t1 = tbb::tick_count::now();
  return (t1-t0).seconds()/num_trials;
}
```

(b) source for the implementation

Figure 17-4. *FG loop per worker: A function that creates just enough parallelism to satisfy the number of workers. Once a worker has stolen its initial task, it will execute the remainder of its tasks from its local deque.*

Unless otherwise noted, all performance results presented in this chapter were collected on a single socket server with an Intel Xeon Processor E3-1230 with four cores supporting two hardware threads per core; the processor has a base frequency of 3.4 GHz, a shared 8 MB L3 cache, and per-core 256 KB L2 caches. The system was running SUSE Linux Enterprise Server 12. All samples were compiled using the Intel C++ Compiler 19.0 with Threading Building Blocks 2019, using the compiler flags "-std=c++11 -O2 -tbb".

We ran these microbenchmarks using N=65,536 and spin-wait times of 100 ns, 1 us, 10 us, and 100 us. We collected their average execution times over 10 trials and present the results in Figure 17-5. From these results, we can see that when the task sizes are very small, 100 nanoseconds for example, the overhead of the flow graph infrastructure leads to degraded performance in all cases. With task sizes of at least 1 microsecond, we begin to profit from parallel execution. And by the time we reach a task size of 100 microseconds, we are able to reach close to perfect linear speedups.

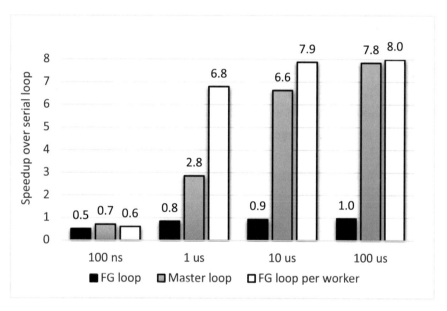

Figure 17-5. *The speedups $T_{serial}/T_{benchmark}$ for different spin wait times*

We can further understand the performance of our microbenchmarks by collecting a trace and viewing the results in Flow Graph Analyzer (FGA) – FGA is described in more detail at the end of this chapter. Figure 17-6 shows per-thread timelines for the different functions when using a spin-wait time of 1 microsecond. These timelines, which are all of the same length, show the work done by each thread over time. The gaps (in gray) in the timelines indicate when a thread is not actively executing a node's body. In Figure 17-6(a), we see the behavior of **FG loop,** which acts like a serial loop. But we can see that the small gap between the try_put in the body and the exit from the task allows the tasks to ping-pong between the threads since they are able to steal each task as it is spawned. This partially explains the fairly large overheads for this microbenchmark shown in Figure 17-5. As we explain later in this chapter, most functional nodes use scheduler bypass to follow their data to the next node when possible (see the discussion on Pipelines and data locality and thread affinity in Chapter 16 for a more detailed discussion of why scheduler bypass improves cache performance). Since a `multifunction_node` puts output messages to its output ports directly inside of the body implementation, it cannot immediately follow the data to the next node using scheduler bypass – it has to finish its own body first! A `multifunction_node` therefore does not use scheduler bypass to optimize for locality. In any case, this makes the performance in Figure 17-6(a) a worst-case overhead, since scheduler bypass is not used.

In Figure 17-6(b), we see the case where the master thread is generating all of the tasks and the workers must steal each task, but tasks can be executed in parallel once they are stolen. Because the worker threads must steal each task, they are much slower at finding tasks than the master thread. The master thread is continually busy in Figure 17-6(b) – it can quickly pop a next task from its local deque – while the worker threads' timelines show gaps during which they are fighting with each other to steal their next task from the master's local deque.

Figure 17-6(c) shows the good behavior of **FG loop per worker**, where each thread is able to quickly pop its next task from its local deque. Now we see very few gaps in the timelines.

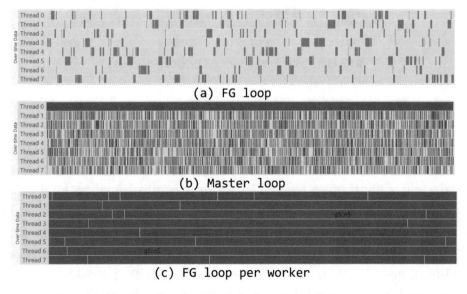

Figure 17-6. Two millisecond regions of the timelines for each microbenchmark when using a spin wait of 1 microsecond

Looking at these extremes of behavior and noting the performance in Figure 17-5, we feel comfortable recommending a similar rule of thumb for flow graph nodes. While a pathological case, like **Master loop**, shows a limited speedup of 2.8 with a 1 microsecond body, it still shows a speedup. If the work is more balanced, such as with **FG loop per worker,** a 1 microsecond body provides a good speedup. With these caveats in mind, we again recommend a 1 microsecond execution time as a crude guideline:

RULE OF THUMB   Flow graph nodes should be at least 1 microsecond in execution time in order to profit from parallel execution. This translates to several thousand CPU cycles – if you prefer using cycles, we suggest a `10,000 cycle` rule of thumb.

Just like with the TBB algorithms, this rule *does not* mean that we must avoid nodes smaller than 1 microsecond at all costs. Only if our flow graph's execution time is dominated by small nodes do we really have a problem. If we have a mix of nodes with different execution times, the overhead introduced by the small nodes may be negligible compared to the execution time of the larger nodes.

What to Do If Nodes Are Too Small

If some of the nodes in a flow graph are smaller than the recommended 1 microsecond threshold, there are three options: (1) do nothing at all if the node does not have significant impact on the total execution time of the application, (2) merge the node with other surrounding nodes to increase granularity, or (3) use the `lightweight` execution policy.

If the node's granularity is small, but its contribution to total execution time is also small, then the node can be safely ignored; just leave it as it is. In these cases, clarity of design may trump any inconsequential efficiency gained.

If the node's granularity has to be addressed, one option is to merge it with surrounding nodes. Does the node really need to be encapsulated separately from its predecessors and successors? If the node has a single predecessor or a single successor and the same concurrency level, it might be easily combined with those nodes. If it has multiple predecessors or successors, then perhaps the operations that are performed by the node can be copied into each of the nodes. In any case, merging the nodes together can be an option if the merging does not change the semantics of the graph.

Finally, the node can be changed to use a lightweight execution policy via a template argument when the node is constructed. For example:

```
tbb::flow::function_node<int, int, lightweight> n(...);
```

This policy indicates that the body of the node contains a small amount of work and should, if possible, be executed without the overhead of scheduling a task.

There are three lightweight policies to choose from: `queueing_lightweight`, `rejecting_lightweight`, and `lightweight`. These policies are described in detail in Appendix B. All of the functional nodes, except `source_node`, support lightweight policies. A lightweight node may not spawn a task to execute the body, but instead execute the body immediately inside of the `try_put` within the context of the calling thread. This means that the overheads of spawning are removed – but there is no opportunity for other threads to steal the task, so parallelism is restricted!

Figure 17-7 shows two simple graphs that we can use to demonstrate the benefits and risks of the lightweight policies: the first is a chain `multifunction_node` objects and the second is a `multifunction_node` object that is connected to two chains of `multifunction_node` objects.

(a) A single chain of multifunction nodes

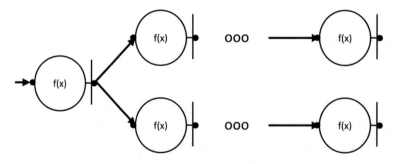

(b) Two chains of multifunction nodes

Figure 17-7. *Flow graph used to examine the impacts of the* `lightweight` *policies*

Figure 17-8 shows the impact of using the `lightweight` policy on the graphs shown in Figure 17-7 using chains of 1000 nodes, all using the same execution policy (`lightweight` or not). We send a single message through each graph and vary the time each node spins from 0 to 1 millisecond. We should note that the single chain does not allow for any parallelism when only one message is sent, while with two chains we can achieve a maximum speedup of 2.

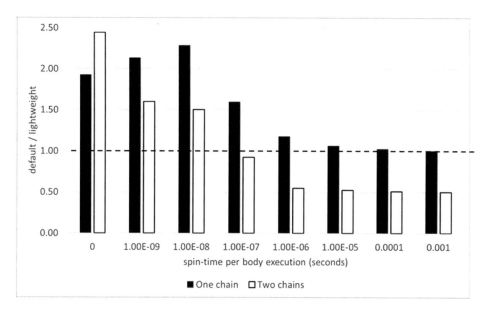

Figure 17-8. *The impact of using a lightweight policy for the one chain and two chains samples. A value greater than 1 means that the lightweight policy improved performance.*

The `lightweight` policy cannot limit parallelism for the one chain case, since there is no parallelism in this graph to begin with. We therefore see in Figure 17-8 that it improves performance for all cases, although its impact becomes less significant as the node granularity increases. For the one chain case, the ratio approaches 1.0 as the overhead of spawning tasks becomes negligible compared to the body's spin time. The two-chain case does have potential parallelism. However, if all of the nodes use a `lightweight` policy, both chains will be executed by the thread that executes the first `multifunction_node` and the potential parallelism will be eliminated. As we might expect then, as we approach our rule of thumb execution time of 1 microsecond, the benefits of the `lightweight` policy are overshadowed by the restricted parallelism. Even if the nodes spin for 0.1 microsecond, the ratio drops below 1. The ratio approaches 0.5

461

as the serialization of the graph results in the complete loss of our expected speedup of 2 when using two chains.

Addressing granularity issues through merging of nodes, or by using the lightweight policy, can decrease overheads, but as we see, they can also limit scalability. These "optimizations" can result in significant improvements, but must be applied judiciously or else they may do more harm than good.

Memory Usage and Data Locality

Unlike the TBB parallel algorithms that iterate over data structures, a flow graph passes data structures from node to node. The messages can be primitive types, objects, pointers or, in the case of a dependence graph, tbb::flow::continue_msg objects. For best performance, we need to consider both data locality and memory consumption. We will discuss both of these issues in this section.

Data Locality in Flow Graphs

Data passes between nodes, and when a node receives a message, it executes its body on the message as a TBB task. The task is scheduled using the same work-stealing dispatchers used by all TBB tasks. In Figure 17-6(a) when a serial loop was executed as a flow graph, we saw that a task spawned by one thread may be executed by another. We noted however that this was due in part to the microbenchmark using multifunction_ node objects, which do not use scheduler bypass to optimize for performance.

In general, the other functional nodes, including source_node, function_node, and continue_node, use scheduler bypass if one of the successors can be immediately run. If the data accessed by one of these nodes fits into a data cache, then it can be reused by the same thread when it executes the successor.

Since we can benefit from locality in a flow graph, it is worth considering data size and even breaking the data into smaller pieces that can benefit from locality through scheduler bypass. For example, we can revisit the matrix transposition kernel that we used in Chapter 16 as an example to demonstrate this effect. We will now pass three pairs of a, b matrices using the FGMsg structure shown in Figure 17-9. You can see the serial, cache oblivious and parallel_for implementations of the matrix transposition kernel in Chapter 16 in Figure 16-6 through Figure 16-13.

Our first implementation that does not break the arrays into small pieces is also shown in Figure 17-9. The source_node, initialize, sends three messages, each being one of three matrix pairs. This node is connected to a single function_node, transpose, that has an unlimited concurrency. The transpose node invokes the simple, serial matrix transposition function from Chapter 16. A final node, check, confirms that the transposition is done correctly.

```cpp
struct FGMsg {
  int N;
  double *a;
  double *b;
  FGMsg() : N(0), a(0), b(0) {}
  FGMsg(int _N, double *_a, double *_b) : N(_N), a(_a), b(_b) {}
};
```

```cpp
double fig_17_9(int N, double *a[3], double *b[3]) {
  tbb::tick_count t0 = tbb::tick_count::now();
  tbb::flow::graph g;
  int i = 0;
  tbb::flow::source_node<FGMsg> initialize{g,
  [&](FGMsg &msg) -> bool {
    if (i < 3) {
      msg = {N, setArray(N, a[i]), setArray(N, b[i])};
      ++i;
      return true;
    } else {
      return false;
    }
  }, false};
  tbb::flow::function_node<FGMsg, FGMsg> transpose{g,
    tbb::flow::unlimited,
    [](const FGMsg &msg) -> FGMsg {
      serialTranspose(msg.N, msg.a, msg.b);
      return msg;
  }};
  tbb::flow::function_node<FGMsg> check{g, tbb::flow::unlimited,
    [](const FGMsg &msg) -> FGMsg {
    checkArray(msg.N, msg.b);
  }};
  tbb::flow::make_edge(initialize, transpose);
  tbb::flow::make_edge(transpose, check);
  initialize.activate();
  g.wait_for_all();
}
```

Figure 17-9. *A graph that sends a series of matrices to transpose, each of which is transposed using the simple serial matrix transposition from Chapter 16*

Our simple implementation sends the full matrices, and these are processed, in a non-cache-oblivious fashion, by transpose. As we might expect, this does not perform well. On our test machine, it was only 8% faster than executing the non-cache-oblivious serial implementation of our matrix transposition from Chapter 16 three times in a row, once on each pair of matrices. This isn't very surprising since the benchmark is memory bound – trying to execute multiple transpositions in parallel doesn't help much when we can't feed one transposition with the data it needs from memory. If we compare our simple flow graph to the serial cache-oblivious transposition from Chapter 16, it looks even worse, taking 2.5 times *longer* to process the three pairs of matrices when executed on our test machine. Luckily, there are many options for improving the performance of this flow graph. For example, we can use a serial cache-oblivious implementation in the transpose node. Or, we can use the parallel_for implementation from Chapter 16 that uses a blocked_range2d and simple_partitioner in the transpose node. We will see shortly that each of these will greatly improve our base case speedup of 1.08.

However, we might also send blocks of the matrices as messages instead of sending each pair of a and b matrices as a single big message. To do so, we extend our message structure to include a blocked_range2d:

```
using RType = tbb::blocked_range2d<int, int>;
struct FGTiledMsg {
  int N;
  double *a;
  double *b;
  RType r;
  FGTiledMsg() : N(0), a(0), b(0), r(0, 0, 0, 0, 0, 0) {}
  FGTiledMsg(int _N, double *_a, double *_b, const RType &_r)
    : N(_N), a(_a), b(_b), r(_r) {}
};
```

We can then construct an implementation in which the initialize node sends blocks of the a and b matrices as messages; sending all of the blocks from one pair of matrices before moving on to the next. Figure 17-10 shows one possible implementation. In this implementation, a stack is maintained by the source_node to mimic the depth-first subdivision and execution of the blocks that would come about through the recursive subdivision of ranges performed by a TBB parallel_for. We will not describe the implementation in Figure 17-10 in depth. Instead, we will simply note that it sends blocks instead of full matrices.

```
double fig_17_10(int N, double *a[3], double *b[3], int gs) {
  tbb::tick_count t0 = tbb::tick_count::now();
  tbb::flow::graph g;
  int i = 0;
  std::vector<RType> stack;
  stack.push_back(RType(0, N, gs, 0, N, gs));
  tbb::flow::source_node<FGTiledMsg> initialize{g,
  [&](FGTiledMsg &msg) -> bool {
    if (i < 3) {
      if (stack.empty()) {
        if (++i == 3) return false;
        stack.push_back(RType(0, N, gs, 0, N, gs));
      }
      RType r = stack.back();
      stack.pop_back();
      while (r.is_divisible()) {
        RType rhs(r, tbb::split());
        stack.push_back(rhs);
      }
      msg = {N, setBlock(r, a[i]), setTransposedBlock(r, b[i]), r};
      return true;
    } else {
      return false;
    }
  }, false};
  tbb::flow::function_node<FGTiledMsg, FGTiledMsg>
  transpose{g, tbb::flow::unlimited,
    [](const FGTiledMsg &msg) {
    double *a = msg.a, *b = msg.b;
    int N = msg.N, ie = msg.r.rows().end(), je = msg.r.cols().end();
    for (int i = msg.r.rows().begin(); i < ie; ++i) {
      for (int j = msg.r.cols().begin(); j < je; ++j) {
        b[j*N + i] = a[i*N + j];
      }
    }
    return msg;
  }};
  tbb::flow::function_node<FGTiledMsg> check{g, tbb::flow::unlimited,
    [](const FGTiledMsg &msg) {
    checkTransposedBlock(msg.r, msg.b);
  }};
  tbb::flow::make_edge(initialize, transpose);
  tbb::flow::make_edge(transpose, check);
  initialize.activate();
  g.wait_for_all();
  return total_time;
}
```

Figure 17-10. *A graph that sends a series of tiles of matrices to transpose, leveraging the blocked_range2d described in Chapter 16 (Advanced Algorithms)*

Figure 17-11 shows the speedup of several variants of matrix transposition when executed on our test machine. We can see that our first implementation, labeled "flow graph," shows the small 8% improvement. The pfor-br2d implementation is the `parallel_for` based implementation from Figure 16-11, with `blocked_range2d` and `simple_partitioner,` executed three times, once on each pair of matrices. The remaining bars all correspond to optimized flow graph versions: "flow graph + oblivious" is similar to Figure 17-9 but calls the serial cache-oblivious implementation of matrix transposition from within the body of the `transpose` node; "flow graph + pfor-br2d" uses a `parallel_for` in the `transpose` body; "tiled flow graph" is our implementation from Figure 17-10; and "tiled flow graph + pfor2d" is similar to Figure 17-10 but uses a `parallel_for` to process its tiles. The tiled flow graph from Figure 17-10 performed the best.

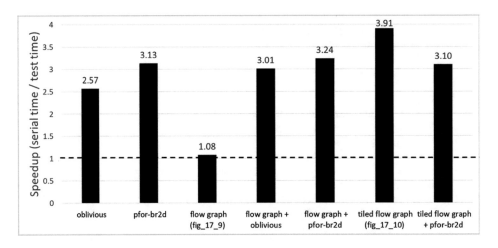

Figure 17-11. *The speedup of the different variants of matrix transposition. We use 32×32 tiles since this performed best on our test system.*

It might be surprising that the tiled flow graph version with nested `parallel_fors` did not perform as well as the tiled flow graph without nested parallelism. In Chapter 9, we claimed that we can use nested parallelism with impunity in TBB – so what went wrong? The harsh reality is that once we start tuning the performance of our TBB applications – we often need to trade away full composability for performance (see the Aspects of Composability Sidebar). In this case, the nested parallelism interfered with the cache optimizations we were carefully trying to implement. Each node was sent a tile to process that was a good fit for its data cache – with nested parallelism, we then undid this perfect fit by sharing the tile with other threads.

ASPECTS OF COMPOSABILITY

We can break down composability into three desires:

(1) Correctness (as an absolute)

(2) Ability to use (as a practical matter)

(3) Performance (as an aspiration)

In the first, we hope we can mix and match code without concerns that it will suddenly malfunction (get the wrong answer). TBB gives us this ability, and it is largely a solved problem – the one wrinkle being that nondeterministic order-of-execution will make answers vary when using finite precision math such as native floating-point arithmetic. We discuss that in Chapter 16 offering approaches to maintain the "correctness" aspects of composability in this light.

In the second, we hope that the program will not crash. This is a practical matter in many cases, because the most common problem (unbounded memory usage) could be theoretically solved with infinite sized memories. ☺ TBB largely solves this aspect of composability, giving it an advantage of programming models that do not (such as OpenMP). TBB does need more help here for the less structured flow graphs, so we discuss using `limiter_nodes` with flow graphs to keep memory usage in check – especially important in large flow graphs.

Finally, for optimal performance, we know of no general solution to full performance composability. The reality is that highly optimized code competing with other code running on the same hardware will interfere with the optimal performance of either code. This means we can benefit from manually tuning the code. Fortunately, TBB gives us control to tune, and tools like Flow Graph Analyzer help give us insights to guide our tuning. Once tuned, it is our experience that code can work well and feel composable – but the technology to blindly use code and get top performance does not exist. "Good enough" performance may happen often, but "great" requires work.

We shouldn't get too focused on the specifics of the results in Figure 17-11 – this is, after all, a single memory-bound microbenchmark. But it does make clear that we can benefit by considering the size of our nodes, not only from a granularity perspective, but also from a data locality perspective. When we moved from a naïve implementation that sent whole arrays and did not implement tuned kernels in the nodes to our more cache-aware tiled flow graph version, we saw a significant performance improvement.

Picking the Best Message Type and Limiting the Number of Messages in Flight

As we allow messages into a graph, or make copies as we split them along multiple paths through a flow graph, we consume more memory. In addition to worrying about locality, we may also need to limit memory growth.

When a message is passed to a node in a data flow graph, it may be copied into the internal buffers in that node. For example, if a serial node needs to defer the spawning of task, it holds incoming messages in a queue until it is legal to spawn a task to process them. If we pass very large objects around in our flow graph, this copying can be expensive! Therefore, when possible, it is better to pass around pointers to large objects instead of the objects themselves.

The C++11 standard introduced classes (in `namespace std`) `unique_ptr` and `shared_ptr`, which are very useful for simplifying memory management of objects passed by pointer in a flow graph. For example, in Figure 17-12, let us assume that a `BigObject` is large and slow to construct. By passing the object using a `shared_ptr`, only the `shared_ptr` is copied into the serial node n's input buffer not the entire `BigObject`. Also, since a `shared_ptr` is used, each `BigObject` is automatically destroyed once it reaches the end of the graph and its reference count reaches zero. How convenient!

```
class BigObject {
  const int id;  // plus some big data not shown
public:
  BigObject() : id(-1) { }
  BigObject(int i) : id(i) { spinWaitForAtLeast(0.001); }
  BigObject(const BigObject &b) : id(b.id) {
    spinWaitForAtLeast(0.001); // simulates copy time
  }
  int get_id() const {return id;}
};

void fig_17_12() {
  tbb::flow::graph g;

  tbb::flow::function_node<std::shared_ptr<BigObject>, int>
  n(g, tbb::flow::serial,
    [](std::shared_ptr<BigObject> b) -> int {
      int id = b->get_id();
      spinWaitForAtLeast(0.01);
      return id;
    }
  );

  for (int i = 0; i < 100; ++i) {
    n.try_put(std::make_shared<BigObject>(i));
  }
  g.wait_for_all();
}
```

Figure 17-12. *Using a* std::shared_ptr *to avoid slow copies while simplifying memory management*

Of course, we need to be careful when we use pointers to objects. By passing pointers and not objects, multiple nodes may have access to the same object at the same time through the shared_ptr. This is especially true if your graph relies on functional parallelism, where the same message is broadcast to multiple nodes. The shared_ptr will correctly handle the increments and decrements of the reference counts, but we need to be sure that we are properly using edges to prevent any potential race conditions when accessing the object that is pointed to.

As we saw in our discussion of how nodes map to tasks, when messages arrive at functional nodes, tasks may be spawned or messages may be buffered. When designing a data flow graph, we should not forget about these buffers and tasks, and their memory footprint.

For example, let's consider Figure 17-13. There are two nodes, serial_node and unlimited_node; both contain a long spin loop. The for loop quickly allocates a large number of inputs for both nodes. Node serial_node is serial and so its internal buffer will grow quickly as it receives messages faster than its tasks complete. In contrast, node unlimited_node will immediately spawn tasks as each message arrives – quickly flooding the system with a very large number of tasks – many more than the number of worker threads. These spawned tasks will be buffered in the internal worker thread queues. In both cases, our graph might quickly consume a large amount of memory because they allow BigObject messages to enter the graph more quickly than they can be processed.

Our example uses an atomic counter, bigObjectCount, to track how many ObjectCount objects are currently allocated at any given time. At the end of the execution, the example prints the maximum value. When we ran the code in Figure 17-13 with A_VERY_LARGE_NUMBER=4096, we saw a "maxCount == 8094". Both the serial_node and the unlimited_node quickly accumulate BigObject objects!

```cpp
tbb::atomic<int> bigObjectCount;
int maxCount = 0;

class BigObject {
    const int id;
    /* And a big amount of other data */
public:
    BigObject() : id(-1) { }
    BigObject(int i) : id(i) {
      int cnt = bigObjectCount.fetch_and_increment() + 1;
      if (cnt > maxCount)
        maxCount = cnt;
    }
    BigObject(const BigObject &b) : id(b.id) { }
    virtual ~BigObject() {
      bigObjectCount.fetch_and_decrement();
    }
    int get_id() const {return id;}
};

using BigObjectPtr = std::shared_ptr<BigObject>;

void fig_17_13() {
  tbb::flow::graph g;
  tbb::flow::function_node<BigObjectPtr, BigObjectPtr>
  serial_node{g, tbb::flow::serial,
    [] (BigObjectPtr m) {
      spinWaitForAtLeast(0.0001);
      return m;
    }};
  tbb::flow::function_node<BigObjectPtr, BigObjectPtr>
  unlimited_node{g, tbb::flow::unlimited,
    [] (BigObjectPtr m) {
      spinWaitForAtLeast(0.0001);
      return m;
    }};
  bigObjectCount = 0;
  for (int i = 0; i < A_VERY_LARGE_NUMBER; ++i) {
    serial_node.try_put(std::make_shared<BigObject>(i));
    unlimited_node.try_put(std::make_shared<BigObject>(i));
  }
  g.wait_for_all();
  std::cout << "maxCount == " << maxCount << std::endl;
}
```

Figure 17-13. *An example with a serial function_node, serial_node, and an unlimited function_node, unlimited_node*

471

There are three common approaches to managing resource consumption in a flow graph: (1) use a limiter_node, (2) use concurrency limits, and/or (3) use a token-passing pattern.

We use a limiter_node to set a limit on the number of messages that can flow through a given point in a graph. A subset of the interface of limiter_node is shown in Figure 17-14.

```
class limiter_node : public graph_node,
  public receiver<T>, public sender<T> {
public:
    limiter_node( graph &g, size_t threshold,
                  int number_of_decrement_predecessors = 0 );
    limiter_node( const limiter_node &src );

    // a continue_receiver
    implementation-dependent-type decrement;

    // receiver<T>
    typedef T input_type;
    bool try_put( const input_type &v );

    // sender<T>
    typedef T output_type;
};
```

Figure 17-14. *The subset of* limiter_node *interface used by the examples*

A limiter_node maintains an internal count of the messages that pass through it. A message sent to the decrement port on a limiter_node decrements the count, allowing additional messages to pass through. If the count is equal to the node's threshold, any new messages that arrive at its input port are rejected.

In Figure 17-15, a source_node source generates a large number of BigObjects. A source_node only spawns a new task to generate a message once its previously generated message is consumed. We insert a limiter_node limiter, constructed with a limit of 3, between source and unlimited_node to limit the number of messages that are sent to unlimited_node. We also add an edge from unlimited_node back to the limiter_node's decrement port. The number of messages sent through limiter will now at most be 3 more than the number of messages sent back through limiter's decrement port.

(a) diagram of the graph

```
void fig_17_15() {
  tbb::flow::graph g;

  int src_count = 0;
  tbb::flow::source_node<BigObjectPtr>
  source{g, [&src_count] (BigObjectPtr &m) -> bool {
      if (src_count < A_VERY_LARGE_NUMBER) {
        m = std::make_shared<BigObject>(src_count++);
        return true;
      }
      return false;
    }, false
  };
  tbb::flow::limiter_node<BigObjectPtr> limiter{g, 3};
  tbb::flow::function_node<BigObjectPtr,
tbb::flow::continue_msg>
  unlimited_node{g, tbb::flow::unlimited,
    [] (BigObjectPtr m) {
      spinWaitForAtLeast(0.0001);
      return tbb::flow::continue_msg();
    }
  };
  tbb::flow::make_edge(source, limiter);
  tbb::flow::make_edge(limiter, unlimited_node);
  tbb::flow::make_edge(unlimited_node, limiter.decrement);

  bigObjectCount = 0;
  maxCount = 0;
  source.activate();
  g.wait_for_all();
  std::cout << "maxCount == " << maxCount << std::endl;
}
```

(b) implementation of the graph

Figure 17-15. *Using a* limiter_node *to allow only three* BigObjects *to reach* unlimited_node *at a time*

We can also use the concurrency limits on nodes to limit resource consumption as shown in Figure 17-16. In the code, we have a node that can safely execute with an unlimited concurrency, but we choose a smaller number to limit the number of tasks that will be spawned concurrently.

(a) diagram of the graph

```cpp
void fig_17_16() {
  tbb::flow::graph g;

  int src_count = 0;
  tbb::flow::source_node< BigObjectPtr > source{g,
    [&] (BigObjectPtr &m) -> bool {
      if (src_count < A_VERY_LARGE_NUMBER) {
        m = std::make_shared<BigObject>(src_count++);
        return true;
      }
      return false;
    }, false};
  tbb::flow::function_node<BigObjectPtr, BigObjectPtr,
                           tbb::flow::rejecting>
  limited_to_3_node{g, 3, [] (BigObjectPtr m) {
      spinWaitForAtLeast(0.0001);
      return m;
    }};
  tbb::flow::make_edge(source, limited_to_3_node);

  bigObjectCount = 0;
  maxCount = 0;
  source.activate();
  g.wait_for_all();
  std::cout << "maxCount == " << maxCount << std::endl;
}
```

(b) implementation of the graph

Figure 17-16. *Using a* `tbb::flow::rejecting` *policy and a* `concurrency_limit` *to allow only three* `BigObjects` *to reach the* `limited_to_3_node` *at a time*

We can turn off the internal buffering for a function_node by constructing it with an execution policy, flow::rejecting or flow::rejecting_lightweight. The source_node in Figure 17-16 continues to generate new outputs only if they are being consumed.

The final common approach for limiting resource consumption in a data flow graph is to use a token-based system. As described in Chapter 2, tbb::parallel_pipeline algorithm uses tokens to limit the maximum number of items that will be in flight in a pipeline. We can create a similar system using tokens and a reserving join_node as shown in Figure 17-17. In this example, we create a source_node source and buffer_node token_buffer. These two nodes are connected to the inputs of a reserving join_node join. A reserving join_node, join_node< tuple< BigObjectPtr, token_t >, flow::reserving >, only consumes items when it can first reserve inputs at each of its ports. Since a source_node stops generating new messages when its previous message has not been consumed, the availability of tokens in the token_buffer limits the number of items that can be generated by the source_node. As tokens are returned to the token_buffer by node unlimited_node, they can be paired with additional messages generated by the source, allowing new source tasks to be spawned.

Figure 17-18 shows the speedup of each approach over a serial execution of the node bodies. In this figure, the spin time is 100 microseconds, and we can see that the token passing approach has a slightly higher overhead, although all three approaches show speedups close to 3, as we would expect.

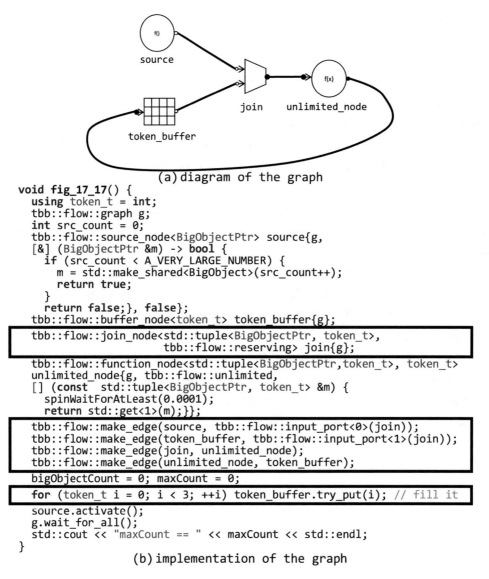

(a) diagram of the graph

```
void fig_17_17() {
  using token_t = int;
  tbb::flow::graph g;
  int src_count = 0;
  tbb::flow::source_node<BigObjectPtr> source{g,
  [&] (BigObjectPtr &m) -> bool {
    if (src_count < A_VERY_LARGE_NUMBER) {
      m = std::make_shared<BigObject>(src_count++);
      return true;
    }
    return false;}, false};
  tbb::flow::buffer_node<token_t> token_buffer{g};
  tbb::flow::join_node<std::tuple<BigObjectPtr, token_t>,
                       tbb::flow::reserving> join{g};
  tbb::flow::function_node<std::tuple<BigObjectPtr,token_t>, token_t>
  unlimited_node{g, tbb::flow::unlimited,
  [] (const  std::tuple<BigObjectPtr, token_t> &m) {
    spinWaitForAtLeast(0.0001);
    return std::get<1>(m);}};
  tbb::flow::make_edge(source, tbb::flow::input_port<0>(join));
  tbb::flow::make_edge(token_buffer, tbb::flow::input_port<1>(join));
  tbb::flow::make_edge(join, unlimited_node);
  tbb::flow::make_edge(unlimited_node, token_buffer);
  bigObjectCount = 0; maxCount = 0;
  for (token_t i = 0; i < 3; ++i) token_buffer.try_put(i); // fill it
  source.activate();
  g.wait_for_all();
  std::cout << "maxCount == " << maxCount << std::endl;
}
```

(b) implementation of the graph

Figure 17-17. *A token passing pattern uses tokens and a* tbb::flow::reserving
join_node to limit the items that can reach node unlimited_node

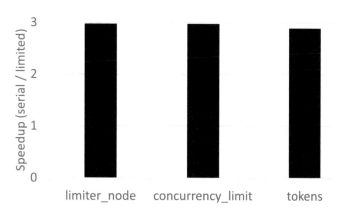

Figure 17-18. *All three approaches limit the speedup since only three items are allowed into node n at a time*

In Figure 17-18, we use int as the token type. In general, we can use any type as a token, even large objects or pointers. For example, we could use BigObjectPtr objects as the tokens if we want to recycle BigObject objects instead of allocating them for each new input.

Task Arenas and Flow Graph

Both implicit and explicit task arenas impact the behavior of TBB tasks and the TBB generic parallel algorithms. The arena in which tasks are spawned controls which threads can participate in executing the tasks. In Chapter 11, we saw how we can use implicit and explicit arenas to control the number of threads that participate in executing parallel work. In Chapters 12–14, we saw that explicit task arenas can be used with task_sheduler_observer objects to set the properties of threads as they join arenas. Because of the impact of task arenas on available parallelism and data locality, in this section, we take a closer look at how task arenas mix with flow graphs.

The Default Arena Used by a Flow Graph

When we construct a tbb::flow::graph object, the graph object captures a reference to the arena of the thread that constructed the object. Whenever a task is spawned to execute work in the graph, the tasks are spawned in this arena, not in the arena of the thread that caused the task to be spawned.

Why?

Well, TBB flow graphs are less structured than TBB parallel algorithms. TBB algorithms use fork-join parallelism and the behavior of TBB task arenas matches this pattern well – each master thread has its own default arena and so if different master threads execute algorithms concurrently, their tasks are isolated from each other in different task arenas. But with a TBB flow graph, there may be one or more master threads explicitly putting messages into the same graph. If the tasks related to these interactions are spawned in each master thread's arena, some tasks from a graph would be isolated from other tasks from the same graph. This is very likely not the behavior we would like.

So instead, all tasks are spawned into a single arena, the arena of the thread that constructed the graph object.

Changing the Task Arena Used by a Flow Graph

We can change the task arena used by a graph by calling the graph's reset() function. This reinitializes the graph, including recapturing the task arena. We demonstrate this in Figure 17-19 by constructing a simple graph with one function_node that prints the number of slots in the arena in which its body task executes. Since the main thread constructs the graph object, the graph will use the default arena, which we initialize with eight slots.

```
void fig_17_19() {
  tbb::task_scheduler_init init{8};
  tbb::task_arena a2{2};
  tbb::task_arena a4{4};

  tbb::flow::graph g;
  tbb::flow::function_node<std::string> f{g, tbb::flow::unlimited,
    [](const std::string &str) {
      int P = tbb::this_task_arena::max_concurrency();
      std::cout << str << " : " << P << std::endl;
    }
  };

  std::cout << "Without reset:" << std::endl;
  f.try_put("default");
  g.wait_for_all();
  a2.execute( [&]() {
    f.try_put("a2");
    g.wait_for_all();
  } );
  a4.execute( [&]() {
    f.try_put("a4");
    g.wait_for_all();
  } );

  std::cout << "With reset:" << std::endl;
  f.try_put("default");
  g.wait_for_all();
  a2.execute( [&]() {
    g.reset();
    f.try_put("a2");
    g.wait_for_all();
  } );
  a4.execute( [&]() {
    g.reset();
    f.try_put("a4");
    g.wait_for_all();
  } );
}
```

Figure 17-19. *Using* graph::reset *to change the task arena used by a graph*

In the first three calls to n.try_put in Figure 17-19, we do not reset that graph g, and we can see that the tasks execute in the default arena with eight slots.

```
Without reset:
default : 8
a2 : 8
a4 : 8
```

But in the second set of calls, we call reset to reinitialize the graph, and the node executes first in the default arena, then in arena a2, and finally in arena a4.

```
With reset:
default : 8
a2 : 2
a4 : 4
```

Setting the Number of Threads, Thread-to-Core Affinities, etc.

Now that we know how to associate task arenas with flow graphs, we can use all of the performance tuning optimizations described in Chapters 11–14 that rely on task arenas. For example, we can use task arenas to isolate one flow graph from another. Or, we can pin threads to cores for a particular task arena using a task_scheduler_observer object and then associate that arena with a flow graph.

Key FG Advice: Dos and Don'ts

The flow graph API is flexible – maybe too flexible. When first working with flow graph, the interface can be daunting since there are so many options. In this section, we provide several dos and don'ts that capture some of our experience when using this high-level interface. However, just like with our rule of thumb for node execution time, these are just suggestions. There are many valid patterns of usage that are not captured here, and we're sure that some of the patterns we say to avoid may have valid use cases. We present these best-known methods, but your mileage may vary.

Do: Use Nested Parallelism

Just like with a pipeline, a flow graph can have great scalability if it uses parallel (flow::unlimited) nodes but can have limited scalability if it has serial nodes. One way to increase scaling is to use nested parallel algorithms inside of TBB flow graph nodes. TBB is all about composability, so we should use nested parallelism when possible.

Don't: Use Multifunction Nodes in Place of Nested Parallelism

As we have seen throughout this book, the TBB parallel algorithms such as `parallel_for` and `parallel_reduce` are highly optimized and include features like Ranges and Partitioners that let us optimize performance even more. We have also seen that the flow graph interface is very expressive – we can express graphs that include loops and use nodes like `multifunction_node` to output many messages from each invocation. We should therefore be on the lookout for cases where we create patterns in our graphs that are better expressed using nested parallelism. One simple example is shown in Figure 17-20.

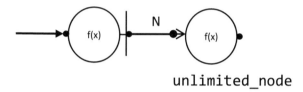

unlimited_node

Figure 17-20. A `multifunction_node` *that sends many messages for each message it receives. This pattern may be better expressed as a nested* `parallel_for` *loop.*

In Figure 17-20, for each message that the `multifunction_node` receives, it generates many output messages that flow into a `function_node` with unlimited concurrency. This graph will act a lot like a parallel loop, with the `multifunction_node` acting as the control loop and the `function_node` as the body. But it will require a lot of stealing to distribute the work like the Master loop from Figures 17-3 and 17-5. While there may be valid uses of this pattern, it is likely more efficient to use a highly optimized parallel loop algorithm instead. This entire graph might be collapsed into a single node that contains a nested `parallel_for`, for example. Of course, whether or not this replacement is possible or desirable depends on the application.

Do: Use `join_node`, `sequencer_node`, or `multifunction_node` to Reestablish Order in a Flow Graph When Needed

Because a flow graph is less structured than a simple pipeline, we may sometimes need to establish an ordering of messages at points in the graph. There are three common approaches for establishing order in a data flow graph: use a key-matching `join_node`, use a `sequencer_node`, or use a `multifunction_node`.

For example, in Chapter 3, the parallelism in our stereoscopic 3D flow graph allowed the left and right images to arrive out of order at the mergeImageBuffersNode. In that example, we ensured that the correct two images were paired together as inputs to the mergeImageBuffersNode by using a tag-matching join_node. A tag-matching join_node is a type of key-matching join_node. By using this join_node type, inputs can arrive in different orders at the two input ports but will still be properly matched based on their tag or key. You can find more information on the different join policies in Appendix B.

Another way to establish order is to use a sequencer_node. A sequencer_node is a buffer that outputs messages in sequence order, using a user-provided body object to obtain the sequence number from the incoming message.

In Figure 17-21, we can see a three-node graph, with nodes first_node, sequencer, and last_node. We use a sequencer_node to reestablish the input order of the messages before the final serial output node last_node. Because function_node first_node is unlimited, its tasks can finish out of order and send their output as they complete. The sequencer_node reestablishes the input order by using the sequence number assigned when each message was originally constructed.

If we execute a similar example without a sequencer node and N=10, the output is scrambled as the messages pass each other on their way to last_node:

```
9 no sequencer
8 no sequencer
7 no sequencer
0 no sequencer
1 no sequencer
2 no sequencer
6 no sequencer
5 no sequencer
4 no sequencer
3 no sequencer
```

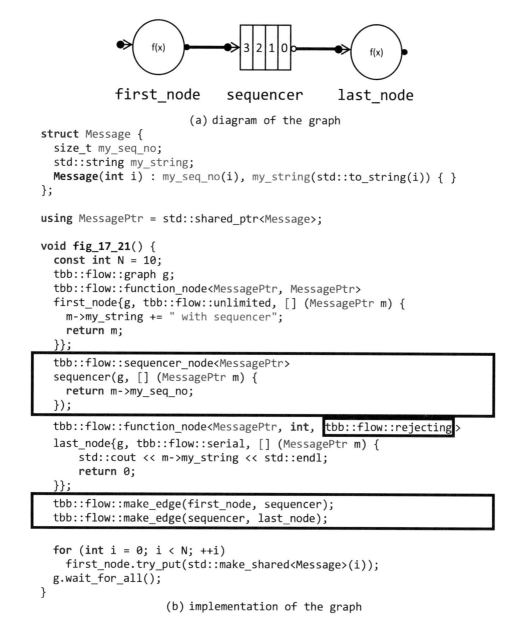

(a) diagram of the graph

```
struct Message {
  size_t my_seq_no;
  std::string my_string;
  Message(int i) : my_seq_no(i), my_string(std::to_string(i)) { }
};

using MessagePtr = std::shared_ptr<Message>;

void fig_17_21() {
  const int N = 10;
  tbb::flow::graph g;
  tbb::flow::function_node<MessagePtr, MessagePtr>
  first_node{g, tbb::flow::unlimited, [] (MessagePtr m) {
    m->my_string += " with sequencer";
    return m;
  }};
  tbb::flow::sequencer_node<MessagePtr>
  sequencer(g, [] (MessagePtr m) {
    return m->my_seq_no;
  });
  tbb::flow::function_node<MessagePtr, int, tbb::flow::rejecting>
  last_node{g, tbb::flow::serial, [] (MessagePtr m) {
      std::cout << m->my_string << std::endl;
      return 0;
  }};
  tbb::flow::make_edge(first_node, sequencer);
  tbb::flow::make_edge(sequencer, last_node);

  for (int i = 0; i < N; ++i)
    first_node.try_put(std::make_shared<Message>(i));
  g.wait_for_all();
}
```

(b) implementation of the graph

Figure 17-21. *A sequencer_node is used to ensure that the messages print in the order dictated by their my_seq_no member variables*

When we execute the code in Figure 17-21, we see the output:

```
0 with sequencer
1 with sequencer
2 with sequencer
3 with sequencer
4 with sequencer
5 with sequencer
6 with sequencer
7 with sequencer
8 with sequencer
9 with sequencer
```

As we can see, a sequencer_node can reestablish the order of the messages, but it does require us to assign the sequence number and also to provide a body to the sequencer_node that can obtain that number from an incoming message.

A final approach to establishing order is to use a serial multifunction_node. A multifunction_node can output zero or more messages on any of its output ports for a given input message. Since it is not forced to output a message for each incoming message, it can buffer incoming messages and hold them until some user-defined ordering constraint is met.

For example, Figure 17-22 shows how we can implement a sequencer_node using a multifunction_node by buffering incoming messages until the next message in sequencer order has arrived. This example assumes that at most N messages are sent to a node sequencer and that the sequence numbers start at 0 and are contiguous up to N-1. Vector v is created with N elements initialized as empty shared_ptr objects. When a message arrives at sequencer, it is assigned to the corresponding element of v. Then starting at the last sent sequence number, each element of v that has a valid message is sent and the sequence number is incremented. For some incoming messages, no output message will be sent; for others, one or more messages may be sent.

```
using MFNSequencer =
  tbb::flow::multifunction_node<MessagePtr,
std::tuple<MessagePtr>>;
using MFNPorts = typename MFNSequencer::output_ports_type;
int seq_i = 0;
std::vector<MessagePtr> v{N, MessagePtr{}};
MFNSequencer sequencer{g, tbb::flow::serial,
[&seq_i, &v](MessagePtr m, MFNPorts &p) {
  v[m->my_seq_no] = m;
  while (seq_i < N && v[seq_i].use_count()) {
    std::get<0>(p).try_put(v[seq_i++]);
  }
}};
```

Figure 17-22. *A* `multifunction_node` *is used to implement a* `sequencer_node`

While Figure 17-22 shows how a `multifunction_node` can be used to reorder messages by sequence order, in general, any user-defined ordering or bundling of messages can be used.

Do: Use the `Isolate` Function for Nested Parallelism

In Chapter 12, we talked about how we may sometimes need to create isolation for performance or correctness reasons when using TBB algorithms. The same is true for flow graphs, and as with the generic algorithms, this can be especially true with nested parallelism. The implementation of the graph in Figure 17-23 shows a simple graph with nodes `source` and `unlimited_node`, and nested parallelism inside node `unlimited_node`. A thread may moonlight (see Chapter 12) while waiting for the nested `parallel_for` loop in node `unlimited_node` to complete, and pick up another instance of node `unlimited_node`. The node `unlimited_node` prints "X started by Y", where X is the node instance number and Y is the thread id.

(a) diagram of the graph

```
void fig_17_23() {
    int P = tbb::task_scheduler_init::default_num_threads();
    tbb::concurrent_vector<std::string> trace;
    double spin_time = 1e-3;
    tbb::flow::graph g;

    int src_cnt = 0;
    tbb::flow::source_node<int> source{g,
        [&src_cnt, P, spin_time](int &i) -> bool {
            if (src_cnt < P) {
                i = src_cnt++;
                spinWaitForAtLeast(spin_time);
                return true;
            }
            return false;
        }, false};
    tbb::flow::function_node<int>
    unlimited_node(g, tbb::flow::unlimited,
        [&trace, P, spin_time](int i) {
            int tid = tbb::this_task_arena::current_thread_index();
            trace.push_back(std::to_string(i) + " started by "
                            + std::to_string(tid));
            tbb::parallel_for(0, P-1, [spin_time](int i) {
                spinWaitForAtLeast((i+1)*spin_time);
            });
            trace.push_back(std::to_string(i) + " completed by "
                            + std::to_string(tid));
    });

    tbb::flow::make_edge(source, unlimited_node);
    source.activate();
    g.wait_for_all();

    for (auto s : trace) std::cout << s << std::endl;
}
```

(b) implementation of the graph

***Figure 17-23.** A graph with nested parallelism*

On our test system with eight logical cores, one output showed that our thread 0 was so bored it pick up not just one, but three different instances of unlimited_node, while waiting for its first parallel_for algorithm to finish as shown in Figure 17-24.

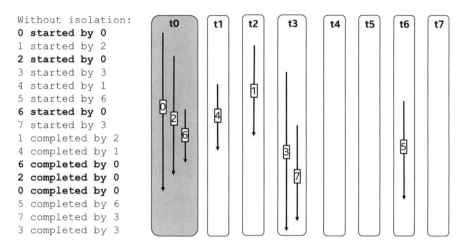

Figure 17-24. *An output from the example in Figure 17-23 is shown on the left, with a diagram showing the overlapped executions on the right. Thread 0 participates in the execution of three different node invocations concurrently.*

As we discussed in Chapter 12, moonlighting is typically benign, which is the case here since we're not computing anything real. But as we highlighted in our previous discussions about isolation, this behavior is not always benign and can lead to correctness issues, or decreased performance, in some cases.

We can address moonlighting in a flow graph just as we did with general tasks in Chapter 12, with the this_task_arena::isolate function or with explicit task arenas. For example, instead of calling the parallel_for directly in the node body, we can invoke it inside of an isolate call:

```
tbb::this_task_arena::isolate([P,spin_time]() {
  tbb::parallel_for(0, P-1, [spin_time](int i) {
    spinWaitForAtLeast((i+1)*spin_time);
  });
});
```

After changing our code to use this function, we see that the threads no longer moonlight and each thread stays focused on a single node until that node is complete as shown in Figure 17-25.

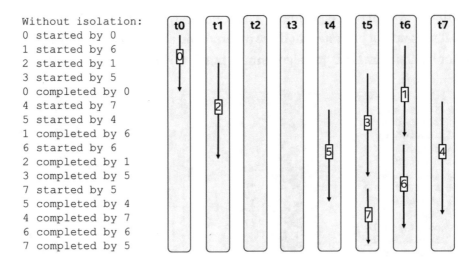

Without isolation:
```
0 started by 0
1 started by 6
2 started by 1
3 started by 5
0 completed by 0
4 started by 7
5 started by 4
1 completed by 6
6 started by 6
2 completed by 1
3 completed by 5
7 started by 5
5 completed by 4
4 completed by 7
6 completed by 6
7 completed by 5
```

Figure 17-25. *None of the nodes execute different node invocations concurrently*

Do: Use Cancellation and Exception Handling in Flow Graphs

In Chapter 15, we discussed task cancellation and exception handling when using TBB tasks in general. Since we are already familiar with this topic, we will only highlight the flow graph related aspects in this section.

Each Flow Graph Uses a Single `task_group_context`

A flow graph instance spawns all of its tasks into a single task arena, and it also uses a single `task_group_context` object for all of these tasks. When we instantiate a graph object, we can pass in an explicit `task_group_context` to the constructor:

```
tbb::task_group_context tgc;
tbb::flow::graph g{tgc};
```

If we don't pass one to the constructor, a default object will be created for us.

Canceling a Flow Graph

If we want to cancel a flow graph, we cancel it using the `task_group_context`, just as we would with the TBB generic algorithms.

```
tgc.cancel_group_excution();
```

And just as with TBB algorithms, the tasks that have already started will complete but no new tasks related to the graph will start. As described in Appendix B, there is also a helper function in the graph class that lets us check the status of a graph directly:

```
if (g.is_cancelled()) {
  std::cout << "My graph was cancelled!" << std::endl;
}
```

If we need to cancel a graph, but do not have a reference to its task_group_context, we can get one from within the task:

```
tbb::task::self().cancel_group_execution();
```

Resetting a Flow Graph After Cancellation

If a graph is canceled, whether directly or due to an exception, we need to reset the graph, g.reset(), before we can use it again. This resets the state of the graph – clearing internal buffers, putting the edges back into their initial states, and so on. See Appendix B for more details.

Exception Handling Examples

To learn about how exceptions work with a flow graph, let's look at the implementation of the graph in Figure 17-26. This figure provides a small, three-node graph that throws an exception in its second node, node2.

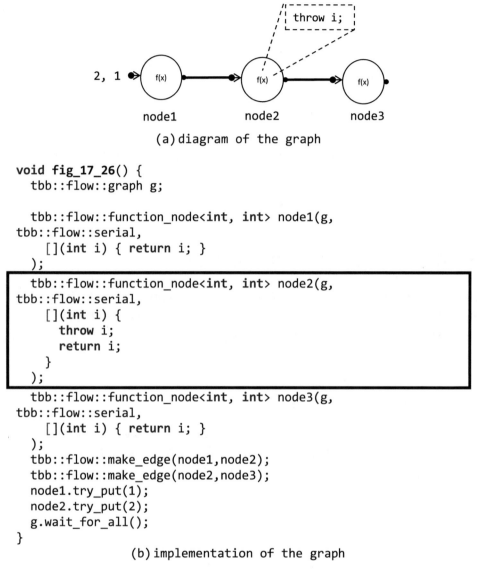

(a) diagram of the graph

```
void fig_17_26() {
  tbb::flow::graph g;

  tbb::flow::function_node<int, int> node1(g,
tbb::flow::serial,
    [](int i) { return i; }
  );
  tbb::flow::function_node<int, int> node2(g,
tbb::flow::serial,
    [](int i) {
      throw i;
      return i;
    }
  );
  tbb::flow::function_node<int, int> node3(g,
tbb::flow::serial,
    [](int i) { return i; }
  );
  tbb::flow::make_edge(node1,node2);
  tbb::flow::make_edge(node2,node3);
  node1.try_put(1);
  node2.try_put(2);
  g.wait_for_all();
}
```

(b) implementation of the graph

Figure 17-26. *A flow graph that throws an exception in one of its nodes*

If we execute this example, we get an exception (hopefully this did not come as a surprise):

`terminate called after throwing an instance of 'int'`

Since we didn't handle the exception, it propagates to the outer scope and our program terminates. We can, of course, modify the implementation of our node node2, so that it catches the exception within its own body, as shown in Figure 17-27.

```
tbb::flow::function_node<int, int> node2(g, tbb::flow::serial,
  [](int i) {
    try {
      throw i;
    } catch (int j) {
      std::cout << "Caught " << j << std::endl;
    }
    return i;
  }
);
```

Figure 17-27. *A flow graph that throws an exception in one of its nodes*

If we make this change, our example will run to completion, printing out the "Caught" messages, in no particular order:

```
Caught 2
Caught 1
```

So far, none of this is very exceptional (pun intended); it's just how exceptions should work.

The unique part of exception handling in a flow graph is that we can catch exceptions at the call to the graph's `wait_for_all` function, as shown in Figure 17-28.

```
try {
  g.wait_for_all();
} catch (int j) {
  std::cout << "Caught " << j << std::endl;
}
```

Figure 17-28. *A flow graph that throws an exception in one of its nodes*

If we re-run our original example from Figure 17-26 but use a try-catch block around the call to `wait_for_all`, we will see only one "Catch" message (either for 1 or 2):

```
Caught 2
```

The exception thrown in node `node2` is not caught in the node's body, so it will propagate to the thread that waits at the call to `wait_for_all`. If a node's body throws an exception, the graph it belongs to is canceled. In this case, we see that there is no second "Caught" message, since `node2` will only execute once.

And of course, if we want to re-execute the graph after we deal with the exception that we catch at the `wait_for_all`, we need to call `g.reset()` since the graph has been canceled.

Do: Set a Priority for a Graph Using `task_group_context`

We can set priorities for all of the tasks spawned by a graph by using the graph's `task_group_context`, for example:

```
if (auto t = g.root_task()) {
  t->group()->set_priority(tbb::priority_high);
}
```

Or we can pass in a `task_group_context` object with a preset priority to the graph's constructor. In either case though, this sets the priorities for all of the tasks related to the graph. We can create one graph with a high priority and another graph with a low priority.

Shortly before the publication of this book, support for relative priorities for functional nodes was added to TBB as a preview feature. Using this feature, we can pass a parameter to a node's constructor to give it a priority relative to other functional nodes. This interface was first provided in TBB 2019 Update 3. Interested readers can learn more details about this new functionality in the online TBB release notes and documentation.

Don't: Make an Edge Between Nodes in Different Graphs

All graph nodes require a reference to a graph object as one of the arguments to their constructor. In general, it is only safe to construct edges between nodes that are part of the same graph. Connecting two nodes in different graphs can make it difficult to reason about graph behaviors, such as what task arenas will be used, if our calls to `wait_for_all` will properly detect graph termination, and so on. To optimize performance, the TBB library takes advantage of its knowledge about edges. If we connect two graphs by an edge, the TBB library will freely reach across this edge for optimization purposes.

We may believe that we have created two distinct graphs, but if there are shared edges, TBB can start mixing their executions together in unexpected ways.

To demonstrate how we can get unexpected behavior, we implemented the class WhereAmIRunningBody shown in Figure 17-29. It prints max_concurrency and priority settings, which we will use to infer what task arena and task_group_context this body's task is using when it executes.

```
struct WhereAmIRunningBody {
  std::string node_name;
  WhereAmIRunningBody(const char *name) : node_name(name) {}

  int operator()(int i) {
    int P = tbb::this_task_arena::max_concurrency();
    std::string priority = "normal";

    if (tbb::task::self().group()->priority() == tbb::priority_high)
      priority = "high";

    std::cout << i << ":" << node_name
              << " executing in arena " << P
              << " with priority " << priority << std::endl;
    spinWaitForAtLeast(0.1);
    return i;
  }
};
```

Figure 17-29. *A body class that lets us infer what task arena and* task_group_ context *are used by a node execution*

Figure 17-30 provides an example that uses the WhereAmIRunningBody to demonstrate an unexpected behavior. In this example, we create two nodes: g2_node and g4_node. The node g2_node is constructed with a reference to g2. The graph g2 is passed a reference to a task_group_context that has priority_normal and g2 is reset() in a task_arena with a concurrency of 2. We should therefore expect g2_node to execute with normal priority in an arena with 2 threads, right? The node g4_node is constructed such that we should expect it to execute with high priority in an arena with four threads.

The first group of calls that include g2_node.try_put(0) and g4_node.try_put(1) match these expectations:

```
0:g2_node executing in arena 2 with priority normal
1:g4_node executing in arena 4 with priority high
```

```cpp
void fig_17_30() {
  tbb::task_arena a2{2};
  tbb::task_group_context tcg2;
  tcg2.set_priority(tbb::priority_normal);
  tbb::flow::graph g2{tcg2};
  a2.execute([&]() {
    g2.reset();
  });

  tbb::task_arena a4{4};
  tbb::task_group_context tcg4;
  tcg4.set_priority(tbb::priority_high);
  tbb::flow::graph g4{tcg4};
  a4.execute([&]() {
    g4.reset();
  });

  tbb::flow::function_node<int, int>
  g2_node{g2, tbb::flow::serial, WhereAmIRunningBody("g2_node")};

  tbb::flow::function_node<int, int>
  g4_node{g4, tbb::flow::serial, WhereAmIRunningBody("g4_node")};
```

```cpp
  g2_node.try_put(0);
  g2.wait_for_all();

  g4_node.try_put(1);
  g4.wait_for_all();
```

```cpp
  tbb::flow::make_edge(g2_node,g4_node);
  g2_node.try_put(2);
  g2.wait_for_all();
  g4.wait_for_all();
```

```cpp
}
```

Figure 17-30. *An example that has unexpected behavior because of cross-graph communication*

But, when we make an edge from g2_node to g4_node, we make a connection between nodes that exist in two different graphs. Our second set of calls that include g2_node.try_put(2) again cause the body of g2_node to execute with normal priority in arena a2. But TBB, trying to reduce scheduling overheads, uses scheduler bypass (see Scheduler Bypass in Chapter 10) when it invokes g4_node due to the edge from g2_node to g4_node. The result is that g4_node executes in the same thread as g2_node, but this thread belongs to arena a2 not a4. It still uses the correct task_group_context when the task is constructed, but it winds up being scheduled in an unexpected arena.

```
2:g2_node executing in arena 2 with priority normal
2:g4_node executing in arena 2 with priority high
```

From this simple example, we can see that this edge breaks the separation between the graphs. If we were using arenas a2 and a4 to control the number of threads, for work isolation or for thread affinity purposes, this edge will undo our efforts. We ***should not*** make edges between graphs.

Do: Use `try_put` to Communicate Across Graphs

In the previous "Don't," we decided that we should not make edges between graphs. But what if we really need to communicate across graphs? The least dangerous option is to explicitly call try_put to send a message from a node in one graph to a node in another graph. We don't introduce an edge, so the TBB library won't do anything sneaky to optimize the communication between the two nodes. Even in this case though, we still need to be careful as our example in Figure 17-31 demonstrates.

Here, we create a graph g2 that sends a message to graph g1 and then waits for both graph g1 and g2. But, the waiting is done in the wrong order!

Since node g2_node2 sends a message to g1_node1, the call to g1.wait_for_all() will likely return immediately since nothing is going on in g1 at the time of the call. We then call g2.wait_for_all(), which returns after g2_node2 is done. After this call returns, g2 is finished but g1 has just received a message from g2_node2 and its node g1_node1 has just started to execute!

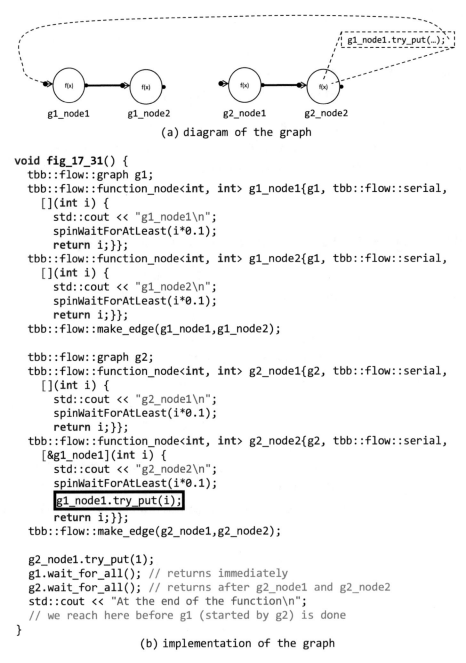

(a) diagram of the graph

```
void fig_17_31() {
  tbb::flow::graph g1;
  tbb::flow::function_node<int, int> g1_node1{g1, tbb::flow::serial,
    [](int i) {
      std::cout << "g1_node1\n";
      spinWaitForAtLeast(i*0.1);
      return i;}};
  tbb::flow::function_node<int, int> g1_node2{g1, tbb::flow::serial,
    [](int i) {
      std::cout << "g1_node2\n";
      spinWaitForAtLeast(i*0.1);
      return i;}};
  tbb::flow::make_edge(g1_node1,g1_node2);

  tbb::flow::graph g2;
  tbb::flow::function_node<int, int> g2_node1{g2, tbb::flow::serial,
    [](int i) {
      std::cout << "g2_node1\n";
      spinWaitForAtLeast(i*0.1);
      return i;}};
  tbb::flow::function_node<int, int> g2_node2{g2, tbb::flow::serial,
    [&g1_node1](int i) {
      std::cout << "g2_node2\n";
      spinWaitForAtLeast(i*0.1);
      g1_node1.try_put(i);
      return i;}};
  tbb::flow::make_edge(g2_node1,g2_node2);

  g2_node1.try_put(1);
  g1.wait_for_all(); // returns immediately
  g2.wait_for_all(); // returns after g2_node1 and g2_node2
  std::cout << "At the end of the function\n";
  // we reach here before g1 (started by g2) is done
}
```

(b) implementation of the graph

Figure 17-31. *A flow graph that sends a message to another flow graph*

Luckily, if we call the waits in the reverse order, things will work as expected:

```
g2.wait_for_all();
g1.wait_for_all();
```

But still, we can see that using explicit try_puts is not without dangers. We need to be very careful when graphs communicate with each other!

Do: Use `composite_node` to Encapsulate Groups of Nodes

In the previous two sections, we warned that communication between graphs can lead to errors. Often developers use more than one graph because they want to logically separate some nodes from others. Encapsulating a group of nodes is convenient if there is a common pattern that needs to be created many times or if there is too much detail in one large flat graph.

In both of these cases, we can use a tbb::flow::composite_node. A composite_node is used to encapsulate a collection of other nodes so they can be used like a first-class graph node. Its interface follows:

```
template< typename... InputTypes, typename... OutputTypes>
class composite_node <tbb::flow::tuple<InputTypes...>,
                      tbb::flow::tuple<OutputTypes...> > {
public:
  /* implementation defined */ input_ports_type;
  /* implementation defined */ output_ports_type;

  composite_node( graph &g );
  virtual ~composite_node();

  void set_external_ports(input_ports_type&& input_ports_tuple,
                          output_ports_type&& output_ports_tuple);
  input_ports_type& input_ports();
  output_ports_type& output_ports();
};
```

Unlike the other node types that we have discussed in this chapter and in Chapter 3, we need to create a new class that inherits from tbb::flow::composite_node to make use of its functionality. For example, let's consider the flow graph in Figure 17-32(a). This graph combines two inputs from source1 and source2, and uses a token passing scheme to limit memory consumption.

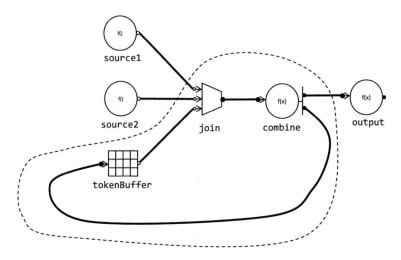

(a) a graph with unneeded detail at the top level

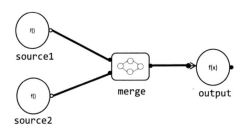

(b) a simplified graph using a `composite_node`

Figure 17-32. *An example that benefits from a* `composite_node`

If this token passing pattern is commonly used in our application, or by members of our development team, it might make sense to encapsulate it into its own node type, as shown in Figure 17-32(b). It also cleans up the high-level view of our application by hiding the details.

Figure 17-33 shows what a flow graph implementation looks like if we have a node that implements the dotted parts of Figure 17-32(a), replacing it with a single merge node. In Figure 17-33, we use the merge node object like any other flow graph node, making edges to its input and output ports. Figure 17-34 shows how we use `tbb::flow::composite_node` to implement our MergeNode class.

```
void fig_17_33() {
  tbb::flow::graph g;

  int src1_count = 0;
  tbb::flow::source_node<BigObjectPtr> source1{g,
  [&] (BigObjectPtr &m) -> bool {
    if (src1_count < A_LARGE_NUMBER) {
      m = std::make_shared<BigObject>(src1_count++);
      return true;
    }
    return false;
  }, false};

  int src2_count = 0;
  tbb::flow::source_node<BigObjectPtr> source2{g,
  [&] (BigObjectPtr &m) -> bool {
    if (src2_count < A_LARGE_NUMBER) {
      m = std::make_shared<BigObject>(src2_count++);
      return true;
    }
    return false;
  }, false};
```

```
  MergeNode merge{g};
```

```
  tbb::flow::function_node<BigObjectPtr> output{g,
    tbb::flow::serial,
    [] (BigObjectPtr b) {
      std::cout << "Received id == " << b->getId()
                << " in final node" << std::endl;
    }
  };
```

```
  tbb::flow::make_edge(source1, tbb::flow::input_port<0>(merge));
  tbb::flow::make_edge(source2, tbb::flow::input_port<1>(merge));
  tbb::flow::make_edge(merge, output);
```

```
  bigObjectCount = 0;
  maxCount = 0;
  source1.activate();
  source2.activate();
  g.wait_for_all();
  std::cout << "maxCount == " << maxCount << std::endl;
}
```

Figure 17-33. *Creating a flow graph that uses a class* MergeNode *that inherits from* tbb::flow::composite_node

```cpp
using BigObjectPtr = std::shared_ptr<BigObject>;
using CompositeType =
  tbb::flow::composite_node<std::tuple<BigObjectPtr, BigObjectPtr>,
                            std::tuple<BigObjectPtr>>;
using MFNode =
  tbb::flow::multifunction_node<std::tuple<BigObjectPtr,
                                           BigObjectPtr, token_t>,
                                std::tuple<BigObjectPtr, token_t>>;


class MergeNode : public CompositeType {
  tbb::flow::buffer_node<token_t> tokenBuffer;
  tbb::flow::join_node<std::tuple<BigObjectPtr, BigObjectPtr, token_t>,
                       tbb::flow::reserving> join;
  MFNode combine;

public:
  MergeNode(tbb::flow::graph &g) :
    CompositeType{g},
      tokenBuffer{g},
      join{g},
      combine{g, tbb::flow::unlimited,
        [] (const MFNode::input_type &in, MFNode::output_ports_type &p) {
          BigObjectPtr b0 = std::get<0>(in);
          BigObjectPtr b1 = std::get<1>(in);
          token_t t = std::get<2>(in);
          spinWaitForAtLeast(0.0001);
          b0->mergeIds(b0->getId(), b1->getId());
          std::get<0>(p).try_put(b0);
          std::get<1>(p).try_put(t);
        }}
    {
      tbb::flow::make_edge(tokenBuffer, tbb::flow::input_port<2>(join));
      tbb::flow::make_edge(join, combine);
      tbb::flow::make_edge(tbb::flow::output_port<1>(combine),
                           tokenBuffer);

      CompositeType::set_external_ports(
        CompositeType::input_ports_type(
          tbb::flow::input_port<0>(join),
          tbb::flow::input_port<1>(join)),
        CompositeType::output_ports_type(
          tbb::flow::output_port<0>(combine))
      );

      for (token_t i = 0; i < 3; ++i) tokenBuffer.try_put(i);
    }
};
```

Figure 17-34. *The implementation of MergeNode*

In Figure 17-34, `MergeNode` inherits from `CompositeType`, which is an alias for

```
tbb::flow::composite_node<std::tuple<BigObjectPtr, BigObjectPtr>,
                          std::tuple<BigObjectPtr>>;
```

The two template arguments indicate that a `MergeNode` will have two input ports, both that receive `BigObjectPtr` messages, and a single output port that sends `BigObjectPtr` messages. The class `MergeNode` has a member variable for each node it encapsulates: a `tokenBuffer`, a `join`, and a `combine` node. And these member variables are initialized in the member initializer list of the `MergeNode` constructor. In the constructor body, calls to `tbb::flow::make_edge` set up all of the internal edges. A call to `set_external_ports` is used to assign the ports from the member nodes to the external ports of the `MergeNode`. In this case, the first two input ports of `join` become the inputs of the `MergeNode` and the output of `combine` becomes the output the `MergeNode`. Finally, because the node is implementing a token passing scheme, the `tokenBuffer` is filled with tokens.

While creating a new type that inherits from `tbb::flow::composite_node` may appear daunting at first, using this interface can lead to more readable and reusable code, especially as your flow graphs become larger and more complicated.

Introducing Intel Advisor: Flow Graph Analyzer

The Flow Graph Analyzer (FGA) tool is available in Intel Parallel Studio XE 2019 and later. It is provided as a feature of the Intel Advisor tool. Instructions for getting the tool can be found at `https://software.intel.com/en-us/articles/intel-advisor-xe-release-notes`.

FGA was developed to support the design, debugging, visualization, and analysis of graphs built using the TBB flow graph API. That said, many of the capabilities of FGA are generically useful for analyzing computational graphs, regardless of their origin. Currently, the tool has limited support for other parallel programming models including the OpenMP API.

For our purposes in this book, we will focus only on how the design and analysis workflows in the tool apply to TBB. We also use FGA to analyze some of the samples in this chapter. However, all of the optimizations presented in this chapter can be done with or without FGA. So, if you have no interest in using FGA, you can skip this section. But again, we believe there is significant value in this tool, so skipping it would be a mistake.

The FGA Design Workflow

The design workflow in FGA lets us graphically design TBB flow graphs, validate that they are correct, estimate their scalability, and, after we are satisfied with our design, generate a C++ implementation that uses the TBB flow graph classes and functions. FGA is not a full Integrated Development Environment (IDE) like Microsoft Visual Studio, Eclipse or Xcode. Instead, it gets us started with our flow graph design, but then we need to step outside of the tool to complete the development. However, if we use the design workflow in a constrained way, as we will describe later, iterative development in the designer is possible.

Figure 17-35 shows the FGA GUI used during the design workflow. We will only briefly describe the components of the tool here as we describe the typical workflow; the Flow Graph Analyzer documentation provides a more complete description.

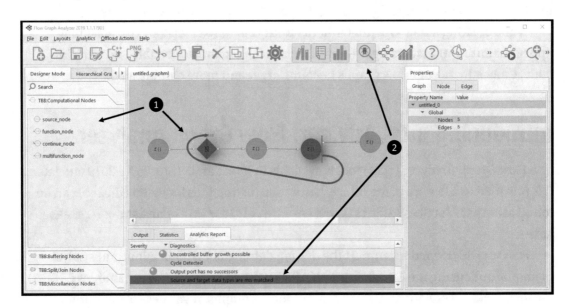

Figure 17-35.   *Using the FGA design workflow*

The typical design workflow starts with a blank canvas and project. As highlighted by the black circle numbered 1 in Figure 17-35, we select nodes in the node palette and place them on the canvas, connecting them together by drawing edges between their ports. The node palette contains all of the node types available in the TBB flow graph interface and provides tooltips that remind us about the functionality of each type. For each node on the canvas, we can modify its type-specific properties; for a `function_node` for example, we can provide the C++ code for the body, set a concurrency limit, and so on. We can also provide an estimated "weight" that represents the computational complexity of the node so that later we can run a Scalability Analysis to see if our graph will perform well.

Once we have drawn our graph on the canvas, we run a Rule Check that analyzes the graph looking for common mistakes and anti-patterns. The Rule Check results, highlighted by the black circle numbered 2 in Figure 17-35, show issues such as unnecessary buffering, type mismatches, suspicious cycles in the graph, and so on. In Figure 17-35, the Rule Check has discovered that there is a type mismatch between the input of our limiter_node and the output of our multifunction_node. In response, we can then, for example, modify the port output type of our multifunction_node to fix this issue.

When we have fixed all correctness issues uncovered by the Rule Check, we can then run a Scalability Analysis. The Scalability Analysis constructs a TBB flow graph in memory, replacing the computational node bodies with dummy bodies that actively spin for a time proportional to their "weight" property. FGA runs this model of our graph on various numbers of threads and provides a table of the speedups, for example:

Graph Name ▼	Graph	Threads	Time(s)	Speedup
▼ simple_g0	Results(4)			
	Scalability projection	1	4.00006	1
	Scalability projection	2	2.00003	2
	Scalability projection	3	2.00004	1.99999
	Scalability projection	4	1.01446	3.94305

Using these features, we can iteratively refine our graph design. Along the way, we can save our graph design in GraphML format (a common standard for representing graphs). When we are satisfied with our design we can generate C++ code that uses the TBB flow graph interface to express our design. This code generator is more accurately viewed as a code wizard than an IDE since it does not directly support an iterative code development model. If we change the generated code, there is no way to reimport our changes into the tool.

Tips for Iterative Development with FGA

If we want to create a design that we can continue to tune from within FGA, we can use a constrained approach, where we specify node bodies that redirect to implementations that are maintained outside of FGA. This is necessary because there is no way to reimport modified C++ code back into FGA.

For example, if we want to make iterative development easier, we should not specify a function_node that exposes its implementation directly in the body code:

```
tbb::flow::function_node<int, std::string>
comp2str(g, tbb::flow::unlimited,
  [](int i) -> std::string {
    // we specified a complete implementation
    // using the node's body property in FGA
    int output_value = i*i;
    return std::to_string(output_value);
  }
);
```

Instead, we should specify only the interface and redirect to an implementation that can be maintained separately:

```
tbb::flow::function_node<int, std::string>
comp2str(g, tbb::flow::unlimited,
  [](int i) -> std::string {
    // we specified a redirected implementation
    // using the node's body property in FGA
    return comp2str_impl(i);
  }
);
```

If we take this constrained approach, we can often maintain the graph design in FGA and its GraphML representation, iteratively tuning the topology and node properties without losing any node body implementation changes we make outside of the tool. Whenever we generate new C++ code from FGA, we simply include the most up-to-date implementation header and the node bodies use these implementations that are maintained outside of the tool.

Flow Graph Analyzer does not require us to use this approach of course, but it is good practice if we want to use the code generation features of FGA as more than a simple code wizard.

The FGA Analysis Workflow

The analysis workflow in FGA is independent of the design workflow. While we can surely analyze a flow graph that was designed in FGA, we can just as easily analyze a TBB flow graph that is designed and implemented outside of the tool. This is possible because the TBB library is instrumented to provide runtime events to the FGA trace collector. A trace collected from a TBB application lets FGA reconstruct the graph structure and the timeline of the node body executions – it does ***not*** depend on the GraphML files developed during the design workflow.

If we want to use FGA to analyze a TBB application that uses a flow graph, the first step is to collect an FGA trace. By default, TBB does not generate traces, so we need to activate trace collection. The FGA instrumentation in TBB was a preview feature prior to TBB 2019. We need to take extra steps if we are using an older version of TBB. We refer readers to the FGA documentation for instructions on how to collect traces for the version of TBB and FGA that they are using.

Once we have a trace of our application, the analysis workflow in FGA uses the activities highlighted by the numbered circles in Figure 17-36: (1) inspect the tree-map view for an overview of the graph performance and use this as an index into the graph topology display, (2) run the critical path algorithm to determine the critical paths through the computation, and (3) examine the timeline and concurrency data for insight into performance over time. Analysis is most commonly an interactive process that moves between these different activities as the performance of the application is explored.

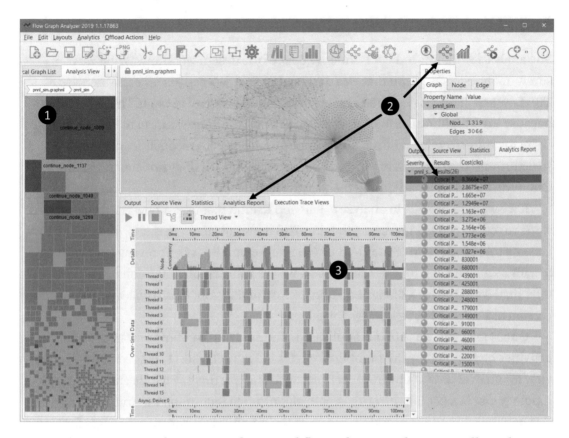

Figure 17-36. *Using the FGA analysis workflow. These results were collected on a system with 16 cores.*

The tree-map view labeled as (1) in Figure 17-36 provides an overview of the overall health of a graph. In the tree map, the area of each rectangle represents the total aggregated CPU time of the node and the color of each square indicates the concurrency observed during the execution of the node. The concurrency information is categorized as poor (red), ok (orange), good (green), and oversubscribed (blue).

Nodes with a large area that are marked as "poor" are hotspots and have an average concurrency between 0% and 25% of the hardware concurrency. These are therefore good candidates for optimization. The tree-map view also serves as an index into a large graph; clicking on a square will highlight the node in the graph and selecting this highlighted node will in turn mark tasks from all instances of this node in the timeline trace view.

The graph topology canvas is synchronized with other views in the tool. Selecting a node in the tree-map view, the timeline, or in a data analytics report will highlight the node in the canvas. This lets users quickly relate performance data to the graph structure.

One of the most important analytic reports provided by FGA is the list of critical paths in a graph. This feature is particularly useful when one has to analyze a large and complex graph. Computing the critical paths results in a list of nodes that form the critical paths as shown in the region labeled (2) in Figure 17-36. As we discussed in Chapter 3, an upper bound on speedup of dependency graphs can be quickly computed by dividing the aggregate total time spent by all nodes in a graph by the time spent on the longest critical path, T_1/T_∞. This upper bound can be used to set expectations on the potential speedup for an application expressed as a graph.

The timeline and concurrency view labeled as (3) in Figure 17-36 displays the raw traces in swim lanes mapped to software threads. Using this trace information, FGA computes additional derived data such as the average concurrency of each node and the concurrency histogram over time for the graph execution. Above the per-thread swim lanes, a histogram shows how many nodes are active at that point in time. This view lets users quickly identify time regions with low concurrency. Clicking on nodes in the timelines during these regions of low concurrency lets developers find the structures in their graph that lead to these bottlenecks.

Diagnosing Performance Issues with FGA

In this chapter, we discussed a number of potential performance issues that can arise when using a flow graph. In this section, we briefly discuss how FGA can be used to explore these issues in a TBB-based application.

Diagnosing Granularity Issues with FGA

Just like with our TBB generic loop algorithms, we need to be concerned about tasks that are too small to profit from parallelization. But we need to balance this concern with the need to create enough tasks to allow our workload to scale. In particular, as we discussed in Chapter 3, scalability can be limited by serial nodes if they become a bottleneck in the computation.

In an example timeline from FGA shown in Figure 17-37, we can see that there is a dark serial task, named m, which causes regions of low concurrency. The color indicates that this task is about 1 millisecond in length – this is above the threshold for efficient scheduling but, from the timeline, it appears to be a serializing bottleneck. If possible, we should break this task up into tasks that can be scheduled in parallel – either by breaking it into multiple independent nodes or through nested parallelism.

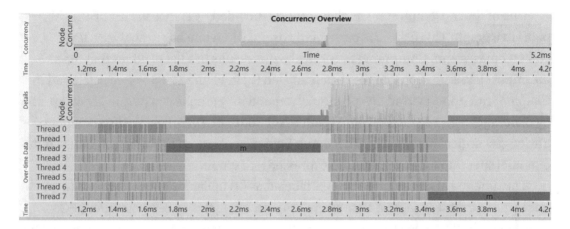

Figure 17-37. *The FGA timeline colors tasks according to their execution times. Lighter tasks are smaller.*

In contrast, there are regions in Figure 17-37 where smaller tasks, named n, are executed in parallel. By their coloring, it appears these are close to the 1 microsecond threshold, and consequently we can see gaps in the timelines during this region, indicating that there may be some non-negligible scheduling overheads involved. In this case, it may benefit us to merge nodes or to use a lightweight policy if possible to decrease overheads.

Recognizing Slow Copies in FGA

Figure 17-38 shows how we might recognize slow copies in FGA. In the figure, we see 100 millisecond segments from the timelines of runs of graphs similar to Figure 17-12, but that pass BigObject messages directly (Figure 17-38(a)) and shared_ptr<BigObject> messages (Figure 17-38(b)). To make the construction appear expensive, we inserted a spin-wait in the BigObject constructor so that it takes 10 milliseconds to construct each object – making the construction time of a BigObject and our function_node body's execution times equal. In Figure 17-38(a), we can see the time it takes to copy the message between nodes appears as gaps in the timeline. In Figure 17-38(b), where we pass by pointer, the message passing time is negligible, so no gaps are seen.

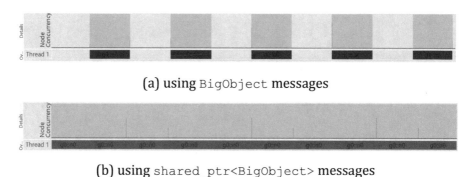

(a) using `BigObject` messages

(b) using `shared_ptr<BigObject>` messages

Figure 17-38. *In FGA, the long copies appear as gaps between the node body executions. Each timeline segment shown is approximately 100 milliseconds long.*

When using FGA to analyze our flow graph applications, gaps in the timeline indicate inefficiencies that need to be further investigated. In this section, they indicated costly copies between nodes and in the previous section they indicated that the overhead of scheduling was large compared to the task sizes. In both cases, these gaps should prompt us to look for ways to improve performance.

Diagnosing Moonlighting using FGA

Earlier in this chapter, we discussed the execution of the moonlighting graph in Figure 17-23 that generated the output in Figure 17-24. FGA provides a Stacked View in its execution timeline that lets us easily detect moonlighting as shown in Figure 17-39.

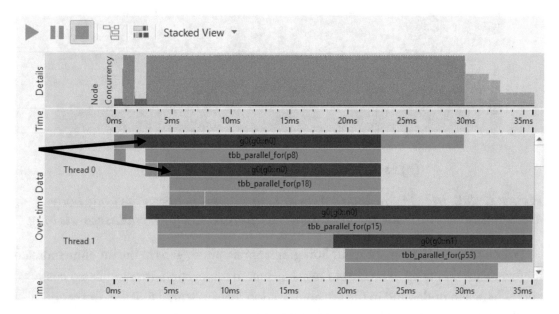

Figure 17-39. *FGA timelines grouped by Node/Region. We can see that thread 0 is moonlighting since it shown as concurrently executing more than one parallel region.*

In a Stacked View, we see all of the nested tasks that a thread is executing, including those that come from flow graph nodes and those that come from TBB Generic Parallel Algorithms. If we see that a thread executes two nodes concurrently, it is moonlighting. In Figure 17-39, for example, we see that Thread 0 starts executing another instance of node n0 inside of an existing instance of n0. In our previous discussions about moonlighting, we know this can happen if a thread steals work while it is waiting for a nested parallel algorithm to complete. The Stacked View in Figure 17-39, lets us easily see that a nested `parallel_for`, labeled p8, is the culprit in this case.

Using the timeline views from FGA, we can identify when threads are moonlighting simply by noticing a thread's overlapped participation in more than one region or node. As developers, and possibly through other interactions with FGA, we then need to determine if the moonlighting is benign or needs to be addressed by TBB's isolation features.

Summary

The flow graph API is a flexible and powerful interface for creating dependency and data flow graphs. In this chapter, we discussed some of the more advanced considerations in using the TBB flow graph high-level execution interface. Because it is implemented on top of TBB tasks, it shares the composability and optimization features supported by TBB tasks. We discussed how these can be used to optimize for granularity, effective cache, and memory use and create sufficient parallelism. We then listed some dos and don'ts that can be helpful when first exploring the flow graph interfaces. Finally, we provided a brief overview of the Flow Graph Analyzer (FGA), a tool available in Intel Parallel Studio XE that has support for the graphical design and analysis of TBB flow graphs.

For More Information

Michael Voss, "The Intel Threading Building Blocks Flow Graph," Dr. Dobb's, October 5, 2011. `www.drdobbs.com/tools/the-intel-threading-building-blocks-flow/231900177`.

Vasanth Tovinkere, Pablo Reble, Farshad Akhbari and Palanivel Guruvareddiar, "Driving Code Performance with Intel Advisor's Flow Graph Analyzer," Parallel Universe Magazine, `https://software.seek.intel.com/driving-code-performance`.

Richard Friedman, "Intel Advisor's TBB Flow Graph Analyzer: Making Complex Layers of Parallelism More Manageable," Inside HPC, December 14, 2017, `https://insidehpc.com/2017/12/intel-flow-graph-analyzer/`.

CHAPTER 18

Beef Up Flow Graphs with Async Nodes

Back in 2005, Herb Sutter wrote "The free lunch is over"[1] paper to warn us about the dawn of the multicore era and its implications on software development. In the multicore era, developers who care about performance can no longer sit back and lazily wait for the next processor generation in order to gleefully see their apps running faster. Those days are long gone. Herb's message was that developers who care about fully exploiting modern processors would have to embrace parallelism. At this point of the book, we certainly know this, so what? Well, we believe that today "Lunch is getting much too expensive." Let's elaborate on this.

In more recent years, strongly spurred by energy constraints, more complex processors have emerged. Nowadays, it is not difficult to find heterogeneous systems comprising one or more GPU, FPGA, or DSP alongside one or more multicore CPUs. Much in the same way that we embraced parallelism to get the most of all CPU cores, now it may also make sense to offload part of the computations to these accelerators. But hey, this is tough! Yep, it is! If sequential programming was once the "free lunch," heterogeneous parallel programming today is more like a feast at a three-star Michelin restaurant – we have to pay, but it is oh so good!

And does TBB help in saving some of the dinner price? Of course! How do you dare doubt it? In this and the next chapter of our book, we walk through the features recently incorporated to the TBB library in order to help make lunch affordable again –we show how to offload computation to asynchronous devices thereby embracing heterogeneous computing. In this chapter, we will pick up the TBB Flow Graph interface and reinforce it with a new type of node: the async_node. In the next chapter, we will go even further and put Flow Graph on OpenCL steroids.

---

[1]"The Free Lunch Is Over: A Fundamental Turn Toward Concurrency in Software," Herb Sutter. www.gotw.ca/publications/concurrency-ddj.htm.

© Intel Corporation 2019

M. Voss, R. Asenjo, J. Reinders, *Pro TBB*, https://doi.org/10.1007/978-1-4842-4398-5_18

Async World Example

Let's start with the simplest example that uses an async_node. We will illustrate why this particular flow graph node is useful, and we will also present a more complex example that will be useful for the next chapter.

Since there is nothing simpler than a "Hello World" code snippet, we propose an "Async World" alternative based on the flow graph API that includes an async_node in the graph. If you have questions about flow graphs in TBB, you may wish to read through Chapter 3 for a solid background and use the "Flow Graph" section in Appendix B as a reference for the APIs. The flow graph that we build in this first example is depicted in Figure 18-1.

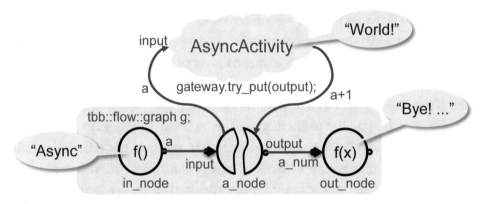

Figure 18-1. *Flow graph for the "Async world" example*

Our goal is to send a message from a source_node, in_node, to an asynchronous node, a_node, but instead of processing the message inside a_node, this task is offloaded to an asynchronous activity that is running somewhere (a different MPI node, an OpenCL capable GPU, an FPGA, you name it). As soon as this asynchronous task finishes, the flow graph engine has to get the control back, read the output of the async activity, and propagate the message to the descendent nodes in the graph. In our very simple "Async World" example, in_node just prints "Async" and passes a=10 to a_node. The a_node receives a=10 as the input and forwards it to an AsyncActivity. In this example, AsyncActivity is a class that just increments the input message and prints "World!". These two actions are carried out in a new thread that simulates here an asynchronous operation or device. Only when the AsyncActivity deigns to respond with output=11, out_node will receive this value and the program finishes.

The code presented in Figure 18-2 includes the `async_world()` function definition where we build the graph g composed of the three nodes of Figure 18-1.

```cpp
void async_world() {
  tbb::flow::graph g;
  bool n = false;

  //Source node:
  tbb::flow::source_node<int> in_node{g,
    [&](int& a) {
      if (n) return false;
      std::cout << "Async ";
      a = 10;
      n = true;
      return true;
    },
    false
  };

  //Async node:
  AsyncActivity asyncAct;
  using activity_node_t = tbb::flow::async_node<int, int>;
  using gateway_t = activity_node_t::gateway_type;
  activity_node_t a_node{g, tbb::flow::unlimited,
    [&asyncAct](int const& input, gateway_t& gateway) {
      asyncAct.run(input, gateway);
    }
  };

  //Output node:
  tbb::flow::function_node<int> out_node{
    g, tbb::flow::unlimited,
    [](int const& a_num){
      std::cout << "Bye! Received: "<< a_num<< '\n';
    }
  };

  //Edges:
  make_edge(in_node, a_node);
  make_edge(a_node, out_node);

  //Run!
  in_node.activate();
  g.wait_for_all();
}
```

Figure 18-2. *Building the flow graph for the "Async World" example*

The source_node interface is described in the first entry of the table in Figure B-37 of Appendix B. In our example, we create the in_node of the source_node type. The argument of the lambda, int& a, is actually the output message that will be sent to its successor node in the graph (the async_node). When the source node is activated near the end of the async_world() function, by using in_node.activate(), the lambda will be executed just once because it returns "true" just for the first invocation (initially n=false, n is set to true inside the lambda, which only returns true if n=true). In this single invocation, a message with a=10 is sent to the next node in the graph. The last argument of the in_node is false so that the source node is created in hibernation mode and only wakes up after the in_node.activate() is called (otherwise the node start sending messages immediately after the output edge is connected).

Next comes the async_node definition. The syntax required for the async_node interface is

```
template<typename InType, typename OutType>
async_node(graph& g, size_t concurrency, Body body);
```

In our example, a_node is constructed here:

```
using activity_node_t = tbb::flow::async_node<int, int>;
using gateway_t = activity_node_t::gateway_type;
activity_node_t a_node{g, unlimited, []… /*lambda*/ };
```

which creates an async_node<int, int> in the graph g with unlimited concurrency. By using unlimited, we instruct the library to spawn a task as soon as a message arrives, regardless of how many other tasks have been spawned. Should we want only up to 4 concurrent invocations of a_node, we can change unlimited to 4. The template parameter <int, int> points out that a message of type int enters a_node and a message of type int leaves a_node. The lambda used in a_node constructor is the following:

```
[&asyncAct](int const& input, gateway_t& gateway) {
  asyncAct.run(input, gateway);
}
```

that captures by reference an AsyncActivity object, asyncAct, and declares the functor that has to be run for each message reaching a_node. This functor has two arguments, input and gateway, passed by reference. But wait, didn´t we say that the template parameter <int, int> means that the node expects an incoming integer and emits an outgoing integer? Shouldn't the functor's prototype be (const int& input) -> int? Well, it would have been that way for a regular function_node, but we are dealing now with an async_node and its particularities. Here, we get const int& input as expected, but also a second input argument, gateway_t& gateway, that serves as an interface to inject the output of the AsyncActivity back into the graph. We will come to this trick when explaining the AsyncActivity class. For the moment, to finish the description of this node let's just say that it basically dispatches the AsyncActivity with asyncAct. run(input, gateway).

The output node, out_node, is a function_node that in this example has been configured as an end node that does not send any output message:

```
tbb::flow::function_node<int> out_node{g, tbb::flow::unlimited,
  [](int const& a_num){
    std::cout << "Bye! Received: "<< a_num<< '\n';
  }
};
```

This node receives the integer that comes from the AsyncActivity through the gateway and finishes off just printing "Bye!" followed by the value of such integer.

In the last lines of our Async World example in Figure 18-2, we find two make_edge calls to create the connections depicted in Figure 18-1, and finally the graph is awakened with in_node.activate() to immediately wait until all messages have been processed with g.wait_for_all().

Here comes the AsyncActivity class, which implements the asynchronous computations in our example as can be seen in Figure 18-3.

```
class AsyncActivity {
public:
  ~AsyncActivity() {
    asyncThread.join();
  }

  using node_t = tbb::flow::async_node<int, int>;
  using gateway_t = node_t::gateway_type;

  void run(int input, gateway_t& gateway) {
    gateway.reserve_wait();
    asyncThread = std::thread{
      [&,input]() {
        std::cout << "World! Input: " << input << '\n';
        int output = input + 1;
        gateway.try_put(output);
        gateway.release_wait();
      }
    };
  }
private:
  std::thread asyncThread;
};
```

Figure 18-3. *Implementation of the asynchronous activity*

The public member function "run" (that was invoked in a_node's functor with
asyncAct.run) first does gateway.reserve_wait(), which notifies the flow graph
that work has been submitted to an external activity so this can be taken into account
by g.wait_for_all() at the end of async_world(). Then, an asynchronous thread is
spawned to execute a lambda, which captures the gateway by reference and the input
integer by value. It is key to pass input by value because otherwise the referenced
variable, a in the source_node, can be destroyed before the thread reads its value (if the
source_node finishes before the asyncThread can read the value of a).

The lambda in the thread constructor first prints the "World" message and then
assigns output=11 (input+1, more precisely). This output is communicated back into
the flow graph by calling the member function gateway.try_put(output). Finally, with
gateway.release_wait(), we inform the flow graph that, as far as the AsyncActivity is
concerned, there is no need to wait any longer for it.

Note   There is no requirement to call member function `reserve_wait()` for each input message submitted to an external activity. The only requirement is that each call to `reserve_wait()` must have a corresponding call to `release_wait()`. Note that `wait_for_all()` will not exit while there are some `reserve_wait()` calls without matching `release_wait()`'s.

The output of the resulting code is

```
Async World! Input: 10
Bye! Received: 11
```

where "Async" is written by in_node, "World! Input: 10" by the asynchronous task and the last line by out_node.

Why and When `async_node`?

Now, there may be readers displaying a conceited smirk and thinking sort of "I don't need an async_node to implement this." Why don't we just rely on the good ol' function_node?

For example, a_node could have been implemented as in Figure 18-4, where we use a function_node that receives an integer, input, and returns another integer, output. The corresponding lambda expression spawns a thread, asyncThread, that prints and generates the output value, and then waits for the thread to finish with the asyncThread. join() to gleefully return output.

```
tbb::flow::function_node<int, int> a_node{g,
  tbb::flow::unlimited,
  [&](const int& input) -> int {
    int output;
    std::thread asyncThread{[&,input]{
      std::cout << "World! Input: "<< input << '\n';
      output = input + 1;
    }};
    asyncThread.join(); // a worker thread blocks here!
    return output;
  }};
```

DANGER DANGER DANGER

Figure 18-4. *A simplest implementation that creates and waits for an asynchronous thread. Did someone say DANGER?*

If you were not one of the smirking readers before, what about now? Because, what is wrong with this much simpler implementation? Why not rely on the same approach to also offload computations to a GPU or an FPGA, and wait for the accelerator to finish its duty?

To answer these questions, we have to bring back one of the fundamental TBB design criteria, namely the composability requirement. TBB is a composable library because performance does not take a hit if the developer decides or needs to nest parallel patterns inside other parallel patterns, no matter how many levels are nested. One of the factors that make TBB composable is that adding nested levels of parallelism does not increase the number of worker threads. That in turn avoids oversubscription and its associated overheads from ruining our performance. To make the most out of the hardware, TBB is usually configured so that it runs as many worker threads as logical cores. The various TBB algorithms (nested or not) only add enough user-level lightweight tasks to feed these worker threads and thereby exploit the cores. However, as we warned in Chapter 5, calling a blocking function inside a user-level task not only blocks the task but it also blocks the OS-managed worker thread processing this task. In such an unfortunate case, if we had a worker thread per core and one of them was blocked, the corresponding core may become idle. In such a case, we would not be fully utilizing the hardware!

In our simple example of Figure 18-4, the asyncThread will use the idle core when it runs the task outside the flow graph control. But what about offloading work to an accelerator (GPU/FPGA/DSP, pick as you please!), and waiting for it? If a TBB task calls blocking functions from OpenCL, CUDA, or Thrust code (to name a few), the TBB worker running this task will inevitably block.

Before `async_node` was available in the flow graph list of nodes, a possible, although not ideal, workaround was to oversubscribe the system with one extra thread. To accomplish this (as described in more detail in Chapter 11), we usually rely on the following lines:

```
int cores = tbb::task_scheduler_init::default_num_threads();
tbb::task_scheduler_init(cores+1);
```

This solution is still viable if we don't require a flow graph in our code and just want to offload work to an accelerator from, say, a `parallel_invoke` or one of the stages of a `parallel_pipeline`. The caveat here is that we should know that the extra thread is going to be blocked most of the time while waiting for the accelerator. However, the glitch with this workaround is that there will be periods of time in which the system is oversubscribed (before and after the offloading operation or even while the accelerator driver decides to block[2] the thread).

To avoid this issue, `async_node` comes to our rescue. When the `async_node` task (usually its lambda) finishes, the worker thread that was taking care of this task switches to work on other pending tasks of the flow graph. This way, the worker thread does not block leaving an idle core. What it is key to remember is that before the `async_node` task finishes, the flow graph should be warned of that an asynchronous task is in flight (using `gateway.reserve_wait()`), and just after the asynchronous task re-injects its result back into the flow graph (with `try_put()`) we should notify that the asynchronous task has finished with `gateway.release_wait()`. Still smirking? If so, please tell us why.

A More Realistic Example

The triad function of the well-known STREAM benchmark[3] is a basic array operation, also called "linked triad," that essentially computes $C = A + \alpha*B$, where A, B, and C are 1D arrays. It is therefore quite similar to the BLAS 1 `saxpy` operation that implements $A=A+\alpha*B$, but writing the result in a different vector. Pictorially, Figure 18-5 helps in understanding this operation.

---

[2]When a thread offloads a kernel to the GPU using a blocking call the driver may not immediately block the calling thread. For example, some GPU drivers keep the thread spinning so that it will respond earlier to lightweight kernels, and finally block the thread after some time to avoid consuming resources while heavyweight kernels finish.

[3]John McCalpin, STREAM benchmark, `www.cs.virginia.edu/stream/ref.html`.

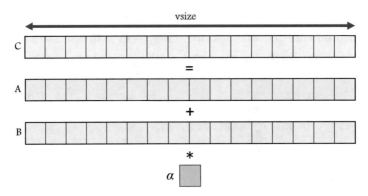

Figure 18-5. *Triad vector operation that computes* $C = A + \alpha * B$ $(c_i = a_i + \alpha * b_i, \forall i)$

In our implementation, we will assume that array sizes are determined by the variable `vsize` and that the three arrays store single precision floats. Coming up with a parallel implementation of this embarrassingly parallel algorithm is not challenging enough for us at this point of the book. Let's go for a heterogeneous implementation.

Okay, so you've got an integrated GPU? That don't impress me much![4] Reportedly, more than 95% of shipped processors come with an integrated GPU, sharing the die along with the multicore CPU. Would you sleep soundly after running the triad code on just one CPU core? Not quite, right? CPU cores shouldn't be sitting idle. Much in the same way, GPU cores shouldn't be sitting idle either. On many occasions, we can leverage the excellent GPU computing capabilities to further speed up some of our applications.

In Figure 18-6, we illustrate the way in which the triad computation will be distributed among the different computing devices.

---

[4]Shania Twain – That Don't Impress Me Much, *Come On Over* album, 1997.

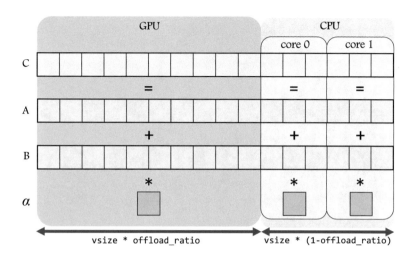

Figure 18-6. *Heterogeneous implementation of the triad computation*

In our implementation, we will rely on the offload_ratio variable, which controls the fraction of the iteration space that is offloaded to the GPU, whereas the rest is processed in parallel on the CPU. It goes without saying that $0 \leq$ offload_ratio ≤ 1.

The code will be based on the flow graph depicted in Figure 18-7. The first node, in_node, is a source_node that sends the same offload_ratio to a_node and cpu_node. The former is an async_node that offloads the computation of the corresponding subregion of the arrays to an OpenCL capable GPU. The latter is a regular function_node that nests a TBB parallel_for to split the CPU assigned subregion of the arrays among the available CPU cores. Execution time on both the GPU, Gtime, and CPU, Ctime, are collected in the corresponding node and converted into a tuple inside the join_node. Finally, in the out_node, those times are printed, and the heterogeneously computed version of array C is compared with a golden version obtained by a plain serial execution of the triad loop.

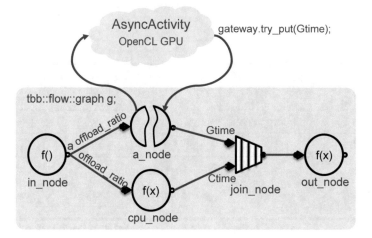

Figure 18-7. *Flow graph that implements heterogeneous triad*

Note   We love to gently introduce new concepts, and we try to toe the line on this, especially when it comes to TBB content. However, OpenCL is outside the scope of the book, so we have to give up our own rule and just comment briefly on the OpenCL constructs that are used in the following examples.

For the sake of simplicity, in this example, we will accept the following assumptions:

1. In order to leverage a zero-copy buffer strategy that reduces the overhead of data movement between devices, we assume that an OpenCL 1.2 driver is available and that there is a common region of memory visible from both the CPU and the GPU. This is usually the case for integrated GPUs. For recent heterogeneous chips, OpenCL 2.0 is also available, and in such a case we can take advantage of the SVM (Shared Virtual Memory) as we will also illustrate next.

2. In order to reduce the number of arguments of the flow graph nodes and that way improve the readability of the code, pointers to CPU and GPU views of the three arrays A, B, and C are globally visible. The variable vsize is also global.

3. In order to skip the aspects less related to TBB, all the OpenCL boilerplate has been encapsulated into a single function opencl_ initialize(). This function takes care of getting the platform, platform, selecting the GPU device, device, creating the GPU context, context, and a command queue, queue, reading the source code of the OpenCL kernel, compiling it to create the kernel, and initializing the three buffers that store the GPU view of arrays A, B, and C. Since the AsyncActivity also needs the command queue and the program handlers, the corresponding variables, queue and program, are also global. We took advantage of the C++ wrappers available for the OpenCL C API. More precisely, we used the cl2.hpp OpenCL C++ header that can be found on https://github.com/KhronosGroup/OpenCL-CLHPP/.

Let's start with the main function of the code; in Figure 18-8, we only show the definition of the two first nodes: in_node and cpu_node.

```cpp
int main(int argc, const char* argv[]) {
  int nth = (argc>1) ? atoi(argv[1]): 4;
  vsize = (argc>2) ? atoi(argv[2]) : 100000000;
  float ratio = (argc>3) ? atof(argv[3]) : 0.5;
  float alpha = 0.5;
  opencl_initialize(); // OpenCL boilerplate
  tbb::task_scheduler_init init{nth};
  auto mp=tbb::global_control::max_allowed_parallelism;
  tbb::global_control gc(mp, nth+1); //One more thread, but sleeping
  tbb::flow::graph g;

  bool n = false;
  tbb::flow::source_node<float> in_node{g,
    [&](float& offload_ratio) -> bool {
    if(n) return false;
    offload_ratio = ratio;
    n = true;
    return true;
  },false};
```

Figure 18-8. *Main function of the heterogeneous triad computation with the first two nodes*

```
tbb::flow::function_node<float, double> cpu_node{g,
  tbb::flow::unlimited,
  [&](float offload_ratio) -> double {
    auto t=tbb::tick_count::now();
    tbb::parallel_for(
      tbb::blocked_range<size_t>{
        static_cast<size_t>(ceil(vsize*offload_ratio)),
        static_cast<size_t>(vsize)
      },
      [&](const tbb::blocked_range<size_t>& r){
        for (size_t i = r.begin(); i < r.end(); ++i)
          Chost[i] = Ahost[i] + alpha * Bhost[i];
      }
    );
    return (tbb::tick_count::now() - t).seconds();
}};
// … to be continued …
```

Figure 18-8. (*continued*)

We first read the program arguments and initialize the OpenCL boilerplate calling opencl_initialize(). From this function, we only need to know that it initializes a GPU command queue, queue, and an OpenCL program, program. The initialization of the number of threads and the reason to initialize a global_control object will be addressed at the end of the section. The source code of the GPU kernel is quite straightforward:

```
kernel void triad(global float* A,
                  global float* B,
                  global float* C) {
  int i=get_global_id(0);
  float alpha = 0.5;
  C[i] = A[i] + alpha * B[i];
}
```

This implements the triad operation, C = A + α*B, assuming α=0.5 and that the arrays of float are stored in global memory. At kernel launching time, we have to specify the range of iterations that the GPU will traverse, and the GPU internal scheduler will pick single iterations from this space with the instruction i=get_global_id(0). For each one of these i's, the computation C[i] = A[i] + alpha * B[i] will be conducted in parallel in the different compute units of the GPU.

Inside the `opencl_initialize()` function, we also allocate the three OpenCL buffers and the corresponding CPU pointers that point to the same buffers from the CPU side (what we call the CPU view of the arrays). Assuming we have OpenCL 1.2, for the input array A, we rely on the OpenCL `cl::Buffer` constructor to allocate a GPU accessible array called `Adevice`:

```
cl::Buffer Adevice;                      // Device view of A
Adevice = cl::Buffer{context, CL_MEM_READ_WRITE |
                     CL_MEM_ALLOC_HOST_PTR, sizeof(float)*vsize};
```

The flag `CL_MEM_ALLOC_HOST_PTR` is key to take advantage of the zero-copy buffer OpenCL feature because it forces the allocation of host-accessible memory. The same call is used for the other two GPU views of the arrays, `Bdevice` and `Cdevice`. To get a pointer to the CPU view of these buffers, the OpenCL `enqueueMapBuffer` is available and used as follows:

```
float* Ahost;                            // Host view of A
Ahost=(float*)queue.enqueueMapBuffer(Adevice, CL_TRUE, CL_MAP_WRITE |
CL_MAP_READ, 0, sizeof(float) * vsize, NULL, NULL, &err);
```

which gives us a float pointer `Ahost` that can be used from the CPU to read and write in the same memory region. Similar calls are needed for pointers `Bhost` and `Chost`. In modern processors with integrated GPUs, this call does not imply data copy overheads and hence the zero-copy buffer name for this strategy. There are additional subtleties regarding OpenCL like the meaning and functionality of `clEnqueueUnmapMemObject()` and potential issues arising of having both the CPU and GPU writing in different regions of the same array, but they fall beyond the scope of this book.

Note   If your device supports OpenCL 2.0, the implementation is easier especially if the heterogeneous chip implements what is called fine-grained buffer SVM. In that case, it is possible to allocate a region of memory that not only is visible by both the CPU and GPU, but that can also be updated concurrently and kept coherent by the underlying hardware. In order to check whether or not OpenCL 2.0 and fine-grained buffer SVM are available, we need to use: `device.getInfo<CL_DEVICE_SVM_CAPABILITIES>();`

To exploit this feature, in the `opencl_initialize()`, we can use `cl::SVMAllocator()` and pass it as the allocator template argument of the `std::vector` constructor. This will give us a `std::vector` A, that is at the same time the GPU view and the CPU view of the data:

```
using svmalloc_t = cl::SVMAllocator<float,
                    cl::SVMTraitFine<cl::SVMTraitReadWrite<>>>;
svmalloc_t svmAlloc;
A=std::vector<float, svmalloc_t>{vsize, 0, svmAlloc};
```

This is, no need for `Ahost` and `Adevice` anymore. Just A. As with any shared data, we are responsible of avoiding data races. In our example, this is easy because the GPU writes in a region of the array C that does not overlap with the region written by the CPU. If this condition is not met, in some cases, the solution is to resort to an array of atomics. Such a solution is usually called platform atomics, or system atomics, since they can be atomically updated by the CPU and the GPU. This feature is optionally implemented and requires that we instantiate the `SVMAllocator` with `cl::SVMTraitAtomic<>`.

The next thing in Figure 18-8 is the declaration of the graph g and definition of the source_node, in_node, which is quite similar to the one explained in Figure 18-2, with the single difference that it passes a message with the value of `offload_ratio`.

The next node in our example is a `function_node`, cpu_node, which receives a `float` (actually, offload_ratio) and sends a `double` (the time required to do the CPU computation). Inside the cpu_node lambda, a `parallel_for` is invoked and its first argument is a blocked range like this:

```
tbb::blocked_range<size_t>{
                    static_cast<size_t>(ceil(vsize*offload_ratio)),
                    static_cast<size_t>(vsize)
                    }
```

which means that only the upper part of the arrays will be traversed. The lambda of this parallel_for computes in parallel `Chost[i]` = `Ahost[i]` + `alpha` * `Bhost[i]` for different chunks of iterations in which the range is automatically partitioned.

We can continue in Figure 18-9 with the next node, a_node, that is an asynchronous node that receives a float (again the offload_ratio value) and sends the time required by the GPU computation. This is accomplished asynchronously in a_node's lambda where the member function run of an AsyncActivity object, asyncAct, is called, similarly to what we already saw in Figure 18-2.

```
using async_node_t = tbb::flow::async_node<float, double>;
using gateway_t = async_node_t::gateway_type;
AsyncActivity asyncAct;
async_node_t a_node{g, tbb::flow::unlimited,
  [&asyncAct](const float& offload_ratio, gateway_t& gateway) {
    asyncAct.run(offload_ratio, gateway);
  }
};
using join_t = tbb::flow::join_node <std::tuple<double,double>,
                                     tbb::flow::queueing>;
join_t node_join{g};

tbb::flow::function_node<join_t::output_type> out_node{g,
  tbb::flow::unlimited,
  [&](const join_t::output_type& times){
    std::vector<float> CGold(vsize);
    std::transform(Ahost, Ahost + vsize, Bhost, CGold.begin(),
                   [&](float a, float b)->float{return a+alpha*b;});
    // Compare golden triad with heterogeneous triad
    if (!std::equal(Chost, Chost+vsize, CGold.begin()))
        std::cout << "Error!!\n";
    std::cout<< "Time cpu: "<< std::get<1>(times)<< " sec."<< '\n';
    std::cout<< "Time gpu: "<< std::get<0>(times)<< " sec."<< '\n';
}};
// … to be continued …
```

Figure 18-9. *Main function of the heterogeneous triad computation with the definition of the last three nodes*

The join_node does not deserve our time here because it was already covered in Chapter 3. Suffice to say that it forwards a tuple, which packs the GPU time and the CPU time, to the next node.

The final node is a function_node, out_node, which receives the tuple with the times. Before printing them, it checks that the resulting C array has been correctly computed partially on the CPU and partially on the GPU. To this end, a golden version of C, CGold, is allocated and then computed serially using the STL algorithm transform. Then, if Chost coincides with CGold, we are all set. The equal STL algorithm comes in handy to implement this comparison.

Figure 18-10 finishes off the main() function with the node connections, thanks to five make_edge calls, followed by the in_node activation to trigger the execution of the graph. We wait for completion with g.wait_for_all().

```
tbb::flow::make_edge(in_node, a_node);
tbb::flow::make_edge(in_node, cpu_node);
tbb::flow::make_edge(a_node, tbb::flow::input_port<0>(node_join));
tbb::flow::make_edge(cpu_node,tbb::flow::input_port<1>(node_join));
tbb::flow::make_edge(node_join, out_node);

auto gt = tbb::tick_count::now();
in_node.activate();
g.wait_for_all();
return 0;
} // End of main()!
```

Figure 18-10. *Last part of the triad main function where nodes are connected and the graph is dispatched*

Finally, in Figure 18-11, we present the implementation of the AsyncActivity class, whose run member function is invoked from the async_node.

```
class AsyncActivity {
  tbb::task_arena a;
public:
  AsyncActivity() {
    a = tbb::task_arena{1,0};
  }
  using async_node_t = tbb::flow::async_node<float, double>;
  using gateway_t = async_node_t::gateway_type;
  void run(float offload_ratio, gateway_t& gateway){
    gateway.reserve_wait();
    a.enqueue([&,offload_ratio]()
      {
        auto t = tbb::tick_count::now();
        // Make triad kernel, NDRange and launch
        auto triad_kernel =
        cl::KernelFunctor<cl::Buffer&, cl::Buffer&, cl::Buffer&>
                          {program, "triad"};
        cl::EnqueueArgs q_args{
          queue,
          cl::NDRange{static_cast<size_t>(ceil(vsize*offload_ratio))}
        };
        triad_kernel(q_args, Adevice, Bdevice, Cdevice).wait();
        gateway.try_put((tbb::tick_count::now()-t).seconds());
        gateway.release_wait();
      });
  }
};
```

Figure 18-11. `AsyncActivity` *implementation, where the actual GPU kernel invocation takes place*

Instead of spawning a thread as we did in the `AsyncActivity` of Figure 18-3, we follow here a more elaborated and efficient alternative. Remember that we postponed the explanation of why we used a `global_control` object in Figure 18-8. In this figure, we initialized the scheduler as follows:

```
tbb::task_scheduler_init init{nth};
auto mp=tbb::global_control::max_allowed_parallelism;
tbb::global_control gc(mp, nth+1); //One more thread, but sleeping
```

If you remember from Chapter 11, the `task_scheduler_init` line will result in the following:

- A default arena will be created with nth slots (one of them reserved
  for the master thread).

- nth - 1 worker threads will be populated in the global thread pool,
  which would occupy the worker slots of the arena as soon as there is
  work pending in such arena.

But later, the global_control object, gc, is constructed so that the actual number of workers in the global thread pool is incremented. This extra thread has no slot available in the default arena so it will be put to sleep.

Now, the AsyncActivity class, instead of spawning a new thread as we did before, it awakes the dormant thread, which is usually faster, especially if we are invoking several times the AsyncActivity. To that end, the constructor of the class initializes a new arena, a = tbb::task_arena{1,0}, that has one worker thread slot since it reserves 0 slots for the master. When the member function run() is invoked, a new task is enqueued in this arena with a.enqueue(). This will result in the dispatch of the dormant thread that will occupy the slot of this new arena and complete the task.

Next, the task spawned in this AsyncActivity follows the usual steps to offload computations to a GPU. First, construct the triad_kernel KernelFunctor informing that the triad kernel has three cl::Buffer arguments. Second, call triad_kernel passing the NDRange, which is calculated as ceil(vsize*offload_ratio), and the GPU view of the buffers, Adevice, Bdevice, and Cdevice.

When running this code on an Intel processor with an integrated GPU, these two lines are generated:

```
Time cpu: 0.132203 sec.
Time gpu: 0.130705 sec.
```

where vsize is set to 100 million elements and we have been playing with offload_ratio until both devices consume approximately the same time in computing their assigned subregion of the arrays.

Summary

In this chapter, we have first introduced the async_node class that enhances the flow graph capabilities when it comes to dealing with asynchronous tasks that escape the flow graph control. In a first simple Async World example, we illustrated the use of this class and its companion gateway interface, useful to re-inject a message from the asynchronous task back into the flow graph. We then motivated the relevance of this extension to the TBB flow graph, which is easily understood if we realize that blocking a TBB task results in blocking a TBB worker thread. The async_node allows for dispatching an asynchronous work outside the flow graph but without blocking a TBB worker thread when waiting for this asynchronous work to complete. We wrapped up the chapter with a more realistic example that puts to work the async_node to offload some of the iterations of a parallel_for to a GPU. We hope we have provided the basis to elaborate more complex projects in which asynchronous work is involved. However, if we usually target an OpenCL capable GPU, we have good news: in the next chapter, we cover the opencl_ node feature of TBB, which provides a friendlier interface to put the GPU to work for us!

For More Information

Here are some additional reading materials we recommend related to this chapter:

- Herb Sutter, "The Free Lunch Is Over: A Fundamental Turn Toward Concurrency in Software," www.gotw.ca/publications/ concurrency-ddj.htm.

- John McCalpin, STREAM benchmark, www.cs.virginia.edu/ stream/ref.html.

- David Kaeli, Perhaad Mistri, Dana Schaa, Dong Ping Zhang. Heterogeneous Computing with OpenCL 2.0. Morgan Kaufmann 2015.

CHAPTER 19

Flow Graphs on Steroids: OpenCL Nodes

Does the `async_node` leave you yearning for more? If so, this is your chapter. Here, we will cover a high-level Flow Graph class, the `opencl_node`, that strives to hide the hardware details and programing nuances of OpenCL capable devices. Why OpenCL? Well, there are many reasons and to name a few: OpenCL is an open standard contributed to by members of a large consortium, it is designed to be a platform-independent API, and it aims to nimbly evolve to meet newer requirements. For instance, OpenCL has been an extension of C (not C++), but the latest OpenCL 2.2 version adds support for a subset of C++14 including classes, lambda expressions, templates, and so on.

Is that not enough? Okay, one more. For us, the mother of all reasons, the one standing out among the others, is the number and variety of platforms on which you can use OpenCL. Starting with the notebook and desktop segment, more than 95% of shipped processors for these systems include an OpenCL capable integrated GPU (usually from Intel or AMD). In the mobile segment, at the heart of most smart phones and tablets, we find a System-on-Chip, SoC, featuring a GPU that supports OpenCL (and yes, from the TBB repository we can get the TBB binaries for Android too). These examples seem to be convincing enough, but there is more! In the embedded arena, for many years running, we have been able to buy and exploit heterogeneous boards including an OpenCL programmable FPGA (from Intel-Altera and Xilinx). In the server domain, at the time of writing these lines, Intel is targeting data centers with both FPGA PCIe cards and Intel Xeon Scalable Processor 6138P that includes on-chip an Intel-Altera Arria 10 FPGA, and of course, OpenCL is one of the supported programming models. Moreover, OpenCL code can also run on many CPUs and other kind of accelerators, like the Xeon Phi.

But if OpenCL does not suit your needs, TBB architects also considered the possibility of supporting other programming models. They abstracted away the low-level details of the accelerator programming model into a module called *factory*. In fact,

M. Voss, R. Asenjo, J. Reinders, *Pro TBB*, https://doi.org/10.1007/978-1-4842-4398-5_19

the opencl_node is the result of instantiating a general class called streaming_node with a particular factory. Then, a factory defines the necessary methods to upload/download data to/from the accelerator and to launch the kernel. That is, the opencl_node is the result of marrying the streaming_node class to an OpenCL factory. Newer programming models can be supported just by developing the corresponding factory.

Now, this is quite a long chapter that covers several concepts (opencl_node, opencl_program, opencl_device, arguments and range of the OpenCL kernel, sub-buffers, etc.) therefore implying a steep learning curve. But we will start easy, on the plains, and progressively ascend to the more complex classes and examples (as we always try to do). As we depict in Figure 19-1, we will start with a simple "Hello World"-like example that uses the opencl_node, to later implement the same triad vector computation that was presented in the previous chapter, but now with our new high-level toy. If you want to save the final climb to the summit, you can stop reading there. If on the other hand you are an experienced climber, at the end of the chapter we give a sneak peek at more advanced features, like fine-tuning the OpenCL NDRange and kernel specification.

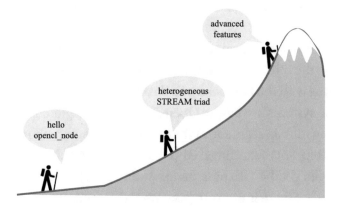

Figure 19-1. *Depicting the learning curve of this chapter*

Hello OpenCL_Node Example

This time let's start at the end. This is the output of our first example:

```
Hello OpenCL_Node
Bye! Received from: OPENCL_NODE
```

These two lines are the result of running the flow graph that is shown in Figure 19-2, where the bubbles identify the string that is printed by each one of the three nodes in the graph.

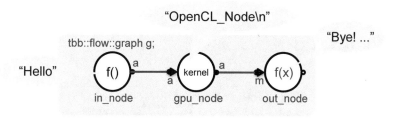

Figure 19-2. *Flow graph for the "Hello OpenCL_Node" example*

The middle node, gpu_node, is an opencl_node that prints out "OpenCL_Node\n". To this end, it will be configured to run the following OpenCL kernel that is stored in an hello.cl file:

```
kernel void cl_print(global char *str) {
  for ( ; *str; ++str ) {
    printf("%c", *str);
    if(*str>96 && *str<123) *str-=32; // a -> A, …
  }
}
```

The hello.cl file includes the definition of the cl_print() kernel that will be executed by a special node of the flow graph, an opencl_node. If we take a closer look at the kernel function, it actually prints whatever array of chars happens to arrive as an input argument. In addition, to exert a noticeable impact, the kernel also changes the string by capitalizing only the lowercase letters. The global keyword preceding the char *str declaration of the argument states that the array of chars should be stored in OpenCL global memory. For what matters here (i.e., oversimplifying), this means that the string is stored in a region of memory that can be "somehow" read and written by the CPU and the GPU. In the common case of an integrated GPU, the global memory just sits on main memory. This means, that the opencl_node should receive as argument an array of chars. In our example, this array of chars contains the characters that read "OpenCL_Node\n". As you are probably guessing, this message comes from the first node, in_node. Right, the pointer to the string (a in Figure 19-2) flies from in_node to gpu_node, and without user intervention, the string initialized on the CPU ends up reaching the GPU. And what message reaches out_node? Again, the pointer a that leaves gpu_node and enters out_node with the name m. Finally, this last node of the graph prints "Bye! Received from: OPENCL_NODE" where we note the change in the string, and also that the string processed on the GPU has somehow become accessible by the CPU. Now, we all crave the details of the actual implementation, so here they are in Figure 19-3.

```
tbb::flow::graph g;
//Source node:
bool n = false;
using buffer_t = tbb::flow::opencl_buffer<cl_char>;
tbb::flow::source_node<buffer_t> in_node{g, [&](buffer_t& a){
  if(n) return false;
  else {
    std::cout << "Hello ";
    char str[] = "OpenCL_Node\n";
    a = buffer_t{sizeof(str)};
    std::copy_n(str, sizeof(str), a.begin());
    n = true;
    return true;
  }
},false};

//GPU node:
tbb::flow::opencl_program<> program{std::string{"hello.cl"}};
tbb::flow::opencl_node<std::tuple<buffer_t>> gpu_node{g,
                                program.get_kernel("cl_print")};
gpu_node.set_range({{1}});

//Output node:
tbb::flow::function_node<buffer_t> out_node{g,
  tbb::flow::unlimited,
  [](buffer_t const& m){
    char *str = (char*) m.begin();
    std::cout << "Bye! Received from: " << str;
  }
};

//Make edges and run!
tbb::flow::make_edge(in_node, gpu_node);
tbb::flow::make_edge(gpu_node, out_node);
in_node.activate();
g.wait_for_all();
```

Figure 19-3. *Building the flow graph for the "Hello OpenCL_Node" example*

And that's it! Note that the GPU node configuration requires only three C++ lines of code. Isn't it neat?

Disclaimer   As of writing this chapter, the latest version of TBB is 2019. In this version, the opencl_node is still a preview feature, which essentially means that

- It is subject to change. If you rely on a preview feature in your code, double check it keeps working when updating to a newer TBB release. In the worst case, a preview feature can even disappear!

- It may have little documentation and support. Indeed, opencl_ node and streaming_node documentation is not abundant on the Web. There are some blog entries[1] illustrating this feature, but they are 3 years old and part of the API has changed since then.

- It has to be explicitly enabled (i.e., by default it is off). To use opencl_node in our codes we have to add these three lines:

```
#define TBB_PREVIEW_FLOW_GRAPH_NODES 1
#define TBB_PREVIEW_FLOW_GRAPH_FEATURES 1
#include <tbb/flow_graph_opencl_node.h>
```

The fringe benefit of using this header is that you don't need to manually include tbb/flow_graph.h nor the OpenCL header files, because they are already included within flow_graph_opencl_node.h. Actually, this header file, along with the blog entries, is nowadays our most reliable source of information about the classes and member functions that this feature provides. This chapter should be considered as a gentle introduction to the one thousand and a half lines of code included in that opencl_node header.

---

[1] https://software.intel.com/en-us/blogs/2015/12/09/opencl-node-overview.

Okay, let's go node by node. The first one, in_node, looks familiar if you remember the examples from the previous chapter. To refresh our minds, suffice to say that (1) the input argument of the lambda ([&](buffer_t& a)) is actually a reference to the message that will be sent to any connected node; (2) only one message leaves in_node because after the first invocation it returns false; and (3) in_node.activate() is in fact awaking the node and triggering that single message. But wait, there is something new in this node that we do have to pay attention to! The message leaving in_node has to end up in a GPU-accessible region of memory and this is why argument a is not just an array of chars, but a reference to a buffer_t. Just before the definition of in_node we see that buffer_t is an opencl_buffer of OpenCL chars (cl_char):

```
using buffer_t = tbb::flow::opencl_buffer<cl_char>;
tbb::flow::source_node<buffer_t> in_node{g, [&](buffer_t& a){
...
```

The opencl_buffer is the first opencl_node helper class that we will see in this chapter, but there are more to come. It is a template class that abstracts a strongly typed linear array and it encapsulates the logic of the memory transactions between the host and the accelerator. We allocate an opencl_buffer<T> using the constructor of the class, like in our example in the line a = buffer_t{sizeof(str)}, or by declaring a new object with

```
buffer_t a{sizeof(str)};
```

In both cases, we end up allocating an opencl_buffer of cl_char. The version of the OpenCL factory that we use now is based on OpenCL 1.2 and leverages the zero-copy buffer approach. This means that, internally, when calling the opencl_buffer constructor, the OpenCL function clCreateBuffer is called, and one of its arguments is CL_MEM_ALLOC_HOST_PTR. As we succinctly explained in the previous chapter, the buffer is allocated on the GPU space but a CPU-accessible pointer (the CPU view of the buffer) can be obtained using a map function (clEnqueueMapBuffer). To return the control of the buffer to the GPU, OpenCL provides an unmap function (clEnqueueUnmapMemObject). On modern chips with integrated GPUs, map and unmap functions are cheap because no actual data copies are required. For these cases, map and unmap functions take care of keeping CPU and GPU caches consistent with the copy stored in the global memory (main memory) which may or may not imply CPU/GPU cache flushes. The good news is that all these low-level chores are none of our business anymore! Newer factories with better features or supporting other accelerators could be developed and we could just use them by simply recompiling our sources. Consider if an OpenCL 2.0 factory were to be disclosed tomorrow and that our accelerator implemented fine-grained buffer SVM. Just by using the new OpenCL 2.0 factory instead of the 1.2 one, we would get for free a boost in performance (because now map and unmap operations are unnecessary and cache coherency between the CPU and GPU is automatically kept by the hardware).

Oops, sorry for letting our minds drift for a while. Let's get back to the point. We were explaining the source_node of our example in Figure 19-3 (yes, several paragraphs ago). This source_node, in_node, just initializes an array of chars, str, with the string "OpenCL_Node\n", allocates the opencl_buffer, a, of the appropriate size, and copies the string to that buffer using the std::copy_n STL algorithm. That's it. When the lambda of this source_node finishes, a message with a reference to the opencl_buffer will fly from in_node to the gpu_node.

Now, remember the lines required to configure the gpu_node:

```
tbb::flow::opencl_program<> program{std::string{"hello.cl"}};
tbb::flow::opencl_node<std::tuple<buffer_t>> gpu_node{g,
                                    program.get_kernel("cl_print")};
gpu_node.set_range({{1}});
```

The first line uses the second opencl_node helper class that we cover in this chapter: the opencl_program class. In this line, we create the program object passing to the constructor the name of the file, hello.cl, where the OpenCL kernel, cl_print, is stored. There are other opencl_program constructors available, should we want to provide a precompiled kernel or the SPIR (OpenCL intermediate representation) version of the kernel. For the sake of keeping drifting minds away and staying focused on our example, we cover these other alternatives later.

The second line creates the gpu_node of type opencl_node<tuple<buffer_t>>. This means that the gpu_node receives a message of type buffer_t and, when done, it emits a message also of type buffer_t. Do we really need a tuple for a single argument/port? Well, the opencl_node is designed to receive several messages from preceding nodes and to send several messages to the following nodes of the graph and theses are packed into a tuple. Currently, there is no special case in the interface for a single input and output, so we need to use a single element tuple in that case. Regarding the correspondence between the opencl_node ports and the kernel arguments, by default, opencl_node binds the first input port to the first kernel argument, the second input port to the second kernel argument, and so on. There are other possibilities that will be covered later.

And do we really need to send an outgoing message for every incoming one? Well, the opencl_node is designed to support this maximum connectivity (one output port per input port) and if there are fewer inputs than outputs, or the other way around, we can always leave the corresponding ports unconnected. And do we really need to use the same data type for the input and the output? Well, with the current factory, yes. If the input port 0 is of type T, the output port 0 is of the same T type (the tuple specifying the argument types do not distinguish between input and output).

Note   The main reason supporting the opencl_node implementation decisions is that each opencl_node's port can potentially be mapped into each OpenCL kernel argument. For an "in-out" argument, having it at both input and output of course makes sense. For an "out" argument, we still need to pass in the object that is to be written, so there is a need for an input to match the output – otherwise the opencl_node would need to allocate the objects, which it doesn't. And finally, for an "in" argument, having it available at the output lets us forward the value, that is, pass it through unchanged to downstream nodes. So, the most practical thing was to just make all arguments in-out. We believe it makes sense if we think of the OpenCL node's tuple as a list of arguments, and we can connect edges to any of the arguments to set/get the value before/after the execution. For an "in" argument, the corresponding emitted value is unchanged. For an "out" argument, we provide the memory to write to and later get the value. And for "in-out," we send the value and receive the modified value.

Remember that OpenCL node is a preview feature. The TBB developers are eager for input on preview features – that's why they're preview features after all. They want to collect input on what's good and what's bad, so they can spend time on perfecting the parts of the library that people care the most about. This preview OpenCL node is supposed to be good enough to try out and provide feedback. If we have strong opinions on what needs to be added – we should speak up!

Now, the constructor of the opencl_node includes as arguments the flow graph object, g, and a handle to the kernel function that should be included in the OpenCL program file. Since the file hello.cl includes the kernel function cl_print, we use the member function: program.get_kernel("cl_print").

This means that we can have several kernel functions in the same OpenCL source file and assign each one to different opencl_nodes. And do we really have to settle just with a single program file? Well, not quite. We can instantiate the desired number of opencl_program objects if we have our OpenCL kernels distributed among several source files.

Finally, the third line of code needed to configure the gpu_node is gpu_node.set_range({{1}}). This member function from opencl_node specifies the iteration space that will be traversed by the GPU. More formally, in the OpenCL jargon, this iteration space is known as the NDRange, but let's not dwell on these details at this point. For now, let's take a leap of faith and just believe that the set_range({{1}}) member function results in the body of the kernel being executed just once.

Now we are done with the source_node (in_node), the opencl_node (gpu_node), and the last one in our example is a regular function_node called out_node. The corresponding code is

```
tbb::flow::function_node<buffer_t> out_node{g,
  tbb::flow::unlimited,
  [](buffer_t const& m){
    char *str = (char*) m.begin();
    std::cout << "Bye! Received from: " << str;
  }
};
```

We see that out_node receives a message, m, of type buffer_t. Because buffer_t is really an opencl_buffer<cl_char>, the call m.begin() results in a CPU visible pointer to the string that was initially set in in_node and was later modified by the GPU kernel. Our last node just prints this string and dies.

The rest of the example is the usual flow graph glue logic that makes the edges between the nodes, wakes up the source node, and waits for all the messages (just one in our example) to pass through the nodes. Nothing new here.

However, before we start climbing the first hills of our ascent, we will do a high level of recap of what we just explained while going deeper into what happens with the message, a, that was born on the CPU, sent to the GPU and modified there, to later pass to the final node where we can see the effect of the GPU kernel execution. We hope Figure 19-4 will serve us well in this regard.

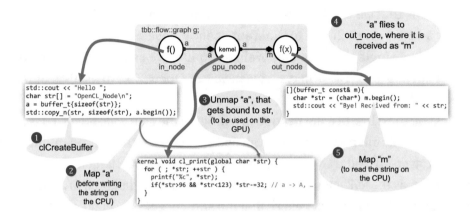

Figure 19-4. Overview of the example with details of message operations

The picture assumes that the OpenCL factory is based on the 1.2 version of this standard. In this case, the message a is allocated, as an opencl_buffer, in the GPU memory space but can also be written on the CPU if we first get the CPU-accessible iterator with a.begin(). The reference to a is a message that leaves in_node and enters port 0 of the gpu_node (which will invariably cause the message – the reference to a – to leave through the port 0 of departure). Port 0 of gpu_node is bound to the first argument of the kernel function that has a compatible type (opencl_buffer<cl_char> can be casted to char *). The kernel can safely access the string without cache coherency issues because before launching the kernel, the OpenCL factory takes care of unmapping the buffer. Finally, the reference to the buffer reaches out_node, where the string is again mapped to be accessed and printed on the CPU.

Before moving on, we would like to underscore here how fortunate we should feel by not having to manually deal with all the OpenCL boilerplate code (platform, devices, context, command queues, kernel reading and compilation, kernel argument setting and launching, OpenCL resources deallocation, etc.). All that is now hidden under the hood thanks to the OpenCL factory. Besides, as we said, new factories can make our code faster or able to work with other accelerators with minor or no changes in the source code.

Where Are We Running Our Kernel?

So far so good, right? But speaking of OpenCL boilerplate code, where is the knob to control on which device we are running our opencl_nodes? In our previous example, we said that the gpu_node was running the specified kernel on the GPU. Where else, right?

But what if we were lying? Disturbing, huh? Okay, let's see first if there are more OpenCL capable devices on our machine. Hopefully there is only a single device and it is a GPU, but I wouldn't bet my fingers on it! We'll have to sniff it out, but we are not emotionally ready to write old-style plain OpenCL code, are we? Mercifully, the TBB OpenCL factory puts in our hands two additional and valuable helper classes (and that makes four of them already). These are the opencl_device and opencl_device_list helper classes. Let's use them first outside the flow graph context, as we can see in Figure 19-5.

```
const tbb::flow::opencl_device_list& devices =
        tbb::flow::interface10::opencl_info::available_devices();
tbb::flow::opencl_device d = *devices.cbegin();
std::cout << "Platform: "          << d.platform_name()    << '\n';
std::cout << "Platform profile: " << d.platform_profile() << '\n';
std::cout << "Platform version: " << d.platform_version() << '\n';
std::cout << "Platform vendor: "   << d.platform_vendor()  << '\n';
for (auto d : devices) {
  std::cout << "Device: "            << d.name() << '\n';
  std::cout << "  Major version: "   << d.major_version();
  std::cout << ";  Minor version: " << d.minor_version() << '\n';
  std::cout << "  Device type: ";
  switch (d.type()) {
    case CL_DEVICE_TYPE_GPU:
      std::cout << "GPU" << '\n';
      break;
    case CL_DEVICE_TYPE_CPU:
      std::cout << "CPU" << '\n';
      break;
    default:
      std::cout << "Unknown" << '\n';
  }
}
```

Figure 19-5. *Simple code to query the OpenCL platform and devices available*

First, an opencl_device_list object, devices, is initialized by calling the function available_devices(). This function returns an iterable container with all the OpenCL enabled devices available in the first platform. Yes, only in the first available platform.[2]

---

[2]Remember again that this is a preview feature. If you need more flexibility in this regard, we will appreciate it if you could file a request to let Intel know that you find the OpenCL node useful but that there are limitations that need to be addressed.

Then, we pop the first `opencl_device`, d, from the list and query the platform name, profile, version, and vendor. All available devices in the platform will share these attributes.

Next, with `for(opencl_device d:devices)`, we iterate through the whole device list to get and print per-device name, major and minor version, and device type. Major and minor version information was already provided by `d.platform_version()`, but this one returns a string, whereas both `d.major_version()` and `d.minor_version()` return an integer. The output resulting of running this code on the MacBook on which we are writing these lines, and where we have run our previous example, can be seen in Figure 19-6.

Note   The function `available_devices()` is in fact not public and that is the reason we had to use this convoluted chain of namespaces:

`tbb::flow::interface10::opencl_info::available_devices()`

We noticed that just before the implementation of this member function inside `flow_graph_opencl_node.h` there is a comment stating that

`// TODO: consider opencl_info namespace as public API`

Since this is a preview feature in TBB, the interface is not yet completely settled. Take this into account in case this consideration eventually becomes a fact.

```
Platform: Apple
Platform profile: FULL_PROFILE
Platform version: OpenCL 1.2 (Feb 22 2019 20:16:07)
Platform vendor: Apple
Device: Intel(R) Core(TM) i7-6700HQ CPU @ 2.60GHz
  Major version: 1;  Minor version: 2
  Device type: CPU
Device: Intel(R) HD Graphics 530
  Major version: 1;  Minor version: 2
  Device type: GPU
Device: AMD Radeon Pro 450 Compute Engine
  Major version: 1;  Minor version: 2
  Device type: GPU
```

Figure 19-6. *Result of running the code of Figure 19-5 on a MacBook Pro*

It may come as some surprise that there may be three OpenCL devices in a laptop! Namely, one Intel CPU and two GPUs, the first one integrated in the Intel Core i7, and the second one a discrete AMD GPU. Remember that OpenCL is a portable programming language that can also be used to implement CPU code. And look, the first OpenCL capable device is not a GPU, is the quad-core Intel CPU. Now, regarding our first example in this chapter, where was the kernel running? You are right, on the first one. The OpenCL factory chooses by default the first available device, irrespective of whether it's a CPU or a GPU. So... we were lying!!! The kernel was running on a CPU disguised as an OpenCL accelerator. What if we have been lying here and there throughout the book? Think about it... that's even more terrifying (unless this is the first chapter you are reading).

Okay, let's fix this minor inconvenience. To save the day, the OpenCL factory comes with two additional features: Device Filter and Device Selector. Device Filters are used to initialize the `opencl_factory` with the set of devices that are available for kernel execution. All filtered devices must belong to the same OpenCL platform. There is a default device filter class, `default_device_filter`, that automatically gathers all available devices from the first OpenCL platform and returns an `opencl_device_list` containing these devices. For its part, a Device Selector, as its name suggests, selects one of the devices in that `opencl_device_list`. It is possible to use different device selectors for different `opencl_node` instances. The selection is done for every kernel execution, so it is also possible to have an `opencl_node` running on different devices for different invocations. The default selector, `default_device_selector`, lazily selects and returns the first device from the list of available devices that was constructed by device filter.

To get our gpu_node running on a real GPU, instead of

```
… gpu_node{g, program.get_kernel("cl_print")};
```

we should use

```
… gpu_node{g, program.get_kernel("cl_print"), gpu_selector};
```

where gpu_selector is an object of our custom class `gpu_device_selector`:

```
gpu_device_selector gpu_selector;
```

and this class is presented in Figure 19-7.

```
class gpu_device_selector{
public:
  template<typename DeviceFilter> tbb::flow::opencl_device
    operator()(tbb::flow::opencl_factory<DeviceFilter>& f) {
      auto it = std::find_if(
        f.devices().cbegin(), f.devices().cend(),
        [](const tbb::flow::opencl_device& d) {
          if (d.type() == CL_DEVICE_TYPE_GPU){
            std::cout << "Found GPU!" << '\n';
            return true;
          }
          return false;
        });

      if (it == f.devices().cend()){
        std::cout << "No GPU found!." << '\n';
        return *f.devices().cbegin(); //Return the first one
      }

      std::cout << "Running on "<< it->name() << '\n';
      return *it;
    }
};
```

Figure 19-7. *Our first custom device selector*

The agreement (more formally, the "Concept") is that the third argument of an
opencl_node is a functor (an object of a class with the operator() member function)
that returns a device. That way, instead of passing the functor we may embed a lambda
expression in its place. The operator() receives an opencl_factory, f, and returns an
opencl_device. Using the find_if STL algorithm, we return the first iterator, it, in the
container devices() that fulfills it->type()==CL_DEVICE_TYPE_GPU. For the sake of
expediency, we declared auto it and delegated to the compiler to find out that the type
of it is actually

tbb::flow::opencl_device_list::const_iterator it = ...

To account for the possibility of not finding a GPU device, we include a fallback
that returns the first device (there should be at least one! ... there is no point in having a
platform without any device). The functor finishes by printing the name of the selected
device and returning it. In our laptop, the output would be:

```
Hello Found GPU!
Running OpenCL code on Intel(R) HD Graphics 530
OpenCL_Node
Bye! Received from: OPENCL_NODE
```

Note that the new messages are printed out by the gpu_node device selector functor when this node is activated. This is, first in_node prints its message "Hello" and passes the message to the gpu_node, which before launching the kernel selects the device (printing the boldface words of the output) and then runs the kernel. That's something to consider: an opencl_node in a flow graph is usually activated several times, so we are better off implementing the lightest possible device selector.

For example, if the lambda expression of the std::find_if algorithm doesn't need to print the "Found GPU!" message, it can be further simplified:

```
auto it = std::find_if(f.devices().cbegin(), f.devices().cend(),
  [](const tbb::flow::opencl_device& d) {
    return  d.type() == CL_DEVICE_TYPE_GPU;
  });
```

Now, if we don't like how our source code looks having to explicitly add the gpu_device_selector class, we can substitute the functor by a lambda expression. It is kind of tricky because the operator() of this class is a templated function, remember?:

```
template<typename DeviceFilter> tbb::flow::opencl_device
        operator()(tbb::flow::opencl_factory<DeviceFilter>& f) {…}
```

The easiest way (that we are aware of) to come up with the lambda implementation is to relay on polymorphic lambdas that are available since C++14. Don't forget to compile the code in Figure 19-8 with the option std=c++14.

```
tbb::flow::opencl_node<std::tuple<buffer_t>> gpu_node{g,
  program.get_kernel("cl_print"),
  [] (auto& f) { //polymorphic lambdas as of C++14
    std::cout << "Available devices:\n";
    int i = 0;
    std::for_each(f.devices().cbegin(), f.devices().cend(),
     [&](const tbb::flow::opencl_device& d) {
      std::cout << i++ << ".- Device: " << d.name() << std::endl;
    });
    tbb::flow::opencl_device d = *(++f.devices().cbegin()); //LOOK!
    std::cout << "Running on " << d.name() << '\n';
    return d;
  }};
```

Figure 19-8. *Using a lambda expression instead of a functor to do the device selection*

Note the **(auto& f)** argument of the lambda, instead of (opencl_factory <DeviceFilter>& f) that we used in the functor-based alternative. This code traverses the devices() container and then returns the second device in the list, resulting in something like

```
Available devices:
0.- Device: Intel(R) Core(TM) i7-6700HQ CPU @ 2.60GHz
1.- Device: Intel(R) HD Graphics 530
2.- Device: AMD Radeon Pro 450 Compute Engine
Running on Intel(R) HD Graphics 530
```

Now that we know our device list and assuming we want to use the integrated GPU, better change the lambda to make it faster:

```
tbb::flow::opencl_node<std::tuple<buffer_t>> gpu_node{g,
    program.get_kernel("cl_print"),
    [] (auto& f) { //polymorphic lambdas as of C++14
        return *(++f.devices().cbegin()); //LOOK!
    }};
```

An even faster alternative would be to cache the opencl_device the first time we invoke the device selector. For example, in Figure 19-9, we sketch a modification of the gpu_device_selector class that was presented in Figure 19-7.

```
class gpu_device_selector {
  bool first_time = true;
  tbb::flow::opencl_device device;
public:
  template<typename DeviceFilter>
  tbb::flow::opencl_device operator()
   (tbb::flow::opencl_factory<DeviceFilter>& f) {
    if(first_time){
      device = *(++f.devices().cbegin());
      first_time = false;
    }
    return device;
  }
};
```

Figure 19-9. *Device selector class that caches the* opencl_device *the first time it is invoked*

The class has now an opencl_device member variable, device. When the operator() is invoked the first time, the device list, f.devices(), is traversed to find the device that we want to use (in the example, the second available device). Then we cache it into the device variable for future uses. Note that further care to avoid data races is required if this operator can be called concurrently from different threads.

We hope you can keep secret how badly we coded the examples of Figures 19-8 and 19-9. In those snippets, we are hardcoding the device to be the second one, which works on our test machine, but it may miserably fail on other platforms. Actually, if there is a single device stored in the f.devices() container, dereferencing *(++f. devices().cbegin()) will trigger a segmentation fault. This is another example of the trade-off between portability and performance. We would be better off using the version of Figure 19-7 (commenting out the print statements) if we don't know where the code can eventually run and the device selection time is negligible in comparison with the OpenCL computation.

Back to the More Realistic Example of Chapter 18

Do you remember the triad vector operation that we introduced in the previous chapter? It was just a basic array operation of the form C = A + α*B where A, B, and C are 1D arrays containing vsize floats, and α is a scalar that we set to 0.5 (because we can). Figure 19-10 is a reminder of the way in which our triad computation will be distributed between the GPU and CPU depending on the variable offload_ratio.

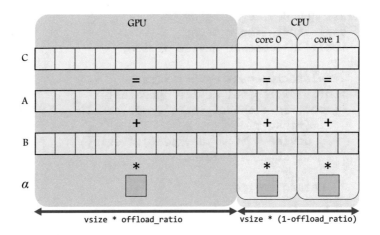

Figure 19-10. *Heterogeneous implementation of the triad computation*

The purpose of re-implementing this example is twofold. First, by re-visiting our old acquaintance but now from the perspective of the opencl_node, we will better appreciate the benefits of this higher-level feature of the TBB flow graph. Second, going beyond the "Hello OpenCL_Node" will allow us to delve into more advanced uses of the opencl_node class and its helper classes. In Figure 19-11, we give an overview of the flow graph that we are about to implement.

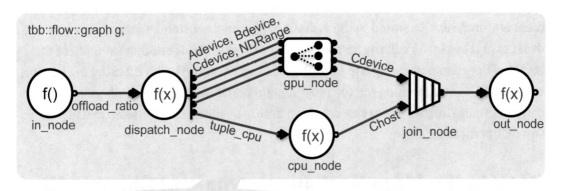

Figure 19-11. *Flow graph that implements triad, now using an OpenCL node*

As in our previous examples, the source_node (in_node) just triggers the execution of the flow graph, in this case passing a single message with the value of offload_ratio. The following node down the stream is a multifunction_node (dispatch_node). This kind of node stands out for its flexibility to send messages to the following nodes in the graph. We see that dispatch_node has five output ports, the first four targeting the gpu_node, and the last port connected to the cpu_node. The gpu_node is an opencl_node that will be configured with the appropriate triad GPU kernel, which expects as input arguments a "GPU view" of arrays A, B, and C (as in the previous chapter, they are called Adevice, Bdevice, and Cdevice). However, the gpu_node has an additional port to receive the number of iterations that will be offloaded, which depends on offload_ratio and that we call NDRange to adhere to the OpenCL notation. The cpu_node is a regular function node that receives the "CPU view" of the three arrays as well as offload_ratio so that the CPU can hold up its end of the bargain. The cpu_node has a single input port, so dispatch_node has to pack into a tuple the four variables required by the CPU. Both the gpu_node and the cpu_node pass their own view of resulting array C to the join_node, which in turn builds a tuple with both views and forwards it to the out_node. This final node will validate that the computation is correct and print out the execution time. Without further ado, let's start with the real implementation, kicking off with data type definitions and buffer allocations in Figure 19-12.

```
tbb::flow::graph g;

using buffer_f = tbb::flow::opencl_buffer<cl_float>;
buffer_f Adevice{vsize};
buffer_f Bdevice{vsize};
buffer_f Cdevice{vsize};
float* Ahost = Adevice.data();
float* Bhost = Bdevice.data();
float* Chost = Cdevice.data();

// Initialize random number generator
std::random_device seed;    // Random device seed
std::mt19937 mte{seed()};   // mersenne_twister_engine
std::uniform_int_distribution<> uniform{0, 256};
// Initialize A and B
std::generate(Ahost, Ahost+vsize, [&]{return uniform(mte);});
std::generate(Bhost, Bhost+vsize, [&]{return uniform(mte);});
```

Figure 19-12. *Data type definition and buffer allocation in triad example*

From now on, a buffer_f is an opencl_buffer of cl_floats (OpenCL counterpart of the regular float data type). With this, we allocate Adevice, Bdevice, and Cdevice as the "GPU views" of our three arrays. The opencl_buffer class also exposes the data() member function, which we see here for the first time. This function returns a CPU-accessible pointer to the GPU buffer and also takes care of mapping the buffer so that the CPU can have access to it. This allows us to initialize the pointers Ahost, Bhost, and Chost. Using the STL generate algorithm we initialize arrays A and B with random numbers between 0 and 255, using a Mersenne Twister generator (as we did in Chapter 5).

The first two nodes of the graph, in_node and dispatch_node, are defined in Figure 19-13.

```
bool n = false;
tbb::flow::source_node<float> in_node {g, [&](float& offload_ratio) {
  if(n) return false;
  offload_ratio = 0.5;
  n = true;
  return true;
},false};

using NDRange = std::array<size_t, 1> ; //1D array of size_t
using tuple_cpu = std::tuple<float*, float*, float*, size_t>;
using mfn_t = tbb::flow::multifunction_node<float,
    std::tuple<buffer_f, buffer_f, buffer_f, NDRange, tuple_cpu>>;
mfn_t dispatch_node {g,
  tbb::flow::unlimited,
  [&](const float& offload_ratio, mfn_t::output_ports_type& ports ){
    t0_p =tbb::tick_count::now();
    // Messages for the GPU
    std::get<0>(ports).try_put(Adevice);
    std::get<1>(ports).try_put(Bdevice);
    std::get<2>(ports).try_put(Cdevice);
    std::get<3>(ports).try_put(
               {static_cast<size_t>(ceil(vsize*offload_ratio))});

    tuple_cpu cpu_vectors;
    std::get<0>(cpu_vectors) = Ahost;
    std::get<1>(cpu_vectors) = Bhost;
    std::get<2>(cpu_vectors) = Chost;
    std::get<3>(cpu_vectors) = ceil(vsize*offload_ratio);
    // Message for the CPU
    std::get<4>(ports).try_put(cpu_vectors);
  }};
```

Figure 19-13. *First two nodes, in_node and dispatch_node, in triad example*

This part of the algorithm is quite straightforward. Our old friend in_node sends offload_ratio=0.5 a single time to dispatch_node. For its part, dispatch_node is of the following type:

```
multifunction_node<float,
            tuple<buffer_f, buffer_f, buffer_f, NDRange, tuple_cpu>>
```

which means that it receives a float (offload_ratio) and has five output ports that send messages that correspond to the five tuple element types. This tuple encapsulates the data type of the five output ports of this multifunction node: three buffer_f (opencl_buffers here) for the three arrays, the NDRange, and a tuple_cpu that packs all the information for the cpu_node.

The two input arguments of the lambda expression that defines the body of dispatch_node are

```
[&](const float& offload_ratio, mfn_t::output_ports_type& ports ){…
```

where we find the input message (offload_ratio) and a handle (ports) that give us access to each one of the five output ports. Now, we use function get<port_number>(ports).try_put(message) to send a message to the corresponding port_number. Four calls to this function are all we need to send the information that the GPU is waiting for. Note that the last one of these four calls puts a 1D array with just one element equal to ceil(vsize*offload_ratio) which corresponds to the iteration space on the GPU. A single message sets out on a trip to the CPU via the last port, using get<4>(ports).try_put(cpu_vectors). Previously, we have conveniently packed the CPU view of the three vectors and the vector partitioning information (ceil(vsize*offload_ratio)) in the cpu_vectors tuple.

Any questions? Sure? We don't want to leave any reader behind. Okay then. Let's move on to see the implementation of the next two nodes, the meat of the matter, where the real computation takes place, in Figure 19-14.

```
gpu_device_selector gpu_selector;
tbb::flow::opencl_program<> program{std::string{"triad.cl"}};
using tuple_gpu = std::tuple<buffer_f, buffer_f, buffer_f, NDRange>;
tbb::flow::opencl_node<tuple_gpu> gpu_node{g,
                                      program.get_kernel("triad"),
                                      gpu_selector};
gpu_node.set_args(tbb::flow::port_ref<0, 2>, alpha);
gpu_node.set_range(tbb::flow::port_ref<3>); //NDRange -> last port


tbb::flow::function_node<tuple_cpu, float *> cpu_node{g,
  tbb::flow::unlimited,
  [&](tuple_cpu cpu_vectors) {
    float* Ahost = std::get<0>(cpu_vectors);
    float* Bhost = std::get<1>(cpu_vectors);
    float* Chost = std::get<2>(cpu_vectors);
    size_t start = std::get<3>(cpu_vectors);
    // Parallel execution on the CPU
    parallel_for(tbb::blocked_range<size_t>{start, vsize},
       [&](const tbb::blocked_range<size_t>& r){
         for (size_t i = r.begin(); i < r.end(); ++i)
           Chost[i] = Ahost[i] + 0.5 * Bhost[i];
       });
    return Chost;
}};
```

Figure 19-14. *The nodes really shouldering the burden in the triad example: gpu_node and cpu_node*

Although cpu_node is the second one in Figure 19-14, we will cover it first since it requires less clarification. The template parameter <tuple_cpu, float*> points out that the node receives a tuple_cpu and sends a pointer to float. The lambda input argument, cpu_vectors, is used in the body to unpack the pointers into the three vectors and the variable start (that gets the value ceil(vsize*offload_ratio) already computed on the dispatch_node). With this information, a parallel_for carries out the triad computation in the range blocked_range<size_t>(start, vsize), which correspond to the second part of the iteration space.

As we said, the GPU is responsible of the first part of this iteration space, known in this context as the NDRange=[0, ceil(vsize*offload_ratio)). The source code of the GPU kernel is the same as we presented in the previous chapter, and it just receives the three arrays and does the triad operation for every i in NDRange:

```
kernel void triad(global float* A, global float* B, global float* C){
  int i = get_global_id(0);
  C[i] = A[i] + 0.5 * B[i];
}
```

These kernel lines are inside the triad.cl file, hence the line:

```
tbb::flow::opencl_program<> program{std::string{"triad.cl"}};
```

at the beginning of Figure 19-14. The custom type tuple_gpu packs the three buffer_f and the NDRange. With this, we declare the gpu_node as

```
tbb::flow::opencl_node<tuple_gpu> gpu_node{g,
                                    program.get_kernel("triad"),
                                    gpu_selector};
```

That selects the "triad" kernel of the program file and specifies our favorite Device Selector, gpu_selector.

Now comes an interesting configuration detail. Four messages reach the gpu_node and we mentioned previously that "opencl_node binds the first input port to the first kernel argument, the second input port to the second kernel argument and so on." But wait! The kernel only has three arguments! Were we lying again!!?? Well, not this time. We also said that this is the default behavior and that it can be modified. Here is how.

With gpu_node.set_args(port_ref<0,2>) we state that the messages arriving at ports 0, 1 and 2 should be bound to the three input arguments of the kernel (A, B and C). And what about the NDRange? In our first example "Hello OpenCL_Node" in Figure 19-3 we just used gpu_node.set_range({{1}}) to specify the smallest possible NDRange with constant value 1. But in this second and more elaborated example, the NDRange is variable and comes from dispatch_node. We can bind the third port of the node, that receives NDRange with the set_range() function, as we did with the line gpu_node.set_range(port_ref<3>). This means that we can pass to set_range() a constant or a variable NDRange that comes through a port. The member function set_args() should support the same flexibility, right? We know how to bind kernel arguments to opencl_node ports, but often times kernel arguments have to be set just once and not for every invocation.

Say for example that our kernel receives the value of α that is now a user-defined argument (not hardwired to 0.5 as before):

```
kernel void triad(global float* A, global float* B,
                  global float* C, float alpha){
  int i = get_global_id(0);
  C[i] = A[i] + alpha * B[i];
}
```

Then we can write the following: gpu_node.set_args(port_ref<0,2>, 0.5f) which binds the three first kernel arguments to the data reaching ports 0, 1, and 2, and the fourth argument to... 0.5 (oh no! hardwired again! More seriously, nothing prevents us from passing a variable, alpha, previously set to... 0.5).

Now, let's go for the last two nodes, node_join and out_node, that are detailed in Figure 19-15.

```
using join_t = tbb::flow::join_node<std::tuple<buffer_f, float*>,
                                    tbb::flow::queueing>;
join_t node_join{g};

tbb::flow::function_node<join_t::output_type> out_node{g,
  tbb::flow::unlimited,
  [&](const join_t::output_type& m){
    std::tie (Cdevice, Chost) = m; //unpack the tuple m

    // Serial execution
    std::vector<float> CGold(vsize);
    std::transform(Ahost, Ahost + vsize, Bhost, CGold.begin(),
            [&](float a, float b)->float{return a+0.5*b;});

    // Check correctness:
    if ( ! std::equal(Chost, Chost+vsize, CGold.begin()))
      std::cout << "Error!!\n";
}};
```

***Figure 19-15.** Last two nodes, node_join and out_node, of the heterogenous triad vector operation*

As indicated in boldface, node_join receives a buffer_f (from gpu_node) and a pointer to float (from cpu_node). This node is created just to join these two messages into a tuple that is forwarded to the next node. Speaking of which, the next node is out_node, a function_node that receives a message of the type join_t::output_type and does not send any output message. Note that join_t is the type of node_join, so join_t::output_type is an alias of tuple<buffer_f, float*>. Actually, the input argument of the lambda, m, has this type. A convenient way to unpack the tuple m is to execute std::tie(Cdevice, Chost) = m, which is completely equivalent to

```
Cdevice = std::get<0>(m);
Chost = std::get<1>(m);
```

The next lines of the body of out_node check that the heterogeneous computation is correct, first serially computing a golden version, CGold, of the triad array operation and then comparing with Chost using the std::equal algorithm. Since Chost, Cdevice.data(), and Cdevice.begin() are all actually pointing to the same buffer, these three comparisons are equivalent:

```
std::equal (Chost, Chost+vsize, CGold.begin())
std::equal (Cdevice.begin(), Cdevice.end(), CGold.begin())
std::equal (Cdevice.data(), Cdevice.data()+vsize, CGold.begin())
```

Time to sign off our code. In Figure 19-16, we add the make_edge calls and trigger the execution of the flow graph.

```
// in_node -> dispatch_node
tbb::flow::make_edge(in_node, dispatch_node);
// dispatch_node -> gpu_node
tbb::flow::make_edge(tbb::flow::output_port<0>(dispatch_node),
                     tbb::flow::input_port<0>(gpu_node));
tbb::flow::make_edge(tbb::flow::output_port<1>(dispatch_node),
                     tbb::flow::input_port<1>(gpu_node));
tbb::flow::make_edge(tbb::flow::output_port<2>(dispatch_node),
                     tbb::flow::input_port<2>(gpu_node));
tbb::flow::make_edge(tbb::flow::output_port<3>(dispatch_node),
                     tbb::flow::input_port<3>(gpu_node));
// dispatch_node -> cpu_node
tbb::flow::make_edge(tbb::flow::output_port<4>(dispatch_node),
                     cpu_node);
// gpu_node -> node_join
tbb::flow::make_edge(tbb::flow::output_port<2>(gpu_node),
                     tbb::flow::input_port<0>(node_join));
// cpu_node -> node_join
tbb::flow::make_edge(cpu_node,tbb::flow::input_port<1>(node_join));
// node_join -> out_node
tbb::flow::make_edge(node_join, out_node);

tbb::tick_count t = tbb::tick_count::now();
in_node.activate();
g.wait_for_all();
```

Figure 19-16. *Last part of the triad main function where nodes are connected and the graph is dispatched*

Note that, although the four input ports of gpu_node are connected to the preceding dispatch_node, only port number 2 of gpu_node goes to node_join. This port carries the resulting Cdevice buffer, so it is the only one we care about. The other three disregarded ports won't feel offended.

It took us a while to explain the whole example, and still we have to add one more thing. How it compares with the async_node version that we presented in the previous chapter? Our async_node version included the OpenCL boilerplate that was hidden in the OpenCL_Initialize() function but was required because it gave us access to the context, command queue and kernel handlers. This async_node version has 287 lines of code (excluding comments and blank lines) if we use the cl.h OpenCL header or 193 lines using the cl.hpp C++ wrapper of the cl.h header. This new version based on the opencl_node feature further reduces the size of the source file to just 144 lines of code.

The Devil Is in the Details

Those of us that have previously developed OpenCL codes, know that we can "enjoy" a considerable degree of latitude if we use the raw OpenCL library directly. This flexibility doesn't show up in the opencl_node at first glance. How can we define a multidimensional NDRange? And how can we also specify the local size in addition to the NDRange global size? And how can we provide a precompiled kernel instead of the OpenCL source? Maybe the problem is that we have not covered all the available configuration knobs yet. Let's jump into the answers to these questions.

The main OpenCL functions needed to launch a kernel are clSetKernelArg (clSetKernelArgSVMPointer if we use OpenCL 2.x Shared Virtual Memory pointers) and clEnqueueNDRangeKernel. These functions are internally called in the OpenCL factory, and we can control which arguments are passed into them. To illustrate how the opencl_node member functions and helper functions are translated to raw OpenCL calls, we zoom in on an opencl_node in Figure 19-17.

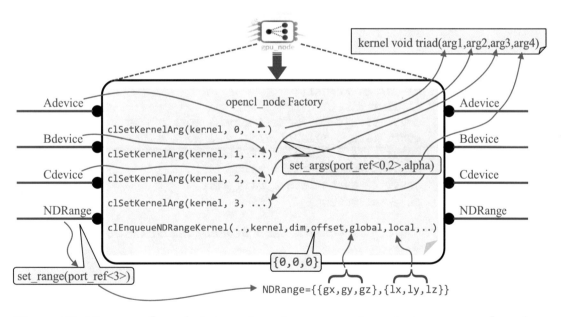

Figure 19-17. *opencl_node internals and correspondence between* opencl_node *functions and native OpenCL calls*

In this figure, we use the gpu_node of the previous triad example, where we configured an opencl_node to receive three opencl_buffers and the NDRange (a total of four ports that enter and leave the node). As we explained a few pages ago, thanks to gpu_node.set_args(port_ref<0,2>, alpha), we clearly state that the first three input ports (0, 1, and 2) that carry A, B, and C vectors should be bound to the first three arguments of the kernel, and the last argument of the kernel (the multiplicative factor α) is statically bounded to a variable alpha, which does not come from previous nodes of the graph. Now, we have all the information that is required to make the four clSetKernelArg() calls that we see in Figure 19-17, which in turn work their magic to get these four arguments to appear as inputs to the kernel void triad(...) OpenCL function.

Now, let's look at how the clEnqueueNDRangeKernel call is appropriately configured. This is one of the most complex OpenCL calls; it requires nine arguments that we list in Figure 19-18. However, this is not an OpenCL primer, and for this chapter it suffices to discuss just the five arguments from the 2nd to the 6th ones. The one identified with the variable "kernel" will be covered later, and to understand the other four we have to delve deeper into one of the fundamental concepts of OpenCL: the NDRange.

```
cl_int clEnqueueNDRangeKernel (
  cl_command_queue command_queue,
  cl_kernel kernel,
  cl_uint dim,
  const size_t *offset, //global_work_offset
  const size_t *global, //global_work_size
  const size_t *local,  //local_work_size
  cl_uint num_events_in_wait_list,
  const cl_event *event_wait_list,
  cl_event *event)
```

Figure 19-18. *Signature of the OpenCL clEnqueueNDRangeKernel call*

The **NDRange** Concept

An NDRange defines an iteration space of independent work items. This space is potentially three-dimensional, but it can be also 2D or 1D. The NDRange in our triad example is 1D. The argument dim in the clEnqueueNDrangeKernel call in Figures 19-17 and 19-18 should contain 1, 2, or 3 accordingly and will be properly set by the gpu_node. set_range() call. In the example of Figure 19-17, this set_range() call points out that the NDRange information arrives to port 3 of the gpu_node from a previous node of the graph. The NDRange information should be in one, or optionally two containers, which provide begin() and end() member functions. Many standard C++ types provide these member functions, including std::initializer_list, std::vector, std::array, and std::list, to name a few. If we only specify one container, the opencl_node just sets the global_work_size argument of the clEnqueueNDRangeKernel() function (identified with the variable global in Figures 19-17 and 19-18). If otherwise, we also specify a second container, the opencl_node sets the local_work_size argument (local in Figures 19-17 and 19-18) as well.

Note   As we said, the NDRange `global_work_size` defines the parallel iteration space that will be executed by the accelerator. Each point in this space is called a work item using the OpenCL slang (if you are familiar with CUDA, it is equivalent to a CUDA thread). Therefore, work items can be processed in parallel on the different accelerator compute units, CUs, and the corresponding computation is defined by the kernel code, that is, if our kernel function includes `C[i]=A[i]+B[i]`, this is the expression that will be applied to each work item i of this 1D iteration space.

Now, work items are grouped into what are called work-groups (or blocks using CUDA notation). Due to architectural implementation details, work items belonging to the same work-group are more tightly related. For instance, on a GPU, it is guaranteed that a work-group will be scheduled on a single GPU compute unit. This implies that we can synchronize the work items of a single work-group with an OpenCL barrier, and these work items share a per-CU memory space called "local memory" which is faster than the global memory.

The argument `local_work_size` specifies the size of the work-groups. OpenCL drivers can automatically compute a recommended `local_work_size` if none is provided. However, if we want to enforce a particular work-group size, we have to set the `local_work_size` argument.

Here is where some examples will make it crystal clear. Say we have 2D arrays A, B, and C, of dimensions h x w and we want to compute the matrix operation C=A+B. Although matrices are two-dimensional, in OpenCL they are passed to the kernel as a pointer to a row-major linearized 1D `cl_mem` buffer. This does not prevent us from computing a 1D index from a 2D one, so the kernel will look like

```
x = get_global_id(0); // column
y = get_global_id(1); // row
C[y*w+x] = A[y*w+x] + B[y*w+x]; // row x width + column
```

although the fancy way to express the same uses the `int2` type and reads as

```
int2 gId = (int2)(get_global_id(0),  get_global_id(1));
C[gId.y*w+gId.x] = A[gId.y*w+gId.x] + B[gId.y*w+gId.x];
```

To get more information about what is going on for each work item during the kernel execution, we will print out some additional information, as seen in Figure 19-19.

```
kernel void cl_print(global float* A,
                     global float* B,
                     global float* C,
                     int w) {
  int2 gId =    (int2)(get_global_id(0),   get_global_id(1));
  int2 lId =    (int2)(get_local_id(0),    get_local_id(1));
  int2 grId =   (int2)(get_group_id (0),   get_group_id(1));
  int2 gSize =  (int2)(get_global_size(0), get_global_size(1));
  int2 lSize =  (int2)(get_local_size(0),  get_local_size(1));
  int2 numGrp = (int2)(get_num_groups (0), get_num_groups(1));
  if (gId.x == 0 && gId.y==0)
     printf("gSize.x=%d, gSize.y=%d, lSize.x=%d, lSize.y=%d,
            numGrp.x=%d, numGrp.y=%d\n",
           gSize.x, gSize.y, lSize.x, lSize.y, numGrp.x,
           numGrp);
  printf("gId.x=%d, gId.y=%d, lId.x=%d, lId.y=%d, grId.x=%d,
         grId.y=%d\n\n",
        gId.x, gId.y, lId.x, lId.y, grId.x, grId.y);
  C[gId.y*w+gId.x] = A[gId.y*w+gId.x] + B[gId.y*w+gId.x];
}
```

Figure 19-19. *Kernel example that adds two matrices and prints out relevant work-item information*

The first three variables, `gId`, `lId`, and `grId` store the global ID, local ID, and group ID of each work item, respectively, in both dimensions x and y. The next three variables `gSize`, `lSize`, and `numGrp` are set to the global size, local size, and number of workgroups. The first if condition is satisfied only by the work item with global ID (0,0).

So only that work item prints out the various sizes and number of groups, which are the same for all work items. The second `printf` statement is executed by every work item and prints the global, local and group IDs for that work item. This results in the output shown in Figure 19-20, when enqueued with `dim = 2`, `global = {4,4}` and `local = {2,2}`.

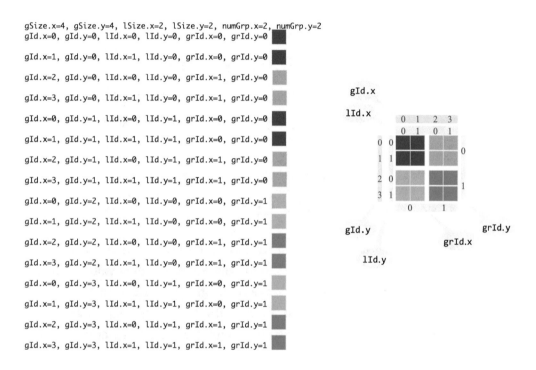

Figure 19-20. *Output of the kernel of Figure 19-19 when configured with* dim=2, global={4,4}, *and* local={2,2} --set_range({{4, 4}, {2, 2}})--

In this figure, we depict every work item with a colored box. There are 16 work items arranged in a 4×4 grid where we identify each work-group using four different colors. Since the local size is {2,2}, each work-group is a 2×2 subspace. It's no wonder that the number of groups is 4, but to give some formalism to this chapter we add here some invariants that we can easily demonstrate:

```
numGrp.x = gSize.x/lSize.x
0 <= gId.x < gSize
0 <= lId.x < lSize
gId.x = grId * lSize.x + lId.x
```

and likewise, for the `.y` coordinate (or even `.z` in a 3D space)

And now, how do we specify the global and local sizes for an opencl_node? So far, we have just used gpu_node.set_range({{<num>}}) in previous examples of the chapter. This would translate into dim=1, global={<num>} and local=NULL which results in a 1D NDRange with local size left to the OpenCL driver discretion.

In the general case, we may need global={gx, gy, gz} and local={lx, ly, lz}. The easiest way to achieve this is to use

```
gpu_node.set_range({{gx, gy, gz},{lx, ly, lz}});
```

However, as we said, any container that can be iterated with a begin() member function will also suit our needs. For instance, a more convoluted way of expressing the same would be

```
std::list<int> list_global = {gx, gy, gz};
std::vector<int> vector_local = {lx, ly, lz};
gpu_node.set_range({list_global, vector_local});
```

The resulting range has as many dimensions as the number of elements in the container, with each dimension size set to the corresponding element value. The caveat here is to specify the same dimensionality for both the global and the local containers.

To make things interesting, we have to add the TBB driver code that can launch the kernel of Figure 19-19. The most concise way we know of is to build a graph with a single opencl_node as shown in Figure 19-21.

```
int h = (argc>1) ? atoi(argv[1]) : 4;
int w = (argc>2) ? atoi(argv[2]) : 4;
size_t vsize = h * w;

tbb::flow::graph g;

using buffer_f = tbb::flow::opencl_buffer<cl_float>;
buffer_f Adevice{vsize};
buffer_f Bdevice{vsize};
buffer_f Cdevice{vsize};
float* Ahost = Adevice.data();
float* Bhost = Bdevice.data();

// Initialize A and B
std::iota(Ahost, Ahost+vsize, 0); // 0, 1, 2, 3, ...
std::iota(Bhost, Bhost+vsize, 0); // 0, 1, 2, 3, ...

//GPU node:
gpu_device_selector s;
tbb::flow::opencl_program<> program{std::string{"fig_19_19.cl"}};
tbb::flow::opencl_node<std::tuple<buffer_f>> gpu_node{g,
                    program.get_kernel("cl_print"), s};
gpu_node.set_range({{w, h}, {w/2, h/2}});
gpu_node.set_args(Adevice, Bdevice, tbb::flow::port_ref<0>, w);
tbb::flow::input_port<0>(gpu_node).try_put(Cdevice);
g.wait_for_all();
```

Figure 19-21. *opencl_node exercised in isolation*

See? Just a handful of lines of code and we are up and running an OpenCL code that adds two matrices A and B. Note that the opencl_node, gpu_node, has only a single port, port<0>, that is bound to the third argument of the kernel, matrix C, that carries the result of the computation conducted in the kernel. The input matrices, A and B, and the matrix width, w, are directly passed using set_args member function. Also note that the opencl_node has to have at least one port and it is activated only if a message lands in this entry port. An alternative to implement the gpu_node would be the following:

```
tbb::flow::opencl_node<std::tuple<buffer_f,tbb::flow::opencl_range>>
            gpu_node{g, program.get_kernel("cl_print"), s};
gpu_node.set_range(tbb::flow::port_ref<1>);
gpu_node.set_args(Adevice, Bdevice, tbb::flow::port_ref<0>, w);
tbb::flow::input_port<0>(gpu_node).try_put(Cdevice);
tbb::flow::input_port<1>(gpu_node).try_put(
                    tbb::flow::opencl_range({{w, h}, {w/2, h/2}}));
```

Where the gpu_node receives Cdevice on port<0>, the NDRange on port<1> and the remaining kernel arguments are specified with the set_range() member function. The type of the message arriving and leaving port<1> of the gpu_node is tbb::flow::opencl_range (the umpteenth opencl_node helper class, so far!), and we rely on try_put() to pass an opencl_range object initialized with the two containers.

Playing with the Offset

There are two other arguments of the clEnqueueNDRangeKernel function that we left behind (see Figure 19-18). One is the offset argument that can be used to skip some of the first work items at the beginning of the iteration space. In the current implementation of the OpenCL factory, this offset is hardwired to {0,0,0}. Not a big deal. There are two possible workarounds to overcome this limitation.

The first one consists in passing the offset to the kernel and add it to the global ID before indexing the arrays. For example, for a one-dimensional C=A+B operation we can write something like

```
kernel void vector-add(global float* A, global float* B,
                       global float* C, int offset ){
    int i = get_global_id(0) + offset ;
    C[i] = A[i] + B[i];
}
```

And of course, we can adapt the NDRange to avoid overrunning the arrays. Although functional, not a super-elegant solution. Which is the super-elegant solution then? Well, we can use the opencl_subbuffer class to achieve the same result. For example, if we want to add just a subregion of vectors A and B, we can keep a simpler version of the vector-add kernel:

```
kernel void vector-add(global float* A, global float* B,
                       global float* C){
    int i = get_global_id(0);
    C[i] = A[i] + B[i];
}
```

but pass the following arguments to the set_args() member function:

```
Adevice.subbuffer(offset, size)
```

and similarly, for Bdevice and Cdevice. Another alternative to create a sub-buffer of Cdevice is to call

```
tbb::flow::opencl_subbuffer<cl_float>(Cdevice, offset, size)
```

Specifying the OpenCL Kernel

Finally, we have to devote some time to the kernel argument (see Figure 19-18). Up to now, we have used OpenCL source files to provide our kernel. In the last example of Figure 19-21, we used again the opencl_program class:

```
tbb::flow::opencl_program<> program{std::string{"fig_19_19.cl"}};
```

which is equivalent to the more explicit constructor:

```
tbb::flow::opencl_program<> program{opencl_program_type::SOURCE,
                                    std::string{"fig_19_19.cl"}};
```

This is the usual approach to provide the kernel function that, on the one hand, requires compiling the source at runtime, but on the other hand, provides portability because the source will be compiled (only once at opencl_program construction) for all the available devices. Internally, the OpenCL factory relies on the OpenCL functions clCreateProgramWithSource and clBuildProgram.

If we are positive we don't need to port our code to any other platform and/or if, for the production version, we require the last drop of performance, we can also precompile the kernel. For example, with the Intel OpenCL tool chain we can run

```
ioc64 -cmd=build -input=my_kernel.cl -ir=my_kernel.clbin
    -bo="-cl-std=CL2.0" -device=gpu
```

which generates the precompiled file my_kernel.clbin. Now, we can create the program object faster using

```
opencl_program<> program{opencl_program_type::PRECOMPILED,
                         std::string{"my_kernel.clbin"}};
```

When passing this type of file to the opencl_program constructor, the factory internally uses the clCreateProgramWithBinary instead. An additional possibility is to provide the SPIR intermediate representation of the kernel, using `opencl_program_type::SPIR`. To generate the SPIR version, we can use

```
ioc64 -cmd=build -input=my_kernel.cl -spir64=my_kernel.spir
      -bo="-cl-std=CL1.2"
```

In both cases, the `ioc64` compiler provides some useful information. The output of the last run will look like

```
Using build options: -cl-std=CL1.2
OpenCL Intel(R) Graphics device was found!
Device name: Intel(R) HD Graphics
Device version: OpenCL 2.0
Device vendor: Intel(R) Corporation
Device profile: FULL_PROFILE
fcl build 1 succeeded.
bcl build succeeded.
my_kernel info:
      Maximum work-group size: 256
      Compiler work-group size: (0, 0, 0)
      Local memory size: 0
      Preferred multiple of work-group size: 32
      Minimum amount of private memory: 0
Build succeeded!
```

This output informs us about, among other things, the maximum work-group size, 256, and the preferred multiple of the work-group size, 32, for this particular kernel.

Even More on Device Selection

In a previous section, we realized that the laptop we are using to conduct our experiments includes two GPUs. Let's see a quick example in which we use both of them in the same flow graph. In Figure 19-22, we link two `opencl_nodes` so that the first computes C=A+B and send C to the following one, that does `C = C - B`. When both nodes are done, we check that `C == A` in a regular `function_node`. Array dimensions are rows × cols.

```
tbb::flow::graph g;
// Initialize A and B
…
tbb::flow::opencl_program<> program{std::string{"fig_19_23.cl"}};
using tuple_gpu = std::tuple<buffer_f>;

//GPU node 1:
tbb::flow::opencl_node<tuple_gpu> gpu_node1{g,
  program.get_kernel("cl_add"),
  [](auto& f){
    auto d = *(f.devices().begin() + 1);
    std::cout << "Running gpu_node1 on " << d.name()<< '\n';
    return d;
  }};
gpu_node1.set_range({{cols, rows}});
gpu_node1.set_args(Adevice, Bdevice, tbb::flow::port_ref<0>);

//GPU node 2:
tbb::flow::opencl_node<tuple_gpu> gpu_node2{g,
  program.get_kernel("cl_sub"),
  [](auto& f){
    auto d = *(f.devices().begin() + 2);
    std::cout << "Running gpu_node2 on " << d.name()<< '\n';
    return d;
  }};
gpu_node2.set_range({{cols, rows}});
gpu_node2.set_args(Adevice, Bdevice, tbb::flow::port_ref<0>);

//Output node:
tbb::flow::function_node<buffer_f> out_node{g, tbb::flow::unlimited,
  [&](buffer_f const& Cdevice){
    float* Chost = Cdevice.data();
    if (! std::equal(Chost, Chost+vsize, Ahost))
      std::cout << "Errors in the heterogeneous computation.\n";
  }
};
make_edge(tbb::flow::output_port<0>(gpu_node1),
          tbb::flow::input_port<0>(gpu_node2));
make_edge(tbb::flow::output_port<0>(gpu_node2), out_node);
tbb::flow::input_port<0>(gpu_node1).try_put(Cdevice);
g.wait_for_all();
```

Figure 19-22. *Example with two* opencl_nodes, *each one configured to use a different GPU*

On our laptop, we already know that the device list f.devices() includes three devices, and the second and third ones are the two GPUs. That way, we can safely use f.devices().begin() +1 and +2 to get the iterator pointing to each GPU, as we see in the boxed statements of Figure 19-22 for the two opencl_node definitions. In addition to targeting different GPUs, each opencl_node is configured to run two different kernels of the program fig_19_23.cl: cl_add and cl_sub. The information flowing from gpu_node1 to gpu_node2 is the opencl_buffer Cdevice. Inside the OpenCL factory, data movement is minimized and if, for example, an opencl_buffer has to be accessed by two consecutive opencl_nodes mapped onto the same GPU, the data allocated on the GPU is not moved to the CPU until the first CPU node of the graph tries to access the corresponding buffer (by using opencl_buffer.begin() or opencl_buffer.data() member functions).

In Figure 19-23, we present the program fig_19_23.cl including the two kernels referenced in the previous code. Note that instead of passing the row width as a fourth argument, we use gSz.x that contains the same value.

```
kernel void cl_add(global float* A,global float* B,global float* C){
  int2 gId = (int2)(get_global_id(0), get_global_id(1));
  int2 gSz = (int2)(get_global_size(0), get_global_size(1));

  if(gId.x == 0 && gId.y==0)
    printf("gSz.x=%d, gSz.y=%d\n",gSz.x,gSz.y);
  C[gId.y*gSz.x+gId.x]=A[gId.y*gSz.x+gId.x]+B[gId.y*gSz.x+gId.x];
}

kernel void cl_sub(global float* A,global float* B,global float* C){
  int2 gId = (int2)(get_global_id(0), get_global_id(1));
  int2 gSz = (int2)(get_global_size(0), get_global_size(1));

  if(gId.x == 0 && gId.y==0)
    printf("gSz.x=%d, gSz.y=%d\n",gSz.x,gSz.y);
  C[gId.y*gSz.x+gId.x]=C[gId.y*gSz.x+gId.x]-B[gId.y*gSz.x+gId.x];
}
```

Figure 19-23. *Content of* fig_19_23.cl *where we see two kernels, each one called from a different* opencl_node

The output resulting from running the code of Figure 19-22 on our laptop is the following:

```
Running gpu_node1 on Intel(R) HD Graphics 530
Running gpu_node2 on AMD Radeon Pro 450 Compute Engine
gSz.x=4, gSz.y=4
gSz.x=4, gSz.y=4
```

It is also possible to have a single opencl_node changing the OpenCL device to which the work is offloaded for every invocation of the node. The example of Figure 19-24 shows an opencl_node that is invoked three times, and for each one a different device is used to run a simple kernel.

```cpp
tbb::flow::graph g;
using buffer_f = tbb::flow::opencl_buffer<cl_int>;
buffer_f Adevice{vsize};
int* Ahost = Adevice.data();
std::iota(Ahost, Ahost+vsize, 0); // 0, 1, 2, 3, ...

//GPU node:
tbb::flow::opencl_program<> program{std::string{"fig_19_24.cl"}};
tbb::atomic<int> device_num{0};
tbb::flow::opencl_node<std::tuple<buffer_f>> gpu_node{g,
  program.get_kernel("cl_inc"),
  [&device_num](auto& f){
    auto d=*(f.devices().begin()+device_num++ % f.devices().size());
    std::cout << "Running on " << d.name() << '\n';
    return d;
  }};
gpu_node.set_range({{static_cast<int>(vsize)}});
gpu_node.set_args(tbb::flow::port_ref<0>);
for(int i=0; i<3; i++){
  std::cout << "Iteration: " << i << '\n';
  tbb::flow::input_port<0>(gpu_node).try_put(Adevice);
}

g.wait_for_all();
std::vector<int> AGold(vsize);
std::iota(AGold.begin(), AGold.end(), 3); // 3, 4, 5, 6, ...
if (! std::equal(Adevice.begin(), Adevice.end(), AGold.begin()))
  std::cout << "Errors in the heterogeneous computation.\n";
```

Figure 19-24. *A single opencl_node can change the target accelerator for every invocation*

The code uses the atomic variable device_num initialized to 0. Each invocation to the gpu_node returns a different device, cyclically traversing all of them (three in our platform). Along with the following kernel:

```
kernel void cl_inc(global int* A) {
  int gId = get_global_id(0);
  A[gId]++;
  if(gId == 0) printf("A[0]=%d\n", A[0]);
}
```

the resulting output is

```
Iteration: 0
Iteration: 1
Iteration: 2
Running on Intel(R) Core(TM) i7-6700HQ CPU @ 2.60GHz
Running on Intel(R) HD Graphics 530
Running on AMD Radeon Pro 450 Compute Engine
A[0]=1
A[0]=2
A[0]=3
```

where we can corroborate that the elements of the array Adevice have been incremented three times in three consecutive invocations of the gpu_node and the corresponding kernel has been executed on three different OpenCL devices.

A Warning Regarding the Order Is in Order!

One final caveat that we should be aware of has to do with the order in which the messages arrive to an opencl_node when it is served from several nodes. For example, in Figure 19-25 we illustrate a flow graph, g, that includes a gpu_node fed from two function nodes, filler0 and filler1. Each "filler" sends 1000 buffers, b, of 10 integers each, of the form {i,i,i,…,i}, with i ranging from 1 to 1000. The receiving gpu_node receives both messages as b1 and b2 and just invokes an OpenCL kernel as simple as this:

```
kernel void mul(global int* b1, global int* b2){
  const int index = get_global_id(0);
  b1[index] *= b2[index];
}
```

As we see, it basically multiplies b1[i]=b1[i]*b2[i]. If b1 and b2 are equal (to {1,1,1,…}, or {2,2,2,…}, etc.), we should get at the output 1000 buffers with squared outputs ({1,1,1,…}, then {4,4,4,…}, and so on). Right? Sure? We don't want to lie, so just in case, let's double check it in the last node of the graph, checker, which validates our assumption.

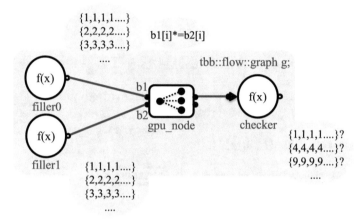

Figure 19-25. *Two function nodes feeding an* opencl_node *with buffers that will be multiplied on the GPU*

The code that implements the previous graph is listed in Figure 19-26. We agree with George Bernard Shaw in that "The liar's punishment is not in the least that he is not believed, but that he cannot believe anyone else." As liar connoisseurs, we use in our code a try-catch construction especially devised to catch liars!

```
using buffer_i = tbb::flow::opencl_buffer<int>;
try {
  constexpr int n = 10;
  tbb::flow::graph g;
  tbb::flow::function_node<int, buffer_i> filler0{g,
    tbb::flow::unlimited,
    [n](int i){
      buffer_i b{n};
      std::fill(b.begin(), b.end(), i);
      return b;
    }};

  tbb::flow::function_node<int, buffer_i> filler1 = filler0;

  tbb::flow::opencl_program<> program{std::string{"mul.cl"}};
  tbb::flow::opencl_node<std::tuple<buffer_i, buffer_i>> gpu_node{g,
                                    program.get_kernel("mul")};
  gpu_node.set_range({{ n }});

  tbb::flow::function_node<buffer_i> checker{g,
    tbb::flow::serial,
    [](const buffer_i& b){
      for (int v : b){
        int r = static_cast<int>(std::sqrt(v) + .5);
        if (r*r != v)
          throw std::runtime_error(std::to_string(v) +
                        " is not a square of any integer number" );
      }
    }};

  tbb::flow::make_edge(filler0, tbb::flow::input_port<0>(gpu_node));
  tbb::flow::make_edge(filler1, tbb::flow::input_port<1>(gpu_node));
  tbb::flow::make_edge(tbb::flow::output_port<0>(gpu_node), checker);

  for (int i = 1; i<=1000; ++i){
    filler0.try_put(i);
    filler1.try_put(i);
  }
  g.wait_for_all();
}
catch (std::exception& e){
  std::cerr << "Liar!!: " << e.what() << std::endl;
}
```

Figure 19-26. *Source code corresponding to the graph depicted in Figure 19-25*

We first define buffer_i as an opencl_buffer of integers. The two "fillers" receive an integer, i, and fill a buffer_i with 10 i's that are sent to the gpu_node. The three lines used to configure the opencl_node are too basic for us now and do not require further elaboration. The last node is the checker that throws an exception if any of the values received in the buffer processed on the GPU is not a squared integer. After making the edges, a 1000 iteration loop puts to work the two fillers. Now, the moment of truth has arrived, and the output is

```
Liar!!: 42 is not a square of any integer number
```

Well, we got caught! Apparently, 6*7 was computed on the GPU, instead of 6*6 or 7*7. Why? The answer is that we have not taken enough measures to ensure that messages arriving to the gpu_node are paired correctly. Remember that the body of the "fillers" is executed by tasks, and we cannot assume any particular order regarding the task execution.

Fortunately, the opencl_node comes with a handy type-specified key matching feature that will save the day. We put that feature to work in Figure 19-27.

```
// previously: using buffer_i = tbb::flow::opencl_buffer<int>;
class buffer_i : public tbb::flow::opencl_buffer<int> {
  int my_key;
public:
  buffer_i() {}
  buffer_i(size_t n, int k) : tbb::flow::opencl_buffer<int>{n},
                              my_key{k} {}
  int key() const {return my_key;}
};
…
    tbb::flow::function_node<int, buffer_i> filler0{g,
      tbb::flow::unlimited,
      [n](int i){
        buffer_i b{n, i};
        std::fill(b.begin(), b.end(), i);
        return b;
      }};

    tbb::flow::function_node<int, buffer_i> filler1 = filler0;

    tbb::flow::opencl_program<> program{std::string{"mul.cl"}};
    tbb::flow::opencl_node<std::tuple<buffer_i, buffer_i>,
                           tbb::flow::key_matching<int> >
                    gpu_node{g, program.get_kernel("mul")};
    gpu_node.set_range({{ n }});
…
```

Figure 19-27. *Fixing the code of Figure 19-26*

Basically, now `buffer_i` is a new class that inherits from `opencl_buffer<cl_int>` and adds an `int my_key` member variable and a `key()` member function that returns that key. Now the fillers have to use a different constructor (`buffer_i b{N,i}`), but more importantly, the `opencl_node` receives a second template argument (`key_matching<int>`). This automatically instructs the `opencl_node` to call the `key()` function and wait for messages with the same key value to be passed to all input ports. Done! If we run our code with these minor modifications, we will see that now we've been acquitted of perjury!

Summary

In this chapter, we presented the `opencl_node` feature of TBB flow graph. We began with a simple `Hello OpenCL_Node` example that represented a first look at the `opencl_node`, covering just the basics of this class. We then started to dive deeper into some of the helper classes, such as the `opencl_device_list` that is a container of `opencl_device` objects, and the Device Filter and Device Selector entities. In order to illustrate other helper classes and to give a more complex example, we also implemented the triad vector operation using an `opencl_node` to take care of part of the computation whereas the rest is processed simultaneously on the CPU cores. While there, we better covered the `opencl_buffer` helper class and the `set_range` and `set_args` member functions of the `opencl_node` class. The `NDRange` concept and how to set the global and local OpenCL sizes required almost a section, where we also explained how to use the `opencl_subbuffer` class and other variants to provide the kernel program (precompiled or the SPIR intermediate representation). We followed up by introducing two examples that illustrate how to map different `opencl_nodes` of the flow graph onto different devices, or even how to change the device to which the `opencl_node` offloads the computation at each invocation. Finally, we described how to avoid ordering issues when an `opencl_node` is fed from different nodes.

One final disclaimer. Maybe we were actually lying in the end. As of writing this chapter, the `opencl_node` is still a preview feature, so it is subject to eventual changes. After 3 years of development, we don't expect major changes, but we cannot promise this. If such changes end up in a future release, we do promise to write an updated edition of this chapter! Do you believe us?

For More Information

Here are some additional reading materials we recommend related to this chapter:

- Alexei Katranov, Opencl_node overview. Series of entries in the Intel Developer Zone blog: `https://software.intel.com/en-us/blogs/2015/12/09/opencl-node-overview`.

- David Kaeli, Perhaad Mistri, Dana Schaa, Dong Ping Zhang. Heterogeneous Computing with OpenCL 2.0. Morgan Kaufmann 2015.

Hiking icon in Figure 19-1 made by Scott de Jonge from `www.flaticon.com`.

CHAPTER 20

TBB on NUMA Architectures

Advanced programmers who care about performance know that exploiting locality is paramount. When it comes to locality, cache locality is the one that immediately springs to mind, but in many cases, for heavy-duty applications running on large shared-memory architectures, Non-Uniform Memory Access (NUMA) locality should also be considered. As you certainly know, NUMA conveys the message that memory is organized in different banks and some cores have faster access to some of the "close" banks than to "far" banks. More formally, a *NUMA node* is a grouping of the cores, caches, and local memory in which all cores share the same access time to the local shared caches and memory. Access time from one NUMA node to a different one can be significantly larger. Some questions arise, such as how the program data structures are allocated on the different NUMA nodes and where the threads that process these data structures are running (are they close or far from the data?). In this chapter, we address these questions, but more importantly, what can be done to exploit NUMA locality within a TBB parallel application.

Tuning for performance on NUMA systems comes down to four activities: (1) discovering what your platform topology is, (2) knowing the costs associated with accessing memory from the different nodes of your system, (3) controlling where your data is stored (data placement), and (4) controlling where your work executes (processor affinity).

In order to prevent you from being disappointed further down the line (i.e., to disappoint you right now!), we shall say the following upfront: currently, TBB does not offer high-level features for exploiting NUMA locality. Or in other words, out of the four activities listed before, TBB offers some help only in the fourth one, where we can rely on

M. Voss, R. Asenjo, J. Reinders, *Pro TBB*, https://doi.org/10.1007/978-1-4842-4398-5_20

the TBB `task_arena` (see Chapter 12) and local `task_sheduler_observer` (see Chapter 13) classes to identify the threads that should be confined in a NUMA node. For all the other activities, and even for the actual pinning of threads to NUMA nodes (which is the essential part of the fourth activity), we need to use either low-level OS-dependent system calls or higher-level third-party libraries and tools. This means, that even if this is a TBB book, this last chapter is not entirely about TBB. Our goal here is to thoroughly elaborate on how we can implement TBB code that exploits NUMA locality, even if most of the required activities are not directly related to TBB.

Now that we have warned the reader, let us break down the sections into which we have organized this chapter. We basically follow, in order, the four activities listed before. The first section shows some tools that can be used to discover the topology of our platform and to check how many NUMA nodes are available. If there is more than one NUMA node, we can move on to the next section. There, we use a benchmark to get an idea of the potential speedup that is at stake when exploiting NUMA locality on our particular platform. If the expected gain is convincing, we should start thinking in exploiting NUMA locality in our own code (not just in a simple benchmark). If we realize that our own problem can benefit from NUMA locality, we can jump into the heart of the matter which consists in mastering data placement and processor affinity. With this knowledge and with the help of TBB `task_arena` and `task_scheduler_observer` classes, we implement our first simple TBB application that exploits NUMA locality and assess the speedup obtained with respect to a baseline implementation. The whole process is summarized in Figure 20-1. We close the chapter sketching more advanced and general alternatives that could be considered for more complex applications.

Figure 20-1. *Activities required to exploit NUMA locality*

Note   If you are wondering why there is no high-level support in the current version of TBB, here are some reasons. First, it is a tough problem, highly dependent on the particular application that has to be parallelized and the architecture on which it will run. Since there is no one-size-fits-all solution, it is left to developers to determine the particular data placement and processor affinity alternatives that best suit the application at hand. Second, TBB architects and developers have always tried to avoid hardware specific solutions inside the TBB library because they can potentially hurt the portability of the code and the composability features of TBB. The library was not developed only to execute HPC applications, where we usually have exclusive access to the whole high-performance platform (or a partition of it). TBB should also do its best in shared environments in which other applications and processes are also running. Pinning threads to cores and memory to NUMA nodes can in many cases leads to suboptimal exploitation of the underlying architecture. Manually pinning has been shown repeatedly to be a bad idea in any application or system that has any dynamic nature in it at all. We strongly advise against taking such an approach, unless you are positive you will improve performance for your particular application on your particular parallel platform and you do not care about portability (or extra effort is made to implement a portable NUMA-aware application).

Considering the task-based nature of TBB parallel algorithms and the work-stealing scheduler that fuels the parallel execution, keeping the tasks running in cores close to the local memory can seem challenging. But that's not going to deter brave and fearless programmer like us. Let's go for it!

Discovering Your Platform Topology

"Know your enemy and yourself, and you shall win a hundred battles without loss." – Sun Tzu in *The Art of War*. This millenarian quote advises us to first strive to meticulously understand what we are facing before tackling it. There are some tools that come in handy to understand the underlying NUMA architecture. In this chapter, we will use hwloc and likwid[1] to gather information about the architecture and code execution. hwloc is a software package that

---

[1] www.open-mpi.org/projects/hwloc and https://github.com/RRZE-HPC/likwid.

provides a portable way to query information about the topology of a system, as well as to apply some NUMA controls, like data placement and processor affinity. likwid is another software package that informs about the hardware topology, can be used to collect hardware performance counters, and also provides a set of useful micro-benchmarks that can be used to characterize systems. We can also use VTune to analyze the performance of our code. Although likwid is only available for Linux, hwloc and VTune can be easily installed on Windows and MacOS as well. However, since the shared memory platforms that will serve to illustrate our codes run Linux, this will be the OS that we assume unless stated otherwise.

Because tuning for NUMA requires a deep understanding of the platforms being used, we will start by characterizing two machines that we will work on throughout this chapter. The two machines that we introduce next are known as **yuca** (from the yucca plant) and **aloe** (from the aloe vera plant). First, we can gather basic information about these machines. On Linux this information can be obtained using the command "lscpu", as we can see in Figure 20-2.

yuca

```
Architecture:          x86_64
CPU op-mode(s):        32-bit, 64-bit
Byte Order:            Little Endian
CPU(s):                64
On-line CPU(s) list:   0-63
Thread(s) per core:    2
Core(s) per socket:    8
Socket(s):             4
NUMA node(s):          4
Vendor ID:             GenuineIntel
CPU family:            6
Model:                 46
Stepping:              6
CPU MHz:               1064.000
BogoMIPS:              3999.02
Virtualization:        VT-x
L1d cache:             32K
L1i cache:             32K
L2 cache:              256K
L3 cache:              18432K
NUMA node0 CPU(s):     0-7,32-39
NUMA node1 CPU(s):     8-15,40-47
NUMA node2 CPU(s):     16-23,48-55
NUMA node3 CPU(s):     24-31,56-63
```

aloe

```
Architecture:          x86_64
CPU op-mode(s):        32-bit, 64-bit
Byte Order:            Little Endian
CPU(s):                32
On-line CPU(s) list:   0-31
Thread(s) per core:    1
Core(s) per socket:    16
Socket(s):             2
NUMA node(s):          2
Vendor ID:             GenuineIntel
CPU family:            6
Model:                 63
Stepping:              2
CPU MHz:               1200.000
BogoMIPS:              4601.10
Virtualization:        VT-x
L1d cache:             32K
L1i cache:             32K
L2 cache:              256K
L3 cache:              40960K
NUMA node0 CPU(s):     0-15
NUMA node1 CPU(s):     16-31
```

Figure 20-2. *Output of* lscpu *on yuca and aloe*

At first glance, we see that yuca has 64 logical cores numbered from 0 to 63, two logical cores per physical core (hyperthreading aka SMT or simultaneous multithreading, available), eight physical cores per socket, and four sockets that are also the four NUMA nodes or NUMA domains. For its part, aloe has 32 physical cores with hyperthreading disabled (only one thread per core), 16 physical cores per socket, and two sockets (NUMA nodes). At the end of the lscpu output, we can see the NUMA nodes and the ids of the logical cores included in each node, but the picture will become clearer if we use the `lstopo` utility from the `hwloc` library. In Figure 20-3, we include the PDF file generated on yuca when executing the command `lstopo --no-io yuca.pdf` (the `--no-io` argument disregards the I/O device topology).

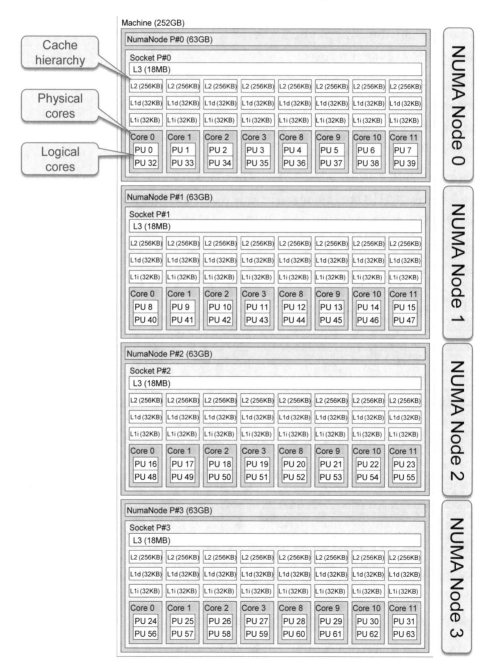

Figure 20-3. *Result of executing* `lstopo` *on yuca*

From this figure, we can get a clear representation of the NUMA organization in yuca. The four NUMA nodes include eight physical cores that are seen by the OS as 16 logical cores (also known as hardware threads). Note that logical core ids depend on the architecture, the firmware (BIOS configuration on PCs), and OS version, so we cannot assume anything from the numbering. For the particular configuration of yuca, logical cores 0 and 32 share the same physical core. Now we better understand the meaning of the last four lines of lscpu on yuca:

```
NUMA node0 CPU(s):      0-7,32-39
NUMA node1 CPU(s):      8-15,40-47
NUMA node2 CPU(s):      16-23,48-55
NUMA node3 CPU(s):      24-31,56-63
```

On yuca, each NUMA node has 63 GB of local memory, or 252 GB in total. Similarly, aloe also features 252 GB but organized in only two NUMA nodes. In Figure 20-4, we see a slightly edited version of the output of lstopo on aloe.

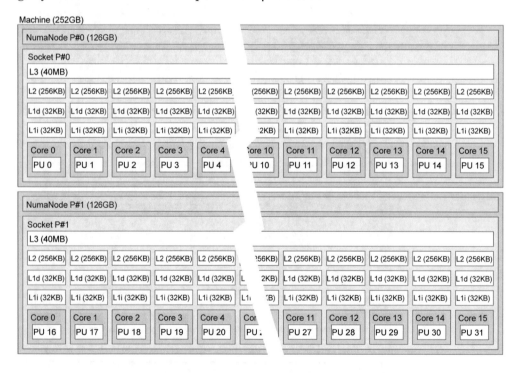

Figure 20-4. *Result of executing* lstopo *on aloe*

We see that on aloe each physical core includes a single logical core, numbered from 0-15 in the first domain and from 16-31 in the second one.

Understanding the Costs of Accessing Memory

Now that we know the topology of our platform, let's quantify the overhead due to nonlocal accesses assuming we already control processor affinity and data placement. Actually, we do control these two aspects on already available benchmarks, like likwid-bench available in the likwid tool. Using this benchmark, we can run the STREAM triad code (see the previous two chapters) using a single command line:

```
likwid-bench -t stream -i 1 -w S0:12GB:16-0:S0,1:S0,2:S0
```

which runs a single iteration (-i 1) of the stream benchmark configured with -w argument so that

- S0: The threads are pinned to the NUMA node 0.

- 12 GB: The three triad arrays occupy 12 GB (4 GB per array).

- 16: 16 threads will share the computation, each one processing chunks of 31,250,000 doubles (this is, 4000 million bytes/8 bytes per double/16 threads).

- 0:S0,1:S0,2:S0: The three arrays are allocated on the NUMA node 0.

On yuca, the result of this command reports a bandwidth of 8219 MB/s. But it is a no-brainer to change the data placement for the three arrays, for example to the NUMA node 1 (using 0:S1,1:S1,2:S1) keeping the computation by 16 threads confined in the NUMA node 0. Not surprisingly, the bandwidth we get now is only 5110 MB/s, which means we are losing a 38% of the bandwidth we measured when exploiting NUMA locality. We get similar results for other configurations that compute local data (data placement on the cores where the threads are pinned) and configurations that do not exploit locality (data placement on cores that do not have the thread affinity). On yuca, all nonlocal configurations result in the same bandwidth hit, but there are other NUMA topologies on which we pay different penalties depending on where the data is placed and where the threads are running.

On aloe we only have two NUMA nodes 0 and 1. Having the data and the computation on the same domain gives us 38671 MB/s, whereas going down the wrong path results in only 20489 MB/s (almost half, exactly 47% less bandwidth). We are certain that a reader like you, eager to read and learn about performance programming topics, is now motivated to exploit NUMA locality in your own projects!

Our Baseline Example

Figure 20-5 shows a parallel version of the triad example that we have been using recently, with just a `parallel_for` algorithm.

```cpp
int main(int argc, const char* argv[]) {

  int nth = (argc>1) ? atoi(argv[1]) : 4;
  size_t vsize = (argc>2) ? atoi(argv[2]) : 100000000;
  float alpha = 0.5;
  tbb::task_scheduler_init init{nth};

  std::unique_ptr<double[]> A{new double[vsize]};
  std::unique_ptr<double[]> B{new double[vsize]};
  std::unique_ptr<double[]> C{new double[vsize]};

  for(size_t i = 0; i < vsize; i++){
    A[i] = B[i] = i;
  }

  auto t=tbb::tick_count::now();
  tbb::parallel_for(tbb::blocked_range<size_t>{0, vsize},
    [&](const tbb::blocked_range<size_t>& r){
      for (size_t i = r.begin(); i < r.end(); ++i)
        C[i] = A[i] + alpha * B[i];
    });
  double ts = (tbb::tick_count::now() - t).seconds();

  std::cout << "Time: " << ts << " seconds; ";
  std::cout << "Bandwidth: "  << vsize*24/ts/1000000.0 << "MB/s\n";
  return 0;
}
```

Figure 20-5. *The baseline algorithm to evaluate and improve*

The last two lines of this code, which is not yet optimized for NUMA, reports the execution time and the obtained bandwidth. For the latter, the total number of bytes accessed is computed as $vsize \times 8$ bytes/double $\times 3$ access per array element (two loads and one store), and this is divided by the execution time and by one million (to convert to Mbytes per second). On yuca, this results in the following output when running with 32 threads and arrays of one giga-element:

```
./fig_20_05 32 1000000000
Time: 2.23835 seconds; Bandwidth: 10722.2MB/s
```

and on aloe:

```
./fig_20_05 32 1000000000
Time: 0.621695 seconds; Bandwidth: 38604.2MB/s
```

Note that the bandwidth obtained with our triad implementation should not be compared with the one reported previously by likwid-bench. Now we are using 32 threads (instead of 16) that, depending on the OS scheduler, can freely run on every core (instead of confined to a single NUMA node). Similarly, arrays are now placed by the OS following its own data placement policy. In Linux, the default policy[2] is "local allocation" in which the thread that does the allocation determines the data placement: in local memory if there is enough space, or remote otherwise. This policy is sometimes called "first touch," because data placement is not done at allocation time, but at first touch time. This means that a thread can allocate a region but the thread that first accesses this region is the one raising the page fault and actually allocating the page on memory local to that thread. In our example of Figure 20-5, the same thread allocates and initializes the arrays, which means that the parallel_for worker threads running on the same NUMA node will have faster access. A final difference is that likwid-bench implements the triad computation in assembly language which prevents further compiler optimizations.

Mastering Data Placement and Processor Affinity

Binding data and computation is not trivial at all. Mainly because it depends on the Operating System and each one has its own system calls. In Linux, the low-level interface is provided by libnuma[3] which includes functions to control the data placement and processor affinity policies implemented in the Linux kernel. A higher-level alternative is the numactl[4] command that tackles the same problem, offering less flexibility though.

However, it is not the best idea in the world to ruin the portability of our TBB application marrying to an OS dependent NUMA library. A portable and widely used alternative is the already mentioned hwloc library. Currently, TBB does not offer its own API to deal with NUMA locality, but as we will see later, there are measures we can take to get our TBB tasks to access local data when possible. At the time of writing this,

---

[2]We can query the enforced NUMA policy using numactl --show.
[3]http://man7.org/linux/man-pages/man3/numa.3.html.
[4]http://man7.org/linux/man-pages/man8/numactl.8.html.

manual control of data placement and processor affinity has to be done via a third-party library, and without loss of generality, we will resort to hwloc in this chapter. This library can be used in Windows, MacOS, and Linux (actually, in Linux hwloc uses numactl/ libnuma underneath).

In Figure 20-6, we present an example that queries the number of NUMA nodes and then allocates some data on each node to later create a thread per node and bind it to the corresponding domain. We are using hwloc 2.0.1 in the following.

```
#include <hwloc.h>
...
int main(void)
{
  hwloc_topology_t topo;
  hwloc_topology_init(&topo);
  hwloc_topology_load(topo);

  //* Print the number of NUMA nodes.
  int num_nodes = hwloc_get_nbobjs_by_type(topo, HWLOC_OBJ_NUMANODE);
  std::cout << "There are " << num_nodes << " NUMA node(s)\n";

  double ** data = new double*[num_nodes];
  //* Allocate some memory on each NUMA node
  long size = 1024*1024;
  alloc_mem_per_node(topo, data, size);

  sout_t sout;
  //* One master thread per NUMA node
  alloc_thr_per_node(topo, sout);

  for (auto &s : sout) {
    std::cout << s.str();
  }
  //* Free the allocated data and topology
  for(int i = 0; i < num_nodes; i++){
    hwloc_free(topo, data[i], size);
  }
  hwloc_topology_destroy(topo);
  delete [] data;
  return 0;
}
```

Figure 20-6. *Using* hwloc *to allocate memory and bind threads to each NUMA node*

A recurrent argument of all hwloc functions is the object topology, topo in our example. This object is first initialized and then loaded with the available information of the platform. After that, we are ready to get information from the topo data structure, as we do with hwloc_get_nbobjs_by_type that returns the number of NUMA nodes when the second argument is HWLOC_OBJ_NUMANODE (several other types are available, as HWLOC_OBJ_CORE or HWLOC_OBJ_PU – logical core or processing unit). This number of NUMA nodes is stored in the variable num_nodes.

The example continues by creating an array of num_nodes pointers to doubles that will be initialized inside the function alloc_mem_per_node. The function call to alloc_thr_per_node creates num_nodes threads, each one pinned to the corresponding NUMA node. These two functions are described in Figures 20-7 and 20-8, respectively. The example finishes by freeing the allocated memory and the topo data structure.

```
void alloc_mem_per_node(hwloc_topology_t topo,
                        double **data,
                        long size){
  int num_nodes = hwloc_get_nbobjs_by_type(topo, HWLOC_OBJ_NUMANODE);
  for(int i = 0; i < num_nodes; i++){ //for each NUMA node
    hwloc_obj_t numa_node = hwloc_get_obj_by_type(topo,
                                        HWLOC_OBJ_NUMANODE, i);
    char *s;
    hwloc_bitmap_asprintf(&s, numa_node->cpuset);

    std::cout<<"NUMA node " << i << " has cpu bitmask: " << s <<'\n';
    free(s);
    hwloc_bitmap_asprintf(&s, numa_node->nodeset);
    std::cout << "Allocate data on node " << i
              << " with node bitmask " << s << '\n';
    free(s);

    data[i] = (double *) hwloc_alloc_membind(topo,
       size*sizeof(double), numa_node->nodeset,
       HWLOC_MEMBIND_BIND, HWLOC_MEMBIND_BYNODESET);
  }
}
```

Figure 20-7. *Function that allocates an array of doubles per NUMA node*

Figure 20-7 shows the implementation of the function alloc_mem_per_node. The key operations are hwloc_get_obj_by_type that returns a handle to the ith NUMA node object, numa_node, when the second and third arguments are HWLOC_OBJ_NUMANODE

591

and i, respectively. This numa_node has several attributes like numa_node->cpuset
(a bitmask identifying the logical cores included in the node) and numa_node->nodeset
(a similar bitmask that identifies the node). The function hwloc_bitmap_asprintf
comes in handy to translate these sets into strings as we will see latter in the output
of the program. Using the nodeset bitmask, we can allocate memory in a node with
hwloc_alloc_membind.

The output we get on yuca when running the code until alloc_mem_per_node returns
to the main function is

```
There are 4 NUMA node(s)
NUMA node 0 has cpu bitmask: 0x000000ff,0x000000ff
Allocate data on node 0 with node bitmask 0x00000001
NUMA node 1 has cpu bitmask: 0x0000ff00,0x0000ff00
Allocate data on node 1 with node bitmask 0x00000002
NUMA node 2 has cpu bitmask: 0x00ff0000,0x00ff0000
Allocate data on node 2 with node bitmask 0x00000004
NUMA node 3 has cpu bitmask: 0xff000000,0xff000000
Allocate data on node 3 with node bitmask 0x00000008
```

where we see the cpuset and nodeset of each NUMA node. If we refresh our memory
looking again at Figure 20-3, we see that in node 0 we have eight cores with 16 logical
cores, numbered from 0 to 7 and from 32 to 39, which are represented in hwloc with the
bitmask 0x000000ff,0x000000ff. Note that the "," separates the two sets of logical cores
sharing the eight physical ones. To compare with a Hyperthreading disabled platform,
this is the corresponding output on aloe:

```
There are 2 NUMA node(s)
NUMA node 0 has cpu bitmask: 0x0000ffff
Allocate data on node 0 with node bitmask 0x00000001
NUMA node 1 has cpu bitmask: 0xffff0000
Allocate data on node 1 with node bitmask 0x00000002
```

In Figure 20-8, we list the function alloc_thr_per_node that spawns a thread per
NUMA node and then bind it using the cpuset attribute.

```
using sout_t = tbb::enumerable_thread_specific<std::stringstream>;
void alloc_thr_per_node(hwloc_topology_t topo, sout_t& sout){
  int num_nodes = hwloc_get_nbobjs_by_type(topo, HWLOC_OBJ_NUMANODE);
  std::vector<std::thread> vth;
  for(int i = 0; i < num_nodes; i++){
    vth.push_back(std::thread{[i, num_nodes, &topo, &sout]()
    {
      int err;
      sout.local() << "I'm masterThread: " << i << " out of "
                   << num_nodes << '\n';
      sout.local() << "Before: Thread: " << i
                   << " with tid " << std::this_thread::get_id()
                   << " on core " << sched_getcpu() << '\n';

      hwloc_obj_t numa_node = hwloc_get_obj_by_type(topo,
                                        HWLOC_OBJ_NUMANODE,i);
      err = hwloc_set_cpubind(topo, numa_node->cpuset,
                       HWLOC_CPUBIND_THREAD);
      assert(!err);
      sout.local() << "After: Thread: " << i
                   << " with tid " << std::this_thread::get_id()
                   << " on core " << sched_getcpu() << '\n';
    }});
  }
  for(auto &th: vth) th.join();
}
```

Figure 20-8. *Function that creates and pins a thread per NUMA node*

This function also queries the number of NUMA nodes, num_nodes, to later iterates this number of times inside a loop that creates the threads. In the lambda expression that each thread executes, we use hwloc_set_cpubind to bind the thread to each particular NUMA node, now relying on the numa_node->cpuset. To validate the pinning, we print the thread id (using std::this_thread::get_id) and the id of the logical core on which the thread is running (using sched_getcpu). The result on yuca is next, also illustrated in Figure 20-9.

```
Before: Thread 0 with tid 873342720 on core 33
After: Thread 0 with tid 873342720 on core 33
Before: Thread 1 with tid 864950016 on core 2
After: Thread 1 with tid 864950016 on core 8
Before: Thread 2 with tid 856557312 on core 33
After: Thread 2 with tid 856557312 on core 16
Before: Thread 3 with tid 848164608 on core 5
After: Thread 3 with tid 848164608 on core 24
```

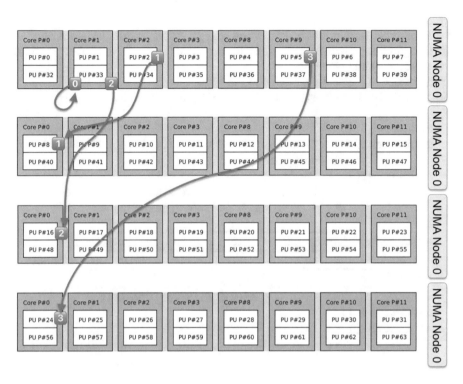

Figure 20-9. *Depicting the movement of threads due to pinning to NUMA nodes on yuca*

Two things are worth mentioning here. First, the threads are initially allocated by the OS on logical cores in the same NUMA node, since it assumes they will collaborate. Threads 0 and 2 are even allocated on the same logical core. Second, the threads are not pinned to a single core, but to the whole set of cores belonging to the same NUMA node. This allows for some leeway if the OS considers it better to move a thread to a different core of the same node. For completeness, here is the equivalent output on aloe:

```
Before: Thread: 0 with tid 140117643171584 on core 3
After: Thread: 0 with tid 140117643171584 on core 3
Before: Thread: 1 with tid 140117634778880 on core 3
After: Thread: 1 with tid 140117634778880 on core 16
```

There are many more features of `hwloc` and `likwid` that the interested reader can learn from the respective documentation and online tutorials. However, what we have covered in this section suffices to move on, roll up our sleeves, and implement a NUMA-conscious version of the triad algorithm using TBB.

Putting `hwloc` and TBB to Work Together

Clearly, the overarching goal is to minimize the number of nonlocal accesses, which implies conducting the computation on the cores nearest to the memory in which the data is stored. A quite simple approach is to manually partition the data on the NUMA nodes and confine the threads that process this data to the same nodes. For educational purposes, we will first describe this solution and in the next section briefly elaborate on more advanced alternatives.

We can rely on the `hwloc` API to accomplish the data placement and processor affinity tasks, but we want a NUMA-aware TBB implementation of the triad benchmark. In this case, the TBB scheduler is the one managing the threads. From Chapter 11, we know that a number of threads are created inside the `tbb::task_scheduler_init` function. Additionally, this TBB function creates a default arena with enough worker slots to allow the threads to participate in executing tasks. In our baseline implementation of triad (see Figure 20-5), a `parallel_for` takes care of partitioning the iteration space into different tasks. All the threads will collaborate on processing these tasks, irrespectively of the chunk of iterations that each task processes and of the core on which the thread is running. But we don't want that on a NUMA platform, right?

Our simplest alternative to the baseline triad implementation will enhance the implementation by performing the following three steps:

- It will partition and allocate the three vectors, A, B, and C, of the triad algorithm on the different NUMA nodes. As the simplest solution, a static block partitioning will do for now. On yuca, this means that four big chunks of A, B, and C will be allocated on each one of the four nodes.

- It will create a master thread on each NUMA node. Each master thread will create its own task arena and its own local `task_scheduler_observer`. Then, each master thread executes its own `tbb::parallel_for` algorithm to process the fraction of A, B, and C that correspond to this NUMA node.

- It will automatically pin the threads that join each arena to the corresponding NUMA node. The local `task_scheduler_observer` that we create for each arena will take care of this.

Let's see the implementation of each one of the described bullet points. For the main function we slightly modify the one we presented for the hwloc example of Figure 20-6. In Figure 20-10, we list the new lines required for this new example, using ellipsis (...) on the lines that do not change.

```
int main(int argc, char** argv)
{
  int thds_per_node = (argc>1) ? atoi(argv[1]) : 4;
  size_t vsize = (argc>2) ? atoi(argv[2]) : 100000000;
  ...
  double **data = new double*[num_nodes];
  times = std::vector<double>(num_nodes);
  //* Allocate some memory on each NUMA node
  long doubles_per_node = vsize*3/num_nodes;
  alloc_mem_per_node(topo, data, doubles_per_node);

  //* One master thread per NUMA node
  tbb::task_scheduler_init init{(thds_per_node-1)*num_nodes};
  auto t = tbb::tick_count::now();
  alloc_thr_per_node(topo, data, vsize/num_nodes, thds_per_node);
  double ts = (tbb::tick_count::now() - t).seconds();
  ...
  delete [] data;
  return 0;
}
```

Figure 20-10. *Main function of the NUMA-conscious implementation of triad*

The program argument, thds_per_node, allows us to play with different number of threads per NUMA node. As in the example of Figure 20-6, num_nodes is the number of NUMA nodes that we obtain using the hwloc API. Consequently, we pass to the TBB scheduler constructor (thds_per_node-1)*(num_nodes) instead of thds_per_node*num_nodes because we will explicitly create the additional num_nodes master threads inside alloc_thr_per_node.

The function alloc_mem_per_node is essentially the same as the one listed in Figure 20-7, but now it is called with a different size argument: doubles_per_node = vsize*3/num_nodes, where vsize is the size of the three vectors, so the total amount of doubles is multiplied by 3, but divided by the number of nodes to implement the block partitioning. For the sake of cleanness, we assume that vsize is a multiple of num_nodes. At the completion of alloc_mem_per_node, data[i] points to the data allocated on the ith NUMA node.

There are other differences in the adapted version of the `alloc_thr_per_node` function as we see in Figure 20-11. It now receives a handle to the data, the size of the local vectors that will be traversed per node, `lsize`, and the number of threads per node set by the user, `thds_per_node`.

```
void alloc_thr_per_node(hwloc_topology_t topo, double** data,
                        size_t lsize, int thds_per_node){
  float alpha = 0.5;
  int num_nodes = hwloc_get_nbobjs_by_type(topo, HWLOC_OBJ_NUMANODE);
  std::vector<std::thread> vth;
  for(int i = 0; i < num_nodes; i++){
    vth.push_back( std::thread {
      [=,&topo](){
        hwloc_obj_t numa_node = hwloc_get_obj_by_type(topo,
                                          HWLOC_OBJ_NUMANODE,i);
        int err = hwloc_set_cpubind (topo, numa_node->cpuset,
                                    HWLOC_CPUBIND_THREAD);
        assert(!err);
        double *A = data[i];
        double *B = data[i] + lsize;
        double *C = data[i] + 2*lsize;

        for(size_t j = 0; j < lsize; j++){
          A[j] = B[j] = j;
        }
        tbb::task_arena numa_arena{thds_per_node};
        PinningObserver p{numa_arena, topo, i, thds_per_node};
        auto t = tbb::tick_count::now();
        numa_arena.execute([&](){
          tbb::parallel_for(tbb::blocked_range<size_t>{0, lsize},
            [&](const tbb::blocked_range<size_t>& r){
              for (size_t i = r.begin(); i < r.end(); ++i)
                C[i] = A[i] + alpha * B[i];
          });
        });
        double ts = (tbb::tick_count::now() - t).seconds();
        times[i] = ts;
      }
    });
  }
  for (auto &th: vth) th.join();
}
```

Figure 20-11. *Function that creates a thread per node to compute the triad computation on each NUMA node*

Note that in the code snippet presented in Figure 20-11, inside the i-loop that traverses the num_nodes, there are three nested lambda expressions: (1) for the thread object; (2) for `task_arena::execute` member function; and (3) for the `parallel_for` algorithm. In the outer one, we first pin the thread to the corresponding NUMA node, i.

The second step is to initialize the pointers to arrays A, B, and C that were allocated in the data[i] array. In Figure 20-10, we call `alloc_thr_per_node` using as the third argument vsize/num_nodes because on each node we traverse just one chunk of the block distribution of the three arrays. Hence, the function's argument `lsize = vsize/ num_nodes`, which is used in the loop that initializes arrays A and B and as the argument to the `parallel_for` that computes C.

Next, we initialize a per NUMA node arena, numa_arena, that is later passed as argument to a `task_scheduler_observer` object, p, and used to invoke a `parallel_for` confined to this arena (using `numa_arena.execute`). Here lies the key of our NUMA-aware implementation of triad.

The `parallel_for` will create tasks that traverse chunks of the local partition of the three vectors. These tasks will be executed by threads running on the cores of the same NUMA node. But up to now, we just have thds_per_node*num_nodes threads, out of which num_nodes have been explicitly spawned as master threads and pinned to a different NUMA node, but the rest are still free to run everywhere. The threads that are available in the global thread pool will each join one of the num_nodes arenas. Conveniently, each numa_arena has been initialized with thds_per_node slots, one already occupied by a master thread and the rest available for worker threads. Our goal now is to pin the first thds_per_node-1 threads that enter each numa_arena to the corresponding NUMA node. To that end, we create a `PinningObserver` class (deriving from `task_scheduler_observer`) and construct an object, p, passing four arguments to the constructor: `PinningObserver p{numa_arena, topo, i, thds_per_node}`. Remember that here, i is the id of the NUMA node for the master thread i.

In Figure 20-12, we see the implementation of the `PinningObserver` class.

```
class PinningObserver : public tbb::task_scheduler_observer {
  hwloc_topology_t topo;
  hwloc_obj_t numa_node;
  int numa_id;
  int num_nodes;
  tbb::atomic<int> thds_per_node;
  tbb::atomic<int> masters_that_entered;
  tbb::atomic<int> workers_that_entered;
  tbb::atomic<int> threads_pinned;
public:
  PinningObserver(tbb::task_arena& arena, hwloc_topology_t& _topo,
                  int _numa_id, int _thds_per_node)
                  : task_scheduler_observer{arena}, topo{_topo},
                    numa_id{_numa_id}, thds_per_node{_thds_per_node}{
    num_nodes = hwloc_get_nbobjs_by_type(topo,
                                         HWLOC_OBJ_NUMANODE);
    numa_node = hwloc_get_obj_by_type(topo,
                                      HWLOC_OBJ_NUMANODE,numa_id);
    masters_that_entered = 0;
    workers_that_entered = 0;
    threads_pinned = 0;
    observe(true);
  }
  void on_scheduler_entry(bool is_worker) {
    if (is_worker) ++workers_that_entered;
    else ++masters_that_entered;
    if(--thds_per_node > 0){
      int err = hwloc_set_cpubind(topo, numa_node->cpuset,
                                  HWLOC_CPUBIND_THREAD);
      assert(!err);
      threads_pinned++;
    }
  }
};
```

Figure 20-12. *Implementation of the local* task_scheduler_observer *for triad*

The task_scheduler_observer class was introduced in Chapter 13. It has a preview feature that allows us to have an observer per task arena – also called a local task_scheduler_observer. This kind of observer is initialized with a reference to the arena, as we do in the initializer list of the PinningObserver constructor using task_scheduler_observer{arena}. This results in the execution of the member function on_scheduler_entry for each thread that enters this particular arena. The constructor of the class also sets the number of NUMA nodes, num_nodes, and the numa_node object that will give us access to the numa_node->cpuset bitmask. The constructor finally calls the member function observe(true) to start tracking whether or not a task enters the arena.

The function on_scheduler_entry keeps track of the number of threads that have been already pinned to the numa_node in the atomic variable thds_per_node. This variable is set in the initializer list of the constructor to the number of threads per node that the user pass as the first argument of the program. This variable is decremented for each thread entering the arena, which will get pinned to the node only if the value is greater than 0. Since each numa_arena was initialized with thds_per_node slots, and the already pinned master thread that creates the arena occupies one of the slots, the thds_per_node - 1 threads that join the arena first will get pinned to the node and work on tasks generated by the parallel_for that this arena is executing.

Note   The implementation of our PinningObserver class is not totally correct. One thread may leave the arena and reenter the same arena, getting pinned twice, but decrementing the number thds_per_node. A more correct implementation would check that the thread entering the arena is a new one that has not been pinned to this arena already. To avoid complicating the example, we leave this correction as an exercise to the reader.

We can now assess on yuca and aloe the bandwidth (in Mbytes per second) of this NUMA optimized version of the triad algorithm. To compare with the baseline implementation in Figure 20-5, we set the vector sizes to 10^9 doubles and set the number of threads per NUMA node so that we end up with 32 threads total. For example, in yuca we call the executables as follows:

```
baseline:           ./fig_20_05 32 1000000000
NUMA conscious:     ./fig_20_10  8 1000000000
```

The results presented in the table of Figure 20-13 are the average of ten runs in which yuca and aloe had a single user that was using the platform exclusively to conduct the experiments.

	baseline	NUMA conscious	
	Bandwidth (MBytes/s)	Bandwidth (MBytes/s)	Speedup
yuca	10722	18652	1.74
aloe	38604	59659	1.54

Figure 20-13. *Speedup due to the NUMA-conscious implementation*

This is 74% faster execution on yuca, and 54% on aloe! Would you ignore this extra amount of performance that we can squeeze out of a NUMA architecture with some extra implementation work?

To further investigate this improvement, we can take advantage of the `likwid-perfctr` application that is able to read out hardware performance counters. Invoking `likwid-perctr -a`, we get a list of groups of events that can be specified using only the group name. In aloe, `likwid` offers a NUMA group, which collects information about local and remote memory accesses. To measure the events in this group on our baseline and NUMA-conscious implementations, we can invoke these two commands:

```
likwid-perfctr -g NUMA ./fig_20_05 32 1000000000
likwid-perfctr -g NUMA ./fig_20_10 16 1000000000
```

This will report plenty of information about the value of some performance counters on all the cores. Among the counted events are

```
OFFCORE_RESPONSE_0_LOCAL_DRAM
OFFCORE_RESPONSE_1_REMOTE_DRAM
```

which give us approximate information (because is based on event-based sampling) of the amount of data accessed in local memory and remote memory. For the baseline triad implementation, the ratio of local data over remote data is only 3.25, but it raises up to 25.5 in the NUMA optimized triad-numa version. This confirms that, for this memory bound application, the effort we made to exploit NUMA locality pays off in terms of both the amount of local accesses and consequently the execution bandwidth.

More Advanced Alternatives

For the regular triad code, the simple solution we have implemented is okay, but TBB's work-stealing scheduler is confined to balancing the load on each NUMA node independently. On yuca, there will be four `parallel_for` algorithms running, each on a NUMA node with eight threads served by eight physical cores. The downside of our simple approach is that the four arenas have been configured with eight slots, which is okay for the steady-state part of the execution, but limits TBB's flexibility if the load is not perfectly balanced between the NUMA nodes.

For example, if one of the `parallel_for` algorithms ends first, eight threads become idle. They come back to the global thread pool but cannot join any of the other three busy arenas because all the slots are already filled. A simple solution for this involves increasing the number of slots of the arenas, while keeping the number of pinned threads to `thds_per_node`. In such a case, if a `parallel_for` finishes first, the eight threads returning to the global pool can be redistributed in the free slots of the other three arenas. Note that these threads are still pinned to the original node, although they will work now in a different arena of a different node and therefore memory accesses will be remote.

We could pin the threads entering the extended arena to the corresponding NUMA node when they occupy its free slots (even if they were pinned to a different NUMA node before). Now these helping threads will also access local memory. However, the node can become oversubscribed, which usually hurts performance (if not, you should oversubscribe every NUMA node from the very beginning). For each particular application and architecture, thorough experimentation should be carried out to decide whether it is advantageous to migrate the thread to the NUMA node or to remotely access the data from the original node. For the simple and regular triad algorithm, none of these discussed approaches significantly improves the performance, but in more complex and irregular applications they might. Not only do remote access have overhead, but also thread migration from one arena to another, as well as pinning the thread once again, represent an overhead that has to be amortized by better load balancing of the work.

Another battle that we can choose to fight concerns the data partitioning. We used a basic block distribution of the three arrays in our simple triad implementation, but we certainly know of better data distributions for more irregular applications. For example, instead of partitioning upfront the iteration space among the NUMA nodes, we can follow a guided scheduling approach. Each master thread leading the computation on each NUMA node can get larger chunks of the iteration space at the beginning of the computation and smaller as we approach the end of the space. The caveat here is to guarantee that chunks have enough granularity to be repartitioned again among the cores of each NUMA node.

A more elaborate alternative consists in generalizing the work-stealing framework in a hierarchical way. In order to allow work stealing both between arenas and within each arena, a hierarchy of arenas can be implemented. A similar idea was implemented for Cilk by Chen and Guo (see the "For More Information" section) who proposed a triple-level work-stealing scheduler that yielded up to 54% of performance improvement over more traditional work-stealing alternatives for memory-bound applications. Note that memory-bound applications will benefit more from NUMA locality exploitation than CPU-bound ones. For the latter, memory access overhead is usually hidden by CPU intensive computations. Actually, for CPU-bound applications, adding extra complexity to the scheduler in order to exploit NUMA locality can result in an extra overhead that ends up not paying off.

Summary

In this chapter, we explored some alternatives to exploit NUMA locality combining TBB and third-party libraries that help in controlling the data placement and processor affinity. We began by studying the enemy that we want to defeat: the NUMA architecture. To that end, we introduced some ally libraries, hwloc and likwid. With them we can not only query the low-level details of the NUMA topology but also control data placement and processor affinity. We illustrated the use of some of the hwloc functions to allocate per-node memory, create one thread per NUMA node and pin threads to the cores of the node. With this template, we re-implemented a baseline version of the triad algorithm, now paying attention to NUMA locality. The simplest solution consisted of distributing the three triad arrays in blocks that are allocated and traversed in the different NUMA nodes. The library hwloc was key to allocate and pin the threads, and the TBB task_arena and task_scheduler_observer classes were instrumental in identifying the threads entering a particular NUMA node. This initial solution is good enough for a code as regular as the triad benchmark, which reports 74% and 54% performance improvement (with respect to the baseline triad implementation) on two different NUMA platforms, respectively. For more irregular and complex applications, more advanced alternatives are sketched in the last section of the chapter.

For More Information

Here are some additional reading materials we recommend related to this chapter:

- Christoph Lameter, NUMA (Non-Uniform Memory Access): An Overview, ACMqueue, Volume 11, issue 7, 2013.

- Ulrich Drepper, What Every Programmer Should Know About Memory, www.akkadia.org/drepper/cpumemory.pdf, 2017.

- Quan Chen, Minyi Guo and Haibing Guan, LAWS: Locality-Aware Work-Stealing for Multi-socket Multi-core Architectures, International Conference on Supercomputing, ICS, 2014.

APPENDIX A

History and Inspiration

In this Appendix, we offer two different complementary perspectives on the history of TBB: first a look at TBB's history, and second a look at what preceded and inspired TBB. We hope you enjoy both, and that they deepen your understanding of why TBB has been called the most important new addition to parallel programming in the past decade, and we would not argue with that.

A Decade of "Hatchling to Soaring"

This first part of the appendix is adapted from a piece that James wrote on the tenth anniversary of TBB (mid-2016).

If you will be so kind as to indulge me, I will share my own thoughts about TBB. I have four things in mind to touch on as I ramble about TBB.

#1 TBB's Revolution Inside Intel

TBB was our first commercially successful software product to embrace open source, and with continued leadership TBB has more recently moved to Apache licensing.

We knew we wanted to open source TBB from the start, but we were not ready when we launched in 2006. Open source projects were new to our small team, and to Intel. We focused first on creating a strong TBB and launching it as a product in mid-2006. After launching, we shifted our attention to revising our build system, cleaning up code (commenting!), and a dozen other things that would help us be inviting to others who would want to understand and contribute to our source code. We had a goal to be open source in mid-2007. A new problem arose – TBB became an immediate hit with customers. We were not secret with our customers about our desire to open source, and this only intensified their interest in TBB. Our success quickly became a problem inside Intel as some of our management asked the question "why give away the source

© Intel Corporation 2019
M. Voss, R. Asenjo, J. Reinders, *Pro TBB*, https://doi.org/10.1007/978-1-4842-4398-5

code to such a successful product?" Armed with facts and figures from our team, I boldly presented a multitude of reasons why we should open up. That was a mistake, and I failed to get the needed permissions before 2006 ended. I licked my wounds, and we eventually realized we only needed to prove one thing: TBB would have far greater adoption if we open sourced it than if we did not. After all, developers bet the very future of their code when they adopt a programming model. Perhaps openness matters more for programming models than it does for most other software. While we understood this point, we had failed to articulate to our management that this was all that really mattered – and that it was all we needed to know to understand that we must open source TBB. Armed with this perspective, I surprised our senior V.P. who had to approve our proposal. I surprised her by showing up with only a single piece of paper with a simple graph on it, which offered a comparison of projected TBB adoption with and without open sourcing. We predicted that TBB would vanish and be replaced within five years if we didn't offer this critical programming model via open source. We predicted great success if we did open source (we actually far underestimated the success, as it turns out). Senior Vice President Renee James listened to my 2-minute pitch, looked at me, and asked "Why didn't you say this the first time? Of course we should do this." I could have pointed out it was exactly slide 7 of the original way-too-long 20 slide presentation that I had presented 2 months earlier. I settled on "Thank you" and the rest is history. We choose the most popular open source licensing at the time: GPL v2 with classpath exception (important for C++ template libraries). Ten years later, we moved TBB to the Apache license. We have received a great deal of feedback from the community of users and contributors that this is the right license to use for TBB in our times.

#2 TBB's First Revolution of Parallelism

The first revolution of parallelism offered by TBB was to fully embrace the task stealing abstraction while giving full C++ support with full composability.

OpenMP is incredibly important, but it is not composable. This is a mistake of epic proportions with long reaching ramifications, and it cannot be changed because OpenMP is so important and committed to compatibility. I am complicit in the OpenMP mistake along with everyone else who helped pull it together, review it, and promote it starting in 1997. We overlooked the importance that nested parallelism would have as the amount of hardware parallelism grew. It simply was not a concern in 1997.

Being composable is the most amazing feature of TBB. I cannot overstate the importance of never worrying about oversubscription, nested parallelism, and so on. TBB is gradually revolutionizing certain communities of developers that demand composability for their applications. The Intel Math Kernel Library (MKL), which has long been based on OpenMP, offers a version built on top of TBB for exactly this reason. And the much newer, and open source, Intel Data Analytics Acceleration Library (DAAL) always uses TBB and the TBB-powered MKL. In fact, TBB is finding use in some versions of Python too.

Of course, the task stealing scheduler at the heart of TBB is the real magic. While HPC customers worry about squeezing out the ultimate performance while running an application on dedicated cores, TBB tackles a problem that HPC users never worry about: how can you make parallelism work well when you share the cores that you run upon? Imagine running on eight cores, but a virus checker happens to run on one core during your application's run. That would never happen on a supercomputer, but it happens all the time on workstations and laptops! Without the dynamic nature of the TBB task stealing scheduler, such a program would simply be delayed by the full time that the virus checker stole... because it would effective delay every thread in the application. When using TBB on eight cores, an interruption, of duration TIME on one core, may delay the application by as little as TIME/8. This real world flexibility matters a lot!

Finally, TBB is a C++ template library that fully embraces bringing parallelism to C++. The dedication of TBB to C++ has helped inspire changes to the C++ standard. Perhaps our biggest dream of all is that TBB will one day only be the scheduler and the algorithms that use it. The many other things in TBB to help parallelize parts of STL, create truly portable locks and atomics, address short comings in memory allocations, and other features to bring parallelism to C++ can and should be part of the standard language eventually. Maybe even more of TBB? Time will tell.

#3 TBB's Second Revolution of Parallelism

The second revolution of parallelism offered by TBB was to offer superior alternatives from bulk synchronous programming.

As much as we can praise the task stealing scheduler of TBB, the algorithms most often used in applications are organized with a lot of synchronization happening at runtime. This is a sign of the times in terms of how parallel programming has been done successfully for years. However, as the amount of parallelism has grown, this has become a great obstacle in the pursuit of scaling. A better approach is to express the flow of data and require a much more minimal level of synchronization. The TBB flow graph addition to TBB, is a leader in this critical new revolution in parallel programming. This type of thinking is required for any parallel programming model to support the future well.

#4 TBB's Birds

On a very different note, I do get asked about the birds we've used. Of course, my original TBB book (2007) was an O'Reilly Nutshell book with its iconic design that always features an animal. O'Reilly made it clear to me, as the author, that they would pick the animal (a mysterious process). Undaunted, I did convey some ideas I had for animals that made sense to me. O'Reilly chose a beautifully drawn canary for the cover, a beautiful bird that was not an animal I had even considered. Everyone can have opinions, but soon our cry around Intel was "embrace the bird." We can thank Belinda Adkisson for that reframe, and for the popular non-infringing "Chirp" bird that we used on t-shirts, stickers, and web sites. A cheery little bird remains our mascot for TBB. We have "embraced the bird."

Embrace the Bird!

The colophon in the original book reads:

> The animal on the cover of *Intel Threading Building Blocks* is a
> wild canary (*Serinus canaria*), a small songbird in the finch family.
> It is also known as an island canary or Atlantic canary because it is
> native to islands off western Europe, particularly Madeira, Azores,

and the Canary Islands, for which the bird was named. The name comes from the Latin *canaria* ("of the dogs"), first used by Pliny the Elder in his *Naturalis Historia* because of the large dogs roaming the Islands. Canaries live in orchards, farmlands, and copses, and make their nests in bushes and trees.

Although the wild canary is darker and slightly larger than the domestic canary, it is otherwise similar in appearance. Its breast is yellow-green and its back is streaked with brown. Like many species, the male is more vibrantly colored than the female. The male also has a sweeter song. When the Spanish conquered the Islands in the 15th century, they domesticated the birds and began to breed them. By the 16th century, canaries were prized as pets throughout Europe. (Samuel Pepys writes about his "canary birds" in a 1661 diary entry.) Five hundred years of selective breeding have produced many canary varieties, including the bright yellow type common today. The small birds are popular pets because they can live up to 10 years, require little special attention, and are considered to have the most melodious song of all birds.

As late as the 1980s, coal miners used canaries as a warning system, with two birds in each coal pit. According to the U.S. Bureau of Mines, canaries were preferred to mice because they are more sensitive to fumes and more visibly show distress in the presence of gas. A canary in a mine would chirp all day, but if the carbon monoxide level rose, it would stop singing and sway on its perch before falling dead – warning the miners to get out fast.

I wrote the TBB book in the Spring of 2007 with a great deal of help from the TBB team. I would very much like to see us do a new TBB book in the upcoming years. I currently do not personally have the time to do it this year, but if enough people wanted to help... well, I think we could figure something out. I'm open to suggestions. *Thank you, Michael and Rafael, for jumping in, first to do a tutorial on TBB together in 2017, and then to collaborate on this book starting in 2018!*

James went on to welcome people to the tenth anniversary special edition of Intel's The Parallel Universe *magazine. It was the published just as James left Intel to become semi-retired (busier than ever). The special issue is available free online at* `https://software.intel.com/parallel-universe-magazine`. *You can read more about the history of TBB in the article "The Genesis and Evolution of Intel Threading Building Blocks" as related by its original architect in the same issue – including his two "regrets" in the initial TBB 1.0 design. Many interesting articles about TBB have been published in the magazine over the years.*

Ten years of TBB – special issue of Intel's *The Parallel Universe* magazine

Inspiration for TBB

This second part of this appendix is adapted from the historical notes that James produced for the first TBB book (2007) when TBB was only 1 year old. This is a look at what preceded and inspired TBB.

James originally titled this chapter of the original TBB book the "Epilogue" and referred to it as a bibliography. The editor at O'Reilly, Andy Oram – who James describes as the best editor on the planet – tempered James' enthusiasm for a technical book having a bibliography or an epilogue and renamed this to be "Chapter 12" in the book and titled it "History and Related Projects."

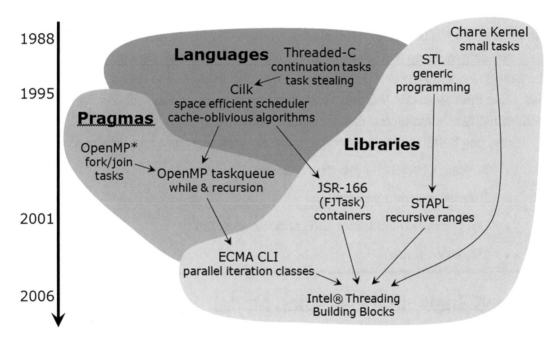

Figure A-1. *Key influences on the design of Threading Building Blocks*

Nothing that follows is required reading to learn how to use Threading Building Blocks. Instead, the following looks at some of the inspirations that shaped our thoughts at Intel and led to the design and implementation of Threading Building Blocks. A list of papers, articles, and books at the end of the chapter forms a bibliography to give some suggested further reading.

> **Note**   The chapter originally contained a brief explanation of lambda functions, whose inclusion in C++ is advocated by Arch Robison, lead developer for Threading Building Blocks. We removed this because the Preface to this book explains lambdas because the C++ standard did add lambdas to the C++ standard a few years later in C++11. This simplified TBB syntax, and hence teaching TBB, exactly as Arch had hoped to do. Of course, it made the original TBB book seem a bit old because all our examples did not use C++11 since we published in 2007.

The information in this bibliography is likely to appeal most to those who want to contribute to Threading Building Blocks. There is much to be pondered in the design of Threading Building Blocks, and this chapter aims to clarify where to start.

Threading Building Blocks draws from a great many sources. Figure A-1 highlights the key influences of the past decade or so. The influences were in the form of inspiration and, other than McRT-Malloc, they have no actual source code connection. Influences prior to 1988 are left as an exercise for other historians.

Threading Building Blocks is unique because it rests on a few key decisions:

- Support general C++ programs with existing compilers

- Relaxed sequential execution

- Use recursive parallelism and generic algorithms

- Use task stealing

Relaxed Sequential Execution Model

TBB implements a relaxed sequential execution model. The word relaxed refers to the notion that serial programs are actually overly constrained by implicit serial dependencies (such as the program counter) and that the concurrent library introduces as much parallelism as possible without removing the ability to run sequentially.

We can think of this model as being as relaxed as possible and still being able to run correctly in a single thread. That is the goal!

Being able to run a program sequentially gives us a tremendous advantage when debugging our applications. It lets us debug common programming errors before dealing with any concurrency issues that need to be debugged. Our advice is simple: start with debugging in a sequential mode, and then run the program in parallel to debug concurrency issues. Programs designed to require concurrency would not give us this option. Furthermore, programs designed to require concurrency will have performance pitfalls when the number of required threads exceeds the number of hardware threads because time-slicing artifacts can hit hard.

Influential Libraries

1988, Chare Kernel, University of Illinois at Urbana-Champaign

> In 1988, it was simply a C library. The key notion was to break a program into small bits of work, called chares, and the scheduler would take care of packing these efficiently (in both space and time) onto processors. Mapping tasks onto threads instead of programming threads directly is an important concept. The Chare Kernel was later extended with some features for marshaling to address distributed memory machines, becoming Charm++.

1993, Standard Template Library (STL) for C++, Hewlett-Packard

> STL was presented in November 1993 to the ANSI/ISO C++ committee and HP made it freely available in 1994. It was adopted into the C++ standard. Arch Robison related: "I once heard Stepanov give a great talk on generic programming, where he went through how to write a really generic greatest-common-factor algorithm. [The paper at is similar to that talk, but with more mathematical emphasis.] In its full glory, generic programming is not just parametric types, but programming with concepts." Works by Stepanov on STL and generic programming are listed later in this chapter. *Note: Alexander Stepanov kindly wrote the foreword for the original book which included praise for the embracing of generic programming in TBB's design.*

1999, Java Specification Request #166 (JSR-166), Doug Lea

> It was actually not standardized until later, but 1999 was the year Lea first introduced it. FJTask was an attempt to put Cilk-style parallelism into the stock Java library. It was proposed for JSR-166, but it did not make it into that standard.

2001, Standard Template Adaptive Parallel Library (STAPL), Texas A&M

> STAPL introduced the notion of recursive parallel ranges ("pRanges") and the concept of using these ranges instead of iterators to bind parallel generic algorithms to parallel containers. STL lacks a recursive range. STAPL is more complex than TBB because it encompasses distributed memory architectures typical of High-Performance Computing (HPC). Furthermore, STAPL supports the specification of arbitrary execution order for parallel task graphs. This allows the use of multiple scheduling policies to optimize execution time.

2004, ECMA CLI parallel profile, Intel

> This ECMA spec for the .NET virtual machine has classes for parallel iteration, designed by Arch Robison.

2006, McRT-Malloc, Intel Research

> A scalable transactional memory allocator, McRT forms the basis of the Scalable Memory Allocator supplied with Threading Building Blocks. Sections 3 and 3.1 of a 2006 paper by Hudson, Saha, Adl-Tabatabai, and Hertzberg (http://doi.acm.org/10.1145/1133956.1133967) describe roughly what is in the Scalable Memory Allocator in TBB.

Influential Languages

1994, Threaded-C, Massachusetts Institute of Technology

> The Parallel Continuation Machine (PCM) was the runtime support for Threaded-C. It was a C-based package that provided continuation-passing-style threads on Thinking Machines Corporation's Connection Machine Model CM-5 Supercomputer and used work stealing as a general scheduling policy to improve the load balance and locality of the computation. This language is not to be confused with the Threaded-C for EARTH from McGill University and the University of Delaware. PCM was briefly mentioned on page 2 of the original Cilk manual.

1995, Cilk, Massachusetts Institute of Technology

> The first implementation of Cilk () was a direct descendent of
> PCM/Threaded-C. Cilk fixed the difficulty of programming
> continuation tasks and came up with methods to tailor task
> allocation to caches without knowing the size of the caches with
> cache-oblivious algorithms. Cilk is an extension of C that supports
> very efficient fork/join parallelism. Its space efficiency is discussed
> in `http://supertech.csail.mit.edu/papers/cilkjpdc96.`
> `pdf`. FFTW (`www.fftw.org`) is an example of a cache-oblivious
> algorithm.

Influential Pragmas

1997, OpenMP, by a consortium of major computer hardware and software vendors

> OpenMP supports multiplatform, shared-memory parallel
> programming in C and Fortran, offering a standard set of compiler
> directives, library routines, and environment variables. Prior to
> OpenMP, many vendors had proprietary compiler directives with
> similar intent, but they lacked portability. OpenMP embodies a
> fork/join philosophy. See `www.openmp.org`.

1998, OpenMP Taskqueue, Kuck & Associates (KAI)

> Proposed extensions for OpenMP to move beyond loops.
> *A refinement of this proposal was adopted and added to OpenMP
> in 2008 (a year after our book) as of OpenMP 3.0.*

Influences of Generic Programming

Bjarne Stroustrup, creator of C++, originally said there were three fundamental styles
supported by C++ – *procedural programming*, *data abstraction*, and *object-oriented
programming* – but later added that *generic programming* had become a fourth style.

We can give credit to the Standard Template Library (STL), created by Alexander
Stepanov, for popularizing this style. It fits very well with the principles of C++, which
favors abstraction and efficiency together.

In STL and Threading Building Blocks, algorithms are separated from containers. This means that an algorithm takes a recursive range and uses it to access elements within the container. The specific type of the container itself is unknown to the algorithm. This clear separation of containers and algorithms is the basic idea of generic programming. Separation of algorithms from containers means that template instantiations result in relatively little added code and generally only that which is actually going to be used.

Threading Building Blocks does embrace the same principles as STL but does it through the use of *recursive ranges*, not *iterators*. Iterators in STL (except for random-access iterators) are fundamentally sequential, and thus inappropriate for expressing parallelism.

Note   C++ Extensions for Ranges became a Technical Specification (ISO/IEC TS 21425:2017) and will almost certainly be part of C++20. The reasons for preferring ranges over iterators include the sequential nature of iterators which caused TBB to reject them in 2006.

Considering Caches

Threading Building Blocks is designed with caches in mind and works to limit the unnecessary movement of tasks and data. When a task has to be passed to a different processor core for execution, Threading Building Blocks moves the task with the least likelihood of having data in the cache for the processor core from which the task is stolen.

It is interesting to note that parallel Quicksort is an example in which caches beat *maximum parallelism*. Parallel Mergesort has more parallelism than parallel Quicksort. But parallel Mergesort is not an in place sort, and thus has twice the cache footprint that parallel Quicksort does. Hence, Quicksort usually runs faster in practice.

Keep data locality in mind when considering how to structure your program. Avoid using data regions sporadically when you can design the application to use a single set of data in focused chunks of time. This happens most naturally if you use data decomposition, especially at the higher levels in a program.

Considering Costs of Time Slicing

Time slicing enables there to be more logical threads than physical threads. Each logical thread is serviced for a time slice – a short period of time defined by the operating system during which a thread can run before being preempted – by a physical thread. If a thread runs longer than a time slice, as most do, it relinquishes the physical thread until it gets another turn. This chapter details the costs incurred by time slicing.

The most obvious cost is the time for *context switching* between logical threads. Each context switch requires that the processor save all its registers for the previous logical thread that it was executing, and load its registers with information for the next logical thread it runs.

A subtler cost is cache cooling. Processors keep recently accessed data in cache memory, which is very fast, but also relatively small compared to main memory. When the processor runs out of cache memory, it has to evict items from cache and put them back into main memory. Typically, it chooses the least recently used items in the cache. (The reality of set-associative caches is a bit more complicated, but this is not a cache primer.)

When a logical thread gets its time slice, as it references a piece of data for the first time, this data is pulled into cache, taking hundreds of cycles. If it is referenced frequently enough not to be evicted, each subsequent reference will find it in cache, and take only a few cycles. Such data is called *hot* in *cache*.

Time slicing undoes this because if Thread A finishes its time slice, and subsequently Thread B runs on the same physical thread, B will tend to evict data that was hot in cache for A, unless both threads need the data. When Thread A gets its next time slice, it will need to reload evicted data, at the cost of hundreds of cycles for each cache miss. Or worse yet, the next time slice for Thread A may be on a different physical thread that has a different cache altogether.

Another cost is *lock preemption*. This happens if a thread acquires a lock on a resource and its time slice runs out before it releases the lock. No matter how short a time the thread intended to hold the lock, it is now going to hold it for at least as long as it takes for its next turn at a time slice to come up. Any other threads waiting on the lock either busy-wait pointlessly or lose the rest of their time slice. The effect is called convoying because the threads end up "bumper to bumper" waiting for the preempted thread in front to resume driving.

617

Further Reading

Acar, U., G. Blelloch, and R. Blumofe (2000). "The Data Locality of Work Stealing." Proceedings of the Twelfth Annual ACM Symposium on Parallel Algorithms and Architectures, 1-12.

Amdahl, G. M. (1967, April). "Validity of the single-processor approach to achieving large scale computing capabilities." AFIP Conference Proceedings, 30. Reston, VA: AFIPS Press, 483-485.

An, P., A. Jula, et al. (2003). "STAPL: An Adaptive, Generic Parallel C++ Library." Workshop on Language and Compilers for Parallel Computing, 2001. Lecture Notes in Computer Science 2624, 193-208.

Austern, M. H., R. A. Towle, and A. A. Stepanov (1996). "Range partition adaptors: a mechanism for parallelizing STL." ACM SIGAPP Applied Computing Review. 4, 1, 5-6.

Blumofe, R. D., and D. Papadopoulos (1998). "Hood: A User-Level Threads Library for Multiprogrammed Multiprocessors."

Blumofe, R. D., C. F. Joerg, et al. (1996). "Cilk: An Efficient Multithreaded Runtime System." Proceedings of the 5th ACM SIGPLAN Symposium on Principles and Practice of Parallel Programming, 207-216.

Boehm, H. (2006, June). "An Atomic Operations Library for C++." C++ standards committee document N2047.

Butenhof, D. R. (1997). Programming with POSIX Threads. Reading, MA: Addison Wesley.

Flynn, M. J. (1972, September). "Some Computer Organizations and Their Effectiveness." IEEE Transactions on Computers, C-21, 9, 948-960.

Garcia, R., J. Järvi, et al. (2003, October). "A Comparative Study of Language Support for Generic Programming." Proceedings of the 2003 ACM SIGPLAN conference on object-oriented programming, systems, languages, and applications.

Gustafson, J. L. (1988). "Reevaluating Amdahl's Law." Communications of the ACM, 31(5), 532-533.

Halbherr, M., Zhou, Y., and C. F. Joerg (1994, March). MIMD-Style Parallel Programming Based on Continuation-Passing Threads, Computation Structures Group Memo 355.

Halbherr, M., Y. Zhou, and C. F. Joerg (1994, September). "MIMD-style parallel programming with continuation-passing threads." Proceedings of the 2nd International Workshop on Massive Parallelism: Hardware, Software, and Applications, Capri, Italy.

Hansen, B. (1973). "Concurrent Programming Concepts." ACM Computing Surveys, 5, 4.

Hoare, C. A. R. (1974). "Monitors: An Operating System Structuring Concept." Communications of the ACM, 17, 10, 549-557.

Hudson, R. L., B. Saha, et al. (2006, June). "McRT-Malloc: a scalable transactional memory allocator." Proceedings of the 2006 International Symposium on Memory Management. New York: ACM Press, 74-83.

Intel Threading Building Blocks 1.0 for Windows, Linux, and Mac OS—Intel Software Network (1996).

"A Formal Specification of Intel Itanium Processor Family Memory Ordering" (2002, October).

ISO/IEC 14882:1998(E) International Standard (1998). Programming languages – C++. ISO/IEC, 1998.

ISO/IEC 9899:1999 International Standard (1999). Programming languages – C, ISO/IEC, 1999.

Järvi, J., and B. Stroustrup (2004, September). Decltype and auto (revision 4). C++ standards committee document N1705=04-0145.

Kapur, D., D. R. Musser, and A.A. Stepanov (1981). "Operators and Algebraic Structures." Proceedings of the 1981 Conference on Functional Programming Languages and Computer Architecture, 59-63.

MacDonald, S., D. Szafron, and J. Schaeffer (2004). "Rethinking the Pipeline as Object-Oriented States with Transformations." Ninth International Workshop on High-Level Parallel Programming Models and Supportive Environments.

Mahmoud, Q. H. (2005, March). "Concurrent Programming with J2SE 5.0." Sun Developer Network.

Massingill, B. L., T. G. Mattson, and B. A. Sanders (2005). "Reengineering for Parallelism: An Entry Point for PLPP (Pattern Language for Parallel Programming) for Legacy Applications." Proceedings of the Twelfth Pattern Languages of Programs Workshop.

Mattson, T. G., B. A. Sanders, and B. L. Massingill (2004). Patterns for Parallel Programming. Reading, MA: Addison Wesley.

McDowell, C. E., and D. P. Helmbold (1989). "Debugging Concurrent Programs." Communications of the ACM, 21, 2.

Meyers, S. (1998). Effective C++, Second Edition. Reading, MA: Addison Wesley, 1998.

Musser, D. R., and A. A. Stepanov (1994). "Algorithm-Oriented Generic Libraries." Software—Practice and Experience, 24(7), 623-642.

Musser, D. R., G. J. Derge, and A. Saini, with foreword by Alexander Stepanov (2001). STL Tutorial and Reference Guide, Second Edition: C++ Programming with the Standard Template Library, Boston, MA: Addison Wesley, 2001.

Narlikar, G., and G. Blelloch (1999). "Space-Efficient Scheduling of Nested Parallelism." ACM Transactions on Programming Languages and Systems, 21, 1, 138-173.

OpenMP C and C++ Application Program Interface, Version 2.5 (May 2005).

Ottosen, T. (2006, September). Range Library Core. C++ standards committee document N2068.

Plauger, P. J., M. Lee, et al. (2000). C++ Standard Template Library, Prentice Hall.

Rauchwerger, L., F. Arzu, and K. Ouchi (1998, May). "Standard Templates Adaptive Parallel Library," Proceedings of the 4th International Workshop on Languages, Compilers, and Run-Time Systems for Scalable Computers (LCR), Pittsburgh, PA. Also Lecture Notes in Computer Science, 1511, Springer-Verlag, 1998, 402-410.

Robison, A. D. (2006). "A Proposal to Add Parallel Iteration to the Standard Library."

Robison, A. (2003, April). "Memory Consistency & .NET." Dr. Dobb's Journal.

Samko, V. (2006, February). "A proposal to add lambda functions to the C++ standard." C++ standards committee document N1958=06-028.

Schmidt, D. C., and I. Pyarali (1998). Strategies for Implementing POSIX Condition Variables on Win32. Department of Computer Science, Washington University, St. Louis, MO.

Schmidt, D. C., M. Stal, et al. (2000). Patterns for Concurrent and Networked Objects. Pattern-Oriented Architecture, 2.

Shah, S., G. Haab, et al. (1999). "Flexible Control Structures for Parallelism in OpenMP." Proceedings of the First European Workshop on OpenMP.

Siek, J., D. Gregor, et al. (2005). "Concepts for C++0x."

Stepanov, A. A., and M. Lee (1995). "The Standard Template Library." HP Laboratories Technical Report 95-11(R.1).

Stepanov, A. A. (1999). "Greatest Common Measure: The Last 2500 Years."

Stroustrup, B. (1994). The Design and Evolution of C++, also known as D&E. Reading, MA: Addison Wesley.

Stroustrup, B. (2000). The C++ Programming Language. Special Edition. Reading, MA: Addison Wesley.

Stroustrup, B., and G. Dos Reis (2005, April). "A Concept Design (rev.1)." Technical Report N1782=05-0042, ISO/IEC SC22/JTC1/WG21.

Stroustrup, B., and G. Dos Reis (2005, October). "Specifying C++ concepts." Technical Report N1886=05-0146, ISO/IEC SC22/JTC1/WG21.

Su, E., X. Tian, et al. (2002, September). "Compiler Support of the Workqueuing Execution Model for Intel SMP Architectures." Fourth European Workshop on OpenMP, Rome.

Sutter, H. (2005, January). "The Concurrency Revolution." Dr. Dobb's Journal.

Sutter, H. (2005, March). "The Free Lunch is Over: A Fundamental Turn Towards Concurrency in Software." Dr. Dobb's Journal.

Voss, M. (2006, December). "Enable Safe, Scalable Parallelism with Intel Threading Building Blocks' Concurrent Containers."

Voss, M. (2006, October). "Demystify Scalable Parallelism with Intel Threading Building Blocks' Generic Parallel Algorithms."

Willcock, J., J. Järvi, et al. (2006). "Lambda Expressions and Closures for C++." N1968-06-0038.

APPENDIX B

TBB Précis

Our book thus far has been focused on teaching – this Appendix completes the picture by fully documenting it in a way that could not be done in the flow of teaching. Throughout the book, we left out some details about interfaces in order to keep the text more readable and manageable. In particular, some advanced concepts like TGC (Task Group Contexts) were not introduced until the second half of the book, so there is no mention of such parameters in the first half of the book.

Therefore, this is where we have placed complete definitions. This appendix is a series of precise summaries (précis) for each category of TBB interfaces. The plural of *précis* is also *précis*, hence the name we chose for this appendix.

We offer terse but complete definitions of the interfaces intended for use in applications. Also, when useful, a "Hello, World" illustrative example is included. It is our hope that the illustrative examples help those readers, who, like the authors, really want to see a simple example in action in order to more fully grasp the API. The example code in this appendix illustrates correct usage of the API, with sample output, without attempting to be awesome parallel programming examples. Keep in mind that code examples from this book, including this appendix, are available for download from the threadingbuildingblocks.org web site, so we encourage you to expand the silly little code examples from this appendix to explore the APIs yourself. The book Index and Table of Contents provide pointers to more detailed discussions regarding each of these items where examples to help with real parallel programming will be found.

Often, we emphasize *possibly parallel* in our terse descriptions, not because we doubt that TBB will give us great parallel execution and scaling, but because parallelism is never guaranteed. For instance, when a program runs on a single core machine the machine cannot give us parallel execution. Or, in a complex pipeline the individual stages (filters) may or may not run in parallel depending on the overall workload. This point about parallelism being only *possible* is subtle but important, and applies to all composable parallel solutions.Debug and Conditional Coding

© Intel Corporation 2019
M. Voss, R. Asenjo, J. Reinders, *Pro TBB*, https://doi.org/10.1007/978-1-4842-4398-5

Debug and Conditional Coding

To aid in debugging, TBB has macros, an environment variable (TBB_VERSION), and a function that reveal version and runtime information for conditional coding and debugging.

Macros
#include <tbb/tbb_stddef.h>
Defines macros related to versioning, as described below. Particularly useful for conditional coding. We should not attempt to redefine these macros.
TBB_INTERFACE_VERSION
Current interface version. The value is a decimal numeral of the form XYYY where X is the major version number and YYY is the minor version number.
TBB_INTERFACE_VERSION_MAJOR
TBB_INTERFACE_VERSION/1000; that is, the major version number
TBB_COMPATIBLE_INTERFACE_VERSION
Oldest major interface version still supported.

Figure B-1. *Précis: Macros*

Environment Variable
Set the environment variable **TBB_VERSION** to 1 to cause the library to print information on stderr.
Each printed line is of the form "TBB: **TAG** value," where **TAG** and value are described below. Debug output can be implementation specific and may change at any time.
VERSION
Intel TBB product version number.
INTERFACE_VERSION
Value of macro TBB_INTERFACE_VERSION when library was compiled.
BUILD_...
Various information about the machine configuration on which the library was built.
USE_ASSERT
Setting of macro TBB_USE_ASSERT
DO_ITT_NOTIFY
1 (one) if library can enable instrumentation for Intel Parallel Studio XE analysis tools; 0 (zero) or undefined otherwise.
ITT
yes if library has enabled instrumentation for Intel Parallel Studio XE analysis tools, no otherwise. Typically, yes only if the program is running under control of Intel Parallel Studio XE analysis tools.
ALLOCATOR
Underlying allocator for tbb::tbb_allocator. It is scalable_malloc if the Intel TBB malloc library was successfully loaded; malloc otherwise.

Figure B-2. *Précis: Environment variable*

> ## Function: `TBB_runtime_interface_version`
> `#include <tbb/tbb_stddef.h>`
>
> Function that returns the interface version of the Intel TBB library that was loaded at runtime. Great for debugging or conditional coding.
>
> ---
>
> `extern "C" int TBB_runtime_interface_version();`
> The value returned by this function may differ from the value `of` `TBB_INTERFACE_VERSION` obtained at compile time. This can be used to identify whether an application was compiled against a compatible version of the Intel TBB headers. In general, the run-time value returned must be greater than or equal to the compile-time value of `TBB_INTERFACE_VERSION`. Otherwise the application may fail to resolve all symbols at run time.

Figure B-3. *Précis: TBB_runtime_interface_version*

Debugging Macros

Four macros control certain debugging features. In general, it is useful to compile with these features on for development code, and off for production code, because the features may decrease performance. The table below summarizes the macros and their default values. A value of 1 enables the corresponding feature; a value of 0 disables the feature.

Macro	Feature	Default Value
`TBB_USE_DEBUG`	Default value for all other macros in this table.	Default is 0, *except* on Windows where it is 1 if `_DEBUG` is defined.
`TBB_USE_ASSERT`	Enable internal assertion checking. Can significantly slow performance.	TBB_USE_DEBUG
`TBB_USE_THREADING_TOOLS`	Enable full support for Intel Parallel Studio XE analysis tools.	
`TBB_USE_PERFORMANCE_WARNINGS`	Enable warnings about performance issues.	

Figure B-4. *Précis: Debugging macros*

Preview Feature Macros

TBB may also include macros to enable "preview features." From time to time, TBB release may include experimental features called "preview features" that will generally be disabled by default. Preview features are included side by side in full releases to enable feedback from users without committing to preserve the API. We do not cover preview features in this book – we refer you to the release notes to learn about any preview features that may be available in a given release of TBB.

Ranges

A Range can be recursively subdivided into two parts. Subdivision is done by calling one of the *splitting constructors* of Range. There are two types of splitting constructors:

1. Basic splitting constructor: It is recommended that the division be done in nearly equal parts in this constructor, but it is not required. Splitting as evenly as possible typically yields the best parallelism.

2. Proportional splitting constructor: This constructor is optional and can be omitted along with the is_splittable_in_proportion class variable. When using this type of constructor, for the best results, follow the given proportion with rounding to the nearest integer if necessary.

Ideally, a range is recursively splittable until the parts represent portions of work that are more efficient to execute serially, rather than split further. The amount of work represented by a Range typically depends upon higher-level context, hence a typical type that models a Range should provide a way to control the degree of splitting. For example, the template class blocked_range has a grainsize parameter that specifies the biggest range considered indivisible.

If the set of values has a sense of direction, then by convention, the splitting constructor should construct the second part of the range, and update its argument to be the first part of the range. This enables parallel_for, parallel_reduce, and parallel_scan algorithms, when running sequentially, to work across a range in the increasing order, typical of an ordinary sequential loop.

Since a Range declares both *splitting* and *copy* constructors, a default constructor for it will not be automatically generated. Therefore, it is necessary to either explicitly define a default constructor, or always use arguments to create an instance of a Range.

Requirements on `range` concept

Class R implementing the concept of range must define:

```
R::R( const R& );
```
Copy constructor
```
R::~R();
```
Destructor
```
bool R::is_divisible() const;
```
True if range can be partitioned into two subranges.
```
bool R::empty() const;
```
True if range is empty.
```
R::R( R& r, tbb::split );
```
A *splitting constructor* - Splits range r into two subranges.
```
R::R( R& r, tbb::proportional_split proportion );
```
Optional. A *splitting constructor* - Proportional splitting constructor. Splits r into two subranges in accordance with proportion.
```
static const bool R::is_splittable_in_proportion;
```
Optional. If true, the proportional *splitting constructor* is defined for the range and may be used by parallel algorithms.

Figure B-5. *Précis: Requirements on range concept*

Partitioners

A partitioner specifies how a loop template should partition its work among threads.

The default behavior of the loop templates `parallel_for`, `parallel_reduce`, and `parallel_scan` tries to recursively split a range into enough parts to keep processors busy, not necessarily splitting as finely as possible. An optional partitioner parameter enables other behaviors to be specified, as shown in the table in Figure B-6. Unlike other partitioners, an `affinity_partitioner` is passed by non-const reference because it is updated to remember where loop iterations run, hence the absence of a `const` qualifier. The template `parallel_deterministic_reduce` supports `simple_partitioner` and `static_partitioner` only because the other partitioners are, by their very nature, nondeterministic.

Partitioners

#include `<tbb/partitioner.h>`

const `auto_partitioner&`
predefined as **tbb::auto_partitioner()**

Default except for parallel_deterministic_reduce.
Performs sufficient splitting to balance load, not necessarily splitting as finely as `Range::is_divisible` permits. When used with classes such as `blocked_range`, the selection of an appropriate grain size is less important, and often acceptable performance can be achieved with the default grain size of 1.

`affinity_partitioner&`
program defines **tbb::affinity_partitioner ap,**
and then passes **ap** (by reference)

Similar to `auto_partitioner`, but improves cache affinity by its choice of mapping subranges to worker threads. It can improve performance significantly when a loop is re-executed over the same data set, and the data set fits in the cache.
`affinity_partitioner` uses proportional splitting when it is enabled for a Range.

const `static_partitioner&`
predefined as **tbb::static_partitioner()**

Distributes range iterations among worker threads as uniformly as possible, without a possibility for further load balancing. Similar to `affinity_partitioner`, maps subranges to worker threads. The work distribution and mapping are deterministic and only depend on the number of range iterations, its grain size and the number of threads.

const `simple_partitioner&`
predefined as **tbb::simple_partitioner()**

Default for parallel_deterministic_reduce.
Recursively splits a range until it is no longer divisible. The `Range::is_divisible` function is wholly responsible for deciding when recursive splitting halts, therefore when used with classes such as `blocked_range`, the selection of an appropriate grain size is critical to enabling concurrency while limiting overheads.

Figure B-6. *Précis: Partitioners*

Algorithms

Chapter 2 introduces TBB algorithms, and Chapter 16 dives deeper.

parallel_while is not documented in this book, as it has been deprecated in favor of the newer parallel_do.

Algorithm: `parallel_do`

Applies a function object body over a sequence [first,last). Items may be processed in parallel. Additional work items can be added if the Body::operator is declared with a second argument of type parallel_do_feeder. The function terminates when body(x) returns for all items x that were in the input sequence or added by method parallel_do_feeder::add. The container form parallel_do(c,body) is equivalent to parallel_do(std::begin(c),std::end(c),body).

```
parallel_do
#include <tbb/parallel_do.h>
template<typename InputIterator,
         typename Body > void
tbb::parallel_do (
     InputIterator  first,
     InputIterator  last,
     Body      body
 [    , tbb::task_group_context &context ]
)
template<typename Container,
         typename Body > void
tbb::parallel_do (
     [const ] Container    &c
     Body      body
 [    , tbb::task_group_context &context ]
)
```

The first version, parallel_do(first,last,body), applies a function object body over a sequence [first,last]. Items may be processed in parallel. Additional work items can be added by body if it has a second argument of type parallel_do_feeder. The function terminates when body(x) returns for all items x that were in the input sequence or added by method parallel_do_feeder::add.

There is no lambda version support for providing a feeder (at least as of TBB 2019).

There are no partitioner options for this template.

Figure B-7. *Précis: Algorithm: parallel_do*

parallel_do – there is no try, Hello, World example

```
/* Does NOT show the POWER of ADDING work during execution of do */
#include <cstdio>
#include <tbb/tbb.h>
#include <array>

tbb::spin_mutex mylock;
// use of an atomic (Chapter 5) instead of
// a simple int for counter would eliminate the need
// for the guarded access with a mutex
int counter;

#define PN(Y) printf( "\nHello, Do (or Do Not) " #Y ":\n\t");
#define PV(X) {                                            \
        int mycount;                                       \
        { tbb::spin_mutex::scoped_lock hello(mylock);      \
          mycount = counter++;                             \
        }                                                  \
        printf(" %02d.%d", X, mycount);                    \
      }

int main( int argc, char *argv[] ) {
  std::array<int,10> myarray    = { 19,13,14,11,15,20,17,16,12,18 };
  std::array<int,10> disarray   = { 23,29,27,25,30,21,26,24,28,22 };

  counter = 0;
  PN(myarray);
  tbb::parallel_do( myarray.begin(),myarray.end(),
                  [](int xyzzy){ PV(xyzzy); }
              );
  printf("\n");

  counter = 0;
  PN(disarray);
  tbb::parallel_do( disarray,
                  [](int xyzzy){ PV(xyzzy); }
              );
  printf("\n\n");
}
```

Note that the order of visits differs from the order in the arrays. This is a sample output - the order can easily vary run to run and machine to machine!

```
Hello, Do (or Do Not) myarray:
       13.0 17.1 20.2 18.3 16.4 12.5 19.6 15.7 11.8 14.9

Hello, Do (or Do Not) disarray:
       29.0 23.1 30.2 27.3 25.5 26.4 21.6 22.7 28.8 24.9
```

Try this for fun (assuming you compile into ./a.out).

```
    for i in `seq 1 1000`;
        do (./a.out; ./a.out; ./a.out; ./a.out & );
    done | grep 29 | sort | uniq
```

```
      26.0 30.1 21.2 29.3 27.4 23.5 22.6 28.7 25.8 24.9
      29.0 23.1 26.2 30.3 21.4 25.5 27.6 22.7 28.8 24.9
      29.0 23.1 30.2 27.3 25.4 21.6 26.5 22.7 28.8 24.9
      29.0 23.1 30.2 27.3 25.4 22.6 24.7 28.8 21.9 26.5
      29.0 23.1 30.2 27.3 25.4 22.6 26.5 21.7 24.8 28.9
      29.0 23.1 30.2 27.3 25.4 26.5 21.6 22.7 24.8 28.9
      29.0 23.1 30.2 27.3 25.4 26.5 21.6 22.7 24.9 28.8
      29.0 23.1 30.2 27.3 25.4 26.5 21.6 22.7 28.8 24.9
      29.0 23.1 30.2 27.3 25.4 26.5 21.6 28.7 24.8 22.9
      29.0 23.1 30.2 27.3 25.4 26.5 21.6 28.8 22.7 24.9
      29.0 23.1 30.2 27.3 25.4 26.5 22.6 21.7 24.8 28.9
      29.0 23.1 30.2 27.3 25.4 26.5 22.6 21.7 28.8 24.9
```

Figure B-8. *Précis: Algorithm: parallel_do example*

Requirements on a `parallel_do body` (and `T`)

Class `Body` implementing the concept of `parallel_do` body must define:

```
Body::operator()(
  [ cv-qualifiers  ] T [ reference ] item,
  [  , parallel_do_feeder<T>& feeder ]
) const
```

Process a work item. `parallel_do` may concurrently invoke `operator()` for the same body object but different items. The operator may accept item by value or by reference, including `rvalue` reference. The signature with feeder permits additional work items to be added. CAUTION: Defining both the one-argument and two-argument forms of `operator()` is *not* permitted.

```
~T::T()
```

Destroy a work item.

```
T( T&& )
```

Optional. Move a work item.

```
T( const T& )
```

Optional. Copy a work item.

Figure B-9. *Précis: Algorithm: `parallel_do` body requirements*

Algorithm: `parallel_for`

The range parameter version provides the most general and efficient form of parallel iteration. It represents a possibly parallel execution of body over each value in range. Type Range must model the Range concept (requirements covered after the upcoming explanation and example code for `parallel_for`). The `first/last/step` version represents a possibly parallel execution of the loop: `for (auto i=first; i<last; i+=step) f();` If `step` is not provided, it is assumed to be one. The optional partitioner specifies a partitioning strategy. The partitioner argument specifies a partitioning strategy, as described in Chapter 12. The `task_group_context` argument specifies the task group context to use for cancellation and exception handling.

```
parallel_for
#include <tbb/parallel_for.h>

template< typename Range, typename Body > void
tbb::parallel_for (const Range     &range,
                    const Body      &body,
          [, tbb::simple_partitioner()        |
     , tbb::auto_partitioner() |
     , tbb::static_partitioner()      |
     , tbb::affinity_partitioner &ap ]
          [, tbb::task_group_context &context ]
)


template< typename Range, typename Func > void
tbb::parallel_for ( Iterator first,
       Iterator last,
               [ Iterator step, ]
               const Func      &func,
          [, tbb::simple_partitioner()        |
     , tbb::auto_partitioner() |
     , tbb::static_partitioner()      |
     , tbb::affinity_partitioner &ap ]
          [, tbb::task_group_context &context ]
)
```

Parallel iteration over items [first,last) or range.

Function func operates on a single Iterator value if the `first,last[,step]` syntax is used for the `parallel_for`.

Function body operates on range if range syntax is used for the `parallel_for`.

Default (auto) partitioner used if no partitioner is specified.

User-supplied context is optional.

Figure B-10. *Précis: Algorithm: parallel_for*

`parallel_for` *(using* `blocked_range`*)* **– 10 x Hello, World example**

```cpp
#include <cstdio>
#include <tbb/tbb.h>

tbb::spin_mutex mylock;
// use of an atomic (Chapter 5) instead of
// a simple int for counter would eliminate the need
// for the guarded access with a mutex
int counter = 0;

int main( int argc, char *argv[] ) {
  tbb::parallel_for(
    tbb::blocked_range<int>( 0, 10 ),
    [](const tbb::blocked_range<int>& r) {
      for( int i=r.begin(); i!=r.end(); ++i ) {
        int mycount;
        { tbb::spin_mutex::scoped_lock hello(mylock);
          mycount = counter++;
        }
        printf("Hello, World (%02d):(%02d)\n",i,mycount);
      }
    } /* end of lambda */
  ); /* end of parallel_for */
}
```

Sample output... will vary run to run and machine to machine!

```
Hello, World (00):(00)
Hello, World (05):(01)
Hello, World (01):(02)
Hello, World (06):(03)
Hello, World (07):(04)
Hello, World (08):(05)
Hello, World (02):(06)
Hello, World (09):(07)
Hello, World (03):(08)
Hello, World (04):(09)
```

Figure B-11. *Précis: Algorithm: example of* `parallel_for` *with* `blocked_range`

`parallel_for` *(using explicit begin end)* **– 10 x Hello, World example**

```
#include <cstdio>
#include <tbb/tbb.h>

tbb::spin_mutex mylock;
// use of an atomic (Chapter 5) instead of
// a simple int for counter would eliminate the need
// for the guarded access with a mutex
int counter = 0;

int main( int argc, char *argv[] ) {
  tbb::parallel_for(
    0,
    10,
    [](int i) {
      int mycount;
      { tbb::spin_mutex::scoped_lock hello(mylock);
        mycount = counter++;
      }
      printf("Hello, World (%02d):(%02d)\n",i,mycount);
    } /* end of lambda */
  ); /* end of parallel_for */
}
```

Sample output… will vary run to run and machine to machine!
```
Hello, World (00):(00)
Hello, World (05):(01)
Hello, World (01):(02)
Hello, World (07):(03)
Hello, World (08):(04)
Hello, World (06):(05)
Hello, World (02):(06)
Hello, World (03):(07)
Hello, World (09):(08)
Hello, World (04):(09)
```

Figure B-12. *Précis: Algorithm: example of parallel_for with first, last*

Requirements on `parallel_for` body

Class `Body` implementing the concept of `parallel_for` body must define:

```
Body::Body( const Body& );
```
Copy constructor
```
Body::~Body();
```
Destructor
```
void Body::operator()( Range& r ) const;
```
Function call operator applying the body to range `r`.

Figure B-13. *Précis: Algorithm: parallel_for body requirements*

Algorithm: `parallel_for_each`

Applies a function object f to each element in a sequence [first,last) or a container c, possibly in parallel.

```
parallel_for_each
#include <tbb/parallel_for_each.h>
template<typename Container, typename Func > void
tbb::parallel_for_each (       Container &c,
                         const Func      &func,
             [, tbb::task_group_context &context ]
)

template<typename Iterator, typename Func > void
tbb::parallel_for_each (Iterator first,
                        Iterator last, ]
                        const Func      &func,
             [, tbb::task_group_context &context ]
)
```
Parallel iteration over sequence [first,last) or elements of a container c.
Function func operates on a single element.
There are no partitioner options for this template.
User-supplied context is optional.

Figure B-14. *Précis: Algorithm: parallel_for_each*

---

parallel_for_each – 10 x Hello, World example

```
#include <cstdio>
#include <array>
#include <tbb/tbb.h>

tbb::spin_mutex mylock;
// use of an atomic (Chapter 5) instead of
// a simple int for counter would eliminate the need
// for the guarded access with a mutex
int counter = 0;
std::array<int, 10> values{ { 11,22,33,44,55,66,77,88,99,42 } };

int main( int argc, char *argv[] ) {
  tbb::parallel_for_each(
    std::begin(values),
    std::end(values),
    [](int i) {
      int mycount;
      { tbb::spin_mutex::scoped_lock hello(mylock);
        mycount = counter++;
      }
      printf("Hello, World (%02d):(%02d)\n",i,mycount);
    } /* end of lambda */
  ); /* end of parallel_for_each */
}
```

Sample output... will vary run to run and machine to machine!

```
Hello, World (11):(00)
Hello, World (66):(01)
Hello, World (33):(02)
Hello, World (22):(03)
Hello, World (88):(04)
Hello, World (77):(05)
Hello, World (44):(06)
Hello, World (99):(07)
Hello, World (55):(08)
Hello, World (42):(09)
```

Figure B-15. *Précis: Algorithm: parallel_for_each example*

Algorithm: `parallel_invoke`

Evaluates $f_1()$, $f_2()$, ..., $f_n()$ possibly in parallel. The arguments can be function objects, lambda expressions, or function pointers. Supports 2 or more arguments. The original TBB was limited to ten parameters, but thanks to variadic templates in C++11, there is no limit now.

```
parallel_invoke

#include <tbb/parallel_invoke.h>

template<         typename FUNC1,
        typename FUNC2
    [ ,          typename FUNCN ]* > void
tbb::parallel_invoke (    const FUNC1 &f01,
                          const FUNC2 &f02
                 [ ,      const FUNCn &fn ]*  )
         [     , tbb::task_group_context &context ]
)
```
Executes a list of (two or more) tasks in parallel and waits for all tasks to complete.
User-supplied context is optional.

Figure B-16. *Précis: Algorithm: parallel_invoke*

```
parallel_invoke – 10 x Hello, World example

#include <cstdio>
#include <tbb/tbb.h>

tbb::spin_mutex mylock;
// use of an atomic (Chapter 5) instead of
// a simple int for counter would eliminate the need
// for the guarded access with a mutex
int counter = 0;

void hw() {
  int mycount;
  { tbb::spin_mutex::scoped_lock hello(mylock);
    mycount = counter++;
  }
  printf("Hello, World (%02d):(%02d)\n",42,mycount);
}

int main( int argc, char *argv[] ) {
  tbb::parallel_invoke( hw,hw,hw,hw,hw, hw,hw,hw,hw,hw );
}
```

Sample output… will vary run to run and machine to machine!

```
Hello, World (42):(00)
Hello, World (42):(01)
Hello, World (42):(02)
Hello, World (42):(03)
Hello, World (42):(04)
Hello, World (42):(05)
Hello, World (42):(06)
Hello, World (42):(07)
Hello, World (42):(08)
Hello, World (42):(09)
```

Figure B-17. *Précis: Algorithm: parallel_invoke example*

Algorithm: `parallel_pipeline`

The `parallel_pipeline` function is a strongly typed lambda-friendly interface for building and running pipelines, possibly in parallel. Because of strong typing and lambda support, it is recommended instead of the `pipeline` class. Flow Graph offers a far more general solution that should be used when that generality is needed.

`parallel_pipeline`
`#include <tbb/pipeline.h>`

`void` `tbb::parallel_pipeline (`
    `size_t max_number_of_live_tokens,`
    `const` `filter_t<`**`void`**`,`**`void`**`>& filter_chain`
`[ ,`   `tbb::task_group_context &context ]`
`)`

Lambda friendly (vs. `tbb::pipeline`), and strongly typed interface for pipelined execution. For more complex flows, an alternative is an explicit Flow Graph (see Chapter 3). User-supplied context is optional.

Figure B-18. *Précis: Algorithm: parallel_pipeline*

`tbb::flow_control` Class
`#include <tbb/pipeline.h>`
`void stop()`
Template function `parallel_pipeline` passes a `flow_control` object `fc` to the input functor of a `filter_t`. When the input functor reaches the end of its input, it should invoke `fc.stop()` and return a dummy value.

Figure B-19. *Précis: Algorithm: parallel_pipeline flow_control*

---

tbb::filter_t Template Class

#include <tbb/pipeline.h>

---

filter _t()

Construct an undefined filter.

CAUTION: The effect of using an undefined filter by `operator&` or `parallel_pipeline` is undefined.

filter_t(const filter_t<T,U>& rhs)

Construct a copy of rhs.

template<typename Func>
filter_t(filter::mode mode, const Func& f)

Construct a `filter_t` that uses a copy of functor f to map an input value t of type T to an output value u of type U.

There are three modes of filters:

- A `parallel` filter can process multiple items in parallel and in no particular order.
- A `serial_out_of_order` filter processes items one at a time, and in no particular order.
- A `serial_in_order` filter processes items one at a time. The order in which items are processed is implicitly set by the first serial_in_order filter and respected by all other such filters in the pipeline.

NOTE: When `parallel_pipeline` uses the `filter_t`, it computes u by evaluating `f(t)`, unless T is void. In the void case u is computed by the expression `u=f(fc)`, where fc is of type `flow_control`.

void operator=(const filter_t<T,U>& rhs)

Update `*this` to use the functor associated with rhs.

~filter_t()

Destroy the `filter_t`.

void clear()

Set `*this` to an undefined filter.

template<typename T, typename U, typename Func> filter_t<T,U>
make_filter(filter::mode mode, const Func& f)

Returns: filter_t<T,U>(mode,f)

template<typename T, typename V, typename U> filter_t<T,U>
operator& (const filter_t<T,V>& left,
**   const filter_t<V,U>& right)**

Returns: A `filter_t` representing the composition of filters left and right. The composition behaves as if the output value of left becomes the input value of right.

Requires: The output type of left must match the input type of right.

Figure B-20. *Précis: Algorithm: parallel_pipeline filter_t*

`parallel_pipeline` – 10 x Hello, World example

```cpp
#include <cstdio>
#include <tbb/tbb.h>

tbb::spin_mutex mylock;
int counter = 0;

void hw(int x, int v) {
  int mycount;
  { tbb::spin_mutex::scoped_lock hello(mylock);
    mycount = counter++;
  }
  printf("Hello, Stage %d (%02d):(%02d)\n",x,mycount,v);
}

int main( int argc, char *argv[] ) {
  int cdown = 3;
  tbb::parallel_pipeline(
    6,
    tbb::make_filter<void,int>(
      tbb::filter::parallel,[&](tbb::flow_control& fc)->int
        { hw(1,0);
          if (!cdown) { fc.stop(); return NULL; }
          return 1000 * cdown--;  }) &
    tbb::make_filter<int,float>(
      tbb::filter::parallel,[](int i)
        { hw(2,i);       return ++i;    }) &
    tbb::make_filter<float,float>(
      tbb::filter::parallel,[](float f)
        { hw(3,(int)f); return f+1.0f;  }) &
    tbb::make_filter<float,int>(
      tbb::filter::parallel,[](float f)
        { hw(4,(int)f); return (int)f+1;}) &
    tbb::make_filter<int,void>(
      tbb::filter::parallel,[](int i)
        { hw(5,i);                      })
  );
}
```

Sample output… will vary run to run and machine to machine!
Full disclosure: to get the run below, we made our machine moderately
busy with other work. Without doing that, the first filter completely
finished before the second began because the example is so trivial – and
the output is boring. We must remember to code (and test) for the various
independent orderings possible with parallel execution.

```
Hello, Stage 1 (00):(00)
Hello, Stage 2 (01):(3000)
Hello, Stage 3 (02):(3001)
Hello, Stage 4 (03):(3002)
Hello, Stage 5 (04):(3003)
Hello, Stage 1 (05):(00)
Hello, Stage 2 (06):(2000)
Hello, Stage 3 (07):(2001)
Hello, Stage 4 (08):(2002)
Hello, Stage 5 (09):(2003)
Hello, Stage 1 (10):(00)
Hello, Stage 2 (11):(1000)
Hello, Stage 3 (12):(1001)
Hello, Stage 4 (13):(1002)
Hello, Stage 5 (14):(1003)
Hello, Stage 1 (15):(00)
```

Figure B-21. *Précis: Algorithm: parallel_pipeline example*

```
Sorted output (from the same exact run as above - but sorted):
Hello, Stage 1 (00):(00)
Hello, Stage 1 (05):(00)
Hello, Stage 1 (10):(00)
Hello, Stage 1 (15):(00)
Hello, Stage 2 (01):(3000)
Hello, Stage 2 (06):(2000)
Hello, Stage 2 (11):(1000)
Hello, Stage 3 (02):(3001)
Hello, Stage 3 (07):(2001)
Hello, Stage 3 (12):(1001)
Hello, Stage 4 (03):(3002)
Hello, Stage 4 (08):(2002)
Hello, Stage 4 (13):(1002)
Hello, Stage 5 (04):(3003)
Hello, Stage 5 (09):(2003)
Hello, Stage 5 (14):(1003)
```

Figure B-21. (*continued*)

Algorithm: `parallel_reduce` and `parallel_deterministic_reduce`

Reductions (possibly in parallel) are supported in a deterministic (slightly slower, but with predictable and repeatable results which are at least useful while debugging!), and a nondeterministic version that will generally be slightly faster. Each reduction type supports template of two forms. A *functional* form is designed to be easy to use in conjunction with lambda expressions. An *imperative* form is designed to minimize copying of data. The functional form `parallel_reduce(range, identity, func, reduction)` performs a parallel reduction by applying `func` to subranges in range and reducing the results using binary operator reduction. It returns the result of the reduction. Parameter `func` and `reduction` can be lambda expressions. The imperative form `parallel_reduce(range,body)` performs parallel reduction of body over each value in range. Type Range must model the Range concept (requirements covered early in this Appendix). The body must model the requirements shown in the table in Figure B-22.

---

parallel_reduce and parallel_deterministic_reduce

`#include <tbb/parallel_reduce.h>`

```
template<typename Range, typename Value,
                        typename Func,
                        typename Reduction >
Value tbb::parallel_[deterministic_]reduce(
                const Range &range,
                const Value &identity,
                const Func        &func,
                const Reduction &joinfunc
        [, tbb::simple_partitioner()        |
    , tbb::auto_partitioner() |
    , tbb::static_partitioner()        |
    , tbb::affinity_partitioner &ap ]
        [, tbb::task_group_context &context ]
)
```

```
template <typename Range, typename Body>
void tbb::parallel_[deterministic_]reduce(
                const Range &range,
                const Body  &body
        [, tbb::simple_partitioner()        |
    , tbb::auto_partitioner() |
    , tbb::static_partitioner()        |
    , tbb::affinity_partitioner &ap ]
        [, tbb::task_group_context &context ]
)
```

Parallel iteration with (optionally deterministic) reduction.

The first form is lambda friendly, because the operation and reduction (join) functions are broken out as separate parameters instead of the second form which requires a body that defines both functions as members.

Default (auto) partitioner used if no partitioner is specified.

When using deterministic reduction, we can only specify simple or static partitioner (the others would not be deterministic).

User-supplied context is optional.

Figure B-22. *Précis: Algorithm: parallel_[deterministic_]reduce*

parallel_reduce – 10 x Hello, World example

```cpp
#include <cstdio>
#include <tbb/tbb.h>

tbb::spin_mutex mylock;
// use of an atomic (Chapter 5) instead of
// a simple int for counter would eliminate the need
// for the guarded access with a mutex
int counter = 0;
int values[] = { 11,22,33,44,55,66,77,88,99,42 };

int main( int argc, char *argv[] ) {
  int howmany =
    parallel_reduce(
      tbb::blocked_range<int*>( values, values+10 ),
      0,
      [](const tbb::blocked_range<int*>& r, int init)->int {
        int rr = init;
        for( int* a=r.begin(); a!=r.end(); ++a ) {
          int mycount;
          { tbb::spin_mutex::scoped_lock hello(mylock);
            mycount = counter++;
          }
          printf("Hello, World (%02d):(%02d)\n",*a,mycount);
          rr += *a;
        } /* end of lambda */
        return rr;
      },
      []( int x, int y )->int {
        return x+y;
      }
    );
  printf("Hello, parallel_reduce(%02d)\n",howmany);
}
```

Sample output… will vary run to run and machine to machine!
```
Hello, World (11):(00)
Hello, World (66):(01)
Hello, World (22):(02)
Hello, World (33):(03)
Hello, World (77):(04)
Hello, World (88):(05)
Hello, World (44):(06)
Hello, World (55):(07)
Hello, World (99):(08)
Hello, World (42):(09)
Hello, parallel_reduce(537)
```

Figure B-23. *Précis: Algorithm: parallel_reduce example*

`parallel_deterministic_reduce` – 10 x Hello, World example

```cpp
/*
    EXACTLY the same code as parallel_reduce...
    except parallel_reduce changed to
    parallel_deterministic_reduce
 */
#include <cstdio>
#include <tbb/tbb.h>

tbb::spin_mutex mylock;
// use of an atomic (Chapter 5) instead of
// a simple int for counter would eliminate the need
// for the guarded access with a mutex
int counter = 0;
int values[] = { 11,22,33,44,55,66,77,88,99,42 };

int main( int argc, char *argv[] ) {
  int howmany =
    parallel_deterministic_reduce(
      tbb::blocked_range<int*>( values, values+10 ),
      0,
      [](const tbb::blocked_range<int*>& r, int init)->int {
        int rr = init;
        for( int* a=r.begin(); a!=r.end(); ++a ) {
          int mycount;
          { tbb::spin_mutex::scoped_lock hello(mylock);
            mycount = counter++;
          }
          printf("Hello, World (%02d):(%02d)\n",*a,mycount);
          rr += *a;
        } /* end of lambda */
        return rr;
      },
      []( int x, int y )->int {
        return x+y;
      }
    );
  printf("Hello, parallel_deterministic_reduce(%02d)\n",howmany);
}
```

Sample output… will vary run to run and machine to machine!
The "deteministic" aspect is the order the joins are done. The
individual computations are still free to occur in any order
because that does not affect the computed value!

```
Hello, World (11):(00)
Hello, World (22):(01)
Hello, World (66):(02)
Hello, World (33):(03)
Hello, World (88):(04)
Hello, World (77):(05)
Hello, World (44):(06)
Hello, World (99):(07)
Hello, World (42):(08)
Hello, World (55):(09)
Hello, parallel_deterministic_reduce(537)
```

Figure B-24. *Précis: Algorithm: parallel_deterministic_reduce example*

> **Requirements on body for**
> **parallel_[deterministic_]reduce**
> Class   Body   implementing   the   concept   of
> parallel_[deterministic_]reduce   body must define:
>
> ---
>
> Body::Body(Body&, split);
> Splitting constructor. Must be able to run concurrently with operator() and method join.
> Body::~Body();
> Destructor
> void Body::operator()(const Range& r);
> Function call operator applying body to range r and accumulating the result.
> void Body::join(Body& b);
> Join results. The result in b should be merged into the result of this.

Figure B-25. *Précis: Algorithm:* parallel_[deterministic_]reduce *body requirements*

Algorithm: `parallel_scan`

The `parallel_scan` template function computes a (possibly parallel) prefix, also known as parallel scan. This computation is an advanced concept in parallel computing that is sometimes useful in scenarios that appear to have inherently serial dependences. A mathematical definition of the parallel prefix is as follows. Let × be an associative operation with left-identity element id_x. The parallel prefix of × over a sequence z_0, z_1, ... z_{n-1} is a sequence y_0, y_1, y_2, ... y_{n-1} where: $y_0 = id_x × z_0$ and $y_i = y_{i-1} × z_i$. Parallel prefix performs this in parallel by reassociating the application of × and using two passes. It may invoke × up to twice as many times as the serial prefix algorithm. Even though it does more work, given the right grainsize the parallel algorithm can outperform the serial one because it distributes the work across multiple hardware threads. To obtain decent speedup, systems with more than two cores are recommended. The `parallel_scan` template function has two forms. The imperative form `parallel_scan(range, body)` implements parallel prefix generically. Type Range must model the Range concept (requirements covered early in this Appendix). The body must model the requirements in the following table.

```
parallel_scan
#include <tbb/parallel_scan.h>

template<typename   range,
         const Body &body > void
tbb::parallel_scan (const Range   &range,
                    const Body    &body,
           [, tbb::simple_partitioner()        |
            , tbb::auto_partitioner()                   ]
           [, tbb::task_group_context &context          ]
)


template<typename   Range,
         typename   Value,
         typename   Scan,
         typename   ReverseJoin > Value
tbb::parallel_scan (const Range   &range,
                    const Value   &identity,
                    const Scan    &scan,
              const ReverseJoin &reverse_join
           [, tbb::simple_partitioner()        |
            , tbb::auto_partitioner()                   ]
           [, tbb::task_group_context &context          ]
)
```

Parallel prefix.
Either supply a body, or value + scan + reverse_join.
Default (auto) partitioner used if no partitioner is specified.
TBB (as of TBB 2019) does not support static or affinity partitioners for `parallel_scan`.
TBB (as of TBB 2019) does not support a user-supplied context to `parallel_scan`.

Figure B-26. *Précis: Algorithm: parallel_scan*

`parallel_scan` – scanning Hello, World example

```
#include <cstdio>
#include <tbb/tbb.h>

tbb::spin_mutex mylock;
// use of an atomic (Chapter 5) instead of
// a simple int for counter would eliminate the need
// for the guarded access with a mutex
int counter = 0;
int in[10] = { 1,2,3,4,5,6,7,8,9,10 };
int out[10];

int main( int argc, char *argv[] ) {
  int re;
  re = tbb::parallel_scan(
        tbb::blocked_range<int>(0,10,1),
        0,
        [](const tbb::blocked_range<int>& r, int gsum,
         bool is_final_scan)->int {
          int psum = gsum;
          int mycount;
          int tst = 0;
          for( int i=r.begin(); i<r.end(); ++i ) {
            psum += in[i];
            tst++;
            if ( is_final_scan ) out[i] = psum;
            { tbb::spin_mutex::scoped_lock hello(mylock);
              mycount = counter++;
            }
          }
          printf("Hello, World (%02d) %02d+[%02d-%02d]=%02d%c\n",
                  mycount,gsum,r.begin(),r.end(),
                  psum,is_final_scan?'F':'-');
          return psum;
        }, /* end of scan lambda */
        []( int left, int right )->int {
          printf("Hello, Scan %02d +  %02d\n",left,right);
          return left + right;
        } /* end of reverse join lambda */
      ); /* end of parallel_scan */
  printf("Hello, Scanned%4d%4d%4d%4d%4d%4d%4d%4d%4d%4d\n",
        in[0],in[1],in[2],in[3],in[4],
        in[5],in[6],in[7],in[8],in[9]);
  printf("      yielding %4d%4d%4d%4d%4d%4d%4d%4d%4d%4d ->%4d\n",
        out[0],out[1],out[2],out[3],out[4],
        out[5],out[6],out[7],out[8],out[9],
        re);
}
```

Sample output… will vary run to run and machine to machine!

```
Hello, Scan 00 +  00
Hello, World (00) 00+[00-01]=01F
Hello, World (01) 01+[01-02]=03F
Hello, World (02) 00+[05-06]=06-
Hello, World (03) 06+[06-07]=13-
Hello, World (04) 00+[02-03]=03-
Hello, World (06) 03+[03-05]=12-
Hello, Scan 03 +  12
Hello, World (09) 03+[02-05]=15F
Hello, World (14) 15+[05-10]=55F
Hello, Scanned    1   2   3   4   5   6   7   8   9  10
     yielding      1   3   6  10  15  21  28  36  45  55 ->  55
```

Figure B-27. *Précis: Algorithm: parallel_scan example*

Requirements on `parallel_scan` body

Class Body implementing the concept of `parallel_scan` body must define:

`Body::Body( Body&, split );`
Splitting constructor. Split b so that this and b can accumulate separately.

`Body::~Body();`
Destructor

`void Body::operator()( const Range& r,`
`                       pre_scan_tag );`
Preprocess iterations for range r.

`void Body::operator()( const Range& r,`
`                       final_scan_tag );`
Do final processing for iterations of range r .

`void Body::reverse_join( Body& a );`
Merge preprocessing state of a into this, where a was created earlier from b by b's splitting constructor.

Figure B-28. *Précis: Algorithm:* `parallel_scan` *body requirements*

Algorithm: `parallel_sort`

Sorts a sequence or a container, possibly in parallel. The sort is *neither* stable *nor* deterministic – relative ordering of elements with equal keys is *not* preserved and *not* guaranteed to repeat if the same sequence is sorted again. The requirements on the iterator and sequence are the same as for `std::sort`. Specifically, `RandomAccessIterator` must be a random-access iterator, and its value type T must model the requirements in the table in Figure B-29. A call `parallel_sort(begin,end,comp)` sorts the sequence [begin, end) using the argument comp to determine relative orderings. If `comp(x,y)` returns true then x appears before y in the sorted sequence. A call `parallel_sort( begin, end )` is equivalent to `parallel_sort(begin,end,std::less<T>)`. A call `parallel_sort(c[,comp])` is equivalent to `parallel_sort(std::begin(c),std::end(c)[,comp])`.

```
parallel_sort
```
```
#include <tbb/parallel_sort.h>
```
```
template<typename Container,
         typename Compare > void
tbb::parallel_sort (
    [const] Container      &c
  [    , const Compare      &comp ]
)
```

```
template<typename RandomAccessIterator,
         typename Compare > void
tbb::parallel_sort (
    RandomAccessIterator first,
    RandomAccessIterator last
  [    , const Compare      &comp ]
)
```

```
template<typename T,
         typename Compare > void
tbb::parallel_sort (
    T *begin,
    T *end
  [    , const Compare      &comp ]
)
```

Sorts the data, in range, [first,last) or [*begin,*end), using the optionally given comparator.
If no comparator is specified, std::less is used as comparator.
There are no partitioner options for this template.
TBB (as of TBB 2019) does not support a user-supplied context to parallel_scan.

Figure B-29. *Précis: Algorithm: parallel_sort*

`parallel_sort` – sorting Hello, World example

```
#include <cstdio>
#include <tbb/tbb.h>
#include <array>

#define PV(X) printf(" %02d", X);
#define PN(Y) printf( "\nHello, Sorted " #Y ":\t");
#define P(N) PN(N); \
        std::for_each(N.begin(),N.end(),[](int x) { PV(x); });
#define V(Z) myvect.push_back(Z);

int main( int argc, char *argv[] ) {
  int myvalues[]            = {  3, 9, 4, 5, 1, 7, 6, 8,10, 2 };
  std::array<int, 10> myarray   = { 19,13,14,11,15,20,17,16,12,18 };
  std::array<int, 10> disarray  = { 23,29,27,25,30,21,26,24,28,22 };
  tbb::concurrent_vector<int> myvect;
  V(40);V(31);V(37);V(33);V(34);V(32);V(34);V(35);V(38) V(36);

  tbb::parallel_sort( myvalues,myvalues+10 );
  tbb::parallel_sort( myarray.begin(), myarray.end() );
  tbb::parallel_sort( disarray );
  tbb::parallel_sort( myvect );

  PN(myvalues); for(int i=0;i<10;i++) PV(myvalues[i]);
  P(myarray);
  P(disarray);
  P(myvect);
  printf("\n\n");
}
```

```
This output is deterministic!
Hello, Sorted myvalues:  01 02 03 04 05 06 07 08 09 10
Hello, Sorted myarray:   11 12 13 14 15 16 17 18 19 20
Hello, Sorted disarray:  21 22 23 24 25 26 27 28 29 30
Hello, Sorted myvect:    31 32 33 34 34 35 36 37 38 40
```

Figure B-30. *Précis: Algorithm: parallel_sort example*

Requirements on iterators for `parallel_sort`.

Requirements on the iterator type `It` and its value type `T` for `parallel_sort`:

```
void iter_swap( It a, It b )
```
Swaps the values of the elements the given iterators a and b are pointing to. It should be a random access iterator.

```
bool Compare::operator()( const T& x, const T& y )
```
True if x comes before y;

Figure B-31. *Précis: Algorithm: parallel_sort iterator requirements*

Algorithm: `pipeline`

A pipeline represents pipelined application of a series of filters to a stream of items, possibly in parallel. Each filter operates in a particular mode: parallel, serial in-order, or serial out-of-order. A pipeline contains one or more filters. Alternatives to `pipeline` are `parallel_pipeline` (recommend because it is strongly typed with a lambda-friendly interface) and Flow Graph (recommended because it is far more general, and should be used when that generality is needed).

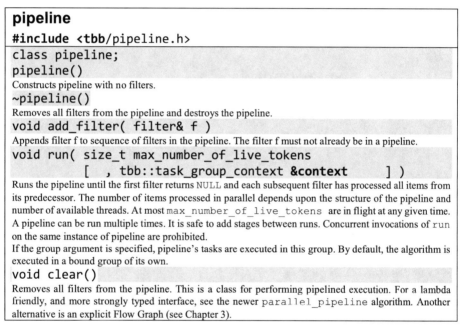

pipeline

`#include <tbb/pipeline.h>`

`class pipeline;`
`pipeline()`
Constructs pipeline with no filters.
`~pipeline()`
Removes all filters from the pipeline and destroys the pipeline.
`void add_filter( filter& f )`
Appends filter f to sequence of filters in the pipeline. The filter f must not already be in a pipeline.
`void run( size_t max_number_of_live_tokens`
`        [  , tbb::task_group_context &context      ] )`
Runs the pipeline until the first filter returns NULL and each subsequent filter has processed all items from its predecessor. The number of items processed in parallel depends upon the structure of the pipeline and number of available threads. At most `max_number_of_live_tokens` are in flight at any given time. A pipeline can be run multiple times. It is safe to add stages between runs. Concurrent invocations of `run` on the same instance of pipeline are prohibited.
If the group argument is specified, pipeline's tasks are executed in this group. By default, the algorithm is executed in a bound group of its own.
`void clear()`
Removes all filters from the pipeline. This is a class for performing pipelined execution. For a lambda friendly, and more strongly typed interface, see the newer `parallel_pipeline` algorithm. Another alternative is an explicit Flow Graph (see Chapter 3).

Figure B-32. *Précis: Algorithm:* `pipeline`

pipeline – 10 x Hello, World example

```cpp
#include <cstdio>
#include <tbb/tbb.h>

class SayIntro : public tbb::filter {
public:
  tbb::spin_mutex firstlock; int first = 0;
  SayIntro(void) : tbb::filter(parallel) {}
  ~SayIntro(void) {};
  void* operator() (void* inp) {
    int *fortytwo = (int*)malloc(sizeof(int));
    { tbb::spin_mutex::scoped_lock hello(firstlock);
      if (first++>1) return NULL;
    }
    *fortytwo = 42 + first*1000;
    printf("Our pipeline begins at %d.\n",*fortytwo);
    return fortytwo;
  }
};

class SayHello : public tbb::filter {
public:
  tbb::spin_mutex mylock;      int counter = 0;
  SayHello(void) : tbb::filter(parallel) {}
  ~SayHello(void) {};
  void* operator() (void* inp) {
    printf("Hello, Pipeline %02d\n",*((int*)inp));
    *(int*)inp += 1;
    return inp;
  }
};

class SayBye : public tbb::filter {
public:
  SayBye(void) : tbb::filter(serial) {}
  ~SayBye(void) {};
  void* operator() (void* inp) {
    printf("Value is finally %d; Good Bye!\n",*((int*)inp));
    return NULL;
  }
};

int main( int argc, char *argv[] ) {
  SayIntro introduction;
  SayHello speaker[5];
  SayBye   conclusion;
  tbb::pipeline mypipe;

  mypipe.add_filter(introduction);
  mypipe.add_filter(speaker[0]);
  mypipe.add_filter(speaker[1]);
  mypipe.add_filter(speaker[2]);
  mypipe.add_filter(speaker[3]);
  mypipe.add_filter(speaker[4]);
  mypipe.add_filter(conclusion);
  mypipe.run(100);
  mypipe.clear();
}
```

Figure B-33. *Précis: Algorithm: pipeline example*

```
Sample output... will vary run to run and machine to machine!
Full disclosure: to get the run below, we made our machine moderately
busy with other work. Without doing that, the first pipeline completely
finished before the second began because the example is so trivial - and
the output is boring. We must remember to code (and test) for the various
independent orderings possible with parallel execution.
```
```
Our pipeline begins at 1042.
Hello, Pipeline 1042
Our pipeline begins at 2042.
Hello, Pipeline 2042
Hello, Pipeline 1043
Hello, Pipeline 2043
Hello, Pipeline 1044
Hello, Pipeline 2044
Hello, Pipeline 1045
Hello, Pipeline 2045
Hello, Pipeline 1046
Value is finally 1047; Good Bye!
Hello, Pipeline 2046
Value is finally 2047; Good Bye!
```

Figure B-33. (*continued*)

Flow Graph

Chapter 3 introduces TBB flow graph, Chapter 17 dives deeper, and Chapters 18 and 19 look at heterogeneous support. Other chapters provide deeper looks at the many controls and considerations in making highly refined use of TBB.

It is possible to create graphs that are highly scalable, but it is also possible to create graphs that are completely sequential. There are three types of components used to implement a graph:

1. Graph object: The owner of the tasks created on behalf of the flow graph. Users can wait on the graph if they need to wait for the completion of all of the tasks related to the flow graph execution. One can also register external interactions with the graph and run tasks under the ownership of the flow graph.

2. Nodes: Invoke user-provided function objects or manage messages flow to/from other nodes. There are predefined nodes that buffer, filter, broadcast, or order items as they flow through the graph.

3. Edges: The connections between the nodes, managed by calls to the make_edge and remove_edge functions.

Flow Graph: **graph class**

graph
#include <tbb/flow_graph.h>
namespace tbb::flow class graph; Note: standard iterators are supported (begin, end, cbegin, cend) but we don't list them below.
graph([task_group_context& group]) Constructs a graph with no nodes. If group is specified the graph tasks are executed in this group. By default, the graph is executed in a bound context of its own. Instantiates a root task of class empty_task to serve as a parent for all of the tasks generated during runs of the graph. Sets ref_count of the root task to one.
~graph() Calls wait_for_all on the graph, then destroys the root task.
void increment_wait_count() Used to register that an external entity may still interact with the graph. Increments the ref_count of the root task.
void decrement_wait_count() Used to unregister an external entity that may have interacted with the graph. Decrements the ref_count of the root task.
void run(Receiver &r, Body body) Use this method to spawn a task that runs a body and puts its output to a specific receiver. The task is created as a child of the graph's root task and therefore wait_for_all will not return until this task completes. Enqueues a task that invokes r.try_put(body()). It does not wait for the task to complete. The spawned task is a child of the root task.
void run(Body body) This method spawns a task that runs as a child of the graph's root task. Calls to wait_for_all will not return until this spawned task completes. Enqueues a task that invokes body(). It does not wait for the task to complete.
void wait_for_all() Blocks until all tasks associated with the root task have completed and the number of decrement_wait_count calls equals the number of increment_wait_count calls. Because it calls wait_for_all on the root graph task, the calling thread may participate in work-stealing while it is blocked.
task *root_task() Returns: a pointer to the root task of the flow graph.
bool is_cancelled() Returns: true if the graph was cancelled during the last call to wait_for_all(), false otherwise.
bool exception_thrown() Returns: true if during the last call to wait_for_all() an exception was thrown, false otherwise. See Chapter 15 for discussion of exception handling.
void reset(reset_flags f = rf_reset_protocol) Flags to reset() can be combined with bitwise-or. See Chapter 15 for discussion of exception handling. The three optional flags are: **rf_reset_protocol:**   All edges are switched to push state, all buffers are emptied, and internal state of all nodes are reinitialized. All calls to reset() perform these actions. **rf_reset_bodies:**   When nodes with bodies are created, the body specified in the constructor is copied and preserved. When rf_reset_bodies is specified, the current body of the node is deleted and replaced with a copy of the body saved during construction. Caution: If the body contains state which has an external component (such as a file descriptor) then the node may not behave the same on re-execution of the graph after body replacement. In this case the node should be re-created. **rf_clear_edges:** All edges are removed from the graph.

Figure B-34. *Précis: Flow Graph:* graph class

Flow Graph: **ports** and **edges**

Flow Graph provides an API to manage connections between the nodes. For nodes that have more than one input or output port (e.g., join_node), making a connection requires that we specify a certain port by using special helper functions.

---

ports and edges
`#include <tbb/flow_graph.h>`

`namespace tbb::flow`

`inline void make_edge(`*output,input*`)`
`inline void remove_edge(`*output,input*`)`
Make (or remove) an edge from:
  1. port 0 of a multi-output predecessor to port 0 of a multi-input successor
  2. port 0 of a multi-output predecessor to a receiver
  3. a sender to port 0 of a multi-input successor
`template<size_t N, typename NT>`
  `typename tuple_element<N,`
    `typename NT::input_ports_type>::type& input_port(NT &n);`
`template<size_t N, typename NT>`
  `typename tuple_element<N,`
    `typename NT::output_ports_type>::type& output_port(NT &n);`
Given a `join_node`, `indexer_node`, or a `composite_node` returns a reference to a specific input/output port.

Figure B-35. *Précis: Flow Graph: ports and edges*

Flow Graph: **nodes**

Functional nodes (Figure B-37) do computations in response to input messages (if any) and send the result or a signal to their successors. The list of types for **Control Flow nodes** is provided in Figure B-38. A special type of control flow node are the **Join nodes**, the different join policies available for join_node are described in Figure B-39. **Buffering nodes** (Figure B-40) are designed to accumulate input messages and pass them to successors in a predefined order, depending on the node type. A pictorial presentation of the node types is given in Figure B-36.

Some nodes create or use messages that are composites of other messages. Multiport nodes use tuples to manage their ports. These include join_node, multifunction_node, split_node, indexer_node and composite_node. Multiport nodes that send or receive tuples are join_node and split_node.

tbb::flow::tuple vs. std::tuple

These days (using C++11 or later compilers), using std::tuple is recommended. TBB introduced tbb::flow::tuple before C++11, and still supports it if needed. However, if std::tuple is available as part of the STL, then tbb::flow::tuple is automatically typedefed to std::tuple.

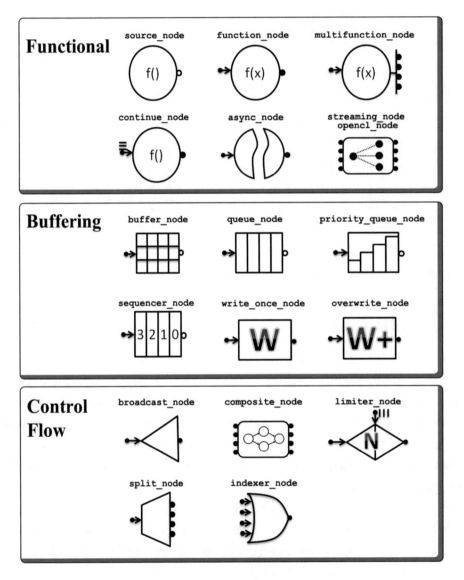

Figure B-36. *Précis: Flow Graph node types (see also Chapters 3, 17, 18, and 19)*

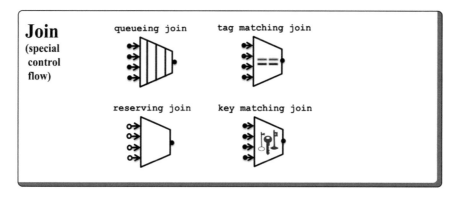

Figure B-36. (*continued*)

Functional Node Types

Source
```
template<typename OutType> class source_node;
```

Example Constructor Signature	**Body Signature**
source_node(graph &g, Body b, bool is_active=true)	[…](OutType& out) -> bool { … }

Generates messages.   If **is_active==true**, a Body task is immediately spawned upon construction. Otherwise, the first Body task is spawned when the **activate** function is called. A new task will be spawned each time a Body execution returns true. If a Body execution returns true but no downstream node accepts the value, the value is stored in a single item buffer at the output and the task spawn is deferred until the buffered value is consumed. The buffer is reservable (see Chapter 17).

Function
```
template<typename InType [,typename OutType=continue_msg]
        [,typename Policy = queueing]
        [,typename Allocator=cache_aligned_allocator<Input>]
    > class function_node;
```

Example Constructor Signature	**Body Signature**
function_node(graph &g, size_t concurrency, Body b)	[…](const InType& in) -> OutType { … }

Applies a function, generating a single output for each input message received. A Body task is spawned if the number of outstanding body tasks is less than the concurrency limit.   If the concurrency limit prevents a body task from being spawned, the incoming message is buffered in the node until the number of outstanding tasks drops below the concurrency limit.

Figure B-37. *Précis: Functional node types available in the TBB flow graph interface. These nodes are discussed in Chapter 3, except* async_node *which is described in Chapter 18.*

Multifunction

```
template<typename InType, typename OutTuple [,typename Policy = queueing]
        [,typename Allocator=cache_aligned_allocator<Input>]
        > class multifunction_node;
```

Example Constructor Signature	**Body Signature**
`multifunction_node(graph &g, size_t` `concurrency, Body b)`	`[…](const InType& in,` `output_ports_type& p) { … }`

Applies a function to each input message received. A Body task is spawned if the number of outstanding body tasks is less than the concurrency limit.   If the concurrency limit prevents a task from being spawned, the incoming message is buffered in the node until the number of outstanding tasks drops below the concurrency limit. The Body also receives a reference to a tuple of output ports. The Body sends output messages by explicitly calling `try_put` on the output ports. This node is useful for implementing conditional paths through the graph and cycles.

Continue

```
template<typename OutType
        [,typename Policy = internal::Policy<void>] > class continue_node;
```

Example Constructor Signature	**Body Signature**
`continue_node(graph &g, size_t` `initial_count, Body b)`	`[…](const continue_msg& in)` `-> OutType { … }`

Used to create dependency graphs. The node counts the number of its in-coming edges and the number of messages it receives.   When the number of messages it has received is equal to the number of predecessors it has, it spawns a task to execute its body and then resets its messages-received count. The node can be constructed with an `initial_count` that increases the number of messages that it must receive before spawning a body.   The `initial_count` is used when the node is expected to receive explicit `try_puts` in addition to messages across edges. The Body receives a single input of type `tbb::flow::continue_msg` and outputs a single output of type OutType.

Asynchronous

```
template<typename InType, typename OutType
        [,typename Policy = queueing_lightweight,
        [,typename Allocator=cache_aligned_allocator<Input>]
        > class async_node;
```

Example Constructor Signature	**Body Signature**
`async_node(graph &g, size_t` `concurrency, Body b)`	`[…](const continue_msg& in)` `-> OutType { … }`

Allows a flow graph to communicate with an external activity managed by the user or another runtime. This node receives messages of type `Input` and invokes the body to submit a message to the external activity. To return a result back and push it to the output port of `async_node`, the `gateway_type` is provided. This node type is explored in detail in Chapter 18.

Streaming and OpenCL

```
template<typename… Args> class streaming_node|opencl_node;
```
or
```
template<typename… Ports, typename JP, typename Factor
        > class streaming_node|opencl_node ;
```

`streaming_node` enables the use of streaming programming models that support submission of kernels and data to devices through queues. `opencl_node` is an example of a model-specific `streaming_node` that enables OpenCL powered devices to be utilized and coordinated by a Flow Graph. Developers may also define custom factories to support different modules. This node type is explored in Chapter 19.

Figure B-37. (*continued*)

Control Flow Node Types
Broadcaster   `template<typename InOutType> class broadcast_node;`
Example Constructor Signature   `broadcast_node(graph &g)`
Broadcasts each incoming message, unchanged, to all of its successors. This node is typically used to provide a single entry-point to a graph or subgraph so that a single explicit `try_put` can broadcast to many nodes. It is rarely used as an internal node in a graph.
Compositer   `template<typename InTuple, typename OutTuple> composite_node;`
Example Constructor Signature   `composite_node(graph &g)`
Encapsulates a subgraph of nodes. Has one or more input ports and one or more output ports. It provides functions that allow its input and output ports to be aliased to the ports of the nodes contained within it.
Indexer   `template<typename T0, ..., typename T9> indexer_node;`
Example Constructor Signature   `indexer_node(graph &g)`
Broadcasts each message received at any of its input ports, tagging the message with the port number on which it arrived.
Limiter   `template<typename InOutType> class limiter_node;`
Example Constructor Signature   `limiter_node(graph &g, size_t limit, size_t initial_count=0)`
Conditionally broadcasts each incoming message, unchanged, to all of its successors. This node counts the messages that pass through it.   When this count reaches `limit`, it no longer broadcasts the incoming messages. The node has a second input port that is used to decrement the count of messages, allowing additional messages to pass through. Examples are provided in Chapter 17.

Splitting
 `template<typename InTuple`
 `        [,typename Allocator=cache_aligned_allocator<TupleType>`
 `    > split_node;`

Example Constructor Signature   `split_node(graph &g)`
Splits a tuple in to its elements. Has a single input port that receives a tuple of values and broadcasts each element of the tuple on a separate output port.

Figure B-38. *Précis: Control flow node types available in the TBB flow graph interface. These nodes are discussed in Chapter 3.*

Join Node Types

Queueing
```
template<typename OutTuple, queueing> class join_node;
```

Example Constructor Signature
```
join_node(graph &g)
```

The node combines one message received at each of its input ports to create a single output that is a tuple of type OutTuple. A queueing `join_node` has queues at each input port and builds tuples by using messages from each port in first-in-first-out order. If a generated tuple is not accepted by a downstream node, it is buffered until it is consumed.

Reserving
```
template<typename OutTuple, reserving> class join_node;
```

Example Constructor Signature
```
join_node(graph &g)
```

The node combines one message received at each of its input ports to create a single output that is a tuple of type OutTuple. A reserving `join_node` is used in concert with buffering nodes.   Each of its input ports must be attached to a buffering node or a **source_node**.   Only when it is able to reserve messages for each port from a preceding buffer does it consume the messages to form a tuple. If a generated tuple is not accepted by a downstream node, it is buffered until it is consumed.

Key Matching
```
template<typename OutTuple,
         key_matching<typename K, class KHash=tbb_hash_compare<K>>
class join_node;
```

Example Constructor Signature
```
template <typename B0, typename B1, ... >
join_node(graph &g, B0 b0, B1 b1, ... )
```

The node combines one message received at each of its input ports to create a single output that is a tuple of type OutTuple. As each input port is put to, a user-provided function object, for example **b0**, is applied to the message to obtain its key. The message is then added to a hash table of the input port. When there is a message at each input port for a given key, the `join_node` removes all matching messages from the input ports, constructs a tuple containing the matching messages and attempts to broadcast it to all successors. If a generated tuple is not accepted by a downstream node, it is buffered until it is consumed.

Tag Matching
```
template<typename OutTuple, tag_matching>
class join_node;
```

Example Constructor Signature
```
template <typename B0, typename B1, ... >
join_node(graph &g, B0 b0, B1 b1, ... )
```

The node combines one message received at each of its input ports to create a single output that is a tuple of type OutTuple. A tag_matching `join_node` is a specialization of **key_matching** that accepts keys of type **size_t**. Otherwise the behavior is the same as **key_matching**. If a generated tuple is not accepted by a downstream node, it is buffered until it is consumed.

Figure B-39. *Précis: Join node policies available in the TBB flow graph interface. These nodes are discussed in Chapter 3.*

Buffering Node Types

Buffering

```
template<typename InOutType
        [,typename Allocator=cache_aligned_allocator<InOutType>]
        > class buffer_node;
```

Example Constructor Signature
```
buffer_node(graph &g)
```

An unordered buffer of elements of type `InOutType`. Supports reservations.

Queueing

```
template<typename InOutType
        [,typename Allocator=cache_aligned_allocator<InOutType>]
        > class queue_node;
```

Example Constructor Signature
```
queue_node(graph &g)
```

A first-in-first-out (FIFO) queue of elements of type `InOutType`. Supports reservations.

Priority Queueing

```
template<typename InOutType[, typename Compare]
        [,typename Allocator=cache_aligned_allocator<InOutType>]
        > class priority_queue_node;
```

Example Constructor Signature
```
priority_queue_node(graph &g)
```

A queue of elements of type `InOutType` that is ordered by using `Compare`. Supports reservations.

Sequencer

```
template<typename InOutType
        [,typename Allocator=cache_aligned_allocator<InOutType>]
        > class sequencer_node;
```

Example Constructor Signature
```
sequencer_node(graph &g, const Sequencer& s)
```

A buffer of elements of type `InOutType` that is ordered by sequence number. The sequencer number is obtained from each message by applying the `Sequencer` functor `s` to the message. Elements are sent in strictly increasing sequence order number – a message will be held in the buffer until all messages with lower sequence number have been received by the buffer and subsequently broadcast. Supports reservations.

Write Once Buffer

```
template<typename InOutType> class write_once_node;
```

Example Constructor Signature
```
write_once_node(graph &g)
```

A single item write-once buffer. Can be reset to allow a new value to be written between phases of an application.   If an edge is made from this node to another node while it contains a value, the value will be sent across the edge to the node.   Otherwise, the node will receive the value when it is set.   The value is sent nondestructively, that is, it remains in the buffer and therefore, can be provided to nodes that subsequently attach to it.   This node is useful in graphs that grow while they are executing. Supports reservations.

Figure B-40.   *Précis: Buffering node types available in the TBB flow graph interface. These nodes are discussed in Chapter 3.*

Overwrite Buffer
```
template<typename InOutType> class overwrite_node;
```

Example Constructor Signature
```
overwrite_node(graph &g)
```

This node is similar to the `write_once_node` but can be written to repeatedly. If an edge is made from this node to another node while it contains a value, the value will be sent across the edge to the node. The value is sent nondestructively, that is, it remains in the buffer.   Nodes that are connected by an edge to the output of this node will receive all values written to the buffer after they are attached. Supports reservations.

Figure B-40. (*continued*)

Graph Policy (namespace)

We can give guidance for scheduling to functional nodes in our graphs. Lightweight policies for functional nodes can help reduce the overhead associated with its execution scheduling. Lightweight policies should only be applied on a per-node basis after careful evaluation. Having multiple successors using the lightweight policy for a particular node can significantly reduce the parallelism available in the graph, and hence severely limit scaling. Cycles in a flow graph consisting *only* of nodes with lightweight policies may possibly result in deadlock.

A `lightweight` policy is used to indicate that the body of the node contains a small amount of work and should, if possible, be executed without the overhead of scheduling a task. All flow graph functional nodes, except for `source_node`, support the `lightweight` policy as a possible value of the optional `Policy` template parameter. To use the `lightweight` policy, specify the `Policy` template parameter of the node to `queueing_lightweight, rejecting_lightweight`, or `lightweight`. For functional nodes that have a default value for the `Policy` template parameter, specifying the `lightweight` policy results in extending the behavior of the default value of `Policy` with the behavior defined by the `lightweight` policy. For example, if the default value of `Policy` is `queueing`, specifying `lightweight` as the `Policy` value is equivalent to specifying `queueing_lightweight`. See Chapter 17 for more discussion of using lightweight Policies.

Policy values are listed in Figure B-41. Note there is a policy `tbb::flow::reserving` that is not listed because it is a special policy exclusively for join node that has no application for async, continue, function and multifunction nodes.

Node Execution Policies
Used with async_node, continue_node, function_node, and multifunction_node

---

`tbb::flow::queueing`

The default policy for all nodes except `async_node`*.* If a message arrives at the node but concurrency limits prevent a new body task from being spawned immediately, the message is buffered until it is legal to spawn a body task.

`tbb::flow::rejecting`

If a message arrives at the node but concurrency limits prevent a new body task from being spawned immediately, the call to `try_put` returns `false` and the message is not buffered. This policy can be used to stop a preceding source_node from generating new values.

`tbb::flow::lightweight`

The `lightweight` policy indicates that the body of the node contains a small amount of work and should, if possible, be executed without the overhead of scheduling a task. Typically, the body is executed during the call to `try_put`. For functional nodes that have a default value for the `Policy` template parameter, specifying the `lightweight` policy results in extending the behavior of the default policy with the behavior defined by the `lightweight` policy. For example, if the default value of Policy is `queueing`, specifying `lightweight` as the Policy value is equivalent to specifying `queueing_lightweight`.

`tbb::flow::queueing_lightweight`

This is the default policy for async_node. If a message arrives at the node but concurrency limits prevent the body from being applied immediately, the message is buffered until it is legal to apply the body to the message. Because this is a lightweight policy, a task is not typically spawned to execute the body.

`tbb::flow::rejecting_lightweight`

If a message arrives at the node but concurrency limits prevent the body from being applied immediately, the call to `try_put` returns `false` and the message is not buffered. If it is legal to execute the body, it is executed within the call to `try_put`.

Figure B-41. *Précis: Flow Graph: policy values*

member operations on `nodes`
`#include <tbb/flow_graph.h>`
`namespace tbb::flow`
Notes: (1) operations return **true** unless stated otherwise (false generally indicates the operation did not complete)   (2) operations do not wait for body executions to complete before returning
`bool activate()`
Supported only for: `source_node`: Sets node to the active state, allowing it to begin generating messages.
`bool try_put( const input_type &v )`
`async_node`: A task is spawned that executes the body(v).   `broadcast_node`: Forwards v to all successors.   `buffer_node`: Adds v to the buffer. If v is the only item in the buffer, a task is also spawned to forward the item to a successor.   `continue_node`: Increments the count of `try_put` calls received. When the count reaches the number of known predecessors, a task is spawned to execute the body and the count of `try_put` calls is reset to zero.   `function_node`: Broadcast is spawned immediately if concurrency limit is not exceeded, otherwise it is queued until concurrency limit allows spawning to do broadcast.   Returns false if the input was rejected (will only happen if concurrency limits reached and `policy==rejecting` instead of the default `policy==queueing`).   `limiter_node`: If the broadcast count (C) is below the threshold, v is broadcast to all successors and C is incremented. If no successor accepts the message, C is decremented. Returns true if the message was successfully broadcast to at least one successor and false otherwise.   `multifunction_node`: Spawns body immediately if concurrency limit is not exceeded, otherwise it rejects the input and returns false.   `overwrite_node` and `write_once_node`: stores v in the internal single item buffer and calls try_put(v) on all successors.   `sequencer_node:` Adds v to the `sequencer_node`. If v's sequence number is the next item in the sequence, a task is spawned to forward the item to a successor.   `split_node:` Broadcasts each element of the incoming tuple to the nodes connected to the `split_node`'s output ports. The element at index i of v will be broadcast through the ith output port.
`bool try_get( output_type &v )`
Not available for `split_node` because it would not know which port to try; technically can be used on a specific `output_port()` of a `split_node`, but since it is non-buffering you'll only get a `false` for your troubles.   Returns `false` for nodes that do not support buffering of output (`async_node, continue_node, function_node, indexer_node, limiter_node`).   Will copy a buffered message into v if available (can be obtained and is not reserved). If none available, and node type has a body, will invoke body to attempt to generate a new message that will be copied into v. Returns `true` if a message is copied to v, `false` otherwise.
`bool try_reserve( output_type &v )`
Returns false for nodes that do not support reservations (async_node, broadcast_node, continue_node, function_node, indexer_node, join_node, limiter_node, split_node).   `overwrite_node` and `write_once_node`: copy internal buffer to v and return true if internal buffer is valid, `false` otherwise.   All other node types: Sets a reservation if possible. This stops additional consumption of any buffers (including sending to successors)   until the reservation is released. If a message can be buffered and the node is not already reserved, the node is reserved for the caller, and the value is copied into v. Returns `true` if the node/buffer is reserved for the caller, `false` otherwise.
`bool try_release( )`
Returns false for nodes that do not support reservations (async_node, broadcast_node, continue_node, function_node, indexer_node, join_node, limiter_node, split_node).   overwrite_node and write_once_node: return true.   All other node types: Releases any reservation held. The message held in the internal buffer is retained. Returns `true` is a reservation did exist, `false` otherwise.

Figure B-42. *Précis: Flow Graph: member operations on nodes*

bool try consume( )
Returns false for nodes that do not support reservations (async_node, broadcast_node, continue_node, function_node, indexer_node, join_node, limiter_node, split_node).
overwrite_node and write_once_node: return true.
All other node types: Releases any reservation held and clears the top item on the internal buffer. Returns `true` is a reservation did exist, `false` otherwise.
bool is_valid( )
Available only for:
overwrite_node and **write_once_node** – returns true if a value is in the buffer, false if not.
bool clear( )
Available only for:
overwrite_node and **write_once_node** – invalidates the value held in the buffer.
input_ports_type &input_ports( )
Available only for:
indexer_node – Returns: a tuple of receivers .
join_node – Returns: a tuple of receivers. The behavior of the ports is based on the selection of buffering policies (`queueing, reserving, key_matching, tag_matching`). See Chapter 3.
input_port(JNT &jn)
Available only for:
composite_node - Returns: A tuple of receivers. Each element is a reference to the actual node or input port that was aliased to that position in `set_external_ports()`. Calling `input_ports()` without a prior call to `set_external_ports()` results in undefined behavior.
join_node – returns the Nth input port for `join_node jn`.
output_ports()
Available only for:
composite_node - Returns: A tuple of receivers. Each element is a reference to the actual node or input port that was aliased to that position in `set_external_ports()`. Calling `input_ports()` without a prior call to `set_external_ports()` results in undefined behavior.
multifunction_node and **split_node** – returns tuple of output ports.
set_external_ports(in_ports_tuple, out_ports_tuple)
Available only for:
composite_node - Creates input and output ports of the `composite_node` as aliases to the ports referenced by `in_ports_tuple` and `out_ports_tuple` respectively. A port referenced at position N in `input_ports_tuple` is mapped as the Nth input port of the `composite_node`, similarly for output ports.

Figure B-42. (*continued*)

Flow graph – Hello, World example

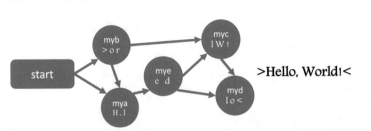

```cpp
#include <cstdio>
#include <tbb/tbb.h>

tbb::spin_mutex mylock;
int counter = 0;

struct hw {
  char myhw1, myhw2, myhw3;
  hw(const char hw1,const char hw2,const char hw3) :
    myhw1(hw1),myhw2(hw2),myhw3(hw3) {}
  void operator()(tbb::flow::continue_msg) const {
    int mycount;
    { tbb::spin_mutex::scoped_lock hello(mylock);
      mycount = counter++;
    }
    printf("%c",
           (mycount < 5) ? myhw1 : (mycount < 10) ? myhw2 : myhw3);
  }
};

int main() {
  tbb::flow::graph g;

  tbb::flow::broadcast_node<tbb::flow::continue_msg> start(g);
#define X tbb::flow::continue_node<tbb::flow::continue_msg>
  X mya(g,hw('H',',','l'));
  X myb(g,hw('>','o','r'));
  X myc(g,hw('l','W','!'));
  X myd(g,hw('l','o','<'));
  X mye(g,hw('e',' ','d'));

  tbb::flow::make_edge(start, mya);
  tbb::flow::make_edge(start, myb);
  tbb::flow::make_edge(myb, mya);
  tbb::flow::make_edge(myb, myc);
  tbb::flow::make_edge(myc, myd);
  tbb::flow::make_edge(mya, mye);
  tbb::flow::make_edge(mye, myc);

  for (int i = 0; i < 3; ++i) {
    start.try_put(tbb::flow::continue_msg());
    g.wait_for_all();
  }
  printf("\n");
  return 0;
}
```

Figure B-43. *Précis: Flow Graph: example*

```
This output is deterministic! In fact, two of the edges are not
needed - and could be left out and still be deterministic. Other
edges are needed to maintain the message - we could play around
and delete a few edges and get non-deterministic output that may
work on some runs, and have spelling issues on other runs.
>Hello, World!<
```

Figure B-43. (*continued*)

Memory Allocation

Chapter 7 covers TBB memory allocators completely within a single chapter; this section of this Appendix is a terse review of the supported APIs, and some notes. Memory allocators supplied by TBB do not depend upon the rest of TBB, and therefore can be used with any threading model.

Memory allocator template classes (there are five)

The first four of these classes model the Allocator concept – all can be used to replace a **std::allocator**. Setting the environment variable TBB_VERSION to 1 enables useful dumps on stderr that can help debugging if the Intel TBB malloc library is being used (see the Debug and Conditional Coding section at the start of this Appendix).

```
#include <tbb/tbb_allocator.h>
template<typename T> class tbb_allocator
```

Template class for scalable memory allocation if available; possibly non-scalable otherwise. A tbb_allocator allocates and frees memory via the TBB malloc library if it is available, otherwise it reverts to using malloc and free.

```
#include <tbb/scalable_allocator.h>
template<typename T> class scalable_allocator
```

Template class for scalable memory allocation (mandatory). A scalable_allocator allocates and frees memory in a way that scales with the number of processors. Using a scalable_allocator in place of std::allocator may improve program performance. Memory allocated by a scalable_allocator should be freed by a scalable_allocator, not by a std::allocator. The scalable_allocator requires the memory allocator library. If the library is missing, calls to the scalable allocator fail. In contrast, if the memory allocator library is not available, tbb_allocator falls back on malloc and free.

```
#include <tbb/cache_aligned_allocator.h>
template<typename T> class cache_aligned_allocator
```

Template class for allocating memory in way that avoids false sharing. A cache_aligned_allocator allocates memory on cache line boundaries, in order to avoid false sharing. False sharing is when logically distinct items occupy the same cache line, which can hurt performance if multiple threads attempt to access the different items simultaneously. Even though the items are logically separate, the processor hardware may have to transfer the whole cache line between the processors even though the precise data locations used differ (but happen to fall within the same cache line) between the processors. The net result can be much more memory traffic than if the logically distinct items were on different cache lines.

It can be used to replace a std::allocator. Used judiciously, cache_aligned_allocator can improve performance by reducing false sharing. However, it can sometimes have a negative effect. The benefit of allocating on a cache line comes at the price that cache_aligned_allocator implicitly adds pad memory. The padding is typically 128 bytes. Hence allocating many small objects with cache_aligned_allocator may increase memory usage.

```
#include <tbb/tbb_allocator.h>
template<typename T> class zero_allocator
```

Template class for allocator that returns zeroed memory. A zero_allocator allocates zeroed memory. A zero_allocator<T,A> can be instantiated for any class A that models the Allocator concept. The default for A is tbb_allocator. A zero_allocator forwards allocation requests to A and zeros the allocation before returning it.

```
#include <tbb/aligned_space.h>
template<typename T [, size_t N=1]> class aligned_space
```

Template class for allocating uninitialized memory space for an array of a given type. Does NOT model the Allocator concept, and therefore cannot be used in place of std::allocator, nor used with zero_allocator. An aligned_space occupies enough memory and is sufficiently aligned to hold an array T[N]. The client is responsible for initializing or destroying the objects. An aligned_space is typically used as a local variable or field in scenarios where a block of fixed-length uninitialized memory is needed.

Figure B-44. *Précis: Memory Allocation: Memory allocator template classes*

Memory allocator functions (C interfaces)

These functions provide a C level interface to the scalable allocator. Each routine `scalable_x` behaves analogously to library function x. The routines form the two families shown in the table below, "C Interface to Scalable Allocator." Storage allocated by a `scalable_x` function in one family must be freed or resized by a `scalable_x` function in the same family, not by a C standard library function. Likewise, storage allocated by a C standard library function should not be freed or resized by a `scalable_x` function. Setting the environment variable `TBB_VERSION` to 1 enables useful dumps for debugging.

`#include <tbb/tbb_allocator.h>`

void **scalable_aligned_free** (void * ptr)
> The "`_aligned_free`" analogue.

void* **scalable_aligned_malloc** (size_t size,
                                    size_t alignment)
> The "`_aligned_malloc`" analogue.

void* **scalable_aligned_realloc** (void * ptr,
                                      size_t size,
                                      size_t alignment)
> The "`_aligned_realloc`" analogue.

void* **scalable_calloc** (size_t nobj, size_t size)
> The "`calloc`" analogue complementing `scalable_malloc`.

void **scalable_free** (void * ptr)
> The "`free`" analogue to discard a previously allocated piece of memory.

void* **scalable_malloc** (size_t size)
> The "`malloc`" analogue to allocate block of memory of size bytes.

size_t **scalable_msize** (void * ptr)
> The analogue of msize/malloc_size/malloc_usable_size. Returns the usable size of a memory block previously allocated by scalable_*, or 0 (zero) if ptr does not point to such a block.

int **scalable_posix_memalign** (void ** memptr,
                                  size_t alignment,
                                  size_t size)
> The "`posix_memalign`" analogue.

void* **scalable_realloc** (void * ptr, size_t size)
> The "realloc" analogue complementing scalable_malloc.

Figure B-45. *Précis: Memory Allocation: Memory allocator functions (C interfaces)*

Memory allocator special controls (C interfaces)

These functions may be used to adjust behavior of the scalable memory allocator.

`#include <tbb/tbb_allocator.h>`

int **scalable_allocation_mode**(int param, intptr_t value)

scalable_allocation_mode(TBBMALLOC_USE_HUGE_PAGES, 1)
tells the allocator to use huge pages if enabled by the operating system Setting TBB_MALLOC_USE_HUGE_PAGES environment variable to 1 has the same effect. The mode set with scalable_allocation_mode() takes priority over the environment variable. **scalable_allocation_mode(TBBMALLOC_USE_HUGE_PAGES, 0)** disables it.

These routines return TBBMALLOC_NO_EFFECT if huge pages are not supported on the platform.

As of 2019, TBB supports huge pages on Linux OS. It works with both explicitly configured and transparent huge pages. Be sure to enable and configure huge pages on the OS in order for TBB to be able to utilize them.

CAUTION: In modes using huge pages, it is not recommended to round up memory request size or alignment to a multiple of the huge page size, as it may result in inefficient use of memory and loss of performance.

scalable_allocation_mode(TBBMALLOC_SET_SOFT_HEAP_LIMIT, size)
sets a threshold of size bytes on the amount of memory the allocator takes from OS. Exceeding the threshold will urge the allocator to release memory from its internal buffers; however it does not prevent it from requesting more memory if needed.

int **scalable_allocation_command** (int cmd, void * param)

The second parameter is reserved and must be set to 0.

scalable_allocation_command(TBBMALLOC_CLEAN_ALL_BUFFERS, 0)
cleans internal memory buffers of the allocator, and possibly reduces memory footprint. It may result in increased time for subsequent memory allocation requests. The command is not designed for frequent use, and careful evaluation of the performance impact is recommended. NOTE: It is not guaranteed that the call will release all unused memory.

scalable_allocation_command(TBBMALLOC_CLEAN_THREAD_BUFFERS, 0)
cleans internal memory buffers but only for the calling thread. It may result in increased time for subsequent memory allocation requests; careful evaluation of the performance impact is recommended.

These routines will return TBBMALLOC_NO_EFFECT if no buffers were released.

Figure B-46. *Précis: Memory Allocation: Memory allocator special controls (C interfaces)*

Allocator Concept

`#include <tbb/tbb_allocator.h>`

tbb_allocator, **scalable_allocator**, and **cache_aligned_allocator**, and **zero_allocator** model the Allocator concept. The Allocator concept for allocators in TBB is similar to the "Allocator requirements" in Table 32 of the ISO C++ Standard (2003), but with further guarantees required by the Standard for use with ISO C++ containers. The table below summarizes the Allocator concept. Here, A and B represent instances of an allocator class.

Figure B-47. *Précis: Memory Allocation: Allocator Concept*

```
typedef T* A::pointer
```
Pointer to T.
```
typedef const T* A::const_pointer
```
Pointer to const T.
```
typedef T& A::reference
```
Reference to T.
```
typedef const T& A::const_reference
```
Reference to const T.
```
typedef T A::value_type
```
Type of value to be allocated.
```
typedef size_t A::size_type
```
Type for representing number of values.
```
typedef ptrdiff_t A::difference_type
```
Type for representing pointer difference.
```
template<typename U> struct rebind
   { typedef A<U> A::other;};
```
Rebind to a different type U
```
A() throw()
```
Default constructor.
```
A( const A& ) throw()
```
Copy constructor.
```
template<typename U> A( const A& )
```
Rebinding constructor.
```
~A() throw()
```
Destructor.
```
T* A::address( T& x ) const
```
Take address.
```
const T* A::const_address( const T& x ) const
```
Take const address.
```
T* A::allocate( size_type n, const void* hint=0 )
```
Allocate space for n values.
```
void A::deallocate( T* p, size_t  n )
```
Deallocate n values.
```
size_type A::max_size() const throw()
```
Maximum plausible argument to method allocate.
```
void A::construct( T* p, const T& value )
```
new(p) T(value)
```
void A::destroy( T* p )
```
p->T::~T()
```
bool operator==( const A&, const B& )
```
Return true.
```
bool operator!=( const A&, const B& )
```
Return false.

Figure B-47. (*continued*)

`memory_pool` and `fixed_pool` template classes

`#define` TBB_PREVIEW_MEMORY_POOL 1

`#include` <tbb/memory_pool.h>

Both `memory_pool` and `fixed_pool` allocate and free memory in a way that scales with the number of processors; both model the Memory Pool concept (see Figure B-49). Template classes for scalable memory allocation are provided by an underlying allocator. For the `fixed_pool`, all memory available for allocation is obtained at construction time from the underlying allocator, and the available pool size will not grow. For `memory_pool`, memory to allocate is obtained as big chunks from an underlying allocator specified by the template argument, and additional memory will be requested as needed. Caution: If the underlying allocator refers to another scalable memory pool, the inner pool (or pools) must be destroyed before the outer pool is destroyed or recycled.

---

explicit **memory_pool**(const Alloc &src = Alloc())

Constructs memory pool with an instance of underlying memory allocator of type Alloc copied from src. Throws bad_alloc exception if runtime fails to construct an instance of the class.

```
// Example of allocation from an extensible memory pool
#define TBB_PREVIEW_MEMORY_POOL 1
#include <tbb/memory_pool.h>
...
char buf[512*1024];
tbb::fixed_pool my_pool(buf, 512*1024);
void* my_ptr = my_pool.malloc(10);
my_pool.free(my_ptr);
```

---

explicit **memory_pool**(const Alloc &src = Alloc())

Constructs memory pool with an instance of underlying memory allocator of type Alloc copied from src. Throws bad_alloc exception if runtime fails to construct an instance of the class.

```
// Example of allocation from a fixed pool
#define TBB_PREVIEW_MEMORY_POOL 1
#include <tbb/memory_pool.h>
...
tbb::memory_pool<std::allocator<char> > my_pool;
void* my_ptr = my_pool.malloc(10);
my_pool.free(my_ptr);
```

Figure B-48. *Précis: Memory Allocation: memory_pool and fixed_pool template classes*

Memory Pool Concept

`#define TBB_PREVIEW_MEMORY_POOL 1`
`#include <tbb/memory_pool.h>`

Memory pools allocate and free memory from a specified region or underlying allocator providing thread-safe, scalable operations. Here, P represents an instance of the memory pool class. Template class **memory_pool** and class **fixed_pool** model the Memory Pool concept.

`~P() throw();`
Destructor. Frees all the memory of allocated objects.
`void P::recycle();`
Frees all the memory of allocated objects.
`void* P::malloc(size_t n);`
Returns pointer to n bytes allocated from memory pool.
`void P::free(void* ptr);`
Reallocates memory object pointed by `ptr` to n bytes.
Frees memory object specified via pointer `ptr`.
`void* P::realloc(void* ptr, size_t n);`
Reallocates memory object pointed by `ptr` to n bytes.

Figure B-49. *Précis: Memory Allocation: Memory Pool Concept*

Containers

Chapter 6 covers TBB highly concurrent container classes completely within a single chapter; this section of the Appendix is a terse review of the supported APIs, and some notes. Highly concurrent container classes supplied by TBB do not depend on the rest of TBB, and therefore can be used with any threading model. Chapter 6 contains usage examples, so none are shown here.

Typical C++ STL containers do not permit concurrent updating; attempts to modify them concurrently often result in corrupting the container. STL containers can be wrapped in a mutex to make them safe for concurrent access, by letting only one thread operate on the container at a time, but that approach eliminates concurrency, thus restricting parallel speedup.

Therefore, TBB offers concurrent containers to allow multiple threads to concurrently access and update items in the container. TBB uses either fine-grained locking, or lock-free techniques, to provide for concurrency. This does come at a cost, typically in the form of slightly higher overheads than regular STL containers. Therefore, we should use highly concurrent containers when the speedup from any additional concurrency will outweigh slower sequential performance.

As with most objects in C++, the constructor or destructor of a container object must not be invoked concurrently with another operation on the same object. Otherwise the resulting race may cause the operation to be executed on an undefined object.

Comparison of Map Classes *and C++11 connection notes*	Concurrent traversal and insertion.	Keys have a value associated with them.	Support concurrent erasure	Built-in locking.	No visible locking (lock-free interface).	Identical items allowed to be inserted.	[] and at accessors
concurrent_hash_map *Predates C++11.*	✓	✓	✓	✓	✗	✗	✗
concurrent_unordered_map *Closely resembles the C++11* unordered_map.	✓	✓	✗	✗	✓	✗	✓
concurrent_unordered_multimap *Closely resembles the C++11* unordered_multimap.	✓	✓	✗	✗	✓	✓	✗
concurrent_unordered_set *Closely resembles the C++11* unordered_set.	✓	✗	✗	✗	✓	✗	✗
concurrent_unordered_multiset *Closely resembles the C++11* unordered_multiset.	✓	✗	✗	✗	✓	✓	✗

Figure B-50. *Précis: Containers: Comparison of Map Classes*

Concurrent Hash Map (Hash Table) Class

#include <tbb/concurrent_hash_map.h>

A tbb::concurrent_hash_map maps keys to values in a way that permits multiple threads to concurrently access values via find, insert and erase methods. It meets the Container Requirements of the ISO C++ standard.

Examples code using concurrent_hash_map is shown in Chapter 6.

Constructor syntax

```
concurrent_hash_map<typename Key,
            typename T,
            [ , typename HashCompare = tbb_hash_compare<Key> ]
            [ , typename A=
                tbb::tbb_allocator<std::pair<Key, T> ] > >
```

Concurrent Access: *accessor*

In order to use the hash map in parallel (from multiple tasks/threads), TBB supplies classes const_accessor *and* accessor *which are called* accessors. *An accessor acts as a smart pointer to a pair in a* concurrent_hash_map. *It holds an implicit lock on a pair until the instance is destroyed or method* release *is called on the accessor.*

Class	value_type	Implicit lock on pair
const_accessor	const std::pair< const Key,T>	Reader lock – permits shared access with other readers.
accessor	std::pair< const Key,T>	Writer lock – permits exclusive access by a thread. Blocks access by other threads.

Member (const_accessor and accessor)	Description
bool **empty**() const	**Returns:** true if instance points to nothing; false if instance points to a key-value pair.
void **release**()	If !empty(), releases the implied lock on the pair, and sets instance to point to nothing. Otherwise does nothing.
const value_type& **operator***() const	Raises assertion failure if empty() and TBB_USE_ASSERT is defined as nonzero. **Returns:** Const reference to key-value pair.
const value_type* **operator->**() const	**Returns:** &operator*()
const_accessor()	Constructs const_accessor that points to nothing.
~const_accessor	If pointing to key-value pair, releases the implied lock on the pair.

Member (accessor *only*)	Description
value_type& **operator***() const	Raises assertion failure if empty() and TBB_USE_ASSERT is defined as non-zero. **Returns:** Reference to key-value pair.
value_type* **operator->**() const	**Returns:** &operator*()

Figure B-51. *Précis: Containers: concurrent hash map (hash table) class*

675

Concurrent Hash Map...	
Whole Table Operations	
Member	**Description**
`~`**`concurrent_hash_map`**`()`	Invokes `clear()`. This method is not safe to execute concurrently with other methods on the same concurrent_hash_map.
`concurrent_hash_map&` **`operator=`** `( concurrent_hash_map& source )`	If source and destination (`this`) table are distinct, clears the destination table and copies all key-value pairs from the source table to the destination table. Otherwise, does nothing. **Returns:** a reference to `*this`.
`concurrent_hash_map&` **`operator=`** `(concurrent_hash_map&& source);`	Moves data from the source table to `*this`. source is left in an unspecified state, but can be safely destroyed. **Returns:** a reference to `*this`.
`concurrent_hash_map&` **`operator=`** `( std::initializer_list<value_type> il )`	Assigns *this to contain data from il. **Returns:** a reference to `*this`.
`void` **`swap`**`( concurrent_hash_map& table )`	Swaps contents and allocators of `this` and `table`.
`void` **`rehash`**`( size_type n = 0 )`	Internally, the table is partitioned into buckets. The rehash method reorganizes these internal buckets in a way that may improve performance of future lookups. Raises number of internal buckets to n if n>0 and n exceeds the current number of buckets. CAUTION: The current implementation never reduces the number of buckets. A future implementation might reduce the number of buckets if n is less than the current number of buckets. Note: The ratio of items to buckets affects time and space usage by a table. A high ratio saves space at the expense of time. A low ratio does the opposite. The default ratio is 0.5 to 1 items per bucket on average.
`void` **`clear`**`()`	Erases all key-value pairs from the table. Does not hash or compare any keys. If `TBB_USE_PERFORMANCE_WARNINGS` is nonzero, issues a performance warning if the randomness of the hashing is poor enough to significantly impact performance.
`allocator_type get_allocator() const`	**Returns:** a copy of allocator used to construct table.

Figure B-51. (*continued*)

Concurrent Hash Map...	
Concurrent Operations	
Member	**Description**
`size_type` **`count`**`( const Key& key )` `const`	CAUTION: This method may invalidate previously obtained iterators. In serial code, you can use equal_range that does not have such problems. **Returns:** 1 if map contains key; 0 otherwise.
`bool` **`find`**`(accessor& result,` `   const Key& key ) const`	Searches table for pair with given key. If key is found, sets result to provide read-only access to the matching pair. CAUTION: This method may invalidate previously obtained iterators. In serial code, you can use equal_range that does not have such problems. **Returns:** True if key was found; false if key was not found.

`[A]`
`bool` **`insert`**`(`
`   accessor& result,`
`   const Key& key )`
`[B]`
`bool` **`insert`**`(`
`   [ accessor& result, ]`
`   const value_type& value )`
`[C]`
`bool` **`insert`**`( const value_type& value )`
	Searches table for pair with given key.
	If not present, inserts
	[A] new `pair(key,T())` into the table.
	or
	[B or C] inserts new `pair` copy-constructed from `value` into the table.
	Sets result to provide read-only access to the matching pair.
	Returns: True if new pair was inserted; false if key was already in the map.
	Tip: If you do not need to access the data after insertion, use the form of insert that does not take an accessor ([C]); it may work faster and use fewer locks.

`bool` **`insert`**`( const value_type& value )`	Searches table for pair with given key. If not present, inserts new pair copy-constructed from value into the table. **Returns:** True if new pair was inserted; false if key was already in the map. Tip: If you do not need to access the data after insertion, use the form of insert that does not take an accessor; it may work faster and use fewer locks.

`template<typename InputIterator> void`
`insert``( InputIterator first,`
`InputIterator last )`
	For each pair `p` in the half-open interval `[first,last)`, does `insert(p)`. The order of the insertions, or whether they are done concurrently, is unspecified.
	CAUTION: The current implementation processes the insertions in order. Future implementations may do the insertions concurrently. If duplicate keys exist in `[first,last)`, be careful to not depend on their insertion order.

`void` **`insert`**`(` `std::initializer_list<value_type> il )`	Inserts a sequence to the map by inserting each element from the initializer list. The order of the insertions, or whether they are done concurrently, is unspecified. CAUTION: The current implementation processes the insertions in order. Future implementations may do the insertions concurrently. If duplicate keys exist in the initializer list, be careful to not depend on their insertion order.
`bool` **`erase`**`( const Key& key )`	Searches table for pair with given key. Removes the matching pair if it exists. If there is an accessor pointing to the pair, the pair is nonetheless removed from the table but its destruction is deferred until all accessors stop pointing to it. **Returns:** True if pair was removed by the call; false if key was not found in the map.

Figure B-51. (*continued*)

bool **erase**(*accessor*& item_accessor)	Requirements: item_accessor.empty()==false Effects: Removes pair referenced by item_accessor. Concurrent insertion of the same key creates a new pair in the table, which can temporarily co-exist with the one being destroyed. If using const_accessor to access, and there is another const_accessor pointing to the pair, the pair is nonetheless removed from the table but its destruction is deferred until all accessors stop pointing to it. Returns: true if pair was removed by this thread; false if pair was removed by another thread.
Concurrent Hash Map…	
Parallel Iteration	
Member	**Description**
const_range_type **range**(size_t grainsize=1) const	Constructs a const_range_type representing all keys in the table. The parameter grainsize is in units of hash table buckets. Each bucket typically has on average about one key-value pair. **Returns:** const_range_type object for the table.
range_type **range**(size_t grainsize=1)	**Returns:** range_type object for the table.
Concurrent Hash Map…	
Capacity	
Member	**Description**
size_type **size**() const	**Returns:** Number of key-value pairs in the table. Note: This method takes constant time, but is slower than for most STL containers.
bool **empty**() const	**Returns:** size()==0. Note: This method takes constant time, but is slower than for most STL containers.
size_type **max_size**() const	**Returns:** Inclusive upper bound on number of key-value pairs that the table can hold.
size_type **bucket_count**() const	**Returns:** Current number of internal buckets. See method rehash for discussion of buckets.
Concurrent Hash Map…	
Iterators	
Member	**Description**
[const_] iterator **begin**()	**Returns:** [const_]iterator pointing to beginning of key-value sequence.
[const_] iterator **end**()	**Returns:** [const_]iterator pointing to end of key-value sequence.
std::pair<iterator, iterator> **equal_range**(const Key& key) std::pair<const_iterator, const_iterator> equal_range(const Key& key) const	**Returns:** Pair of iterators (i,j) such that the half-open range [i,j) contains all pairs in the map (and only such pairs) with keys equal to key. Because the map has no duplicate keys, the half-open range is either empty or contains a single pair. Tip: These methods are serial alternatives to concurrent count and find methods.

Figure B-51. (*continued*)

Concurrent Hash Map...	
Global Functions	
Member	**Description**
`template<typename Key, typename T, typename HashCompare, typename A1, typename A2> bool` **`operator==`** `( const concurrent_hash_map<Key,T,HashCompare,A1>& a, const concurrent_hash_map<Key,T,HashCompare,A2>& b)`	**Returns:** true if a and b contain equal sets of keys and for each pair (k,v1) ∈a and (k,v2) ∈b, the expression `bool(v1==v2)` is true.
`template<typename Key, typename T, typename HashCompare, typename A1, typename A2> bool` **`operator!=`** `(const concurrent_hash_map<Key,T,HashCompare,A1> &a, const concurrent_hash_map<Key,T,HashCompare,A2> &b)`	**Returns:** `!(a==b)`
`template<typename Key, typename T, typename HashCompare, typename A> void` **`swap`**`( concurrent_hash_map<Key, T, HashCompare, A> &a, concurrent_hash_map<Key, T, HashCompare, A> &b)`	`a.swap(b)`

Figure B-51. *(continued)*

Concurrent Unordered Map, Multimap, Set, and Multiset Classes

`#include <tbb/concurrent_unordered_map.h>`
`#include <tbb/concurrent_unordered_set.h>`

These classes support concurrent insertion and traversal. Sets are collections of items (keys), maps are collections of items (keys) which map to a value. Each key must be unique for a map or set; multiple items with the same key are supported by multimap and multiset.

Constructor syntax

```
concurrent_unordered_map<typename Key,
            typename Element,
            typename Hasher = tbb_hash<Key>,
            typename Equality = std::equal_to<Key>,
            typename Allocator =
                tbb::tbb_allocator<std::pair<const Key, Element> >
```

concurrent_unordered_multimap< *same as concurrent_unordered_map* >

```
concurrent_unordered_set<typename Key,
            typename Hasher = tbb_hash<Key>,
            typename Equality = std::equal_to<Key>,
            typename Allocator =
                tbb::tbb_allocator<Key> >
```

concurrent_unordered_multiset< *same as concurrent_unordered_set* >

Figure B-52. *Précis: Containers: Concurrent Unordered Map, Multimap, Set, and Multiset Classes*

Differences Between STL and TBB unordered [multi]sets	
• Some methods requiring C++11 language features (e.g. `rvalue` references) are omitted.	
• The erase methods are prefixed with `unsafe_`, to indicate that they are not concurrency safe.	
• Bucket methods are prefixed with `unsafe_` as a reminder that they are not concurrency safe with respect to insertion.	
• For `concurrent_unordered_set`, insert methods may create a temporary item that is destroyed if another thread inserts the same item concurrently.	
• Like `std::list`, insertion of new items does not invalidate any iterators, nor change the order of items already in the map. Insertion and traversal may be concurrent.	
• The iterator types `iterator` and `const_iterator` are of the forward iterator category.	
• Insertion does not invalidate or update the iterators returned by `equal_range`, so insertion may cause non-equal items to be inserted at the end of the range.	

Concurrent Unordered Set and Multiset...

Destroy and Copy

Member	Description
`~concurrent_unordered_[multi]set()`	Destroys the set.
`concurrent_unordered_[multi]set& operator=` `(const concurrent_unordered_[multi]set& m);`	Assigns contents of m to `*this`. **Returns:** a reference to `*this`.
`concurrent_unordered_[multi]set& operator=` `(concurrent_unordered_[multi]set&& m);`	Moves data from m to `*this`. m is left in an unspecified state, but can be safely destroyed. **Returns:** a reference to `*this`.
`concurrent_unordered_[multi]set& operator=` `(std::initializer_list<value_type> il);`	Assigns contents of il to `*this`. **Returns:** a reference to `*this`.
`allocator_type get_allocator() const;`	**Returns:** a copy of the allocator associated with `*this`.

Concurrent Unordered Set and Multiset...

Size and Capacity

Member	Description
`bool empty() const`	**Returns:** size()!=0.
`size_type size() const`	**Returns:** Number of items in *this. **CAUTION:** Though the current implementation takes time O(1), possible future implementations might take time O(P), where P is the number of hardware threads.
`size_type max_size() const`	**Returns:** Upper bound on number of **items that *this can hold.** **CAUTION:** The upper bound may be much higher than what the container can actually hold.

Concurrent Unordered Set and Multiset...

Iterators

Member	Description
`[const_] iterator begin()`	Returns: `[const_] iterator` pointing to first item in the set.
`[const_] iterator end()`	Returns: `[const_] iterator` pointing to immediately past last item in the set.
`const_iterator cbegin() const`	Returns: `const_iterator` pointing to the first item in the set.
`const_iterator cend() const`	Returns: `const_iterator` pointing to immediately after the last item in the set.

Figure B-52. (*continued*)

Concurrent Unordered Set and Multiset...	
Modifiers	
Member	**Description**
`std::`**`pair`**`<iterator, bool>` `insert(const value_type& x)`	Constructs copy of `x` and attempts to insert it into the set. If the attempt fails because an item with the same key already exists, the copy is destroyed. **Returns:** `std::pair(iterator,success)`. The value iterator points to an item in the set with a matching key. The value of success is true if the item was inserted; false otherwise.

`iterator` **`insert`**`(`
`  const_iterator hint,`
`  const value_type& x)`
	Same as `insert(x)`.
	Note: The current implementation ignores the hint argument. Other implementations might not ignore it. It exists for similarity with the C++11 classes unordered_set and unordered_multiset. It hints to the implementation about where to start searching. Typically it should point to an item adjacent to where the item will be inserted.
	Returns: Iterator pointing to inserted item, or item already in the set with the same key.

`std::`**`pair`**`<iterator, bool>` `  insert(value_type&& x)`	Moves x into new instance of `value_type` and attempts to insert it into the set. If the attempt fails because an item with the same key already exists, this instance is destroyed. **Returns:** the same as `insert(const value_type& x)` version.

`iterator` **`insert`**`(`
`  const_iterator hint,`
`  value_type&& x)`
	Same as `insert(x)`.
	Note: The current implementation ignores the hint argument. Other implementations might not ignore it. It exists for similarity with the C++11 classes `unordered_set` and `unordered_multiset`. It hints to the implementation about where to start searching. Typically it should point to an item adjacent to where the item will be inserted.
	Returns: the same as `insert(const_iterator hint, const value_type& x)` version.

`template<class InputIterator>`
`  void` **`insert`**`(`
`  InputIterator first,`
`  InputIterator last)`
	Does `insert(*i)` where i is in the half-open interval `[first,last)`.

`void` **`insert`**`(`
`  std::initializer_list`
`  <value_type> il)`
	Inserts a sequence to the set by inserting each element from the initializer list.

`template<typename... Args>`
`  std::pair<iterator, bool>`
`  `**`emplace`**`(Args&&... args);`
	Constructs new instance of value_type from args and attempts to insert it into the set. If the attempt fails because an item with the same key already exists, this instance is destroyed.
	Returns: the same as `insert(const value_type& x)` version.

`template<typename... Args>`
`  iterator`
`  `**`emplace_hint`**`(`
`    const_iterator hint,`
`    Args&&... args);`
	Same as emplace(args).
	Note: The current implementation ignores the hint argument. Other implementations might not ignore it. It exists for similarity with the C++11 classes `unordered_set` and `unordered_multiset`. It hints to the implementation about where to start searching. Typically it should point to an item adjacent to where the item will be inserted.
	Returns: Iterator pointing to inserted item, or item already in the set with the same key.

`iterator` **`unsafe_erase`**`(` `  const_iterator position)`	Removes the item pointed to by position from the set. **Returns:** Iterator pointing to item that was immediately after the erased item, or `end()` if erased item was the last item in the set.
`size_type` **`unsafe_erase`**`(` `  const key_type& k)`	Removes item with key k if such an item exists. Returns: 1 if an item was removed; 0 otherwise.

`iterator` **`unsafe_erase`**`(`
`  const_iterator first,`
`  const_iterator last)`
	Removes `*i` where i is in the half-open interval `[first,last)`.
	Returns: last

Figure B-52. (*continued*)

void **clear**()	Removes all items from the set.
void **swap**(concurrent_unordered_[multi]set& m)	Swaps contents of *this and m

Concurrent Unordered Set and Multiset...

Observers

Member	Description
hasher **hash_function**() const()	**Returns:** Hashing functor associated with the set.
key_equal **key_eq**() const	**Returns:** Key equivalence functor associated with the set.

Concurrent Unordered Set and Multiset...

Lookup

Member	Description
iterator **find**(const key_type& k)	**Returns:** iterator pointing to item with key equivalent to k, or end() if no such item exists.
const_iterator **find**(const key_type& k) const	**Returns:** const_iterator pointing to item with key equivalent to k, or end() if no such item exists.
size_type **count**(const key_type& k) const	**Returns:** Number of items with keys equivalent to k.
std::pair<iterator, iterator> **equal_range**(const key_type& k)	**Returns:** Range containing all keys in the set that are equivalent to k.
std::pair<const_iterator, const_iterator> **equal_range**(const key_type& k) const	**Returns:** Range containing all keys in the set that are equivalent to k.

Concurrent Unordered Set and Multiset...

Parallel Iteration

Member	Description
const_range_type **range**() const	**Returns:** const_range_type object representing all keys in the table.
range_type **range**()	**Returns:** range_type object representing all keys in the table.

Concurrent Unordered Set and Multiset...

Bucket Interface

Member	Description
size_type **unsafe_bucket_count**() const	**Returns:** Number of buckets.
size_type **unsafe_max_bucket_count**() const	**Returns:** Upper bound on possible number of buckets.
size_type **unsafe_bucket_size**(size_type n)	**Returns:** Number of items in bucket n.
size_type **unsafe_bucket**(const key_type& k) const	**Returns:** Index of bucket where item with key k would be placed.
local_iterator **unsafe_begin**(size_type n)	**Returns:** local_iterator pointing to first item in bucket n.
const_local_iterator **unsafe_begin**(size_type n) const	**Returns:** const_local_iterator pointing to first item in bucket n.
local_iterator **unsafe_end**(size_type n)	**Returns:** local_iterator pointing to immediately after the last item in bucket n.
const_local_iterator **unsafe_end**(size_type n) const	**Returns:** const_local_iterator pointing to immediately after the last item in bucket n.
const_local_iterator **unsafe_cbegin**(size_type n) const	**Returns:** const_local_iterator pointing to first item in bucket n.
const_local_iterator **unsafe_cend**(size_type n) const	**Returns:** const_local_iterator pointing to immediately past last item in bucket n.

Figure B-52. (*continued*)

Concurrent Unordered Set and Multiset...	
Hash Policy	
Member	**Description**
`float` **`load_factor`**`() const`	**Returns:** Average number of elements per bucket.
`float` **`max_load_factor`**`() const`	**Returns:** Maximum size of a bucket. If insertion of an item causes a bucket to be bigger, the implementation may repartition or increase the number of buckets.
`void` **`max_load_factor`**`(float z)`	Set maximum size for a bucket to `z`.
`void` **`rehas`**`h(size_type n)`	Effects: No effect if current number of buckets is at least `n`. Otherwise increases number of buckets to n. Note: n must be a power of two.

Figure B-52. *(continued)*

Requirements on *Container Range* concept

Classes `concurrent_hash_map` *and* `concurrent_vector` *both have member types* `range_type` *and* `const_range_type` *that model a Container Range.*

Use the range types in conjunction with `parallel_for`, `parallel_reduce`, *and* `parallel_scan` *to iterate over items in a container.*

Class R implementing the concept of container range must define:

From Range concept	`R::R( const R& );`
	Copy constructor
	`R::~R();`
	Destructor
	`bool R::is_divisible() const;`
	True if range can be partitioned into two subranges.
	`bool R::empty() const;`
	True if range is empty.
	`R::R( R& r, split );`
	Split range r into two subranges.
	`R::R( R& r, proportional_split proportion );`
	Optional. Proportional splitting constructor. Splits r into two subranges in accordance with proportion.
	`static const bool R::is_splittable_in_proportion;`
	Optional. If true, the proportional splitting constructor is defined for the range and may be used by parallel algorithms.
Additional requirements for Container Range	`R::value_type`
	Item type
	`R::reference`
	Item reference type
	`R::const_reference`
	Item const reference type
	`R::difference_type`
	Type for difference of two iterators
	`R::iterator`
	Iterator type for range
	`R::iterator R::begin()`
	First item in range
	`R::iterator R::end()`
	One past last item in range
	`R::size_type R::grainsize() const`
	Grain size

Figure B-53. *Précis: Containers: Requirements on Container Range Concept*

Concurrent Queue Class

#include <**tbb**/concurrent_queue.h>

A `tbb::concurrent_queue` is a first-in first-out data structure that permits multiple threads to concurrently push and pop items. Its capacity is unbounded, subject to memory limitations on the target machine. The interface is similar to std::queue except where it must differ to make concurrent modification safe.

Examples code using queues are shown in Chapter 6 (Figures 6.7 – 6.9).

Differences Between STL and TBB queues

Feature	`std::queue`	`tbb::concurrent_queue`
Access to `front` and `back`	Methods `front` and `back`	Not present. They would be unsafe while concurrent operations are in progress.
Requires type `T` to be default-constructible	No	Yes
`unsafe_size()`	Returns number of items in queue	Returns number of items in queue. May return incorrect value if any `push` or `try_pop` operations are concurrently in flight.

Copy and pop item unless queue `q` is empty.	`bool b=!q.empty();`
	`if(b) {`
	`    x=q.front();`
	`    q.pop();`
	`}`
		`bool b = q.try_pop(x)`

Member	Description
concurrent_queue([const allocator_type& a])	Constructs empty queue.

concurrent_queue(
  const concurrent_queue& src
  [, const allocator_type& a])
	Constructs a copy of `src`.

template<typename InputIterator>
concurrent_queue(
  InputIterator first,
  InputIterator last,
  [const allocator_type& a])
	Constructs a queue containing copies of elements in the iterator half-open interval `[first,last)`.

concurrent_queue(
  concurrent_queue&& src
  [, const allocator_type& a])
	Constructs new queue by moving content from `src` using the optionally specified allocator. `src` is left in an unspecified state, but can be safely destroyed.

~concurrent_queue()	Destroys all items in the queue, and the container itself, so that it can no longer be used.
void **push**(const T& source)	Pushes a copy of `source` onto back of the queue.
void **push**(T&& elem)	Pushes given element into the queue by utilizing element's move constructor (if available).
template<typename... Arguments> void **emplace**(Arguments&&... args)	Pushes a new element into the queue. The element is constructed with given arguments.
bool **try_pop**(T& destination)	If value is available, pops it from the queue, assigns it to destination, and destroys the original value. Otherwise does nothing. **Returns**: `true` if value was popped; `false` otherwise.
void **clear**()	Clears the queue. Afterwards `size() == 0`. Supported for `concurrent_queue` *only*.
size_type **unsafe_size**() const	**Returns:** Number of items in the queue. If there are concurrent modifications in flight, the value might not reflect the actual number of items in the queue. Supported for `concurrent_queue` *only*.
bool **empty**() const	**Returns**: `true` if queue has no items; `false` otherwise.
allocator_type **get_allocator**() const	**Returns**: Copy of allocator used to construct the queue.

Figure B-54. *Précis: Containers: Concurrent Queue Class*

Concurrent *Bounded* Queue Class

#include <**tbb**/concurrent_queue.h>

A tbb::concurrent_bounded_queue is similar to a tbb::concurrent_queue, but adds the ability to specify a capacity and modifies certain operations in reaction to that change (push can wait, a waiting pop is providing, size()/size_type differ, and an abort is added to cancel waiting push/pop operations.)

Examples code using queues are shown in Chapter 6 (Figures 6.7 – 6.9).

Only methods that differ from **tbb::concurrent_queue** are shown here.

Refer to prior concurrent_queue table for constructors and destructor (same other than name change to concurrent_bounded_queue), and the members which remain the same (try_pop, clear, get_allocator).

Member	Description
void **push**(const T& source)	*Behavior differs to comprehend capacity:* Waits until size()<capacity, and then pushes a copy of source onto back of the queue.
void **push**(T&& source)	*Behavior differs to comprehend capacity:* Waits until size()<capacity, and then moves source onto back of the queue.
template<typename... Arguments> void **emplace**(Arguments&&... args);	*Behavior differs to comprehend capacity:* Waits until size()<capacity, and then pushes a new element into the queue. The element is constructed with given arguments.
void **pop**(T& destination)	*In addition to try_pop method – this is a waiting pop:* Waits until a value becomes available and pops it from the queue. Assigns it to destination. Destroys the original value.
void **abort**()	*Additional method:* Wakes up any threads that are waiting on the queue via the push and pop operations and raises the tbb::user_abort exception on those threads. This feature is unavailable if TBB_USE_EXCEPTIONS is not set.

bool **try_push**(
  { const T& source |
    T&& source
  }
)
	Additional method: If size()<capacity, pushes a copy of source onto back of the queue.
	Returns: true if a copy was pushed; false otherwise.

template<typename... Arguments>
  bool
  try_emplace(Arguments&&... args)
	Behavior differs to comprehend capacity: If size()<capacity, constructs an item with given arguments and moves it onto back of the queue.
	Returns: True if an item was moved; false otherwise.

size_type **size**() const	*Behavior differs to comprehend capacity:* **Returns:** Number of pushes minus number of pops. The result is negative if there are pop operations waiting for corresponding pushes. The result can exceed capacity() if the queue is full and there are push operations waiting for corresponding pops.
bool **empty**() const	*Behavior differs to comprehend capacity:* **Returns:** size()<=0
size_type **capacity**() const	*Additional method:* **Returns**: maximum number of values that the queue can hold.
void **set_capacity**(size_type capacity)	*Additional method:* Sets the maximum number of values that the queue can hold.

***Figure B-55.** Précis: Containers: Concurrent Bounded Queue Class*

Concurrent *Priority* Queue Class

#include <**tbb**/concurrent_priority_queue.h>

A tbb::concurrent_priority_queue is a container that permits multiple threads to concurrently push and pop items. Items are popped in priority order as determined by a template parameter. Its capacity is unbounded, subject to memory limitations on the target machine. The interface is similar to std::priorty_queue except where it must differ to make concurrent modification safe.

Examples code using queues are shown in Chapter 6 (Figures 6.7 – 6.9).

Differences Between STL and TBB priority queues

Feature	`std::priority_queue`	`tbb::concurrent_priority_queue`
Choice of underlying container	Sequence template parameter	No choice of underlying container; allocator choice is provided instead
Access to highest priority item	`const value_type& top() const`	Not available. Unsafe for concurrent container

Copy and pop	`bool b=!q.empty();`
	`if(b){ x=q.top();`
	`       q.pop();`
	`}`
		`bool b = q.try_pop(x)`

Get number of items in queue	`size_type size() const`	Same, but may be inaccurate due to pending concurrent push or pop operations
Check if there are items in queue	`bool empty() const`	Same, but may be inaccurate due to pending concurrent push or pop operations

***Figure B-56.** Précis: Containers: Concurrent Priority Queue Class*

Concurrent Priority Queue	
Member	**Description**

`concurrent_priority_queue(`
`    [ size_type init_capacity ]`
`    [ comma if needed ]`
`    [ const allocator type& a ] )`
	Constructs an empty queue, optionally with an initial capacity. *Comma needed between parameters if both optional parameters are used.*

`concurrent_priority_queue(`
`    const concurrent_priority_queue& src`
`    [ , const allocator type& a ] )`
	Constructs a copy of `src`.

`template<typename InputIterator>`
`concurrent_priority_queue(`
`    InputIterator first,`
`    InputIterator last,`
`    [ const allocator type& a ] )`
	Constructs a queue containing copies of elements in the iterator half-open interval `[first,last)`.

`concurrent_priority_queue(`
`    std::initializer_list<T> il`
`    [ const allocator type& a ] )`
	Equivalent to `concurrent_priority_queue(`
	`il.begin(), il.end(),a)`.

`concurrent_priority_queue(`
`    concurrent_priority_queue&& src`
`    [, const allocator_type& a ] )`
	Constructs new queue by moving content from `src` using the optionally specified allocator. `src` is left in an unspecified state, but can be safely destroyed.

`~concurrent_priority_queue()`	Destroys all items in the queue, and the container itself, so that it can no longer be used.
`concurrent_priority_queue& operator=` `(const concurrent_priority_queue& src)`	Assigns contents of `src` to `*this`. This operation is not thread-safe and may result in an error or an invalid copy of src if another thread is concurrently modifying src. **Returns:** a reference to `*this`.
`concurrent_priority_queue& operator=` `(concurrent_priority_queue&& src)`	Moves data from `src` to `*this`. `src` is left in an unspecified state, but can be safely destroyed. This operation is unsafe if there are pending concurrent operations on the `src` queue. Returns: a reference to `*this`.
`concurrent_priority_queue& operator=` `(std::initializer_list<T> il)`	Assigns contents of the initializer list `il` to `*this`. **Returns:** a reference to `*this`.

`template <typename InputIterator>`
`void assign(InputIterator begin,`
`            InputIterator end,`
`            const allocator type&)`
	Assigns contents of the iterator half-open interval [begin, end) to `*this`.

`void assign(` `std::initializer_list<T> il)`	Equivalent to `assign(il.begin(), il.end())`.
`bool empty() const`	**Returns:** `true` if queue has no items; `false` otherwise. May be inaccurate when concurrent `push` or `try_pop` operations are pending. This operation reads shared data and may trigger a race condition in race detection tools when used concurrently.

Figure B-56. (*continued*)

`size_type` **`size`**`() const`	**Returns:** Number of items in the queue. May be inaccurate when concurrent push or `try_pop` operations are pending. This operation reads shared data and may trigger a race condition in race detection tools when used concurrently.
`void` **`push`**`(const_reference elem)`	Pushes a copy of elem into the queue. This operation is thread-safe with other `push`, `try_pop` and `emplace` operations.
`void` **`push`**`(T&& elem)`	Pushes a given element into the queue using move constructor. This operation is thread-safe with other `push`, `try_pop` and `emplace` operations.
`template<typename... Args>` `void` **`emplace`**`(Args&&... args)`	Pushes a new element into the queue. The element is constructed with given arguments. This operation is thread-safe with other `push`, `try_pop` and `emplace` operations.
`bool` **`try_pop`**`(reference elem)`	If the queue is not empty, copies the highest priority item from the queue and assigns it to elem, and destroys the popped item in the queue; otherwise, does nothing. This operation is thread-safe with other `push`, `try_pop` and `emplace` operations. **Returns:** true if an item was popped; false otherwise.
`void` **`clear`**`()`	Clears the queue; results in `size()==0`. This operation is not thread-safe.
`void` **`swap`**`(concurrent_priority_queue& other)`	Swaps the queue contents with those of other. This operation is not thread-safe.
`allocator_type get_allocator``() const`	**Returns:** A copy of allocator used to construct the queue.

Figure B-56. (*continued*)

Concurrent Vector Class

#include <tbb/concurrent_vector.h>

A concurrent_vector<T, [A]> is a dynamically growable array of T with allocator A (allocator defaults to tbb::cache_aligned_allocator<T>). It is safe to grow a concurrent_vector while other threads are also operating on elements of it, or even growing it themselves. For safe concurrent growing, concurrent_vector has three methods that support common uses of dynamic arrays: push_back, grow_by, and grow_to_at_least.

A concurrent_vector meets all requirements for a Container and a Reversible Container as specified in the ISO C++ standard. It does not meet the Sequence requirements due to absence of methods insert() and erase().

Unlike a std::vector, a concurrent_vector never moves existing elements when it grows. The container allocates a series of contiguous arrays. The first reservation, growth, or assignment operation determines the size of the first array. Using a small number of elements as initial size incurs fragmentation across cache lines that may increase element access time. The method shrink_to_fit() merges several smaller arrays into a single contiguous array, which may improve access time.

Examples code using the vector class is shown in Chapter 6.

Concurrent Vector Class...

Construction Methods

These operations must not be invoked concurrently on the same vector.

Member	Description

concurrent_vector(
    [size_type n
    [, const_reference t=T()]]
    [comma if needed]
    [const allocator_type& a]
)
	Constructs a vector of n copies of t, using optionally specified allocator instance.
	If n is not specified, an empty vector is created.
	If t is not specified, each element is default-constructed instead of copied.

template<typename InputIterator>
concurrent_vector(
  InputIterator first,
  InputIterator last
  [, const allocator_type& a]
)
	Constructs a vector that is a copy of the sequence [first,last), making only N calls to the copy constructor of T, where N is the distance between first and last.

concurrent_vector(
  std::initializer_list<T> il
  [, const allocator_type& a]
)
	Equivalent to
	concurrent_vector(il.begin(), il.end(), a)

concurrent_vector(const concurrent_vector& src)	Constructs a copy of src.

concurrent_vector(
  concurrent_vector&& src
  [, const allocator_type& a]
)
	Constructs a new vector by moving content from src, optionally using allocator a. src is left in an unspecified state, but can be safely destroyed.

concurrent_vector& operator= (const concurrent_vector& src)	Assigns the contents of src to *this. **Returns:** a reference to *this.
concurrent_vector& operator= (concurrent_vector&& src)	Moves data from src to *this. src is left in an unspecified state, but can be safely destroyed. **Returns:** a reference *this.
template<typename M> **concurrent_vector**& operator= (const concurrent_vector<T, M>& src)	Assigns the contents of src to *this. **Returns:** a reference *this.
concurrent_vector& operator= (std::initializer_list<T> il)	Sets *this to contain data from il. **Returns:** a reference *this.

Figure B-57. *Précis: Containers: Concurrent Vector Class*

Concurrent Vector Class...	
Whole Vector Methods: Copy, Assignment, Destruction	
Concurrent invocation of these operations on the same instance is not safe.	
Member	**Description**
`void assign( size_type n,` `   const_reference t )`	Assigns `n` copies of `t` to `*this`.

`template<class InputIterator>`
`void assign( InputIterator first,`
`   InputIterator last )`
	Assigns the contents of the sequence `[first,last)`, making only `N` calls to the copy constructor of `T`, where `N` is the distance between `first` and `last`.

`void assign(` `   std::initializer_list<T> il )`	Equivalent to `assign(il.begin(), il.end())`.
`void reserve( size_type n )`	Reserves space for at least n elements. Throws `std::length_error if n>max_size()`. It can also throw an exception if the allocator throws an exception. Safety: If an exception is thrown, the instance remains in a valid state.
`void shrink_to_fit()`	Compacts the internal representation to reduce fragmentation.
`void swap( concurrent_vector& x )`	Swap contents of two vectors. Takes `O(1)` time.
`void clear()`	Erases all elements. Afterwards, `size()==0`. Does not free internal arrays. **Tip:** To free internal arrays, call `shrink_to_fit()` after `clear()`.
`~concurrent_vector()`	Erases all elements and destroys the vector.

Figure B-57. (*continued*)

Concurrent Vector Class...	
Concurrent Growth Methods	
The methods described in the following table may be invoked concurrently on the same vector.	
Member	**Description**

`iterator grow_by( size_type delta )`
 	
`iterator grow_by(`
`  size_type delta,`
`  const_reference t )`
	Appends a sequence comprising delta new elements to the end of the vector. If the second parameter `t` is specified, the new elements are initialized by copying `t`; otherwise, the new elements are default-constructed.
	Returns: Iterator pointing to the beginning of the appended sequence.

`template<typename ForwardIterator>`
`iterator grow_by(`
`  ForwardIterator first,`
`  ForwardIterator last )`
	Appends a sequence to the vector by copying each element in the sequence `[first,last)`.
	Returns: Iterator pointing to the beginning of the appended sequence.

`iterator grow_by(` `  std::initializer_list<T> il )`	Appends a sequence to the vector by copying each element from the initializer list. **Returns:** Iterator pointing to the beginning of the appended sequence.

`iterator grow_to_at_least(`
`  size_type n )`
 	
`iterator grow_to_at_least(`
`  size_type n, const_reference t )`
	Appends minimal sequence of elements such that `vector.size()>=n`. If the second parameter `t` is specified, the new elements are initialized by copying `t`; otherwise, the new elements are default-constructed. Blocks until all elements in range `[0..n)` are allocated (but not necessarily constructed if they are under construction by a different thread).
	Tip: If a thread must know whether construction of an element has completed, consider the following technique. Instantiate the `concurrent_vector` using a `zero_allocator`. Define the constructor `T()` such that when it completes, it sets a field of `T` to non-zero. A thread can check whether an item in the `concurrent_vector` is constructed by checking whether the field is non-zero.
	Returns: Iterator that points to the beginning of the appended sequence, or a pointer to `(*this)[n]` if no elements were appended.

`iterator push_back(` `  const_reference value )`	Appends copy of value to the end of the vector. **Returns:** Iterator that points to the copy.
`iterator push_back( T&& value )`	Moves value to a new element appended at the end of the vector. **Returns:** Iterator that points to the new element.
`template<typename... Args> iterator` `emplace_back( Args&&... args );`	Appends a new element to the end of the vector. The element is constructed with given arguments. **Returns:** Iterator that points to the new element.

Figure B-57. (*continued*)

Concurrent Vector Class...

Access Methods

The methods described in this section may be concurrently invoked on the same vector as methods for concurrent growth. However, the returned reference may be to an element that is being concurrently constructed.

Member (optional const appears twice or not at all below)	Description
[const_]reference **operator[]** (size_type index) [const]	**Returns:** [Const] Reference to element with the specified index.
[const_]reference **at**(size_type index) [const]	**Returns:** [Const] Reference to element at specified index. **Throws:** std::out_of_range if index >= size() or index is for broken portion of vector.
[const_]reference **front**() [const]	**Returns:** (*this)[0]
[const_]reference **back**() [const]	**Returns:** (*this)[size()-1]

Concurrent Vector Class...

Parallel Iteration Methods

Types const_range_type and range_type model the Container Range *concept. The types differ only in that the bounds for a* const_range_type *are of type* const_iterator, *whereas the bounds for a* range_type *are of type* iterator.

Member	Description
[const_]range_type **range** (size_t grainsize=1) [const]	**Returns:** Range over entire concurrent_vector that permits, read-only (if const type) or read-write, access.

Concurrent Vector Class...

Capacity Methods

Member	Description
size_type **size**() const	**Returns:** Number of elements in the vector. The result may include elements that are allocated but still under construction by concurrent calls to any of the growth methods.
bool **empty**() const	**Returns:** size()==0
size_type **capacity**() const	**Returns:** Maximum size to which vector can grow without having to allocate more memory. **Note:** Unlike a std::vector, a concurrent_vector does not move existing elements if it allocates more memory.
size_type **max_size**() const	**Returns:** The highest possible size of the vector could reach.

Concurrent Vector Class...

Iterator Methods

Template class concurrent_vector<T> supports random access iterators of the ISO C++ Standard. Unlike a std::vector, the iterators are not raw pointers. A concurrent_vector<T> meets the reversible container requirements of the ISO C++ Standard.

Member (optional const appears twice or not at all below)	Description
[const_]iterator **begin**() [const]	Returns: [const_] iterator iterator pointing to beginning of the vector.
[const_]iterator **end**() [const]	Returns: [const_] iterator iterator pointing to end of the vector.
[const_]reverse_iterator **rbegin**() [const]	Returns: [const_] iterator reverse iterator pointing to beginning of reversed vector.
[const_]iterator **rend**() [const]	Returns: [const_] iterator reverse_iterator pointing to end of reversed vector.

Figure B-57. (*continued*)

Synchronization

Chapter 5 covers TBB synchronization in a single chapter; this section of this Appendix is a terse review of the supported APIs, and some notes. Thread Local Storage, which is also covered in Chapter 5, is reviewed after this section. TBB supplies a platform independent mutual exclusion and atomic operations. These predate support in the C++ standard. With the addition of similar capabilities in the C++ standard, TBB supports C++11 interfaces (defined in namespace `std`, not `tbb`) for condition variables and scoped locking, with a few differences:

- TBB support is available regardless of whether full C++11 language support is available or not on a given system.

- The implementation uses the `tbb::tick_count` interface instead of the C++11 `<chrono>` interface.

- The implementation will throw `std::runtime_error` if C++11 `std::system_error` is not available.

- The implementation omits or approximates features requiring C++11 language support such as `constexpr` or explicit operators.

- The implementation works in conjunction with `tbb::mutex` wherever the C++11 specification calls for a `std::mutex`.

- `notify_all_at_thread_exit()` is not supported.

Mutexes							
class name	#include<tbb/?>	Scalable	Fair	Reentrant	Long Wait	Use TSX	Size
mutex	mutex.h	OS dependent		No	blocks	no	>=3 words
recursive_mutex	recursive_mutex.h			Yes		no	>=3 words
spin_mutex	spin_mutex.h	No	No		yields	no	1 byte
speculative_spin_mutex	spin_mutex.h	Hardware dependent		No		yes	2 cache lines
queuing_mutex	queuing_mutex.h	Yes	Yes	No		no	1 word
spin_rw_mutex	spin_rw_mutex.h	No	No			no	1 word
speculative_spin_rw_mutex	spin_rw_mutex.h	Hardware dependent		No		yes	3 cache lines
queuing_rw_mutex	queuing_rw_mutex.h	Yes	Yes	No		no	1 word
null_mutex	null_mutex.h	-	Yes	Yes	never	no	empty
null_rw_mutex	null_rw_mutex.h			Yes			

Figure B-58. *Précis: Synchronization: comparison of various mutexes*

C++11 Compatibility

See the C++11 standard for a detailed description of the members for C++11 standard mutexes. Classes `mutex`, `recursive_mutex`, `spin_mutex`, and `spin_rw_mutex` support the C++11 interfaces described here:

Pseudo-Signature	Semantics
`void M::lock()`	Acquire lock.
`bool M::try_lock()`	Try to acquire lock on mutex. Return true if lock acquired, false otherwise.
`void M::unlock()`	Release lock.
`class lock_guard<M>`	Refer to C++ standard for complete documentation. The
`class unique_lock<M>`	`std::lock_guard` class keeps its associated mutex locked during the entire life time by acquiring the lock on construction and releasing the lock on destruction. The `std::unique_lock` class offers more flexible when dealing with mutex locks. It has the same interface as `std::lock_guard` but provides additional methods for explicitly locking and unlocking mutexes and deferring locking on construction.
Classes mutex and recursive mutex also provide the C++11 idiom for accessing their underlying OS handles, as described here (M is mutex or recursive_mutex):	
`M::native_handle_type`	Native handle type. For Windows operating system, `LPCRITICAL_SECTION` is the Native handle type. For all other operating system, it is (`pthread_mutex`).
`native_handle_type M::native_handle()`	Get underlying native handle of mutex M.

Figure B-59. *Précis: Synchronization: C++11 mutex support*

Mutexes

#include `<see below>`

TBB mutexes provide portable MUTual EXclusion of threads from sections of code by wrapping OS calls for mutual exclusion. TBB interfaces enforce the scoped locking pattern, which is widely used in C++ libraries because they do not require that we remember to release a lock, and they release the lock if an exception is thrown which takes execution outside the mutual exclusion region protected by the lock.

Speculative interfaces will use speculative locking (TSX on Intel processors) on systems that support hardware speculative locking. Speculative locking allows multiple threads to acquire the same lock, as long as there are no conflicts that may generate different results than non-speculative locking. These mutexes are scalable when working with low conflict rate, i.e. mostly in speculative locking mode.

Figure B-60. *Précis: Synchronization: mutex examples*

```
#include <cstdio>
#include <tbb/tick_count.h>
#include <tbb/mutex.h>
#include <tbb/recursive_mutex.h>
#include <tbb/spin_mutex.h>
#include <tbb/queuing_mutex.h>
#include <tbb/spin_rw_mutex.h>
#include <tbb/queuing_rw_mutex.h>
#include <tbb/null_mutex.h>
#include <tbb/null_rw_mutex.h>

int main( int argc, char *argv[] ) {
  tbb::mutex                        my_mutex_01;
  tbb::recursive_mutex              my_mutex_02;
  tbb::spin_mutex                   my_mutex_03;
  tbb::speculative_spin_mutex       my_mutex_04;
  tbb::queuing_mutex                my_mutex_05;
  tbb::spin_rw_mutex                my_mutex_06;
  tbb::speculative_spin_rw_mutex    my_mutex_07;
  tbb::queuing_rw_mutex             my_mutex_08;
  tbb::null_mutex                   my_mutex_09;
  tbb::null_rw_mutex                my_mutex_10;
  {
    tbb::mutex::scoped_lock                     mylock01a(my_mutex_01);
    // the following would stall because already locked the mutex
    // tbb::mutex::scoped_lock                  mylock01b(my_mutex_01);
    tbb::recursive_mutex::scoped_lock           mylock02a(my_mutex_02);
    // recursion is allowed... so this does not stall...
    tbb::recursive_mutex::scoped_lock           mylock02b(my_mutex_02);
    // recursion is allowed... so this does not stall...
    tbb::recursive_mutex::scoped_lock           mylock02c(my_mutex_02);
    tbb::spin_mutex::scoped_lock                mylock03a(my_mutex_03);
    tbb::speculative_spin_mutex::scoped_lock    mylock04a(my_mutex_04);
    // reader...
    tbb::spin_rw_mutex::scoped_lock             mylock06a(my_mutex_06);
    // the following would stall, really!
    // we already have locked the mutex from this thread
    // RW allows one lock per thread - this is not a recursive lock!
    // tbb::spin_rw_mutex::scoped_lock          mylock06c(my_mutex_06);
    tbb::speculative_spin_rw_mutex::scoped_lock mylock07a(my_mutex_07);
    // writer...
    tbb::queuing_rw_mutex::scoped_lock          mylock08a(my_mutex_08,true);
    tbb::null_mutex::scoped_lock                mylock09a(my_mutex_09);
    // null does nothing... so this does not stall...
    tbb::null_mutex::scoped_lock                mylock09b(my_mutex_09);
    tbb::null_rw_mutex::scoped_lock             mylock10a(my_mutex_10);
    // null does nothing... so this does not stall...
    tbb::null_rw_mutex::scoped_lock             mylock10b(my_mutex_10);
    // null does nothing... so this does not stall...
    tbb::null_rw_mutex::scoped_lock             mylock10c(my_mutex_10);

    printf("Locks acquired!\nHello, World!\n");
  }
}
```

Assuming you do not uncomment the lines which will cause a stall… the output on any machine should be:

```
Locks acquired!
Hello, World!
```

Figure B-60. (*continued*)

Mutex Concepts	
Mutex concept for a mutex type M.	
Pseudo-Signature	**Semantics**
`M()`	Construct unlocked mutex.
`~M()`	Destroy unlocked mutex. The effect of destroying a locked mutex is undefined.
`typename M::scoped lock`	Corresponding scoped-lock type.
`M::scoped lock()`	Construct lock without acquiring mutex.
`M::scoped lock(M&)`	Construct lock and acquire lock on mutex.
`M::~scoped lock()`	Release lock (if acquired).
`M::scoped lock::acquire(M&)`	Acquire lock on mutex.
`bool M::scoped_lock::try_acquire(M&)`	Try to acquire lock on mutex. Return true if lock acquired, false otherwise.
`M::scoped lock::release()`	Release lock.
`static const bool M::is rw mutex`	True if mutex is reader-writer mutex; false otherwise.
`static const bool M::is_recursive_mutex`	True if mutex is recursive mutex; false otherwise.
`static const bool M::is fair mutex`	True if mutex is fair; false otherwise.
The ReaderWriterConcept concept extends the Mutex concept (*all the above requirements apply also*). Classes `spin_rw_mutex`, `speculative_spin_rw_mutex` and `queuing_rw_mutex` model the ReaderWriterMutex concept. Additional ReaderWriterConcept requirements for a mutex type RW are:	
`RW::scoped_lock(RW&, bool write=true)`	Construct lock and acquire lock on a given mutex. The lock is a writer lock if *write* is true; a reader lock otherwise.
`RW::scoped_lock::acquire(RW&, bool write=true)`	Acquire lock on a given mutex. The lock is a writer lock if *write* is true; a reader lock otherwise.
`bool RW::scoped_lock::try_acquire(RW&, bool write=true)`	Try to acquire lock on a given mutex. The lock is a writer lock if *write* is true; a reader lock otherwise. Return true if lock acquired, false otherwise.
`bool RW::scoped_lock::upgrade_to_writer()`	Change reader lock to writer lock. The effect is undefined if no reader lock is held. Return false if lock was released and reacquired; true otherwise.
`bool RW::scoped_lock::downgrade_to_reader()`	Change writer lock to reader lock. The effect is undefined if no writer lock is held. Return false if lock was released and reacquired; true otherwise.

Figure B-61. *Précis: Synchronization: Mutex Concepts*

`atomic<T>` Class

`#include <tbb/atomic.h>`

An `atomic<T>` supports atomic read, write, fetch-and-add, fetch-and-store, and compare-and-swap. Type T may be an integral type, enumeration type, or a pointer type. When T is a pointer type, arithmetic operations are interpreted as pointer arithmetic. For example, if x has type `atomic<float*>` and a float occupies four bytes, then ++x advances x by four bytes. Arithmetic on `atomic<T>` is not allowed if T is an enumeration type, `void*`, or `bool`.

Sequential consistency is the default memory semantics for all atomic operations per the C++ standard, but with TBB a modification of that default is possible.

```
#include <tbb/atomic.h>
int main( int argc, char *argv[] ) {
  double value = 9.9;
  tbb::atomic<double> y(value); // Not atomic
  tbb::atomic<double> z;
  z=value;                      // Atomic assignment
}
```

Member	Description
enum **memory_semantics**	Defines values used to select the template variants that permit more selective control over visibility of operations (see below).

Kind (enum)	Description	Default For
acquire	Operations after the atomic operation never move over it.	read
release	Operations before the atomic operation never move over it.	write
full_fence	Sequentially consistent. Operations on either side never move over it and furthermore, the sequentially consistent atomic operations have a global order.	`fetch_and_store,` `fetch_and_add,` `compare_and_swap`
relaxed	No ordering.	none

`atomic() = default`	Default constructor generated by compiler. This constructor behaves same as if there were no user defined constrcutors declared at all.
`constexpr atomic(` `value_type arg)`	Initialize `*this` with value of arg. If the argument is a translation time constant, then initialization is performed during translation time, overwise initialization is performed at run time.
`template<memory_semantics M>` `value_type fetch_and_add(` `value_type addend )`	Let x be the value of `*this`. Atomically updates $x = x +$ addend. **Returns**: Original value of x.
`template<memory_semantics M>` `value_type fetch_and_increment()`	Let x be the value of `*this`. Atomically updates $x = x + 1$. **Returns**: Original value of x.
`template<memory_semantics M>` `value_type fetch_and_decrement()`	Let x be the value of `*this`. Atomically updates $x = x - 1$. **Returns**: Original value of x.
`template<memory_semantics M>` `value_type compare_and_swap` `value_type compare_and_swap(` `value_type new_value,` `value_type comparand )`	Let x be the value of `*this`. Atomically compares x with comparand, and if they are equal, sets x=new_value. **Returns**: Original value of x.
`template<memory_semantics M>` `value_type fetch_and_store(` `value_type new_value )`	Let x be the value of `*this`. Atomically exchanges old value of x with new_value. **Returns**: Original value of x.
`template<memory_semantics M>` `value_type load()`	**Returns**: Value of x.
`template<memory_semantics M>` `void store(value_type new_value)`	Atomically stores new_value.

Figure B-62. *Précis: Synchronization: `atomic<T>` class*

Thread Local Storage (TLS)

Chapter 5 covers TBB thread local storage as part of the broader coverage of synchronization; this section of the Appendix is a terse review of the supported APIs. Thread local storage, for our purposes here, refers to having privatized copies of data on each thread. An important aspect of TBB is that we do not know how many threads are being used at any given time, so thread local storage is presented in a manner that automatically matches the number of threads created at runtime by the TBB library – a number that can vary greatly depending on the platform our program runs upon.

TBB provides two template classes for thread local storage. Both provide a thread local element per thread. Both lazily create the elements on demand. They differ in their intended use models:

- `combinable` provides thread local storage for holding per-thread subcomputations that will later be reduced to a single result.

- `enumerable_thread_specific` provides thread local storage that acts like an STL container with one element per thread. The container permits iterating over the elements using the usual STL iteration idioms.

Template class `flatten2d` assists a common idiom where an `enumerable_thread_specific` represents a container partitioner across threads. This is supplied because it is very useful when debugging code.

combinable

#include <tbb/combinable.h>

Template class combinable<T> provides each thread with its own instance of type T, presumably to hold per-thread subcomputations that will later be reduced to a single result. It is useful to note that combine and combine_each run serially, and that is intentional. Typically, there is not many thread-local values to combine, and not much computation either. Therefore, the methods of class combinable are not thread-safe, except for local.

Examples of how to use in code are shown in Chapter 5.

combinable Member	Description
combinable()	Constructs combinable such that thread-local instances of T will be default-constructed.
template<typename FInit> explicit **combinable**(FInit finit)	Constructs combinable such that thread-local elements will be created by copying the result of finit(). The expression finit() must be safe to evaluate concurrently by multiple threads. It is evaluated each time a new thread-local element is created.
combinable(const combinable& other);	Constructs a copy of other, so that it has copies of each element in *other* with the same thread mapping.
combinable(combinable&& other);	Constructs combinable by moving the content of other intact. other is left in an unspecified state but can be safely destroyed.
~combinable()	Destroys all elements in *this.
combinable& **operator=** (const combinable& other)	Sets *this to be a copy of other.
combinable& **operator=** (combinable&& other)	Moves the content of *other* to *this intact. other is left in an unspecified state but can be safely destroyed.
void **clear**()	Removes all elements from *this.
T& **local**([bool& exists])	An element is created if it does not exist for the current thread. Additionally, if an exists parameter was specified, then *exists* is set to true if an element was already present for the current thread; false if it had to be created. **Returns**: Reference to thread-local element.
template<typename BinaryFunc> T **combine**(BinaryFunc f)	Computes a reduction over all elements using binary functor f. All evaluations of f are done sequentially in the calling thread. If there are no elements, creates the result using the same rules as for creating a new element. **Returns**: Result of the reduction.
template<typename UnaryFunc> void **combine_each**(UnaryFunc f)	Evaluates f(x) for each thread-local element x in *this. All evaluations are done sequentially in the calling thread.

Figure B-63. *Précis: TLS: combinable example*

combinable - example

```cpp
#include <tbb/parallel_for.h>
#include <tbb/combinable.h>
#include <iostream>
#include <stdio.h>

#define HOWMANY 10

void dump(tbb::combinable<int> *pTLS) {
  tbb::parallel_for( 0, HOWMANY, [&](int i){
      bool truth;
      int val;
      val = pTLS->local(truth);
      printf("%d%c ",val,truth ? 'T':'F');
    } );
  printf("\n");
}

int main() {
  int gval;
  tbb::combinable<int> myTLS([](){return 0;});
  tbb::combinable<int> mycopiedTLS([](){return 6;});

  dump( &myTLS );

  myTLS.clear();
  printf("cleared\n");

  dump( &myTLS );  dump( &myTLS );
  tbb::parallel_for( 0, HOWMANY, [&](int i){
      myTLS.local() += i;
    } );
  printf("added local values into local sums\n");
  dump( &myTLS );

  gval = myTLS.combine([](int a,int b){return a+b;});
  printf("global value = %d\n",gval);
  mycopiedTLS = myTLS;
  gval = mycopiedTLS.combine([](int a,int b){return a+b;});
  printf("global copied value = %d\n",gval);

  myTLS.clear();
  printf("cleared\n");

  gval = myTLS.combine([](int a,int b){return a+b;});
  printf("global value = %d\n",gval);
  gval = mycopiedTLS.combine([](int a,int b){return a+b;});
  printf("global copied value = %d\n",gval);
  mycopiedTLS.combine_each([](int a){printf("%d ",a);});
  printf("<< values from combine_each\n");
  gval = mycopiedTLS.combine([](int a,int b){return a+b;});
  printf("global copied value = %d\n",gval);
  return 0;
}
```
Sample output… will vary run to run and machine to machine!

Figure B-64. *Précis: TLS: combinable example*

```
0F 0T 0T 0T 0T 0T 0F 0F 0T 0T
cleared
0F 0T 0T 0T 0T 0T 0F 0F 0T 0T
0T 0T 0T 0T 0F 0T 0T 0T 0T 0T
added local values into local sums
45T 45T 45T 45T 45T 0T 0T 0T 0T 45T
global value = 45
global copied value = 45
cleared
global value = 0
global copied value = 45
0 0 45 0 << values from combine_each
global copied value = 45
```

Figure B-64. (*continued*)

enumerable_thread_specific	
#include <tbb/enumerable_thread_specific.h>	
Template class enumerable_thread_specific <T> provides each thread with storage of type T that acts like an STL container with one element per thread. The container permits iterating over the elements using the usual STL iteration idioms.	
enumerable_thread_specific Member	**Description**
Constructors...	
enumerable_thread_specific()	Constructs an enumerable_thread_specific where each thread-local element will be default-constructed.
template<typename Finit> explicit **enumerable_thread_specific**(Finit finit)	Constructs an enumerable_thread_specific such that any thread-local element will be created by copying the result of finit(). The expression finit() must be safe to evaluate concurrently by multiple threads. It is evaluated each time a thread-local element is created. This constructor is only available (i.e. participates in overload resolution) if finit() is a valid expression.
explicit **enumerable_thread_specific**(const T& exemplar) explicit **enumerable_thread_specific**(T&& exemplar)	Constructs an enumerable_thread_specific where each thread-local element will be copy-constructed from exemplar. Move constructor of T can be used to store exemplar internally, however thread-local elements are always copy-constructed.
template <typename... Args> **enumerable_thread_specific**(Args&&... args);	Constructs enumerable_thread_specific such that any thread-local element will be constructed by invoking T(args...). This constructor does not participate in overload resolution if the type of the first argument in args... is T, or enumerable_thread_specific<T>, or foo() is a valid expression for a value foo of that type.
enumerable_thread_specific (const enumerable_thread_specific& other) template<typename Alloc, ets_key_usage_type Cachetype> **enumerable_thread_specific**(const enumerable_thread_specific <T, Alloc, Cachetype>& other)	Constructs an enumerable_thread_specific as a copy of other. The values are copy-constructed from the values in other and have same thread correspondence.
enumerable_thread_specific (enumerable_thread_specific&& other)	Constructs an enumerable_thread_specific by moving the content of other intact. other is left in an unspecified state, but can be safely destroyed.
template<typename Alloc, ets_key_usage_type Cachetype> **enumerable_thread_specific**(enumerable_thread_specific <T, Alloc, Cachetype>&& other)	Constructs an enumerable_thread_specific using per-element move construction from the values in other, and keeping their thread correspondence. other is left in an unspecified state, but can be safely destroyed.

Figure B-65. *Précis: TLS: enumerable_thread_specific*

Whole Container Operation	
These operations must not be invoked concurrently on the same instance of enumerable_thread_specific.	
`~enumerable_thread_specific()`	Destroys all elements in *this. Destroys any native TLS keys that were created for this instance.

`enumerable_thread_specific& operator=`
`( const enumerable_thread_specific&`
`other );`
	Copies the content of *other* to *this.

`template<typename Alloc,`
`  ets_key_usage_type Cachetype>`
`enumerable_thread_specific&`
`operator=(`
`  const enumerable_thread_specific`
`  <T, Alloc, Cachetype>& other );`
	Copies the content of *other* to *this.
	The allocator and key usage specialization is unchanged by this call.

`enumerable_thread_specific& operator=`
`( enumerable_thread_specific&&`
`    other );`
	Moves the content of *other* to *this intact. *other* is left in an unspecified state, but can be safely destroyed.

`template<typename Alloc,`
`  ets_key_usage_type Cachetype>`
`enumerable_thread_specific&`
`operator=(`
`  enumerable_thread_specific`
`  <T, Alloc, Cachetype>&& other );`
	Moves the content of *other* to *this using per-element move construction and keeping thread correspondence. *other* is left in an unspecified state, but can be safely destroyed.
	The allocator and key usage specialization is unchanged by this call.

`void clear()`	Destroys all elements in *this. Destroys and then recreates any native TLS keys used in the implementation.
Concurrent Operations	
`reference local( [ bool& exists ] )`	An element is created if it does not exist for the current thread. Additionally, if an *exists* parameter was specified, then *exists* is set to true if an element was already present for the current thread; false if it had to be created. **Returns**: Reference to thread-local element.
`size_type size() const`	**Returns**: The number of elements in *this. The value is equal to the number of distinct threads that have called local() after *this was constructed or most recently cleared. See Caution below.
`bool empty() const`	**Returns**: size()==0
Combining Operations	
These methods iterate across the entire container sequentially in the calling thread.	
`template<typename BinaryFunc> T` `combine(BinaryFunc f)`	Computes reduction over all elements using binary functor *f*. If there are no elements, creates the result using the same rules as for creating a thread-local element. **Returns**: Result of the reduction.
`template<typename UnaryFunc> void` `combine_each(UnaryFunc f)`	Evaluates $f(x)$ for each instance *x* of T in *this.
Parallel Iteration	
`[const_range_type] range(` `  size_t grainsize=1 ) [const]`	**Returns**: A [const_]range_type representing all elements in *this. The parameter grainsize is in units of elements.
Iterators	
Access iterators, which enable iteration over the set of all elements in the container.	
`[ const_]iterator begin() [ const ]`	**Returns**: [const_]iterator pointing to the beginning of the set of elements.
`[ const_]iterator end() [ const ]`	**Returns**: [const_]iterator pointing to the end of the set of elements.

Figure B-65. (*continued*)

`enumerable_thread_specific` - **example**

```cpp
#include <cstdio>
#include <utility>
#include <tbb/task_scheduler_init.h>
#include <tbb/enumerable_thread_specific.h>
#include <tbb/parallel_for.h>
#include <tbb/blocked_range.h>

typedef tbb::enumerable_thread_specific< std::pair<int,int> > CounterType;
CounterType MyCounters (std::make_pair(0,0));

struct Body {
  void operator()(const tbb::blocked_range<int> &r) const {
    CounterType::reference my_counter = MyCounters.local();
    ++my_counter.first;
    for (int i = r.begin(); i != r.end(); ++i)
      ++my_counter.second;
    }
};

int main() {
  tbb::parallel_for(
    tbb::blocked_range<int>(0, 100000000), Body());

  for (CounterType::const_iterator i = MyCounters.begin();
       i != MyCounters.end(); ++i) {
    printf("Thread stats:\n");
    printf("    calls to operator(): %d", i->first);
    printf("    total # of iterations executed: %d\n",
         i->second);
  }
  std::pair<int,int> sum =
    MyCounters.combine([](std::pair<int,int> x,
                          std::pair<int,int> y) {
      return std::make_pair(x.first+y.first,
                            x.second+y.second);
    });
  printf("Total calls to operator() = %d, "
         "total iterations = %d\n", sum.first, sum.second);
}
```

Sample output… will vary run to run and machine to machine!

```
Thread stats:
    calls to operator(): 63      total # of iterations executed: 7812500
Thread stats:
    calls to operator(): 63      total # of iterations executed: 9375000
Thread stats:
    calls to operator(): 256     total # of iterations executed: 81250000
Thread stats:
    calls to operator(): 21      total # of iterations executed: 1562500
Total calls to operator() = 403, total iterations = 100000000
```

Figure B-66. *Précis: TLS: enumerable_thread_specific example*

flatten2d

#include <tbb/enumerable_thread_specific.h>

Template class flatten2d assists a common idiom where an enumerable_thread_specific represents a container partitioner across threads. A flattened2d provides a flattened view of a container of containers as an aid for debugging applications.

flatten2d Member	Description
explicit flattened2d(const Container& c)	Constructs a flattened2d representing the sequence of elements in the inner containers contained by outer container c.
flattened2d(const Container& c, typename Container::const_iterator first, typename Container::const_iterator last)	Constructs a flattened2d representing the sequence of elements in the inner containers in the half-open interval [*first, last*) of Container c.
size_type size() const	**Returns**: The sum of the sizes of the inner containers that are viewable in the flattened2d.
iterator begin()	**Returns**: iterator pointing to the beginning of the set of local copies.
iterator end()	**Returns**: iterator pointing to the end of the set of local copies.
const_iterator begin() const	**Returns**: const_iterator pointing to the beginning of the set of local copies.
const_iterator end() const	**Returns**: const_iterator pointing to the end of the set of local copies.

template <typename Container>
    flattened2d<Container>
        flatten2d(const Container &c,
        const typename
        Container::const_iterator b,
        const typename
        Container::const_iterator e)
	Returns: Constructs and returns a flattened2d that provides iterators that traverse the elements in the containers within the half-open range [b, e) of Container c.

template <typename Container> flattened2d(const Container &c)	**Returns**: Constructs and returns a flattened2d that provides iterators that traverse the elements in all of the containers within Container c.

Figure B-67. *Précis: TLS:* flatten2d *example*

flatten2d - example

```cpp
#include <iostream>
#include <utility>
#include <vector>
#include <tbb/task_scheduler_init.h>
#include <tbb/enumerable_thread_specific.h>
#include <tbb/parallel_for.h>
#include <tbb/blocked_range.h>
// A VecType has a separate std::vector<int> per thread
typedef
  tbb::enumerable_thread_specific< std::vector<int> >
  VecType;

VecType MyVectors;
int k = 10000000; // made 10X larger to keep sample output short for the book

struct Func {
    void operator()(const tbb::blocked_range<int>& r) const {
        VecType::reference v = MyVectors.local();
        for (int i=r.begin(); i!=r.end(); ++i)
            if( i%k==0 )
                v.push_back(i);
    }
};

int main() {
    tbb::parallel_for(
tbb::blocked_range<int>(0, 100000000), Func());

    tbb::flattened2d<VecType> flat_view =
 tbb::flatten2d( MyVectors );

    for( tbb::flattened2d<VecType>::const_iterator
        i = flat_view.begin(); i != flat_view.end(); ++i)
        std::cout << *i << std::endl;

    return 0;
}
```

Sample output… will vary run to run and machine to machine!

```
0
10000000
20000000
50000000
60000000
30000000
80000000
40000000
70000000
90000000
```

Figure B-68.   *Précis: TLS: flatten2d example*

Timing

TBB supplies a platform independent, thread-aware, manner to get a high-resolution time stamp (TBB implementations seek to utilize the highest resolution timing available on any given platform). This was included in TBB to assist with debugging and tuning activities that are natural for any programmer to do when adding and tuning parallel code.

`tick_count` Class for reliably computing wall-clock time.

`#include <tbb/tick_count.h>`

A `tbb:tick_count` is an absolute timestamp. Two `tbb:tick_count` objects may be subtracted to compute a relative time `tbb:tick_count::interval_t`, which can be added, differenced, and converted to seconds. On Linux, you may need to add `-lrt` to the linker command when you use `tbb::tick_count` class.

```
#include <cstdio>
#include <unistd.h>
#include <tbb/tick_count.h>
volatile int foo = 4;
int main( int argc, char *argv[] ) {
  tbb::tick_count t0 = tbb::tick_count::now();
  while (foo--) sleep(1);
  tbb::tick_count t1 = tbb::tick_count::now();
  printf("resolution for timing on this platform is =\n%12.8f seconds\n",
    tbb::tick_count::resolution() );
  printf("time for action =\n%12.8f seconds\n", (t1-t0).seconds() );

}
```

Sample output… will vary run to run and machine to machine!

```
resolution for timing on this platform is =
  0.00000100 seconds
time for action =
  4.00328800 seconds
```

Class	vlalue_type	Implicit lock on **pair**
const_accessor	const std::pair< const Key, T>	Reader lock – permits shared access with other readers.
accessor	std::pair< const Key, T>	Writer lock – permits exclusive access by a thread. Blocks access by other threads.

tbb:tick_count Member	Description
static tick count **now**()	Current wall clock timestamp.
static double **resolution**()	The resolution of the clock in seconds.
tick_count::interval_t **operator-**(const tick_count& t1, const tick_count& t0)	Relative time that t1 occurred after t0.

tbb::interval_t Member	Description
interval_t()	Constructs interval_t representing zero time duration.
interval_t(double sec)	Constructs interval_t representing specified number of seconds.
double **seconds**() const	**Returns:** Time interval measured in seconds.
operations: += -= + -	Addition or differences of interval_t values.

Figure B-69. *Précis: Timing:* `tick_count class`

Task Groups: Use of the Task Stealing Scheduler

This section ("Task Groups") is a summary of the supported high-level APIs to the TBB task scheduler, while the next section ("Task Scheduler") covers the more numerous low-level APIs. The high-level APIs let us easily create groups of potentially parallel tasks from functors or lambda expressions (Preface, Chapters 1-3). Collectively, the TBB task scheduler forms the basis of all TBB algorithms (Chapters 2 and 16) and TBB flow graph (Chapters 3 and 17–19).

Functor arguments for the various methods in this section should supply at a minimum, a copy constructor, a destructor, and have an evaluate functor.

`task_group` and `structured_task_group` Classes `#include <tbb/task_group.h>`	
Member	**Description**
`template<typename Func> void run(` `Func&& f )`	Spawns a task to compute `f()` and returns immediately.
`template<typename Func> void run (` `task_handle<Func>& handle );`	Spawns a task to compute `handle()` and returns immediately.
`template<typename Func> task_group_status` `run_and_wait( const Func& f )`	Equivalent to `{run(f); return wait();},` but guarantees that `f()` runs on the current thread. **Note:** Template method `run_and_wait` is intended to be more efficient than separate calls to `run` and `wait`.
`template<typename Func> task_group_status` `run_and_wait( task_handle<Func>& handle );`	Equivalent to `{run(handle); return wait();},` but guarantees that `handle()` runs on the current thread. **Note:** Template method `run_and_wait` is intended to be more efficient than separate calls to `run` and `wait`.
`task_group_status wait()`	Waits for all tasks in the group to complete or be cancelled. **Returns**: The status of `task_group`:

<pre>enum task_group_status {
  not_complete, // Not cancelled and not all tasks in group have completed.
  complete,   // Not cancelled and all tasks in group have completed
  canceled   // Task group received cancellation request
};</pre>	

`bool is_canceling()`	**Returns**: True if this task group is cancelling its tasks.
`void cancel()`	Cancels all tasks in this `task_group`.
`tbb::is_current_task_group_canceling()` True if innermost task group executing on this thread is cancelling its tasks.	
A **structured_task_group** is like a `task_group`, but has only a subset of the functionality. It may permit performance optimizations in the future. The restrictions are: • Methods `run` and `run_and_wait` take only `task_handle` arguments, not general functors. Class `task_handle` exists to be used in conjunction with class `structured_task_group`. For sake of uniformity, class `task_group` also accepts `task_handle` arguments. • Methods `run` and `run_and_wait` do not copy their `task_handle` arguments. The caller must not destroy those arguments until after `wait` or `run_and_wait` returns. • Methods `run`, `run_and_wait`, `cancel`, and `wait` should be called only by the thread that created the `structured_task_group`. • A `task_handle` is created from a function or functor with the template function task_handle: `template<typename TFunc> task_handle<Func> make_task( TFunc&& f );` Method `wait` (or `run_and_wait`) should be called only once on a given instance of `structured_task_group`.	

Figure B-70. *Précis: Task Groups: [`structured_`]`task_group`*

```
task_group and structured_task_group Classes
```

```
#include <stdio.h>
#include <tbb/task_group.h>
#define FIB(X) printf("Fib(%d) = %d\n",X,Fib(X))
int Fib(int n) {
  if( n<2 ) {
    return n;
  } else {
    int x, y;
    tbb::task_group g;
    g.run([&]{x=Fib(n-1);}); // spawn a task
    g.run([&]{y=Fib(n-2);}); // spawn another task
    g.wait();                // wait for both tasks to complete
    return x+y;
  }
}
int main( int argc, char *argv[] ) {
  FIB(1);
  FIB(2);
  FIB(3);
  FIB(11);
  FIB(20);
  printf(tbb::is_current_task_group_canceling() ?
    "Cancelling\n" : "Not cancelling.\n");
}
```

```
Fib(1) = 1
Fib(2) = 1
Fib(3) = 2
Fib(11) = 89
Fib(20) = 6765
Not cancelling.
```

Figure B-71. *Précis: Task Groups: task_group example*

Task Scheduler: Fine Control of the Task Stealing Scheduler

This section ("Task Scheduler") is a summary of the (numerous) supported low-level APIs to the TBB task scheduler, while the prior section ("Task Groups") covers the high-level APIs. The key four concepts in this section are the task scheduler, task arenas, tasks, and floating-point controls. The low-level interfaces permit more detailed control, such as control over exception propagation (Chapter 15), priorities (Chapter 4), isolation (Chapter 12), and affinity (Chapters 13 and 20). Collectively, the TBB task scheduler forms the basis of all TBB algorithms (Chapters 2 and 16) and TBB flow graph (Chapters 3 and 17–19).

Task Scheduler (task_scheduler_init) Class
#include <tbb/task_scheduler_init.h>

Constructor

```
class task_scheduler_init(
  int max_threads=automatic
[ , stack_size_type thread_stack_size ]
)
```

Class **tbb::task_scheduler_init** explicitly represents a thread's interest in task scheduling services. TBB automatically creates a task scheduler the first time that a thread uses task scheduling services and destroys it when the last such thread exits, which means that any explicit call to intialize to non-default settings must happen in a thread before any task scheduling service is invoked indirectly. Also, it means that explicit initialization should only be used for debugging, or when a special need to control initialization exists.

The parameter max_threads can be a positive integer to request that up to max_threads-1 worker threads work on behalf   of   the   calling   thread   at   any   one   time.   Two   special   values   can   be   used   as   well: tbb::task_scheduler_init::automatic has TBB automatically determine max_threads based on hardware configuration, this is the default for max_threads; tbb::ask_scheduler_init::deferred defers activation until either a call to method initalize() or an automatic initialization triggered by use of a TBB algorithm that uses the TBB scheduler.

It is meaningful for the parameter max_threads to differ for different calling threads. For example, if thread A specifies max_threads=4 and thread B specifies max_threads=12, then A is limited to having 4 workers, but B can have up to 11 workers. Since workers may be shared between A and B, the total number of worker threads created by the scheduler could be 11.

The optional parameter thread_stack_size specifies the stack size of each worker thread. A value of 0 specifies use of a default stack size. The first active task_scheduler_init establishes the stack size for all worker threads.

Initialization member

```
void initialize( int max_threads=automatic )
```
Activates a task_scheduler_init which has not been previoulsy activated.

Destruction

```
~task_scheduler_init
```
If the task_scheduler_init is inactive, nothing happens. Otherwise, the task_scheduler_init is deactivated as follows. If the thread has no other active task_scheduler_init objects, the thread deallocates internal thread-specific resources required for scheduling task objects. If no existing thread has any active task_scheduler_init objects, then the internal worker threads are terminated.

Deactivation

```
void terminate()
```
Deactivates the task_scheduler_init without destroying it. The description of the destructor specifies what deactivation entails.

Inquiries

```
static int default_num_threads()
```
Returns: One more than the number of worker threads that task_scheduler_init creates by default.

```
bool is_active() const
```
Returns: true if the task_scheduler_init item has been initialized, otherwise false.

Figure B-72. *Précis: Task Scheduler:* task_scheduler_init class

---

Task Scheduler (task_scheduler_init) Class

```
#include <tbb/task_scheduler_init.h>

#define XYZZY(FLAG) \
    printf(FLAG " default threads = %d; ", \
            tbb::task_scheduler_init::default_num_threads()); \
    printf(my_init.is_active()?"TBB activate\n":"TBB not active\n");

int main( int argc, char *argv[] ) {
  {
    tbb::task_scheduler_init
      my_init(tbb::task_scheduler_init::deferred);
    XYZZY("AA");   my_init.initialize(10);
    XYZZY("AB");
  }
  {
    tbb::task_scheduler_init my_init;
    XYZZY("BB");
    // if this is used:
    // my_init.initialize(24);
    // the runtime will fault, printing something like this:
    // Assertion !my_scheduler failed...
    // Detailed description: task_scheduler_init already initialized
    // Abort trap: 6
    XYZZY("BC");   my_init.terminate();
    XYZZY("BD");   my_init.initialize(90);
    XYZZY("BE");
  }
}
```
```
AA default threads = 4; TBB not active
AB default threads = 4; TBB activate
BB default threads = 4; TBB activate
BC default threads = 4; TBB activate
BD default threads = 4; TBB not active
BE default threads = 4; TBB activate
```

Figure B-73. *Précis: Task Scheduler: task_scheduler_init example*

Task Arenas (`task_arena`) Class
`#include <tbb/task_arena.h>`

A `task_arena` class represents a place where threads may share and execute tasks.

The number of threads that may simultaneously execute tasks in a task_arena is limited by its concurrency level. The concurrency level affects only that arena, and is not affected by previous task_scheduler_init specifications. The total number of threads that the scheduler may use is limited by whichever is largest: the default number of threads for the machine or the value specified for the first task scheduler initialization. Therefore the number of threads assigned to a task_arena will never exceed that maximum value, regardless of its concurrency level. Moreover, a task_arena might not get the specified number of threads even if it is lower than the allowed maximum. A `task_arena` instance also holds a reference to such internal representation, but does not fully control its lifetime. The internal representation cannot be destroyed while it contains tasks or other threads reference it.

The `task_arena` constructors do not create an internal arena object. It may already exist in case of the "attaching" constructor, otherwise it is created by explicit call to task_arena::initialize or lazily on first use.

The namespace `this_task_arena` contains global functions for interaction with the arena (either explicit `task_arena` or implicit arena object) currently used by the calling thread.

`static const int automatic`	When passed as max_concurrency to the constructor, arena concurrency will be automatically set based on the hardware configuration.
`static const int not_initialized`	When returned by a method or function, indicates that there is no active arena or that the arena object has not yet been initialized.

Constructors, Destructor

Member	Description

`task_arena(`
  `int max_concurrency = automatic,`
  `unsigned reserved_for_masters = 1)`
	Creates a task_arena with a certain concurrency limit (`max_concurrency`). Some portion of the limit can be reserved for application threads with reserved_for_masters. The amount for reservation cannot exceed the limit.
	If max_concurrency and reserved_for_masters are explicitly set to be equal and greater than 1, Intel TBB worker threads will never join the arena. As a result, the execution guarantee for enqueued tasks is not valid in such arena. Do not use `task_arena::enqueue()` and `task::enqueue()` with an arena set to have no worker threads.

`task_arena(const task_arena&)`	Copies settings from another `task_arena` instance.
`explicit task_arena(task_arena::attach)`	Creates an instance of task_arena that is connected to the internal arena currently used by the calling thread. If no such arena exists yet, creates a `task_arena` with default parameters. Unlike other constructors, this one automatically initializes the new task_arena when connecting to an already existing arena.

`void initialize()`
 	
`void initialize(`
  `int max_concurrency,`
  `unsigned reserved_for_masters = 1)`
 	
`void initialize(task_arena::attach)`
	Performs actual initialization of internal arena representation. If arguments are specified, they override previous arena parameters. If an instance of class task_arena::attach is specified as the argument, and there exists an internal arena currently used by the calling thread, the method ignores arena parameters and connects `task_arena` to that internal arena. The method has no effect when called for an already initialized arena. After the call to initialize, the arena parameters are fixed and cannot be changed.

`void terminate()`	Removes the reference to the internal arena representation without destroying the `task_arena` object, which can then be re-used. Not thread safe with respect to concurrent invocations of other methods.
`~task_arena()`	Removes the reference to the internal arena representation, and destroys the `task_arena` instance. Not thread safe with respect to concurrent invocations of other methods.

Figure B-74. *Précis: Task Scheduler:* `task_arena class`

Query, Enqueue, Execute	
Member	Description
bool **is_active**() const	Returns true if the arena has been initialized, false otherwise.
int **max_concurrency**() const	Returns the concurrency level of the arena. Does not require the arena to be initialized and does not perform initialization.
template<F> void **enqueue**(F&& f)	Enqueues a task into the arena to process the specified functor (which is copied or moved into the task), and immediately returns. The method does not require the calling thread to join the arena; i.e., any number of threads outside of the arena can submit work to it without blocking. There is no guarantee that tasks enqueued into an arena execute concurrently with respect to any other tasks there. An exception thrown and not caught in the functor results in undefined behavior.
template<F> void **enqueue**(F&& f, priority_t)	Enqueues a task with specified task priority. Is similar to enqueue(f) in all other ways.
template<F> auto **execute**(F&) -> decltype(f()) template<F> auto **execute**(const F&) -> decltype(f())	Executes the specified functor in the arena. The function returns the value returned by the functor. The calling thread joins the arena if possible, and executes the functor. Upon return it restores the previous task scheduler state and floating-point settings. If joining the arena is not possible, the call wraps the functor into a task, enqueues it into the arena, waits using an OS kernel synchronization object for another opportunity to join, and finishes after the task completion. An exception thrown in the functor will be captured and re-thrown from execute. If exact exception propagation is unavailable or disabled, the exception will be wrapped into tbb::captured_exception even for the same thread.

Figure B-74. (*continued*)

Information on the members of the namespace `this_task_arena`.	
`int current_thread_index()`	Returns the thread index in a task arena currently used by the calling thread, or `task_arena::not_initialized` if the thread has not yet initialized the task scheduler. A thread index is an integer number between 0 and the arena concurrency level. Thread indexes are assigned to both application (master) threads and worker threads on joining an arena and are kept until exiting the arena. Indexes of threads that share an arena are unique - i.e., no two threads within the arena may have the same index at the same time - but not necessarily consecutive. Since a thread may exit the arena at any time if it does not execute a task, the index of a thread may change between any two tasks, even those belonging to the same task group or algorithm. Threads that use different arenas may have the same current index value. Joining a nested arena in `execute()` may change current index value while preserving the index in the outer arena which will be restored on return. This method can be used, for example, by the preview extension of `task_scheduler_observer` to pin threads entering an arena to specific hardware.
`int max_concurrency()`	Returns the concurrency level of the task arena currently used by the calling thread. If the thread has not yet initialized the task scheduler, returns the concurrency level determined automatically for the hardware configuration.
`template<F> auto isolate(F&) -> decltype(f())` `template<F> auto isolate(const F&) -> decltype(f())`	Runs the specified functor in isolation by restricting the calling thread to process only tasks scheduled in the scope of the functor (also called the isolation region). The function returns the value returned by the functor. The object returned by the functor cannot be a reference. `std::reference_wrapper` can be used instead. Asynchronous parallel constructs such as a flow graph or a task_group should be used with care within an isolated region. For `graph::wait_for_all` or `task_group::wait` executed in isolation, tasks scheduled by calling try_put for a flow graph node or by `task_group::run` are only accessible if scheduled in the same isolation region or in a task previously spawned in that region. Otherwise, performance issues and even deadlocks are possible.

Figure B-75. *Précis: Task Scheduler:* `this_task_arena` *members*

Task (task) Class
#include <tbb/task.h>
Class task is the base class for tasks. class empty_task is a subclass of task that represents doing nothing. It is useful as a continuation of a parent task when the continuation should do nothing except wait for its predecessors to complete.

Task Attributes

Each instance of task has associated task attributes, which are not directly visible but are important in understanding how task objects are used. In general, the allocation methods must be called before any of the tasks allocated are spawned. The exception to this rule is allocate_additional_child_of(t), which can be called even if task t is already running.

Attribute	Description
successor	Either null, or a pointer to another task whose refcount field will be decremented after the present task completes. Typically, the successor is the task that allocated the present task, or a task allocated as the continuation of that task. Methods of class task call the successor "parent" and its preceding task the "child", because this was a common use case. But the library has evolved such that a child-parent relationship is no longer required between the predecessor and successor.
refcount	The number of Tasks that have this as their parent. Increments and decrement of refcount are NOT atomic. In the early days of TBB, this might not have been a concern but it is now. In modern TBB, all routines, except allocate_additional_child_of, are made more efficient by assuming that they will only be used for setup prior to spawning. Since this is the normal usage model, we gain efficiency and everything will work well as long as we adhere to "first allocate, then spawn." Once running, additional additions shoud be done with allocate_additional_child_of.

Task Allocation

Always allocate memory for task objects using one of the special overloaded new operators. The allocation methods do not construct the task. Instead, they return a proxy object that can be used as an argument to an overloaded version of operator new provided by the library.

Member	Description
new(task::**allocate_root**(task_group_context& group)) T	Allocate a task of type *T* with the specified cancellation group. Use method spawn_root_and_wait to execute the task.
new(task::**allocate_root**()) T	Like new(task::allocate_root(task_group_context&)) except that cancellation group is the current innermost cancellation group.
new(x.**allocate_continuation**()) T	Allocates and constructs a task of type *T*, and transfers the *successor* from *x* to the new task. No reference counts change.
new(x.**allocate_child**()) T	Allocates a task with this as its *successor*. If using explicit continuation passing, then the continuation, not the *successor*, should call the allocation method, so that successor is set correctly. If the number of tasks is not a small fixed number, consider building a task_list of the predecessors first, and spawning them with a single call to task::spawn. If a task must spawn some predecessors before all are constructed, it should use task::allocate_additional_child_of(*this) instead, because that method atomically increments *refcount*, so that the additional predecessor is properly accounted. However, if doing so, the task must protect against premature zeroing of *refcount* by using a blocking-style task pattern.

new(
  task::**allocate_additional_child_of**(
    y)
) T
	Allocates a task as a predecessor of another task *y*. Task y may be already running or have other predecessors running. Because *y* may already have running predecessors, the increment of *y.refcount* is atomic (unlike the other allocation methods, where the increment is not atomic). When adding a predecessor to a task with other predecessors running, it is up to the programmer to ensure that the successor's *refcount* does not prematurely reach 0 and trigger execution of the successor before the new predecessor is added.

Figure B-76. *Précis: Task Scheduler: task class*

Task Destruction (Explicit)

Usually, a task is automatically destroyed by the scheduler after its method execute returns. But sometimes task objects are used idiomatically (such as for reference counting) without ever running `execute`. Such tasks should be disposed with method `destroy`.

Member	Description
`static void ` **`destroy`** ` ( task& victim )`	Calls destructor and deallocates memory for victim. If victim.parent is not null, atomically decrements victim.parent->refcount. The parent is not put into the ready pool if its refcount becomes zero. The figure below summarizes the state transition.

Task Recycling

It is often more efficient to recycle a task object rather than reallocate one from scratch. Often the parent can become the continuation, or one of the predecessors. Overlap rule: A recycled task q must not be put in jeopardy of having `t.execute()` rerun while the previous invocation of `t.execute()` is still running. The debug version of the library detects some violations of this rule. These `recycle_*` methods must be called only while method execute() is running

Member	Description
`void ` **`recycle_as_continuation`** `()`	The `refcount` for the recycled task should be set to n, where n is the number of predecessors of the continuation task. The caller must guarantee that the task's `refcount` does not become zero until after method `execute()` returns, otherwise the overlap rule is broken. If the guarantee is not possible, use method `recycle_as_safe_continuation()` instead, and set the `refcount` to $n+1$. The race can occur for a task t when: t.`execute()` recycles t as a continuation. The continuation has predecessors that all complete before t.`execute()` returns. Hence the recycled t will be implicitly respawned with the original t.`execute()` still running, which breaks the overlap rule. Patterns that use `recycle_as_continuation()` typically avoid the race by making t.`execute()` return a pointer to one of the predecessors instead of explicitly spawning that predecessor. The scheduler implicitly spawns that predecessor after t.`execute()` returns, thus guaranteeing that the recycled t does not rerun prematurely. **Effects**: Causes `this` to not be destroyed when method `execute()` returns.
`void ` **`recycle_as_safe_continuation`** `()`	The `refcount` for the recycled task should be set to $n+1$, where n is the number of predecessors of the continuation task. The additional +1 represents the task to be recycled. **Effects**: Causes `this` to not be destroyed when method `execute()` returns. This method avoids the race discussed for recycle_as_continuation because the additional +1 in the `refcount` prevents the continuation from executing until the original invocation of `execute()` completes.
`void ` **`recycle_as_child_of`** `(` `  task& new_successor )`	**Effects**: Causes `this` to become a predecessor of `new_successor`, and not be destroyed when method `execute()` returns.

Task Synchronization

Spawning a task t either causes the calling thread to invoke `t.execute()`, or causes t to be put into the ready pool. Any thread participating in task scheduling may then acquire the task and invoke `t.execute()`.

Some calls distinguish between spawning root tasks and non-root tasks. A root task is one that was created using method `allocate_root`.

Note: A task should not spawn any predecessor task until it has called method `set_ref_count` to indicate both the number of predecessors and whether it intends to use one of the "`wait_for_all`" methods.

Figure B-76. (*continued*)

Member	Description
`void ` **`set_ref_count`**`( int count )`	**Requirements**: *count>=0*. If the intent is to subsequently spawn *n* predecessors and wait, then *count* should be *n+1*. Otherwise count should be *n*. **Effects**: Sets the *refcount* attribute to `count`.
`int ` **`add_ref_count`**`( int count )`	Atomically adds `count` to *refcount* attribute. **Returns**: New value of *refcount* attribute.
`void ` **`increment_ref_count`**`();`	Atomically increments *refcount* attribute.
`int ` **`decrement_ref_count`**`();`	Atomically decrements *refcount* attribute. **Returns**: New value of *refcount* attribute.
`void ` **`wait_for_all`**`()`	Executes tasks in ready pool until *refcount* is 1. Afterwards, leaves *refcount=1* if the task's `task_group_context` specifies `concurrent_wait`, otherwise sets *refcount* to 0. Also, `wait_for_all()` automatically resets the cancellation state of the `task_group_context` implicitly associated with the task , when all of the following conditions hold: • The task was allocated without specifying a context. • The calling thread is a user-created thread, not an Intel® Threading Building Blocks worker thread. • It is the outermost call to `wait_for_all()` by the thread.
`static void ` **`spawn`**`( task& t )`	Puts task *t* into the ready pool and immediately returns. If the *successor* of t is not null, then `set_ref_count` must be called on that *successor* before spawning any child tasks, because once the child tasks commence, their completion will cause *successor.refcount* to be decremented asynchronously. The debug version of the library often detects when a required call to `set_ref_count` is not made, or is made too late.
`static void ` **`spawn`**`( task_list& list )`	Equivalent to executing spawn on each task in *list* and clearing *list*, but may be more efficient. If *list* is empty, there is no effect.
`void ` **`spawn_and_wait_for_all`**`( task& t )`	Similar to `{spawn(t); wait_for_all();}`, but often more efficient. Furthermore, it guarantees that *task* is executed by the current thread. This constraint can sometimes simplify synchronization. The figure below illustrates the state transitions. It is similar to the figure above, with task *t* being the *n*th task.
`void ` **`spawn_and_wait_for_all`**`( task_list& list )`	Similar to `{spawn(list); wait_for_all();}`, but often more efficient.
`static void ` **`spawn_root_and_wait`**`( task& root )`	Sets *parent* attribute of *root* to an undefined value and execute root as described in Section Processing of execute(). Destroys *root* afterwards unless *root* was recycled.
`static void ` **`spawn_root_and_wait`**`( task_list& root_list )`	For each `task` object *t* in root_list, performs `spawn_root_and_wait(t)`, possibly in parallel. Section static void spawn_root_and_wait(task& root) describes the actions of `spawn_root_and_wait(t)`.

Figure B-76. (*continued*)

`static void` **`enqueue`** `( task& )`	The task is scheduled for eventual execution by a worker thread even if no thread ever explicitly waits for the task to complete. If the total number of worker threads is zero, a special additional worker thread is created to execute enqueued tasks. Enqueued tasks are processed in roughly, but not precisely, first-come first-serve order. Using enqueued tasks for recursive parallelism can cause high memory usage, because the recursion will expand in a breadth-first manner. Use ordinary spawning for recursive parallelism. Explicitly waiting on an enqueued task should be avoided, because other enqueued tasks from unrelated parts of the program might have to be processed first. The recommended pattern for using an enqueued task is to have it asynchronously signal its completion, for example, by posting a message back to the thread that enqueued it.

Task Context

The methods detailed in the following table expose relationships between task objects, and between task objects and the underlying physical threads.

Member	Description
`static task&` **`self`**`()`	**Returns**: Reference to innermost *task* that the calling thread is running. A task is considered running if its methods `execute()`, `note_affinity()`, or destructor are running. If the calling thread is a user-created thread that is not running any task, `self()` returns a reference to an implicit dummy task associated with the thread.
`task*` **`parent`**`() const`	**Returns**: Value of the attribute *successor*. The result is an undefined value if the task was allocated by `allocate_root` and is currently running under control of `spawn_root_and_wait`.
`void` **`set_parent`**`(task* p)`	**Requirements**: Both tasks must be in the same task group except for p == NULL. For example, for `task t`, `t.group() == p->group()` **Effects**: Sets parent task pointer to specified value p.
`bool` **`is_stolen_task`**`() const`	**Returns**: *true* if task is running on a thread different than the thread that spawned it. **Note** Tasks enqueued with `task::enqueue()` are never reported as stolen.
`task_group_context*` **`group`**`()`	**Returns**: Descriptor of the task group, which this task belongs to.
`void` **`change_group`**`(` `  task_group_context& ctx )`	Moves the task from its current task group into the one specified by the `ctx` argument.

Task Cancellation

A task is a quantum of work that is cancelled or executes to completion. A cancelled task skips its method `execute()` if that method has not yet started. Otherwise cancellation has no direct effect on the task. A task can poll `task::is_cancelled()` to see if cancellation was requested after it started running.

Member	Description
`bool` **`cancel_group_execution`**`()`	Requests cancellation of all tasks in its group and its subordinate groups. **Returns**: False if the task's group already received a cancellation request; true otherwise.
`bool` **`is_cancelled`**`() const`	**Returns**: True if task's group has received a cancellation request; false otherwise.

Figure B-76. (*continued*)

Task Priorities

Priority levels can be assigned to individual tasks or task groups. The library supports three levels {low, normal, high} and two kinds of priority: (1) Static priority for enqueued tasks, (2) Dynamic priority for task groups.

The former is specified by an optional argument of the `task::enqueue()` method, affects a specific task only, and cannot be changed afterwards. Tasks with higher priority are dequeued before tasks with lower priorities. The latter affects all the tasks in a group and can be changed at any time either via the associated `task_group_context` object or via any task belonging to the group. The priority-related methods, in `task_group_context`, are described in Section `task_group_context`. The task scheduler tracks the highest priority of ready tasks (both enqueued and spawned), and postpones execution of tasks with lower priority until all higher priority task are executed. By default, all tasks and task groups are created with normal priority.

Member	Description
`void enqueue ( task& t, priority_t p ) const`	Enqueues task t at the priority level p. **Note** The priority of an enqueued task does not affect priority of the task group, from the scope of which `task::enqueue()` is invoked. That is, the group, which the task returned by `task::self()` method belongs to.
`void set_group_priority ( priority_t )`	Changes priority of the task group, which this task belongs to.
`priority_t group_priority () const`	**Returns**: Priority of the task group, which this task belongs to.

Task Affinity

These methods enable optimizing for cache affinity. They enable you to hint that a later task should run on the same thread as another task that was executed earlier.

Member	Description
`affinity_id`	The type `task::affinity_id` is an implementation-defined unsigned integral type. A value of 0 indicates no affinity. Other values represent affinity to a particular thread. Do not assume anything about non-zero values. The mapping of non-zero values to threads is internal to the TBB library implementation.
`virtual void note_affinity ( affinity_id id )`	The task scheduler invokes `note_affinity` before invoking `execute()` when: • The task has no affinity, but will execute on a thread different than the one that spawned it. • The task has affinity, but will execute on a thread different than the one specified by the affinity. You can override this method to record the id, so that it can be used as the argument to `set_affinity(id)` for a later task. **Effects**: The default definition has no effect.
`set_affinity ( affinity_id id )`	Sets affinity of this task to id. The id should be either 0 or obtained from `note_affinity`.
`affinity_id affinity() const`	**Returns**: Affinity of this task as set by set_affinity.

Task List (class task_list)

List of task objects.

Member `tbb::task::task_list::`	Description
`task_list()`	Constructs an empty list.
`~task_list()`	Destroys the list. Does not destroy the task objects.
`bool empty() const`	**Returns**: True if list is empty; false otherwise.
`push_back( task& task )`	Inserts a reference to *task* at back of the list.
`task& task pop_front()`	Removes a *task* reference from front of list. **Returns**: The reference that was removed.
`void clear()`	Removes all *task* references from the list. Does not destroy the task objects.

Figure B-76. (*continued*)

Task Debugging	
These methods are useful for debugging. They may change in future implementations.	
Member	**Description**
`state_type` **`state`**`() const`	Current state of the task. The table below describes valid states. Any other value is the result of memory corruption, such as using a task whose memory has been deallocated.

Value	Description
`allocated`	Task is freshly allocated or recycled.
`ready`	Task is in ready pool, or is in process of being transferred to/from there.
`executing`	Task is running, and will be destroyed after method execute() returns.
`freed`	Task is on internal free list, or is in process of being transferred to/from there.
`reexecute`	Task is running, and will be respawned after method execute() returns.

`int` **`ref_count`**`() const`	The value of the attribute refcount.

Figure B-76. (*continued*)

Floating-Point Settings

For applications that need to control CPU-specific settings for floating-point computations, there are two ways to propagate desired settings to tasks executed by the TBB task scheduler:

- When a task_arena or the task scheduler for a given application thread is initialized, it captures the current floating-point settings of the thread.

- The class task_group_context has a method to capture the current floating-point settings.

By default, worker threads use the floating-point settings captured during initialization of an application thread's implicit arena or explicit task_arena. These settings are applied to all parallel computations within the task_arena or started by the application thread, until that thread terminates its task scheduler instance. If the thread later re-initializes the task scheduler, new settings are captured.

For finer control over floating point behavior, a thread may capture the current settings in a task group context. It can be done at context creation if a special flag is passed to the constructor:

```
task_group_context ctx(
   task_group_context::isolated,
   task_group_context::default_traits |
   task_group_context::fp_settings );
```

or by a call to the method `capture_fp_settings`:

```
task_group_context ctx;
ctx.capture_fp_settings();
```

The task group context can then be passed to most Intel TBB parallel algorithms (including `tbb::flow::graph`) to ensure that all tasks related to this algorithm use the specified floating-point settings. It is possible to execute parallel algorithms with different floating-point settings captured to separate contexts, even at the same time.

Floating-point settings captured to a task group context prevail over the settings captured during task scheduler initialization. Thus, if a context is passed to a parallel algorithm then floating-point settings captured to the context are used. Otherwise, if floating-point settings are not captured to the context, or a context is not explicitly specified, then the settings captured during task scheduler initialization are used.

In a nested call to a parallel algorithm not using a task group context with explicitly captured floating-point settings, the settings from the outer level are used. If neither of the outer level contexts captured floating-point settings, then the settings captured during task scheduler initialization are used.

It is guaranteed that

- Floating-point settings captured to a task group context or at the moment of task scheduler initialization are applied to all tasks executed by the task scheduler.

- An invocation of an Intel TBB parallel algorithm does not visibly modify the floating-point settings of the calling thread, even if the algorithm is executed with different settings.

These guarantees *only* apply in the following conditions:

- The user code inside a task either does not change floating-point settings, or any modifications are reverse by restoring the previous settings before the end of the task.

- Intel TBB task scheduler observers are not used to set or modify floating-point settings.

Otherwise, the stated guarantees are not valid and the behavior related to floating-point settings is undefined.

Exceptions

Chapter 15 covers exception handling; this section of this Appendix is a terse review of the exceptions which can be thrown by TBB components, and the subclass of `std::exception` called `tbb::tbb_exception`, which TBB uses to propagate exceptions between TBB tasks to make exception handling seamless within a program using TBB.

TBB propagates exceptions along logical paths in a tree of tasks. Because these paths cross between thread stacks, support for moving an exception between stacks is necessary.

When an exception is thrown out of a task, it is caught inside the Intel TBB runtime and handled as follows:

1. If the cancellation group for the task has already been canceled, the exception is ignored.

2. Otherwise, the exception is captured and the group is canceled.

3. The captured exception is rethrown from the root of the cancellation group after all tasks in the group have completed or have been successfully canceled.

An exact exception is captured in modern versions of TBB (built with compilers with C++11 support). When supporting non-C++11 compilers, TBB has backward compatibility support via `tbb::captured_exception` to approximate the original exception, which is no longer relevant and therefore not covered in this book.

Exceptions thrown within TBB components `#include <tbb/tbb_exception.h>`	
Exceptions name...	Thrown when...
`bad_last_alloc`	1. A pop operation on a `concurrent_queue` or `concurrent_bounded_queue` corresponds to a push that threw an exception. 2. An operation on a `concurrent_vector` cannot be performed because a prior operation threw an exception.
`improper_lock`	A thread attempts to lock a `critical_section` or `reader_writer_lock` that it has already locked.
`invalid_multiple_scheduling`	A `task_group` or `structured_task_group` attempts to run a `task_handle` twice.
`missing_wait`	A `task_group` or `structured_task_group` is destroyed before method `wait()` is invoked.
`user_abort`	A push or pop operation on a `concurrent_bounded_queue` was aborted by the user.

Figure B-77. *Précis: Exceptions that can be thrown by TBB*

Exception handling example

```
#include <tbb/tbb_exception.h>
#include <tbb/parallel_for.h>
#include <vector>
#include <iostream>

std::vector<int> Data;

struct Update {
  void operator()( const tbb::blocked_range<int>& r ) const {
    for( int i=r.begin(); i!=r.end(); ++i )
      Data.at(i) += 1;
  }
};

int main( int argc, char *argv[] ) {
  int vecsize = 1000;
  int vecwalk = (argc > 1) ? atoi(argv[1]) : vecsize;
  Data.resize(vecsize);
  printf("Vector of size %d being traversed up to element %d\n",
    vecsize,vecwalk);
  try {
    tbb::parallel_for( tbb::blocked_range<int>(0, vecwalk), Update());
  } catch( std::out_of_range& ex ) {
    std::cout << "Exception caught was out_of_range: " <<
      ex.what() << std::endl;
    exit(0);
  }
  printf("No exception detected.\n");
  return 0;
}
```
```
$ ./example 1000
Vector of size 1000 being traversed up to element 1000
No exception detected.
$ ./example 1001
Vector of size 1000 being traversed up to element 1001
Exception caught was out_of_range: vector
```

Figure B-78. *Précis: Exceptions: Exception handling example*

---

tbb_exception and movable_exception classes

#include <tbb/tbb_exception.h>

In a parallel environment, exceptions sometimes have to be propagated across threads. Class **tbb::tbb_exception** subclasses **std::exception** add support for such propagation. Class **tbb::movable_exception** provides a convenient way to implement a subclass of tbb_exception that propagates arbitrary copy-constructible data.

```
namespace tbb {
  class tbb_exception: public std::exception {
    virtual tbb_exception* move() = 0;
    virtual void destroy() throw() = 0;
    virtual void throw_self() = 0;
    virtual const char* name() throw() = 0;
    virtual const char* what() throw() = 0;
  };
}
```

```
Derived classes should define the abstract virtual methods as follows:
```
- **move**() should create a pointer to a copy of the exception that can outlive the original. It may move the contents of the original.
- **destroy**() should destroy a copy created by move().
- **throw_self**() should throw *this.
- **name**() typically returns the RTTI name of the originally intercepted exception.
- **what**() returns a null-terminated string describing the exception.

Members for movable exception	Description
movable_exception(const ExceptionData& src)	Construct movable_exception containing copy of src.
ExceptionData& data() **throw**()	**Returns**: Reference to contained data.
const ExceptionData& **data**() const throw()	**Returns**: const reference to contained data.

Figure B-79. *Précis: Exceptions:* tbb_exception *and* movable_exception *classes*

Threads

TBB supports a portable "thread" API which is nothing more than a wrapper for whatever native threads a platform supports. This predates the existence of std::thread in C++, and offers no advantage over std::thread.

Several mentions are made of the evils of oversubscription in this book, and a short mention in the Preface is made to the virtues of careful oversubscription. This is because TBB is designed to support tasks for computationally intensive code. It is important to note that concurrency may be used effectively to hide latency of operations such as I/O. TBB tasks are a poor place to put I/O, because TBB does not preempt threads that are stalled for I/O – that is a function already supplied by modern operating systems. For this reason, TBB did add a portable API for adding additional threads for work which is not computationally intensive and which would benefit from oversubscription. The TBB developers were among those who lobbied for the addition of this capability into C++, which happened in the C++11 standard.

For a related discussion of controlling the number of threads used by TBB, we recommend reading Chapter 11.Here are a few notes about TBB's implementation of `std::thread`, for support of legacy TBB applications. We advise the use of the standard C++11 `std::thread` in all new code.

Differences between C++11 and TBB Thread Classes	
Both named `std::thread` – depends on which `#include` is used	
C++11 `std::thread`	**TBB Threads**
`#include <thread>`	`#include <tbb/compat/thread.h>`

`template<class Rep, class Period>`
`  std::this_thread::sleep_for(`
`    const std::chrono::duration`
`    <Rep, Period>& rel_time)`
	`std::this_thread::sleep_for(`
	`  const tbb::tick_count::interval_t& )`

`std::thread::id` can be hashed with `std::hash` template class.	`std::thread::id` can be hashed with `tbb::tbb_hash_compare` and `tbb::tbb_hash` template classes.
`rvalue` reference parameters	Parameter changed to plain value, or function removed, as appropriate.
constructor for `std::thread` takes arbitrary number of arguments.	constructor for `std::thread` takes 0-3 arguments.
destructor for `std::thread` calls `terminate()`, if the thread is `joinable()`.	destructor for `std::thread` calls `detach()`, if the thread is `joinable()`.

Figure B-80. *Précis: Threads: comparison of C++11 and TBB Thread Classes*

Parallel STL

Chapter 4 discusses Parallel STL; this section of this Appendix summarizes Parallel STL.

Since Parallel STL is an emerging part of C++17, implementations are relatively new and optimized versions are relatively new as we are finishing this book. Intel has produced an implementation of Parallel STL that is available as a part of Intel Parallel Studio XE and Intel System Studio, and is included with the binary distributions of TBB.

The Parallel STL available with TBB already includes support for Parallel STL that includes C++17 as well as features likely to make it into C++2x (specifically the unsequenced execution policy specified in C++ committee's Parallelism Technical Specification (TS) version 2 dated February 2018). Parallel STL offers efficient support for both parallel and vectorized execution of algorithms. For sequential execution, it relies on an available implementation of the C++ standard library. As time passes, and C++2x takes shape, Parallel STL support will be adjusted and expanded as needed.

As we go to publication with this book, Intel has been maintaining source code for Parallel STL as open source on github (`https://github.com/intel/parallelstl`), and

Parallel STL is being openly discussed for possible inclusion in libstdc++ (gnu) and libc++ (LLVM).

For now, the optimized Parallel STL has us add #include <pstl/execution> to our code and then add a subset of the following set of lines, depending on the type of STL algorithm we intend to use:

- **#include** <pstl/algorithm>

- **#include** <pstl/numeric>

- **#include** <pstl/memory>

```
// original code
#include <algorithm>
using namespace std;
sort(v.begin(), v.end());

// parallel execution policy of 'par' (parallel)
// can be added easily as follows:
#include <algorithm>
#include <pstl/execution>
#include <pstl/algorithm>  // because of std::sort
using namespace pstl::execution; // vs. std::execution
sort(par, v.begin(), v.end());
```

Figure B-81. *Précis: Parallel STL: simplistic code snippet*

Unsequenced ("unseq" and "par_unseq") is a strange beast: An unsequenced execution policy means that function calls are completely *unsequenced* with respect to each other – the key implication being that they *can* be interleaved on a single thread of execution. In all other situations in C++, the standard requires that they are indeterminately sequenced (cannot interleave on a single thread of execution). Because of that, code should not perform any other vectorization-unsafe operations. In general, any action in one invocation which sets up a synchronization need with a different invocation would be vectorization-unsafe, including memory alloc/free and mutex acquisition.

Parallel STL execution policies

Parallel STL extends the C++ STL by adding an execution policy argument to specify the degree of threading and vectorization for each algorithm.

Execution Policy, Class Name	Standard	Meaning	In simplistic terms	May use
seq, sequenced_policy	C++17	Sequential execution **required**.	serial (no parallelism)	n/a
unseq, unsequenced_policy	Proposed for C++2x	Unsequenced SIMD execution **permitted**. This policy requires that all functions provided are SIMD-safe.	vectorized	Compilers for SIMD
par, parallel_policy	C++17	Parallel execution by multiple threads **permitted**. This policy requires that all functions provided are concurrency safe.	threaded	TBB for tasks
par_unseq, parallel_unsequenced_policy	C++17	Combination of unseq and par. Policy requirements combine requirements of unseq and par.	threaded and vectorized	TBB for tasks Compilers for SIMD
vec is a promising proposal, but it is not yet supported (as of book publication) in Parallel STL with TBB because this proposed addition remains an area of active standards development				
vec, vector_policy	Proposed for C++2x	Similar to unseq, but allows for forward dependencies (with some distance).	vectorized	Compilers for SIMD

Figure B-82. *Précis: Parallel STL: execution policies*

Glossary

Abstraction: In the case of TBB, abstraction serves to separate the work into work appropriate for a programmer and work best left to a runtime. The goal of such an abstraction is to deliver scalable high performance on a variety of multicore and many-core systems, and even heterogeneous platforms, without requiring rewriting of the code. This careful division of responsibilities leaves the programmer to expose opportunities for parallelism, and the runtime responsible for mapping the opportunities to the hardware. Code written to the abstraction will be free of parameterization for cache sizes, number of cores, and even consistency of performance from processing unit to processing unit.

Affinity: The specification of methods to associate a particular software thread to a particular hardware thread usually with the objective of getting better or more predictable performance. Affinity specifications include the concept of being maximally spread apart to reduce contention(scatter), or to pack tightly (compact) to minimize distances for communication. OpenMP supports a rich set of affinity controls at various levels from abstract to full manual control. Fortran 2008 does not specify controls, but Intel reuses the OpenMP controls for "do concurrent." Threading Building Blocks (TBB) provides an abstract loop-to-loop affinity biasing capability.

Algorithm is a term that TBB has used in association with general, reusable solution to a common parallel programming problems. TBB, and this book, therefore uses the term 'parallel algorithm' when 'parallel pattern' would also be an appropriate description.

Amdahl's Law: Speedup is limited by the nonparallelizable serial portion of the work. A program where two thirds of the program can be run in parallel and one third of the original nonparallel program cannot be sped up by parallelism will find that speedup can only approach 3× and never exceed it assuming the same work is done. If scaling the problem size places more demands on the parallel portions of the program, then Amdahl's Law is not as bad as it may seem. See **Gustafson's law**.

© Intel Corporation 2019
M. Voss, R. Asenjo, J. Reinders, *Pro TBB*, https://doi.org/10.1007/978-1-4842-4398-5

Atom is touted as a hackable text editor for the twenty-first century, and it is open source. Rafa says "I also love emacs, but now Atom is winning this space on my Mac." Compare to the vi and emacs editors.

Atomic operation is an operation that is guaranteed to appear as if it occurred indivisibly without interference from other threads. For example, a processor might provide a memory increment operation. This operation needs to read a value from memory, increment it, and write it back to memory. An atomic increment guarantees that the final memory value is the same as would have occurred if no other operations on that memory location were allowed to happen between the read and the write.

Barrier: When a computation is broken into phases, it is often necessary to ensure that all threads complete all the work in one phase before any thread moves onto another phase. A barrier is a form of synchronization that ensures this: threads arriving at a barrier wait there until the last thread arrives, then all threads continue. A barrier can be implemented using atomic operations. For example, all threads might try to increment a shared variable, then block if the value of that variable does not equal the number of threads that need to synchronize at the barrier. The last thread to arrive can then reset the barrier to zero and release all the blocked threads.

Block can be used in two senses: (1) a state in which a thread is unable to proceed while it waits for some synchronization event and (2) a region of memory. The second meaning is also used in the sense of dividing a loop into a set of parallel tasks of a suitable granularity.

Cache is a part of memory system that stores copies of data temporarily in a fast memory so that future uses for that data can be handled more quickly than if the request had to be fetched again from a more distant storage. Caches are generally automatic and are designed to enhance programs with temporal locality and/or spatial locality. Caching systems in modern computers are usually multileveled.

Cache friendly is a characteristic of an application in which performance increases as problem size increases but then levels off as the bandwidth limit is reached.

Cache lines are the units in which data are retrieved and held by a cache, which in order to exploit spatial locality are generally larger than a word. The general trend is for increasing cache line sizes, which are generally large enough to hold at least two double-precision floating-point numbers, but unlikely to hold more than eight on any current design. Larger cache lines allow for more efficient bulk transfers from main memory but worsen certain issues including false sharing, which generally degrades performance.

Cache oblivious algorithm is any algorithm which performs well, without modification, on multiple machines memory organization such as different levels of cache having different sizes. Since such algorithms are carefully designed to exhibit compact memory reuse, it seems like it would have made more sense to call such algorithms cache agnostic. The term *oblivious* is a reference to the fact that such algorithms are not aware of the parameters of the memory subsystem, such as the cache sizes or relative speeds. This is in contrast with earlier efforts to carefully block algorithms for specific cache hardware.

Cache unfriendly is a characteristic of an application in which the memory footprint of the workloads needs to be optimal. In this case, we see that performance stays constant or increases as problem size reaches the optimal size and then performance decreases as problem size increases. In these workloads, there is a definite "sweet spot."

Clusters are a set of computers with distributed memory communicating over a high-speed interconnect. The individual computers are often called **nodes**. TBB is used at the node level within a cluster, although multiple nodes are commonly programmed with TBB and then connected (usually with MPI).

Communication: Any exchange of data or **synchronization** between software tasks or threads. Understanding that communication costs are often a limiting factor in scaling is a critical concept for parallel programming.

Composability: The ability to use two components in concert with each other without causing failure or unreasonable conflict (ideally no conflict). Limitations on composability, if they exist, are best when completely diagnosed at build time instead of requiring any testing. Composability problems that manifest only at runtime are the biggest problem with non-composable systems. Can refer to system features, programming models, or software components.

Concurrent means that things are logically happening simultaneously. Two tasks that are both logically active at some point in time are considered to be concurrent. This is in contrast with **parallel**.

Core: A separate subprocessor on a multicore processor. A core should be able to support (at least one) separate and divergent flow of control from other cores on the same processor.

Data parallelism is an approach to parallelism that attempts to be oriented around data rather than tasks. However, in reality, successful strategies in parallel algorithm development tend to focus on exploiting the parallelism in data, because data decomposition (generating tasks for different units of data) scales, but functional decomposition (generation of heterogeneous tasks for different functions) does not. See Amdahl's Law and Gustafson-Barsis' law.

Deadlock is a programming error. Deadlock occurs when at least two tasks wait for each other and each will not resume until the other task proceeds. This happens easily when code requires locking multiple mutexes. For example, each task can be holding a mutex required by the other task.

Deterministic refers to a deterministic algorithm which is an algorithm that behaves predictably. Given a particular input, a deterministic algorithm will always produce the same output. The definition of what is the "same" may be important due to limited precision in mathematical operations and the likelihood that optimizations including parallelization will rearrange the order of operations. These are often referred to as "rounding" differences, which result when the order of mathematical operations to compute the answer differ between the original program and the final concurrent program. Concurrency is not the only factor that can lead to **nondeterministic** algorithms but in practice it is often the cause. Use of programming models with sequential semantics and eliminating data races with proper access controls will generally eliminate the major effects of concurrency other than the "rounding" differences.

Distributed memory is memory that is physically located in separate computers. An indirect interface, such as message passing, is required to access memory on remote computers, while local memory can be accessed directly. Distributed memory is typically supported by clusters which, for purposes of this definition, we are considering to be a collection of computers. Since the memory on attached coprocessors also cannot typically be addressed directly from the host, it can be considered, for functional purposes, to be a form of distributed memory.

DSP (Digital Signal Processor) is a computing device designed specifically for digital signal processing tasks such as those associated with radio communications including filters, FFTs, and analog to digital conversions. The computational capabilities of DSPs alongside CPUs gave rise to some of the earliest examples of heterogeneous platforms and various programming languages extensions to control and interact with a DSP. OpenCL is a programming model that can help harness the compute aspects of DSPs. See also, heterogeneous platforms.

EFLOP/s (ExaFLOP/s) = 10^{18} Floating-Point Operations per second.

732

EFLOPs (ExaFLOPs) = 10^{18} Floating-Point Operations.

emacs is the best text editor in the world (according to James), and it is open source. Compare to the vi editor. "emacs" is the first package James installs on any computer that he uses.

Embarrassing parallelism is a description of an algorithm if it can be decomposed into a large number of independent tasks with little or no synchronization or communication required.

False sharing: Two separate tasks in two separate cores may write to separate locations in memory, but if those memory locations happened to be allocated in the same cache line, the cache coherence hardware will attempt to keep the cache lines coherent, resulting in extra interprocessor communication and reduced performance, even though the tasks are not actually sharing data.

Far memory: In a NUMA system, memory that has longer access times than the near memory. The view of which parts of memory are near vs. far depends on the process from which code is running. We also refer to this memory as nonlocal memory (in contrast to local memory) in Chapter 20.

Floating-point number is a format for numbers in computers characterized by trading a higher range for the numbers for a reduced precision by using the bits available for a number (mantissa) and a shift count (exponent) that places the point to the left or right of a fixed position. In contrast, fixed-point representations lack an explicit exponent thereby allowing all bits to be used for number (mantissa).

Floating-point operation includes add, multiply, subtract, and more, done to floating-point numbers.

FLOP/s = Floating-Point Operations per second.

FLOPs = Floating-Point Operations.

Flow Graph is a way to describe an algorithm using graph notation. Use of graph notation means that a flow graph consists of computational nodes connected by edges denoting possible control flow.

Forward scaling is the concept of having a program or algorithm scalable already in threads and/or vectors so as to be ready to take advantage of growth of parallelism in future hardware with a simple recompile with a new compiler or relink to a new library. Using the right abstractions to express parallelism is normally a key to enabling forward scaling when writing a parallel program.

FPGA (Field Programmable Array) is a device that integrates a large number of gates (and often higher-level constructs such as DSPs, floating-point units, or network controllers) that remain unconnected to each other until the device is programmed. Programming was originally a whole chip process that was intended to be done once when a system was started, but modern FPGAs support partial reconfigurability and are often dynamically loaded with new programs as a matter of course. Traditionally, FPGAs were viewed as a way to consolidate a large number of discrete chips in a design into a single FPGA – usually saving board space, power, and overall cost. As such, FPGAs were programmed using tools similar to those used to design circuitry at a board or chip level – called high-level description languages (e.g., VHDL or Verilog). More recent use to harness FPGAs as compute engines has used the OpenCL programming model.

future-proofed: A computer program written in a manner so it will survive future computer architecture changes without requiring significant changes to the program itself. Generally, the more abstract a programming method is, the more **future-proof** that program is. Lower level programming methods that in some way mirror computer architectural details will be less able to survive the future without change. Writing in an abstract, more **future-proof** fashion may involve tradeoffs in efficiency, however.

GFLOP/s (GigaFLOP/s) = 10^9 Floating-Point Operations per second.

GFLOPs (GigaFLOPs) = 10^9 Floating-Point Operations.

GPU (Graphic Processing Unit) is a computing device designed to reform calculations associated with graphics such as lighting, transformations, clipping, and rendering. The computational capabilities of GPUs were originally designed solely for use in a "graphical pipeline" sitting between a general-purpose compute device (CPU) and displays. The emergence of programming support for using the computation without sending results to the display, and subsequent extensions to the designs of the GPU, lead to a more generalized compute capability being associated with many GPUs. OpenCL and CUDA are two popular programming models utilized to harness the compute aspects of GPUs. See also, heterogeneous platforms.

Grain, as in *coarse-grained parallelism* or *fine-grained parallelism, or grain size*, all refer to the concept of "how much work" gets done before moving to a new task and/or potentially synchronizing. Programs scale best when grains are as large as possible (so threads can run independently) but small enough to keep every compute resource fully busy (load-balancing). These two factors operate somewhat at odds with each other, which creates the need to consider grain size. TBB works to automate partitioning, but there is never a perfect world in which a programmer cannot help tune for the best performance based on knowledge of their algorithms.

Gustafson-Barsis' law is a different view on **Amdahl's Law** that factors in the fact that as problem sizes grow, the serial portion of computations tend to shrink as a percentage of the total work to be done.

Hardware thread is a hardware implementation of a task with a separate flow of control. Multiple hardware threads can be implemented using multiple cores, or can run concurrently or simultaneously on one core in order to hide latency using methods such as hyper-threading of a processor core. In the latter case (hyperthreading or simultaneous multithreading, SMT), it is said that a physical core features several logical cores (or hardware threads).

Heterogenous platforms consist of a mixture of compute devices instead of a homogeneous collection of only CPUs. Heterogenous computing is usually employed to provide specific acceleration via an attached device, such as a GPU, DSP, FPGA, and so on. See also **OpenCL**.

High-Performance Computing (HPC) refers to the highest performance computing available at a point in time, which today generally means at least a petaFLOP/s of computational capability. The term HPC is occasionally used as a synonym for supercomputing, although supercomputing is probably more specific to even higher performance systems. While the use of HPC is spreading to more industries, it is generally associated with helping solve the most challenging problems in science and engineering. High-performance data analytics workloads, often using Artificial Intelligence (AI) and Machine Learning (ML) techniques, qualify as HPC workloads in their larger instantiations and often combine well with long standing (traditional) HPC workloads.

Hyper-threading refers to multithreading on a single processor core with the purpose of more fully utilizing the functional units in an out-of-order core by bringing together more instructions than executable by one software thread. With hyper-threading, multiple hardware threads may run on one core and share resources, but some benefit is still obtained from parallelism or concurrency. Typically, each hyper-thread has, at least, its own register file and program counter, so that switching between hyper-threads is relatively lightweight. Hyper-threading is associated with Intel, see also simultaneous multithreading.

Latency is the time it takes to complete a task; that is, the time between when the task begins and when it ends. Latency has units of time. The scale can be anywhere from nanoseconds to days. Lower latency is better in general.

Latency hiding schedules computations on a processing element while other tasks using that core are waiting for long-latency operations to complete, such as memory or disk transfers. The latency is not actually hidden, since each task still takes the same time to complete, but more tasks can be completed in a given time since resources are shared more efficiently, so throughput is improved.

Load balancing assigns tasks to resources while handling uneven sizes of tasks. Optimally, the goal of load balancing is to keep all compute devices busy with minimal waste due to overhead.

Locality refers to utilizing memory locations that are closer, rather than further, apart. This will maximize reuse of cache lines, memory pages, and so on. Maintaining a high degree of locality of reference is a key to scaling.

Lock is a mechanism for implementing **mutual exclusion**. Before entering a mutual exclusion region, a thread must first try to acquire a lock on that region. If the lock has already been acquired by another thread, the current thread must **block**, which it may do by either suspending operation or spinning. When the lock is released, then the current thread is free to acquire it. Locks can be implemented using **atomic operations**, which are themselves a form of mutual exclusion on basic operations, implemented in hardware.

Loop-carried dependence if the same data item (e.g., element [3] of an array) is written in one iteration of a loop and is read in a different iteration of a loop, there is said to be a loop-carried dependence. If there are no loop-carried dependencies, a loop can be vectorized or parallelized. If there is a loop-carried dependence, the direction (prior iteration vs. future iteration, also known as backward or forward) and the distance (the number of iterations separating the read and write) must be considered.

Many-core processor is a **multicore** processor with so many cores that in practice we do not enumerate them; there are just "lots." The term has been generally used with processors with 32 or more cores, but there is no precise definition.

Megahertz era is a historical period of time during which processors doubled clock rates at a rate similar to the doubling of transistors in a design, roughly every 2 years. Such rapid rise in processor clock speeds ceased at just under 4 GHz (four thousand megahertz) in 2004. Designs shifted toward adding more cores marking the shift to the **multicore era**.

Moore's Law is an observation that, over the history of semiconductors, the number of transistors in a dense integrated circuit has doubled approximately every 2 years.

Message Passing Interface (MPI) is an industry-standard message-passing system designed to exchange data on a wide variety of parallel computers.

Multicore is a processor with multiple subprocessors, each subprocessor (known as a **core**) supporting at least one hardware thread.

Multicore era is the time after which processor designs shifted away from rapidly rising clock rates and shifted toward adding more cores. This era began roughly in 2005.

Node (in a cluster) refers to a shared memory computer, often on a single board with multiple processors, that is connected with other nodes to form a **cluster** computer or supercomputer.

Nondeterministic: Exhibiting a lack of deterministic behavior, so results can vary from run to run of an algorithm. Concurrency is not the only factor that can lead to nondeterministic algorithms, but in practice it is often the cause. See more in the definition for **deterministic**.

Non-Uniform Memory Access (NUMA): Used to categorize memory design characteristics in a distributed memory architecture. NUMA = memory access latency is different for different memories. UMA = memory access latency is same for all memory. Compare with UMA. See Chapter 20.

Offload: Placing part of a computation on an attached device such as an FPGA, GPU, or other accelerator.

OpenCL (Open Computing Language) is a framework for writing programs that execute across heterogeneous platforms. OpenCL provides host APIs for controlling offloading and attached devices, and extensions to C/C++ to express code to run on the attached accelerator (GPUs, DSPs, FPGAs, etc.) with the ability to use the CPU as a fallback if the attached device is not present or available at runtime.

OpenMP is an API that supports multiplatform shared memory multiprocessing programming in C, C++, and Fortran, on most processor architectures and operating systems. It is made up of a set of compiler directives, library routines, and environment variables that influence runtime behavior. OpenMP is managed by the nonprofit technology consortium OpenMP Architecture Review Board and is jointly defined by a group of major computer hardware and software vendors (`http://openmp.org`).

Parallel means actually happening simultaneously. Two tasks that are both actually doing work at some point in time are considered to be operating in parallel. When a distinction is made between concurrent and parallel, the key is whether work can ever be done simultaneously. Multiplexing of a single processor core, by multitasking operating systems, has allowed concurrency for decades even when simultaneous execution was impossible because there was only one processing core.

Parallelism is doing more than one thing at a time. Attempts to classify types of parallelism are numerous.

Parallelization is the act of transforming code to enable simultaneous activities. The parallelization of a program allows at least parts of it to execute in parallel.

Pattern is a general, reusable solution to a common problem. Historically, TBB has used the term parallel algorithm when parallel pattern would also be an appropriate description.

PFLOP/s (PetaFLOP/s) = 10^{15} Floating-Point Operations per second.

PFLOPs (PetaFLOPs) = 10^{15} Floating-Point Operations.

Race conditions are nondeterministic behaviors in a parallel program that is generally a programming error. A race condition occurs when concurrent tasks perform operations on the same memory location without proper synchronization, and one of the memory operations is a write. Code with a race may operate correctly sometimes and fail other times.

Recursion is the act of a function being reentered while an instance of the function is still active in the same thread of execution. In the simplest and most common case, a function directly calls itself, although recursion can also occur between multiple functions. Recursion is supported by storing the state for the continuations of partially completed functions in dynamically allocated memory, such as on a stack, although if higher-order functions are supported a more complex memory allocation scheme may be required. Bounding the amount of recursion can be important to prevent excessive use of memory.

Scalability is a measure of the increase in performance as a function of the availability of more hardware to use in parallel.

Scalable: An application is **scalable** if its performance increases when additional parallel hardware resources are added. The term **strong-scaling** refers to scaling that occurs while a problem size does not need to be changed as more compute is available in order to achieve scaling. **Weak-scaling** refers to scaling that occurs only when a problem size is scaled up when additional compute is available. See **scalability**.

Serial means neither concurrent nor parallel.

Serialization occurs when the tasks in a potentially parallel algorithm are executed in a specific serial order, typically due to resource constraints. The opposite of parallelization.

Shared memory: When two units of parallel work can access data in the same location. Normally doing this safely requires synchronization. The units of parallel work, processes, threads, and tasks can all share data this way, if the physical memory system allows it. However, processes do not share memory by default and special calls to the operating system are required to set it up.

SIMD: Single-instruction-multiple-data referring to the ability to process multiple pieces of data (such as elements of an array) with all the same operation. SIMD is a computer architecture within a widely used classification system known as Flynn's taxonomy, first proposed in 1966.

Simultaneous multithreading refers to multithreading on a single processor core. See also, hyper-threading.

Software thread is a virtual hardware thread; in other words, a single flow of execution in software intended to map one for one to a hardware thread. An operating system typically enables many more software threads to exist than there are actual hardware threads, by mapping software threads to hardware threads as necessary. Having more software threads than hardware threads is known as **Oversubscription**.

Spatial locality: Nearby when measured in terms of distance (in memory address). Compare with temporal locality. Spatial locality refers to a program behavior where the use of one data element indicates that data nearby, often the next data element, will probably be used soon. Algorithms exhibiting good spatial locality in data usage can benefit from cache lines structures and prefetching hardware, both common components in modern computers.

Speedup is the ratio between the latency for solving a problem with one processing unit vs. the latency for solving the same problem with multiple processing units in parallel.

SPMD: Single-program-multiple-data refers to the ability to process multiple pieces of data (such as elements of an array) with the same program, in contrast with a more restrictive SIMD architecture. SPMD most often refers to message passing programming on distributed memory computer architectures. SPMD is a subcategory of MIMD computer architectures within a widely used classification system known as Flynn's taxonomy, first proposed in 1966.

STL (Standard Template Library) is a part of the C++ standard.

Strangled scaling refers to a programming error in which the performance of parallel code is poor due to high contention or overhead, so much so that it may underperform the nonparallel (serial) code.

Symmetric Multiprocessor (SMP) is a multiprocessor system with shared memory and running a single operating system.

Synchronization: The coordination, of tasks or threads, in order to obtain the desired runtime order. Commonly used to avoid undesired race conditions.

Task: A lightweight unit of potential parallelism with its own control flow, generally implemented at a user-level as opposed to OS-managed threads. Unlike threads, tasks are usually serialized on a single core and run to completion. When contrasted with "thread" the distinction is made that tasks are pieces of work without any assumptions about where they will run, while threads have a one-to-one mapping of software threads to hardware threads. Threads are a mechanism for executing tasks in parallel, while tasks are units of work that merely provide the *opportunity* for parallel execution; tasks are not themselves a mechanism of parallel execution.

Task parallelism: An attempt to classify parallelism as more oriented around tasks than data. We deliberately avoid this term, task parallelism, because its meaning varies. In particular, elsewhere "task parallelism" can refer to tasks generated by functional decomposition *or* to irregular tasks that still generated by data decomposition. In this book, any parallelism generated by data decomposition, regular or irregular, is considered data parallelism.

TBB: See Threading Building Blocks (TBB).

Temporal locality means nearby when measured in terms of time. Compare with spatial locality. Temporal locality refers to a program behavior in which data is likely to be reused relatively soon. Algorithms exhibiting good temporal locality in data usage can benefit from data caching, which is common in modern computers. It is not unusual to be able to achieve both temporal and spatial locality in data usage. Computer systems are generally more likely to achieve optimal performance when both are achieved hence the interest in algorithm design to do so.

Thread could refer to a *software* or *hardware* thread. In general, a "software thread" is any software unit of parallel work with an independent flow of control, and a "hardware thread" is any hardware unit capable of executing a single flow of control (in particular, a hardware unit that maintains a single program counter). When "thread" is compared with "task" the distinction is made that tasks are pieces of work without any assumptions about where they will run, while threads have a one-to-one mapping of software threads to hardware threads. Threads are a mechanism for implementing tasks. A multitasking or multithreading operating system will multiplex multiple software threads onto a single hardware thread by interleaving execution via software created time slices. A multicore or many-core processor consists of multiple cores to execute at least one independent software thread per core through duplication of hardware. A multithreaded or hyper-threaded processor core will multiplex a single core to execute multiple software threads through interleaving of software threads via hardware mechanisms.

Thread parallelism is a mechanism for implementing parallelism in hardware using a separate flow of control for each task.

Thread local storage refers to data which is purposefully allocated with the intent to only access from a single thread, at least during concurrent computations. The goal is to avoid need for synchronization during the most intense computational moments in an algorithm. A classic example of thread local storage is creating partial sums when working toward adding all numbers in a large array, by first adding subregions in parallel into local partial sums (also known as privatized variables) that, by nature of being local/private, require no global synchronization to sum into.

Threading Building Blocks (TBB) is the most popular abstract solution for parallel programming in C++. TBB is an open source project created by Intel that has been ported to a very wide range of operating systems and processors from many vendors. OpenMP and TBB seldom compete for developers in reality. While more popular than OpenMP in terms of the number of developers using it, TBB is popular with C++ programmers whereas OpenMP is most used by Fortran and C programmers.

Throughput is defined as the rate at which those tasks are completed, given a set of tasks to be performed. Throughput measures the rate of computation, and it is given in units of tasks per unit time. See **bandwidth** and **latency**.

TFLOP/s (TeraFLOP/s) = 10^{12} Floating-Point Operations per second.

TFLOPs (TeraFLOPs) = 10^{12} Floating-Point Operations.

Tiling is when you divide a loop into a set of parallel tasks of a suitable granularity. In general, tiling consists of applying multiple steps on a smaller part of a problem instead of running each step on the whole problem one after the other. The purpose of tiling is to increase reuse of data in caches. Tiling can lead to dramatic performance increases when a whole problem does not fit in cache. We prefer the term "tiling" instead of "blocking" and "tile" instead of "block." Tiling and tile have become the more common term in recent times.

TLB is an abbreviation for Translation Lookaside Buffer. A TLB is a specialized cache that is used to hold translations of virtual to physical page addresses. The number of elements in the TLB determines how many pages of memory can be accessed simultaneously with good efficiency. Accessing a page not in the TLB will cause a TLB miss. A TLB miss typically causes a trap to the operating system so that the page table can be referenced and the TLB updated.

Trip count is the number of times a given loop will execute ("trip"); same thing as *iteration count.*

Uniform Memory Access (UMA): Used to categorize memory design characteristics in a distributed memory architecture. UMA = memory access latency is same for all memory. NUMA = memory access latency is different for different memories. Compare with NUMA. See Chapter 20.

Vector operations are low-level operations that can act on multiple data elements at once in SIMD fashion.

Vector parallelism is a mechanism for implementing parallelism in hardware using the same flow of control on multiple data elements.

Vectorization is the act of transforming code to enable simultaneous computations using vector hardware. Multiprocessor instructions such as MMX, SSE, AVX, AVX2, and

AVX-512 instructions utilize vector hardware, but vector hardware outside of CPUs may come in other forms that are also targeted by vectorization. The vectorization of code tends to enhance performance because more data is processed per instruction than would be done otherwise. See also **vectorize**.

Vectorize refers to converting a program from a scalar implementation to a vectorized implementation to utilize vector hardware such as SIMD instructions (e.g., MMX, SSE, AVX, AVX2, AVX-512). Vectorization is a specialized form of parallelism.

vi is a text-based editor that was shipped with most UNIX and BSD systems written by Bill Joy, popular only to those who have yet to discover emacs (according to James). Yes, it is open source. Compares unfavorably to emacs and Atom. Yes, Ron, James did look at the "vi" nutshell book you gave to him... he still insists on using vi just long enough to get emacs downloaded and installed.

Virtual memory decouples the address used by software from the physical addresses of real memory. The translation from virtual addresses to physical addresses is done in hardware that is initialized and controlled by the operating system.

Index

© Intel Corporation 2019
M. Voss, R. Asenjo, J. Reinders, *Pro TBB*, https://doi.org/10.1007/978-1-4842-4398-5

T

W, X, Y

Z

Printed in the United States
By Bookmasters